PROPERTY OF
BARNEY WELLS

THE KINGDOM OF THE CULTS

OTHER WORKS BY THE SAME AUTHOR . . .

Jehovah of the Watch Tower
The Christian Science Myth
The Rise of the Cults
The Christian and the Cults
The Maze of Mormonism
The Truth About Seventh-day Adventism
Essential Christianity

Booklets

Jehovah's Witnesses
Christian Science
Mormonism
Unity

THE KINGDOM

OF THE CULTS

An Analysis of the Major Cult Systems
in the Present Christian Era

by

WALTER R. MARTIN, M.A.

Director, The Christian Research Institute, Wayne, N. J.

BETHANY FELLOWSHIP, INC., PUBLISHERS
Minneapolis, Minnesota

THE KINGDOM OF THE CULTS
Copyright 1965
Walter R. Martin
Oakland, N. J.

Library of Congress Catalog Card Number 64-22840
ISBN 0-87123-300-2

First printing — 1965
Second printing — March, 1966
Third printing — November, 1968
Fourth printing (REVISED EDITION) — July, 1968
Fifth printing — March, 1969
Sixth printing — January, 1970
Seventh printing — November, 1970
Eighth printing — July, 1971
Ninth printing — October, 1971
Tenth printing — June, 1972
Eleventh printing — October, 1972
Twelfth printing — March, 1973
Thirteenth printing — August, 1973
Fourteen printing — October, 1973
Fifteenth printing — January, 1974

Printed in the United States of America

To
PETER DE VISSER

my friend and brother in the common faith. His help and encouragement made this volume possible.
If you seek his monument, consult
the libraries of the informed.

ACKNOWLEDGMENTS

I wish to express my deep gratitude to Pierson Curtis, senior master of the Stony Brook School, who helped edit and correct the manuscript; the Messrs. Anthony Collarile, Herbert Jacobsen, Robert Smith and John Carter, who offered valuable insights and research data; and Mr. Walter Bjorck, Jr., of the American Tract Society, who made many helpful manuscript suggestions which were adopted in a number of instances.

My wife, Elaine, also contributed much from the perennial woman's point of view, an effort noted and gratefully appreciated.

CONTENTS

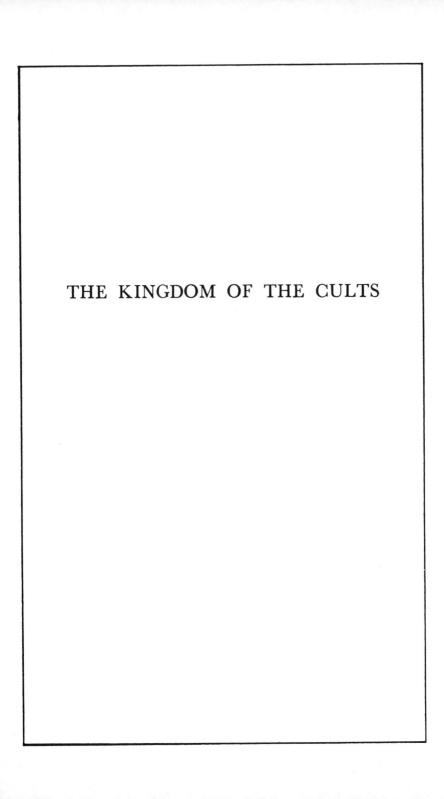

THE KINGDOM OF THE CULTS

Chapter 1

THE KINGDOM OF THE CULTS

It has been said of the United States that it is "the great melting pot" for the people of the world. And the contents of that pot would not be complete unless it also included the religions of those masses that now make up the populace of America. The writer has spent the last twelve years of his life in research and field work among the religions of America, and this volume, limited as it is by the vastness and complexity of the problem itself, constitutes his evaluation of that vibrant brand of religion which has come to be recognized by many as the "Kingdom of the Cults."

In his study of modern American cults and minority religious movements as found in his text, *These Also Believe,* Dr. Charles Braden, professor of History and Literature of Religions at Northwestern University, has made a number of observations with which this writer agrees. In regard to the term "cult," for instance, Dr. Braden states:

"By the term 'cult' I mean nothing derogatory to any group so classified. A cult, as I define it, is any religious group which differs significantly in some one or more respects as to belief or practice, from those religious groups which are regarded as the normative expressions of religion in our total culture" (Preface, xii). I may add to this that a cult might also be defined as a group of people gathered about a specific person or person's interpretation of the Bible. For example, Jehovah's Witnesses are, for the most part, followers of the interpretations of Charles T. Russell and J. F. Rutherford. The Christian Scientist of today is a disciple of Mary Baker Eddy and her interpretations of Scripture. The Mormons, by their own admission, adhere to those interpretations found in the writings of Joseph Smith and Brigham Young. It would be possible to go on citing many others, including the Unity School of Christianity, which follows the theology of Charles and Myrtle Filmore. We mention Moral Re-Armament, which continues to honor its founder, Dr. Frank Buchman. From a theological viewpoint, the cults contain not a few major deviations from historic Christianity. Yet paradoxically, they continue to insist that they are entitled to be classified as Christians.

It is my conviction that the reader is entitled to know the theological position from which this volume is written so that there will be no misconceptions as to the ground for my evaluation. I am a Baptist minister of the conservative school of thought, and teach in the fields of Biblical Theology and Comparative Religions at the King's College in Briarcliff Manor, New York. It is impossible for me to say with Dr. Braden that "I am an unrepentant liberal to the present," or that I "hold no brief for any particular cult, nor am violently opposed to any." While I am in agreement that "in general the cults represent the earnest attempt of millions of people to find the fulfillment of deep and legitimate needs of the human spirit, which most of them seem not to have found in the established churches," I feel there is still much more to be said. It has been wisely observed by someone that "a man who will not stand for something is quite likely to fall for almost anything." So I have elected to stand on the ramparts of Biblical Christianity as taught

11

by the apostles, defended by the church fathers, rediscovered by the reformers, and embodied in what is sometimes called Reformed Theology.

It is the purpose of this book then, to evaluate the so-called cults and isms which today are found in abundance in America and, in quite a number of cases, on the great mission fields of the world. My approach to the subject then is threefold: (1) historical analysis of the salient facts connected with the rise of the cult systems; (2) the theological evaluation of the major teachings of those systems; and (3) an apologetic contrast from the viewpoint of Biblical theology, with an emphasis upon exegesis and doctrine.

It is not my desire in any sense to make fun of adherents of cult systems, the large majority of whom are sincere, though I am not adverse to humor when it can underscore a contrast. A study of the cults is a serious business. They constitute a growing trend in America — a trend which is away from the established Christian churches and the historic teachings of the Bible — an emphasis upon autosoteric efforts, or the desire to save one's self apart from Biblical revelation.

It is most significant that, with the exceptions of Van Baalen's *Chaos of the Cults,* and Gerstner's *Theology of the Major Sects* (the only two major works of evangelical import), those who have written on the cults have never stressed the authority of the Scriptures as a criterion for measuring either the truth or falsity of cultic claims. Dr. Marcus Bach, who has written extensively from a liberal viewpoint on the cults, summed up this attitude of tolerance apart from Scriptural authority when he wrote:

> Somehow I felt I must become a representative of the average church-goer everywhere in America, whose heart was with me in my seeking. If the Jehovah's Witnesses have some

heavenly tip-off that the world is coming to an end in 1973, we want to tell our friends about it in plenty of time! If Father Divine is really God, we want to know about it! If Unity is building a new city down in Missouri, we Americans want to get in on the ground floor! If that man in Moscow, Idaho, talked with God, actually and literally, we have a right to know how it's done! Certainly these modern movements suggest that there was a vital, if not always coherent, moving force back of them, giving luster and drive to their beliefs. I decided that I would not concern myself so much with the rivalry among groups as with their realization. I would devote myself more to the *way* than to the *why* of their doctrine. Let others turn ecclesiastical microscopes on them, or weigh them in the sensitive scale of final truth; I would content myself with the age-old verdict of Gamaliel: "If this work be of men, it will come to naught; but if it be of God, we cannot overthrow it."

> I decided to set forth on my own, with no strings attached, and no stipend from any university, no commission from any church, no obligation to any individual or group, no bias, no preconceived judgment, no illusions.

> "All roads that lead to God are good." As I began my adventure the fervor of this naive and youthful conviction rushed over me once more. (*They Have Found a Faith,* pages 19, 20,21).

Dr. Bach admits more in this statement than perhaps he intended, for though it is a laudable aim to become "representative of the average church-goer everywhere in America," the use of the word "if" in the reference to the teachings of the cults indicates that the final truth, grounded in the authority of Scripture and the revelation of Jesus Christ, has not been obtained by the Christian Church, and that other sources must be investigated in order to ascertain the whole truth of the Christian message. We are in full agreement that "these modern movements suggest that there was a vital, if not always coherent, moving force back of them, giving luster and drive to their beliefs." But since most, if not all the cult systems vigorously oppose the Christian Church, particularly in the realm of Christology and Soteriology, perhaps it is not at all out of order to suggest that "that force" is the same as that which opposed our Lord and the apostles, and has consistently opposed the efforts of the Christian Church, the force described by our Lord as "the god of this world."

Liberal scholars then, have devoted themselves more to "the way" than to "the why" of the doctrines of the cults, and they have adopted the statement of Gamaliel as their creed. It will be remembered that Gamaliel counseled the Jews not to oppose the Christians for "if this work be of men, it will come to nought: but if it be of God, ye cannot overthrow it" (Acts 5:38-39).

Let it not be forgotten that Gamaliel's advice is not Biblical theology; and if it were followed in the practical realm of experience as steadfastly as it is urged, then we would have to recognize Islam as "of God," because of its rapid growth and reproductive virility throughout the world. We would have to acknowledge Mormonism (six people in 1830 to 2,000,000 in 1964) in the same category as Islam, something which most liberals are unwilling to do, though some have not hesitated to so declare themselves. We do not suggest that we "turn ecclesiastical microscopes" on the cults, but rather, that they be viewed in the light of what we know to be divine revelation, the Word of God, which itself weighs them, "in the sensitive scale of final truth," for it was our Lord who taught, "If you believe not that I am, you will die in your sins." And the final criterion today as always, must remain, "What think ye of Christ, whose son is He?"

I must dissent from the view that "all roads that lead to God are good" and believe instead the words of our Lord, "I am the way, the truth and the life. No man cometh unto the Father, but by me" (John 14:6). It should be carefully noted that Jesus did not say "I am one of many equally good ways," or, "I am a better way than the others. I am an aspect of truth; I am a fragment of the life." Instead, His claim was absolute, and allegiance to Him, as the Saviour of the world, was to take precedence over all the claims of men and religions.

I should like to make it clear that in advancing criticism of some of the views of liberal scholars in the field of cults and isms, I do not discount their many valuable contributions. And no one study, regardless of the time involved and the thoroughness of the investigation, can review all the data and evaluate all the facts necessary to completely understand the origin and development of cultism. My approach is quite honestly theological in its orientation, with the aim of contrast and reaffirmation in view. Dr. Van Baalen is correct when he says that "the cults are the unpaid bills of the church" (*Chaos of Cults, p. 14*). They are this and more, for they are a challenge to the church to affirm once again the great principles and foundations of the Gospel of Christ, and to make them meaningful to the present generation. There can be no doubt that the great trend in religion is synchretistic, or a type of homogenization of religions, such as the great historian Arnold Toynbee has more than once suggested.

We are consistently being told in books, articles, council pronouncements and ecumenical conclaves, that we must "play down the things that divide us and emphasize those things which make for unity." This is all well and good, if we are speaking about a firm foundation of doctrinal, as well as of moral and ethical truth, and if we are speaking about true unity within the body of Christ. But if, as some suggest, this be broadened to include those who are not in agreement with the essentials of Biblical Christianity, we must resolutely oppose it. It is most interesting to note that the National Council of Churches, and the World Council of Churches, which constitute the spearhead of the ecumenical movement throughout the world, have consistently denied membership to the cults under study in this volume on the ground that they do not recognize or worship Jesus Christ as God and Saviour. In 1959 *The Christian Century* printed a series of articles on the subject of "The Major Cults in Our Land," which were written by Dr. Marcus Bach. Dr. Bach's presentation was so sympathetic that the then editor of *The Christian Century,* Theodore Gill, was compelled to write an editorial, pointing out that "we are the Church" and that the sects and cults were not entitled to that classification, because they willingly choose to stand outside the pale of Biblical Christianity. The reason for Dr. Gill's concern was that the series provoked not an inconsiderable amount of mail from readers who wanted to get the mailing addresses of the various cults under discussion, because they liked the doctrines, and wanted more data, preparatory to leaving established churches and joining them! We can sympathize with Dr. Gill's concern, since any series of articles which presents the cults in such a favorable light, though it indicates objectivity, does little or nothing for Christianity, except to encourage weaker Christians to dabble in what is a dangerous hobby.

Biblical Perspectives

The age which saw the advent of Jesus Christ was an age rich in religion, stretching from the crass animism and sex worship of the great majority of the world, to the Roman pantheon of gods and the Greek mystery religions. One need only pursue Gibbon's *Decline and Fall of the Roman Empire* to become acutely aware of the multiplicity of gods and goddesses, as well as of philosophical and ethical systems which pervaded the religious horizon in that era of history. Judaism had withdrawn itself from any extensive missionary activity, burdened as the Jews were by the iron rule of an unsympathetic Roman paganism. The law of God had been interpreted and reinterpreted through commentaries and rabbinical emendations to the place where our Lord had to say to the religious leaders of His day: "Why do ye also transgress the commandment of God by your tradition? . . . Ye made the commandment of God of none effect by your tradition" (Matthew 15:3, 6).

Into this whirlpool of stagnant human philosophy and perverted revelation, came the Son of God who, through His teachings and example, revealed that there was such a thing as divine humanity, and through His miraculous powers, vicarious death and bodily Resurrection, cut across the maze of human doubts and fears, and was lifted up, to draw all men unto Him. It has been wisely observed that men are at liberty to reject Jesus Christ and the Bible as the Word of God; they are at liberty to oppose Him; they are at liberty to challenge it. But they are not at liberty to alter the essential message of the Scriptures, which is the good news that God does care for the lost souls of His children, and so loved us as to send His only Son that we might live through Him.

In keeping with this gospel of God's grace, our Lord not only announced it, but He prophesied the trials and tribulations which would encompass His followers, both within the Church and without, and one of the greatest of all these trials would, our Lord taught, be the challenge of false prophets and false christs, who would come in His name and deceive many (Matthew 24:5). So concerned was Christ in this area that He at one time declared:

> Beware of false prophets which come to you in sheep's clothing, but inwardly they are ravening wolves. Ye shall know them by their fruits. Do men gather grapes of thorns, or figs of thistles? Even so every good tree bringeth forth good fruit; but a corrupt tree bringeth forth evil fruit. A good tree cannot bring forth evil fruit, neither can a corrupt tree bring forth good fruit. Every tree that bringeth not forth good fruit is hewn down, and cast into the fire. Wherefore, by their fruits ye shall know them. Not every one that saith to me, Lord, Lord, shall enter into the kingdom of heaven, but he that doeth the will of My Father which is in heaven. Many will say to me in that day, Lord, Lord, have we not prophesied in Thy name? and in Thy name have cast out devils? in Thy name done many wonderful works? And then will I profess unto them, I never knew you! depart from me, ye that work iniquity (Matthew 7:15-23).

Christ pointed out that the false prophets would come. There was not a doubt in the mind of the Son of God that this would take place, and the history of the heresies of the first five centuries of the Christian Church bear out the accuracy of His predictions. Christ further taught that the fruits of the false prophets would also be apparent, and that the Church would be able to detect them readily. Let us never forget that "fruits" from a corrupt tree can also be doctrinal, as well as ethical and moral, and a person may be ethically and morally "good" by human standards, but if he sets his face against Jesus Christ as Lord and Saviour, and rejects Him, his fruit is corrupt and he is to be rejected as counterfeit. The Apostle John understood this when he wrote: "They went out from us, but they were not of us; for if they had been of us, they would no doubt have continued with us: but they went out that they might be made

manifest that they were not all of us" (I John 2:19).

The Bible then, does speak of false prophets, false christs, false apostles and "Deceitful workers, transforming themselves into the apostles of Christ. And no marvel, for Satan himself is transformed into an angel of light. Therefore, it is no great thing if his ministers be transformed as the ministers of righteousness; whose end shall be according to their works" (II Corinthians 11:13-15).

We cannot afford then, to have any concept of the purveyors of erroneous doctrines different from that held by our Lord and the apostles, and agree with the Apostle Paul that we must "abhor that which is evil, cleave to that which is good" (Romans 12:9). It is extremely difficult for this writer to understand how it is possible in the light of Paul's teaching, to cleave to that which is good, without an abhorrence of that which is evil.

The Biblical perspective then, where false teachers and false teachings are concerned, is that we are to have compassion and love for those who are enmeshed in the teachings of the false prophets, but we are to vigorously oppose the teachings, with our primary objective the winning of the soul, and not so much the argument. It must never be forgotten that cultists are souls for whom Jesus Christ died, for "he is the propitiation for our sins, and not for ours only, but for the sins of the whole world" (I John 2:2).

Today, the kingdom of the cults stretches throughout the world, its membership in excess of ten million, and Dr. Bach has not hesitated to raise that figure to 15,000,000, which may not be far from the truth. The Church of Jesus Christ has badly neglected both the evangelizing and refuting the various cult systems, but there is cause for some optimism. Recently the World Council of Churches set up a special study group to report on the development of non-Christian cults on Christian mission fields and throughout the world, with the aim in mind of taking definite steps to educate their constituencies to the aberrations of the cults and thus to rescue some of those potentially destined for cult membership. The National Association of Evangelicals, on the conservative side, is now seriously considering a similar type of study, and there is evidence on the local church level that concern has at last bred action, both evangelical and apologetic.

But the problem faces us all the same and continues to grow: The kingdom of the cults is expanding, and when it is remembered that the rate of growth for the Mormon Church in the United States in 1961 was 7.2 per cent, greater than the combined growth of all the Protestant denominations and the Roman Catholic Church on a percentage basis, the issue comes clearly into focus.

Our purpose in this volume is to awaken interest further to this tremendously important field of Christian missionary effort among the cults, to point out the flaws in the various cult systems, and to provide the information which will enable Christians both to answer cultists and to effectively present to them the claims of the Gospel of Christ, with a deep concern for the redemption of their souls. It is also the aim of this book to so familiarize the reader with the refreshing truths of the Gospel of Christ, that he may see the great heritage which is ours in the Christian faith, and be challenged both to more effectively live and to witness for the Saviour.

The American Banking Association has a training program which exemplifies this aim of the author. Each year it sends hundreds of bank tellers to Washington in order to teach them to detect counterfeit money, which is a great source of a loss of revenue to the Treasury Department. It is most interesting that during the entire two-week training program, no teller touches counterfeit money. Only the original passes through his hands. The reason for this is that the American Banking Association is convinced that if a man is thoroughly familiar with the original, he will not be deceived by the counterfeit bill, no matter how much like the original it appears. It is the contention of this writer that if the average Christian would become familiar once again with the great foundations of his faith, he would be able to detect those counterfeit elements so apparent in the cult systems, which set them apart from Biblical Christianity.

Charles W. Ferguson, in his provocative volume, *The New Books of Revelation,* describes the advent of modern cult systems as "the modern Babel," then goes on to state that:

> It should be obvious to any man who is not one himself, that the land is overrun with messiahs. I refer not to those political quacks, who promise in one election to rid the land of evil, but rather, to those inspired fakirs who promise to reduce the diaphragm, or orient the soul through the machinery of a cult religion. Each of these has made himself the center of a new theophany, has surrounded himself with a band of zealous apostles, has hired a hall for a shrine and then set about busily to rescue truth from the scaffold, and put it on the throne (page 1).

Ferguson did the Christian Church a great service in the late 1920's by focusing attention upon the rise of the cults. His observations were pithy and to-the-point, and though they cannot always be endorsed from a Biblical standpoint, there can be little doubt that he put his finger upon the cults as a vital emergent force in American Protestantism, with which the Church of Jesus Christ must reckon. It is with this force that we now come to deal, confident that, on the authority of the Scriptures, the Christian Church has the answers, and in the Gospel of Christ, the Saviour who can provide the cultist with something no cult system has ever been able to originate — peace with God and fellowship with the Father and with His Son, Jesus Christ. The cults have capitalized upon the failure of the Christian Church to understand their teachings and to develop a workable methodology to both evangelize and refute cult adherents. Within the theological structure of the cults there is considerable truth, all of which, it might be added, is drawn from Biblical sources, but so diluted with human error as to be more deadly than complete falsehood. The cults have also emphasized the things which the Church has forgotten, such as divine healing (Christian Science, Unity, New Thought), prophecy (Jehovah's Witnesses and Mormonism), and a great many other things which in the course of our study we will have opportunity to observe. But let it never be forgotten that where the Gospel of Jesus Christ is proclaimed in power and with what Dr. Frank E. Gaebelein has called "a compelling relevancy," cults have made little or no headway. This has led Dr. Lee Belford, Professor of Comparative Religions at New York University, to state,

> The problem is essentially theological where the cults are concerned. The answer of the Church must be theological and doctrinal. No sociological or cultural evaluation will do. Such works may be helpful, but they will not answer the Jehovah's Witness or Mormon, who is seeking Biblical authority for either the acceptance or rejection of his beliefs.

The problem then, is complex. There is no simple panacea, but it constitutes a real challenge to Christianity which cannot be ignored nor neglected any longer. For the challenge is here, and the time is now.

Chapter 2

SCALING THE LANGUAGE BARRIER

The scientific age in which we live has, in the very real sense of the term, given rise to a new vocabulary, which, unless it is understood, can create enormous problems in the realm of communication. The revolutions in culture which have taken place in the vocabularies of technology, psychology, medicine and politics have not left untouched the religions of the world in general, and the theology of Christianity in particular. Writing in *Eternity* Magazine, the noted theologian Dr. Bernard Ramm calls attention to this particular fact, when evaluating the theological system of Dr. Paul Tillich, leading theological luminary of our day and Professor of Theology at the University of Chicago's Divinity School. Dr. Ramm charges that Tillich has so radically re-defined standard theological terms that the effect upon Christian theology is nothing short of cataclysmic. ". . . Such Biblical notions of sin, guilt, damnation, justification, regeneration, etc., all come out retranslated into a language that is foreign to the meaning of these concepts in the Scriptures themselves."[1]

Dr. Ramm is quite right in his observations, for any student of Paul Tillich's theology, and, for that matter, the theology of contemporary Neo-liberalism and Neo-orthodoxy, will concede immediately that, in the theological framework of these two systems of thought, the vocabulary of what has been rightly termed by Dr. Edward Carnell "classical orthodoxy," undergoes what can only be termed radical redefinition. Just how this is effected is worthy of another chapter, but no one

informed on the subject seriously questions that this is what has occurred.

It is therefore possible for the modern theologians to use the terminology of the Bible and historic theology, but in an entirely different sense from that intended by the writers of Scripture.

Before attempting to examine the non-Christian cult systems contained in this volume, one must face the fact that the originators and promulgators of cult theology have done exactly the same thing to the semantic structure of Christian Theology as did the modern theologians. So it is possible for a Jehovah's Witness, a Christian Scientist or a Mormon, for example, to utilize the terminology of Biblical Christianity with absolute freedom, having already redesigned these terms in a theological framework of his own making and to his own liking, but almost always at direct variance with the historically accepted meanings of the terms.

The student of cultism then, must be prepared to scale the language barrier of terminology. First, he must recognize that it does exist, and second, he must acknowledge the very real fact that unless terms are defined when one is either speaking or reading cult theology, the semantic jungle which the cults have created will envelop him, making difficult, if not impossible, a proper contrast between the teachings of the cults and those of orthodox Christianity.

On countless occasions, the author has been asked, "Why is it, that when I am talking with a cultist, he seems to be in full agreement with what I am saying; but, when we have finished talking,

[1]November 1963, page 33.

18

I am aware of a definite lack of communication, almost as though we were not talking the same language?"

The answer to this question is, of course, that we have not been communicating, because the vocabulary of the cults is not the vocabulary of the Bible by definition. Only the Lord knows how many fruitless hours have been spent attempting to confront cultists with the claim of the Gospel, when five short minutes of insistence upon definitions of the terms employed in conversation, (particularly concerning the nature of God and the Person, nature and work of Jesus Christ), would have stripped the cult theology of one of its most potent tools, that of theological term-switching. Through the manipulation of terminology, it is therefore obvious that the cultist has the Christian at a distinct disadvantage, particularly in the realm of the great fundamental doctrines of Biblical theology. The question then is, how can the interested Christian solve that problem, if indeed it can be solved at all? In short, is there some common denominator that one can use when faced with a cultist of any particular variety, and, if so, how does one put this principle into practice?

The cults capitalize on the almost total inability of the average Christian to understand the subtle art of redefinition in the realm of Biblical theology. Human nature being what it is, it is only natural that Christian ministers as well as laymen should desire a panacea to the irritating and, at times, frustrating problem of cult terminology. Unfortunately, however, no such panacea exists. But lest we become discouraged with the prospect of facing the ever-multiplying bodies of non-Christian cults unprepared for this conflict, (and make no mistake, this *is* spiritual conflict), proper usage of definitions as a practical tool will rob the cultist of at least two of his advantages: surprise and confusion.

THE RIDDLE OF SEMANTICS

The problem of semantics has always played an important part in human affairs, for by its use, or abuse, whichever the case may be, entire churches, thrones and even governments for that matter, have been erected, sustained or overthrown. The late George Orwell's stirring novel, *1984,* in which he points out that the redefinition of common political terms can lead to slavery when it is allowed to pass unchallenged by a lethargic populace, is a classic illustration of the dangers of perverted semantics. It should be of no particular surprise to any student of world history that trick terminology is a powerful propaganda weapon. The communist dictatorship of China, which even the Russian theorists have rejected as incalculably brutal and inept, dares to call itself the People's Democratic Government. As history testifies, the people have very little, if any, say in the actual operation of communism, and if democracy is to be understood as the rule of the people, the Chinese communists have canonized the greatest misnomer of all time!

Both the Chinese communists and the Russians have paid a terrible price for not defining terminology, and for listening to the siren song of Marxism without carefully studying and analyzing the atheistic collectivism through which the music came.

Applying this analogy to the field of cults, it is at once evident that a distinct parallel exists between the two systems. For cultism, like communism, plays a type of hypnotic music upon a semantic harp of terminological deception. And there are many who historically have followed these strains down the broad road to spiritual eternal judgment. There is a common denominator then, and it is inextricably connected with language and the precise definition of terminology. It is what we might call the key to understanding cultism.

Precisely how to utilize the key which will help unlock the jargon of cult semantics is best illustrated by the following facts, drawn from almost a decade of research and practical field work with cultists of every variety.

The average non-Christian cult owes its very existence to the fact that it has utilized the terminology of Christianity, has borrowed liberally from the Bible, almost always out of context, and sprinkled its format with evangelical cliches and terms wherever possible or advantageous. Up to now this has been a highly successful attempt to represent their respective systems of thought as "Christian."

On encountering a cultist then, always remember that you are dealing with a person who is familiar with Christian terminology, and who has carefully redefined it to fit the system of thought he or she now embraces.

A concrete example of a redefinition of terms can be illustrated in the case of almost any of the Gnostic cult systems which emphasize healing, and hold in common a pantheistic concept of God (example: Christian Science, New Thought, Unity, Christ Unity Science, Metaphysics, Religious Science, Divine Science, etc.).

In the course of numerous contacts with this type of cultist, the author has had many opportunities to see the semantic maze in full operation, and it is awesome to behold. Such a cult adherent will begin talking at length about God and Christ. He will speak especially about love, tolerance, forgiveness, the Sermon on the Mount and, as always, the out-of-context perversion of James' "faith without works is dead."

It should be noted that hardly ever in their discourses will such cultists discuss the essential problem of evil, the existence of personal sin, or the necessity of the substitutionary atonement of Christ as the sole means of salvation from sin, through the agency of divine grace and the exercise of faith. In fact, they conscientiously avoid such distasteful subjects like the proverbial plague, and discuss them only with great reluctance. Of course, there are exceptions to this rule, but on the average, it is safe to assume that reticence will characterize any exploration of these touchy issues. Both Christian Science and Unity talk of God as Trinity; but their real concept of God is a pantheistic abstraction (Life, Truth and Love constitute the Trinity divine principles — Christian Science).

The historic doctrine of the Trinity is seldom, if ever, considered without careful redefinition. If the reader consults the *Metaphysical Bible Dictionary,* published by the Unity School of Christianity, he will see the masterpiece of redefinition for himself. For in this particular volume, Unity has redefined exhaustively many of the cardinal terms of Biblical theology, much as Mrs. Eddy did, in her Glossary of Terms in the book, *Science and Health.* The reader will be positively amazed to find what has happened to Biblical history, the person of Adam, the concept of human sin, spiritual depravity and eternal judgment. One thing however will emerge very clearly from this study, and that is the fact that Unity may *use* the terminology of the Bible, but by no stretch of the imagination can the redefinition be equated with the thing itself.

Another confusing aspect of non-Christian cultists' approach to semantics is the manner in which they will surprise the Christian with voluminous quotations from no less authority than the Bible, and give the appearance of agreeing with nearly every statement the Christian makes in attempting to evangelize the cultist. Such stock phrases as, "We believe that way too; we agree on this point," or the more familiar, Mrs. Eddy or Mr. or Mrs. Fillmore, Mr. Evans, Dr. Buchman, Joseph Smith or Brigham Young, etc.

"says exactly the same thing; we are completely in agreement." All such tactics based upon the juggling of terms usually have the effect of frustrating the average Christian, for he is unable to put his finger upon what he knows is error, and is repeatedly tantalized by seeming agreement which, as he knows, does not exist. He is therefore often forced into silence, because he is unaware of what the cultist is actually doing. Often, even though he may be aware of this, in a limited sense, he hesitates to plunge into a discussion for fear of ridicule because of an inadequate background or a lack of Biblical information.

The solution to this perplexing problem is far from simple, but once the Christian realizes that for every Biblical or doctrinal term *he* mentions, a redefinition light flashes on in the mind of the cultist, and a lightning-fast redefinition is accomplished, thus allowing the cultist apparently to agree with the doctrine under discussion, while firmly disagreeing in reality with the historical and Biblical concept. Then the Christian is on his way to dealing effectively with cult terminology. This amazing operation of terminological redefinition works very much like a word-association test in psychology.

It is simple for a cultist to spiritualize and redefine the clear meaning of Biblical text and teachings so as to be in apparent harmony with the historic Christian faith. However, such a harmony is at best a surface agreement, based upon double meanings of words which cannot stand the test of Biblical context, grammar, or sound exegesis. Language is, to be sure, a complex subject; all are agreed on this. But one thing is beyond dispute, and that is that in context, words mean just what they say. Either we admit this, or we must be prepared to surrender all the accomplishments of grammar and scholastic progress, and return to writing on cave walls with charcoal sticks in the tradition of our alleged stone-age ancestors. To illustrate this point more sharply, the experience of everyday life points out the absurdity of terminological redefinitions in every way of life.

An attorney who is retained by his client must know the laws which govern trial procedure, cross-examination and evidence. But above all else he must believe in the innocency of his client. A client who tells his attorney that he is guilty of a misdemeanor but not a felony is using the vocabulary of law. But if his attorney finds out that his client has perverted that vocabulary, so that the terms are interchangeable, he will either refuse to defend him, or will clarify the terminology before the court, because by definition, a misdemeanor is a misdemeanor, and a felony is a felony. A man who says he only stole ninety dollars (petty theft), but who really means that it was ninety dollars more or less, and in reality knows that it was in excess of one hundred dollars (grand theft) is playing a game that the law will not tolerate. He will most certainly be punished for such perversions of standard legal terms. In the realm of medicine, a doctor who announces that he will perform an open-heart operation, then proceeds in the presence of his colleagues to remove the gall bladder, and then attempts to defend his action by the claim that open-heart surgery actually means removal of the gall bladder in his vocabulary, could not practice medicine for long! Open-heart surgery is a delicate, surgical repair of the heart muscle. Removal of the gall bladder is, by definition, surgery of another type. In law and in medicine therefore, terms are what they are by definition. On the business and professional level also this holds true. But to the cultists, words do not always mean what they have always meant by definition in specific context. And just as the American Bar Association will not tolerate confusion of terminology in the trial of cases, and as the American Medical Association will not tolerate redefinition of terminology in diagnostic and surgical medicine, so also the Church of Jesus Christ has every right not to tolerate the gross perversions and redefinitions of historical, Biblical terminology, simply to accommodate a culture and a society which cannot tolerate an absolute standard or criterion of truth, even if it be revealed by God in His Word and through the true witness of His Spirit.

The major cult systems, then, change the definition of historic terms without a quibble. They answer the objections of Christian theologians with the meaningless phrase, "You interpret it your way, I'll interpret it in mine. Let's be broad-minded. After all, one interpretation is as good as another."

Is it any wonder then, that orthodox Christians feel called upon to openly denounce such perversions of clearly defined and historically accepted Biblical terminology, and claim that the cults have no rights, scholastically, Biblically or linguistically to redefine Biblical terms as they do?

We ought never to forget for one moment that things are what they are by definition. Any geometric figure whose circumference is $2 \pi r$ is by definition circular. Any two figures whose congruency can be determined by the application of angle-side-angle, side-angle-side, or side-side-side is, by definition, a triangle. To expand this, we might point out that any formula which expresses hydrogen to be in two parts and oxygen to be in one, is water, and hydrogen to be in two parts, sulfur in one part and oxygen in four parts is sulfuric acid. H_2O can never be H_2SO_4. Nor can atonement become at-one-ment, as the theology of the Gnostic cults, (Christian Science, Unity, New Thought, etc.) explains it. It simply cannot be, if language means anything.

To spiritualize texts and doctrines, or attempt to explain them away on the basis of the nebulous phrase, "interpretation," is scholastic dishonesty, and it is not uncommonly found in leading cult literature. Cultists are destined to find out that the power of Christianity is not in its terminology, but in the relationship of the individual to the historic Christ of revelation. The divine-human encounter must take place. One must become a new creation in Christ Jesus, and the emptying of Christian terminology of all its historic meanings serves only the purpose of confusion, and can never vitiate the force of the Gospel, which is the Person of the Saviour, performing the historic function of redeeming the sinner by grace.

The Christ of Scripture is an eternal, divine personality who cannot be dismissed by a flip of the cultist's redefinition switch, regardless of how deftly it is done. The average Christian will do well to remember the basic conflict of terminology which he is certain to encounter when dealing with cultists of practically every variety.

SUMMARY

Whenever a Christian encounters a cultist then, certain primary thoughts must be paramount in his mind: (1) he must strive to direct the conversation to the problem of terminology and maneuver the cult adherent into a position where he must define his usage of terms and his authority, if any, for drastic, un-Biblical redefinitions, which are certain to emerge; (2) the Christian must then compare these "definitions" with the various contexts of the verses upon which the cultist draws for support of his doctrinal interpretations; (3) he must define the words "interpretation," "historic orthodoxy," and standard doctrinal phrases, such as "the new birth," "atonement," "context," "exegesis," "eternal judgment," etc., so that no misunderstanding will exist when these things come under discussion as they inevitably will; (4) the Christian must attempt to lead the cultist to a review of the importance of properly defining terms for all important doctrines involved, particularly the doctrine of personal redemption from sin, which most cult systems define in a markedly un-Biblical manner; (5) it is the responsibility of the Christian to present a clear testimony to his own regenerative experience with Jesus Christ, in terminology which has been carefully clarified, regarding the necessity of such regeneration on the part of the cultist, in the light of the certain reality of God's inevitable justice. It may be necessary also, in the course of discussing terminology and its dishonest recasting by cult systems, to resort to occasional polemic utterances. In such cases, the Christian should be certain that they are tempered with patience and love, so that the cultist appreciates that such tactics are motivated by one's personal concern for his eternal welfare, and not just to "win the argument."

Let it never be forgotten that cultists are experts at lifting texts out of their respective contexts, without proper concern for the laws of language, or the established principles of Biblical interpretation. There are those of whom Peter warns us, who "wrest the Scriptures unto their own destruction" (II Peter 3:16). This is an accurate picture of the kingdom of the cults in the realm of terminology.

Looking back over the picture of cult semantics, the following facts emerge:

1. The average cultists know their own terminology very thoroughly. They also have a historic knowledge of Christian usage, and are therefore prepared to discuss not a few areas of Christian theology intelligently.

2. The well-trained cultist will carefully avoid definition of terms concerning cardinal doctrines such as the Trinity, the Deity of Christ, the Atonement, the Bodily Resurrection of our Lord, the process of salvation by grace and justification by faith. If pressed in these areas, he will redefine the terms to fit the semantic framework of orthodoxy, unless he is forced to define his terms explicitly.

3. The informed Christian must seek for a point of departure, preferably the authority of the Scriptures, which can become a powerful and useful tool in the hands of a good Christian, if properly exercised.

4. The concerned Christian worker must familiarize himself to some extent with the terminology of the major cult systems if he is to enjoy any measure of success in understanding the cultist's mind when bearing a witness for Christ.

We have stressed heavily the issue of terminology and a proper definition of terms throughout this entire chapter. It will not have been wasted effort if the reader has come to realize its importance, and will be guided accordingly when approaching the language barrier, which is an extremely formidable obstacle both to evangelizing cultists, and to giving a systematic and effective defense of the Christian faith against their perversions.

Chapter 3

THE PSYCHOLOGICAL STRUCTURE OF CULTISM

It is extremely difficult, when approaching the study of the field of non-Christian cults, to accurately appraise such groups without some knowledge of the psychological factors involved in both their formation and growth.

Each cult has what might be called its own "belief system" which follows a distinct pattern and, allowing for obvious differences of personality which exist in any group, can be analyzed and understood in relation to its particular theological structure. Since very little, if anything, has been written on the subject relative to the cults, considerable research was necessary in order to bring this matter under discussion. That it must be discussed and understood as an integral part of the whole complex of the development of American cult systems, no thorough student will deny.

In the course of working with cultists it has been the observation of this writer that each cultist though different as an individual does share certain psychological traits in common with his fellow members, and a careful study of these similarities has revealed some provocative and unusual findings.

It is not possible in one chapter to cover all of the cult systems so we have limited our observations to Jehovah's Witnesses, Mormonism and Christian Science. The Jehovah's Witnesses represent those cult systems which put strong emphasis upon eschatology and prophecy, the Mormons those which emphasize priestly authority, secret rituals and symbols, and Christian Science, the gnostic cults which ground their experience in metaphysical pantheism and physical healing (a fact which contains within itself enough material to merit an entire book on the problem of psychosomatic medicine and healing).

Dr. Milton Rokeach in his illuminating book, *The Open and Closed Mind,* notes that there are three regions or levels that psychologists generally recognize in any belief or disbelief system. The first or central region is that which encompasses the individual's basic primitive outlook on the world in which he lives and asks such questions as, "Is the world a threatening place, or is it an accepting place?"

The second or intermediate region is the area of authority. In other words, whose authority is a person willing to accept in matters pertaining to the functions of life?

Finally there is the peripheral region which penetrates into the details of the structure of living. The details may vary or change according to the specific content which the authority, once accepted, may invoke.

There is no doubt in my mind that the belief systems of the cults share much in common, and that some of these common factors are worth noting.

First and foremost, the belief systems of the cults are characterized by closed-mindedness. They are not interested in a rational cognitive evaluation of the facts. The organizational structure interprets the facts to the cultist, generally invoking the Bible and/or their respective founders as the ultimate source of their pronouncements. Such belief systems are in isolation, they never shift to logical consistency. They exist in what we might describe as separate compartments in the cultist's mind and are almost incapable of penetration or disruption if the individual cultist is completely committed to the authority pattern of his organization.

Secondly, cultic belief systems are characterized by genuine antagonism on a personal level since the cultist almost always identifies his dislike of the Christian message with the messenger who holds such opposing beliefs.

The identification of opposing beliefs with the individual in the framework of antagonism leads the cultist almost always to reject the individual as well as the belief, a problem closely linked with closed-mindedness and one that is extremely difficult to deal with in general dialogue with cultists.

Theoretically speaking, if one could drive a wedge between the individual (or the personality of the individual toward whom the cultist is antagonistic) and the theology (which is the real source of the antagonism) it would be possible to deal with the individual cultist by becoming in his or her eyes a neutral objective source of data. The Christian would then become a person who maintains a system of theology opposed to theirs but not necessarily involved on a level of personal antagonism toward the cultist. Experience has shown me that when this is accomplished it is the first step in a systematic under-cutting of one of the basic problems all cultists face in inter-personal contact, the problem of hostility toward those who reject their interpretations.

Such a procedure can go a long way toward allaying hostility, for once a cultist, who has been thoroughly "brainwashed" psychologically by his own authority system (The Watch Tower Society, Mrs. Eddy's books, the writings of Joseph Smith and Brigham Young, etc.), is confronted by a Christian whom he can learn to accept on a personal basis apart from differences of theological opinion, the possibility of communication improves markedly.

In effect, the cultist is faced with a dilemma, "How can this person (the Christian) be such an acceptable personality yet not share his (the cultist's) theology?"

The cultist then quite often begins to wonder how it is possible for the Christian to accept him as a person and yet not accept his beliefs. This can be the beginning of rapport in the realm of personal evangelism.

Since almost all systems of authority in cult organizations indoctrinate their disciples to believe that anyone who opposes their beliefs cannot be motivated by anything other than satanic force or blind prejudice and ignorance, a cultist's encounter with Christians who do not fit this pattern can produce startling results. A discerning Christian who gives every indication of being unprejudiced, reasonably learned and possessed of a genuine love for the welfare of the cultist himself (which is easily detectable in the Christian's concern for his soul and spiritual well-being generally) can have a devastating effect upon the conditioning apparatus of any cult system.

Above all else Christians must learn that most cults consider that they have freed their adherents from religious exploitation which they almost always accuse historic Christianity of practicing. In this connection it becomes a vital necessity to demonstrate genuine interest in the cultist as a person for the sake of himself and his personal redemption, rather than as a possible statistic for any given denomination.

The prime task of Christians who would be effective witnesses for Christ in the midst of the kingdom of the cults is that they be free from all appearance of guile and ulterior motivation, remembering that our main task is to communicate to those who are by their very adherence to cultic systems of belief in virtual isolation from the Christian message.

Thirdly, almost without exception cultic belief systems all manifest a type of institutional dogmatism and a pronounced intolerance for any position but their own. This no doubt stems from the fact that in the case of non-Christian cult systems which wish to be identified with Christianity the ground for their claims is almost always supernatural.

We do not wish to imply that there is no such thing as an authoritative dogmatism which is valid and true (such as the teachings of Jesus Christ), but rather that cult systems tend to invest with the authority of the supernatural whatever pronouncements are deemed necessary to condition and control the minds of the faithful.

Thus it is that when Joseph Smith, Jr., the Mormon prophet, and his successor, Brigham Young, wished to implement doctrines or changes of practice in the Mormon Church they prefaced their remarks with proclamations that God had revealed to them the necessity of such doctrines or practices among the "saints."

No less an example of this was Charles Taze Russell's bold claim that his writings were indispensable to the study of the Bible for Jehovah's Witnesses, and that to study the Bible apart from his inspired comments was to go into spiritual darkness. Russell also taught that concentration upon his writings even at the expense of studying the Bible would most certainly lead one into deeper spiritual illumination within five years.

Mary Baker Eddy also conformed to this pattern by requiring her followers to regard her book *Science and Health with Key to the Scriptures* as a divine revelation, and her religion as a "higher, clearer and more permanent revelation than that given eighteen centuries ago!" Mrs. Eddy did not hesitate to state that she would "Blush to write of *Science and Health* as she did if she apart from God were its author."

The history of cultism generally begins with an authoritarian pronouncement on the part of the founder or founders. This in turn is institutionalized during their lifetime or after their death into a dogmatic system which requires absolute faith in the supernatural authority of those who received the initial revelation and whose writings and pronouncements are alleged to have transmitted it.

Some interesting studies of institutional dogmatism can be found in such books as George Orwell's *1984*, Eric Hoffer's *The True Believer* and Crossman's volume *The God That Failed*.

The problem of intolerance is closely linked to institutional dogmatism or authoritarianism, and those systems which embody this line of reasoning are resistant to change and penetration since the cults thrive on conformity, ambiguity and extremeness of belief.

The fourth and final point in any analysis of the belief system of cults is the factor of isolation.

Within the structure of non-Christian cult systems one can observe the peaceful coexistence of beliefs that are beyond a question of a doubt logically contradictory and which in terms of psychological analysis would come under the heading of "compartmentalization." In his classic book, *1984,* George Orwell describes this as "double think." Rokeach commenting on this illustrates the point admirably:

> In everyday life we note many examples of double "think"; expressing an abhorrence of violence and at the same time believing it is justifiable under certain conditions; affirming a faith in the common man and at the same time believing that the masses are stupid; being for democracy but also advocating a government run by an intellectual elite; believing in freedom for all but also believing that certain groups should be restricted; believing that science makes no value judgments but also knowing a good theory from a bad theory and a good experiment from a bad experiment. Such expressions of clearly contradictory beliefs will be taken as one indication of isolation in the belief system . . . a final indicator of isolation is the outright denial of contradiction. Contradictory facts can be denied in several ways: on grounds of face absurdity ("it is absurd on the face of it"), "chance," "the exception

that proves the rule," "the true facts are not accessible, and the only available sources of information are biased."[1]

I do not believe it could be stated with greater clarity where the belief system of cults is concerned for Dr. Rokeach has hit the proverbial nail squarely on the head. Jehovah's Witnesses are well aware of the fact that the Watch Tower organization under the leadership of Judge Rutherford maintained that Abraham, Isaac and Jacob would return to earth before the close of the 1920's and even bought a home for the patriarchs to dwell in (San Diego, California, Beth Sarim, "the house of princes"). At the same time Jehovah's Witnesses are fully aware of the fact that the patriarchs did not materialize on schedule, yet they cling tenaciously to the same principles of prophetic interpretation which conceived and brought forth the now defunct interpretations of previous Watch Tower leaders.

Well-informed Mormon historians and theologians are equally aware that the first edition of *The Book of Mormon* and the present edition of *The Book of Mormon* are quite different in a number of places, the first issue having been revised and corrected by Joseph Smith after numerous errors were pointed out. Yet both the errors and the revisions of *The Book of Mormon* are heralded as divine revelation by Mormons. This is another example of the peaceful co-existence of logical contradiction within the belief system of Mormonism which permits the isolation or compartmentalization of conflicting evidence or concepts.

Still another example of contradiction is the fact that the Christian Science Church has known for many years that though Mary Baker Eddy spoke vigorously against doctors and drugs as well as vigorously affirming the unreality of pain, suffering and disease, she herself was frequently attended in her

declining years by doctors, received injections of morphine for the alleviation of pain, wore glasses, and had her teeth removed when they became diseased. However, despite this the Christian Science Church insists upon the validity of Mrs. Eddy's teachings which deny the very practices Mrs. Eddy herself exemplified. Here is a classic example of isolation which might justly come under the heading of "physician heal thyself!"

It would be possible to point out many other instances of psychological aberration in the belief systems of the major cults, but it is apparent that we are confronted with those whom the Apostle Paul described as victims of the master psychologist and propagandist of the ages, described by our Lord as "the prince of this world" and by the Apostle Paul as "the god of this age" — the one who by the sheer force of his antagonism to the truth of divine revelation in the person of Jesus Christ has psychologically "blinded the minds" of those who believe not the Gospel, "lest the light of the glorious gospel of Christ, who is the image of God, should shine unto them" (II Corinthians 4:4).

This, of course, is not only a psychological blindness but a spiritual blindness brought about by the isolation of man from God through the rebellion of human nature and the repeated violation of divine law. These are factors which cannot be ignored for they are a direct reflection of the forces which from "the heavenlies" dominate the world in which we live (Ephesians 6:10-12).

The Psychological Conditioning Process

To conclude our observations in this seldom considered area of cultic analysis let us consider examples of just how the cult systems of Jehovah's Witnesses, Mormonism, and Christian Science condition their adherents to respond to the "outside world" of unbelievers.

[1]*The Open and Closed Mind,* pages 36 and 37.

In the case of Jehovah's Witnesses the literature of the Watch Tower is replete with examples of a psychological conditioning which elicits a definite pattern of religious reflexes in response to a given stimuli. As Pavlov's dog salivated at the sound of a bell which represented food, so a true Jehovah's Witness will spiritually and emotionally salivate whenever the Watch Tower rings the conditioning bell of Russellite theology. The example which I believe best demonstrates this is taken in context from Watch Tower publications and speaks for itself.

. . . In Christendom as surprising as as it may seem to some the false religious teachings create traditions, and commands of men are both directly and indirectly responsible for the physical and spiritual miseries of the poor, notwithstanding Christendom's showy display of charity.[2]

. . . Christendom's pretended interest in the poor is sheer hypocrisy . . . her priests have done violence to my law and have profaned my holy things . . . her princes in the midst thereof are like wolves ravening the prey to shed blood and to destroy souls that they may get dishonest gain . . and her prophets have daubed them with untempered mortar seeing false visions in divining lies unto them saying thus says Jehovah when Jehovah hath not spoken . . . the people of the land have used oppression and exercised robbery, yea they have vexed the poor and needy and have oppressed the sojourners wrongfully . . . oh wicked Christendom why have you forsaken God's clean worship? Why have you joined forces and become part of Satan's wicked organization that oppresses the people? Why have you failed to show concern for the poor as Jehovah commands?[3]

The little charitable help the poor get from Christendom is like the crumbs that beggar Lazarus picked up from the rich man's table while the dog licked his ulcerous sores. Neither the crumbs nor the licking remedied the beggarly condition. Only Jehovah can effect a rescue. How comforting then for the dejected, down-trodden people of the earth to learn that there is One higher than the highest of Christendom's moguls . . . yes, Jehovah the Almighty hears the cries of the half dead ones and in hearing He answers their prayers and sends His good samaritans to the rescue even the witnesses who are despised by Christendom.[4]

Haters of God and His people are to be hated, but this does not mean that we will take any opportunity of bringing physical hurt to them in the spirit of malice or spite, for both malice and spite belong to the devil, whereas, pure hatred does not.

We must hate in the truest sense which is to regard with extreme and active aversion, to consider as loathsome, odious, filthy, to detest. Surely any haters of God are not fit to live on His beautiful earth. The earth will be rid of the wicked and we shall not need to lift a finger to cause physical harm to come to them, for God will attend to that, but we must have a proper perspective of these enemies. His name signifies recompense to the enemies.

Jehovah's enemies are recognized by their intense dislike for His people and the work these are doing. For they would break it down and have all of Jehovah's Witnesses sentenced to jail or concentration camps if they could. Not because they have anything against the Witnesses personally but on account of their work. They publish blasphemous lies and reproach the holy name Jehovah. Do we not hate those who hate God? We cannot love those hateful enemies for they are fit only for destruction. We utter the prayer of the Psalmist, "How long, oh God, shall the adversary reproach, shall the enemy blaspheme thy name forever? Why drawest thou back thy hand, even thy right hand? Pluck it out of thy bosom and consume them" (Psalm 74:10, 11).

We pray with intensity and cry out this prayer for Jehovah to delay no longer and plead that His anger be made manifest, oh Jehovah, God of hosts . . . be not merciful to any wicked transgressors. . . . Consume them in wrath, consume them so that they shall be no more (Psalm 59, verses 4 through 6, 11 through 13). These are the true sentiments, desires and prayers of the

---

[2]*Watch Tower*, December 1, 1951, page 731
[3]*Ibid.*, page 732 and 733.
[4]*Ibid.*, page 733.

righteous ones today. Are they yours . . . how 'we despise the workers of iniquity and those who would tear down God's organization! ". . . Oh, Jehovah. Let them be put to shame and dismayed forever, yea, let them be confounded and perish that they may know that Thou alone whose name is Jehovah art the most high over all the earth" (Psalm 83:9 through 18).
. . . The near neighbors of Judah . . . have been the opposers of the Israelites right from the time when refusal was given by them to supply provisions to Israel as they journeyed to the promised land. Moab hired Baalam to curse Israel . . . they had much contempt for Jehovah's people and prided themselves in their own lofty city, her counterpart today being that rich, lofty city, the mighty religious organization standing for the whole of Satan's organization. The modern-day Moabites are the professing Christians whose words and actions are as far removed from Christianity and true worship of Jehovah as Moab was removed from true worship in the covenant of Jehovah. Jehovah had warned Moab of His proposed punishment for her iniquity and opposition.

The modern-day Moabites have opposed Jehovah's Witnesses with a hatred not born of righteousness but from the devil and against all righteousness. Their hatred for God's true people increases as they see upon us the very plain evidence of Jehovah's favor in the obvious disfavor they themselves are in. They put forth every effort to prevent the people of goodwill from entering the new world. They are richer than Jehovah's Witnesses in material things and with it they have much pride and arrogance . . .

The modern-day Moabites will be brought low for Jehovah has completely finished with them. Hear just a part of the punishment:

"For in this mountain will the hand of Jehovah rest and Moab shall be trodden down in his place, even as straw is trodden down in the water of the dung hill. He shall spread forth his hands in the midst thereof as he that swimmeth spreadeth forth his hands to swim, but Jehovah will lay low his pride together with the craft of his hands."

It is a sure thing that one cannot have much pride left when one is being pressed down into a manure pile, showing the utter contempt Jehovah has for modern-day Moab, keeping her wallowing in the mire of shame.

"For thou has made of a city a heap of a fortified city a ruin a palace of strangers to be no city; it shall never be built."

He hath put down them that dwell on high the lofty city, he layeth it low, he layeth it low even to the ground, he bringeth it even to the dust. The foot shall tread it down, even the feet of the poor and the steps of the needy . . .

When this happens what a tremendous change will take place, the tables will be turned! Brought down will be the lofty from dwelling on high as the great, high influential ones of this world to the lowest possible place imaginable, so low and degraded they can only be compared to being trampled under foot by the poor like straw in a manure heap. Christendom's lofty looks, boastful words, bragging tongue are superior attitude toward the holy Word of God, her trust in idols, men and riches such as belong to this world will not provide her with security or any safety from Jehovah's storm and blast. They have no defense nor disgrace . . .

Christendom's defenses are of no value but Jehovah's Witnesses have a strong city and this is something to sing about. There are millions who want a safe place and are in need of security, let them know we have a strong city! "Thou shalt call thy wall salvation and thy gates praise" (Isaiah 60:18). Only God's Kingdom offers such protection and salvation for inside the city one is safe. Those desiring salvation must make for God's organization and find entrance into it and remain there permanently.

God has been grossly misrepresented by the clergy. If this statement is true then that alone is proof conclusive that the clergy do not in fact represent God in Christ but do represent God's enemy the devil . . . torture is repulsive even to the imperfect man. Only a selfish heart, cruel and wicked one, could inflict conscious eternal torment upon another . . . the theory of eternal torment in hell is the outgrowth of . . . satanic lies. These doctrines originated with the devil. They have long been taught by his representatives . . . the clergy have been his instruments freely used to instill these false doctrines into the minds of men. Whether the clergy have willingly done this or not does not alter the fact . . . the clergy have at all times posed as the representatives of

God on earth. But Satan overreached the minds of these clergymen and injected into their minds doctrines . . . which . . . the clergy have taught the people concerning Jesus and His sacrifice. These doctrines have brought great confusion.[5]

The clergy have ever held to this senseless, God-dishonoring doctrine . . . if you ask a clergyman what is meant by the trinity, he says: That is a mystery. He does not know and no one else knows . . . they are willingly or unwillingly the instruments of the hands of Satan, the devil, who has used them to blind the minds of the people to prevent the people from understanding God's great plan of salvation and reconciliation.[6]

The clergy of Christendom are obviously the villains and are the object of "pure hatred." Just how pure hatred differs from good old-fashioned hatred the Watch Tower never gets around to explaining, but it is clear that Christendom (all historic communions) led by the allegedly corrupt clergy has foisted the "satanically conceived" trinity doctrine, and the doctrines of hell and eternal punishment upon the unsuspecting masses of mankind. Clergymen are therefore always suspect and their theology is to be regarded as untrustworthy and inspired by Satan.

Is it any wonder that the usually calm and detached Stanley High writing in *The Reader's Digest* of June, 1940, could state:

"Jehovah's Witnesses hate everybody and try to make it mutual. . . . Jehovah's Witnesses make hate a religion."

The doctrines of hell and eternal punishment which stimulate fear of judgment are "unreasonable" and not in accord with the Watch Tower's concept of the character of God, therefore, it and the doctrine of the trinity are satanic in origin and all must be rejected and hated as false.

What the Watch Tower does in essence is attach polemic significance to certain common theological terms (Holy Trinity, Deity of Christ, Hell, Eternal Punishment, Christendom, immortal soul, etc.), thus every time these terms are mentioned by anyone the reflex action on the part of the Jehovah's Witnesses is instantaneous and hostile.

If we couple this with the Watch Tower's heavy emphasis upon the fulfillment of prophecy and a distorted eschatology, the sense of urgency they radiate about Armageddon (which they believe will solve all these problems by annihilating the clergy and all organized religion), then begins to make sense and the reason for their actions becomes clear.

When dealing with the average Jehovah's Witness this entire pattern of preconditioning must be understood so that the Christian can avoid, where possible, direct usage of terms that will almost certainly evoke a theologically conditioned reflex and sever the lines of communication.

Another important point where Jehovah's Witnesses are concerned is the fact that an intricate part of their belief system is the conviction that Christians will always attack Jehovah's Witnesses on a personal as well as a religious level, hence the Witnesses readily assume a martyr or persecution complex the moment any antagonism is manifested toward Russell, Rutherford, their theology, the Watch Tower or themselves. It is apparently a comfortable, somewhat heroic feeling to believe that you are standing alone against the massed forces of "the devil's organization" (A Watch Tower synonym for Christendom!) and this illusion is made to seem all the more real when unthinking Christians unfortunately accommodate the Witnesses by appearing overly aggressive toward the Watch Tower theology or the Witnesses personally.

In the light of Jehovah's Witnesses

[5]*Reconciliation*, J. F. Rutherford, Watch Tower Bible and Tract Society, 1928, pages 85, 91, 100, 101 and 125.

[6]*Ibid.*, Rutherford, page 125.

insistence upon "pure hatred" one wonders how they live with their own New World Translation of Matthew, chapter 5, verses 43 through 45 which reads:

> You heard that it was said you must love your neighbor and hate your enemy. However, I say to you continue to love your enemies and pray for those persecuting you that you may prove yourselves sons of your father who is in heaven . . . but I say to you who are listening, continue to love your enemies and do good to those hating you, to bless those cursing you, to pray for those who do you injury.

The Watch Tower then does not hesitate to accuse the clergy and Christendom of provoking all kinds of evil; in fact, they have not hesitated to suggest that Christendom encouraged and did nothing to prevent the two great world wars:

> "Had Christendom chosen to do so she could easily have prevented World Wars 1 and 2."[7]

Some of the basic motivations of the Watch Tower are clearly seen in stark contrast with the teachings of Holy Scripture and reveals that there is more than a spiritual disorder involved. Indeed there exists deep psychological overtones which cannot be considered healthy in any sense of the term.

Whereas Jehovah's Witnesses are occupied with Armageddon, the theocracy, the end of the ages, and "pure hatred" the Mormons have quite different psychological and theological emphases.

At the very core of Mormon theology there is a tremendous emphasis upon authority as it is invested in the priesthood, rituals and symbols presided over by the hierarchy of the Mormon Church. Mormons are taught from their earliest days that the priesthood has the key to authority, and that one of the marks which identifies the "restoration" of the true church of Jesus Christ on earth is the fact that this priesthood exists and perpetuates that authority.

A devout Mormon will wear symbolic underclothing which perpetually reminds him of his responsibility and duties as a Mormon. When this is coupled with Mormonism's tremendous emphasis upon baptism for the remission of sins, tithing and voluntary missionary service, it is seen to bind its followers into a tight, homogeneous circle, escape from which, apart from severe spiritual as well as economic penalties, is virtually impossible.

Every Mormon is indoctrinated with the concept that his is the true Christian religion or to use their terms, "the restoration of Christianity to earth." The secret rites in the Mormon temples, the rituals connected with baptism for the dead, and the secret handshakes, signs and symbols bind the average Mormon and his family into what might be called in psychological terms the "in group." Apart from acceptance by this group the average Mormon can find no peace, or for that matter, community status or prestige.

Instances of discrimination against Mormons who have experienced true Christian conversion are not infrequent in Mormon dominated areas where a man can lose his business very easily by incurring the disfavor of the Mormon Church.

The social welfare program of the Mormons is another excellent inducement to Mormons to remain faithful, since if the "bread winner" of the family is injured, loses his job, or dies, the church undertakes the care and support of his family. So effective is this work that during the great depression of the 1930's no Mormon families went hungry and no soup kitchens or bread lines disfigured the domain of Mormondom.

The Mormons also conscientiously invoke the Biblical principle of helping each other. They lend to each other, work for each other, and cooperate toward the common goal of bringing

[7]*The Watch Tower*, December 1, 1951, page 731.

"restored Christianity" to the masses of mankind. These and other forces make Mormonism a family-centered religion which ties the faith of the church to the indissoluble bonds of family unity and loyalty. This forges an incredibly complex system of pressures and intertwining values over which is superimposed the theological structure of the Mormon Church, which stands between the *average* Mormon and the attainment of "exaltation" or progression to godhood. (See chapter on Mormonism for a discussion of this.)

With such great psychological, economic and religious forces concentrated upon him, it is a courageous person indeed who shakes off these varied yokes and steps into the freedom of a genuine experience with the Son of God. But a growing number are doing just this as the Spirit of God continues to call out the Church which is Christ's Body.

Christian Science, unlike the two other cults we have considered, is neither interested in bestowing godhood (Mormonism) on its adherents or pushing the eschatological panic button of Armageddon incorporated (Jehovah's Witnesses).

Christian Science is an ingenious mixture of first century gnostic theology, eighteenth century Hegelian philosophy, and nineteenth century idealism woven into a redefined framework of Christian theology with an emphasis upon the healing of the body by the highly questionable practice of denying its objective material reality!

In Christian Science there is a complete separation between the objective world of physical reality (matter) and the spiritual world of supernatural existence (mind). Mrs. Eddy taught that "man in God's idea is already saved with an everlasting salvation."

Hence it is unnecessary for Christian Scientists to think of themselves as sinners in need of a salvation they believe is already theirs by virtue of the fact that "man is already saved" because he

is a reflection of the divine mind. However, in Christian Science there are disturbing psychological aberrations. Mrs. Eddy demanded of her followers that they abstain from any critical contact with the non-spiritual elements of the illusory material world. She forbade the reading of "obnoxious literature" lest Christian Scientists become convinced that the physical body and its diseases, suffering and inevitable death was real.

There is in Christian Science a subconscious repression, a disassociation or conscious putting out of one's mind certain things which are disconcerting to the entire configuration of psychological patterns of conditioning. Christian Scientists are conditioned to believe in the non-existence of the material world even though their senses testify to its objective reality. They continually affirm that matter has no true existence, and thus, in a very real sense, entertain a type of religious schizophrenia. One side of their personality testifies to the reality of the material world and its inexorable decay, while the conditioning process of Christian Science theology hammers relentlessly to suppress this testimony and affirm that the only true reality is spiritual or mental.

In Margaret Mitchell's classic novel, *Gone With the Wind,* Scarlet O'Hara, the heroine, when confronted with the harsh realities of life in the wake of the Civil War repeatedly states, "I'll think about that tomorrow," as if not thinking about it today would eliminate the reality of its claim at that moment.

When working with sensory data Christian Scientists totally disassociate their religious convictions, for, if they did not, they would not continue to feed, clothe or house their bodies. But in still another sense, they attempt to master the all too obvious frailties of the body by the application of a religion which denies the material reality of that body. A psychologist of the behaviorist school in one sense does the same thing. In the office he may talk about "conditioning" and may associate everything, including his home, with mechanistic psychology; however, at home he still loves his wife and children, and doesn't respond in that same manner. This is one of the chief reasons why Christian Scientists sometimes appear to be almost immune to the conviction of personal guilt as a result of sin. Guilt implies the threat of judgment and a standard which is the basis of that judgment; hence the reality of the concept of sin which is transgression of the law of God. Christian Scientists desperately want only a "good" world, a pleasant place full of happiness, life, love and security. This they can have only if they deny the empirical evidence of the opposites of those concepts. In effect they affirm the reality of "good" at the expense of the antithesis of "good," as if by denying the existence of evil one had annihilated evil!

There can be no doubt that there is "selective perception" in the mind of the Christian Scientist which enables him to select those things which are of a metaphysical nature, disassociate them from the sense perception of the physical world, and still maintain his idealistic philosophy and gnostic theology. This he accomplishes by repressing or suppressing any evidence to the contrary.

By following Mrs. Eddy's advice and avoiding what she would call "obnoxious literature," i.e., evidence which controverts the idealism of Christian Science philosophy, Christian Scientists avoid facing the damaging data of physical reality. It is in effect an act of unconscious suppression utilized in order to escape the data. Concluding our thoughts in this area we might say that in the kingdom of the cults we are actually seeing a mosaic of abnormal conditioned behavior patterns that express themselves in a theological framework, utilizing Christian terms perverted by re-definition and represented as "new insight" when in truth they are only old errors with new faces. The defense mechanisms on a psychological level are apparent when one considers the background and vocabulary of the cult systems. There exists, beyond a question of a doubt, an abnormal behavior syndrome operating in the mentality of most cultists, which causes the cultist (in the case of Christian Scientists) to build his theological system upon a preconditioned and artificially induced criterion of evaluation, i.e., the divine mission and inspiration of Mary Baker Eddy. In the case of other cultists, the names Joseph Smith, "Pastor" Russell, Brigham Young, or any other cult authority figure could be supplied and the conditioned reflex would be virtually the same.

There are many more observations which could be made but space will not permit. It is my hope that in observing and analyzing the facets of cult behavior patterns already discussed, the reader may obtain a deeper insight and appreciation of the psychological structure of cultism as it continues to influence a growing segment of professing Christendom which is ill prepared for the subtleties and dangers of such psychological and theological deviations.

Chapter 4

JEHOVAH'S WITNESSES AND THE WATCH TOWER

A BRIEF HISTORY OF THE WATCH TOWER BIBLE AND TRACT SOCIETY, — JEHOVAH'S WITNESSES

Charles Taze Russell was the founder of what is now Jehovah's Witnesses and the energetic administrator that brought about its far-flung organization. The name Jehovah's Witnesses, incidentally, was taken at Columbus, Ohio, in 1931, to differentiate between the Watch Tower and the true followers of Russell as represented by The Dawn Bible Students.[1] C. T. Russell was born on February 16, 1852, the son of Joseph L. and Anna Eliza Russell, and spent most of his early years in Pittsburgh and Allegheny, Pennsylvania, where at the age of 25 he was known to be manager of several men's furnishings stores. At an early age he rejected the doctrine of eternal torment, probably because of the severe indoctrination he had received as a Congregationalist, and as a result of this act entered upon a long and varied career of denunciation aimed at "Organized Religions." In 1870, at the age of 18, Russell organized a Bible class in Pittsburgh which in 1876 elected him "Pastor" of the group. From 1876 to 1878 the "Pastor" was assistant editor of a small Rochester, New York, monthly magazine, but resigned when a controversy arose over Russell's counter arguments on "the atonement" of Christ.

Shortly after leaving his position, Russell founded "Zion's Watch Tower" (1879) which is known today as "The Watch Tower Announcing Jehovah's Kingdom." From 6,000 in 1879 to the staggering figure of nearly 64,000,000[2] as of February, 1963 (approximation), this magazine has grown until it has surpassed even Russell's fondest dreams. In the year 1884 "Pastor" Russell incorporated "Zion's Watch Tower Tract Society" at Pittsburgh, Pennsylvania, which in 1886 published the first in a series[3] of seven books (Russell wrote six) entitled, *Studies in the Scriptures.* The sixth volume was published in 1904 and the seventh in 1917 after his death. The seventh volume, *The Finished Mystery,* caused a split in the organization, which culminated in a clean division, the larger group following J. F. Rutherford, the smaller remaining by itself. This group subsequently became "The Dawn Bible Students Association," which sponsors the coast-to-coast radio program, "Frank and Ernest," publishes *The Dawn* magazine (circulation over 20,000 per month), and has its headquarters and publishing plant in East Rutherford, N. J. Meanwhile, under Rutherford's leadership, the "Society" became known by its present name "Jehovah's Witnesses."

By July, 1963, The Watch Tower Bible and Tract Society founded (1896), which is the focal point of the organization, had known branches in more than

---

[1]And The Layman's Home Missionary Movement.

[2]*Awake* magazine, the other Watch Tower publication, has a yearly circulation of over 55 million copies, and is fast approaching

the circulation of *The Watch Tower. Awake* is circulated in 20 languages, *The Watch Tower* in 46.

[3]Originally titled "The Millennial Dawn."

34

92 lands, and missionary works and Kingdom preaching in over 214. Its literature is distributed in 110 languages, and it has become a great disseminator of propaganda and a challenge to the zeal of every Christian.

In the year 1908 the headquarters of the movement were transferred to Brooklyn, New York, where property was purchased (17 Hicks Street) and became known as "The Brooklyn Tabernacle." Large tracts of property were purchased by the Society on Columbia Heights, as it grew and prospered, until today whole blocks are in their possession. Among the other things the Society owns are: a large up-to-date printing plant which has produced more than *one and one-half billion* pieces of literature since its inauguration in 1928 and expansions in 1949 and 1957, a modern apartment building and office quarters; three "Kingdom Farms," which supply food, wood for furniture, etc.; a Bible school, "Gilead," which since its opening in 1943 has sent out approximately 8,000[4] missionaries of the Kingdom; and many more enterprises of like character. All employees in the factory are allowed $14.00 a month, receive room and board, and work for nothing — no salaries are paid.

During the years 1942-1952, the membership of Jehovah's Witnesses doubled in North America, multiplied fifteen times in South America, twelve times in the Atlantic islands, five times in Asia, seven times in Europe and Africa, and six times in the islands of the Pacific. By 1962 these figures had almost doubled. Such is the evolution of "Pastor" Russell's "Zion."

Russell continued his teachings until his death on October 31, 1916, aboard a transcontinental train in Texas. The erstwhile pastor had a remarkable life highly colored with legal entanglements, but not without success in his chosen field. In fairness to the reader and in the interest of truth, the following account is quoted from *The Brooklyn Daily Eagle,* November 1, 1916 (Obit. Column), and has been inserted at this point to authenticate beyond doubt the true history of Russell so that even his most devoted followers may realize the character of the man to whose teachings they have entrusted their eternal destiny.

A year after this publication, *The Watch Tower,* had been established Russell married Maria Ackley in Pittsburgh. She had become interested in him through his teachings, and she helped him in running the Watch Tower.

Two years later, in 1881, came "The Watch Tower Bible and Tract Society," the agency through which in later years "Pastor" Russell's sermons were published (as advertisements) in newspapers throughout the world. This Society progressed amazingly under the joint administration of husband and wife, but in 1897 Mrs. Russell left her husband. Six years later, in 1903, she sued for separation. The decree was secured in 1906 following sensational testimony and "Pastor" Russell was scored by the courts. There was much litigation then that was quite undesirable from the "Pastor's" point of view regarding alimony for his wife, but it was settled in 1909 by the payment of $6,036 to Mrs. Russell. The litigation revealed that "Pastor" Russell's activities in the religious field were carried on through several subsidiary societies and that all of the wealth which flowed into him through these societies was under the control of a holding company in which the "Pastor" held $990 of the $1,000 capital and two of his followers the other $10.

Thus Russell apparently controlled the entire financial power of the Society and was not accountable to anyone.

The *Eagle* column goes on to say:

After the "work" had been well started here, "Pastor" Russell's Watch Tower publication advertised wheat seed for sale at $1.00 a pound. It was styled "Miracle Wheat," and it was asserted that it would grow five times as much as any other

---

[4]The Watch Tower recently started special classes for women ministers at Gilead for the first time.

brand of wheat. There were other claims made for the wheat seed, and the followers were advised to purchase it, the proceeds to go to the Watch Tower and be used in publishing the "Pastor's" sermons.

The *Eagle* first made public the facts about this new venture of the Russellites and it published a cartoon picturing the "Pastor" and his "Miracle Wheat" in such a way that "Pastor" Russell brought suit for libel, asking $100,000 damages. Government departments investigated the wheat for which $1.00 a pound was asked, and agents of the Government were important witnesses at the trial of the libel suit in January, 1913. The "Miracle Wheat" was low in the Government tests, they said. The *Eagle* won the suit.

Prior to entering court the *Eagle* had said,

The *Eagle* goes even further and declares that at the trial it will show that "Pastor" Russell's religious cult is nothing more than a money-making scheme.

The court's decision vindicated the *Eagle's* statement and proved its reliability.

All during this time the "Pastor's" sermons were being printed in newspapers throughout the world, notably when he made a tour of the world in 1912 and caused accounts to be published in his advertised sermons telling of enthusiastic greetings at the various places he visited. It was shown in many cases that the sermons were never delivered in the places that were claimed.

For the benefit of any naïve Jehovah's Witness who may think that the "Miracle Wheat" fraud is an invention of the "jealous religionists" who are trying to defame the "Pastor's" memory, we document the scandal, trial, and verdict as follows:

From *The Brooklyn Daily Eagle,* obtainable at the Montague Street branch of the Brooklyn Public Library —

(1) January 1, 1913, pages 1, 2. Miracle Wheat Scandal.

(2) January 22, 1913, page 2. Testimony of Russellite beliefs.
(3) January 23, 24, 1913, page 3. Testimony on wheat.
(4) January 25, 1913, page 16. Financial statements proving Russell's absolute control, made by Secretary-Treasurer Van Amberg.
(5) *Van Amberg's statement*:
"... We are not responsible to anyone for our expenditures. We are responsible only to God."
(6) January 27, 1913, page 3. Government experts testify on "Miracle Wheat" and ascertain beyond doubt that it is not miraculous or overly excellent.
(7) January 28, 1913, page 2. Prosecution and Defense sum-up. Russell assailed, but not present to hear it.
(8) January 29, 1913, page 16, Russell loses libel suit.[5]

The Brooklyn *Eagle* led the fight to expose the hypocrisy of "Pastor" Russell and nothing could be more appropriate than their on-the-spot testimony as to his many fraudulent claims.[6] The following documentary evidence is taken from *The Brooklyn Daily Eagle,* page 18, February 19, 1912, and is titled "Pastor Russell's Imaginary Sermons — Printed Reports of Addresses in Foreign Lands that He Never Made — One at Hawaii, a Sample." These excerpts concern the Pastor's "World Tour" and are very enlightening with respect to his reliability and truthfulness.

"Pastor" Russell, who has found the atmosphere of Brooklyn uncongenial ever since the *Eagle* published the facts concerning his methods and morals, is making some new records in the far parts of the world. He is delivering sermons to imaginary audiences on tropical islands and completing "searching investigations" into the missions of China and Japan by spending a few hours in each country.

---

[5] In recent years *The Watch Tower* has maintained that Russell never made a cent on the "Miracle Wheat," and that it was a contribution to the Society — "as open and above board as a church cake sale." They characteristically omit the fact that Russell controlled the Watch Tower, owning 990 of the 1,000 shares of its stock; therefore, any

contributions to it were actually to him. This fact explodes nicely another Watch Tower attempt to dodge the issue.

[6] Some Watch Tower adherents deny the documentation of the above listed newspaper editions, but they are on microfilm and are available for confirmation.

Following the *Eagle's* exposing "Pastor" Russell's "Miracle Wheat" enterprise and the publication of the testimony on the basis of which Mrs. Russell obtained a separation and alimony, the "Pastor" developed the "world tour" idea. He set his printing plant to work to get out advance literature, huge bundles of which were sent to every place where he intended to appear. Then he contracted for advertising space in many American newspapers to print his imaginary sermons.

His first stop after sailing from the Pacific Coast was Honolulu. And Presto! — the newspapers in which advertising space had been engaged printed long cable dispatches which presented the "Pastor's" discourses. In one paper which printed the advertisement the opening sentences read "Honolulu Hawaiian Islands:

"The International Bible Students Committee of Foreign Mission investigation stopped at Honolulu and made observations. Pastor Russell, Chairman of the Committee, delivered a public address. He had a large audience and attentive hearing."

Then follows the sermon, full of local color and allusions to the "Paradise of the Pacific":

"I can now well understand [the printed report makes the 'Pastor' say] why your beautiful island is 'The Paradise of the Pacific.' I note your wonderful climate and everything which contributes to bring about this Paradise likeness."

And so on for two columns.

It has long been known that "Pastor" Russell has a strong imagination, but now it appears that he is even capable of delivering imaginary sermons. *Pastor Russell never spoke in Honolulu during the few hours that his ship stopped there to take on coal.* In the hope of securing an accurate report of his sermon, the *Eagle* wrote to the editor of the *Hawaiian Star*, which is published in Honlulu.

The following reply was shortly thereafter received:

"In answer to your inquiry of December 19th concerning Pastor Russell, I would say that he was here for a few hours with a Bible students' committee of foreign mission investigation, but did not make a public address as was anticipated." Walter G. Smith, Editor, *Star*.

(On page 18 of the same edition of the *Eagle*, February 19, 1912, photographically reproduced evidence of the

"imaginary sermon" and Editor Smith's letter branding it a *lie* can be found by the interested reader and leave no doubt as to "Pastor" Russell's character.

Tour of Orient branded huge advertising scheme.

As to the "Pastor's" methods of carrying Russellism to the heathen and the speed with which his searching investigations into the missions of the world are being conducted, the *Japan Weekly Chronicle* of January 11 supplies some interesting information. After explaining how the office of the paper had for weeks been bombarded with Russell literature and advance agents with contracts "just as if the reverend gentleman were an unregenerate theatrical company" the *Chronicle* says:

"These gentlemen arrived in Japan on Saturday the 30th December. On the following day 'Pastor' Russell delivered a sermon in Tokyo entitled 'Where are the Dead?' which, though the title is a little ambiguous, does not seem to have any special connection with the mission work. On Monday it is assumed that the mission work in Japan was begun and finished, for the next day seems to have been devoted to traveling, and on Wednesday 'Pastor' Russell and his co-adjutors left Kobe for China in the same vessel in which they had arrived in Yokohama . . . the truth is that the whole expedition is merely a huge advertising scheme!"

(See *The Brooklyn Daily Eagle*, January 11, 1913.)

Russell carried on many such advertising stunts, and despite his protestations about earthly governments and laws being organizations of the devil, he was always the first to claim their protection when it was convenient for him to do so.

To mention one instance in addition to the *Eagle* suit, Russell brought suit for "defamatory libel" against the Reverend J. J. Ross, pastor of the James Street Baptist Church of Hamilton, Ontario, when the fearless minister wrote a blistering pamphlet denouncing Russell's theology and personal life. Russell lost this attempt (see *The Brooklyn Daily Eagle*, January 11, 1913) with J. F. Rutherford as his attorney. For the benefit of the interested reader, at this time we recount the facts concerning the libel suit as it actually occurred.

In June, 1912, the Reverend J. J. Ross, Pastor of the James Street Baptist Church, Hamilton, Ontario, published a pamphlet entitled, "Some facts about the Self-Styled 'Pastor' Charles T. Russell" which minced no words in its denunciation of Russell, his qualifications as a minister, or his moral example as a "Pastor." Russell promptly sued Ross for "defamatory libel" in an effort to silence the courageous minister before the pamphlet could gain wide circulation and expose his true character and the errors of his theology. Mr. Ross, however, was unimpressed by Russell's action and eagerly seized upon the opportunity as a means of exposing Russell for the fraud he was. In his pamphlet, Ross assailed Russell's teachings as revealed in "Studies in the Scriptures" as "the destructive doctrines of one man who is neither a scholar nor a theologian" (page 7). Mr. Ross scathingly denounced Russell's whole system as "anti-rational, anti-scientific, anti-Biblical, anti-Christian, and a deplorable perversion of the gospel of God's Dear Son" (page 7).

Continuing his charges in the pamphlet, Ross exposed Russell as a pseudo-scholar and philosopher who "never attended the higher schools of learning; knows comparatively nothing of philosophy, systematic or historical theology, and is totally ignorant of the dead languages" (pages 3,4). It must be clearly understood at this point by the reader that in a libel suit of the type pursued by Russell, the plaintiff (Russell) had to *prove* that the charges lodged against him by the defendant (Ross) were not true. It is significant to note that Russell lost his suit against Ross when the High Court of Ontario, in session March, 1913, ruled that there were no grounds for libel; and "the case was thrown out of Court by the evidence furnished by 'Pastor' Russell himself" (page 15).[7]

"Pastor" Russell refused to give any evidence to substantiate his "case" and the only evidence offered was Russell's own statements, made under oath and during cross examination by Ross's lawyer, Counsellor Staunton. By denying Ross's charges, Russell automatically claimed high scholastic ascendancy, recognized theological training (systematic and historical), working knowledge of the dead languages (Greek, Hebrew, etc.), and valid ordination by a recognized body (page 18).[8] To each part of Mr. Ross's pamphlet (and all was read) Russell entered vigorous denials, with the exception of the "Miracle Wheat Scandal" which he affirmed as having "a grain of truth in a sense" to it (page 17).[9] "Pastor" Russell had at last made a serious mistake. He had testified under oath before Almighty God, and had sworn to tell "the truth, the whole truth, and nothing but the truth." He was soon to regret his testimony and stand in jeopardy as a perjurer, an unpleasant experience for the "Pastor" which more than explains his aversion to the witness chair.

In order to clarify the evidence as irrefutable, I refer any curious doubters to the files of the High Court of Ontario — Russell vs. Ross — "defamatory libel," March 17, 1913. Jehovah's Witnesses cannot deny this documentary evidence; it is too well substantiated. This is no "religionist scheme" to "smear" the "Pastor's" memory; I offer it as open proof of their founder's inherent dishonesty and lack of morals, that they may see the type of man to whose doctrines they have committed their eternal souls.

[7]*Some Facts and More Facts About the Self-Styled Pastor—Charles T. Russell.* Mr. Ross's second pamphlet.

[8]*Ibid.*

[9]*Ibid.*

The following reference quotations are taken in part from Mr. Ross's second pamphlet entitled *Some Facts and More Facts About the Self-Styled Pastor — Charles T. Russell:*

But now what are the facts as they were brought out by the examination on March 17, 1913? As to his scholastic standing he (Russell) had sworn that what was said about it was not true. Under the examination, he admitted that at most he had attended school only seven years of his life at the public school, and that he had left school when he was about fourteen years of age . . .

The cross examination of Russell continued for five hours. Here is a sample of how the "Pastor" answered. The following reproduction of the Russell vs. Ross transcript relative to the perjury charge made against Russell is taken from a copy on file in the headquarters of the cult in Brooklyn and is presented in the interests of thorough investigation.

Question: (Attorney Staunton) — "Do you know the Greek alphabet?"
Answer: (Russell) — "Oh yes."
Question: (Staunton) — "Can you tell me the correct letters if you see them?"
Answer: (Russell)—"Some of them, I might make a mistake on some of them."
Question: (Staunton)—"Would you tell me the names of those on top of the page, page 447 I have got here?"
Answer: (Russell) — "Well, I don't know that I would be able to."
Question: (Staunton) — "You can't tell what those letters are, look at them and see if you know?"
Answer: (Russell)—"My way . . ." [he was interrupted at this point and not allowed to explain]
Question: (Staunton) — "Are you familiar with the Greek language?"
Answer: (Russell) — "No."

It should be noted from this record of the testimony that Russell frequently contradicted himself, claiming first to "know" the Greek alphabet, then claiming under pressure that he might make mistakes in identifying the letters, and then finally admitting that he couldn't read the alphabet at all

when confronted with a copy of it.

From this it is easy to see that Russell did not "know" the Greek alphabet in any proper sense of the term, since it is assumed that when we say we "know" the English alphabet, for example, we shall be able upon request to name the letters by their correct titles.

"Pastor" Russell in failing to name the letters of the Greek alphabet, therefore, proved himself a perjurer, for he had previously stated that he "knew" them, thereby implying the ability to recite them, which he could *not* do.

It makes very little difference, therefore, whether the Watch Tower wants to admit Russell's guilt or not since their own transcript shows that Russell said he "knew" what was later proved he did not know.

Here is conclusive evidence; the "Pastor" under oath perjured himself beyond question. Can one sincerely trust the teachings of a man who thought nothing of such evidence?

This, however, was not all of Russell's testimony, and as Counselor Staunton pressed him further the "Pastor" admitted that he knew *nothing* about Latin and Hebrew, and that he had never taken a course in philosophy or systematic theology much less attended schools of higher learning. Bear in mind now that Russell a short time before had sworn he *did* have such knowledge by denying Mr. Ross's allegations. But there was no way out now; the "Pastor" was caught in a bold-faced fabrication and he knew it. However, all was not over yet. It will be remembered that Russell claimed "ordination" and equal if not superior status to ordained and accredited ministers. Counselor Staunton next smashed this illusion by demanding that Russell answer "Yes" or "No" to the following questions:

Question: (Ross' lawyer) — "Is it true you were never ordained?"
Answer: (Russell)—"It is not true."

It was necessary at this point for

Counselor Staunton to appeal to the magistrate in order to make Russell answer the question directly. The magistrate presiding ruled that Russell must answer the questions put to him. Here is the result of the cross-examination.

Question: (Counselor Staunton) — "Now, you never were ordained by a bishop, clergyman, presbytery, council, or any body of men living?"
Answer: (Russell, after a long pause) — "I never was."

Once again Russell's "unswerving" honesty received a rude blow; the situation was out of his hands and Russell stood helpless as Counselor Staunton wrung statement after statement from him which established him beyond doubt as a pre-meditated perjurer. Russell further swore that his wife had not divorced him, and that the Court had not granted alimony from him, a statement he soon regretted when Counselor Staunton forced him to admit that the Court did divorce[10] him from his wife, and did award his wife alimony. The evidence was in; the case was clear; Russell was branded a perjurer by the Court's verdict "No Bill." As a result of the Court's action Mr. Ross's charges were proven true and the real character of Russell was revealed, that of a man who had no scruples about lying under oath and whose doctrines were admittedly based on no sound educational knowledge of the subject in question. Much evidence is available concerning Russell's moral life, but I see no reason to inject lewdness into the text. The character of the man is evident for all to see.

The easily offended "Pastor" might have practiced what he preached for once and heeded Christ's injunction concerning the patient enduring of "reviling and persecution" (Matthew 5: 11, 12), but in Russell's case it is not at all applicable. However, Russell took every opportunity to make money, and legal clashes were frequent as a

result. He maneuvered masterfully just one jump ahead of the law and had it not been for Rutherford, who was a clever lawyer, the "Pastor" might not have been so fortunate. Russell hid, whenever cornered, behind the veil of a martyr for religious toleration, and despite the denunciation of churches and ministers he somehow succeeded in escaping the effects of damaging publicity. The Christian Church fought him openly but without the unified effort needed to squelch his bold approach. Some churches and pastors were united (see *The Brooklyn Daily Eagle,* January 2, 1913, page 18) and called for Russell's silencing as a menace. The "Pastor" was also deported from Canada because he hindered mobilization (see *The Daily Standard Union,* November 1, 1916), and in the early stages of World War I he was a prominent conscientious objector as all of his followers (Jehovah's Witnesses) still are today.

As a speaker, Russell swayed many; as a theologian, he impressed no one competent; as a man, he failed before the true God. Russell traveled extensively, spoke incessantly, and campaigned with much energy for "a great awakening" among the people of the world. In the course of his writings and lectures Russell denied many of the cardinal doctrines of the Bible — the Trinity, the Deity of Christ, the physical Resurrection and Return of Christ, eternal punishment, the reality of Hell, the eternal existence of the soul and the validity of the infinite Atonement, to state a few. The honest fact is that Russell had no training or education to justify his interpretation of Scripture. By this it is not meant that great education is a necessary qualification for exegesis, but when a man contradicts practically every major doctrine of the Bible he ought to have the education needed to defend (if that is pos-

[10]Neither party, however, obtained an absolute decree.

sible) his arguments. "Pastor" Russell did not have that knowledge, or even the qualifications for ordination by any recognized body. The title "Pastor" was assumed, not earned, and to document this fact we quote from the November 1, 1916, edition of *The Brooklyn Daily Eagle.* "Although he styled himself a 'pastor' and was so addressed by thousands of followers all over the world, he had never been ordained and had no ministerial standing in any other religious sect than his own."

Psychologically, the man was an egotist whose imagination knew no bounds and who is classed (by his followers) along with St. Paul, Wycliff and Luther as a great expounder of the Gospel. These are trite words for a man who proffered his writings as necessary for a clear understanding of the Scriptures and who once declared that it would be better to leave the Scriptures unread and read his books, rather than to read the Scriptures and neglect his books.

For the benefit of those so naïve as to believe that the "Pastor" did not make such a claim, we document the above assertion from *The Watch Tower,* September 15, 1910, page 298, where the "Pastor" makes the following statement concerning his "Studies in the Scriptures" and their "indispensable" value when examining the Bible.

If the six volumes of "Scripture Studies" are practically the Bible, topically arranged with Bible proof texts given, we might not improperly name the volumes "The Bible in an Arranged Form." That is to say, they are not mere comments on the Bible, but *they are practically the Bible* itself. Furthermore, not only do we find that *people cannot see the divine plan in studying the Bible by itself,* but we see, also, that if anyone lays the "Scripture Studies" aside, even after he has used them, after he has become familiar with them, after he has read them for ten years — if he then lays them aside and ignores them and goes to the Bible alone, though he has understood his Bible for ten years, our experience shows that within two years *he goes into darkness.* On the other hand, if he had merely read the "Scripture Studies" with their references and *had not read a page of the Bible as such,* he would be in the *light* at the end of two years, because he would have the light of the Scriptures.[11]

Nowhere was Russell's egotism or boldness better revealed than in that statement. Think of it — according to the "Pastor" it is impossible to understand God's plan of salvation independent of Russellite theology, and to relegate one's study to the Bible alone void of Russell's interpretations is to walk in darkness at the end of two years. But there is a ray of hope for all those foolish enough to study God's Word alone. If all will adopt Russellism as a guide in Biblical interpretation, mankind will enter into a "new" Kingdom Age; for then, by virtue of the "Pastor's" expositions, true understanding of the Bible's basic doctrines will have been arrived at. To quote Mr. Ross: "This inspiration has its origin in the pit" (page 42).

Jehovah's Witnesses pursue this same line of theological interpretation today. Russellism did not die with Charles Taze Russell; it lives under the new title "The Watch Tower Announcing Jehovah's Kingdom." The "Pastor's" dream has survived its author and remains today a living challenge to all Christians everywhere. Let us recognize it for what it is and unmask the unsound principles upon which it stands.

Upon Russell's death the helm of leadership was manned by Judge Joseph Franklin Rutherford, who acquitted himself nobly in the eyes of the Society by attacking the doctrines of "organized religion" with unparalleled vigor, and whose radio talks, phonograph recordings, numerous books, and resounding blasts against Christendom reverberated down the annals of the organization until his death on January

11Emphasis is ours.

8, 1942, from cancer, at his palatial mansion, "Beth Sarim," in San Diego, California. He was 72. Rutherford's career was no less amazing than Russell's, for the Judge was an adversary of no mean proportions, whether in action against "organized religion" which he termed "rackets" or against those who questioned his decisions in the Society.

Throughout the years following Russell's death, Rutherford rose in power and popularity among the "Russellites" and to oppose him was tantamount to questioning the authority of Jehovah Himself. An example of this one-man sovereignty concerns the friction that occurred in the movement when Rutherford denounced Russell's pyramid prophecies scheme as an attempt to find God's will outside the Scriptures (1929). Many followers of Russell's theory left the Society as a result of this action by Rutherford, only to be witheringly blasted by the vituperative Judge, who threatened that they would "suffer destruction" if they did not repent and recognize Jehovah's will as expressed through the Society. (*See The Kingdom*, page 14, by J. F. Rutherford, 1933.)

Rutherford also approached at times the inflated egotism of his predecessor Russell, and especially when, in his textbook *Why Serve Jehovah?* (page 62) he declared in effect that he was the mouth-piece of Jehovah for this age and that God had designated His words as the expression of divine mandate. It is indeed profitable to observe that Rutherford, as do all would-be "incarnations of infallibility," manifested unfathomable ignorance of God's express injunctions, especially against the preaching of "any other gospel" (Galatians 1:8,9).

Fear of retaliation or rebuke was never characteristic of Judge Rutherford, and quite often he displayed complete contempt for all "religions" and their leaders. Lashing out against

the persecution of "The Witnesses" in 1933, the tireless Judge challenged the Pope or any qualified representative of the Roman Catholic Church to debate with him on the plight of "Jehovah's Witnesses" (*Religious Intolerance — Why?*, page 41, by J. F. Rutherford). Needless to say, he was ignored. Rutherford also battled against the Federal Council of the Churches of Christ in the U.S.A. and even offered to pay half the time cost for a radio debate on the subject of persecution (*Jehovah's Witnesses — Why Persecuted?*, page 41). When ignored, Rutherford abated for a time. Few things, however, were allowed to dampen the Judge's vociferous thunderings and even a term in Atlanta Federal Penitentiary for violation of the "Espionage Act" in 1918, failed to silence the Judge's attacks. Rutherford was released from Atlanta in March, 1919, and returned to the Witnesses fold a martyr-hero, a complex readily appropriated by all Witnesses upon the slightest pretext. Indeed they enjoy greatly playing the role of persecuted saints. One only regrets that some of our less prudent administrators have so obligingly accommodated them.

The person of J. F. Rutherford, then, in the light of these facts, cannot be ignored in any true evaluation which seeks valid data concerning the Society's history. The great personal magnetism and the air of mystery which surround the man account most probably for his success as a leader, for he was almost a legendary figure even during his lifetime. The Judge shunned photographs, although he was most photogenic and presented both an imposing and impressive figure when attired in his familiar wing collar, bow tie and black suit. Reading glasses, which hung on a string across his honor's portly profile, accentuated the illusion of dignified importance, along with the title of Judge, which, contrary to popular opinion, he did hold from the days of his early legal career, when he was a special judge of the Eighth Judicial Circuit Court of Boonville, Missouri. Rutherford also possessed a deep, powerful voice which was capable of holding large audiences with its crescendo-like effect — but he seldom appeared in public and lived a closely guarded private life. Toward the end of his life, Rutherford's reign was not overly smooth, notably when the deposed head of the Witnesses' legal staff, Mr. Olin Moyle, sued Rutherford and several members of the Watch Tower's Board of Directors in 1939 for libel and won his case, a judgment of $25,-000, in 1944, two years after Rutherford's demise.

In comparing Russell and Rutherford it must be noted that the former was a literary pygmy compared to his successor. Russell's writings (approximation) were distributed, some fifteen or twenty million copies of them, over a period of sixty years, but Rutherford's in half that time were many times that amount. The prolific Judge wrote over one hundred books and pamphlets and his works as of 1941 had been translated into eighty languages. This, then, was the Society's second great champion, who, regardless of his many failings, was truly an unusual man by any standards. Russell and Rutherford are the two key figures in the Society's history, and without them no doubt the organization would never have come into existence. But conjecture never eliminated a problem, and Jehovah's Witnesses are now a problem with which every intelligent Christian must cope.

The new president of the combined organization is Nathan H. Knorr, who was elected president after Rutherford's death. Mr. Knorr is responsible for the Gilead Missionary Training School in South Lansing, New York, and has

addressed 252,000 persons at the International Convention of Jehovah's Witnesses in Yankee Stadium and the Polo Grounds in New York City, held August, 1958. Mr. Knorr is following diligently in the footsteps of Russell and Rutherford, and under his tutelage Christianity can expect much opposition in the future.

One of the most distressing traits manifested in the literature and teachings of Jehovah's Witnesses is their seemingly complete disregard for historical facts and dependable literary consistency. At the same time, however, they condemn all religious opponents as "enemies of God"[12] and perpetrators of what they term "a racket."[13]

For some time now the author has been considerably disturbed by Jehovah's Witnesses' constant denial of any theological connection whatsoever with "Pastor" Charles T. Russell, their admitted founder and first president of The Watch Tower Bible and Tract Society. Since Russell was long ago proven to be a perjurer under oath, a sworn adversary of historic Christianity, and a scholastic fraud, it is obvious why the Witnesses seek to avoid his influence and memory whenever possible. Be that as it may, however, some light should be thrown on the repeated self-contradictions which are committed by the Witnesses, in their zeal to justify their position and the ever-wavering doctrines to which they hold. It is my contention that they are following the basic teachings of Charles T. Russell in relation to many Biblical doctrines which he denied, and from their own publication I shall document this accusation.

In their eagerness to repudiate the charge of "Russellism," the Witnesses dogmatically say: ". . . but who is preaching the teaching of Pastor Russell? *Certainly not* Jehovah's Witnesses!

---

[12] J. F. Rutherford, *Deliverance*, p. 91; also *Religion*, pp. 263, 268.

[13] *Religion*, pp. 88, 104, 133, 137, 140, 141, etc.

They cannot be accused of following him, for they *neither quote him as an authority nor publish nor distribute his writings.*"[14] This is the statement of the Witnesses' magazine. Now let us compare this with history, and the truth will be plainly revealed.

Historically, Jehovah's Witnesses have quoted "Pastor" Russell numerous times since his death in 1916. The following is a token sample of what we can produce as concrete evidence. In 1923, seven years after the "Pastor's" demise, Judge J. F. Rutherford, then heir apparent to the Russellite throne, wrote a booklet some fifty-odd pages in length, entitled *World Distress — Why and the Remedy.* In this informative treatise, the new president of The Watch Tower Bible and Tract Society and the International Bible Students quoted "Pastor" Russell no less than *sixteen* separate times; referred to his books, *Studies in the Scriptures* over *twelve* times; and devoted *six* pages at the end of the booklet to advertising these same volumes. Further than this, in a fifty-seven-page pamphlet published in 1925 and entitled *Comfort for the People,* by the same Rutherford, "his honor," in true Russellite character, defines clergymen as "dumb dogs (D.D.)," proceeds to quote "Pastor" Russell's prophetical chronology (1914 A.D.),[15] and then sums up his tirade against Christendom universal by recommending Russell's writing in *four* pages of advertisements at the rear of the book.

The dark specter of historical facts thus begins to creep across the previously happy picture of a "Russell-free"[16] movement. But let us further consult history. In the year 1927, The

Watch Tower Bible and Tract Society published Judge Rutherford's "great" literary effort entitled *Creation,* which was circulated into the millions of copies, and in which this statement appeared concerning "Pastor" Russell:

The second presence of Christ dates from about 1874.

From that time forward many of the truths long obscured by the enemy began to be restored to the honest Christian.

As William Tyndale was used to bring the Bible to the attention of the people, so the Lord used Charles T. Russell to bring to the attention of the people an understanding of the Bible particularly of those truths that had been taken away by the machinations of the devil and his agencies. Because it was the Lord's due time to restore these truths, he used Charles T. Russell to write and publish books known as *Studies in the Scriptures* by which the great fundamental truths of the divine plan are clarified. Satan has done his best to destroy these books because they *explain* the Scriptures. Even as Tyndale's Version of the Bible was destroyed by the clergy, so the clergy in various parts of the earth have gathered together thousands of volumes of *Studies in the Scriptures* and burned them publicly. But such wickedness has only served to advertise the truth of the divine plan.

Please consider, if you will, this statement by the then president of the Jehovah's Witnesses organization. Rutherford plainly quotes Russell and his writings as authoritative material, yet *The Watch Tower* today claims *that Jehovah's Witnesses are free* from the taint of "Russellism"!

Concluding this brief historical synopsis of the Watch Tower Society's past, we quote the grand finale of J. F. Rutherford's funeral oration over the

---

[14]*Awake,* May 8, 1951, page 26.

[15]Jehovah's Witnesses still hold today and teach it as dogma.

[16]In recent years, Jehovah's Witnesses have been forced openly to acknowledge Russell owing to the effect of my book *Jehovah of the Watch Tower,* which gave the true history of Russell's infamous doings, thus necessitating an answer from the Witnesses, even if it was an unreliable one in many respects and highly colored. The historical series was run in *The Watch Tower* for some months and was entitled "A Modern History of Jehovah's Witnesses." It was a very weak apologetic.

prostrate remains of "dear brother Russell" who, according to the floral sign by his casket, remained "faithful unto death." Said the Judge: "Our brother sleeps not in death, but was instantly changed from the human to the divine nature, and is now forever with the Lord." This episode in Jehovah's Witnesses' history is cited for its uniqueness, to show the adoration in which Russell was once held by the theological ancestors of those who deny his influence today.

Leaving the past history of the Witnesses, I shall now answer those who say: "The Society may have quoted him in the past, but that was before Judge Rutherford's death. We do not do it now, and after all, didn't we say 'neither quote . . . publish . . . nor distribute his writings'? This is in the *present* tense, not the past." This would, we agree, be a splendid refutation of our claims if it were true, but as we shall now conclusively prove, it is not! Not only did Jehovah's Witnesses quote the "Pastor" as an authority in the past, before Rutherford's death in 1942, but they have done it right up until 1953, eleven years *after* his death.

In the July 15, 1950, edition of *The Watch Tower* (page 216), the Witnesses quoted "Pastor" Russell as an authority regarding his chronology on the 2,520-year-reign of the Gentiles, which reign allegedly ended, according to his calculations (and Jehovah's Witnesses), in A.D. 1914. To make it an even more hopeless contradiction, they listed as their source, *The Watch Tower* of 1880, of which "Pastor" Russell was editor-in-chief! Now if they "do not consider his writings authoritative and do not circulate them," why (1) publish his chronology, (2) quote his publication as evidence and (3) admit his teachings on this vital point in their theology?

To shatter any misconception as to their literary shortcomings, I refer the interested reader to a pamphlet published by the Watch Tower, entitled *Jehovah's Witnesses, Communists or Christians?* (1953). Throughout the major content of this comparatively recent propaganda, Jehovah's Witnesses defend the thesis that they are not communists (which they are not), but, in their zeal to prove "their skirts clean," they quote "Pastor" Russell's writings no less than *five times,* refer to them with apparent pride *twice* (pages 4,5), and even mention *two* of his best-known works, *The Plan of the Ages* (1886), and *The Battle of Armageddon* (1897). Further than this, *The Watch Tower* of October 1, 1953, quotes "Pastor" Russell's *Studies in the Scriptures* (Vol. IV, page 554) (and Judge Rutherford's *Vindication* [Vol. II, page 311] —), convincing evidence indeed that *The Watch Tower* still follows the Russellite theology of its much denied founder. All this despite the fact that they say, in their own words, "Jehovah's Witnesses . . . neither quote him [Russell] as an authority nor publish nor distribute his writings" (*Awake.* page 26).

Through a careful perusal of these facts, it is a simple matter to determine that Jehovah's Witnesses have never stopped being "Russellites," no matter how loudly they proclaim the opposite. To those who are enmeshed in the Watch Tower's web, we can only say that you are *not* following a "new" Theocratic organization; you are following the old teachings of Charles Taze Russell, a bitter antagonist of historic Christianity, who has bequeathed to you a gospel of spiritual confusion. Those who are contemplating becoming members of the Watch Tower Society, we ask to weigh the evidence found here and elsewhere[17] and to judge for your-

[17]*Jehovah of the Watch Tower,* Martin and Klann (Grand Rapids: Zondervan Publishing House, 1956), Chapter I.

selves whether it is wiser to trust the plain teachings of the Scripture and the guidance of the Holy Spirit and the Christian Church or to cast your lot with a group of zealous but misled people who are "blindly leading the blind down the broad way which leads to destruction." These persons, it should be remembered have abandoned practically every cardinal doctrine of Biblical Christianity for the dogmatic doctrinal deviations of Charles Taze Russell and J. F. Rutherford. In the light of Holy Scripture, however, Russellism is shown to be a snare from whose grip only Jesus Christ can deliver.

This then is the history of Jehovah's Witnesses, the product of Charles Taze Russell, who, because he would not seek instruction in the Word of God, dedicated his unschooled talents to a lone vain search without the guidance of the Holy Spirit. This attempt has produced a cult of determined people who are persuaded in their own minds and who boldly attempt to persuade all others that the Kingdom of God is "present," and that they are Jehovah's Witnesses, the only *true* servants of the living God.

SOME OF THE DOCTRINES OF JEHOVAH'S WITNESSES

I. There is one solitary being from all eternity, Jehovah God, the Creator and Preserver of the Universe and of all things visible and invisible.

II. The Word or Logos is "a god," a mighty god, the "beginning of the Creation" of Jehovah, and His active agent in the creation of all things. The Logos was made human as the man Jesus and suffered death to produce the ransom or redemptive price for obedient men.

III. The Bible is the inerrant, infallible, inspired Word of God as it was originally given, and has been preserved by Him as the revealer of His purposes.

IV. Satan was a great angel who rebelled against Jehovah and challenged His Sovereignty. Through Satan, sin and death came upon man. His destiny is annihilation with all his followers.

V. Man was created in the image of Jehovah but willfully sinned, hence all men are born sinners and are "of the earth." Those who follow Jesus Christ faithful to the death will inherit the heavenly Kingdom with Him. Men of good will who accept Jehovah and His Theocratic Rule will enjoy the "new earth"; all others who reject Jehovah will be annihilated.

VI. The atonement is a ransom paid to Jehovah God by Christ Jesus and is applicable to all who accept it in righteousness. In brief, the death of Jesus removed the effects of Adam's sin on his offspring and laid the foundation of the New World of righteousness including the Millennium of Christ's reign.

VII. The man Christ Jesus was resurrected a divine spirit creature after offering the ransom for obedient man.

VIII. The soul of man is not eternal but mortal, and it can die. Animals likewise have souls, though man has the pre-eminence by Special creation.

IX. Hell, meaning a place of "fiery torment" where sinners remain after death until the resurrection, does not exist. This is a doctrine of "Organized Religion," not the Bible. Hell is the common grave of mankind, literally *sheol* (Hebrew), "a place of rest in hope" where the departed sleep until the resurrection by Jehovah God.

X. Eternal Punishment is a punishment or penalty of which there is no end. It does not mean "eternal torment" of living souls. Annihilation, the second death, is the lot of all those who reject Jehovah God and it is eternal.

XI. Jesus Christ has returned to earth A.D. 1914, has expelled Satan from Heaven and is proceeding to overthrow Satan's organization, establish the Theocratic Millennial Kingdom, and vindicate the name of Jehovah God. He did not return in a physical form and is invisible as the Logos.

XII. The Kingdom of Jehovah is Supreme, and as such cannot be compatible with present Human Government ("Devil's Visible Organization") and any allegiance to them in any way which violates the allegiance owed to Him, is a violation of the Scripture.

THE HOLY TRINITY

1 ". . . Such doctrine is not of God." *Let God Be True* (Rev. 1952). Published by Watch Tower Bible and Tract Society, Inc.; International Bible Students Association, Brooklyn, New York, U.S.A. Page 100.

2 "The obvious conclusion is . . . that Satan is the originator of the trinity doctrine." *Ibid.* Page 101.

3 ". . . Sincere persons who want to know the true God and serve Him find it a bit difficult to love and worship a complicated, freakish - looking, three-headed God." *Ibid.* Page 102.

4 "The trinity doctrine was not conceived by Jesus or the early Christians." *Ibid.* Page 111.

5 "The plain truth is that this is another of Satan's attempts to keep God-fearing persons from learning the truth of Jehovah and His Son, Christ Jesus. No, there is no trinity!" *Ibid.* Page 111.

6 "Such doctrine is altogether foreign to true Christianity." *What Has Religion Done for Mankind?* (Copyright 1951). Published as noted above. Page 268.

7 "Any trying to reason out the Trinity teaching leads to confusion of mind. So the Trinity teaching confuses the meaning of John 1:1, 2; it does not simplify it or make it clear or easily understandable." *"The Word" Who Is He? According to John* (Copyright 1962). Published as before noted. Page 7.

DEITY OF CHRIST

1 "Who ran the universe during the three days that Jesus was dead and in the grave . . . If Jesus was God, then during Jesus' death God was dead and in the grave . . . If Jesus was the immortal God, He could not have died." *Let God Be True* (Rev. 1952). Published as noted. Page 109.

2 " 'My Father is greater than I.' . . . means 'greater' not only as to office but also as to person." *Ibid.* Page 110.

3 "Being God's first creation, he was with the Father in heaven from the beginning of all creation. Jehovah God used him in the creating of all other things that have been created." *From Paradise Lost to Paradise Regained* (Copyright 1958). Pub. by W. T. B. & T. Soc. of New York, Inc.; I.B.S.A., Brooklyn, U.S.A. Pages 126, 127.

4 ". . . The Bible shows that there is only one God . . . 'greater than His Son.' . . . And that the Son, as the First-born, Only-begotten and 'the creation by God,' had a beginning. That the

Father is greater and older than the Son is reasonable, easy to understand and is what the Bible teaches." *Ibid.* Page 164.

5 ". . . Jesus was 'the Son of God.' Not God himself!" *"The Word" Who Is He?* Etc., as before noted. Page 20.

6 "The very fact that he was sent proves he was not equal with God but was less than God the Father." *Ibid.* Page 41.

7 "Certainly the apostle John was not so unreasonable as to say that someone ('the Word') was with some other individual ('God') and at the same time was that other individual ('God')." *Ibid.* Page 53.

THE HOLY SPIRIT

1 ". . . The holy spirit is the invisible active force of Almighty God which moves his servants to do his will." *Let God Be True,* as noted. Page 108.

2 ". . . The 'Holy Ghost' or Holy Spirit is God's active force . . . There is no basis for concluding that the Holy Spirit is a Person . . . (Page 24). *Watch Tower* article (Jan. 1, 1953). "The Scriptures, Reason, and the Trinity," quoted in *Jehovah of the Watch Tower,* as noted. Page 134.

3 "Far from teaching equality with Jehovah, the Scriptures show that the holy spirit is not even a person." *The Watch Tower,* July 15, 1957. Pub. by the Watch Tower Bible and Tract Society of Pennsylvania. Page 431.

4 "The fact is that the truth about the holy spirit has been beclouded by the prejudices of Bible translators." *Ibid.* Page 432.

5 ". . . God's holy spirit is not a God, not a member of a trinity, not coequal, and is not even a person . . . It is God's *active force,* not Jehovah's power residing within himself, but his energy when projected out from himself . . . It is not a blind, uncontrolled force, such as the forces of 'nature,' lightning, hurricanes and the like, but . . . is at all times under his control . . . and therefore may be likened to a radar beam." *Ibid.* Pages 432, 433.

THE VIRGIN BIRTH

1 "Mary was a virgin . . .

". . . When Joseph learned that Mary was going to have a child, he did not want to take her as his wife. But God's angel . . . said: '. . . That which has been begotten in her is by holy spirit . . .' . . . He took Mary his wife home. 'But he had no relations with her until she gave birth to a son.' — Matthew 1: 20-25." (NW) *From Paradise Lost to Paradise Regained,* as before noted. Pages 122, 123.

2 ". . . Jesus was conceived by a sinless, perfect Father, Jehovah God . . .

". . . The perfect child Jesus did not get human life from the sinner Adam, but received only a human body through Adam's descendant, Mary. Jesus' life came from Jehovah God, the Holy One.

". . . Jehovah took the perfect life of his only-begotten Son and transferred it from heaven to . . . the womb of the unmarried girl Mary . . . Thus God's Son was conceived or given a start as a human creature. It was a miracle. Under Jehovah's holy power the child Jesus, conceived in this way, grew in Mary's womb to the point of birth." *Ibid.* Pages 126, 127.

3 ". . . Jesus' birth on earth was not an incarnation . . . He emptied himself of all things heavenly and spiritual, and God's almighty spirit transferred his Son's life down to the womb of the Jewish virgin of David's descent. By this miracle he was born a man . . . He was not a spirit-human hybrid, a man and at the same time a spirit person. . . . He *was* flesh." *What Has Religion Done for Mankind?* as noted before. Page 231.

THE ATONEMENT

1 "The atonement is a ransom paid to Jehovah God by Christ Jesus and is applicable to all who accept it in righteousness. In brief, the death of Jesus removed the effects of Adam's sin on his offspring and laid the foundation of the New World of righteousness including the Millennium of Christ's reign." *Jehovah of the Watch Tower* by Martin & Klann (1963). Approved by Watch Tower. Page 30.

2 "That which is redeemed or bought back is what was lost, namely, perfect human life, with its rights and earthly prospects." *Let God Be True,* as noted before. Page 114.

3 ". . . Jesus as the glorified High Priest, by presenting in heaven this redemptive price, is in position to relieve the believing ones of Adam's descendants from the inherited disability under which all are born." *Ibid.* Page 119.

4 "The human life that Jesus Christ laid down in sacrifice must be exactly equal to that life which Adam forfeited for all his offspring. It must be a perfect human life, no more, no less . . . This is just what Jesus gave . . . for men of all kinds." *You May Survive Armageddon Into God's New World.* Pub. W. T. B. & T. S., Inc.; I.B.S.A., Brooklyn, N. Y., U.S.A., (Copyright 1955). Page 39.

SALVATION BY GRACE

1 "Those who follow Jesus Christ faithful to the death will inherit the heavenly Kingdom with Him. Men of good will who accept Jehovah and His Theocratic Rule will enjoy the 'new earth'; all others who reject Jehovah will be annihilated." *Jehovah of the Watch Tower* by Martin and Klann, as before noted. Statement approved by Watch Tower. Page 30.

2 "Immortality is a reward for faithfulness. It does not come automatically to a human at birth." *Let God Be True,* as noted. Page 74.

3 "Those people of good will today who avail themselves of the provision and who steadfastly abide in this confidence will find Christ Jesus to be their 'everlasting Father' (Isaiah 9:6)." *Ibid.* Page 121.

4 ". . . You must love Jehovah's universal sovereignty . . .; you must uphold it and proclaim it and remain true to it at all costs until it is vindicated. Only then may you survive Armageddon . . ." *You May Survive Armageddon, Etc.,* as noted. Page 30.

5 "We have learned that a person could fall away and be judged unfavorably either now or at Armageddon, or during the thousand years of Christ's reign, or at the end of the final test . . . into everlasting destruction." *From Paradise Lost to Paradise Regained,* as noted. Page 241.

THE RESURRECTION OF CHRIST

1 "This firstborn from the dead was raised from the grave, not a human creature, but a spirit." *Let God Be True,* as noted. Page 276.

2 ". . . Jehovah God raised him from the dead, not as a human Son, but as a mighty immortal spirit Son . . . For forty days after that he materialized, as angels before him had done, to show himself alive to his disciples . . ." *Ibid.* Page 40.

3 ". . . Jesus did not take his human body to heaven to be forever a man in heaven. Had he done so, that would have left him ever lower than the angels . . . God did not purpose for Jesus to be humiliated thus forever by being a fleshly man forever. No, but after he had sacrificed his perfect manhood, God raised him to deathless life as a glorious spirit creature." *Ibid.* Page 41.

4 "To sacrifice something means to give it up . . . Hence Jesus . . . could not have that body back again . . .

"Almighty God raised his son Jesus Christ from the dead an immortal spirit person . . . So to make himself visible and appear to his disciples for the forty days after his resurrection that they might be his witnesses, Jesus materialized different bodies on various occasions to show he was alive but no longer a human creature." *What Has Religion Done for Mankind?* as noted. Pages 259, 260.

5 "Usually they could not at first tell it was Jesus, for he appeared in different bodies. He appeared and disappeared just as angels had done, because he was resurrected as a spirit creature. Only because Thomas would not believe did Jesus appear in a body like that in which he had died . . ." *From Paradise Lost to Paradise Regained,* as noted. Page 144.

THE RETURN OF CHRIST AND HUMAN GOVERNMENT

1 "Christ Jesus came, not as a human, but as a glorious spirit creature." *Let God Be True.* Page 185.

2 "Some wrongfully expect a literal fulfillment of the symbolic statements of the Bible. Such hope to see the glorified Jesus coming seated on a white cloud where every human eye will see him . . . Since no earthly men have ever seen the Father . . . neither will they see the glorified Son." *Ibid.* Page 186.

3 "It does not mean that he [Christ][18] is on the way or has promised to come, but that he has already arrived." *Ibid.* Pages 187, 188.

4 "Jehovah's Witnesses do not salute the flag of any nation." *Ibid.* Page 234.

5 "Any national flag is a symbol or image of the sovereign power of that nation." *Ibid.* Page 235.

6 "All such likenesses (symbols of a national power, eagle, sun, lion, etc.) are forbidden by Exodus 20:2-6 (the commandment of idolatry)." *Ibid.* Page 235.

7 "Therefore, no witness of Jehovah, who ascribes salvation *only* to Him, may salute any flag or any nation without a violation of Jehovah's commandment against idolatry as stated in His Word— I John 5:21." *Ibid.* Page 236.

THE EXISTENCE OF HELL AND ETERNAL PUNISHMENT

1 . . . God dishonoring religious doctrine . . . *Let God Be True.* Page 68.

2 It is so plain that the Bible Hell is the tomb, the grave, that even an honest little child can understand it, but not the religious theologians. *Ibid.* Pages 72, 73.

3 "And now, who is responsible for this God-dishonoring doctrine, and what is his purpose? *The promulgator of it is Satan Himself;* and his purpose in introducing it has been to frighten the people away from studying the Bible and to make them hate God." *Ibid.* Page 79.

4 "Imperfect man does not torture even a mad dog, but kills it; and yet clergymen attribute to God, who is love (I John 4:16), the *Wicked Crime* of torturing human creatures merely because they had the misfortune to be born sinners." *Ibid.* Page 79.

5 "The doctrine of a burning hell where the wicked are tortured eternally after death cannot be true, mainly for four reasons: (1) Because it is wholly unscriptural; (2) Because it is unreasonable; (3) Because it is contrary to God's love; and (4) Because it is repugnant to justice." *Ibid.* Page 80.

MAN THE SOUL, HIS NATURE AND DESTINY

1 ". . . Man is a combination of two things, namely, the 'dust of the ground' and 'the breath of life.' The combining of these two things (or elements) produced a living soul or creature called man." *Let God Be True.* Page 59.

2 "Thus we see that the claim of religionists that man has an immortal soul, and therefore differs from the beast, is not Scriptural." *Ibid.* Pages 59, 60.

3 "The fact that the human soul is mortal can be amply proved by a careful study of the Scriptures. An immortal soul could not die, but God's Word, at Ezekiel 18:4 says, 'Behold all souls are mine; . . . the soul that sinneth it shall die.' " *Ibid.* Page 61.

4 ". . . It is clearly seen that even the man Christ Jesus was mortal. He did not have an immortal soul: Jesus, the human soul, died." *Ibid.* Page 63.

5 "Thus it is seen that the serpent (the Devil) is the one who originated the doctrine of the inherent immortality of the soul." *Ibid.* Page 66.

6 ". . . He (man) enters into unconsciousness." *Ibid.* Page 67.

7 "Thus do the Scriptures show that the natural destiny of the sinner man is death." *Ibid.* Page 67.

[18]Emphasis is ours; brackets are ours.

8 "But the Bible also offers a ray of hope . . . If a man turns to God through Jesus Christ and seeks meekness and righteousness that man can gain eternal life — Zephaniah 2:3." *Ibid.* Page 67.

THE KINGDOM OF HEAVEN (A HEAVENLY ONE)

1 "Who, and how many, are able to enter the Kingdom? Revelation limits the number to 144,000 that become a part of the Kingdom and stand on Mount Zion—Revelation 14:1,3; 7:4-8." *Let God Be True.* Page 121.

2 "In the capacity of priests and kings of God they reign for a thousand years with Jesus Christ." *Ibid.* Page 121.

3 "He (Christ) went to prepare a heavenly place for his associate members, the body of Christ, for they too will be invisible creatures." *Ibid.* Page 123.

4 "If it is to be a heavenly Kingdom who will be the subjects of its rule? In the invisible realm angelic hosts, myriads of them, will serve as faithful messengers of the King. And on earth the faithful men of ancient times, being resurrected, will be 'princes in all the earth' (Psalm 45:16; Isaiah 32:1) . . . Also the 'great multitude' of Armageddon survivors will continue to 'serve him day and night' (Revelation 7:9-17). In faithfulness these will 'multiply, and fill the earth' and their children will become obedient subjects of the Higher Powers. And finally the 'unjust' ones that are resurrected, in proving their integrity, will joyfully submit themselves to Theocratic rule (Acts 24:15). Those who prove rebellious or who turn unfaithful during Satan's loosing at the end of Christ's thousand year reign will be annihilated with Satan the Devil — Revelation 20:7-15." *Ibid.* Pages 123, 124.

5 "Even the Creator so loved the New World that he gave his only begotten Son to be its King — John 3:16." *Ibid.* Page 128.

6 "The undefeatable purpose of Jehovah God to establish a righteous kingdom in these last days was fulfilled A.D. 1914." *Ibid.* Page 128.

7 "Obey the King Christ Jesus and flee, while there is still time, to the Kingdom mountains (Matthew 24:15-20). The time is short, for 'The Kingdom of Heaven is at Hand.' " *Ibid.* Page 129.

Jehovah's Witnesses become intensely disturbed whenever they are referred to as "Russellites" or their theology as "Russellism." After a thorough examination of the doctrines of the Society and a lengthy comparison with the teachings of "Pastor" Russell its founder, the author is convinced that the two systems are basically the same, and whatever differences do exist are minute and affect in no major way the cardinal beliefs of the organization. I believe, however, that in any research project substantiating evidence should be produced for verification whenever possible. I have attempted to do this and as a result have listed below five of the major doctrines of Jehovah's Witnesses paralleled with the teachings of Charles Taze Russell their late great "Pastor." I am sure that the interested reader will recognize the obvious relationship between the two systems for it is inescapably evident that Russell is the author of both.

THE TEACHINGS OF CHARLES TAZE RUSSELL OR "RUSSELLISM"	THE DOCTRINES OF JEHOVAH'S WITNESSES

I. TRIUNE GODHEAD

1 "This view [the Trinity][19] suited well the dark ages it helped to produce." *Studies in the Scriptures.* Vol. V, page 166.

(Speaking of John 1:1-3)
1 "Does this mean that Jehovah God (Elohim) and the . . . Son are two persons but at the same time one God and members of a so called 'trinity' or 'triune god'? When religion so teaches it violates the Word of God, wrests the Scriptures to the destruction of those who are misled, and insults God-given intelligence and reason." *The Truth Shall Make You Free,* page 45.

[19]Brackets are ours.

2 "This . . . theory is as unscriptural as it is unreasonable." *Ibid.* Vol. V, page 166.

2 "Only the religious 'trinitarians' are presumptuous enough to claim, without Scripture basis, that two other persons are equal with Jehovah God; but Jesus does not himself claim to be one of such persons." *The Kingdom Is at Hand,* page 507.

3 ". . . If it were not for the fact that this trinitarian nonsense was drilled into us from earliest infancy and the fact that it is so soberly taught in Theological Seminaries by gray haired professors, . . . nobody would give it a moment's serious consideration." *Ibid.* Vol. V, page 166.

3 "The obvious conclusion, therefore, is that Satan is the originator of the 'Trinity' doctrine." *Let God Be True,* page 827.

4 "How the great adversary [Satan] ever succeeded in fostering it [The Triune Godhead] upon the Lord's people to bewilder and mystify them and render much of the Word of God of none effect is the real mystery . . ." *Ibid.* Vol. V, page 166.

II. THE DEITY OF JESUS CHRIST

1 ". . . Our Lord Jesus Christ is a God . . . still the united voice of the Scriptures must emphatically assert that there is but one Almighty God, the Father of all." *Studies in the Scriptures.* Vol. V, page 55.

1 ". . . The true Scriptures speak of God's Son, the Word, as 'a god.' He is a 'mighty god,' but not 'the Almighty God, who is Jehovah' — Isaiah 9:6." *The Truth Shall Make You Free,* page 47.

2 "Our Redeemer existed as a spirit being before he was made flesh and dwelt amongst men. At that time, as well as subsequently, he was properly known as 'a god' —a mighty one." *Ibid.* Vol. V, page 84.

2 "At the time of his beginning of life he was created by the everlasting God, Jehovah, without the aid or instrumentality of any mother. In other words, he was the first and direct creation of Jehovah God . . . He was the start of God's creative work. He was not an incarnation in flesh but was flesh, a human Son of God, a perfect man, no longer a spirit, although having a spiritual or heavenly past and background." *The Kingdom Is at Hand,* pages 46,47,49.

3 ". . . The Logos [Christ] himself was 'the beginning of the creation of God.'" *Ibid.* Vol. V, page 86.

3 "This One was not Jehovah God, but was existing in the form of God . . . he was a spirit person . . . he was a mighty one although not Almighty as Jehovah God is; . . . he was a God, but not the Almighty God, who is Jehovah." *Let God Be True,* pages 34,35.

4 "As chief of the angels and next to the Father, he [Christ] was known as the Archangel (highest angel or messenger), whose name, Michael, signifies, 'Who as God' or 'God's Representative.'" *Ibid.* Vol. V, page 84.

4 "Being the only begotten Son of God, . . . the Word would be a prince among all other creatures. In this office he [Christ] bore another name in heaven, which name is 'Michael' . . . Other names were given to the Son in course of time." *The Truth Shall Make You Free,* page 49.

III. THE RESURRECTION OF CHRIST

1 ". . . Our Lord was put to death in flesh, but was made alive in spirit; he was put to death a man, but was raised from the dead a spirit being of the highest order of the divine nature." *Studies in the Scriptures,* Vol. V, page 453.

2 ". . . It could not be that the man Jesus is the second Adam, the new father of the race instead of Adam; for the Man Jesus is dead, forever dead." *Ibid.* Vol. V, page 454.

3 ". . . He [Christ] instantly created and assumed such a body of flesh and such clothing as he saw fit for the purpose intended." *Ibid.* Vol. II, page 127.

4 "Our Lord's human body . . . did not decay or corrupt . . . whether it was dissolved into gases or whether it is still preserved somewhere . . . no one knows." *Ibid.* Vol. II, page 129.

1 ". . . In his resurrection he was no more human. He was raised as a spirit creature, . . ." *The Kingdom Is at Hand,* page 258.

2 ". . . Jehovah God raised him from the dead, not as a human son, but as a mighty immortal spirit son . . . So the King Christ Jesus was put to death in the flesh, and was resurrected an invisible spirit creature." *Let God Be True,* pages 43,122.

3 "Therefore the bodies in which Jesus manifested himself to his disciples after his return to life were not the body in which he was nailed to the tree. They were merely materialized for the occasion, resembling on one or two occasions the body in which he died . . ." *The Kingdom Is at Hand,* page 259.

4 "The Firstborn one from the dead was not raised out of the grave a human creature, but he was raised a spirit." *Let God Be True,* page 272.

IV. THE PHYSICAL RETURN OF CHRIST

1 "And in like manner as he went away (quietly, secretly, so far as the world was concerned, and unknown except to his followers), so in this manner, he comes again." *Studies in the Scriptures.* Vol. II, page 154.

2 "[Russell's idea of what Christ is saying, and his teaching on the matter.] . . . He comes to us in the early dawn of the Millennial Day (Jesus seems to say . . . 'Learn that I am a spirit being, no longer visible to human sight." *Ibid.* Vol. II, page 191.

3 "He [Christ] does not come in the body of his humiliation, a human body which he took for the suffering of death . . . but in his glorious spiritual body . . ." *Ibid.* Vol. II, page 108.

1 "Christ Jesus comes, not as a human but as a glorious spirit creature." *Let God Be True,* page 185.

2 "Since no earthly men have ever seen the Father . . . neither will they see the glorified Son . . ." *Ibid.* Page 186.

3 "It is a settled Scriptural truth, therefore, that human eyes will not see him at his second coming, neither will he come in a fleshy body." *The Truth Shall Make You Free,* page 295.

4 ". . . Christ Jesus came to the Kingdom in A.D. 1914, but unseen to men." *Ibid.,* page 300.

V. THE EXISTENCE OF HELL OR A PLACE OF CONSCIOUS TORMENT AFTER DEATH

1 "Many have imbibed the erroneous idea that God placed our race on trial for life with the alternative of eternal torture, whereas nothing of the kind is even hinted at in the penalty." *Studies in the Scriptures*, Vol. I, page 127.

2 "Eternal torture is nowhere suggested in the Old Testament Scriptures, and only a few statements in the New Testament can be so misconstrued as to appear to teach it." *Ibid.*, Vol. I, page 128.

1 ". . . The Bible hell is the tomb, the grave . . ." *Let God Be True*, page 72.

2 ". . . God-dishonoring doctrine . . ." *Ibid.*, page 79.

3 "The doctrine of a burning hell where the wicked are tortured eternally after death cannot be true . . ." *Ibid.*, page 80.

In concluding this comparison it is worthwhile to .note that as far as the facts are concerned "Jehovah's Witnesses" is simply a pseudonym for "Russellism" or "Millennial Dawnism." The similarity of the two systems is more than coincidental or accidental regardless of the Witnesses' loud shouts to the contrary. The facts speak for themselves. Inquisitive persons may ask at this point why the organization assumed the name of "Jehovah's Witnesses." The answer is more than understandable.

After Russell's death Judge Rutherford, the newly elected president of the Society, saw the danger of remaining Russellites and over a period of fifteen years he labored to cover up the "Pastor's" unpleasant past, which did much to hinder the organization's progress. In 1931 Rutherford managed to appropriate the name—"Jehovah's Witnesses" from Isaiah 43:10, thus escaping the damaging title "Russellites." Clever man that he was, Rutherford thus managed to hide the unsavory background of Russellistic theology and delude millions of people into believing that Jehovah's Witnesses was a "differ-

ent" organization. Rutherford's strategy has worked well for the Russellites, and as a result today those trusting souls and millions like them everywhere sincerely believe that they are members of a "New Kingdom Order" under Jehovah God, when in reality they are deluded believers in the theology of *one* man, Charles Taze Russell, who was proven to be neither a Christian nor a qualified Bible student. Jehovah's Witnesses who have not been in the movement any great period of time deny publicly and privately that they are Russellites; and since few of the old-time members of "Pastor" Russell's personal flock are still alive, the Society in safety vehemently denounces any accusations which tend to prove that Russell's theology is the basis of the entire Watch Tower system. Proof of this is found in a personal letter from the Society to the author dated February 9, 1951, wherein, in answer to my question concerning Russell's influence, they stated — "We are not 'Russellites' for we are not following Charles T. Russell or any other imperfect man. Honest examination of our literature today would quickly reveal that it differs widely from that of Russell's, even though he was the first President of our Society."

Further than this, the Society in another letter dated November 6, 1950, and signed by Nathan H. Knorr, its legal President, declared that "the latest publications of The Watch Tower Bible and Tract Society set out the doctrinal views of this organization, and I think any information you want in that regard you can find yourself without an interview." So then it is evident from these two official letters that we must judge the faith of the Jehovah's Witnesses by their literature, for they are reluctant to grant personal interviews for clarification of doctrine.

A REFUTATION OF WATCH TOWER THEOLOGY

The Triune Deity.[20]

One of the greatest doctrines of the Scriptures is that of the Triune Godhead *(tes theotetos)* or the nature of God Himself. To say that this doctrine is a "mystery" is indeed inconclusive and no informed minister would explain the implications of the doctrine in such abstract terms. Jehovah's Witnesses accuse "The Clergy" of doing just that, however, and it is unfortunate to note that they are as usual guilty of misstatement in the presentation of the•facts, and even in their definition of what Christian clergymen believe the Deity to be.

First of all, Christian ministers and Christians as a whole do not believe that there are "three gods in one" (*Let God Be True,* page 81) but *do* believe that there are three Persons all of the same Substance, co-equal, co-existent and co-eternal. There is ample ground for this belief in the Scriptures,

where plurality in the Godhead is very strongly intimated if not expressly declared. Let us consider just a few of these references.

In Genesis 1:26 Jehovah is speaking of creation and He speaks in the plural number, "Let *us* create man in our image after *our* likeness." Now it is obvious that God would not create man in His image and the angels' images if He were talking to them, so He must have been addressing someone else and who, but His Son and the Holy Spirit who are equal in Substance could He address in such familiar terms? Since there is no other god but Jehovah (Isaiah 43:10, 11), not even "a lesser mighty god" as Jehovah's Witnesses affirm Christ to be, there must be a unity in plurality and Substance or the passage is not meaningful. The same is true of Genesis 11:7, at the tower of Babel, when God said, "Let *us* go down," and also of Isaiah 6:8, "who will go for *us* . . ." These instances of plurality indicate something deeper than an impersonal relationship; they strongly suggest what the New Testament fully develops, namely, a Tri-Unity in the One God. The claim of Jehovah's Witnesses that Tertullian and Theophilus propagated and introduced the threefold unity of God into Christianity is ridiculous and hardly worth refuting. Any unbiased study of the facts will convince the impartial student that before Tertullian or Theophilus lived the doctrine was under study and considered sound. No one doubts that among the heathens (Babylonians and Egyptians) demon gods were worshiped, but to call the Triune Godhead doctrine "of the devil" (*Let God Be True,* page 82) as Je-

---

[20]Jehovah's Witnesses take great delight in pointing out that the word "Trinity" does not appear as such in the Bible. They further state that since it is not a part of Scripture, it must be of pagan origin and should be discounted entirely. What the Witnesses fail to understand is that the very word "Jehovah," which they maintain is the only true

name for God, also does not appear as such in the Bible, but is an interpolation of the Hebrew consonants YHWH or JHVH, any vowels added being arbitrary. Thus it is seen that the very name by which they call themselves is just as unbiblical as they suppose the Trinity to be.

hovah's Witnesses do, is blasphemy and the product of untutored and darkened souls.

In the entire chapter "Is there a Trinity?" *(Let God Be True,* pages 81-93) the whole problem as to why the Trinity doctrine is "confusing" to Jehovah's Witnesses lies in their interpretation of "death" as it is used in the Bible. To Jehovah's Witnesses death is the cessation of consciousness, or *destruction.* However, no single or collective rendering of Greek or Hebrew words in any reputable lexicon or dictionary will substantiate their view. Death in the Scriptures is "separation" from the body as in the case of the first death (physical), and separation from God for eternity as in the second death (the lake of fire, Revelation 20.) Death never means annihilation and Jehovah's Witnesses cannot bring in one word in the original languages to prove it does. A wealth of evidence has been amassed to prove it does not. I welcome comparisons on this point.

The rest of the chapter is taken up with childish questions some of which are painful to record. "Who ran the universe the three days Jesus was dead and in the grave? (death again portrayed as extinction of consciousness) is a sample of the nonsense perpetrated on gullible people. "Religionists" is the label placed on all who disagree with the organization's views regardless of the validity of the criticism. Christians do not believe that the Trinity was incarnate in Christ and that they were "three in one" during Christ's ministry. Christ voluntarily limited Himself in His earthly body, but heaven was always open to Him. At His baptism the Holy Spirit descended like a dove, the Father spoke and the Son was baptized. What further proof is needed to show a three-

fold unity? Compare the baptism of Christ (Matthew 3:16, 17) with the commission to preach in the threefold Name of[21] God (Matthew 28:19) and the evidence is clear and undeniable. Of course it is not possible to fathom this great revelation completely but this we do know: there is a unity of Substance, not three gods, and that unity is One in every sense, which no reasonable person can doubt after surveying the evidence. When Jesus said, "My Father is greater than I" He spoke the truth, for in the form of a servant (Philippians 2:7) and as a man, the Son was subject to the Father willingly; but upon His Resurrection and in the radiance of His glory taken again from whence He veiled it (Verses, 7, 8) He showed forth His Deity when He declared, "All authority is surrendered to me in heaven and earth" (Matthew 28:18); proof positive of His intrinsic Nature and Unity of Substance. It is evident then that the Lord Jesus Christ was never inferior, spiritually speaking, to His Father during His sojourn on earth.

JEHOVAH'S WITNESSES VS. THE SCRIPTURES, REASON, AND THE TRINITY

Every major cult and non-Christian religion which seeks to deride orthodox theology continually attacks the doctrine of the Trinity. Jehovah's Witnesses (the Russellites of today) are the most vehement in this endeavor, and because they couch their clever misuse of terminology in Scriptural contexts, they are also the most dangerous. Throughout the whole length and breadth of the Watch Tower's turbulent history, one "criterion" has been used in every era to measure the credibility of any Biblical doctrine. This "criterion" is *reason*. During the era of "Pastor" Russell and right

21Note: In the incarnation itself, Luke 1:35, where the Trinity appears (also John 14:16 and 15:26).

through until today, *reason* has always been "the great god" before whom all followers of the Millennial Dawn[22] movement bow with unmatched reverence. In fact, the "great paraphraser," as Russell was once dubbed, even went so far as to claim that reason[23] opened up to the intellect of man the very character of God Himself! Think of it, according to the "Pastor," God's nature is actually openly accessible to our feeble and erring reasoning powers. In the first volume of the "Millennial Dawn" series[24] (page 41), "Pastor" Russell makes God subject to our powers of reasoning. Wrote the "Pastor": ". . . let us examine the character of the writings claimed as inspired (The Bible) *to see whether their teachings* correspond with the character we have reasonably imputed to God." Here it is plain to see that for Russell man's understanding of God's character lies, not in God's revelation of Himself to be taken by faith, but in our ability to reason out that character subject to the laws of our reasoning processes. Russell obviously never considered Jehovah's Word as recorded in the fifty-fifth chapter of Isaiah the Prophet, which discourse clearly negates man's powers of reasoning in relation to the divine character and nature of his Creator.

"For my thoughts are not your thoughts, neither are your ways my ways, saith the Lord, for as the heavens are higher than the earth, so are my ways higher than your ways, and my thoughts than your thoughts" (Isaiah 55:8,9). By this statement God certainly did not say reason and thought should be abandoned in the process of inquiry, but merely that no one can know the mind, nature, or thoughts of God in all their fullness, seeing that

man is finite and He is infinite. The term "reason" and derivatives of it (reasonable, reasoning, reasoned, etc.) are used eighty-eight times in the English Bible, and only *once* in all these usages (Isaiah 1:18) does God address man. Jehovah's Witnesses maintain that since God said, "Come now and let us reason together . . ." that He therefore gave reason a high place, even using it Himself to commune with His creatures. While this is true, it is only so in a limited sense at best. God never said, "Reason out the construction of my Spiritual Substance and Nature," or "limit my character to your reasoning powers." Nevertheless, Jehovah's Witnesses, by making Christ (The Logos, John 1:1) "a god" or a "mighty god," but not "Jehovah God," have done just these things. In the reference quoted above (Isaiah 1:18), Jehovah showed man the way of salvation and invited him to be redeemed from sin. God never invited him to explore His deity or probe into His mind. The Apostle Paul says, "For who hath known the mind of the Lord? or who hath been his counselor? or who hath first given to him, and it shall be recompensed unto him again? For of him, and through him, and to him, are all things: to whom be glory for ever" (Romans 11:34-36).

But now let us examine this typical propaganda from the Watch Tower's arsenal and see if they really do follow "Pastor" Russell and his theory of reason. In this article, "The Scriptures, Reason, and the Trinity," the Witnesses constantly appeal to *reason* as the standard for determining what God thinks. The following are quotations which we believe illustrate this point beyond doubt.

1. "To hold that Jehovah God the Father and Christ Jesus His Son are

---

[22]Name originally given to the movement by Russell in 1886.

[23]"The ability to think and draw conclusions."

[24]Later changed to "Studies in the Scriptures" when the orthodox clergy exposed the "Pastor's" false theology and shady character.

co-eternal is to fly in the face of reason" (page 22). Notice that reason is used as the "yardstick" to determine the validity of a Scriptural doctrine.

2. "Jehovah God says: 'Come now, and let us reason together' (Isaiah 1:18). The advocates of the Trinity admit that it is not subject to *reason*[25] or logic, and so they resort to terming it a 'mystery.' *But the Bible contains no divine mysteries. It contains 'sacred secrets.' Every use of the word 'mystery' and 'mysteries' in the King James Version comes from the same Greek root word meaning 'to shut the mouth,' that is to keep secret. There is a vast difference between a secret and a mystery. A secret is merely that which has not been made known, but a mystery is that which cannot be understood."*

Once again the interested reader must pay close attention to the Witnesses' favorite game of term-switching. *The Watch Tower* makes a clever distinction between the term "mystery" and the term "secret" and declares that ". . . the Bible contains no divine mysteries." It is affirmed that "a secret is merely that which has not been made known, but a mystery is that which cannot be understood." In view of the seriousness of this Watch Tower exercise in semantics, we feel obliged to destroy their *manufactured* distinction between "secret" and "mystery," by the simple process of consulting the dictionary. "Mystery" is defined as: "1. Secret, something that is hidden or unknown." "Secret" is defined as: "1. Something secret or hidden; mystery." Surely this is proof conclusive that the Bible contains "divine mysteries" as far as the meaning of the term is understood. It must also be equally apparent that Jehovah's Witnesses obviously have no ground for rejecting the word "mystery" where either the Bible or the dictionary are concerned. We fail to note any "vast difference"

between the two words, and so does the dictionary. The truth is that the Watch Tower rejects the Trinity doctrine and other cardinal doctrines of historic Christianity, not because they are mysterious, but because Jehovah's Witnesses are determined to reduce Jesus, the Son of God, to a creature or "a second god," all Biblical evidence notwithstanding. They still follow in "Pastor" Russell's footsteps, and one needs no dictionary to substantiate that.

3. "Jehovah God by His Word furnishes us with ample *reasons* and logical bases for all regarding which he expects us to exercise faith. . . . We can make sure of what is right *only* by a process of *reasoning* on God's Word" (page 24).

Here indeed is a prime example of what Jehovah's Witnesses continually represent as sound thinking. They cannot produce even one shred of evidence to bolster up their unscriptural claim that God always gives us reasons for those things in which He wants us to "exercise faith." Biblical students (even "International"[26] ones) really grasp at theological straws in the wind when they attempt to prove so dogmatic and inconclusive a statement. A moment of reflection on the Scriptures will show, we believe, that this attempt to over-emphasize *reason* is a false one.

First, does God give us a reason for creating Lucifer the author of sin? Is such a reason found in the Scripture? It is not, and yet we must believe that he exists, that he opposes God and that all references in the Scripture to Satan are authoritative. God demands that we exercise faith in their objective truth, yet He *never* gives us a reason for it.

Second, does God anywhere give to man a fathomable *reason* for choosing one person to salvation and rejecting another to eternal punishment? No. Never in the Scripture does He give a

---

[25]Emphasis is ours (page 24).

[26]International Bible students is one of the other names for Russellism.

"reasonable" answer to this power of choice He exercises. As a matter of fact, He even politely tells us to mind our own business, as recorded in the ninth chapter of Romans: "I will have mercy on whom I will have mercy, and I will have compassion on whom I will have compassion." So it depends not upon man's will or exertion, but upon God's mercy. He has mercy upon whomsoever He wills, and He hardens the heart of whomever He wills. "O man, who art thou that repliest against God? Shall the thing formed say to him that formed it, Why hast thou made me thus? Hath not the potter power over the clay; of the same lump to make one vessel unto honour, and another unto dishonour?" (9:15,20,21). *All* this God requires us to believe still on faith — no human reasons needed.

Third, does God anywhere give man a reason for children being born dead, blind, crippled or diseased? Does He anywhere clearly give understandable reasons for the suffering of circumstantially innocent people during war time, for the death of an only son, or for untold human misery and suffering for apparently no good reasons? But through it all God asks us to believe that these seemingly indescribable evils will ultimately work out His divine plan, and He asks us at times to believe in Him *against reason* and with the eyes of faith.

Much, much more could be said along the same lines, but enough has been shown to refute adequately the contention of Jehovah's Witnesses that God *always* gives us "reasons and logical bases" for all regarding which He expects us to exercise faith.

Let us also remember the falsity of their other claim in the same paragraph: "We can make sure of what is right only by a process of reasoning on God's Word." But Jesus said: "The

Comforter, which is the Holy Ghost, whom the Father will send in my name, he shall teach you all things, and bring all things to your remembrance, whatsoever I have said unto you!" (John 14:26). Now if only by a process of reasoning on God's Word we can make sure of what is right, as Jehovah's Witnesses contend, then Jesus and they are at direct variance, for they do not have the guidance of the Holy Spirit, since they deny His person and deity. In a controversy of this nature we prefer to choose God and His Word to the Watch Tower's jumbled Russellism.

Fourth, "God, through His Word, appeals to our reason. The Trinity doctrine is a negation of both the Scriptures and reason." Like so many other of the Watch Tower's clever examples of phraseology, this statement contains a mixture of truth and error, with just enough of the former to make good sense, and just enough of the latter to confuse the gullible reader. It is unquestionably true that God through His Word appeals to our reason; were it not so we could not understand His desires. But by the same token, God does not invite our inquiry into His nature or character. Jehovah's Witnesses, however, if their views are rightly understood, assume that human *reason* is capable of doing just that.

The Watch Tower has never failed to echo the old Arian heresy,[27] since it is upon this one long-exploded theological myth that the entire Jehovah's Witness movement unsteadily rests.

Jehovah's Witnesses know beyond doubt that if Jesus is Jehovah-God then every one of them is going to a flaming hereafter; and hell they fear above all else. This no doubt explains a great deal of their antagonism to the doctrines of the Trinity and Hell. The Witnesses, it must be remembered, consistently berate the Trinity doctrine as "of the

[27]A theory popularized by Arius of Alexandria (Egypt) in the fourth century, A.D.. which taught that Jesus was the first crea-

ture, made "a second god," inferior to Jehovah.

Devil," and never tire proclaiming that "the Bible Hell is the grave." The thought of being punished in unquenchable fire for their disobedience to God is probably the strongest bond that binds the Watch Tower's flimsy covers together.

Let us further pursue the Watch Tower's logic. In *The Watch Tower's* various articles, two other terms are repeated constantly by Jehovah's Witnesses. These terms are "equal" and "co-eternal." The terms are used some six times in this particular article and each time it is denied that Jesus Christ is either equal to or co-eternal with God His Father. Says *The Watch Tower:*

"We see God in heaven as the Superior One . . . We see his Son on earth expressing delight to do his Father's will; clearly two separate and distinct personalities and *not* at all equal. Nothing here (Matthew 28:18-20) to indicate that it (The Holy Spirit) is a person, let alone that it is equal with Jehovah God [page 21]. The very fact that the Son received his life from the Father proves that *he could not be co-eternal with him.* (John 1:18; 6:57) . . . Nor can it be argued that God was superior to Jesus only because of Jesus' then being a human, for *Paul makes clear that Christ Jesus in his pre-human form was not equal with his father.* In Philippians 2:1-11 (N.W.T.)[28] he counsels Christians not to be motivated by egotism but to have lowliness of mind, even as Christ Jesus had, who, although existing in God's form before coming to earth was not *ambitious* to become equal with his Father [page 22] . . . Jesus did not claim to be *The God,* but *only* God's Son. That Jesus is inferior to his Father, is also apparent . . . etc. [page 23] . . . The 'Holy Ghost' or Holy Spirit is God's active force . . . There is no basis for concluding that the Holy Spirit is a Person

. . . Yes, the Trinity finds its origin in the pagan concept of a multiplicity, plurality, or pantheon of Gods. The law Jehovah God gave to the Jews stated diametrically the opposite. 'Jehovah our God is *one* Jehovah' (Deuteronomy 6:4 [page 24]."

Briefly let us examine these statements of Jehovah's Witnesses and see if they have any rational content where the Bible is concerned. The Watch Tower maintains that Christ and His Father are "not at all equal," which has been their boldest insult to Christianity since Russell and Rutherford concocted and promoted the whole Watch Tower nightmare. This type of unbelief where Christ's true deity is concerned has gladdened the hearts of intellectual hill-billies the country over, who find it easier to mock the Trinity than to trust God's Word and His Son. Concerning His relationship with the Father, the Apostle John in the fifth chapter of his gospel, the eighteenth verse, when speaking of Jesus and the Jews said "Therefore the Jews sought the more to kill him, because he not only had broken the sabbath, but said also God was his Father, making himself *equal* with God" (A.V.). The Greek word for equal is *ison,* which acording to Thayer's Greek Lexicon (page 307), an acknowledged authority, means "equal in quality as in quantity, to claim for one's self the *Nature,* rank, authority, which belong to God" (John 5:18). Dr. Thayer, Jehovah's Witnesses might take notice, was a Unitarian who denied Christ's Deity even as they themselves do; yet, being honest, he gave the true meaning of the Biblical terms even though they contradicted his views. Thus God's Word directly contradicts Jehovah's Witnesses and this they dare not deny.

The Watch Tower further contends that since Christ received life from His Father — "I live by the Father" (John

[28]*New World Translation,* Watch Tower Bible and Tract Society, Revised, 1951.

6:57) — he could not be co-eternal with Him. At first glance this seems plausible, especially when coupled with John 5:26: "As the Father hath life in himself, so hath he given to the Son to have life in himself." Taking this text in its context we readily see that it cannot mean that Christ derived "eternal existence" from the Father. John 1:1 bears witness that "the Word was God," therefore eternity was inherent in His makeup by Nature. The logical conclusion must be that the indwelling "Life" of "God The Word" entered time in the form of "the Son of Man" and by this operation the Father through the agency of the Holy Spirit gave the "Son of Man" to have "Life in himself," the same Life that was eternally His as the eternal Word. But it takes more than a glance to support this garbled Watch Tower polytheism as we shall soon see. Unwittingly, Jehovah's Witnesses answer their own Scriptural doubletalk when they quote Philippians 2:5-11 on page 22 of their article. In this passage of Scripture Paul claims full Deity for Christ and maintains that in His pre-incarnate life He "existed in a form of God" and "thought it not something to be grasped at to be *equal* with God, but took upon Himself the *form* of a servant and was made in the likeness of men." The term *equal* here is another form of *ison,* namely *isa,* which again denotes *absolute sameness of Nature,* thus confirming Christ's true Deity. Further, this context reveals beyond reasonable doubt that *all* reference to Christ's being subject to His Father (John 5: 26; 6:57) pertain to His earthly existence, during which "he emptied Himself" to become as one of us. This in no way affected His true Deity or unity with the Father, for Jesus claimed Jehovahistic identity (John 8:58) when He announced Himself to the unbelieving Jews as The "I Am" of Exodus 3: 14. Twice then in the same terms Jehovah's Witnesses deny what the

Scriptures specifically testify, that Christ *is equal* with God in Essence, Character, and Nature, which truths the Watch Tower's term-switching campaigns can never change. I should also like to call attention to an extremely bold example of misquoting so commonly found in Watch Tower propaganda. On page 22 the Russellite oracle declares, ". . . . *Paul makes clear that Christ Jesus in his pre-human form was not equal to his father.* Philippians 2:1-11 (N.W.T.) he counsels Christians not to be motivated by egotism but to have lowliness of mind even as Christ Jesus had, who, although existing in God's form before coming to earth *was not ambitious to become equal with his Father."*

Now as far as the original Greek text of Philippians 2:1-11 is concerned, this is an absurd and plainly dishonest statement. Paul never even mentions Christ's being ambitious to attain anything at all or even his lack of ambition, since no Greek term there can be translated "ambition." Jehovah's Witnesses themselves do not use the word ambition in their own New World Translation, nor does any other translator that we know of. Despite this, however, they introduce the term which clouds the real meaning of the Greek terms. Further than this, and worse, the Watch Tower plainly attempts to use Paul's declaration of Christ's Deity as a means of confusing the issue. They maintain that Paul here taught that Jesus was inferior in Nature to His Father, when in reality Paul's entire system of theology says the opposite. If we are to believe the Greek text, Paul declares that Jesus did *not* consider equality with God something "to be grasped after, or robbed" (Greek *arpazo*) since He previously existed as the eternal Word of God (John 1:1) prior to His incarnation (John 1:14), and as such shared the Father's prerogatives and attributes. Hence He had no desire to strive for what was His by Nature and inheritance.

Paul elsewhere calls Christ "all the fullness of the Deity in the flesh" (Colossians 2:9), "The great God and our Saviour" (Titus 2:13), and "God" (Hebrews 1:3, 8). These are just a few of the references; there are at least twenty-five more which could be cited from his writings and over seventy-five from the balance of the New Testament. Contrary to the Watch Tower, then, Paul never wrote their Russellite interpretational paraphrase as recorded on page twenty-two, since even the Greek text bears witness against them.

Jehovah's Witnesses sum up their latest blast at the Trinity doctrine by informing us that John 1:1 should be rendered, "In the beginning was the Word and the Word was with God and the Word was *a god.*" This is another example of the depths to which the Watch Tower will descend to make Jesus *"a second god"* and thus introduce polytheism into Christianity. Needless to say, no recognized translators in the history of Greek exegesis have ever sanctioned such a grammatical travesty as the Watch Tower translation and the Watch Tower translators know it. Such a rendition is an indication of markedly inferior scholarship and finds no basis whatsoever in New Testament Greek grammar. Both James Moffat and Edgar Goodspeed, liberal translators, render John 1:1: ". . . the Word was Divine"; but Mantey translates it "The Word was Deity," as does every acknowledged authority. Moffat and Goodspeed, however, admit that Scripture teaches the full and *equal* Deity of Jesus Christ, something Jehovah's Witnesses vehemently deny. Beyond doubt the Watch Tower of Jehovah's Witnesses presents a strange dilemma, "ever learning, and never able to come to a knowledge of the truth." The Russellite movements (there are other small branches) all cry loudly the old Jewish Scripture, "Hear, O Israel, the Lord our God is *one Lord"* (or, "The Lord is One"), and attempt to use it against

the doctrine of the Trinity. But once again language betrays the shallowness of their resources. The term *Echod,* "One" in Hebrew, does *not* denote *absolute* unity in many places throughout the Old Testament, and often it definitely denotes *Composite Unity,* which argues for the Trinity of the Deity (Jehovah). In the *second chapter* and the *twenty-fourth* verse of Genesis, the Lord tells us that "a man leaves his father and his mother and cleaves to his wife, and they become one flesh" (in Hebrew, *Bosor Echod*). Certainly this does not mean that in marriage a man and his wife become one *person,* but that they become *one* in the unity of their substance and are considered as *one* person in the eyes of God. Please note, this is true unity; yet *not solitary,* but *composite unity.* Let us further consider composite unity. Moses sent twelve spies into Canaan (Numbers 13:23) and when they returned they brought with them a great cluster of grapes (in Hebrew *Eschol Echod*). Now since there were hundreds of grapes on this one stem, it could hardly be absolute or solitary unity, yet again *Echod* (one) is used to describe the cluster. This shows conclusively that the grapes were considered one in the sense of their being of the same origin, hence *composite unity* is again demonstrated. Jehovah's Witnesses continually ask, "If Jesus when on the cross was truly an incarnation of Jehovah, then who was in heaven?" This is a logical question to which the eighteenth chapter of Genesis gives fourteen answers, each reaffirming the other. As recorded in the eighteenth chapter of Genesis, Abraham had three visitors. Two of them were angels (Genesis 19:1), but the third he addressed as *Jehovah God, fourteen times!* Abraham's third visitor stayed and conversed with him and then departed, saying concerning Sodom, "I will go down and see whether they have done altogether according to the outcry which has come to me, and if not, I will know"

(18:21). And so, "The Lord went his way when he had finished speaking to Abraham, and Abraham returned to his place" (verse 33). Now if John is to be believed without question, and Jehovah's Witnesses agree that he must be, then "No man hath seen God [the Father] at any time; the only begotten Son [Jesus Christ] who is in the bosom of the Father, he hath revealed him" (John 1:18). To further confuse the Witnesses' peculiar view of God as a *solitary unit,* Jesus Himself said concerning His Father, ". . . you have not at any time either heard his voice *or* seen his form . . . for God is a Spirit, and they that worship him must worship him in Spirit and in truth" (John 4:24; 5:37). Now, then, here is the evidence. Moses declares that God spoke face to face with Abraham (Genesis 18:26) and Jesus, and John, say, "No man hath seen God at any time." But Jesus makes it clear that He is referring to *the Father,* and so does John. The nineteenth chapter of Genesis, the twenty-fourth verse, solves then this problem for us once and for all, as even Jehovah's Witnesses will eventually be forced to admit. Moses here reveals a glimpse of the *composite unity* in the Triune God. "Then Jehovah rained on Sodom and Gomorrah brimstone and fire *from Jehovah* out of heaven." This unquestionably is the only solution to this dilemma. God the Father rained fire on Sodom and Gomorrah, and God the Son spoke and ate with Abraham and Sarah. Two persons (the third Person of the Trinity is revealed more fully in the New Testament: John 14:26; 16:7-14; etc.) are both called Jehovah (Genesis 18:21; 19:24; cf. Isaiah 9:6; Micah 5:2), and both are *One* (*Echod*) with the Holy Spirit in *composite unity* (Deuteronomy 6:4). God the Father was in heaven, God the Son died on the cross, God the Holy Spirit comforts the Church till Jesus shall come again. This is the Triune God whom Jehovah's Witnesses are committed to ridicule, berate, and blas-

pheme in the name of "human reason." God said in Genesis 1:26, "Let us make man in *our* image after *our* likeness," not in *my* image, after *my* likeness. Here plurality is seen, obviously, God speaking to His co-eternal Son (Christ) and addressing *Him* as an *equal.* Genesis 11:7, 9, with reference to the Tower of Babel, also lends strong support to the Triune God Doctrine, where God, speaking as an *equal* to His Son, declares, "Let *us* go down and there confound their language" — again plurality and *equal* discourse. In the face of all these texts, the Watch Tower is strangely silent. They, however, rally afresh to the attack on page 23 of their article and declare that "there is no basis for concluding that the Holy Spirit is a person." This is so immature and unskilled an attack that it hardly justifies an effort to refute it. The fact that the Holy Spirit is referred to as a Person in the masculine gender throughout the New Testament, that He also is described as possessing an active *will* ("If I go not away, he will not come to you," John 16:7), which is the most concrete trait of a distinct personality, and that He is said to exercise the characteristics of a *teacher* (John 16:8), apparently all falls on deaf ears where the Watch Tower is concerned. The literature of Jehovah's Witnesses is also consistently filled with nonsensical questions such as, "How could the one hundred and twenty persons at Pentecost be baptized with a Person," etc.? (Acts 1:5, 2:1-4). In answer to this, it evidently escapes the ever-zealous Russellites that the fulfillment of Jesus' prophecy as recorded in Acts 1:5 was explained in chapter two, verse four. Luke here says, "And they were all filled (Greek *eplesthesan*) with the Holy Spirit," etc. Jesus all too obviously did not mean that the apostles would be "immersed" in a Person, but filled with and immersed in the power of His Presence as symbolized in the tongues like unto fire. If Jehovah's Witnesses ever studied the Scriptures in the open with good scholars and stopped masquerading as Biblical authorities, which they are not, it might be interesting to see the results. Of course, great scholarship is not necessary to obtain a saving knowledge of Jesus Christ from God's Word; but when people deny the historic Christian faith and berate those who profess it, they ought to have some scholastic support, and Jehovah's Witnesses have none. The Watch Tower widely cries that they will meet all persons with an open Bible, but to this date not one of their alleged authorities has materialized despite our numerous invitations. We of orthodox Christianity do not desire maliciously to attack any one's faith for the "joy" of doing it; but we must be faithful to our Lord's command to "preach the word and contend for the faith." As long as the Watch Tower continues to masquerade as a Christian movement and attack without Biblical provocation or cause orthodox Christian theology with such articles as "The Scripture, Reason, and the Trinity," etc., so long will our voice be raised in answer to their consistent misrepresentations. God granting us the grace, we can do no other but be faithful to Him "who is the faithful and true witness, the *source* through whom God's creation came" (Revelation 3:14, Knox), His eternal Word and beloved Son, Jesus Christ our Lord.

Author's note:

JEHOVAH'S WITNESSES AND THE HOLY SPIRIT

Though it is rudimentary to any study of the Bible, the Personality and Deity of the Holy Spirit must constantly be defended against the attacks of the Watch Tower.

The Watch Tower, as has been seen (page 32), denies His Personality and Deity, but the following references, a few of many in Scripture, refute their stand completely:

(1) Acts 5:3,4 — In verse 3 Peter accuses Ananias of lying *to* the Holy Spirit, and in verse 4 he declares the Holy Spirit

to be God, an equation hard for the Watch Tower to explain, much less deny. Who else but a Person can be lied to?

(2) Acts 13:2,4 — In the context the Holy Spirit speaks and sends, as He does in 21:10,11, where He prophesies Paul's imprisonment. Only a Personality can do these things, *not* "an invisible active force," as the Jehovah's Witnesses describe Him.

(3) Finally, such references as John 14:16,17,26 and 16:7-14 need no comment. *He* is a divine Person and He is God (Genesis 1:2).

THE NEW WORLD TRANSLATIONS OF THE BIBLE

In any dealings one may have with the Watch Tower or its numerous representatives, it is a virtual certainty that sooner or later in the course of events the Watch Tower's "translations" of the Bible will confront the average prospective convert. These "translations" at present cover the entire New Testament and the first seventeen books of the Old Testament and are respectively titled, *The New World Translation of the Christian Greek Scriptures* and *The New World Translation of the Hebrew Scriptures.*[29]

First published in 1950 and later revised in 1951, the New Testament version of these "translations" sold over 480,000 copies before its initial revision, and at this writing the latest forecast for its sale, including international distribution, is calculated in seven figures. The Old Testament version of the first eight books, titled, "The Octateuch," had a first edition of 500,000 copies and bids fair to rival its older brother in distribution. These books sell for one dollar and fifty cents each and possess a veneer of scholarship unrivaled for its daring and boldness in a field that all informed scholars know Jehovah's Witnesses are almost totally unprepared to venture into.

Be that as it may, however, the "translations" exist and, as has been shown, have had and are having wide distribution both in the continental United

[29]Watch Tower Bible and Tract Society, Brooklyn, New York, Publishers.

States, Canada and all of the six continents. Jehovah's Witnesses boast that their "translations" are "the work of competent scholars" and further that they "give a clarity to the Scriptures that other translations have somehow failed to supply." Such stupendous claims by the Watch Tower involves the necessity of a careful examination of their translations so that they may be weighed by the standards of sound Biblical scholarship. Any exhaustive analysis of these works is impossible in this limited space, but we have selected some of the outstanding examples of fraud and deceit from the New Testament version. These examples should discourage any fairminded individual from placing much value upon the Jehovah's Witnesses' Bible.

In their Foreword to the New World Translation of the Christian Greek Scriptures, the translation committee of the Watch Tower cleverly claims for itself and its translation a peculiar freedom from what they define as "the misleading influence of religious traditions which have their roots in paganism." This "influence," the Watch Tower insists, has colored the inspired Word of God, so it is necessary for them, Jehovah's chosen theocratic representatives, to set aright the numerous alleged examples of "human traditionalism" evidenced in all translations from John Wycliffe to the Revised Standard Version. Should anyone question that this arrogant attitude is the true Watch Tower position regarding other translations, the following quote from their Foreword will dismiss all doubt:

> But honesty compels us to remark that, while each of them has its points of merit, they have fallen victim to the power of human traditionalism in varying degrees. Consequently, religious traditions, hoary with age, have been taken for granted and gone unchallenged and uninvestigated. These have been interwoven into the translations to color the thought. In support of a preferred religious view, an inconsistency and unreasonableness have been insinu-ated into the teachings of the inspired writings.
> The Son of God taught that the traditions of creed-bound men made the commandments and teachings of God of no power and effect. The endeavor of the New World Bible Translation Committee has been to avoid this snare of religious traditionalism.

From this pompous pronouncement it is only too evident that the Watch Tower considers its "scholars" the superiors of such great scholars as Wycliffe and Tyndale, not to mention the hundreds of brilliant, consecrated Christian men who produced the King James, American Standard, and Revised Standard Versions of the Bible. Such a pretext is of course too absurd to merit refutation, but let it be remembered that the Watch Tower Translation Committee, comparatively speaking, had but a handful of "scholars" who hold degrees in New Testament Greek exegesis, or Hebrew for that matter; yet these egotistical pseudo-scholars dare to challenge the record of translations which have had hundreds of the greatest Greek and Hebrew scholars in the world as contributors.

However, the Watch Tower translation speaks for itself and shows more clearly than pen can, the scholastic dishonesty and lack of scholarship so rampant within its covers. In order to point out these glaring inconsistencies, the authors have listed five prime examples of the Watch Tower's inaccuracies in translating the New Testament.

(1) The first major perversion that Jehovah's Witnesses attempt to foist upon the minds of the average reader is that it has remained for them as God's true Witnesses to restore the divine name "Jehovah" to the text of the New Testament. But let us observe this pretext as they stated it in their own words.

> The evidence is, therefore, that the original text of the Christian Greek Scriptures has been tampered with, the same as the text of the LXX [The Septuagint—a Greek translation of the Old Testament] has been. And, at least

from the third century A.D. onward, the divine name in tetragrammaton [the Hebrew consonants YHWH, usually rendered "Jehovah"] form has been eliminated from the text by copyists. . . . In place of it they substituted the words *kyrios* (usually translated "the Lord") and *theos,* meaning "God" (page 18).

The "evidence" that the Witnesses refer to is a recently discovered papyrus roll of the LXX which contains the second half of the book of Deuteronomy and which does have the tetragrammaton throughout. Further than this, the Witnesses refer to Aquila (A.D. 128) and Origen who both utilized the tetragrammaton in their respective Version and Hexapla. Jerome in the fourth century also mentioned the tetragrammaton as appearing in certain Greek volumes even in his day. On the basis of this small collection of fragmentary "evidence" Jehovah's Witnesses conclude their argument thusly:

> It proves that the original LXX did contain the divine name wherever it occurred in the Hebrew original. Considering it a sacrilege to use some substitute such as *kyrios* or *theos,* the scribes inserted the tetragrammaton at its proper place in the Greek version text (page 12).

The whole case the Witnesses try to prove is that the original LXX and the New Testament autographs all used the tetragrammaton (page 18) but owing to "tampering" all these were changed; hence their responsibility to restore the divine name. Such is the argument, and a seemingly plausible one to those not familiar with the history of manuscripts and the Witnesses' subtle use of terms.

To explode this latest Watch Tower pretension of scholarship completely is indeed an elementary task. It can be shown from literally thousands of copies of the Greek New Testament that not *once* does the tetragrammaton appear, not even in Matthew, possibly written in Hebrew or Aramaic originally, and therefore more prone than all the rest to have traces of the divine name in it yet it does not! Beyond this, the roll

of papyrus (LXX) which contains the latter part of Deuteronomy and the divine name only proves that one copy did have the divine name (YHWH), whereas all other existing copies use *kyrios* and *theos,* which the Witnesses claim are "substitutes." The testimonies of Aquila, Origen and Jerome, in turn, only show that *sometimes* the divine name was used, but the general truth, upheld by all scholars, is that the Septuagint with minor exceptions always uses *kyrios* and *theos* in place of the tetragrammaton, and the New Testament never uses it at all. Relative to the nineteen "sources" the Watch Tower uses (pages 30-33) for restoring the tetragrammaton to the New Testament, it should be noted that they are all translations from Greek (which uses *kyrios* and *theos,* not the tetragrammaton) back into Hebrew, the earliest of which is A.D. 1385 and therefore they are of no value as evidence.

These cold logical facts unmask once and for all the shallow scholarship of Jehovah's Witnesses, whose arrogant pretension that they have a sound basis for restoring the divine name (Jehovah) to the Scriptures, while inferring that orthodoxy suppressed it centuries ago, is revealed to be a hollow scholastic fraud.

No reasonable scholar, of course, objects to the use of the term Jehovah in the Bible. But since only the Hebrew consonants YHWH appear without vowels, pronounciation is at best uncertain, and dogmatically to settle on *Jehovah* is straining at the bounds of good linguistics. When the Witnesses arrogantly claim then to have "restored" the divine name (Jehovah), it is almost pathetic. All students of Hebrew know that any vowel can be inserted between the consonants (YHWH or JHVH) so that theoretically the divine name could be any combination from JoHeVaH to JiHiViH without doing violence to the grammar of the language in the slightest degree. So much then for this, another empty claim of the Watch Tower's pseudo-scholars.

(2) *Colossians 1:16* — "By means of him all *other* things were created in the heavens and upon the earth, the things visible and the things invisible, no matter whether they are thrones or Lordships or governments or authorities" (N.W.T.).

In this particular rendering, Jehovah's Witnesses attempt one of the most clever perversions of the New Testament texts that the author has ever seen. Knowing full well that the word *other* does not occur in this text, or for that matter in any of the three texts (verses 16,17, 19), the Witnesses deliberately insert it into the translation in a vain attempt to make Christ a creature and one of the "things" He is spoken of as having created.

Attempting to justify this unheard of travesty upon the Greek language and simple honesty, the New World Translation committee inserts a footnote, marked (a) after each use of the word "other," which refers the reader to Luke 13:2,4, "and elsewhere," for apparent support of their ungrammatical rendering. Upon turning to Luke 13:2,4, however, the elementary Greek student can see that the Witnesses plainly do not have any grammatical leg to stand on as is shown by their immature reasoning. The verses utilized by the Watch Tower to cover up their scholastic dishonesty are as follows:

> So in reply, he said to them: "Do you imagine that these Galileans were proved worse sinners than all *other* Galileans because they have suffered these things?" (verse 2, N.W.T.).
>
> "Or those eighteen upon whom the tower of Siloam fell, thereby killing them, do you imagine that they were proved greater debtors than all *other* men inhabiting Jerusalem?" (verse 4, N.W.T.).

In the translation of these verses, the Watch Tower translators also inserted the word "other," not present in the Greek text, on the ground that it is im-

plied in the context, owing to the comparison made by Jesus. It is admissible, of course, that Jesus was drawing a contrast between certain Galileans and their fellow countrymen; but it is *not* admissible to insert terms in order to prove a doctrinal point, and in Colossians 1: 15-17 no such comparison or contrast is being made anyway; unless, as is the case with Jehovah's Witnesses, one assumes that Christ Himself was a "creature" or a "thing," which would necessitate inserting the word "other" in order to conform Scripture to a preconceived theology. It is incorrect grammar, no reputable translation dares tamper with doctrinal texts in this way, and not one single competent Greek authority can be cited for this deliberate attempt to reduce the Son of God from Creator to creature.

The entire context of Colossians 1: 15-22 is filled with superlatives in its description of the Lord Jesus as the "image of the invisible God, the first-begetter [or 'original bringer forth' — Erasmus] of every creature." The Apostle Paul lauds the Son of God as *creator* of all things (verse 16) and describes Him as existing "before all things" and "holding together all things" (verse 17). This is in perfect harmony with the entire picture Scripture paints of the eternal Word of God (John 1:1) who was made flesh (John 1:14) and of whom it was written: "All things were made by him, and without him was nothing made that was made" (John 1:3). The writer of the book of Hebrews also pointed out that God's Son "upholds all things by the word of his power" (Hebrews 1:3) and that He is Deity in all its fullness, even as Paul wrote to the Colossians: "For . . . in him should all the fullness [of God] dwell" (Colossians 1.19 A.S.V.).

The Scriptures, therefore, bear unmistakable testimony to the creative activity of God's Son, distinguishing Him from among the "things" created, as *the* Creator and Sustainer of "all things."

Jehovah's Witnesses have no conceivable ground, then, for this dishonest rendering of Colossians 1:16, 17 and 19 by the insertion of the word "other" since they are supported by no grammatical authorities, nor do they dare dispute their perversions with competent scholars lest they further parade their obvious ignorance of Greek exegesis.

(3) *Matthew 27:50*—"Again Jesus cried out with a loud voice, and ceased to breathe" (N.W.T.).

Luke 23:46—"And Jesus called with a loud voice and said: Father, into your hands I entrust my spirit" (N.W.T.).

For many years the Watch Tower has been fighting a vain battle to redefine Biblical terms to suit their own peculiar theological interpretations. They have had some measure of success in this attempt in that they have taught the rank and file a new meaning for tried and true Biblical terms, and it is this trait of their deceptive system that we analyze now in connection with the above quoted verses.

The interested student of Scripture will note from Matthew 27:50 and Luke 23:46 that they are parallel passages describing the same event, namely the crucifixion of Jesus Christ. In Matthew's account, the Witnesses had no difficulty substituting the word "breath" for the Greek spirit (*pneuma*), for in their vocabulary this word has many meanings, none of them having any bearing upon the general usage of the term, Biblically, i.e., that of an immaterial cognizant nature, inherent in man by definition and descriptive of angels through creation. Jehovah's Witnesses reject this immaterial nature in man and call it "breath," "life," "mental disposition" or "something wind like." In fact they will call it anything but what God's Word says it is, an invisible nature, eternal by creation, a spirit, made in the image of God (Genesis 1:27). Sometimes and in various contexts, spirit (*pneuma*) can mean some of the things the Witnesses hold, but context determines translation,

along with grammar, and their translations quite often do not remain true to either.

Having forced the word "breath" into Matthew's account of the crucifixion, to make it appear that Jesus only stopped breathing and did not yield up His invisible nature upon dying, the Witnesses plod on to Luke's account, only to be caught in their own trap. Luke, learned scholar and master of Greek that he was, forces the Witnesses to render his account of Christ's words using the correct term "spirit" (*pneuma*), instead of "breath" as in Matthew 27:50. Thus in one fell swoop the entire Watch Tower fabric of manufactured terminology collapses, because Jesus would hardly have said: "Father into thy hands I commit my *breath"* — yet if the Witnesses are consistent, which they seldom are, why did they not render the identical Greek term (*pneuma*) as "breath" both times, for it is a parallel account of the same scene!

The solution to this question is quite elementary as all can clearly see. The Witnesses could not render it "breath" in Luke and get away with it, so they used it where they could and hoped nobody would notice it, or the different rendering in Matthew. The very fact that Christ dismissed His spirit proves the survival of the human spirit beyond the grave, or as Solomon so wisely put it: "Then shall the dust return to the earth as it was: and the spirit [*pneuma* — LXX] shall return unto God who gave it" (Ecclesiastes 12:7).

(4) *Philippians 1:21-23* — "For in my case to live is Christ, and to die, gain. Now if it be to live on in the flesh, this is a fruitage of my work — and yet which thing to choose I do not know. I am under pressure from these two things; but what I do desire is the releasing and the being with Christ, for this, to be sure, is far better" (N.W.T.).

In common with other cults that teach soul-sleep after the death of the body, Jehovah's Witnesses translate texts contradicting this view to suit their own ends, a prime example of which is their rendering of Philippians 1:21-23. To anyone possessing even a cursory knowledge of Greek grammar the translation "but what I do desire is the releasing. . . ." (verse 23) signifies either a woeful ignorance of the rudiments of the language or a deliberate, calculated perversion of terminology for a purpose or purposes most questionable.

It is no coincidence that this text is a great "proof" passage for the expectation of every true Christian who after death goes to be with the Lord (II Corinthians 5:8). Jehovah's Witnesses realize that if this text goes unchanged or unchallenged it destroys utterly their Russellite teaching that the soul becomes extinct at the death of the body. This being the case, and since they could not challenge the text without exploding the myth of their acceptance of the Bible as the final authority, the Watch Tower committee chose to alter the passage in question, give it a new interpretation, and remove this threat to their theology.

The rendering, "but what I do desire is the releasing . . .," particularly the last word, is a gross imposition upon the principles of Greek exegesis because the untutored Russellites have rendered the first aorist active infinitive of the verb *analuoo* (*analusai*) as a substantive ("the releasing"), which in this context is unscholarly and atrocious Greek. In order to translate it "the releasing," the form would have to be the participle construction (*analusas*), which when used with the word "wish" or "desire" denotes "a great longing" or "purpose" and must be rendered "to depart" or "to unloose." (See Thayer, Liddell and Scott, Strong, Young and A. T. Robertson.)

Quite frankly, it may appear that I have gone to a great deal of trouble just to refute the wrong usage of a Greek form, but in truth this simple switching of terms is used by the Witnesses in an attempt to teach that Paul meant something entirely different than what he wrote to the Philippians. To see just how the Watch Tower manages this, I quote from their own Appendix to the New World Translation which appears on pages 780, 781.

The verb *a-na-ly'sai* is used as a verbal noun here. It occurs only once more in the Christian Greek Scriptures, and that is at Luke 12:36, where it refers to Christ's return. The related noun *(a-na'-ly-sis)* occurs but once, at II Timothy 4:6, where the apostle says: "The due time for my realeasing is imminent." . . . But here at Philippians 1:23 we have not rendered the verb as "returning" or "departing," but as "releasing." The reason is, that the word may convey two thoughts, the apostle's own releasing to be with Christ at His return and also the Lord's releasing Himself from the heavenly restraints and returning as He promised.

In no way is the apostle here saying that immediately at his death he would be changed into spirit and would be with Christ forever. . . . It is to this return of Christ and the apostle's releasing to be always with the Lord that Paul refers at Philippians 1:23. He says there that two things are immediately possible for him, namely, (1) to live on in the flesh and (2) to die. Because of the circumstances to be considered, he expressed himself as being under pressure from these two things, not knowing which thing to choose as proper. Then he suggests a third thing, and this thing he really desires. There is no question about his desire for this thing as preferable, namely, the releasing, for it means his being with Christ.

The expression to *a-na-ly'sai*, or *the releasing* cannot therefore be applied to the apostle's death as a human creature and his departing thus from this life. It must refer to the events at the time of Christ's return and second presence, that is to say, his second coming and the rising of all those dead in Christ to be with him forevermore.

Here, after much grammatical intrigue, we have the key as to why the Witnesses went to so much trouble to render "depart" as "releasing." By slipping in this grammatical error, the Watch Tower hoped to "prove" that Paul wasn't really discussing his impending death and subsequent reunion with Christ at all (a fact every major Biblical scholar and translator in history has held), but a *third* thing, namely, "the events at the time of Christ's return and second presence." With breathtaking dogmatism, the Witnesses claim that "the releasing cannot therefore be applied to the Apostle's death. It *must* refer to the events at the time of Christ's return. . . ."

Words fail the trained mind when confronted with this classic example of unparalleled deceit, which finds no support in any Greek text or exegetical grammatical authority. Contrary to the Watch Tower's statement that "the word may convey two thoughts, the Apostle's 'releasing' to be with Christ at his return, and also the Lord's 'releasing' himself from the heavenly restraints and returning as he promised" (page 781), the Greek text offers no such thought. As a matter of plain exegetical fact, Christ's return is not even the subject of discussion — rather it is the Apostle's death and his concern for the Philippians that is here portrayed. That Paul never expected to "sleep" in his grave until the resurrection as Jehovah's Witnesses maintain is evident by the twenty-first verse of the chapter literally — "For me to live is Christ, and to die is gain." There would be no gain in dying if men slept till the resurrection, for "God is not the God of the dead but of the living" (Mark 12:27). Clearly then, Paul was speaking of but two things: his possible death and subsequent presence with the Lord (II Corinthians 5:8), and also the possibility of his continuing on in the body, the latter being "more needful" for the Philippian Christians. His choice in his own words was between these two (verse 23), and Jehovah's Witnesses have gone to great trouble for nothing; the Greek text still records faithfully what the inspired Apostle said —not what the Watch Tower maintains he said, all their deliberate trickery to the contrary.

Concluding our comments upon these verses in Philippians, we feel constrained to point out a final example of Watch Tower dishonesty relative to Greek translation.

On page 781 of the New World Translation, it will be recalled that the Committee wrote: "The expression to *a-na-ly'-sai* or *the releasing* cannot therefore apply to the apostle's death as a human creature and his departing thus from this life."

If the interested reader will turn to page 628 of the same Watch Tower Translation, he will observe that in II Timothy 4:6 the Witnesses once more use the term "releasing" (*analuseos*), where all translators are agreed that it refers to Paul's impending *death*. The Revised Standard Version, often appealed to by Jehovah's Witnesses, puts it this way:

"For I am already on the point of being sacrificed, the time of my departure has come." (See also — An American Translation [Goodspeed], Authorized Version, J. N. Darby's Version, James Moffatt's Version, J. B. Rotherham's Version, Douay Version [Roman Catholic], etc.).

Jehovah's Witnesses themselves render the text: "For I am already being poured out like a drink offering, and the due time of my *releasing* is imminent" (II Timothy 4:6, N.W.T.).

Now since it is admitted by the Witnesses under the pressure of every translator's rendering of his text, that it refers to Paul's death, and further, since the noun form of the Greek word (*analuseos*) is here used and translated "releasing," why is it that they claim on page 781 that this expression "the releasing" (*analusai* — Philippians 1:23) ". . . cannot therefore apply to the apostle's death as a human creature and his departing thus from this life"? The question becomes more embarrassing when it is realized that Jehovah's Witnesses themselves admit that these two forms (*analusai* and *analuseos*) are "related" (page 781). Hence they have no excuse for maintaining in one place (Philippians 1:23) that "the releasing" cannot refer to the apostle's death, and in another place (II Timothy 4:6) using a form of the same word, and allowing that it does refer to his death. This one illustration alone should serve to warn all honest people of the blatant deception employed in the Watch Tower's "translations," a name not worthy of application in many, many places.

(5) *Matthew 24:3*—"While he was sitting upon the mount of Olives, the disciples approached him privately, saying: 'Tell us, When will these things be, and what will be the sign of your presence and of the consummation of the system of things?' " (N.W.T.).

Since the days of "Pastor" Russell and Judge Rutherford, one of the favorite dogmas of the Watch Tower has been that of the *parousia*, the second coming or "presence" of the Lord Jesus Christ. Jehovah's Witnesses, loyal Russellites that they are, have tenaciously clung to the "Pastor's" theology in this respect and maintain that in the year 1914 when the "times of the gentiles" ended (according to Russell) the "second presence" of Christ began. (See *Make Sure of All Things*, page 319—Watch Tower Bible and Tract Society.)

From the year 1914 onward, the Witnesses maintain,

Christ has turned his attention toward earth's affairs and is dividing the peoples and educating the true Christians in preparation for their survival during the great storm of Armageddon, when all unfaithful mankind will be destroyed from the face of the earth (*op. cit.*, page 319).

For Jehovah's Witnesses, then, Christ is not coming; He is here! (A.D. 1914) — only invisibly — and He is directing His activities through His theocratic organization in Brooklyn, New York. In view of this claim, it might be well to hearken unto the voice of Matthew who wrote:

Then if any man shall say to you. Lo, here is Christ, or there; believe it not. For there shall arise false Christs, and false prophets, and shall shew great signs and wonders; insomuch that, if it were possible, they shall deceive the very elect. Behold I have told you before. Wherefore if they shall say unto you, Behold he is in the desert; go not forth; behold, he is in the secret chambers; believe it not. For as the lightning cometh out of the east, and shineth even unto the west; so shall also the coming of the Son of man be (Matthew 24:23-27).

Jehovah's Witnesses in their New World Translation on page 780 list the twenty-four occurrences of the Greek word *parousia*, which they translate each time as "presence." They give the following defense found on page 779:

The tendency of many translators is to render it here "coming" or "arrival." But throughout the twenty-four occurrences, the Greek word *parousia* . . . we have rendered it "presence." From the comparison of the parousia of the Son of man with the days of Noah at Matthew 24:37-39, *it is very evident that the meaning of the word is as we have rendered it*. And from the contrast that is made between the presence and the absence of the apostle both at II Corinthains 10:10-11 and at Philippians 2:12, *the meaning of parousia is so plain that it is beyond dispute by other translators*.

Following this gigantic claim, namely, that their translation of the word *parousia* is "beyond dispute by other translators," the theocratic authorities proceed to list the verses in question.

Now the main issue is not the translation of *parousia* by "presence" because in some contexts it is certainly allowable (see I Corinthians 16:16, II Corinthians 7:6,7; 10:10 and Philippians 1:26; 2:12). But there are other contexts where it cannot be allowed in the way Jehovah's Witnesses use it, because it not only violates the contextual meaning of the word, but the entire meaning of the passages as always held by the Christian Church.

Jehovah's Witnesses claim scholarship

for this blanket translation of *parousia*, yet not one great scholar in the history of Greek exegesis and translation has ever held this view. Since 1871, when "Pastor" Russell produced this concept, it has been denounced by every competent scholar upon examination.

The reason this Russellite rendering is so dangerous is that it attempts to prove that *parousia* in regard to Christ's second advent really means that His return or "presence" was to be invisible and unknown to all but "the faithful" Russellites, of course). (See *Make Sure of All Things,* pages 319, 320-323).

The New World Translators, therefore, on the basis of those texts where it is acceptable to render *parousia* "presence," conclude that it must be acceptable in all texts. But while it appears to be acceptable grammatically, no one but Jehovah's Witnesses or their sympathizers accepts the New World blanket use of "presence," be the translators Christian or not. It simply is not good grammar, and it will not stand up under comparative exegesis as will be shown. To conclude that "presence" necessarily implies invisibility is also another flaw in the Watch Tower's argument, for in numerous places where they render *parousia* "presence" the persons spoken of were hardly invisible. (See I Corinthians 16:17; II Corinthians 7:6 and 10:10, also Philippians 1:26 and 2:12.)

If the Watch Tower were to admit for one moment that *parousia* can be translated "coming" or "arrival," in the passages which speak of Christ's return the way all scholarly translators render it, then "Pastor" Russell's "invisible presence" of Christ would explode in their faces. Hence their determination to deny what all recognized Greek authorities have established.

Dr. Joseph F. Thayer, a Unitarian scholar, author of one of the best lexicons of the Greek New Testament (who, incidentally, denied the visible second coming of Christ), says on page 490

of that work, when speaking of *parousia:* ". . . a return (Philippians 1:26) . . . In the New Testament especially of the Advent, i.e., the future visible return from heaven of Jesus, the Messiah, to raise the dead, hold the last judgment, and set up formally and gloriously the Kingdom of God." (For further references, see Liddell and Scott, Strong and any other reputable authority.)

Dr. Thayer, it might be mentioned, was honest enough to say what the New Testament Greek taught, even though he didn't believe it. One could wish that Jehovah's Witnesses were at least that honest, but they are not!

In concluding this discussion of the misuse of *parousia* we shall discuss the verses Jehovah's Witnesses use to "prove" that Christ's return was to be an invisible "presence" instead of a visible glorious, verifiable event.

The following references and their headings were taken from the book, *Make Sure of All Things,* published by the Watch Tower as an official guide to their doctrine.

(1) *Angels Testified at Jesus' Ascension as a Spirit that Christ Would Return in Like Manner, Quiet, Unobserved by the Public* (page 320).

And after he had said these things while they (only the disciples) were looking on, he was lifted up and a cloud caught him up from their vision. . . . "Men of Galilee, why do you stand looking into the sky? This Jesus who was received up from you into heaven will come thus in the same manner as you have beheld him going into heaven" (Acts 1:9, 11, N.W.T.).

It is quite unnecessary to refute in detail this open perversion of a clear Biblical teaching because as John 20:27 clearly shows, Christ was not a spirit, and did not ascend as one. The very text they quote shows that the disciples were "looking on" and saw him "lifted up and a cloud caught him from their vision" (verse 9). They could hardly have been looking at a spirit, which by definition is incorporeal,* not with human eyes at least, and Christ had told them once before, "Behold my hands and my feet, that it is I myself: handle me, and see; for a Spirit hath not flesh and bones, as ye see me have" (Luke 24:39).

So it remains for Christ Himself to denounce the Russellite error that He "ascended as a spirit." Moreover, since He left the earth visibly from the Mount of Olives it is certain that He will return visibly even as the Scriptures teach (see Matthew 26:63, 64; Daniel 7:13, 14; Revelation 1:7, 8; Matthew 24:7, 8, 30).

(2) *Christ's Return Invisible, as He Testified that Man Would Not See Him Again in Human Form* (page 321).

A little longer and the world will behold me no more (John 14:19, N.W.T.).

For I say to you, You shall by no means .see me from henceforth until you say, "Blessed is he that comes in Jehovah's name!" (Matthew 23:39, N.W.T.).

These two passages in their respective contexts give no support to the Russellite doctrine of an invisible "presence" of Christ for two very excellent reasons:

(a) John 14:19 refers to Christ's anticipated death and resurrection — the "little longer" He made reference to could only have referred to His resurrection and subsequent ascension (Acts 1:9, 11), before which time and during the period following His resurrection He appeared only to believers, not the world (or unbelievers), hence the clear meaning of His words. Jesus never said that *no* one would ever "see Him Again in Human Form" as the Watch Tower likes to make out. Rather in the same chapter He promised to *"come again* and receive you unto myself, that where I am, there you may be also" (verse 3). The Bible also is quite clear in telling us that one day by His grace alone "we shall be like him, for we shall *see* him as he is" (I John 3:2-). So the Watch

Tower once more is forced to silence by the voice of the Holy Spirit.

(b) This second text, Matthew 23:39, really proves nothing at all for the Watch Tower's faltering arguments except that Jerusalem will never see Christ again until it blesses Him in repentance as the anointed of God. Actually the text hurts the Russellite position, for it teaches that Christ will be *visible* at His coming, else they could not see Him to bless Him in the name of the Lord. Christ also qualified the statement with the word "until," a definite reference to His visible second advent (Matthew 24:30).

(3) *Early Christians Expected Christ's Return to Be Invisible. Paul Argued There Was Insufficient Evidence in Their Day* (page 321).

However, brothers, respecting the presence of our Lord Jesus Christ and our being gathered together to him, we request of you not to be quickly shaken from your reason nor to be excited either through an inspired expression or through a verbal message or through a letter as though from us, to the effect that the day of Jehovah is here. Let no one seduce you in any manner, because it will not come unless the falling away comes first and the man of lawlessness gets revealed, the son of destruction (II Thessalonians 2:1-3).

This final example from II Thessalonians most vividly portrays the Witnesses at their crafty best, as they desperately attempt to make Paul teach what in all his writings he most emphatically denied, namely that Christ would come invisibly for His saints.

In his epistle to Titus, Paul stressed the importance of "looking for that blessed hope, the glorious appearing of the great God and our Saviour Jesus Christ" (2:13), something he would not have been looking for if it was to be a secret, invisible *parousia* or "presence."

Paul, contrary to Jehovah's Witnesses, never believed in an invisible return, nor

*Even angels have to take a human form in order to be seen (Genesis 19:1, 2).

did any bona fide member of the Christian Church up until the fantasies of Charles Taze Russell and his *parousia* nightmare, as a careful look at Paul's first epistle to the Thessalonians plainly reveals. Said the inspired Apostle:

> For this we say unto you by the word of the Lord, that we which are alive and remain unto the *coming* of the Lord shall not prevent them which are asleep.
>
> For the Lord himself shall *descend* from heaven [visible] with a shout [audible], with the voice of the archangel, and with the trump of God; and the dead in Christ shall rise first (4:15, 16).

Here we see that in perfect accord with Matthew 26 and Revelation 1, Christ is pictured as *coming* visibly, and in this context no reputable Greek scholar alive will allow the use of "presence"; it must be "coming." (See also II Thessalonians 2:8.)

For further information relative to this subject, consult any standard concordance and Greek lexicon available, and trace Paul's use of the word *"Coming,"* etc. This will convince any fair-minded person that Paul never entertained the Watch Tower's fantastic view of Christ's return.

These things being clearly understood, the interested reader should give careful attention to those verses in the New Testament which do not use the word *parousia* but are instead forms of the verb *elthon* and related to the word *erchomai*. (See Thayer, page 250ff) and which refer to the Lord's coming as a visible manifestation. These various texts cannot be twisted to fit the Russellite pattern of "presence," since *erchomai* means "to come," "to appear," "to arrive," etc., in the most definite sense of the term. (For reference, check Matthew 24:30 in conjunction with Matthew 26:64 — *erchomenon;* also John 14:3 — *echomai;* and Revelation 1:7 — *erchetai.*)

Once it is perceived that Jehovah's Witnesses are only interested in what they can make the Scriptures say, and not in what the Holy Spirit has already perfectly revealed, then the careful student will reject entirely Jehovah's Witnesses and their Watch Tower translations. These are as "blind leaders of the blind" (Matthew 15:14) who have "turned the grace of God into lasciviousness, and denied our only Master and Lord Jesus Christ" (Jude 4). Further, that they "wrest the scriptures to their own destruction" (II Peter 3:16), the foregoing evidence has thoroughly revealed for all to judge.

The Deity of Jesus Christ

Throughout the entire content of inspired Scripture the fact of Christ's identity is clearly taught. He is revealed as Jehovah-God in human form, (Isaiah 9:6; Micah 5:2; Isaiah 7:14; John 1:1; 8:58; 17:5; cf. Exodus 3:14; and Hebrews 1:3; Philippians 2:11; Colossians 2:9; and Revelation 1:8, 17, 18; etc.). The Deity of Jesus Christ is one of the cornerstones of Christianity, and as such has been attacked more vigorously throughout the ages than any other single doctrine of the Christian faith. Adhering to the old Arian heresy, which Athanasius the great Church Father refuted in his famous essay "On the Incarnation of the Word," many individuals and all cults steadfastly deny the equality of Jesus Christ with God the Father, and hence the Triune Deity. Jehovah's Witnesses, as has been observed, are no exception to this infamous rule. However, the testimony of the Scriptures standeth sure and the above mentioned references alone put to silence forever this blasphemous heresy, which in the power of Satan himself deceives many with its "deceitful handling of the Word of God."

The Deity of Christ then is a prime answer to Jehovah's Witnesses, for if the Trinity is a reality, which it is, if Jesus and Jehovah are "One" and the Same, then the whole framework of the cult collapses into a heap of shattered disconnected doctrines incapable of even a semblance of congruity. We will now consider the verses in question, and their bearing on the matter.

    1. (a) Isaiah 7:14 — "Therefore the Lord [Jehovah] himself shall give you a sign; Behold, a virgin shall conceive, and bear a son, and shall call his name Immanuel" (lit., God or Jehovah with us, since Jehovah is the *only* God).

    (b) Isaiah 9:6 — "For unto us a child is born, unto us a son is given: and the government shall be upon his shoulder: and his name shall be called Wonderful, Counsellor, The mighty God, The everlasting Father, The Prince of Peace."

    (c) Micah 5:2 — "But thou, Bethlehem Ephratah, though thou be little among the thousands of Judah, yet out of thee shall he come forth unto me that is to be ruler in Israel; whose goings forth have been from of old, from everlasting."

Within the realm of Old Testament Scripture Jehovah, the Lord of Hosts, has revealed His plan to appear in human form and has fulfilled the several prophecies concerning this miracle in the Person of Jesus Christ. Examination of the above listed texts will more than convince the unbiased student of Scripture that Jehovah has kept His promises and did become man, literally "God with us" (Matthew 1:23; Luke 1:32, 33; John 1:14).

The key to Isaiah 7:14 is the Divine Name "Immanuel," which can only be rightly rendered "God with us"; and since there is no other God but Jehovah by His own declaration (Isaiah 43:10, 11), therefore Jesus Christ and Jehovah God are of the same Substance in power and eternity, hence equal. This prophecy was fulfilled in Matthew 1:22, 2, 3; thus there can be no doubt that Jesus Christ is the "son of the virgin" so distinctly portrayed in Isaiah 7:14. Jehovah's Witnesses can present no argument to refute this plain declaration of Scripture, namely that

Jehovah and Christ are "One" and the Same, since the very term "Immanuel" (God or Jehovah with us) belies any other interpretation.

Isaiah 9:6 in the Hebrew Bible is one of the most powerful verses in the Old Testament, in proving the Deity of Christ, and incontestably declares that Jehovah Himself planned to appear in human form. The verse clearly states that all government will rest upon the "Child born" and the "Son given" whose identity is revealed in the very terms used to describe His attributes. Isaiah under the inspiration of the Holy Spirit describes Christ as "Wonderful, Counsellor, The mighty God, The everlasting Father, The Prince of Peace," all attributes of God alone. The term "mighty God" is in itself indicative of Jehovah since not only is He the only God (Isaiah 43:10, 11), but the term "mighty" is applied to Him alone in relation to His Deity. Jehovah's Witnesses dodge this verse by claiming that Christ is "a Mighty God,"[30] but not the Almighty God (Jehovah). This argument is ridiculous on the face of the matter. However, Jehovah's Witnesses argue that since there is no article in the Hebrew text, "mighty," therefore, does not mean Jehovah. The question then arises, are there two "mighty Gods"? This we know is absurd; yet Jehovah's Witnesses persist in the fallacy, despite Isaiah 10:21, where Isaiah (without the article) declares that "Jacob shall return" unto the "mighty God," and we know that Jehovah is by His own word to Moses "the God of Jacob" (Exodus 3:6). In Jeremiah 32:18 (with the article) the prophet declares that He (Jehovah) is "the great, and the Mighty God" (two forms of saying the same thing). (Cf. Isaiah 9:6; 10:21; Jeremiah 32:18.) If we are to accept Jehovah's Witnesses' view, there must be two "Mighty Gods"; and that is impossible, for

---

[30]See *The Truth Shall Make You Free*, page 47.

there is only One True and Mighty God (Isaiah 45:22).

The prophet Micah, writing in Micah 5:2, recording Jehovah's words, gives not only the birthplace of Christ (which the Jews affirmed as being the City of David, Bethlehem), but he gives a clue as to His identity—namely God in human form. The term "goings forth" can be rendered *origin* (reference—Brown, Driver and Briggs, *Hebrew Lexicon of the Old Testament*, 426 [a] Item [2]), and we know that the only one who fits this description, whose origin is "from everlasting" must be God Himself, since He alone is "the eternally existing One" (Isaiah 44:6, 8). The overwhelming testimony of these verses alone ascertains beyond reasonable doubt the Deity of the Lord Jesus Christ, who became man, identified Himself with us in that incarnation, and offered Himself "once for all" a ransom for many, the eternal sacrifice who is able to save to the uttermost whoever will appropriate His cleansing power.

    2. John 1:1 — "In the beginning [or 'origin,' Greek, *Arche*] was the Word [*Logos*] and the Word was with God [*Ton Theon*] and the Word was God [*Theos*]."

Contrary to the translations of *The Emphatic Diaglott* and the *New World Translation* the Greek grammatical construction leaves no doubt whatsoever that this is the only possible rendering of the text. The subject of the sentence is *Word (Logos)*, the verb, *was*. There can be no direct object following *was* since according to grammatical usage intransitive verbs take no objects but take instead predicate nominatives which refer back to the subject, in this case, *Word (Logos)*.[31] It is therefore easy to see that no article is needed for *Theos* (God) and to translate it "a god" is both incorrect

grammar and poor Greek since *Theos* is the predicate nominative of *was* in the third sentence-clause of the verse and must refer back to the subject, *Word (Logos)*. Christ then if He is the Word "made flesh" (John 1:14) can be no one else except God unless the Greek text and consequently God's Word be denied.

Jehovah's Witnesses in their *New World Translation* Appendix 773-777 attempt to discredit the Greek text on this point, for they realize that if Jesus and Jehovah are "One" in nature their theology cannot stand, since they deny that unity of nature. The refutation of their arguments on this point is conclusive.[32]

The claim is that since the definite article is used with *Theon* in John 1:1c and not with *Theos* in John 1:1d, therefore the omission is designed to show a difference; the alleged difference being that in the first case the One True God (Jehovah) is meant, while in the second "a god," other than, and inferior to, the first is meant, this latter "god" being Jesus Christ.

On page 776b the claim is made that the rendering "a god" is correct because ". . . all the doctrine of sacred Scriptures bears out the correctness of this rendering." This remark focuses attention on the fact that the whole problem involved goes far beyond this text. Scripture does in fact teach the full and equal Deity of Christ. Why then is so much made of this one verse? It is probably because of the surprise effect derived from the show of pseudo-scholarship in the use of a familiar text. Omission of the article with *Theos* does not mean that "a god" other than the one true God is meant. Let one examine these passages where the article is not used with *Theos* and see if the rendering "a god" makes

---

[31]Colwell's rule clearly states that a definite predicate nominative (*Theos* — God) *never* takes an article when it precedes the verb (*was*) as in John 1:1.

[32]Remarks on Appendix note to John 1:1, pages 773-777. *New World Translation of the Christian Greek Scriptures.*

sense (Matthew 5:9; 6:24; Luke 1:35, 78; 2:40; John 1:6, 12, 13, 18; 3:2, 21; 9:16, 33; Romans 1:7, 17, 18; I Corinthians 1:30; 15:10; Philippians 2:11, 13; Titus 1:1 and many, many more). The "a god" contention proves too weak and is inconsistent. To be consistent in this rendering of "a god" Jehovah's Witnesses would have to translate every instance where the article is absent as "a god (nominative), of a god (genitive), to or for a god (dative)," etc. This they do not do in Matthew 5:9; 6:24; Luke 1:35, 78; John 1:6, 12, 13, 18; Romans 1:7, 17, etc. (See *New World Translation* and *Emphatic Diaglott* at above mentioned references.)

You cannot honestly render *Theos* "a god" in John 1:1, and then *Theou* "of God" (Jehovah), in Matthew 5:9, Luke 1:35, 78; John 1:6, etc., when *Theou* is the genitive case of the *same* noun (second declension), *without* an article and *must* be rendered (following Jehovah's Witnesses' argument) "of *a* god" not "of God" as both *The Emphatic Diaglott* and *New World Translation* put it. We could list at great length, but suggest consultation of the Greek New Testament by either D. Erwin Nestle or Westcott & Hort, in conjunction with *The Elements of Greek* by Francis Kingsley Ball (Macmillan, 1948, pages 7, 14) on noun endings, etc. So then if Jehovah's Witnesses must persist in this fallacious "a god" rendition they can at least be consistent, which *they are not,* and render every instance where the article is absent in the same manner. The truth of the matter is this, that Jehovah's Witnesses use and remove the articular emphasis whenever and *wherever* it suits their fancy regardless of grammatical laws to the contrary. In a translation as important as God's Word every law must be observed. Jehovah's Witnesses have not been consistent in their observances of those laws.

The writers of the claim have ex-

hibited another trait common to Jehovah's Witnesses, that of half quoting or misquoting a recognized authority to bolster their ungrammatical renditions. On page 776 (N.W.T.) when quoting Dr. Robertson's words, "among the ancient writers *O Theos* was used of the god of the absolute religion in distinction from the mythological gods," they fail to note that in the second sentence following, Dr. Robertson says, "In the New Testament, however, while we have *pros ton Theon* (John 1:1, 2) it is far more common to find simply *Theos,* especially in the Epistles."

In other words, the writers of the New Testament frequently do not use the article with *Theos* and yet the meaning is perfectly clear in the context, namely that the One True God is intended. Let one examine the following references where in successive verses and even in the same sentence the article is used with *one* occurrence of *Theos* and *not* with another form, and it will be absolutely clear that no such drastic inferences can be drawn from John's usage in John 1:1, 2. (Matthew 4:3, 4; 12:28; 28:43; Luke 20:37, 38; John 3:2; 13:3; Acts 5:29, 30; Romans 1:7, 8, 17-19; 2:16, 17; 3:5, 22, 23; 4:2, 3, etc.)

The doctrine of the article is important in Greek; it is *not* used indiscriminately. But we are *not* qualified to be sure in *all* cases what is intended. Dr. Robertson is careful to note that "it is only of recent years that a really scientific study of the article has been made" (page 755, A. T. Robertson). The facts are not all known and no such drastic conclusion as the writers of the appendix note draw should be dogmatically affirmed.

It is nonsense to say that a simple noun can be rendered "divine," and that one without article conveys merely the idea of quality (pages 773, 774, N. W. T.). The authors of this note themselves later render the same noun

Theos as "a god" not as "a quality." This is a self-contradiction in the context.

In conclusion, the position of the writers of this note is made clear at page 774 (N. W. T.); according to them it is "unreasonable" that the Word (Christ) should be the God with whom He was (John 1:1). Their own manifestly erring reason is made the criterion for determining Scriptural truth. One need only note the obvious misuse in their quotation from "Dana and Mantey" (pages 774, 775). Mantey clearly means that the "Word was Deity" in accord with the overwhelming testimony of Scripture, but the writers have dragged in the interpretation "a god" to suit their own purpose, which purpose is the denial of Christ's Deity, and as a result a denial of the Word of God.

3. John 8:58—"Jesus said unto them . . . before Abraham was [born], *I am.*"

In comparing this with the Septuagint translation of Exodus 3:14 and Isaiah 43:10-13, we find that the translation is identical. In Exodus 3:14, Jehovah, speaking to Moses, said, *"I am,"* which any intelligent scholar recognizes as synonymous with God. Jesus literally said to them, *"I am* Jehovah" *(I am),* and it is clear that they understood Him to mean just that, for they attempted, as the next verse reveals, to stone Him. Hebrew law on this point states five cases in which stoning was legal — and bear in mind that the Jews were legalists. Those cases were: (1) Familiar spirits, Leviticus 20:27; (2) Cursing (Blasphemy), Leviticus 24:10-23; (3) False Prophets who lead to idolatry, Deuteronomy 13:5-10; (4) Stubborn son, Deuteronomy 21:18-21; and (5) Adultery and Rape, Deuteronomy 22:21-24 and Leviticus 20:10. Now any

honest Biblical student must admit that the only legal ground the Jews had for stoning Christ (and actually they had none at all) was the second violation — namely, blasphemy. Many zealous Jehovah's Witnesses maintain that the Jews were going to stone Him because He called them children of the devil (John 8:44). But if this were true, why did they not stone Him on other occasions (Matthew 12:34; 23:33; etc.) when He called them sons of vipers? The answer is very simple. They could not stone Christ on that ground because they were bound by the law which gives only five cases, and would have condemned them on their own grounds had they used "insult" as a basis for stoning. This is not all, however, for in John 10:33, the Jews again attempted to stone Christ and accused Him of making Himself God, (not *a god,* which subject has already been treated at length).[33] Let us be logical then; if the Jews observed the laws of stoning on other occasions when they might have been insulted, why would they violate the law as they would have had to do if Jehovah's Witnesses are right in John 8:58? Little more need be said. The argument is ridiculous in its context; there is only *one "I am"* in the Scriptures (Isaiah 48:12; 44:6; Revelation 1:8 and 17), and Jesus laid claim to that Identity for which the Jews, misinterpreting the law, set about to stone Him.

Jehovah's Witnesses (page 312 of the N. W. T., footnote "c") declare that the Greek rendering of *Ego Eimi (I am)* in John 8:58 is "properly rendered in the 'perfect indefinite sense' (I have been), not ' I am.' To unmask this bold perversion of the Greek text we shall now examine it grammatically to see if it has any valid grounds for being so translated.

It is difficult to know what the author

---

[33]Jehovah's Witnesses point to the *New English Bible's* rendering of this as "a god" as proof of the validity of their translation.

The fact is, however, that the *NEB* mistranslated this passage and is correcting it.

of the note on page 312 means since he *does not* use standard grammatical terminology, nor is his argument documented from standard grammars. The aorist infinitive as such does *not* form a clause. It is the adverb *Prin* which is significant here, so that the construction should be called *Prin* clause. The term "perfect indefinite" is an invention of the author of the note, so it is impossible to know what is meant. The real problem in the verse is the verb *"Ego Eimi."* Dr. Robertson, who is quoted as authoritative by the N. W. T., page 775, states (page 880) that *Eimi* is "absolute." This means there is *no* predicate expressed with it. This usage occurs four times (in John 8:24; 8:58; 13:19; 18:5). In these places the term is the same used by the Septuagint at Deuteronomy 32:39; Isaiah 43:10; 46:4; etc., to render the Hebrew phrase "I (am) He." The phrase occurs *only* where Jehovah's Lordship is reiterated. The phrase then is a claim to full and equal Deity. The incorrect and rude rendering of the N. W. T. only serves to illustrate the difficulty of evading the meaning of the phrase and the context.

The meaning of the phrase in the sense of full Deity is especially clear at John 13:19 where Jesus says that He has told them things before they came to pass, that when they do come to pass the disciples may believe that *Ego Eimi (I am)*. Jehovah is the only One who knows the future as a present fact. Jesus is telling them beforehand that when it does come to pass in the future, they may know that *"I am" (Ego Eimi)*, i.e. that *He is Jehovah!*

In conclusion, the facts are self-evident and undeniably clear — the Greek allows no such impositions as "I have been."[34] The term is translated correctly *"I am"* and since Jehovah is the only

"I am" (Exodus 3:14; Isaiah 44:6) He and Christ are "One" in Nature, truly the fullness of the "Deity" in the flesh.

The Septuagint translation of Exodus 3:14 from the Hebrew EHYEH utilizes *Ego Eini* as the equivalent of *"I am,"* Jehovah, and Jesus quoted the Septuagint to the Jews frequently, hence their known familiarity with it, and their anger at His claim (8:59).

> 4. Hebrews 1:3 — "He [Christ][35] is the reflection of His [Jehovah's] glory, and the image imprinted by His [Jehovah's] Substance, and He [Christ] sustains all things by the word of His power . . . " (New World Translation).

This passage of Scripture, I believe, clarifies beyond doubt the Deity of Jesus Christ. It would be illogical, and unreasonable to suppose that Christ, who is the image imprinted by Jehovah's *Substance,* is not *of* the Substance of Jehovah and hence God, or the second Person of the Triune Deity. No creation is ever declared to be of God's very "Substance" or "Essence" (Greek *upostaseos*); therefore the eternal Word, who is "the fullness of the Godhead [Deity] bodily" (Colossians 2:9), cannot be a creation, or a created being. The writer of the book of Hebrews clearly intended to portray Christ as Jehovah, or he never would have used such explicit language as "the image imprinted by His Substance," and as Isaiah 7:14 clearly states, the Messiah was to be Immanuel, literally "God with us." Jehovah's Witnesses attempt the articular fallacy of "a god" instead of God, in reference to Immanuel; but if there has been "no god formed before or after Me" (Jehovah speaking in Isaiah 43:10) then it is impossible on that ground alone, namely God's declaration, for any other god ("a God"

---

[34] The Watch Tower's contention on this point is that the phrase in question is a "historical present" used in reference to Abraham, hence permissible. This is a classic example of Watch Tower double talk. Jesus was not

narrating but arguing, and the "historical present" is used in narrative not argument as any standard grammar reveals.

[35] Brackets are ours.

included) to exist. Their argument, based on a grammatical abstraction, fails to stand here; and the Deity of the Lord Jesus as always remains unscathed.

5. Philippians 2:11 — ". . . And every tongue should confess that Jesus Christ is Lord, to the glory of God the Father."

If we compare this verse of Scripture with Colossians 2:9 and Isaiah 45:23 we cannot help but see the full Deity of the Lord Jesus in its true light.

Jehovah spoke in Isaiah 45:23 and said, "I have sworn by myself, the word is gone out of my mouth in righteousness, and shall not return. That unto *me* every knee shall bow, every tongue shall swear." In Colossians 2:9 the Apostle Paul writing under the inspiration of the Holy Spirit declares, "For in Him [Christ] dwelleth all the fullness of the Godhead bodily." The literal translation of the Greek word *Theotetos* (Godhead) is *Deity*, so in Christ all the fullness (*pleroma*) of the Deity resides in the flesh (*somatikos*).

In Thayer's *Greek-English Lexicon of the New Testament*, which is referred to as being "comprehensive" (page 19, N.W.T.), a complete analysis of *Theotetos* (Godhead, Deity) is given, especially its interpretation in the context of Colossians 2:9. Jehovah's Witnesses will do well to remember that Thayer was a Unitarian (one who denies the Deity of Christ) and therefore more prone to accept their interpretations than those of evangelical Christianity. But despite his theological views Thayer was a Greek scholar whose integrity in the presentation of honest facts, despite their disagreement with his beliefs, is the trait exemplified in all good critics and honest scholars. On page 288 of the edition of 1886, Thayer states that *Theotetos* [Godhead, Deity] is a form of *Theot* [Deity] or in his own words "i.e., the state of Being God, Godhead" (Colossians 2:9)! In other words Christ was the fullness of "The

Deity" (Jehovah) in the flesh! *The Emphatic Diaglott* correctly translates *Theotetos* "Deity"; but the N.W.T. erroneously renders it "the divine quality," which robs Christ of His Deity. Jehovah's Witnesses arrive at this inaccurate translation by substituting the word *Theiotes*, a form of *Theiot* (divinity) and thus escaping the condemning evidence of "The Deity" (Jehovah) *tes Theotetos*. However, documentary evidence reveals that they cannot rightfully do this for in Thayer's own words (page 288), *"Theot* (Deity) *differs* from *theiot* (divinity) as essence differs from quality or attribute." This fact again exposes the deception employed by Jehovah's Witnesses to lead the unwary Bible student astray into the paths of blasphemy against the Lord Jesus. It is improper, it *cannot* be so translated, the substitution of one word for another in translation is pure scholastic dishonesty and Jehovah's Witnesses can produce no authority for this bold mistranslation of the Greek text. Jesus Christ, according to the words themselves, is the same "Essence" and "Substance" as Jehovah, and as the Essence (Deity) differs from the *quality* (divinity) so He is God — *tes Theotetos* (The Deity) — Jehovah manifest in the flesh.

That Jesus and Jehovah are "One" in nature dare not be questioned from these verses which so clearly reveal the plan and purpose of God. Paul sustains this argument in his epistle to the Philippians (before quoted) when he ascribes to the Lord Jesus the identity of Jehovah as revealed in Isaiah 45:23. Paul proclaims boldly, "That at the name of *Jesus* every knee should bow . . . and every tongue confess that Jesus Christ is Lord to the glory of God the Father." It is a well-known Biblical fact that the highest glory one can give to God is to acknowledge and worship Him in the Person of His Son, and as Jesus Himself said, "No man cometh unto the Father, but by *Me*" (John 14:6) and "all men should honor the Son even as they honor the Father" (John 5:23).

It is therefore clear from the context that the wonder of the Godhead is specifically revealed in Jesus Christ to the fullest extent, and it is expedient for all men to realize the consequences to be met if any refuse the injunctions of God's Word and openly deny the Deity of His Son, who is "the true God and eternal life" (I John 5:20).

6. Revelation 1:7, 8, 17, 18; 2:8; 22: 13; Matthew 24:30 and Isaiah 44: 6 — "I am Alpha and Omega [Greek — First and Last — A to Z][36] says *Jehovah God*, the One who is and who was and who is coming, the Almighty" (Revelation 1:8, New World Translation).

In the seventh, eighth, seventeenth and eighteenth verses of the first chapter of Revelation a unique and wonderful truth is again affirmed — namely, that Jesus Christ and Jehovah God are of the same "Substance," hence co-equal, co-existent and co-eternal, in short, "One" Nature in its fullest sense. We shall pursue that line of thought at length in substantiating this doctrine of Scripture.

Comparing Matthew 24:30 with Revelation 1:7 it is inescapably evident that Jesus Christ is the "One coming with clouds" in both the references mentioned.

And then shall appear the sign of the Son of man in heaven: and then shall all the tribes of the earth mourn, and they shall *see* the Son of man coming *in the clouds of heaven with power* and great glory (Matthew 24:30).

Behold, he cometh with clouds; and every eye shall see him, and they also which pierced him: and all kindreds of the earth shall wail because of him. Even so, Amen (Revelation 1:7).

Following this train of thought, we find that Jehovah declares in Isaiah 44: 6 that He alone is the First and the Last and the *only* God, which eliminates forever any confusion as to their being *two*

Firsts and Lasts. Since Jehovah is the only God, then how can the *Logos* be "a god," a lesser god than Jehovah, as Jehovah's Witnesses declare in John 1:1? (*Emphatic Diaglott* and *New World Translation.*) Many times Jehovah declares His existence as the "Only" God and Saviour (Isaiah 41:4; 43:11-13; 44:6; 45:5; 48:12; etc.). This is indeed irrefutable proof, since Christ could not be our Saviour or Redeemer if He were not Jehovah, for Jehovah is the only Saviour (Isaiah 43:11). However, despite the testimony of Scripture that ". . . before me there was no God formed, neither shall there be after me" (Isaiah 43:10) and "a god" fallacy is pursued and taught by Jehovah's Witnesses in direct contradiction to God's Word.[37]

Revelation 1:17, 18 and 2:8 add further weight to the Deity of Christ, for they reveal Him as the First and the Last, who became dead and lives forever. Now since Jehovah is the only First and Last (cf. Isaiah references) either He and Christ are "One," or to claim otherwise Jehovah's Witnesses must deny the authority of Scripture.

In order to be consistent we must answer the arguments advanced by Jehovah's Witnesses concerning the use of First and Last (Greek, *Protos*) in Revelation 1:17 and 2:8.

By suggesting the translation of *Protokos* (First Born) instead of *Protos* (First) in these passages (see footnotes in N.W.T. and *Emphatic Diaglott*), Jehovah's Witnesses attempt to rob Christ of His Deity and make Him a created being with "a beginning" (*Let God Be True*, page 88). When approached on this point they quickly refer you to Colossians 1:15 and Revelation 3:14 "proving" that the Logos had "a beginning" (see John 1:1, *Emphatic Diaglott* and N.W.T.). To any informed Bible student this argument is fallacious. A

---

[36]Brackets are ours.

[37]See I Corinthians 8:4-6, where Paul points out that an idol is nothing and, even though

men worship things (idols, position, material possessions, etc.) as gods, there is only one true and living God. Cf. Acts 5:3,4 and John 1:1 — Trinity.

Greek-English Lexicon of the New Testament by J. H. Thayer, edition of 1886, which on page 19 of the N.W.T. is quoted as authoritative and reliable, states that the only correct rendering of *protos* is "First" and in Thayer's own words *"The Eternal One"* [Jehovah] (Revelation 1:17). Here again the Deity of Christ is vindicated.

Further proof of this synthesis is the fact that the best and most authoritative manuscripts (Sinaiticus, Vaticanus, etc.) have *protos* "First." The Alexandrinian Manuscript, since it possesses no accent marks, should be translated "Original Bringer Forth"[38] (Erasmus) in keeping with the laws of textual criticism (Colossians 1:15). In short the whole problem is one of accentuation. Since there are no marks of punctuation or accent in the Alexandrinian Manuscript wording of Revelation 1:17; 2:8; etc., and since all the other manuscripts have *protos* "First" it is a contradiction to accentuate *prototokos* so as to make Christ a created being instead of the Creator. The correct accentuation of *prototokos* agrees with all the other manuscripts in portraying Christ as "The pre-eminent one" which is as it should be. These truths coupled with the fact that all reliable translations and translators bear out the rendering "First" in preference to "First Born" expose one more of the many clever attempts to pervert the Word of God by mistranslations and linguistic manipulation.

Jesus said: "I am Alpha and Omega the First and the Last, the Origin and the End" (Revelation 22:13), and not only this but it is He who is revealing the mysteries to John (Revelation 1:1 and 22:16) and declaring Himself to be the "Faithful Witness" (Revelation 1:5) who testifies "I come quickly" (Revelation 22:20). It is evident then that Jesus is the One testifying and the

"One" coming (Revelation 1:2, 7) throughout the book of Revelation since it is by His command (Revelation 22:16) that John records everything. So in honesty we must acknowledge His Sovereignty as the "First and Last" (Isaiah 48:12, Revelation 1:17 and 22:13), the Lord of all and the Eternal Word of God incarnate (John 1:1).

Revelation 3:14 asserts that Christ is the "beginning of the creation of God" and Colossians 1:15 states that Christ is "First Born of all creation." These verses in no sense indicate that Christ was a created being except in the physical sense (John 1:14) at His incarnation (Luke 1:35). The Greek word *arche* (Revelation 3:14) can be correctly rendered "origin" and is so translated in John 1:1 of Jehovah's Witnesses' own *New World Translation* (edition 1950). Revelation 3:14 then declares that Christ is the faithful and true witness, the "origin"[39] of the creation of God. This corroborates Hebrews 1:2 and Colossians 1:16, 17 in establishing Christ as the Creator of all things and hence God (Genesis 1:1). Christ is the Firstborn of all creation since He is the new Creation, conceived without sin (Luke 1:35), the second Adam (I Corinthians 15:45 and 47) who is the fulfillment of the divine Promise of the God-man (Isaiah 7:14; 9:6; Micah 5:2) and the Redeemer of the world (Colossians 1:14). John 3:13 states that no one has ascended into heaven but Christ who came down; Philippians 2:11 declares that He is Lord (Greek, *Kurios*), and as such is "The Lord from heaven" of I Corinthians 15:47, hence God, and not a created being or "a god."

The Lord Jesus is also the "First Born" of the dead (Revelation 1:5) — that is, the First one to rise in a glorified body (*not* a spirit form — see Luke 24:39,40), which type of body Chris-

---

[38] Or more literally, "First Begetter" — see Hebrews 1:2.

[39] Or "source" — see Bishop Ronald Knox's translation (Roman Catholic). Also *An American Translation* by E. J. Goodspeed.

tians will someday possess as in the words of the Apostle John, ". . . it does not yet appear what we shall be [but] we know that when He shall appear we shall be like [similar to] Him for we shall see Him as He is" (I John 3:2). We know that these promises are sure, for He is faithful who promised (Hebrews 10:23), and all who deny the Deity of Christ might well take cognizance of His warning and injunction when He said,

> For I testify unto every man that heareth the words of the prophecy of this book, If any man shall add unto these things, God shall add unto him the plagues that are written in this book: And if any man shall take away from the words of the book of this prophecy, God shall take away his part out of the book of life, and out of the holy city, and from the things which are written in this book (Revelation 22:18, 19).
> 7. John 17:5 — And now, O Father, glorify thou me with thine own self *with the glory which I had with thee before the world was* (Jesus Christ).

This passage of Scripture in cross reference with Isaiah 42:8 and 48:11 proves conclusively the identity of the Lord Jesus, and is a fitting testimony to the Deity of Christ.

In Isaiah 42:8 Jehovah Himself is speaking and He emphatically declares "I am the Lord, that is my name: and my glory will I not give to another, neither my praise, nor to graven images." Again in Isaiah 48:11 Jehovah is speaking and He declares "For mine own sake even for mine own sake, will I do it: for how should my name be polluted? *And I will not give my glory unto another.*"

It is plain to see from these references in Isaiah that Jehovah has irrevocably declared His divinely inherent glory,

which is of His own Nature, cannot and will not be given to any person other than Himself. There is *no* argument Jehovah's Witnesses can erect to combat the truth of God as revealed in these passages of Scripture. The inherent glory of God belongs to God alone and by His own mouth He has so ordained it to be.[40]

The Lord Jesus Christ, when He prayed in John 17:5, likewise irrevocably revealed that He would be glorified with *the glory of the Father* and that the glory of the Father (Jehovah) was not new to Him, since He affirmed that He possessed it, *with* (Greek, *para*) the Father (". . . the glory which I *had with* thee") even before the world came into existence. Jehovah's Witnesses attempt to answer this by saying that if He were God where was His glory while He walked the earth?

In answer to this question the Scriptures list at least four separate instances where Christ manifested His glory and revealed His power and Deity. On the Mount of Transfiguration (Matthew 17:2) Christ shone with the inherent glory of God, which glory continued undiminished when in John 18:6 the Lord applied to Himself the *"I am"* of Jehovahistic identity that radiated glory enough to render His captors powerless at His will. The seventeenth chapter of John, the twenty-second verse, also confirms the manifestation of Jehovah's glory when Jesus, looking forward to the cross, prays for His disciples and affirms the origin of His glory as being the Substance of God. The resurrection glory of Christ also serves to illustrate His Deity and reveal it as of God Himself.

So it is plain to see that the argument Jehovah's Witnesses advance, to the ef-

---

[40]God, however, bestowed upon the incarnate Word a certain glory manifested in the presence of the Holy Spirit through whose power and agency Christ worked while in the flesh and Jesus in turn bestowed this upon his followers (John 17:22), but it was *not* the glory of God's Nature but instead the abiding presence of His Spirit

and the two should not be confused. Jesus prayed to receive *back* again the glory He had with the Father "before the world was" (17:5) and it was *not* the glory given to Him as the Messiah, which glory Christ promised to share with His disciples (verse 22). Nowhere are the two equated.

fect that Christ did not manifest the glory of Himself, is invalid and finds no basis in the Scriptures. The truth of the whole matter is that the Lord Jesus did reveal the true glory of His Nature in the very works He performed, and as John says (1:14): "We beheld his glory . . . full of grace and truth."

St. Paul in the second chapter of Philippians removes all doubt on this question when he writes, guided by the Holy Spirit, that Christ never ceased to be Jehovah even during His earthly incarnation. It is interesting to note that the Greek term *uparchon,* translated "being" in Philippians 2:6, literally means "remaining or not ceasing to be" (see also I Corinthians 11:7), hence in the context Christ never ceased to be God, and "remained" in His basic Substance; He was truly "God manifest in the flesh."

An average Jehovah's Witness interviewed recently, in attempting to escape the obvious declaration of Christ's Deity as revealed in this text, reverted to the old Greek term-switching routine of the Society and asserted that the word "with" (Greek, *para*) in John 17:5, really means "through," and therefore the glory that is spoken of is not proof of Christ's Deity since the glory is Jehovah's and is merely shining "through" the Son; it is not His own but a manifestation of Jehovah's glory.

Once again we are confronted with the problem of illogical exegesis, the answer to which must be found in the Greek text itself. We must believe that the grammar of the Bible is inspired by God if we believe that God inspired the writers, or how else could He have conveyed His thoughts without error? Would God commit His inspired words to the failing grammatical powers of man to record? No! He could not do this without risking corruption of His message; therefore, as the wise and prudent Lord that He is, He most certainly inspired the grammar of His servants that their words might transmit His

thoughts without error, immutable and wholly dependable. With this thought in mind, let us consider the wording and construction of the verse.

The Greek word *para* (with) is used in the dative case in John 17:5 and is not translated "through" (Greek *dia*) but is correctly rendered according to Thayer's Lexicon as "with," and Thayer quotes John 17:5, the very verse in question, as his example of how *para* (with) should be translated.

Never let it be said that *para* in this context indicates anything less than possessive equality — "the glory which I had *with* thee before the world was." The Lord Jesus Christ clearly meant that He as God the Son was the possessor of divine glory along with the Father and the Holy Spirit before the world was even formed. Christ also declared that He intended to appropriate that glory in all its divine power once again, pending the resurrection of His earthly temple which by necessity, since it was finite, veiled as a voluntary act His eternal power and Deity (Philippians 2:5-8). The glory He spoke of did not only shine through the Father; it was eternally inherent in the Son, and since John, led by the Holy Spirit, deliberately chose *para* (literally "with") in preference to *dia* (through), the argument that Jehovah's Witnesses advance cannot stand up. The Lord Jesus claimed the same glory of the Father as His own, and since Jehovah has said that He will not give His inherent glory to another (Isaiah 42:9) the unity of Substance between Him and Christ is undeniable; they are One in all its wonderful and mysterious implications which, though we cannot understand them fully, we gladly accept, and in so doing remain faithful to God's Word.

8. John 20:28 — Thomas answered and said unto him, My Lord and my God!

No treatment of the Deity of Christ would be complete without mentioning the greatest single testimony recorded in the Scriptures. John 20:28 presents that testimony.

Beginning at verse 24 the disciple Thomas is portrayed as being a thorough-going skeptic in that he refused to believe that Christ had risen and appeared physically in the *same* form which had been crucified on the cross. In verse 25 Thomas stubbornly declares that "Except I shall see in his hands the print of the nails, and put my finger into the print of the nails, and thrust my hand into his side I will not believe." Following through the sequence of events in verses 26 and 27, we learn that the Lord appeared to Thomas together with the other disciples and presented His body bearing the wounds of Calvary to Thomas for his inspection. This was no spirit or phantom, no "form" assumed for the occasion as Jehovah's Witnesses maintain. This was the very body of Christ which bore the horrible imprints of excruciating torture and the pangs of an ignominious death. Here displayed before the eyes of the unbelieving disciple was the evidence which compelled him by the sheer power of its existence to adore the One who manifested the Essence of Deity. "Thomas answered and said to him, My Lord and my God." This was the only answer Thomas could honestly give; Christ had proved His identity; He was truly "The Lord God." Let us substantiate this beyond doubt.

Jehovah's Witnesses have vainly striven to elude this text in the Greek (*Emphatic Diaglott* and *New World Translation*), but they have unknowingly corroborated its authority beyond refutation as a brief survey of their sources will reveal.

In *The Emphatic Diaglott* (John 20:28, page 396) *o Theos mou,* literally "The God of me, or my God," signifies Jehovahistic identity, and since it is in possession *of the definite article,* to use Jehovah's Witnesses' own argument, it must therefore mean "the only true God" (Jehovah), not "a god." On page 776 of the *New World Translation* (Ap-

pendix) the author of the note states, "So too John 1:1, 2 uses *o Theos* to distinguish Jehovah God from the Word (Logos) as 'a god,' 'the only begotten God, as John 1:18 calls him." Now let us reflect as sober individuals. If Thomas called the risen Christ, Jehovah (definite article) (*o Kurios mou kai o Theos mou*), and Christ did not deny it but confirmed it by saying (verse 29), "Because thou hast seen me, thou hast believed; Blessed are they not having seen yet having believed," then no juggling of the text in context can offset the basic thought — namely, that Jesus Christ is Jehovah God!

The N.W.T. carefully evades any explanation of the Greek text on the aforementioned point, but just as carefully inserts in the margin (page 350) under symbol some five or six references to Christ as "a god" which they attempt to slip by the unwary Bible student. These references as usual are used abstractly and four of them (Isaiah 9:6; John 1:1; 1:18; and 10:35) have been mentioned already in previous points. The question then is, is there any other god beside Jehovah which Jehovah's Witnesses affirm to be true by their reference to Christ as "a god" (John 1:1; Isaiah 9:6)? The Scriptures give but one answer: Emphatically *NO!* There is no god but Jehovah. (See Isaiah 45:21-23; 44:68; 37:16, 20; etc.).

To be sure, there are many so-called gods in the Scriptures, but they are not gods by identity and self-existence, but by human acclamation and adoration. Satan also falls into this category since he is the "god of this world," who holds that position only because unregenerate and ungodly men have accorded to him service and worship belonging to God.

The Apostle Paul seals this truth with his clear-cut analysis of idolatry and false gods in I Corinthians 8:4-6, where he declares that an idol is nothing in itself and there is no god but Jehovah in heaven or earth regardless of the inventions of man.

The picture then is clear. Thomas adored Christ as the risen incarnation of the Deity (Jehovah); John declared that Deity from all eternity (John 1:1); and Christ affirmed it irrefutably — "If ye believe not that I Am [Jehovah] ye shall die in your sins" (John 8:24; cf. Exodus 3:14). All of the pseudo-scholastic and elusive tactics ever utilized can never change the plain declarations of God's Word. Jesus Christ is Lord of all; and like it or not, Jehovah's Witnesses will never destroy or remove that truth. Regardless of what is done to God's Word on earth, it remains eternal in the glory, as it is written, "Forever, O Lord, thy Word is settled in heaven" (Psalm 119:89).

9. John 5:18 — He said that God was his Father, making himself equal with God.

Concluding our chapter on this vital topic is this verse that is self-explanatory. The Greek term "equal" (*ison*) cannot be debated; nor is it contextually or grammatically allowable that John is here recording *what the Jews said about Jesus,* as Jehovah's Witnesses lamely argue. The sentence structure clearly shows that *John said it* under the inspiration of the Holy Spirit, and *not* the Jews! Anyone so inclined can diagram the sentence and see this for himself. No serious scholar or commentator has ever questioned it. In the Jewish mind, for Jesus to claim to be God's Son was a claim to equality with God, a fact Jehovah's Witnesses might profitably consider!

We see, then, that our Lord was equal with God the Father and the Holy Spirit in His divine nature, though inferior (as a man) by choice in His human nature as the last Adam (John 14:28; I Corinthians 15:45-47). This text alone is of enormous value and argues powerfully for our Lord's Deity.

The Resurrection of Christ

Jehovah's Witnesses, as has been observed, deny the bodily resurrection of the Lord Jesus Christ and claim instead that He was raised a "divine spirit being," or as an "invisible spirit creature." They answer the objection that He appeared in human form by asserting that He simply took human forms as He needed them, which enabled Him to be seen, for as the Logos He would have been invisible to the human eye. In short, Jesus did not appear in the *"same"* form which hung upon the cross since that body either "dissolved in gases or is preserved somewhere as a memorial to God's love."[41]

The Scriptures, however, tell a completely different story, as will be evident when their testimony is considered. Christ Himself prophesied His own bodily resurrection, and John tells us "He spoke of the temple of His body" (John 2:21).

In John 20:25, 26, the disciple Thomas doubted the literal physical resurrection of Christ only to bitterly repent (verse 28) after Jesus (verse 27) offered His body, the same one that was crucified and still bore the prints and spear wound, to Thomas for his examination. No reasonable person will say that the body the Lord Jesus displayed was not His crucifixion body, unless he either ignorantly or willfully denies the Word of God. It was no other body "assumed" for the time by a spiritual Christ; it was the identical form that hung on the tree — the Lord Himself; He was alive and undeniably tangible, not a "divine spirit creature." The Lord foresaw the unbelief of men in His bodily resurrection and made an explicit point of saying that He was not a spirit but flesh and bones (Luke 24:39-44), and He even went so far as to eat human food to prove that He was identified

[11]*Studies in the Scriptures,* Volume 2, page 129. Russell and the Watch Tower have also stated that "the man Jesus is dead, forever dead" (*Ibid.* volume V, page 454), a view

directly refuted by the Apostle Paul in I Timothy 2:5 where he calls Christ "the Mediator" thirty years after the Resurrection, and He mediates as a Man!

with humanity as well as Deity. Christ rebuked the disciples for their unbelief in His physical resurrection (Luke 24: 25) and it was the physical resurrection that confirmed His Deity, since only God could voluntarily lay down and take up life at will (John 10:18).[42]

Jehovah's Witnesses utilize, among other unconnected verses, I Peter 3:18, as a defense for their spiritual resurrection doctrine. Peter declares that Christ was "put to death in the flesh, made alive by the Spirit." Obviously He was made alive[43] in the Spirit and by the Spirit of God, for the Spirit of God, the Substance of God Himself, raised up Jesus from the dead, as it is written, "But if the Spirit of Him that has raised up Jesus from among the dead dwell in you . . ." (Romans 8:11). The meaning of the verse then is quite clear. God did not raise Jesus a Spirit but raised Him by His Spirit, which follows perfectly John 20:27 and Luke 24:39-44, in establishing the physical resurrection of the Lord.

The Watch Tower quotes Mark 16: 12 and John 20:14-16 as proof that Jesus had "other bodies" after His resurrection. Unfortunately for them the reference in Mark is noncanonical and worthless! (See the RSV Oxford Annotated Bible.) The reason that Mary and the Emmaus disciples (Luke 24) did not recognize Him is explained in Luke 24:16 (RSV): "Their eyes were kept from recognizing him," but it was Jesus Himself (verse 15).

Jehovah's Witnesses also try to undermine our Lord's bodily resurrection by pointing out that "the doors were shut" (John 20:26) when Jesus appeared in the upper room. However, Christ had

a "spiritual body" (I Corinthians 15: 50, 53) in His glorified state, identical in form to his earthly body, but immortal, and thus capable of entering either the dimension of earth or heaven with no violation to the laws of either one.

St. Paul states in Romans 4:24; 6:4; I Corinthians 15:15; etc., that Christ is raised from the dead; and Paul preached the physical resurrection and return of the God-Man, not a "divine spirit being" without a tangible form. Paul also warned that if Christ is not risen then our faith is vain; to us who believe God's Word there is a Man in the Glory who showed His wounds as a token of His reality and whose question we ask Jehovah's Witnesses — "Has a Spirit flesh and bones as you see me have?"

The Atonement of Christ

The infinite atonement of the Lord Jesus Christ is one of the most important doctrines of the Bible since it is the guarantee of eternal life through the complete forgiveness of sins to whomever appropriates its cleansing power. The Old Testament clearly teaches that, "it is the *blood* that makes an atonement for the soul." Leviticus 17:11 and Hebrews 9:22 corroborate this beyond doubt, for in truth "without shedding of blood is no remission." The Lord Jesus Christ became the one blood sacrifice for sin that insures everlasting life, as John said upon seeing Jesus — "Behold the Lamb of God which taketh away the sin of the world" (John 1:29). The Apostle John writing in Revelation 13:8 declares that the Lamb (Christ) slain from the foundation of the world is God's own eternal sacrifice that cleanses from all sin and provides redemption for lost souls who trust in its efficacy. The

---

[42]We must never let it be forgotten that Christ prophesied not only His resurrection but the nature of that resurrection, which He said would be bodily (John 2:19-21). He said He would raise up "the temple" in three days (verse 19) and John tells us, "He spoke of the temple of His *body*" (verse 21). The Greek word (*soma*) always means body, never soul (*psuche*) or spirit (*pneu-*

ma), and Jehovah's Witnesses are hard put to answer this; in fact, never have.

[43]*The Emphatic Diaglott* renders the Greek *pneumati* as "in spirit," but neglects to mention that it is the *agency* of the Holy Spirit being spoken of, for it was through the operation of His power that Jesus rose again (Romans 8:11).

writer of the epistle to the Hebrews goes to great length to show that the sacrifices of the Old Testament were types designed to show forth the coming sacrifices of Christ on Calvary (Hebrews 9 and 10). The Hebrew term *kaphar* (covering) and the Greek term *katallage,* which literally means reconciliation, are used in reference to payment of an obligation or exchange. The picture then portrays Christ as bearing our sins in His own body on the tree (I Peter 2:24) and giving us peace with God through the *blood* of His cross (Colossians 1:20) which blood is the everlasting covenant that is able to make us perfect, in that God through it empowers us to do His will (Hebrews 13: 20, 21). The Scriptures give vast testimony to the redeeming power of the Lamb's blood (Romans 3:25; 5:9; Colossians 1:14; Hebrews 9:22; I Peter 1:19; I John 1:7; Revelation 5: 9; 12:11) which *alone* can save and cleanse (Hebrews 9:22).

Charles Taze Russell resigned from a position he once held as assistant editor of a Rochester, New York, newspaper because he disagreed with the editor's view of the Atonement. Whether Russell was right in that disputation or wrong we do not know, but his doctrine of the Atonement and Jehovah's Witnesses' doctrine we do have knowledge of and know it to be completely unscriptural. Jehovah's Witnesses argue that the Atonement is not wholly of God, despite II Corinthians 5:20, but rather half of God and half of man. Jesus, according to their argument, removed the effects of Adam's sin by His sacrifice on Calvary, but the work will not be fully completed until the survivors of Armageddon return to God through free will and become subject to the Theocratic rule of Jehovah. For Jehovah's Witnesses the full realization of the matter is reconciliation with God, which will be completed in relation to the Millennial Kingdom. This utterly

unreasonable and illogical interpretation of Scripture does away with the validity of the "infinite Atonement" unconditionally administered by God and through God for man. Russell and Jehovah's Witnesses have detracted from the blood of Christ by allowing it only partial cleansing power, but the truth still stands; it is either all-sufficient or insufficient; and if the latter be the case, man is hopelessly lost in an unconnected maze of irrelevant doctrines which postulate a finite sacrifice and, by necessity, a finite god.

The Physical Return of Christ

Jehovah's Witnesses declare that Christ returned to the temple in 1914 and cleansed it by 1918 for judgment upon sinful men and Satan's organizations. They affirm that since He did not rise physically, neither did He return physically, nor will He.[44]

The first claim is that Jesus said ". . . the world seeth me no more" (John 14:19); therefore, no mortal eye shall see Him. The second claim is the intimation that *parousia* (Greek for presence, coming, advent, etc. — Thayer, Greek Lexicon) in Matthew 24:26-28, can only be rendered "exactly" as *presence;* therefore, Christ is now present, not coming.

These arguments are another example of the half-truths used by Jehovah's Witnesses to lead people astray. To begin with, Thayer, who is esteemed reliable in the field of scholarship, clearly states on page 490 of his *Greek-English Lexicon of the New Testament* that *parousia,* especially in the New Testament, refers to the second coming of Christ in *visible* form to raise the dead, hold the last judgment and set up the Kingdom of God. Christ is present; His "Presence" is always near ("I will never leave you . . ." Hebrews 13:5. ". . . I am with you always . . . to the consummation of the age," Matthew 28: 20) for as God He is omnipresent, everywhere. But that does not mean He is here physically as the Scriptures attest He will be at the Second Advent. The physical return of Christ is the "Blessed Hope" of Christendom (Titus 2:13) and the language used to portray its visible certainty is most explicit. In Titus 2:13 the Greek word *epiphaneia* ("Appearing") is more correctly translated "Manifestation" or "Visible" from *phanero,* "to make manifest, or visible, or known" (Thayer's *Greek-English Lexicon of the New Testament,* page 648). The language is self-explanatory. When the Lord returns with His saints "every eye shall see Him" (Matthew, 24:30, cf. Revelation 1:7.) How then can Jehovah's Witnesses claim that He has already returned but is invisible? The answer is they cannot and still remain honest Scripturally. To further establish these great truths the Apostle Paul writing to Timothy in I Timothy 6:14 clearly states that the Lord Jesus will appear physically by using *epiphaneia,* another form of *phanero* which also denotes visibility or manifestations. In I Thessalonians 4:16, 17 the Lord's return is revealed as being visible and audible, not invisible as Jehovah's Witnesses affirm contrary to Scripture.

The Old Testament bears out the physical return of Messiah, also a wonderful testimony to the consistency of God's Word. Comparing Zechariah 12:10; 14:4 with Revelation 1:7; Matthew 24:30; and Acts 1:9-12 it is obvious that the Lord's ascension was visible, for the disciples *saw* Him rise, and in like fashion (Greek, *tropos*) the angels declared He would return. Zechariah 12:10 quotes Jehovah (further proof of Christ's Deity), "And they shall look upon *Me* whom they have pierced." Revelation 1:7 states that Christ is the One pierced, and *visible* to human eyes. Zechariah 14:4 reveals Christ as touching the Mount of Olives at His visible return, and the Scriptures teach that this literally corroborates the angelic proclamation of Acts 1:9-12 even to the Lord's return to the exact location of His ascension, the Mount of Olives (Verses 12). The doctrine of the physical return of Christ cannot be denied in the Scriptures unless a denial of God's Word also be entered which would exhibit unfathomable ignorance.

Jehovah's Witnesses and Human Government

Jehovah's Witnesses refuse to pay homage in any way to the flag of any nation or even to defend their own individual nation from assault by an enemy. Patriotism as displayed in bearing arms is not one of their beliefs, since they claim to be ambassadors of Jehovah and as such deem themselves independent of allegiance to any government other than His. In this age of uncertainty, sincerity is a priceless gem and no doubt Jehovah's Witnesses believe themselves sincere, but all their arguments avail nothing when in Romans 13:1-7 St. Paul clearly outlines the case for human government as instituted by God. Paul goes to great length to stress that the "Higher Powers" (human governmental rules) are allowed and sanctioned by God. As supposed followers of His Word the Witnesses ought to heed both Christ and Paul and "render unto Caesar what is Caesar's," which in the context of Romans 13:1-7 clearly means subjugation of governmental rule. Paul settles the question decisively and in conclusion we quote his teaching:

> Let every soul be subject unto the higher powers. For there is no power but of God: the powers that be are ordained of God. Whosoever therefore resisteth the power, resisteth the ordinance of God: and they that resist shall receive to themselves damnation. For rulers are not a terror to good works, but to the evil. Wilt thou then not be afraid of the power? do that which is good, and thou shalt have praise of the same: For he is the minister of God to thee for good. But if thou do that which is evil, be afraid; for he beareth not the sword in vain; for he is the minister of God, a revenger to execute wrath upon

him that doeth evil. Wherefore ye must needs be subject, not only for wrath, but also for conscience sake. For for this cause pay ye tribute also: for they are God's ministers, attending continually upon this very thing. Render therefore to all their dues: tribute to whom tribute is due; custom to whom custom, fear to whom fear; honour to whom honour (Romans 13:1-7).

The Existence of Hell and Eternal Punishment

The question of the existence of hell and eternal punishment presents no problem to any Biblical student who is willing to practice honest exegesis unhindered by the teachings of any organizations of man. Jehovah's Witnesses use emotionally loaded words such as "hell fire screechers" and "religionists," etc., to describe the theological views of anyone who disagrees with their philosophy. In order to understand their views it must first be established that their beliefs are based upon no sound or valid knowledge of the original languages, and it should be remembered that this one factor influences practically every major phase of semantic study. However, we will now consider this problem in its context, and contrast it with Jehovah's Witnesses' interpretation which professes to have solved the problem, though on what grounds it is difficult to ascertain.

1. To begin with, grammatically Jehovah's Witnesses use poor reasoning in their construction, and from the evidence seldom check the original scripts beyond the Dictionary and Lexicon stage. I document to prove the point and reveal this shortcoming. On pages 69 and 70 of *Let God Be True* (ed. 1946) the following statement appears:

> If you were to translate a book from a foreign language into English and there you found the foreign word for bread 65 times, would you translate it 31 times bread, 31 times fish, and 3

times meat? Of course not. Why? Because if you did your translation would not be correct. For what is bread cannot at the same time be fish or meat and vice versa. The same holds true with the word Sheol. If Sheol is the grave, it is impossible at the same time to be a place of fiery torture and at the same time a pit.[45]

To the average Jehovah's Witness then Hell (Sheol) is literally "the grave," the place where mortals wait the resurrection. Their chief argument is that a Greek or Hebrew word means one thing and has no area of meaning. This is a typical Jehovah's Witness approach and again reveals the linguistic failings of the Organization. First of all, the very example the author of the chapter uses concerning bread, fish and meat, etc., is a reality in the text of the Bible, and if words do not have areas of meaning in different context he stands accused of defaming God's Word. A little research would have revealed this truth. In the Hebrew text, the word *lechem* is translated bread 238 times, one time as "feast," 21 times as "food," one time as "fruit," 5 times as "loaf," 18 times as "meat," one time as "provision," twice as "victuals," and once as "eat." This puts to silence the argument that Sheol *always* means the grave. It is clear that it has an area of meaning which must be decided from the context, not by the conjectures of misinformed authors.

2. In the second place, Jehovah's Witnesses have conceived of death as being unconsciousness or extinction, which definition cannot be found in the Bible. Death in the Biblical sense never means extinction or annihilation, and not one word, Greek or Hebrew, in either Testament will be found to say that it does. Death in the Bible is portrayed as separation. "The soul that sinneth . . . it shall be *separated*" (Ezekiel 18:4) is a better rendition in the sense that the

---

[45] It is most interesting to note in passing that in their revision of this book, April, 1952, the Watch Tower carefully omitted this paragraph, so thorough was our exposé of their shallow scholasticism.

word conveys. When Adam sinned, his soul became separated from God in the sense of fellowship—and consequently as a result of sin all men die or are separated from God by Adam's as well as their own sins. But God has provided a reconciliation for us in the person of His Son and we are "born again," regenerated and reconciled to God by the sacrifice of His Son "in whom we have redemption through his blood even the forgiveness of sins" (cf. John 3:3-7, 15, 16; II Corinthians 5:17-21; Colossians 1:14). So then we see that death in reality is not extinction but conscious existence, as was demonstrated in Matthew 17:1-3, when Moses and Elijah talked with Christ. Moses' body was dead—no one will deny; his soul was also dead according to Jehovah's Witnesses. Then what or who was it talking to Christ? The answer is simple. Moses as a living soul spoke to Christ, and he was alive and conscious! Substantiating all this is Christ's own declaration, "I am the resurrection and the life; he that believes on me, though he were dead, yet shall he live; and whosoever liveth and believeth on me shall never die" (John 11:25). Therefore, death is only the separation between, not the extinction of personalities (Isaiah 59:1, 2; see also II Corinthians 5:8 and Philippians 1:21-23).

3. Jehovah's Witnesses claim on page 77 of *Let God Be True* that—"In all places where "hell" is translated from the Greek word *Gehenna* it means everlasting destruction or extinction."

This is indeed a bold-faced misrepresentation of the Greek language and certainly ranks next to the "a god" fallacy of John 1:1 as an outstanding example of complete falsehood. There is no evidence that Gehenna ever means annihilation in the New Testament but rather abundant evidence to the contrary. In Matthew 5:22 Gehenna is portrayed as literally "The Hell of fire," in 10:28 coupled with *apolesai* "to be delivered up to eternal misery" (see Thayer, page

64). It indicates everlasting misery, and in Matthew 18:9 the same words corroborate 5:22, "The Hell of fire." If we are to follow through with Jehovah's Witnesses argument, then Gehenna simply means the smoldering furnaces of Hinnon. But is that fire everlasting? No! For today the valley of Hinnon is not burning, so unless Jesus meant the example for just those living at that time, and this not even Jehovah's Witnesses will affirm, then Gehenna must be what it is, the symbol of eternal separation in conscious torment by a flame which is unquenchable (Isaiah 66:24).

4. It is fruitless to pursue this analysis of the Greek any further for it must be clear from the contexts that more than the grave or extinction is portrayed in Sheol, Hades and Gehenna. Without benefit of any complicated textual exegesis we shall let God's Word speak its own message and commit to the honest reader the decision as to whether or not eternal punishment, rather than annihilation, is Scriptural doctrine. The following verses collectively refer to a place of everlasting conscious torment where Satan and his followers must remain in future everlasting wounding or misery, separated from God's Presence and "the glory of His power" (II Thessalonians 1:9; cf. Thayer, page 443 [A] on *olethros* and Latin Vulnus—*to wound*).

1. And I say unto you, that many shall come from the east and the west, and shall sit down with Abraham, and Isaac, and Jacob, in the kingdom of heaven. But the children of the kingdom shall be cast out into outer darkness: there shall be weeping and gnashing of teeth (Matthew 8:11, 12).

2. And shall cast them into the furnace of fire: there shall be wailing and gnashing of teeth (Matthew 13:42, 50).

3. Then said the king to the servants, Bind him hand and foot, and take him away, and cast him into outer darkness; there shall be weeping and gnashing of teeth (Matthew 22:13).

4. Strive to enter in at the strait gate: for many, I say unto you, will seek to enter in, and shall not be able. When once the master of the house is risen up, and hath shut to the door, and ye begin to stand without, and to knock at the door saying, Lord, Lord, open unto us; and he shall answer and say unto you, I know you not whence ye are: Then shall ye begin to say, We have eaten and drunk in thy presence, and thou hast taught in our streets. But he shall say, I tell you, I know you not whence ye are; depart from me, all ye workers of iniquity. There shall be weeping and gnashing of teeth, when ye shall see Abraham, and Isaac, and Jacob, and all the prophets, in the kingdom of God, and you yourselves thrust out (Luke 13:24-28).

5. These are wells without water, clouds that are carried with a tempest; to whom the mist of darkness is reserved for ever (II Peter 2:17).

6. Raging waves of the sea, foaming out their own shame; wandering stars, to whom is reserved the blackness of darkness for ever (Jude 13).

7. And the third angel followed them, saying with a loud voice, if any man worship the beast and his image, and receive his mark in his forehead, or in his hand, the same shall drink of the wine of the wrath of God, which is poured out without mixture into the cup of his indignation; and he shall be tormented with fire and brimstone in the presence of the holy angels, and in the presence of the Lamb: And the smoke of their torment ascendeth up for ever and ever: and they have no rest day nor night, who worship the beast and his image, and whosoever receiveth the mark of his name (Revelation 14:9-11).
And the beast was taken, and with him the false prophet that wrought miracles before him, with which he deceived them that had received the mark of the beast, and them that worshipped his image. These both were cast alive into a lake of fire burning with brimstone (Revelation 19:20).

These verses are conclusive proof that everlasting conscious separation from God and real torment exist, and no possible confusion of terminology can change their meaning in context. Revelation 20:10 is perhaps the most descriptive of all the verses in the Greek. John positively states that "the devil who deceived them was cast into the lake of fire and brimstone where the beast and the false prophet are and they will be tormented (*basanisthesontai*) day and night into the everlasting (*aionas*) of the everlasting." The Greek word *basanizo* literally means "to torment," "to be harassed," "to torture," or "to vex with grievous pains" (Thayer, page 96 [b]), and is used throughout the New Testament to denote great pain and conscious misery, not annihilation, cessation of consciousness, or extinction. Further proof of the reality of conscious torment, not annihilation, is found in the following verses where *basanizo* is utilized to exhibit the truth of God's eternal justice.

1. Matthew 8:6 — The one tormented (suffering) with palsy (*basanizomenos*).

2. Matthew 8:29 — The demons addressing Jesus admit the certainty of future torment (*basanisai*). "Art thou come here before (the) time to *torment* us?"

3. Mark 5:7 — Again the demon cries out, "Torment [*basanisas*] me not." He obviously feared conscious pain, not extinction.

4. Luke 8:28 — A demon once more reveals his knowledge of coming torment (*basanisas*): "do not torment me" is his supplication to Christ.

5. Revelation 14:10, 11 — "He [the believer in the beast] shall be tormented [*basanistheasetai*] with fire and brimstone, in the presence of the holy angels, and in the presence of the Lamb. And the smoke of their torment rises up into the everlasting of the everlasting; and they have no intermission, cessation or relief [*anapausis* — Thayer, page 40 (B), also Liddell & Scott] day and night who worship the Beast and his image and if any one receive the mark of his name.

The Scriptures then clearly teach eternal conscious punishment and torment for those who reject Christ as Lord, and the language of the texts leaves no room for doubt that the apostles intended that confirmation. Jehovah's Witnesses think God a "Fiend" because He executes eternal righteous judgment. They make much to-do about God being Love but forget that because He is Love, He is also Justice and must require infinite vengeance from anyone who treads underfoot the precious blood of Christ, who is the Lamb slain for lost sinners from the foundation of the World. Death is not extinction, hell is not an illusion, and everlasting conscious punishment is a terrifying reality of God's infinite justice upon the souls of unbelieving men. The Apostle Paul summed up this certainty in Romans 2:8, 9, when he declared that God's indignation (*thumos*) and wrath (*orges*) are upon all who work unrighteousness. These two words have identical usage in Revelation 14:10, where John speaks of the eternal torment of those who serve the beast, ". . . that wine of the wrath (*orges*) of God, which is mingled undiluted in the cup of His indignation (*thumou*). . ." So then the picture is clear. God is both Love and Justice and it is not He who condemns man, but man who condemns himself. As it is written—"For by thy words wilt thou be justified and by thy words wilt thou be condemned" (Matthew 12:37).

5. In *Let God Be True*, page 74, Jehovah's Witnesses again exhibit their lack of knowledge as to what fundamental Christians believe, where, when speaking of the "religious theologians" they declare—"But do they not say that Satan the Devil with his demons are in hell keeping up the fires and making it hard for those who are therein? Yes, that is what is taught by the religious leaders." It is nonsense to suppose that the Devil and his demons "are in hell keeping up the fires" and no responsible clergyman or Christian would make so childish a statement. Jehovah's Witnesses attribute to Christianity the same

caliber of reasoning that appeals to their untutored minds and to claim that "religionists" teach such doctrines is to reveal ignorance of the facts, a symptom not at all healthy in the processes of logical analysis. Further comment is not justified. Further examination is superfluous.

6. Luke 16:19-31 is claimed to be a parable in the text, by Jehovah's Witnesses, but nowhere is this substantiated in Luke's account. It is pure conjecture. Jehovah's Witnesses claim that the "parable" portrays a coming event which was fulfilled in A.D. 1918. The rich man represents the clergy and Lazarus the "faithful body of Christ." The clergy is constantly tormented by the truth proclaimed through the faithful remnant (*Let God Be True,* page 79). Comment on this interpretational travesty is senseless since Jehovah's Witnesses twist the Scriptures to suit their own ends regardless of the textual background. The Lord Jesus in this account portrayed the condition of a lost soul (the rich man) who rejected God, and the beggar who partook of the Lord's mercy. The rich man went into conscious torment after physical death (Greek, *basanois*), verse 24, and even proclaimed his spiritual conscious anguish (Greek, *odunomai*), "I am being tormented" (see Thayer, page 438 [B]) There can be no doubt; he was suffering and knew it. Jehovah's Witnesses believe that in order to suffer you must exist physically, but this is naïve to say the least since souls suffer, as is demonstrated in this account. It must also be remembered that Christ, in parables, never used personal names, such as *Lazarus.* The language, although literal, is forceful in depicting spiritual suffering.

We must conclude then that Luke's account is a record of an actual case, a historical fact in which a soul suffered after death and was conscious of that torment. Regardless of what conjectures are injected at this point, the conclusion is sure: there is conscious punishment after death; and whether it is accepted or not by Jehovah's Witnesses it still remains a Scriptural doctrine substantiated by God's Word.

Satan — The Devil

In Ezekiel 28:16-19 quoted in *Let God Be True,* page 56, Jehovah's Witnesses maintain Satan's annihilation, but in the light of the Scriptures before discussed, the area of meanings of the Hebrew words must be considered. The word for "destroy" (*'abad*) does not convey the meaning of annihilation or extinction. The term here used may be validly rendered "to reckon as lost, given up as lost, or cast away" (cf. Ecclesiastes 3:6b, and also Gesenius' *Hebrew-English Lexicon*). If Ezekiel, chapter 28, verse 19, is as translated in *Let God Be True,* page 56 "never shalt thou *be* anymore" the Hebrew word *'ayin*[46] may properly be rendered "to fail" or "to be gone," *not* to cease to exist (cf. Isaiah 44:12; I Kings 20:40). The use of *'ayin* in Hebrew sentence structure is the standard means employed when negating noun clauses. In I Kings 20:40, for example, where the man is spoken of as "gone" the term *'ayin* is utilized to show the man's absence or escape, *not* his extinction. If Jehovah's Witnesses persist in their annihilation doctrine where Satan is concerned they must also believe that the man was annihilated, and the context rules out that interpretation as absurd. The picture then is clear in the light of language interpretation. Satan *must* and *will* endure everlasting torment with his followers, and to this truth God's Word bears irrefutable testimony.

Man the Soul, His Nature and Destiny

Any critical thinker in examining this problem cannot escape the confusion of terms utilized by Jehovah's Witnesses to substantiate their argument that the soul is not an eternal entity. To carry this argument to any great length is foolish, for the Hebrew word (*nephesh*) and the Greek (*psuche*) possess great areas of meaning impossible to fathom without exhaustive exegesis of the original sources. The root of the problem lies in Jehovah's Witnesses' misconception of the soul as merely a principle of life, not an entity. The Bible clearly teaches in numerous places (Genesis 35:18; I Kings 17:21, 22; Revelation 6:9-11 to state a few) that the soul departs at the death of the body, that it is not destroyed by physical death, and that it can be restored by God at His discretion.

In an exegetical study it is impossible to emphasize too much the importance of defining terms, and in the problem at hand it is of the utmost importance. Therefore, before we can decide who or what has immortality, we must know what the term immortality itself means. Due to the evolution of any language, we must realize that the area of meanings of words changes as time goes on. The English word "immortal" has, among others, a peculiar meaning of "not mortal." However, in most circles and also in theology, the word generally carries the meaning of "exemption from death." The question that will arise then is "When the Scriptures use the term 'immortal,' is this definition all that is meant?" Contrary to the belief of some, there is *no reference* in Scripture that can be given to show that man or his soul is immortal.

To go even one step farther, there is nothing in Scripture that states anything or anyone is immortal but God Himself. Let us analyze this problem. There are two words in the Greek text that are translated "immortality." The first is *athanasia,* and it appears three times and is translated "immortality" each time. The other term is *aphthartos,* and is translated "immortality" twice and "in-

---

[46]See Strong's *Exhaustive Concordance, Hebrew and Chaldee Dictionary,* page 11. The

Hebrew letters are Aleph (A), Yod (Y), Nun (N), transliterated *AYIN*.

corruption" four times. Now let us examine the use of these words. The former word *athanasian* is used in I Timothy 6:16 and is speaking of God "Who *alone* has immortality (*athanasian*) dwelling in the light which *no man* can approach unto." In I Corinthians 15:53, 54, we again have *athanasia* used twice, but in the same verse we have *aphthartos* used twice also. Paul here is speaking of the second coming of Christ, and declares (verse 53) "For this corruption must put on incorruption (*aphtharsian*) and this mortal must put on immortality (*athanasian*)." "So when this corruption *shall have put on* [Aorist middle subjunctive of the verb *enduo*] incorruption (*aphtharian*) and this mortal *have put on* immortality (*athanasian*) *then* shall be brought to pass the saying that is written, *Death* is swallowed up in victory" (verse 54). We see here that in the two places where *athanasian* is used in reference to man, it is clear that it is an immortality to be given in the future, not one possessed at the present time.

Similarly, when an *aphtharsian* is used here and in Romans 2:7, "Something sought for," and I Peter 1:4, "reserved in heaven for you," it is speaking of the incorruption of man to be given at some future date, not possessed at the present time. Only when immortality or incorruption is used with God, is it in the present tense (I Timothy 6:16, 1:17; Romans 1:23). Therefore, to say that the saints are immortal (if by immortality we mean *athanasian* or *aphtharsian*), we are not Scriptural. We must say the saints *will be* immortal. It is also plain to see in I Corinthians 15:53, 54, that this immortality (*athanasian*) and this incorruption (*aphtharsian*) *will be put on* (*endusetai*) as one puts on a garment. Just as Paul exhorts us to put on (*endusasthe*) Christ (Romans 13:14; Galatians 3:27), the armor of light (Romans 13:12), the new man (Ephesians 4:24), and the armor or panoply of God (Ephesians 6:11),

we must conclude then that *athanasian* or *aphtharsian* have a larger and broader meaning than to be "everlasting." It must be seen that immortality and incorruption, *when given,* will mean a change, not simply the giving and receiving of the attribute — "exemption from death." Jehovah's Witnesses have badly misconstrued the usage of immortality, and that error, coupled with their famous practice of term-switching has resulted in confusion and poor exegesis.

Now as to the eternity of the human soul, we must consult the existing language sources. When we use the term "eternal" in association with the soul of man, we mean that the human soul *after* its creating by God will (future) exist somewhere into the eternal, into the everlasting. Since there is only one place where the honest seeker can find pure information on the eternal existence of the soul, and that place is in the revelation which God, who created the soul, has given to man, namely His Word, let us turn to it and consider therein His revealed Will.

Revelation does show first that God can be known, and secondly that man's soul is eternal. In Hebrews 1:1, we read, "God who at sundry times and in divers manners spake in time past unto the fathers by the prophets, hath in these last days spoken unto us by a Son, whom he hath appointed heir of all things, by whom also he made the worlds." All through history God has manifested Himself to man in different ways, and at no time in history has man been left without a witness of God. In the Old Testament, God manifested Himself and His Will to man by the prophets, visions, and direct oral contact. However, when the fullness of time was come, God sent forth His Son in the likeness of sinful flesh and completed His progressive revelation. Man, since the time of his creation upon the earth, has always been able to know God and His will, if he so desired, and consequently since the day of Adam, men who know not God are without excuse.

God's revelation is not only a manifestation of God to man, but it also is the answer to the question, "Where did man come from? Is he a spiritual as well as natural being? What is his worth? and Where is he going?"

God's revelation shows that man is a creation of God, created in God's spiritual image, Genesis 1:26; Genesis 5:1; I Corinthians 11:7. He was created to have pre-eminence over other creatures, Genesis 1:28; Psalm 8:6; Psalm 82:6; Matthew 6:26; and Matthew 12:12. He is definitely a spiritual being, Job 32:8; Psalm 51:10; Ecclesiastes 12:7; Acts 7:59; and II Corinthians 4:13. He is an object of God's love, John 3:16; Revelation 1:5. He sinned and lost God's favor, Genesis 3:1-19. Adam's sin passed upon all mankind, Romans 5:12. God sent His Son to redeem man, John 3:16. This redemption is by the vicarious death of Christ, Matthew 26:28; Acts 20:28; Romans 5:9; Hebrews 9:14; I Peter 1:18, 19; I John 1:7; Revelation 1:5; Revelation 7:14; Colossians 1:20. This salvation is obtained by a new birth through faith in Jesus Christ, John 3:3 through 16.

We must then conclude that since "God is Spirit" (John 4:24) and as such is incorporeal, He must have imparted to man a spiritual nature created in His own image, or else Genesis 1:26 is not meaningful.

Now the question arises, "If Jesus redeemed those who accept His salvation, what is the difference between those who are redeemed and those who are not?" It is clear that redemption is not simply favor with God here upon earth. This brings us to the Scriptural teaching of the eternal existence of the soul. First of all, there is much evidence that the soul does exist as a conscious

entity after it departs from the body, and there is no Scriptural evidence to the contrary. In Luke 20:37, 38, the Lord Jesus there speaking of the revelation God gave to Moses, makes it clear that when God said, "I am the God of Abraham, Isaac, and Jacob," that God was not the God of the dead, but of the living, though Abraham, Isaac, and Jacob had long since been physically dead. The only reasonable conclusion then is that these great Old Testament saints of God possessed spiritual natures that transcended physical death.

In the 17th chapter of Matthew we see Moses and Elijah on the Mount of Transfiguration with Christ, and communing with Him, yet we know that Moses had been physically dead for centuries,[47] and no record of his resurrection exists in Scripture.

In Luke 16:19 through 31, Jesus here (and this is not a parable) shows the difference between the state of the soul of the redeemed and the state of the soul of the wicked after death. In Revelation 6:9, we see the souls of those who had been martyred for Christ crying out for vengeance. In II Corinthians 5:1-9, Paul makes it clear that to be absent from the body is to be consciously "present" or "at home" with the Lord. But the Scriptures go even further, for they speak of a resurrection of the body, Job 19:25; I Thessalonians 4:16, 17; I Corinthians 15:35-57. In this last reference, I Corinthians 15, in verses 35-49, is found the answer to this question which the Jehovah Witnesses are laboring under, that is (verse 35), "How are the dead raised up? and with what body do they come?" We notice that in verse 36 Paul addresses those who labor under this question as "(thou) fool."

Now that we have considered the problem of the soul's existence after

---

[47] Jehovah's Witnesses claim that this was a vision, not a "real" evidence of the soul's existence beyond the grave, and they point to Matthew 17:9, where the English rendition to the Greek (*orama*) is "Vision." However, this Greek term literally reads, "that which is seen — a spectacle" (see Thayer's Lexicon, page 451), not mere "vision"; hence the occurrence was real and therefore sufficient evidence to indicate the conscious survival of the soul or spirit after physical death.

death, and the resurrection of the body, we find Scripture is clear in its teaching that those who reject God's salvation will suffer throughout eternity in outer darkness, Matthew 8:11, 12; 13:42-50; 22:13; II Peter 2:17; Jude 13; Revelation 14:9-11; 19:20, and those who accept God's salvation will dwell with Christ throughout eternity in joy and peace, John 14:1-3; 17:24; Luke 20:36; I Thessalonians 4:17; Revelation 22:5. Here is revealed what we believe is the true meaning of the Scriptural terms "immortality and incorruption" (*athanasian, aphtharsian*). We must also realize that these words do not apply to God the Father in the same sense that they apply to God the Son. When we come "with" Him from heaven (I Thessalonians 4:14), we shall be made like Him in the sense that we shall have a soul and body *incapable* of sin, not earthly but heavenly. We shall put on *aphtharsian* and *athanasian* and abide with Christ into the eternal.

As I stated at the beginning of this point, it would be futile to refute all the errors of thought in Jehovah's Witnesses theology. Therefore, I have presented what I feel is sufficient evidence to show that man has an eternal soul and will abide somewhere either in conscious joy or sorrow eternally, and that those who believe and trust in Christ as their personal Saviour will "put on" that immortality when Jesus returns.

Regarding the Jehovah's Witnesses, we can only say as Paul said to the Corinthians in II Corinthians 4:3, 4, "But if our gospel be hid, it is hid to them that are lost: in whom the God of this world hath blinded the minds of them which believe not, lest the light of the glorious gospel of Christ, who is the image of God should shine unto them," and as he again states in II Thessalonians 2:10b, 11, "because they received not the love of the truth that they might be saved. And for this cause God shall send them strong delusion, that they should believe a lie."

Honest study of this problem will reveal to any interested Bible student that man does possess an eternal immaterial nature which was fashioned to occupy an everlasting habitation whether in conscious bliss or torment. This then is the nature and certain destiny of man.

Author's Note

The following partial list of references to the soul and spirit of man as drawn from the Old and New Testaments will, we believe, furnish the interested reader with ample evidence that man is not just a combination of body and breath forming a living soul, as the Jehovah's Witnesses teach, but rather a soul, or spirit, possessing a corporeal form.

The Hebrew equivalent for soul as used in the Old Testament is *nephesh,* and for spirit *ruach.* The Greek equivalent for soul is *psuche* and for spirit *pneuma.*

1. It is an entity possessing the attributes of life (Isaiah 55:3). It is also separate from the body (Matthew 10:28; Luke 8:55; I Thessalonians 5:23; Hebrews 4:12; Revelation 16:3), *ie.,* it exists independent of material form.
2. A soul departs at the death of the form (Genesis 35:18).
3. The soul is conscious after death (Matthew 17:3; Revelation 6:9-11).
4. The soul of Samuel was conscious after death (I Samuel 28:18, 19).
5. Stephen had a spirit which he committed to Christ at his death (Acts 7:59).
6. There is definitely a spirit and soul of man (Isaiah 57:16).
7. The spirit is independent of the body (Zechariah 12:1).
8. The spirit, the soul of man, does that which only a personality can do; it "wills" [*prothumon*] (Matthew 26:41).
9. We are instructed to worship in the spirit (John 4:23; Philippians 3:3) since God is a spirit.
10. The spirit of man has the attribute of personality, the ability to testify (Romans 8:16, 26); also the faculty of "knowing" (I Corinthians 2:11).
11. The spirit can be either saved or lost (I Corinthians 5:5); it belongs

to God, and we are instructed to glorify Him in it (I Corinthians 6: 20).

12. The spirit or soul goes into eternity and is a conscious entity (Galatians 6:8).

13. Christ is with our spirit (II Timothy 4:22), for the spirit is the life of the body (James 2:26).

14. We are born of God's Spirit, and as such spirits ourselves (John 3:5, 6).

These references will suffice to show that the immaterial nature of man is far from the combination of breath and flesh as Jehovah's Witnesses maintain.

The Kingdom of Heaven

The human soul, marred and stained as it is by the burden of inherent sin, seeks constant escape from the reality of that sin and the sure penalty due because of it. Once the reality of eternal punishment is clouded by idealistic concepts of everlasting bliss without the fear of personal reckoning, the soul can relax, so to speak, and the sinner, unconscious of the impending doom, God's Justice, rests secure in the persuasion that "God is Love." Laboring under this delusion it is no wonder that Jehovah's Witnesses can so calmly construct "The Kingdom of Heaven" for to them God's infinite justice does not exist and eternal retribution is only an invention of "hell fire screechers."

The Biblical kingdom of heaven has many aspects, none of which includes the invented hierarchal construction so vividly outlined in *Let God Be True*. In Luke 17:20, 21 the Lord reveals the kingdom of heaven as within the believer in one aspect but clearly states that the heavenly aspect will be visible and observable at His return (verses 23-26). In Matthew 13, the Lord Jesus portrays the kingdom of heaven symbolically in parables yet always it is pictured as reality, not invisible phantom government. Jehovah's Witnesses arrive at the year A.D. 1914 as the end of the Gentile times and the beginning of the reign of the invisible heavenly King Christ Jesus. How they arrived at

this arbitrary date no one can reasonably or chronologically ascertain, but valuable evidence to the effect that "Pastor" Russell formulated the whole hoax is obtainable from the July 15, 1950, copy of *The Watch Tower Announcing Jehovah's Kingdom*, where, on pages 216, 217, the following statements are found.

Away back in 1880 the columns of *The Watch Tower* had called notice to Bible Chronology marking A.D. 1914 as the year for the 2,520 year period to end and referred to by Jesus as "the times of the Gentiles" in his prophecy on the world's end (Luke 21:24). In harmony with this it was expected that in 1914 the kingdom of God by Christ Jesus in the heavens would be fully established, while the world would be involved in an unprecedented time of trouble. The religious leaders and the systems of Christendom were all set to laugh at Brother Russell and his fellow witnesses of Jehovah over failure of his announced predictions concerning A.D. 1914. But it was no laughing matter when, at the end of July, World War I broke out and by October it had become global in its scope. Christendom's religious mouths were silenced at this frightening turn of events, but not Brother Russell's. October 1, 1914, on taking his place at the breakfast table in the Brooklyn Bethel dining-room, he in a strong voice denoting conviction announced:

"The Gentile Times have ended."

Knowing that the world had now reached the time for its dissolution he refused to heed the plea of U. S. President Wilson for all clergymen and preachers to join in nation wide prayer for peace, ...

Thus it was, that at the words of one colossally egotistical and unschooled haberdasher, the Times of the Gentiles ended.

To follow through Jehovah's Witnesses' interpretation of the Kingdom it is necessary to understand that only 144,000 faithful servants will rule with King Jesus in the heavenly sphere. They quote Revelation 7:4 and 14:1, 3 but neglect to notice that the 144,000 are of the tribes of Israel (Jews), 12,000 of each tribe, and are in no sense to be construed as anything else. This is not figurative; this is actual, since the tribes are listed by name. To follow out their own argument Jehovah's Witnesses must believe that only 144,000 Jewish members of their organization will be privileged to reign with Christ Jesus. The argument that they are spiritual Jews is invalid since even if they were, which they aren't, they would be "Children of Abraham" not Israel, and there is a vast difference in interpretation at this point (Galatians 3:29). Ishmael, the father of the Arab race, the ancestor of Mohammed, the founder of Islam, was a son of Abraham (Genesis 16) after the flesh even as Isaac the father of Jacob, so it can be seen that Abraham's seed differs from the selection of Israel's stock, as it is written ". . . for in Isaac shall thy seed be called" (Genesis 21:12). The texts are then clear that Israel after the flesh is mentioned and not spiritual symbolism; therefore, the 144,000 conjecture pertaining to kingdom rule as advanced by Jehovah's Witnesses crumbles under the light of Scriptural truth.

In concluding this point it is imperative to remember that there can be no kingdom without the King and the Scripture is clear when it states that the true kingdom will be instituted at Christ's visible return.

The Old and New Testaments corroborate each other in establishing the certainty of the visible return and reign of Christ. (Cf. Zechariah 14:4, Amos 9:8-15, Isaiah 11 and 12, Ezekiel 37: 20-28, Luke 17:22ff and Matthew 24: 26-31 to mention just a few). Jehovah's Witnesses unknowingly fulfill the prophecy of Christ in Matthew 24:23ff, where the Lord warns of false Christs and prophets who shall say Christ is here, Christ is there (in the desert, in the secret places, etc.), and shall deceive many with their deceit. Jehovah's Witnesses say He is here now but the Lord said He would be visible at His return, and every eye should see Him (Revelation 1:7; cf. Matthew 24:27-30). How then can we doubt His testimony when He Himself has said:

> And the sign of the Son of Man will then appear in heaven and all the tribes of the earth will wail — *and they will see* [visible] the Son of Man coming on the clouds of heaven, with great majesty and power (Matthew 24:30).

To this we can only say with John: "Even so come, Lord Jesus."

In drawing this portion of our study of Jehovah's Witnesses to a close it is expedient and vitally necessary that a clear picture of what this cult means to all Christians be presented. This organization has mushroomed from a meager beginning in 1881 until now it extends to every part of the globe and continues to grow each year in strength and popularity. Because the cult does away with the doctrine of eternal retribution for sin[48] it appeals greatly to those who believe they see in it an escape from the penalty of personal transgression. Jehovah's Witnesses offer an illusionary "Kingdom" to the personalities who desire importance, and most of all an outlet to vent their wrath upon religious leaders and organizations whose doctrines they assail as "of the Devil."[49] We do not believe for one moment that the greater body of these people know the true implications of Russell's doctrines; however, let no Jehovah's Witness ever disclaim Russellistic origin. Charles Taze Russell founded, operated, propagated and gave his life to furthering this cult, and his teachings permeate every major

---

[48]"Eternal torture is nowhere taught in the Bible," (Volume I, page 128) *Studies in Scriptures* — C. T. Russell.

[49]*Deliverance* — pages 91, 222, 226, 230 by J. F. Rutherford. Page 91, "Clergymen form-ing a part of the World are therefore Enemies of God." Pages 222, 226, 230, "The ecclesiastical systems Catholic and Protestant are under the supervision of the Devil . . . and therefore, constitute the Antichrist."

phase of its doctrines despite the intense aloofness they manifest when his past is mentioned. But now the question arises — "How can so many people be deceived by so obviously fraudulent a type of religion?" To understand this, the teachings and methods of propagation of the cult must be analyzed.

To begin with, no member of the Society is ever allowed to think independently for himself.

All religious leaders and organizations are false and anything they say is to be discounted as the "vain philosophies of men." The Scriptures are always made to conform to Jehovah's Witnesses' beliefs, never Jehovah's Witnesses' beliefs to the Scriptures. Rutherford's legal mind made most of this conjecture and linguistic chicanery reasonable to the minds of the people to whom he addressed it, and his books are masterpieces of illogical and invalid premises and conclusions.

To trace the logic and reasoning processes of Rutherford is the task of a logician, since for Russell or Rutherford a contradictory statement can be a premise which, regardless of the steps, always has a valid conclusion in their system of thinking. Jehovah's Witnesses' doctrine is a mass of half-truths and pseudo-scholastic material which to the untutored mind appears as "wonderful revelation."

Recently, when I was speaking to an ardent Jehovah's Witness, the following statement fell unashamedly from his lips: "I have never met anyone who knows more about Greek than the Society." In all probability he was right, for had he met someone who did know Greek he would never have become a member of the cult. The Society, to our knowledge, does not have any Greek scholars of any repute in their ranks, and if they do I would welcome any opportunity for them to come out from behind their lexicons and explain their rendition of John 1:1, 8:58 and Colossians 2:9, to mention just a few. He-

brew scholars are also included in this invitation.

Another trait of the Society is their aversion to signing literary efforts such as *Let God Be True, The Truth Shall Make You Free, The New World Translation,* etc. By not committing persons to their signatures the Society escapes the unpleasant task of having to answer for their numerous blunders. Their standard answer is, "Many persons worked on the books, not just one particular person," etc. In their predicament, having no recognized scholarship behind them, they have chosen the wisest possible course — silence. The plain truth of the matter is that the "new" books are just rephrases of Russell's and Rutherford's works and contain no originality other than up-to-date information on world conditions and new approaches to old material.

One of the distinguishing characteristics of an ardent Jehovah's Witness is his (or her) ability to handle the Scriptures. *The Emphatic Diaglott* with its interlinear readings of the Greek facilitates their progress in this project. Any good Jehovah's Witness, sad to say, can cause the average Christian untold trouble in the Scriptures, though the trouble in most cases has an elementary solution. The Christian is bewildered by the glib manner in which they repeat Scripture verses (usually entirely out of context) and sprinkle their discourses with Greek or Hebrew grammatical terms of which they have no knowledge beyond their *Diaglott.* The boldness with which they collar the unwary pedestrian, intrude on the quiet of a restful evening, attend their conventions, and propagate their literature, is a danger signal that Evangelical Christianity would do well to heed and take definite steps to combat. As has been observed, the answer to Jehovah's Witnesses, or "Russellism" if you will, is the Deity of Jesus Christ, and in teaching that one cardinal doctrine of the Christian faith, all energy ought to be expended to the uttermost. All ministers, Sunday-school supervisors, Bible and Tract Societies and teachers should drill their charges in Biblical memorization and doctrinal truths, that a united Christian front may be thrown up against this ever-growing menace to sound reasoning in Biblical exposition and study. The plan is not difficult, and only procrastination hinders its adoption. This problem is also the task of Christian colleges, seminaries and Bible schools, who too long have neglected the institution of strong cult courses in their curricula. The fruit of their neglect is before us today. Must we stand by in silence while the Word of God is defamed, the Lordship of Christ blasphemed, and the faith of generations still unborn is threatened by a group of people who will not listen to honest Biblical truths, and dare not contest them in scholastic discussion? It is frustrating and exasperating to carry on a discussion with a person or persons who argue in circles and dodge artfully from one refutation to another. These tactics characterize the preaching and argumentation of Jehovah's Witnesses, which must be met by calm dispositions and truthful Scriptural exegesis on the part of well-grounded Christians. Information in the form of documentary evidence and cold facts has met and can meet their perversions and emerge triumphant over them. We as Christians must perform this task without delay; we can ill afford to wait any longer.

The end product of this whole cult is the denial of the Lord Jesus Christ as "very God" and despite their protests that they honor Christ, they do indeed dishonor and "crucify Him afresh" since they deny His Deity and Lordship. Regardless of their Biblical names and proficiency in the Scriptures, they constantly reveal their true character in their actions, which are the diametric opposite of Scriptural teachings. The following old adage is most appropriate in describing the doctrines of Jehovah's Witnesses: "No matter how you label

it or what color bottle you put it in, poison is still poison." "He that has ears, let him hear." On the cover of *The Watch Tower Announcing Jehovah's Kingdom,* Isaiah 35:15 and 43:12 are quoted, and throughout all of their publications they boast themselves as "Jehovah's Witnesses."

There can be no kingdom without the King, however, and His return is visible, with power and glory (Matthew 24:30). Their kingdom has come (1914-1918 A.D.), but with no visible king, power or glory. Jehovah of the Watch Tower is a conjectural myth, a creation of the reactionary theology of Charles Taze Russell, and is conformed to the pattern of Russell's mind and education, which continued through Rutherford and now continues through Knorr to the ever-increasing blindness of those misguided souls foolish enough to trust in the Russellite delusion. In comparison to the Scriptures this picture is infinite darkness, for its author is the "Prince of Darkness," and the Word of God clearly and incontestably reveals that "Jehovah of the Watch Tower" is not the Jehovah of the Bible, for Jehovah of the Bible is Lord of all — "The great God and our Saviour Jesus Christ" (Titus 2:13).

SELECTED TERMS AND TEXTS MISAPPLIED BY JEHOVAH'S WITNESSES

To review all the terms and texts which Jehovah's Witnesses have misinterpreted and misapplied to bolster up their fractured system of theology would be impossible in the space here available. Therefore, I have chosen to survey six of their worst perversions of common Biblical terms, and various texts which the Watch Tower has mauled and mangled almost beyond recognition with little or no regard for hermeneutical principles, contexts, or the laws of sound exegesis.

These examples of Watch Tower deceptions are found all neatly cataloged in their handbook of doctrinal subjects, entitled, *Make Sure of All Things* (Watch Tower Bible and Tract Society, Brooklyn, New York, 1953) upon which this study is principally based, should any care to check further their authenticity, etc.

Misapplied Terms

1. "Only begotten" (Greek: Monogenes) — Jehovah's Witnesses in their zeal to establish the Christology of Arius of Alexandria have seized upon this Greek term, translated "only begotten" in the New Testament, and unfortunately they have been most successful in hoodwinking many uninformed persons into believing that "only begotten" really means "only generated." From this erroneous view they therefore suggest that since the term is applied to Jesus Christ five times in the New Testament Christ is but a creature, or as they love to quote Codex Alexandrinus, "The only begotten God" (John 1:18).

It should be noted in this connection, therefore, that the most authoritative lexicons and grammar books, not to mention numerous scholarly works, all render "monogenes" as "only or unique 'the only member of a kin or kind, hence generally only,' " (Liddell and Scott's *Greek-English Lexicon,* Vol. 2, page 1144). Moulton and Milligan in their vocabulary of the Greek New Testament, pages 416 and 417, render "monogenes" as "one of a kind, only, unique," facts that establish beyond scholarly doubt the truth of the contention that in both classical and Koine Greek the term "monogenes" carries the meaning of "only," "unique," or "the only member of a particular kind." The Septuagint translation of the Old Testament also utilizes the term "monogenes" as the equivalent in translation of the Hebrew adjective "yachid" translated "solitary" (Psalm 68:6), etc. This interesting fact reveals that the translators understood "monogenes" to have the meaning of uniqueness attached to it, emphasis obviously being placed on

"only" and decidedly not in "genus" or "kind."

In other places in the New Testament, such as Luke 7:11-18; 8:42; 9:38; Hebrews 11:17, etc., the rendering "only begotten" in the sense that Jehovah's Witnesses attempt to employ it in their translations and propaganda is an exegetical impossibility; especially in the instance of Hebrews 11:17, where Isaac is called the "only begotten" son of Abraham. Certainly he was not the eldest child, but rather he was the *sole* or *only* precious son in the sense that Abraham loved him in a unique way.

Dr. Thayer in his *Greek-English Lexicon of the New Testament,* page 417, referring to "monogenes," states, "single of its kind, only . . . used of Christ, denotes the only Son of God." Unfortunately in ancient literature "monogenes" became connected with the Latin term "unigenitus." However, such a translation is basically incorrect, as any lexicographical study will quickly reveal.

The early church fathers were in essential agreement that Jesus Christ pre-existed from all eternity in a unique relationship to God the Father. In the year 325 at the Council of Nicaea it was officially proclaimed that Jesus Christ was of the same substance or nature as the Father, and those who differed with this pronouncement which the Church had always held were excommunicated. Among them was Arius of Alexandria, a learned Presbyter and the Christological father of Jehovah's Witnesses. Arius held that Jesus Christ was a created being, the first and greatest creation of God the Father, that He did not pre-exist from all eternity and that His only claim to Godhood was the fact that He had been created first and then elevated to the rank of a deity.

Arius derived many of his ideas from his teacher, Lucien of Antioch, who in turn borrowed them from Origen, who himself had introduced the term "eternal generation" or the concept that God from all eternity generates a second person like Himself, ergo the "eternal Son." Arius of course rejected this as illogical and unreasonable, which it is, and taking the other horn of the dilemma squarely between his teeth reduced the eternal Word of God to the rank of a creation! It is a significant fact, however, that in the earliest writings of the church fathers dating from the first century to the year 230 the term "eternal generation" was never used, but it has been this dogma later adopted by Roman Catholic theology which has fed the Arian heresy through the centuries and today continues to feed the Christology of Jehovah's Witnesses.

In the year A.D. 328, in his private creed, Arius interestingly enough applies the term "gegennemenon" in reference to Christ, not the terms "monogenes" or "ginomai." "Gegennemenon" is a derivative of the word "gennao" which is translated "begotten" and rightly so; further than this, Eusebius of Caesarea, a follower of Arius about 325 also utilized the term "gegennemenon" not "monogenes," a fact which throws a grammatical monkey wrench into the semantic machinations of the Watch Tower.

We may see, therefore, that a study of this term "monogenes" reveals that in itself it is understood in both the classical and Koine vocabulary to be a term emphasizing uniqueness; i.e. the only one, the beloved, etc.; and there is no good grammatical ground for insist-ing as Jehovah's Witnesses do that it *must* mean "only generated," i.e. "only created."

Regarding the five times in the New Testament where the term "monogenes" is applied to Jesus Christ (John 1:14, 18; 3:16, 18; I John 4:9) it can easily be seen by the interested reader that the proper rendering "only" or "unique" in keeping with the historic usage of the term in no way disturbs the context but in fact makes it clearer Christologically, eliminating the concept fostered by the Arians and carried on by Jeho-vah's Witnesses that "only begotten" must infer creation which it most certainly does not!

The Eternal Word

As we mentioned before, the doctrine of eternal generation relative to the pre-existence of the Lord Jesus Christ is one of the great stumbling blocks in any intelligent approach to the Christological problems of the New Testament. This fact being true, the authors feel it is wiser to return to the original language of Scripture in its description of the Lord Jesus and His preincarnate existence, where He is never referred to except prophetically in the Bible as the "eternal Son" but as the Word of God (John 1:1) who "was" from all eternity and who "became" flesh (John 1:14), taking upon Himself the nature of man, and as such was "begotten" of the Virgin Mary by the power of the Holy Spirit. The "unique," "only" Son of God, then, whose uniqueness stems from the fact that of all men He was the most precious in the Father's sight, beloved above all His brethren, so much that the Father could say of Him when He sent Him into the world, "Thou art my Son, this day have I begotten thee" (Hebrews 1:5), is not a creature or a demi-god but ". . . God over all, blessed forever. Amen." (Romans 9:5, RSV Footnote).

The Bible clearly teaches, then, that Jesus Christ before His incarnation was the eternal Word, Wisdom, or Logos, of God, pre-existent from all eternity, co-equal, co-existent, co-eternal with the Father, whose intrinsic nature of deity He shared, and even though clothed in human form He never ceased to be deity, "God manifest in the flesh" (I Timothy 3:16) or as Paul put it so directly, "in him dwells all the fulness of the Godhead bodily" (Colossians 2:9).

By insisting upon the correct title of the pre-existent Christ, orthodox Christianity can successfully undercut the emphasis Jehovah's Witnesses place upon "monogenes," showing in contrast that "only begotten" is a term of time which can have no meaning outside of the sphere that man knows as recorded experience; and further, that Jesus Christ is not called by Scripture the "eternal Son," the error passed on from Origen under the title "eternal generation," but rather He is the Living Word of God (Hebrews 4:12), Creator of the Universe (II Peter 3:5), Sustainer of all things (II Peter 3:7), First Begotten from the dead (Acts 13:33), and our "Great High Priest, who has passed into the heavens, Jesus the Son of God . . . who can be touched with the feelings of our infirmities and who was in all points tempted like as we are, yet without sin." Let us fix these things in our minds, then: (a) the doctrine of "eternal generation" or the eternal Sonship of Christ, which springs from the Roman Catholic doctrine first conceived by Origen in A.D. 230, is a theory which opened the door theologically to the Arian and Sabellian heresies which today still plague the Christian Church in the realms of Christology.

(b) The Scripture nowhere calls Jesus Christ the eternal Son of God, and He is never called Son at all prior to the incarnation, except in prophetic passages in the Old Testament.

(c) The term "Son" itself is a functional term, as is the term "Father" and has no meaning apart from time. The term "Father" incidentally never carries the descriptive adjective "eternal" in Scripture; as a matter of fact, only the Spirit is called eternal[50] ("the eternal Spirit" — Hebrews 9:14), emphasizing the fact that the words Father and Son are purely functional as previously stated.

(d) Many heresies have seized upon the confusion created by the illogical "eternal Sonship" or "eternal generation" theory of Roman Catholic theology, unfortunately carried over to some aspects of Protestant theology.

(e) Finally; there cannot be any such thing as eternal Sonship, for there is a logical contradiction of terminology due to the fact that the word "Son" predicates time and the involvement of creativity. Christ, the Scripture tells us, as the Logos, is timeless, ". . . the Word *was* in the beginning" *not* the Son!

Summary

The Lord Jesus Christ, true God and true man, is now and for all eternity Son of God and Son of Man; therefore in this sense He is the eternal Son. But to be Biblical in the true sense of the term we must be willing to admit that He was known prior to His incarnation as the eternal Word, and knowledge of this fact cuts across the very basic groundwork and foundation of the Arian system of theology espoused by Jehovah's Witnesses. For if "only begotten" means "unique" or "only one of its kind" there cannot be any ground for rendering it "only generated" as Jehovah's Witnesses often attempt to do in a vain attempt to rob Christ of His Deity.

If then we relegate the terms "Father" and "Son" to the sphere of time as functional vehicles for the conveyance of the mysterious relationship which existed from all eternity between God and His Word, we will be probing deeper into the truth of the Scripture, which seems to teach us that God calls Christ His Eternal Word, lest we should ever forget that He is intrinsic Deity (for never was there a moment when God had a thought apart from His Logos or Reason). Further than this God calls Christ His "Son," lest we should think of the Word as being an impersonal force or attribute instead of a substantive entity existing in a subject-object relationship, the Eternal God "who is the Saviour of all men, especially those who believe."

1. Since the word "Son" definitely

---

[50]The Trinity as such is, however, spoken of as "the everlasting God" (Romans 16:26).

suggests inferiority and derivation it is absolutely essential then that Christ as the Eternal Word be pointed up as an antidote to the Arian heresy of Jehovah's Witnesses, and in this light we can understand quite plainly the usages of the term "monogenes" not in the Jehovah's Witnesses' sense of Creatureliness but in the true Biblical sense of "uniqueness," i.e. "the unique or only Son of God," generated in the womb of a woman by the direct agency of the Holy Spirit, "God manifest in the flesh." "The great God and our Saviour, Jesus Christ" (Titus 2:13).

2. "Greater" — (Greek: "Meizon"). Another principal term utilized by Jehovah's Witnesses is the term "greater" translated from the Greek, "Meizon" as it appears in the gospel of John, chapter 14, verse 28, "Ye have heard how I said unto you, I go away, and come again unto you. If ye loved me, ye would rejoice, because I said I go unto the Father: for my Father is greater than I." From this particular text, lifted conveniently out of its context by the ever-zealous Russellites, the Watch Tower attempts to "prove" that since Jesus in His own words while He was on earth stated that His Father was "greater" than He was, therefore Christ could not be equal with God or one of the members of the Trinity which Jehovah's Witnesses deny so vehemently.

On the face of the matter this appears to be a good argument from Christ's usage of the word "greater," but a closer examination of the context and of the hermeneutical principles which govern any sound exegetical study of the New Testament quickly reveals that theirs is a shallow case indeed and one which rests rather unsteadily upon one Greek word in a most restricted context.

The refutation of this bit of Watch Tower semantic double talk is found in a comparison with Hebrews, the first chapter, verse 4, "Being made so much *better* than the angels that he hath by his inheritance obtained a more excel-

lent name than they."

The careful student of Scripture will recognize immediately that in the first chapter of Hebrews, the verse previously cited, an entirely different word is utilized when comparing Christ and the angels. This word is "kreitton" and is translated "better" in the King James Version. Paralleling these two comparisons, then, that of Jesus with His Father in John 14:28, and Jesus with the angels in Hebrews 1:4, one startling fact immediately attracts attention. In the fourteenth chapter of John, as the Son of Man who had emptied Himself of His prerogatives of deity, Philippians 2:8-11, and taken upon Himself the form of a slave, the Lord Jesus Christ could truthfully say, "My Father is greater than I," greater being a *quantitative* term descriptive of *position*. Certainly in no sense of the context could it be construed as a comparison of nature or quality.

In the first chapter of Hebrews, however, the comparison made there between the Lord Jesus Christ and angels is clearly one of nature. The Greek "kreitton" being a term descriptive of quality, ergo, Christ was *qualitatively* better than the angels because He was their Creator (Colossians 1:16, 17) and as such He existed before all things and through Him all things hold together (Colossians 1:17-19). Since His intrinsic Nature is that of deity (John 8:58, compare Colossians 2:9), therefore *qualitatively* He was God manifest in the flesh, while *quantitatively* speaking He was limited as a man and could in all truthfulness state "My Father is greater than I." When this comparison of position in John 14:28 and the comparison of *nature* in Hebrews 1 are clearly understood the argument Jehovah's Witnesses attempt to raise in order to rob Christ of His deity is reduced to rubble before one of the greatest of all truths revealed in Scripture, i.e., that "God who made the world and all things therein" so loved us as to appear in our form (John 1:1, 14) that the sons of men might through His measure-less grace at length become the sons of God.

We should be quick to recognize, however, that had the Lord Jesus said in John 14:28 that his Father was *better* than He was and had used the proper Greek word denoting this type of comparison, another issue would be involved, but in actuality the compari-son between Christ and His Father in that context and verse clearly indicates that Jesus was speaking as a man and not as the second person of the Trinity (John 1:1). Therefore it is perfectly understandable that He should humble Himself before His Father and declare that in the present form in which He found Himself, His Father most cer-tainly was "greater," positionally, than He. One might be willing to admit that the President of the United States is a *greater* man by virtue of his present po-sition, authority and recognition, etc., but it would be a far different matter to assent to the proposition that the Presi-dent of the United States is a *better* man than his fellow Americans in the sense of *quality,* because such a comparison then involves a discussion of funda-mental natures, attributes, etc. In like manner, then, Jesus as the Incarnate Son of God who had by His own volun-tary act of will divested Himself of His prerogatives of intrinsic deity could speak of His Father as being *positionally* greater than He was without in any sense violating His true deity or humanity.

Hebrews 1:4 clearly teaches that Christ is better than the angels *quali-tatively* from all eternity and that even while He walked the earth, though He was made lower than the angels *po-sitionally* for the suffering of death in the form of a man, never for an instant did He ever cease to be the Lord of glory who could say with confident as-surance "Before Abraham was I AM" (John 8:58).

Let us be constantly aware of these facts when discussing the nature of Christ with Jehovah's Witnesses, for once the distinction is made between "greater" and "better" their entire ar-gument based upon John 14:28 melts into nothingness, and the deity of our Lord is completely vindicated by the whole testimony of Scripture.

3. "Born again" — Many times in their contacts with Christians Jehovah's Witnesses utilize the evangelical termi-nology of the gospel of John, chapter 3, where Christ speaking to Nicodemus said, "Except a man be born again he cannot see the kingdom of God." The Witnesses utilize such terminology be-cause they realize that contemporary evangelical efforts, especially those of Dr. Billy Graham, have popularized this term, and the Watch Tower is quick to capitalize on any popularization of a Biblical term, especially if it can be twisted to serve its own end! The defini-tion which Jehovah's Witnesses give to the new birth or the act of being "born again" is found on page 48 of their text book *Make Sure of All Things* and is as follows: "Born again means a birth-like realization of prospects and hopes for spirit life by resurrection to heaven. Such a realization is brought about through the water of God's truth in the Bible and God's holy spirit, his active force."

The interested student can see from this definition that the Witnesses reject flatly the concept of the new birth as taught in the New Testament. The Bible teaches us that when we are born again it is through repentance, the washing of water by the Word, and the direct agency of the third Person of the Trinity, God the Holy Spirit. (John 3, Ephe-sians 5:26, I Peter 1:23, etc.) There is not one verse that may be cited in either the Old or New Testaments to prove that the new birth means "a birth-like realization of prospects and hopes for spirit life by resurrection to heaven," as Jehovah's Witnesses so brazenly misrepresent it. On the contrary, the new birth guarantees eternal life to *all* believers, entrance into the kingdom of Heaven, and a resurrection to immortality in a deathless, incorruptible form similar to that of the Lord Jesus Christ's form when He rose from among the dead.

The theology of Jehovah's Witnesses relevant to the new birth is that there will be only 144,000 "spiritual brothers" who will reign with Christ in heaven for a thousand years; and, further, that only these 144,000 will have a resurrection to heaven and a "spirit life" such as that now allegedly enjoyed by "Pastor" Charles Taze Russell and Judge J. F. Rutherford, who are carrying on the work of the Society "within the veil," according to Watch Tower teaching.

In direct contrast to this the Lord Jesus Christ made a universal statement when He stated "Except a man be born again he cannot see the kingdom of God," and we find no record of either Christ, the disciples, or the apostles ever promulgating the 144,000 "spirit brothers" idea espoused so zealously by the Watch Tower. A doctrine of such momentous importance, the author feels, would certainly have been carefully defined in the New Testament; yet it is not, and the only support Jehovah's Witnesses can garner for this weird Russellite interpretation is from the book of Revelation and the mystical number "144,000," which, incidentally, the Bible teaches, refers to the twelve tribes of Israel, twelve thousand out of each tribe, and therefore certainly *not* to members of the Watch Tower's Theocracy.

Christians should therefore be on guard continually against the Watch Tower's perversion of common Biblical terms drawn from evangelical sources, for in 90% of the cases which the author has analyzed, the Witnesses *mean* just the opposite of what they *appear* to say. The new birth, Peter tells us, is a *past* event in the lives of those who have experienced the regenerating power of God's Spirit (Greek — "having been born again," I Peter 1:23); it is not something to be constantly experiencing or to be looking forward to in a type of ethereal spiritual resurrection as the Witnesses would have us believe. Rather it is a fact to be rejoiced in that we "have been born again" and are new creations in Christ Jesus (II Corinthians 5:17), joint heirs in the glory of the Kingdom which is yet to be revealed.

The Watch Tower Bible and Tract Society most decidedly has its "new birth" but it is not the new birth of Scripture, nor is their theory taught anywhere within the pages of the Bible. It is instead the theological brain child of Charles Taze Russell, to which the Witnesses cling so tenaciously, and which in the end will be found to have originated with "the god of this world" who has blinded their eyes "lest the glorious light of the Gospel of Christ, who is the image of God should shine unto them."

4. "Death" — In common with other deviant systems of theology Jehovah's Witnesses espouse a peculiar and definitely unbiblical concept of death, both in regard to the physical body and the soul and spirit of man.

According to the Watch Tower publication, *Make Sure of All Things,* page 86, death is defined in the following manner: "Death — loss of life; termination of existence; utter cessation of conscious intellectual or physical activity, celestial, human, or otherwise."

Reverting to their basic trait of text-lifting and term-switching, Jehovah's Witnesses garner a handful of texts from the Old and New Testaments which speak of death as "sleep" or "unconsciousness," and from these out-of-context quotations attempt to prove that at the death of the physical form, man, like the beasts, ceases to exist until the resurrection.

Seizing upon such texts as Ecclesiastes 9:5, 6 and 10; Psalm 13:3; Daniel 12:2, etc., the Witnesses loudly contend that until the resurrection, the dead remain unconscious and inactive in the grave, thus doing away in one fell swoop with the doctrine of hell and the true Biblical teaching regarding the soul of man.

It is impossible in the time allotted here to place all the verses Jehovah's Witnesses lift out of their contexts back into their proper contextual-hermeneutical position, and by so doing to show that their theory is an exegetical nightmare, but the following observation can be made:

Despite the fact that in the Old Testament the term "sleep" is used to denote death, never once is such a term used to describe the immaterial nature of man, which the Scriptures teach was created in the image of God (Genesis 1:26, 27). This fact also holds true in the New Testament, as any cursory study of either Strong's or Young's concordances will reveal. The term "sleep" is always applied to the body, since in death the body takes on the appearance of one who is asleep, but the term "soul sleep" or "the sleep of the soul" is never found in Scripture and nowhere does it state that the soul ever sleeps or passes into a state of unconsciousness. The only way that Jehovah's Witnesses can infer such a doctrine is by assuming beforehand that death *means* sleep or unconsciousness; hence, every time they are confronted with the term "death" they assign the meaning of the temporary extinction of consciousness to it, and by so doing remove from Scripture the doctrine which they fear and hate the most — that of conscious punishment after death for unregenerate souls, continuing on into the everlasting ages of eternity (Jude 10-13; II Peter 2:17).

Since we have already covered the doctrine of hell in a previous section, the simplest refutation of Jehovah's Witnesses' perverted terms such as "death" can be found in the Scriptures themselves, where it can easily be shown that death does not mean "termination of existence"; "utter cessation of conscious intellectual . . . activity" as the Watch Tower desperately attempts to establish.

The interested reader is referred to the following references: Ephesians 2: 1-5; John 11:26; Philippians 1:21, 23; and Romans 8:10. The usage of death in these passages clearly indicates a state of existence solely in opposition to the definition which the Watch Tower assigns to the word "death," and the reader need only substitute the Watch Tower's definition in each one of these previously enumerated passages to see how utterly absurd it is to believe that the body has experienced "the loss of life" or "termination of existence" in such a context where Paul writes, "If Christ be in you the body is dead because of sin" (Romans 8:10). The inspired apostle here obviously refers to a spiritual condition of separation — certainly not to "termination of existence," as the Watch Tower's definition states.

We see, therefore, that death is a separation of the soul and spirit *from* the body, resulting in physical inactivity and a general *appearance* of sleep; however, in the spiritual sense death is the separation of soul and spirit from God as the result of sin, and in no sense of the term can it ever be honestly translated "unconsciousness" or "termination of existence" as Jehovah's Witnesses would like to have it.

In his epistle to the Thessalonians, the fourth chapter, the Apostle Paul spoke of the return of the Lord Jesus Christ and most pointedly made use of the term "sleep" as a metaphor for death (I Thessalonians 4:13-18), and it is interesting to note his concept: "But I would not have you to be ignorant, brethren, concerning them which are asleep, that ye sorrow not even as others which have no hope; for if we believe that Jesus died and rose again, even so them also which sleep in Jesus will God bring *with* him. For this we say unto you by the word of the Lord, that we which are alive and remain unto the coming of the Lord shall not prevent them which are asleep. For the Lord himself shall descend from heaven with a shout, with the voice of the archangel, and with the trump of God: and the dead in Christ shall rise first: Then we which are alive and remain shall be caught up together with them in the clouds, to meet the Lord in the air; and so shall we ever be with the Lord. Wherefore comfort one another with these words."

Verse 14 of this previously quoted section indicates that Paul, while using the metaphor "sleep" to describe physical death, clearly understood that when Jesus comes again He will bring *with* (Greek *sun*) Him those whose bodies are sleeping. To be more explicit, the souls and spirits of those who are with Christ now in glory (II Corinthians 5:8; Philippians 1:22, 23) will be reunited with their resurrection bodies (I Corinthians 15); that is, they will be clothed with immortality, incorruptibility, exemption from physical decay and they will be coming *with* Jesus. The Greek "sun" indicates in a "side by side" position, and the bodies that are sleeping will in that instant be quickened, raised to immortality and reunited with the perfected spirits of the returning saints.

This passage alone would be enough to convince any exegetical scholar that those "sleeping in Jesus" must refer to their *bodies,* since they are in the same verse spoken of as coming *with* Jesus, and by no possible stretch of the imagination could one honestly exegete the passage so as to teach anything to the contrary.

Jehovah's Witnesses are justly afraid of the "everlasting fire" prepared for the devil and his followers (Matthew 25:41), and their entire system of theology is dedicated to a contradiction of this important Biblical teaching of God's eternal wrath upon those who perpetrate the infinite transgression of

denying His beloved Son. Rightly, then, does the Bible say that "The wrath of God continues to abide upon them" (John 3:36—literal translation) (Revelation 20:10; Mark 9:43, 48; Daniel 12:2).

For the Christian, then, physical death involves only the sleep of the body, pending the resurrection to immortality, when our resurrection bodies will be joined to our perfected souls and spirits; but in the intermediate state, should we die before the Lord comes, we have the assurance that we shall be *with Him* and that we shall return *with Him,* or as the Apostle Paul stated it, "To be absent from the body is to be at home (or present) with the Lord."

5. "First born" (*prototokos*—Greek) — The author feels it necessary to include a brief resumé of Jehovah's Witnesses misuse of the Greek term "prototokos" (Colossians 1:15), which the Watch Tower lays much emphasis upon since it is used descriptively of the Lord Jesus Christ, and so in their Arian theology it is construed to teach that Christ is the first creature since the word "first born" implies that of the *first* child.

In Colossians 1 the Apostle Paul speaks of the Lord Jesus Christ as the first born of every creature or of all creation. And the Witnesses, always eager to reduce Christ to the rank of an angel, have seized upon these passages of Scripture as indicative of His creaturehood. The Watch Tower teaches that since Christ is called the "first born of all creation," therefore He must be the *first one* created, and they cross-reference this with Revelation 3:14 which states that the faithful and true witness (Christ) is "the beginning of the creation of God."

On the surface the argument the Watch Tower erects appears to be fairly sound, but underneath it is found to be both shallow and fraudulent. The term first-born (*prototokos*) may also rightfully be rendered "first begetter" or "original bringer forth" (Erasmus), a term of preeminence, and in Colossians 1 it is a term of comparison between Christ and created *things*. In the first chapter of Colossians Paul points out that Christ is "before all things" and clearly establishes the fact that the eternal Word of God (John 1:1) existed before all creation (Hebrews 1), that He is preeminent over all creation, by virtue of the fact that He is Deity; and beyond this, that He is the Creator of all "things," which to any rational person indicates that if He is Creator of all things, He Himself is not one of the "things" created! In the eighth chapter of Romans, verse 29, the word "first born" is applied to Christ, clearly denoting His preeminence — not the concept that He is "the first creature made by Jehovah God," as the Witnesses would like us to believe — and in Colossians 1:18 we learn that Christ is "first born" from the dead, that is, the first one to rise in a resurrection body. Again the meaning is that of preeminence, not of creation.

Revelation 3:14, "The beginning of the creation of God" is easily harmonized with the rest of Scripture, which teaches the absolute deity of the Lord Jesus Christ when we realize that the Greek word "arche," which is translated "beginning," is translated by the Witnesses themselves as "originally" in John 1:1 of their own *New World Translation* — and this is a good translation at this point — so applying it to Revelation 3:14 Christ becomes the "origin" or the "source" of the creation of God (Knox), and not the very beginning of it Himself in the sense that He is the *first* creation, a fact which Scripture most pointedly contradicts.

Christ is therefore "first born" or preeminent by virtue of the fact that He is Deity, and by virtue of the fact that He is the first one to rise in a glorified body. He is therefore preeminent

over all creation, and through His power all things consist or hold together. He is not one of the "things" (Colossians 1:16, 17) but He is the Creator of *all things*, the eternal Word who possesses the very nature of God (Hebrews 1:3).

6. "Soul and spirit" (Greek: *Psuche, Pneuma*) — Jehovah's Witnesses delight in the assertion that man does not possess an immaterial, deathless[51] nature, and they never tire of proclaiming such teaching to be "a lie of the Devil" and a dogma derived from pagan religions (Egyptian, Babylonian, Greek, etc.). The literature of Jehovah's Witnesses is filled with condemnations of the doctrine of the immaterial nature of man. According to the Watch Tower the soul is "a living, breathing, sentient creature, animal or human," and Jehovah's Witnesses also define a spirit as "a life force, or something wind-like" (page 357, *Make Sure of All Things*).

By so defining these two common Biblical terms, the Watch Tower seeks to avoid the embarrassing Scriptural truth that since man is created in the image of God, and God is Spirit, man must possess a cognizant spiritual entity formed in the image of his Creator (Genesis 1:26, 27). To explode this Watch Tower mythology is an elementary task when we realize that when the Lord Jesus Christ died upon the cross He said, "Father, into thy hands I commend my spirit," a fact Jehovah's Witnesses are hard put to explain, since if the spirit is nothing but breath or wind, and certainly not a conscious entity as the Bible teaches it is, then it would be fruitless for Christ to commit His breath to the Father; yet He did precisely that! The truth of the matter is that the Lord Jesus Christ committed to His Father His immaterial nature as a man, proving conclusively that the spirit and soul of man goes into eternity as a conscious entity (Galatians 6:8).

---

[51] In the sense of extinction that is, for the soul is spoken of as being extinct or unconscious.

It will also be remembered that when Stephen was stoned, he fell asleep in death, but not before he said, "Lord Jesus, receive my spirit," and in that particular context it is rather obvious that he was not referring to the exhalation of carbon dioxide from his lungs! However, we may safely say that the meanings Jehovah's Witnesses give to soul and spirit will not stand the test of systematic exegesis in either the Old or New Testament, and no competent Hebrew or Greek scholar today has ever espoused their cause in open scholastic discussion.

Conclusion

Concluding this synopsis of the misapplications and misinterpretations of Jehovah's Witnesses where Biblical terms and texts are concerned, the author feels constrained to state that by no means has he thoroughly covered this vast subject.

Jehovah's Witnesses thrive on the confusion they are able to create, and in their door-to-door canvassing they accentuate this trait by demonstrating extreme reluctance to identify themselves as emissaries of the Watch Tower until they have established a favorable contact with the prospective convert. To put it in the terms of the vernacular, until they have "made the pitch" they are careful to conceal their identity. To illustrate this particular point more fully, the *New Yorker Magazine,* June 16, 1956, carried a lengthy article by one of its feature writers, Richard Harris, in which Mr. Harris recounts his experiences with Jehovah's Witnesses. In this article, Mr. Harris relates that the Witesses never identified themselves to prospective converts as Jehovah's Witnesses at first, when Mr. Harris accompanied a team of Witnesses on one of their daily canvassing routes in Brooklyn. Mr. Harris also pointed out in the article that the Witnesses openly admitted to him that it was necessary for them first to make a successful contact before they fully identified themselves. In short, they fly under false colors: "A representative of Radio Station WBBR," "A Bible student," or "a minister," but seldom if ever as a Jehovah's Witness.

The late Judge J. F. Rutherford has well taught his followers to "advertise, advertise, advertise!" And today throughout the world Jehovah's Witnesses are advertising, advertising, and selling, selling, the theocracy of Charles Taze Russell and J. F. Rutherford under any label that is convenient, and that will gain for them a hearing.

If evangelical Christianity continues to virtually ignore today the activities of Jehovah's Witnesses it does so at the peril of countless souls. Therefore let us awaken to their perversions of Scripture and stand fast in the defense of the faith "once delivered unto the saints."

AUTHOR'S NOTE

Nowhere is this point more forcefully demonstrated than in a book written by a former member of the Watch Tower Society, W. J. Schnell ("Thirty Years a Watch Tower Slave," Baker Book House, 1956). In this particular reference Schnell succinctly states the Watch Tower methodology in the following words:

"The Watch Tower leadership sensed that within the midst of Christendom were many millions of professing Christians who were not well grounded in 'the truths once delivered to the saints,' and who would be rather easily pried loose from the churches and led into a new and revitalized Watch Tower organization. The Society calculated, and that rightly, that this lack of proper knowledge of God and the widespread acceptance of half-truths in Christendom would yield vast masses of men and women, if the whole matter were wisely attacked, the attack sustained and the results contained, and then re-used in an ever-widening circle" (Page 19).

Chapter 5

CHRISTIAN SCIENCE AND NEW THOUGHT

HISTORICAL PERSPECTIVES

Of all the persons destined for religious prominence and success in the nineteenth century, none has eclipsed Mary Ann Morse Baker, — better known among the band of faithful Christian Scientists as Mary Baker Eddy, "Mother" and our Leader, the "Discoverer and Founder" of Christian Science.

Mary Baker was born in Bow, New Hampshire, in the year 1821 in the humble surroundings of a New Hampshire farm house, and was reared a strict Congregationalist by her parents, Mark and Abigail Baker. The life of young Mary Baker until her twenty-second year was marked with frequent illnesses of both emotional and physical nature,[1] and the then infant science of mesmerism was not infrequently applied to her case with some success.

In December of 1843, at the age of 22, the future Mrs. Eddy was married to George W. Glover, a neighboring business man, whose untimely death of yellow fever in Wilmington, South Carolina, some seven months later, reduced his pregnant wife to an emotional and highly unstable invalid, who, throughout the remaining years of her life, relied from time to time upon the drug morphine as a medication.[2]

To be sure, no informed person believes that Mrs. Eddy was a "dope addict," but much evidence from incontrovertible sources is available to show beyond doubt that throughout her life Mrs. Eddy made repeated use of this drug.[3]

A decade passed in the life of Mrs. Glover during which she had many trying experiences, and then on June 21st, 1853 she married Dr. Daniel M. Patterson, a dentist, who, contrary to the advice of Mrs. Glover's own father, Mark Baker, took the emotionally unstable Mary Glover for his bride.

The advice of Mark Baker was indeed ominously accurate, for some years later Mrs. Eddy divorced Dr. Patterson, who, she claimed, had abandoned her, and thus her second attempt at matrimony met with crushing disaster.

The third and last marriage of Mary Baker Glover Patterson was to one Asa G. Eddy when Mrs. Eddy was fifty-six years of age, although, claiming the prerogative of woman-kind, she demurely inserted the age as forty years on her third marriage form. She thus proved once again that far from being the saint of current Christian Science mythology, she was indeed a very human if not vain member of the female sex. Asa Eddy's death of a coronary thrombosis prompted Mrs. Eddy to commit a nearly fatal mistake where Christian Science was concerned. She contested the autopsy report and the physician she chose confirmed her conviction that Asa died of "arsenic poisoning mentally administered." Such a radical report prompted an inquiry into the credentials of Mrs. Eddy's physician, Dr. C. J. Eastman, Dean of the Bellview Medical College, outside Boston. It was found that "Doctor" Eastman was running a virtual abortion mill, had no medical credentials whatever to justify his title. He was

---

[1] E. F. Dakin, *Mrs. Eddy,* page 19.

[2] *New York World,* October 30, 1906.

[3] E. F. Dakin, *Mrs. Eddy,* pages 19, 149, especially pages 513, 514; also *New York World,* May 8, 1907.

sentenced to ten years in prison upon his conviction, and the Bellview Medical College closed. Mrs. Eddy had contradicted her own advice concerning autopsies.[4] And she would have been far better off to have practiced in this instance what she preached and to have abandoned Asa's remains to the scrap heap of mental malpractice, but the error was virtually unavoidable since Mrs. Eddy was not to be outdone by any medical doctor. She was an expert healer by her own admissions; the autopsy was therefore inevitable.

Mrs. Eddy's letter to the *Boston Post* dated June 5, 1882, in which she accused some of her former students of mentally poisoning Asa Eddy with malicious mesmerism in the form of arsenic mentally administered is one of the most pathetic examples of Mrs. Eddy's mental state ever recorded and one which the Christian Science Church would like to forget she ever wrote.

The real history of Christian Science, however, cannot be told unless one P. P. Quimby of Portland, Maine, be considered, for history tells us that as Mrs. Eddy was the mother of Christian Science, so Phineas Parkhurst Quimby was undoubtedly its father. "Dr." Quimby in the late 1850's entitled his system of mental healing "The Science of Man," and had used the terms "The Science of Christ" and "Christian Science" for some time before Mrs. Eddy gratuitously appropriated the terminology as her own, something she dared not do while the old gentleman was alive and her relationship to him known to all.

Mrs. Eddy's relationship to Dr. Quimby began when she arrived in Portland, Maine, in 1862 and committed herself to his care for treatment of "spinal inflammation." In November of that same year Mrs. Eddy noised

abroad to all men that P. P. Quimby had healed her of her infirmity. Said the then adoring disciple of Quimby, "I visited P. P. Quimby and in less than one week from that time I ascended by a stairway of 182 steps to the dome of the City Hall and am improving ad infinitum."[5]

In later years Mrs. Eddy's recollection of Quimby was somewhat different from her earlier echoes of praise, and she did not hesitate to describe him as a very "unlearned man," etc. Dr. Quimby termed his ideas "Science of Health." Mrs. Eddy entitled her book *Science and Health,* and published it in 1875, filled with numerous plagiarisms from the manuscripts of P. P. Quimby and from the writings of Francis Lieber, distinguished German-American publisher and authority on the philosophy of Hegel. For full documentation on Mrs. Eddy's plagiarism from Quimby the reader is urged to study the first four chapters of my book *The Christian Science Myth,*[6] which documents exhaustively the entire controversy and proves beyond a shadow of a doubt that Mrs. Eddy plagiarized a great part of her work from other sources, and then had it all copiously edited by the Rev. J. H. Wiggin, a retired Unitarian minister, who revealed his part in her deceptive plan via the posthumus publication of an interview he gave to one Livingstone Wright, later published as a pamphlet, entitled *How Reverend Wiggin Rewrote Mrs. Eddy's Book.*

Returning to Mrs. Eddy and the writings of Dr. Lieber for a moment, it is a simple matter to document her plagiarisms where this good man's writings were concerned. It is demonstrably true that Mrs. Eddy copied *thirty-three pages verbatim* and *one hundred pages in substance* into *Science and Health, with Key to the Scriptures,* Edition 1875, from

---

[4]"A medi-physician never gives medicine, recommends or trusts in hygiene, or believes in the ocular or post-mortem examination of patients." *Science and Health* edition 1881, page 261.

[5]Portland *Evening Courier,* November 7, 1862.

[6]Zondervan Publishing House, 1955.

Dr. Lieber's manuscript on the writings of Hegel, a manuscript antedating *Science and Health* and now in the possession of the Princeton Theological Seminary in Princeton, New Jersey, and certified as accurate by Arthur E. Overberry, authority on Dr. Lieber's writings, and by a special research committee of Johns Hopkins University who in 1940 pronounced the Lieber-Hegel document "unimpeachably authentic."

It is a proven fact that the Lieber Document is above challenge by any Christian Scientist. Our authority for exposing this plagiarism on the part of "Mother" Eddy is none other than Mrs.

Eddy herself, who wrote, "When needed tell the truth concerning a lie. The evasion of truth cripples integrity, and casts thee down from the pinnacle . . . A dishonest position is far from Christianly scientific" (*Science and Health,* page 448). In addition to this statement on the subject of plagiarism, Mrs. Eddy wrote in her book *Retrospection and Introspection* the following: "There is no warranted common law, and no permission in the Gospel for plagiarizing an author's ideas and their works . . ." So it appears that out of her own mouth Mrs. Eddy has condemned plagiarism, a practice from which she seemed to have extreme difficulty abstaining.

THE METAPHYSICAL RELIGION OF HEGEL
by Francis Lieber

1. "For Hegel and his true disciples there is no truth, substance, life or intelligence in matter; all is Infinite Mind. Thus matter has no reality; it is only the manifestation of spirit . . . therefore science is spiritual, for God is Spirit" (page 85).

2. "Hegel science brings to light truth and its supremacy, universal harmony, God's entirety, and matter's nothingness. For him there are but two realities, God and the ideas of God, in other words spirit and what it shadows forth. Properly, there is no physical science. The Principle of science is God, intelligence and not matter. Therefore science is spiritual, for God is Spirit and the Principle of the universe is (man). We learn from Hegel that Mind is universal the first and only cause of all that really is. Embryology affords no instance of one species producing another, the serpent germinating a bird, or a lion a lamb. The difference is not as great between the opposite species as between matter and spirit, so utterly unlike in substance and intelligence. That spirit propagates matter or matter spirit, is morally impossible. Hegel repudiates the thought" (pages 85, 86).

3. "To conclude that Life, Love, and Truth are attributes of personal deity implies there is something in Person superior to Principle. What, then, is the Person of God? Hegel makes clear that He has no personality as we now

SCIENCE AND HEALTH WITH KEY TO THE SCRIPTURES
by Mary Baker Eddy

1. "There is no life, truth, intelligence nor substance in matter. All is Infinite Mind and its infinite manifestation, for God is all in all . . . Spirit is God, and man is His image and likeness. Therefore man is not material; he is spiritual" (page 468, paragraphs 9-15).

2. "Christian Science brings to light Truth and its supremacy, universal mind, the entireness of God, good, and the nothingness of evil" (page 293, paragraphs 28-31).

"There is no physical science, the principle of science is God, intelligence and not matter; therefore science is spiritual for God is Spirit and the Principle of the universe and man. We learn from science mind is universal, the first and only cause of all that really is."

"Embryology affords no instance of one specie producing another; of a serpent germinating a bird, or a lion a lamb. . . . The difference is not as great between opposite species as between matter and spirit, so utterly unlike in substance and intelligence. That spirit propagates matter, or matter spirit, is morally impossible; science repudiates the thought" (pages 10, 264).

3. "To conclude, Life, Love, and Truth are attributes of a personal deity, implies there is something in Person superior to Principle."

"What is the Person of God? He has no personality, for this would imply Intelligence in matter; the body of God is know personality, for this would imply intelligence and matter.

The body of God is the Idea given of Him, harmonious order of the universe and in man (male and female) formed by Him" (page 82).

4. "Beauty is also eternal. The beauty of matter passes away, fading at length into decay and ugliness. But beauty itself is a thing of Life, exempt from age or decay. To be this must be a thing of spirit" (page 83).

5. "Hegel science brings to light Truth and its supremacy, universal harmony, God's entirety, and man's nothingness" (page 85).

6. "As music is harmoniously controlled by its Principle, so man governed by his Principle and Being, by Soul and not senses, is harmonious, sinless, and immortal" (page 91).

7. "The first step to understand Hegel is the Idea. He says the world would collapse without intelligence and Idea" (page 74).

8. "These Ideas of God never amalgamate but retain their distinct identities, and are controlled only by the Principle that evokes them. The mineral, vegetable, and animal kingdoms have their distinct identities, wherein one does not create or control the other, but all are created and controlled by God, Spirit" (page 76).

the idea given of Him in the harmonious universe, and the male and female formed by Him" (page 44, paragraphs 5-7; page 221, paragraph 24; page 222, paragraph 2).

4. "Beauty is eternal; but the beauty of matter passes away, fading at length into decay and ugliness."

"But beauty is a thing of Life, exempt from age or decay, and to be this it must be a thing of spirit" (page 212, paragraph 7; page 212, paragraph 10).

5. "Science brings to light Truth, and its supremacy, universal harmony, God's entirety, and matter's nothingness" (page 28, paragraph 6).

6. "As music is harmoniously controlled by its Principle, so man governed by his Principle and Being, by Soul and not sense, is harmonious, sinless, and immortal" (page 117, paragraph 29).

7. "This world would collapse without Intelligence and its Idea" (page 185, paragraph 23).

8. "The ideas of God never amalgamate but retain their distinct identities, and are controlled only by the Principle that evoked them. The mineral, vegetable, and animal kingdoms have their distinct identities, wherein one creates not nor controls the other, all are created and controlled by God" (page 71, paragraph 4-10).

The interested reader can observe for himself that Mrs. Eddy plagiarized from the Lieber manuscript almost at will, and it is a historical fact that she had access to this manuscript at the home of Hiram S. Crafts, where she lived for at least a year, during which time Crafts was admittedly her disciple avidly propagating the face-lifted teachings of Phineas Parkhurst Quimby.

Lest any should doubt the historical validity of these facts, the reader is referred to Sybil Wilbur's authorized *Life of Mrs. Eddy,* wherein the said Hiram Crafts is referred to as a "Kantian Transcendentalist," and further as "Mrs. Eddy's First Student." Dr. Lieber originally forwarded his manuscript "Metaphysical Religion of Hegel" to Hiram Crafts, a friend of his, with the express intent that it should be read before the "Kantian Society" in Boston. History does not tell us whether or not this ever

took place, but one thing history has beyond doubt revealed for all to see and that is the fact that Mary Baker Eddy both saw and plagiarized from this manuscript, and therefore her claim to originality where "Science and Health" is concerned is shown to be a sham.

The reader may wonder why we have gone to such great lengths to discuss Mary Baker Eddy and her plagiarisms, but the answer is really quite simple. Christian Science has historically from its very inception depended wholly and solely upon the authority conferred upon it by its now extinct high priestess, and in order to expose the claims of Christion Scientists relative to the inspiration of Mrs. Eddy — and for that matter Mrs. Eddy's own claims — it is virtually essential that her writings be shown in their true light, a light clouded and studded with plagiarisms.

Two other instances of Mrs. Eddy's plagiarisms are worth documenting. The first is found on page 147 of her book *Miscellaneous Writings* and was "her" annual message to her church [1895]. Only a short introduction and the elimination of a few words in the text serves to differentiate it from *Murray's Reader*.

Murray's Reader, p. 89.	*Miscellaneous Writings, p. 147.*
. . . the man of integrity . . . is one who makes it his constant rule to follow the road of duty, according as the word of God, and the voice of his conscience, point it out to him. He is not guided merely by affections, which may sometimes give the colour of virtue to a loose and unstable character.	The man of integrity is one who makes it his constant rule to follow the road of duty, according as Truth and the voice of his conscience point it out to him. He is not guided merely by affections which may some time give the color of virtue to a loose and unstable character.
2. The upright man is guided by a fixed principle of mind, which determines him to esteem nothing but what is honourable; and to abhor whatever is base or unworthy, in moral conduct. Hence we find him ever the same; at all times, the trusty friend, the affectionate relation, the conscientious man of business, the pious worshipper, the public-spirited citizen.	The upright man is guided by a fixed Principle, which destines him to do nothing but what is honorable, and to abhor whatever is base or unworthy; hence we find him ever the same — at all times the trusty friend, the affectionate relative, the pious worker, the public-spirited citizen.
3. He assumes no borrowed appearance. He seeks no mask to cover him, for he acts no studied part; but he is indeed what he appears to be, full of truth, candour, and humanity. In all his pursuits, he knows no path but the fair and direct one; and would much rather fail of success, than attain it by reproachful means.	He assumes no borrowed appearance. He seeks no mask to cover him, for he acts no studied part; but he is indeed what he appears to be, — full of truth, candor and humanity. In all his pursuits, he knows no path but the fair, open, and direct one, and would much rather fail of success than attain it by reproachable means. He never shows us a smiling countenance while he meditates evil against us in his heart. We shall never find one part of his character at variance with another. Lovingly yours,
4. He never shows us a smiling countenance, while he meditates evil against us in his heart. He never praises us amongst our friends; . . . We shall never find one part of his character at variance with another. . . . —*Blair.*	*Mary Baker Eddy* Sept. 30, 1895

The final illustration of Mrs. Eddy's plagiarism comes from *The New York Times* of July 10, 1904, which published parallel columns of Mrs. Eddy and P. P. Quimby writings proving Quimby to be at least a partial source of her "revelation" of science and health.

From Quimby's *Science of Man,* expounded by Mrs. Eddy at Stoughton, 1868, 1869, 1870.	From Mrs. Eddy's *Science and Health,* the textbook of the "Christian Science" she now claims to have discovered in 1866.
If I understand how disease originates in the mind and fully believe it, why cannot I cure myself?	Disease being a belief, a latent delusion of mortal mind, the sensation would not appear if *this error was met and destroyed by Truth.* — page 61, edition of 1898.
Disease being made by our belief or by our parents' belief or by public opinion there is no formula of argument to be adopted, but every one must fit in their particular case. There it requires great shrewdness or wisdom to get the better of the error. . .	Science not only reveals the origin of all disease as wholly mental, but it also declares that all disease is cured by mind. — page 62 — edition of 1898.
I know of no better counsel than	When we come to have more faith in

Jesus gave to his disciples when he sent them forth to cast out devils and heal the sick, and thus in practice to preach the Truth, "Be ye wise as serpents and harmless as doves." Never get into a passion, but in patience possess ye your soul, and at length you weary out the discord and produce harmony by your Truth destroying error. Then you get the case. Now, if you are not afraid to face the error and argue it down, then you can heal the sick.

The patient's disease is in his belief. Error is sickness. Truth is health.

In this science the names are given; thus God is Wisdom. This Wisdom, not an Individuality but a principle every idea — form, of which the idea, man, is the highest — hence the image of God, or the Principle.

Understanding is God.

All sciences are part of God.

Truth is God.

There is no other Truth but God.

God is Wisdom.

God is Principle.

Wisdom, Love, Truth are the Principle.

Error is matter.

Matter has no intelligence.

To give intelligence to matter is an error which is sickness.

Matter has no intelligence of its own, and to believe intelligence is in matter is the error which produced pain and inharmony of all sorts; to hold ourselves we are a principle outside of matter, we would not be influenced by the opinions of man, but held to the workings only of a principle, Truth, in which there are not inharmonies of sickness, pain or sin.

For matter is an error, there being no substance, which is Truth, in a thing which changes and is only that which belief makes it.

Christ was the Wisdom that knew Truth dwelt not in opinion that could be formed into any shape which the belief gave to it and that the life which moved it came not from it but was outside of it.

the Truth of Being than we have in error, more faith in spirit than in matter, then no material conditions can prevent us from healing the sick, *and destroying error through Truth.* — page 367 — edition of 1898.

We classify disease as error which nothing but Truth or Mind can heal. — page 427, edition of 1898.

Discord is the nothingness of error. Harmony is the somethingness of Truth. — page 172 — edition of 1898.

Sickness is part of the error which Truth casts out. — page 478 — edition of 1898.

God is the principle of man; and the principle of man remaining perfect, its idea or reflection — man remains perfect. — page 466 — edition of 1898.

Man was and is God's idea. — page 231 — edition of 1898.

Man is the idea of Divine Principle. — page 471 — edition of 1898.

What is God? Jehovah is not a person. God is Principle. — page 169 — edition of 1881.

Understanding is a quality of God. — page 449 — edition of 1898.

All Science is of God. — page 513, edition of 1898.

Truth is God. — page 183 — edition of 1898.

Truth, God, is not the Father of error. — page 469, edition of 1898.

How can I most rapidly advance in the understanding of Christian Science? Study thoroughly the letter and imbibe the spirit. Adhere to its divine Principle, and follow its behests, abiding steadily in Wisdom, Love and Truth. — page 491, edition of 1898.

Matter is mortal error. — page 169, edition of 1881.

The fundamental error of mortal man is the belief that matter is intelligent. — page 122, edition of 1881.

Laws of matter are nothing more or less than a belief of intelligence and life in matter, which is the procuring cause of all disease; whereas God, Truth, is its positive cure. — page 127, edition of 1881.

There is no life, truth, intelligence, or substance in matter. — page 464, edition of 1898.

Wrote Mrs. Eddy in the *Christian Science Journal,* January, 1901, regarding her teachings:

"I should blush to write of *Science*

and *Health, With Key to the Scriptures* as I have, were it of human origin and I apart from God its author, but as I was only a scribe echoing the harmonies of heaven in divine metaphysics, I cannot be super-modest of the Christian Science textbook."

In a letter to a personal friend dated in 1877, Mrs. Eddy stated concerning Christian Science, "The idea given by God this time is higher, clearer and more permanent than before." [*The Life of Mary Baker G. Eddy,* George I. Milmine, page 73].

Let it not be thought by anyone that Mrs. Eddy did not personally aspire to equality with Christ as some of her eager followers contend, for in the *Christian Science Journal* of April, 1889, Mrs. Eddy allowed the claim made in her behalf to the effect that she was the equal, as chosen successor, to Christ.

In a book entitled *Christ and Christmas* [1884] both the language and a picture depicting Mrs. Eddy and Christ directly infers in unmistakable context language the claim that she is Jesus Christ's equal.

The evidence of the Leiber document and the Quimby manuscripts with emendations in Mrs. Eddy's own handwriting added to the previously cited evidence of her total lack of ethics in borrowing what was not hers, indicates that the Deity had no part in the authorship of *Science and Health.* One would be foolish indeed to accept her claim at face value in the face of such incontrovertible evidence.

The Figment of Divine Authorship

Let us return, however, to Mrs. Eddy's explanation of how she "discovered" Christian Science.

According to an authorized statement published by the Christian Science Publishing Society of Boston, Mrs. Eddy after a fall on a slippery sidewalk February 1, 1866, was pronounced "incurable" and given three days to live by the attending physician (Dr. Alvin M.

Cushing). The third day, allegedly her last on earth, Mrs. Eddy (the statement makes out) cried for a Bible, read Matthew 9:2 and rose completely healed. Thus the statement claims "she discovered" Christian Science.

Corroborating this new story, Mrs. Eddy in her book, *Retrospection and Introspection,* declares that in February of 1886 (one month after Quimby's death), she was mortally injured in a sidewalk fall and was not expected to live. She, however, vanquished the angel of death in this skirmish, and on the third day emerged triumphant over her bodily infirmity. These two statements, the interested reader will note, substantiate each other in every detail; it is therefore most unfortunate that they should both be deliberate falsehoods. Mrs. Eddy never discovered Christian Science in the manner claimed, never was in danger of losing her life in the manner described, and never "rose the third day healed and free" as she maintained. Two incontrovertible facts establish these truths beyond doubt. They are as follows: (1) Dr. Alvin M. Cushing, the attending physician at this "illness" of Mrs. Eddy, denied under oath in a 1,000-word statement that he ever believed or said that she was in a precarious physical condition.[7] Moreover Dr. Cushing stated (contrary to the claims of Christian Scientists that Mrs. Eddy always enjoyed robust health) that he further attended her in August of the same year four separate times and administered medicine to her for bodily ailments. (2) Mr. Julius Dresser (pupil of the late "Dr." Quimby) received a letter from Mrs. Eddy dated February 15, 1866, two weeks *after* her alleged "recovery" from the fall on an icy sidewalk. In this letter Mrs. Eddy alludes to the fall and claims Dr. Cushing resigned her to the life of a cripple. Mrs. Eddy wrote:

[7]The author has this statement in its entirety, should it ever be necessary to substantiate this fact further.

Two weeks ago I fell on the sidewalk and struck my back on the ice and was taken for dead, came to consciousness, admitted a storm of vapors from cologne, chloroform, ether, camphor, etc., but to find myself the helpless cripple I was before I saw Dr. Quimby. The physician attending said I had taken the last step I ever should but in two days I got out of my bed alone and will walk, but yet I confess I am frightened . . . now can't *you* help me? I think I could help another in my position . . . yet I am slowly failing. . . .[8]

Barring the obvious medical error of a doctor administering chloroform and ether to an unconscious person, Mrs. Eddy's account once again demonstrates her ability to think in paradoxes and contradict all reason and logical expression. The accounts are therefore spurious and complete fabrications.

Mr. Horace T. Wentworth, whose mother Mrs. Eddy lived with in Stoughton while she was teaching from the *Quimby Manuscripts* (1867-1870), has made the following statement, and no Christian Scientist has ever refuted it:

As I have seen the amazing spread of this delusion and the way in which men and women are offering up money and the lives of their children to it, I have felt that it is a duty I owe to the public to make it known.

I have no hard feelings against Mrs. Eddy, no axe to grind, no interest to serve; I simply feel that it is due the thousands of good people who have made Christian Science the anchorage of their souls and its founder the infallible guide of their daily life, to keep this no longer to myself. I desire only that people who take themselves and their helpless children into Christian Science shall do so with the full knowledge that this is not divine revelation but simply the idea of an old-time Maine healer.

Further than this statement Mr. Wentworth has also recorded as incontestable evidence the *very* copy of P. P. Quimby's *Manuscripts* from which Mrs. Eddy taught during the years 1867-

1870, which copy also contains corrections in Mrs. Eddy's *own* handwriting.[9] Note, please, all this is undeniable fact — yet Mrs. Eddy maintains that she *alone* "discovered and founded" the Christian Science religion. What a historical perversion the prophetess of Christian Science has attempted to perpetrate. Let it also be remembered that Mrs. Eddy claimed for Quimby's theories, which she expanded, Divine import, owning that she only copied what God Almighty spoke.[10]

Let us return then to the personal history of the central figure of this analysis, Mary Baker Eddy — the still reigning Sovereign of Christian Science.

From the home of the Wentworths in Stoughton, Massachusetts, where she taught from the Quimby manuscripts, Mrs. Eddy went on to Lynn, Massachusetts, where she completed her "writing" of *Science and Health,* which she published in 1875. After leaving Lynn largely because of the revolt of most of her students, Mrs. Eddy came to Boston and opened what later became "The Massachusetts Metaphysical College" (571 Columbus Ave.) where she allegedly taught some 4,000 students at $300.00 per student for a period of eight years (1881-1889). One cannot help but wonder what would induce a reasonably-intelligent person to spend that amount of money for a course which never lasted the length of a college half-semester and which was taught by a staff hardly qualified intellectually to instruct the ninth grade. Mrs. Eddy herself knew comparatively nothing of Biblical history, theology, philosophy or the ancient languages. Christian Science sources have attempted for years to prove that Mrs. Eddy was a scholar in these fields, but the Rev. J. H. Wiggin, her literary adviser for some years, and himself an excellent scholar, has gone on record as saying that she was grossly

[8]F. W. Peabody, *The Religio-Medical Masquerade,* pages 80-81.

[9]Photostatic copies of this manuscript are

also in the possession of the author if verification is desired.

[10]*Christian Science Journal,* January, 1901.

ignorant of the subjects in question.

When Mrs. Eddy left the thankless community of Lynn, Massachusetts, she was then 61 years old and possessed less than 50 persons she could call "followers." As the calendar neared 1896, however, the indomitable will and perseverance of Mary Baker Eddy had begun to pay sizable dividends. Her churches and societies numbered well over 400 and the membership in them eventually increased from 800 to 900 per cent. Considering what she had to work with, Mrs. Eddy accomplished a financial miracle and a propaganda goal unrivaled for its efficiency and ruthlessness.[11] From her ceaseless efforts for deification and wealth, there flowed continual revisions of *Science and Health,* which the "faithful" were commanded to purchase and sell, or stand in danger of excommunication from the Eddy Autocracy. Should the skeptical reader wish proof on this point of history, and on Mrs. Eddy's insatiable greed for the comforts of financial security and power, we quote her announcement to that effect in its entirety:

Christian Scientists in the United States and Canada are hereby enjoined not to teach a student of Christian Science for one year, commencing on March 14, 1897.

Miscellaneous Writings is calculated to prepare the minds of all true thinkers to understand the Christian Science textbook more correctly than a student can.

The Bible, *Science and Health, With Key to the Scriptures* and my other published works are the only proper instructors for this hour. It shall be the *duty* of all Christian Scientists to *circulate* and to *sell* as many of these books as they can.

If a member of the First Church of Christ, Scientist shall fail to *obey* this *injunction* it will render him liable to *lose* his *membership* in this church. — Mary Baker G. Eddy.[12]

Please pay close heed to what Mrs. Eddy said. She did not ask, she commanded all Scientists as their duty to her church to "circulate" and "sell" her works and "obey" her "injunction" under penalty of loss of membership. If, perchance, a method of blackmail is ever rendered legal, it could not be stated in more compelling terminology than this encyclical from the Eddy throne.

But let it be observed that her religious pandering was not limited to just one edition of *Science and Health* alone — no, Mrs. Eddy even extended her tactics to other fields. For example, in February, 1908, she "requested" all Christian Scientists to read the "new" edition of *Science and Health* which contained on page 442, beginning at line 30, information she affirmed to be of "great importance." Said Mrs. Eddy:

TAKE NOTICE

I request Christian Scientists universally to read the paragraph beginning at line 30 on page 442 in the edition of *Science and Health* which will be issued February 29. I consider the information there given to be of *great importance* at this state of the workings of Animal Magnetism, and it will *greatly aid* the students in their individual experiences. — Mary Baker G. Eddy.

One would assume from the tone of the language she used that here was a new revelation imperative to the defense against "Animal Magnetism" (the Fiend all Christian Scientists continually ward off mentally), but such was not the case; instead Mrs. Eddy merely wrote what she had written a hundred times previously in different language. Said the material of "great importance":

Christian Scientists, be a law to yourselves, that mental malpractice can harm you neither when asleep nor when awake.

Imagine $3.00 for these two sentences, the same old volume excepting this "new" sage advice, and countless loyal Scientists obliged her wish by dutifully

---

[11]See Chapter VII, *Christian Science Propaganda and Censorship.*

[12]*Christian Science Journal,* March, 1897.

pouring their money into the Eddy Treasury. It is no wonder that at her death Mrs. Eddy's personal fortune exceeded three million dollars. *None* of this, unfortunately, was left to charity.

Mrs. Eddy's reign had very little internal opposition and hence went unchallenged during her lifetime, but after her decease a definite scramble for control of her Empire ensued. All but the most exacting students of Christian Science history have overlooked this battle for the vacated throne of Christian Sciencedom, but it is an important historical conflict and one that deserves consideration. Upon the death of Mrs. Eddy the Christian Science Board of Directors, in good business fashion, assumed control of her thriving empire and consolidated this coup by obtaining from the Massachusetts Supreme Court authority for their self-perpetuating directorate. It was over this issue that a schism appeared in the ranks of Christian Science, and after assuming the title "The Christian Science Parent Church," under the leadership of Mrs. Annie C. Bill of London, the struggle commenced hot and heavy. John V. Dittemore, a member of the Christian Science Board of Directors, left the Boston camp and joined Mrs. Bill in editing the *Christian Science Watchman* and acclaimed her as Mrs. Eddy's successor. It was the contention of "The Parent Church" that Mrs. Eddy intended to have a successor within a half century of her demise and never intended a self-perpetuating Board of Directors. The directors, no doubt for good financial reasons, stoutly rejected this view and defended their new-found gold mine. On February 6, 1924, Mrs. Eddy's name was taken off *The Manual's* list of active officers and thus *The Watchman* claimed the Board had proven its original intentions by fully occupying the most powerful position in the Christian

Science Church and forever eliminating the danger of a successor to Mrs. Eddy.[13] The claim by Mrs. Bill and Mr. Dittemore that the directors had usurped the authority of Mrs. Eddy and acted contrary to her expressed wishes went unchallenged for the most part by the Christian Science Board of Directors, for Mr. Dittemore had strong evidence from *The Memoirs of Adam Dickey,* which the Board suppressed, and excerpts from the unpublished writings of Mrs. Eddy's secretary, Calvin A. Frye, that she expected a personal successor within fifty years. Wrote Mrs. Eddy:

> In answer to oncoming questions will say: I calculate that about one-half century more will bring to the front the man that God has equipped to lift aloft His standard of Christian Science (Vol. 4, No. 5, January, 1928).

It should also be noted that Mrs. Eddy herself said in a newspaper interview, May 1, 1901:

> No present change is contemplated in the relationship. You would ask, perhaps, whether my successor will be a woman or a man. I can answer that. It will be a man.
> Q. Can you name that man?
> A. I cannot answer that now.[14]

But, Mrs. Eddy never picked her successor, and with the advancing years the Christian Science Parent Church and *The Watchman* faded into obscurity and the controversy has long since been forgotten.

Continuing further into the Eddy legend, we are once again confronted with the cold, impartial testimony of history where Mrs. Eddy's boundless "generosity" and "selflessness" are concerned. Shortly after the famous "Woodbury Suit" wherein Mrs. Eddy was accused of slandering a former disciple, the Christian Science treasury showed a marked decrease in volume, the result of large legal fees due in consideration of services rendered during

---

[13]*The Christian Science Watchman,* Vol. 4, No. 7, March, 1928, pages 153-154.

[14]The Christian Science Church maintains

that she later amended this statement, saying that it referred to "generic man," or the human race, etc.

the case. As a result of this, Mrs. Eddy perpetrated on the "faithful" the infamous "Teajacket swindle" calculated to draw from her gullible followers the revenue with which to further strengthen her treasury. In line with this scheme she drafted the following "request" to her Church universal which appeared in the *Christian Science Journal,* December 21, 1899:

Beloved, I ask this favor of all Christian Scientists. Do not give me on, before, or after the forthcoming holiday aught material except three teajackets. *All may contribute to these.* One learns to value material things only as one needs them, and the costliest things are the ones that one needs most. Among my present needs material are these — three jackets, two of darkish, heavy silk, the shade appropriate to white hair; the third of heavy satin, lighter shade, but sufficiently sombre. Nos. 1 and 2 to be common-sense jackets for Mother to work in, and not over-trimmed by any means. No. 3 for best, such as she can afford for her dressing room. — Mary Baker Eddy.

The key to this whole financial angle is to be found in five short words, *"All may contribute to these."* Notice Mrs. Eddy does not request two hundred thousand teajackets,[15] merely "contributions" toward them. No one was to send them — only send the money to buy them. "Mother" Eddy must have enjoyed this neat trick of replenishing her gold reserve, and none can deny that it was carried off with a finesse that rivals any confidence game ever conceived. All this, mind you, in the name of Jesus Christ and under the banner of Christian Science, allegedly the true religion. Judge Rutherford of Jehovah's Witnesses could not have had Christian Science too far out of mind when he said, "Religion is a racket." Compared to Mrs. Eddy, "Pastor" Russell and

Judge Rutherford of The Watch Tower were rank amateurs at collecting money. She played for the highest stakes at all times, and with Mary Baker Eddy it was always "winner take all," and she did!

THEOLOGICAL STRUCTURE OF CHRISTIAN SCIENCE

In outlining this chapter on Christian Science, it is the conviction of the author that a series of primary quotations taken directly from official Christian Science books will prove far more useful to the average reader than any number of statements made by a non-Christian Scientist. Therefore to enable the reader to have this valuable source material at his fingertips, I have listed sixteen of the major doctrines of historic Christianity, and under each of their respective headings placed contradictory quotations derived from Mrs. Eddy's writings, which will I believe provide more than sufficient documentation should any dispute ever arise concerning the proper classification of Christian Science as an anti-Christian cult.[16]

I. THE INSPIRATION OF THE BIBLE

1. Referring to Genesis 2:7: "Is this addition to His creation real or unreal? Is it the truth? Or is it a lie, concerning man and God? It must be the latter . . ." (*Science and Health,* page 517).

2. ". . . the manifest mistakes in the ancient versions; the thirty thousand different readings in the Old Testament, and the three hundred thousand in the New — these facts show how a mortal and material sense stole into the divine record, darkening, to some extent, the inspired pages with its own hue" (*Science and Health,* page 33).

II. THE DOCTRINE OF THE TRINITY AND THE DEITY OF CHRIST

1. "The theory of three persons in one God (that is, a personal Trinity or Triunity) suggests heathen gods, rather than

[15]Estimated Christian Science Church membership in 1899.

[16]All quotations from the book *Miscellaneous Writings* are from the edition of 1897; and all quotations from *Science and Health*

are from the edition of 1895, unless specifically designated otherwise. This is a Copyright precaution and the above quoted statements are still in print in current editions, though on different pages. Consult concordance of Christian Science publications for verification.

the one ever-present I Am" (*Science and Health*, page 152).

2. "The Christian who believes in the First Commandment is a monotheist. Thus he virtually unites with the Jews' belief in one God and recognizes that Jesus Christ *is not*[17] God as Jesus Himself declared, but is the Son of God" (*Science and Health*, [1914], page 361).

3. "The spiritual Christ was infallible; Jesus, as material manhood, *was not* Christ" (*Miscellaneous Writings*, page 84).

III. THE DOCTRINE OF GOD AND THE HOLY SPIRIT

1. "In that name of Jehovah the true idea of God seems almost lost. He becomes 'a man of war,' a tribal god to be worshiped — rather than Love, the divine Principle to be lived and loved" (*Science and Health*, page 517).

2. "God; Principle, Life, Truth, Love, Soul, Spirit, Mind" (*Science and Health*, page 9).

3. "God is all . . . the soul, or mind, of the spiritual man *is* God, the divine Principle of all being" (*Science and Health* [1914], page 302).

IV. THE VIRGIN BIRTH OF CHRIST

1. "A portion of God could not enter corporeal mortal man; neither could His feelings be reflected by Him, or God would be manifestly finite, lose the deific character, and become less than God" (*Science and Health*, page 231).

3. "Jesus, the Galilean prophet, was born of the virgin Mary's spiritual thoughts of life and its manifestation" (*The First Church of Christ, Scientist and Miscellany*, page 261).

V. THE DOCTRINE OF MIRACLES

1. "The sick are not healed merely by declaring there is no sickness, but by knowing that there is none" (*Science and Health* [1914], page 447).

2. "A mere request that God will heal the sick has no power to gain more of the divine presence than is always at hand" (*Science and Health*, page 317).

3. "The so-called miracles contained in Holy Writ are neither supernatural or preternatural . . . Jesus regarded good as the normal state of mind and evil as the abnormal. . . . The so-called pains and pleasures of matter were alike unreal to Jesus; for He regarded matter as only a vagary of mortal belief, and subdued it with this

understanding" (*Miscellaneous Writings*, pages 200-201).

VI. THE ATONEMENT OF JESUS CHRIST

1. "The material blood of Jesus was no more efficacious to cleanse from sin, when it was shed upon 'the accursed tree,' than when it was flowing in His veins, as He went daily about His Father's business" (*Science and Health*, page 330).

2. "The real atonement — so infinitely beyond the heathen conception that God requires human blood to propitiate His justice and bring His mercy — needs to be understood. . . . He (Jesus) suffered, to show mortals the awful price paid by sin and how to avoid paying it. He atoned for the terrible unreality of a supposed existence apart from God. He suffered because of the shocking human idolatry that presupposes Life, Substance, Soul and Intelligence in matter . . ." (*No and Yes* [1893], pages 44-45).

VII. THE DEATH AND RESURRECTION OF CHRIST

1. "Jesus' students, not sufficiently advanced to understand fully their Master's triumph, did not perform many wonderful works until they saw Him after His crucifixion, and learned that *He had not died*" (*Science and Health*, pages 350, 351).

2. "His disciples believed Jesus dead while He was hidden in the sepulchre, whereas He was alive, demonstrating, within the narrow tomb, the power of Spirit to destroy human, material sense" (*Science and Health*, page 349).

VIII. THE ASCENSION AND SECOND COMING OF CHRIST

1. "Through all the disciples beheld, they became more spiritual, and understood better what the Master had taught. . . . They needed this quickening, for soon their dear Master would rise again in the spiritual scale of existence, and fly far beyond their apprehension. As the reward for His faithfulness He would disappear to material sense, in that change which has since been called the Ascension" (*Science and Health*, page 339).

IX. SATAN AND THE EXISTENCE OF EVIL

1. "The beliefs of the human mind rob and enslave it, and then impute this result to another elusive personification, named Satan" (*Science and Health*, page 81).

2. "There was never a moment in which evil was real" (*No and Yes*, page 33).

---

[17]Italics mine.

X. THE NATURE AND EXISTENCE OF HELL

1. "The sinner makes his own hell by doing evil, and the saint his own heaven by doing right" (*Science and Health* [1914], page 266).

2. "The olden opinion that hell is fire and brimstone, has yielded somewhat to the metaphysical fact that suffering is a thing of mortal mind instead of body; so, in place of material flames and odor, mental anguish is generally accepted as the penalty for sin" (*Miscellaneous Writings*, page 237).

XI. THE KINGDOM OF HEAVEN — ITS REALITY AND SIGNIFICANCE

1. Definition: "Heaven. Harmony; the reign of Spirit; government by Principle; spirituality; bliss; the atmosphere of Soul" (*Science and Health*, page 578).

2. "Heaven is harmony — infinite, boundless bliss. . . . Heaven is the reign of Divine Science" (*First Church of Christ, Scientist and Miscellany*, page 267).

XII. THE DOCTRINE OF ETERNAL SALVATION

1. "Man as God's idea is already saved with an everlasting salvation" (*Miscellaneous Writings*, page 261).

2. "Final deliverance from error — whereby we rejoice in immortality, boundless freedom, and sinless sense — is neither reached through paths of flowers, nor by pinning one's faith to another's vicarious effort" (*Science and Health*, page 327).

XIII. THE DOCTRINE OF PRAYER

1. "Prayer can neither change God, nor bring his designs into mortal modes . . . I have no objection to audible prayer of the right kind; but inaudible is more effectual" (*No and Yes*, pages 48 and 50).

2. "If prayer nourishes the belief that sin is cancelled, and that man is made better by merely praying, it is an evil. He grows worse, who continues in sins because he thinks himself forgiven" (*Science and Health*, page 311).

XIV. THE CREATION OF MATTER AND ITS REALITY

1. "There is . . . no intelligent sin, evil mind or matter; and this is the only true philosophy and realism" (*No and Yes*, page 47).

2. "There is no Life, Truth, Intelligence or Substance in matter but all is infinite Mind and its infinite manifestation for God is All in all" (*Science and Health* [1914], page 468)

XV. MAN, THE SOUL, HIS TRUE NATURE AND DESTINY

1. "Man originated not from dust, materially, but from Spirit, spiritually" (*Miscellaneous Writings*, page 57).

2. "Man is God's image and likeness; whatever is possible to God, is possible to man as God's reflection" (*Miscellaneous Writings*, page 183).

XVI. THE EXISTENCE OF SIN, SICKNESS AND DEATH

1. "Being destroyed, sin needs no other form of forgiveness. . . . Since God is All, there is no room for His opposite . . . therefore evil, being the opposite of goodness, is unreal . . . for the sinner is making a reality of sin — making that real which is unreal. . . . Only those who repent of sin, and forsake all evil, can fully understand the unreality of evil. . . . To get rid of sin, through Science, is to divest sin of any supposed mind or reality, and never to admit that sin can have intelligence or power, pain or pleasure. You can conquer error by denying its verity" (*Science and Health*, page 234).

2. "Death. An illusion, for there is no death; the unreal and untrue, the opposite of Good, God, or Life. . . . Any material evidence of death is false, for it contradicts the spiritual facts of Being" (*Science and Health*, page 575).

3. "To put down the claim of sin you must detect it, remove the mask, point out the illusion, and thus get the victory over sin, and prove its unreality" (*Science and Health*, page 444).

As the preceding quotations indicate, the teachings of Christian Science are vastly different than those generally understood to comprise the fundamental teaching of historic Christianity. And it would be a foolish student indeed who did not take cognizance of these severe deviations from Biblical theology, and mark them well as evidence of another gospel, the product of plagiarism, the amalgamation of sources suitably doctored by a professional literary adviser, and made palatable to the average mind by the semantic manipulations of Mary Baker Eddy.

The philosophy of Christian Science is basically syllogistic[18] embodying all the logical mazes that the confused and untrained mind of Mrs. Eddy wandered through. Theoretically Mrs. Eddy was an Absolute Idealist who denied outright the existence of matter from the tiniest insect to the most gigantic star in the celestial galaxies. But practically speaking Mrs. Eddy was a calculating materialist, an individual who thoroughly enjoyed all the material comforts derived from denying their existence. Hundreds of thousands of faithful Christian Scientists supplied their "leader" with all that money could buy, and every material benefit available, yet Mrs. Eddy continually affirmed the non-existence of these material blessings by teaching in effect that they really did not exist to be enjoyed — they were "illusions of mortal mind," she said. In Mrs. Eddy's philosophy all that exists is "Mind" (God) and "It" is "Good"; matter has no "real" existence at all. It should be mentioned here that Mrs. Eddy never defined matter, to the satisfaction of any qualified logician, that is; so it must be assumed that she meant those elements which were recognizable to the five senses of man, etc.

According to Mrs. Eddy "there is no pain in Truth, and no truth in pain; no matter in Mind, and no mind in matter, etc." (page 7) and this is "proved" metaphysically by the rule of inversion. However Mrs. Eddy's vaunted metaphysical allegiance to this alleged rule crumbles weakly under the relentless hammering of sound logical principles. Let us see if the rule of inversion is always valid by applying it to similar constructions.

All rabbits are quadrupeds — (inverted) all quadrupeds are rabbits. Now of course any intelligent person can easily see that this inversion leads to a false conclusion since dogs, cats, horses and elephants are all quadrupeds and it is obvious they have no relation to the rabbit family. No rational person could therefore long entertain such logical absurdity, but it is exactly this kind of reasoning that forms the basis of Mrs. Eddy's philosophy and the entire foundation of Christian Science practice. Sin, sickness and death are equally relegated to these peculiar logical dungeons of Christian Science reasoning processes and then represented as "illusions of Mortal Mind." Regarding this phantom "Mortal Mind" Mrs. Eddy wrote:

> At best, matter is only a phenomenon of mortal mind which evil is the highest degree; but really there is no such thing as mortal mind, — though we are compelled to use the phrase in the endeavor to express the underlying thought (*Unity of Good*, page 50).

These are strange words indeed, are they not — giving a name to an illusion that does not exist, representing it as evil which is equally non-existent, and then blaming it for all physical woes which cannot exist, since there is no reality or existence apart from Mind, or God? This type of reasoning is considered sound thinking by Christian Scientists the world over; however, the reader is urged to form his own conclusions dictated by the obvious facts that matter is demonstrably "real" and its decay and death are an ever-present problem.

The syllogism — (1) God is all, God is Mind, therefore Mind is all, and (2) Mind is all, matter is not mind, therefore matter has no existence; these are only escape mechanisms from the objective world of material reality to the subjective world of idealism which can never answer the problems of evil, sin, sickness, or material death since they are negated by the assumption that only Mind exists and it is immaterial, therefore not included in material categories. By denying even that portion of the mind which recognizes these phys-

---

[18]Syllogism (in logic) — "a form of argument or reasoning, consisting of two statements and a conclusion drawn from them" (dictionary).

ical realties, and calling it "Mortal Mind," Mrs. Eddy has forever isolated herself and Christian Science from the realm of objective reality, since the mind that truly rejects the existence of matter must never allow the limitations of matter which constitute physical existence. But in practice no Christian Scientist holds these tenets as an Absolute — they all clothe, feed, and house the illusion of Mortal Mind called their bodies and many go to dentists and surgeons for the filling of imaginary cavities and the setting of non-existent bones. If these facts are not proof positive that the entire philosophy of Christian Science in principle and practice is a huge philosophic hoax, then the author despairs of man's ability to analyze available evidence and arrive at logical conclusions. Even in its basic propositions the Eddy philosophy is a sorry foundation for faith by all standards and an almost unbelievable imposition upon the principles of sound logic.

Inspiration and Authority of the Bible

Christian Science, as a theology, and all Christian Scientists, for that matter, both affirm that the Bible is God's Word and quote Mrs. Eddy to "prove" that their whole religion is based upon the teachings of Scripture. Mrs. Eddy said:

> The Bible has been my only authority. I have had no other guide in the 'straight and narrow' way of truth (*Science and Health*, page 126).

However Mrs. Eddy and Christian Science have repudiated and contradicted this affirmation numerous times (see *Miscellaneous Writings*, pages 169-170, and *Science and Health*, pages 517, 537, etc.) and in reality have perverted the clear teachings of the Bible to serve their own ends.

In Psalm 119 we read: "Forever, O Lord, thy *Word* is settled in heaven . . . thy *Word* is very pure . . . thy *Word* is true from the beginning." The prophet

Isaiah reminds us: "The *Word* of our God shall stand for ever" (Isaiah 40:8), and Christ Himself confirmed these great truths when He said: "The Scripture *cannot* be broken . . . Heaven and earth shall pass away but my Words shall never pass away" (John 10:35; Matthew 24:35). It will be remembered also that St. Paul stamped with divine authority the testimony of the Scriptures when he wrote: "All scripture is given by inspiration of God, and is profitable for doctrine, for reproof, for correction, for instruction in righteousness" (II Timothy 3:16).

Coupled with these unassailable voices of testimony as to the Bible's authority, it is evident from the words of Jesus Himself and the writings of His disciples and apostles that He believed in the authority of the Old Testament most emphatically, and even alluded to Old Testament characters and events, thus establishing the authenticity and trustworthiness of the Old Testament.

The Bible declares that *It,* not Mrs. Eddy and Christian Science, is the supreme authority on the activities of God and His relationship to man. Christian Science employs every art and method of paradoxical reasoning to escape the dilemma with which it is faced. It switches terminology about until the terms in question lose all logical meaning and spiritualizes texts until they are literally milked dry of any divine revelation whatsoever. To the average Christian Scientist the Bible is a compilation of ancient writings "full of hundreds of thousands of textual errors . . . its divinity is . . . uncertain, its inspiration . . . questionable . . . It is made up of metaphors, allegories, myths and fables . . . It cannot be read and interpreted literally . . ."[19] Consequently Christian Scientists believe, owing to the utter and hopeless confusion that the Bible allegedly engenders without a qualified interpreter, that it is necessary

[19]I. M. Haldeman, *Christian Science in the Light of Holy Scripture,* page 377.

to have someone interpret the Bible for them. Mrs. Eddy is the divinely appointed person to fulfill this task. Through *Science and Health,* she, they affirm, "rediscovered the healing principle of Jesus and his disciples, lost since the early Christian era," and has *blessed the world* with Christian Science—the "Divine Comforter." To all Christian Scientists then, since they swear allegiance to Mrs. Eddy, "the material record of the Bible . . . is no more important to our well-being than the history of Europe and America" (*Miscellaneous Writings,* page 170).

The reader is asked to compare this supposedly "Christian" view with the foregoing Scriptural references and the words of Christ and St. Paul, who said and wrote respectively:

> Sanctify them through thy truth; thy *Word* is truth (John 17:17).
> But continue thou in the things which thou hast learned and hast been assured of, knowing of whom thou hast learned them; and that from a child thou has known the *holy scriptures,* which are able to make thee wise unto salvation through faith which is in Christ Jesus (II Timothy 3:14, 15).

We are told in the words of Peter:

> Knowing this first, that no prophecy of the Scripture is of any private interpretation. For the prophecy came not in old time by the will of man; but holy men of God spake as they were moved by the Holy Ghost (II Peter 1:20, 21).

By these things of course we do not mean that God dictated or mechanically reproduced the Bible, or even that He wrote tangibly, using the hands of men as an adult guides the hand of a child, but that God spoke and caused to be recorded truly and without error those things necessary for our salvation and an understanding of His sovereign purposes and love. The Bible is the inspired Word of God, and is wholly dependable in whatever fields it speaks. This of course holds true only for the original manuscripts of the Bible of which we have excellent reproductions. No scholar

to our knowledge, however, holds to the infallibility of copies or translations which sometimes suggest textual difficulties. The Bible, therefore, stands paramount as God's revelation to man, the simple presentation of infinite values and truths clothed in the figures of time and space. Christian Science, by denying many of these truths and the veracity of the Bible itself in favor of Mrs. Eddy's "interpretations," disobeys directly the injunction of God to "study" and "believe" His Word which alone is able to make us "wise unto salvation through faith in Christ Jesus."

The Doctrine of the Trinity and the Deity of Christ

One prominent trait of all non-Christian religions and cults is their pointed denial of the Scriptural doctrine of the Trinity and the Deity of Jesus Christ. Christian Science ranges high in this category on the basis that it unequivocally denies the true deity of our Lord and the triunity of the Godhead (Colossians 2:9). Mrs. Eddy said, and most decisively so, that "the theory of three persons in one God (that is, a personal trinity or triunity) suggests heathen gods, rather than the one ever-present I Am" (*Science and Health,* page 152). Going beyond this declaration Mrs. Eddy also wrote: "Jesus Christ is not God as Jesus Himself declared but is the son of God" (*Science and Health,* page 361), and she then crowned this travesty with the astounding "revelation" that "Life, Truth, Love constitute the triune God" (*Science and Health,* pages 226, 227). Thus it was that with one sweep of an unblushing pen a vindictive, ignorant, untrained and egocentric old woman banished the God of the Bible from her religion forever. It is hardly necessary to examine at length the doctrine of the Trinity and the deity of Christ to refute Mrs. Eddy's vague ramblings, but it is profitable, we believe, to review those passages of Scripture which so thoroughly unmask the pronounced shallowness of the

Christian Science contentions.

In Genesis 1:26 — "Let *us* make man in *our* image, after *our* likeness."

11:7 — "Let *us* go down, and there confound their language."

Isaiah 6:8 — "Who will go for *us?*

Then we could mention Genesis 18 where Abraham addresses God personally as Lord (Jehovah) over ten times; the obvious plurality of the Godhead is strongly implied if not expressly declared. The fact that God intended to beget a Son after the flesh and of the line of David by virgin birth (Isaiah 7:14; 9:6; Micah 5:2; Matthew 1:23; Luke 1:35; cf. Psalm 2:7 and Hebrews 1:5; 5:5 and Acts 13:33), that this Son in the likeness of flesh was His eternal *Word* or *Wisdom* (John 1:1, 14, 18), and that He is true Deity (Colossians 2:9; Philippians 2:8-11; Revelation 1: 8, 17, 18; Hebrews 1:1-4, etc.) and a separate Person from God the Father, is all indicative of the truth that Jesus Christ was truly the God-Man of prophecy and the *personal* Messiah of Israel. It is fruitful to note also that Mrs. Eddy recognizes the "true" God not as Jehovah but as "I Am" (*Science and Health,* page 152), apparently oblivious of the fact that the word "Jehovah" is itself taken from the Hebrew verb form "to be" (Exodus 3:14), literally "I was, I am, I continue to be" or as the Jews render it "the Eternal" — (*Yhwh* — the tetragrammaton). Keeping with this vein of thought it will be easily recognized that Jesus identified Himself with the same "I Am" or Jehovah — and in fact claimed in no uncertain terms that He was that I Am (John 8:58) for which the Jews were ready to stone Him to death on the grounds of blasphemy (John 8:59 and 10:30-33).

As to Mrs. Eddy's argument that Jesus was God's Son, *not* God, the answer is painfully simple, when thoroughly analyzed. The solution is briefly this: Christ was God's Son by Nature, not creation, as we are, hence His intrinsic character was that of Deity — His at-

tributes were divine — He possessed "all power," etc. (Matthew 28:18). He therefore could *not* be a true Son unless He were truly divine; therefore He could not be the Son of God at all without at once being "God the Son," i.e., of the very Nature of His Father. The Scriptures declare God's Son is Deity—"The mighty God . . . the Everlasting Father, or the Image of God . . . Impress of His Substance . . . Radiance of His glory" . . . etc. Innumerable testimonies as to His divinity are given, far too exhaustive to record here but evidence nonetheless, and beyond disputation. To reduce the Trinity so evident at Christ's baptism and the Great Commission ("In the name of the Father and of the Son and of the Holy Spirit," Matthew 28: 19) to three of Mrs. Eddy's choice terms, "Life, Truth and Love," and declare all else "suggestive of heathen gods" (*Science and Health,* page 152) is a prime demonstration of crass indifference to Biblical terminology and historical theology—an emphatic Christian Science attitude instituted by Mrs. Eddy.

John tells us that Christ was by His own admission *equal* in Deity to God the Father (John 5:18; cf. Philippians 2:8-11; Colossians 2:9; Hebrews 1:3), yet inferior in position and form during His earthly ministry (John 14:28) as a man. The Eternal Word voluntarily humbled Himself, became human and subject to our limitations even to the death of the cross, the Bible tells us, but *never* for a moment did He cease to be what by Nature and inheritance He always was and will be, God the Son, Second Person of the Trinity, Eternal Creator and Saviour of the sons of men.

Therefore let us remember most clearly that Christian Science offers a dual Christ, a great man inspired by the "Christ idea" as Mrs. Eddy would have it, one who never really "died" at all for our sins.

The Scriptures hold forth as a ray of inextinguishable light the Deity of our Lord and the Trinity of God. We must therefore be ever vigilant in our defense of the *personal* Jesus who is our *personal* Saviour, lest the *impersonal* Christ of Christian Science be allowed further opportunity to counterfeit the Christ of the Bible. This counterfeit so widely taught in Christian Science is merely another false theory that masquerades under the banner of the Christian religion and attempts to subvert the true Christian faith.

The Personality of God the Father and the Holy Spirit

In Christian Science theology, if it be properly understood, the term "God" is merely a relative one and bears no resemblance whatsoever to the Deity so clearly revealed in the Bible. As has been amply shown, Mrs. Eddy interchanges the terms "Life," "Truth," "Love," "Principle," "Mind," "Substance," "Intelligence," "Spirit," "Mother," etc. with that of God; thus Christian Science contends that God is *impersonal,* devoid of any personality at all. Biblically speaking, of course, this is a theological and historical absurdity since the core of Jehovah's uniqueness was His personal nature — I Am — indicative of a reflective and constructive Mind. Jesus repeatedly addressed His Father as a direct object, "I" and "Thou," postulating a logical subject-object relation in intercourse and at least twice the Father answered Him (see Matthew 3:17 and Luke 17:5) establishing His independence of person. This would have been impossible if God were circumscribed by Mrs. Eddy's theology, for only a personality or cognizant ego can think reflectively, carry on conversation and use the personal pronouns "I" or "he," etc. The God of the Old Testament and the New is a personal transcendent Being, not an impersonal spirit or force, and man is created in His image, that of a personal, though finite, being. The higher animals, to whatever degree they "think," are incapable of rationality and, also unlike man, of the faculty of "knowing," as Descartes once put it "cogito ergo sum" ("I think, therefore I am").

But far surpassing this elementary distinction between the God of Christianity and that of Christian Science, is the inescapable fact that the God of the Bible does what only a personality can do, and these traits forever separate Him from the pantheistic god of Christian Science which is incapable by definition of performing these things. Briefly, God is described as capable of doing the following things:

1. *God remembers* — "I, even I, am he that blotteth out thy transgressions for mine own sake, and will not *remember* thy sins" (Isaiah 43:25; also compare Psalm 79:8; Jeremiah 31:20; Hosea 8:13, etc).

2. *God speaks* — "I am the Lord: that is my name: and my glory will I not give to another, neither my praise to graven images" (Isaiah 42:8. See also Genesis 1:26; Isaiah 43:10-13; 44:6; Matthew 17:5; Hebrews 1:1; etc.).

3. *God hears, sees and creates* —
   A. "And God saw that the wickedness of man was great in the earth" (Genesis 6:5).
   B. "God *heard* their groaning" (Exodus 2:24), "and the people complained . . . and . . . the Lord *heard* it . . ." (Numbers 11:1).
   C. "In the beginning God *created* the heaven and the earth" (Genesis 1:1).

4. *God "knows," i.e., He has a Mind* —
   A. "The Lord knoweth them that are his" (II Timothy 2:19).
   B. "God is greater than our heart, and knoweth all things" (I John 3:20).
   C. "For I *know* the thoughts that I think toward you, saith the Lord . . ." Jeremiah 29:11).

5. *God will judge the world* —
   A. "Therefore I will *judge* you

... saith the Lord God" (Ezekiel 18:30).

B. "Therefore thus saith the Lord God unto them; Behold, I, even I, will *judge* . . ." (Ezekiel 34:20).

C. "For we must all appear before the *judgment* seat of Christ" (II Corinthians 5:10).

6. *God is a personal Spirit* —

A. "God is a *Spirit:* and they that worship him must worship him in spirit and in truth" (John 4:24).

B. "I am the Almighty God; walk before me, and be thou perfect" (Genesis 17:1).

C. God's Son is declared to be the "express image of his *person*" (Hebrews 1:3), therefore God is a Person.

7. *God has a will* —

A. "Thy *will* be done in earth, as it is in heaven" (Matthew 6:10).

B. ". . . prove what is that good, and acceptable, and perfect, *will* of God" (Romans 12:2).

C. "He that doeth the *will* of God abideth for ever" (I John 2:17).

D. "Lo, I come to do thy *will, O God*" (Hebrews 10:7, 9).

From this brief resumé of some of God's attributes, the interested reader can doubtless see the vast difference between the God and Father of our Lord Jesus Christ and the "Divine Principle" of Mrs. Eddy's Christian Science. Psychologically speaking, a Principle cannot remember; "Life, Truth and Love" cannot speak audibly; nor can "Substance, Mind or Intelligence" hear, see, create, know, judge or will. The God of the Bible does these things; the god of Christian Science cannot. It is admitted, of course, that *a* mind or *an* intelligence can do those things, but then Mrs. Eddy does not recognize the existence of personality in the Deity and only *a* personality has *a* mind or *an* intelligence.

Mrs. Eddy's god (Principle) cannot create nor can *it* exert a will because Principle or even *a* Principle, if you desire, does not possess a will, by any logical definition. The God of Christian Science is there an *It,* a neuter gender — merely a name — incapable of metaphysical definition or understanding outside of the maze which is Christian Science theology. St. Paul triumphantly reminds us, "I know *whom* I have believed, and am persuaded that *he* is able to keep that which I have committed unto *him* against that day" (II Timothy 1:12). The true Christian has a personal relationship with his Lord; he prays through Christ and the power of the Holy Spirit; he asks that it might be given; indeed, *personal* contact is the very source of the Christian's life and spiritual peace. Christian Scientists have no such contact, and consequently no real spiritual life or peace, only the riddles and incoherencies of Mrs. Eddy and a basic uncertainty about good health.

Concerning the doctrine of the Holy Spirit and the attitude of Christian Science toward it, little need be said since Mrs. Eddy's attitude was so obvious, but at the risk of repetition a short review may be profitable. As a matter of course, Mrs. Eddy denied both the personality and office of the Holy Spirit and for His exalted ministry substituted "Divine Science" (*Science and Health,* page 55). She defined the Holy Spirit as "Divine Science — the development of Life, Truth and Love" and further added, "That influx of Divine Science" (*Science and Health,* pages 348 and 579).[20]

To refute such a decided perversion of Scripture and historical theology one need only recall who the writers of the Bible, and Christ Himself, considered the Holy Spirit to be in respect to personality and powers. In the sixteenth chapter of John's gospel Jesus instruct-

---

[20]Those quotations not found in the standard edition of *Science and Health* on the pages enumerated here are to be found in the edition of 1895, and also in the modern editions although on different pages. The author has used the edition of 1895 primarily because it best reveals some of the vagaries of Mrs. Eddy's early philosophic evolution.

ed His disciples about their new ministry and duties and promised them a "Comforter" who would strengthen and guide them after His ascension. To quiet their fears Jesus told them that it was essential to the coming of the Comforter, who issued forth from the Father, that *He* go away. The Lord said:

"If I go not away, the Comforter will *not* come unto you; but if I depart, I will send *him* unto you. And when *he* is come, *he* will reprove the world of sin, and of righteousness, and of judgment" (verses 7 and 8).

It is useful to observe that the Greek text uses the masculine pronoun *"He"* and also *"Him"* for the Holy Spirit and ascribes to Him a *Will* (verse 7) and the power to "convince" the world of "sin, righteousness and judgment" (verse 8). "Divine Science" has not, will not, and cannot do any of these things since it denies the reality of sin, hence excluding the need for righteousness, and teaches in place of judgment the pernicious un-Biblical doctrine of man's *inherent* goodness. The Holy Spirit therefore is a Person with a Will and divine power to regenerate the soul of man (John 3) and glorify Jesus Christ. It should also be remembered that He does what only a person can do — He teaches us (Luke 12:12), He speaks to us (Acts 13:2), He thinks and makes decisions (Acts 15:28), and He moves us to do the will of God as He has moved holy men of God to serve in the past (II Peter 1:21). Further than this the Holy Spirit can be lied to (Acts 5:3), He can be grieved (Ephesians 4:30), and He is often resisted (Acts 7:51). All these things denote dealings with a personality, not an impersonal force, and certainly not "Divine Science." Beyond these things the Holy Spirit sanctifies and separates us from sin and prays to the Father for us that we might be freed from great temptations (Romans 8:26).

Certainly these points of evidence disprove the meager attempts of Christian Science to reduce the Third Person of the Trinity to a metaphysical catchword ("Divine Science"), and reveal clearly for all to see the semantic deception Mrs. Eddy has utilized in attempting to undermine this great Scriptural truth.

The Miracles of Christ

The doctrine of the virgin birth of Jesus Christ is indissolubly joined with that of the validity of Old Testament prophecy concerning the Messiah of Israel. Isaiah the prophet tells us that "a virgin shall conceive, and bear a son, and shall call his name Immanuel" (7:14), and that this child was to be miraculous in every sense of the word. Indeed, so unique was this child to be that to Him alone of all the sons of men is the name God applied, the "mighty God" 'to be specific, the "everlasting Father," the "Prince of peace" (9:6). We are told that He shall reign forever (verse 7) and that the zeal of God Himself will bring this to pass. Unfolding further the panorama of Old Testament prophecy we are told that the child in question will be the Son of David (9:7), of royal lineage, that He will be born in Bethlehem of Judea (Micah 5:2). Even more remarkable than these rays of light from God, the Scriptures further tell us that He was to be crucified for the sins of Israel and the world (Isaiah 53, cf. Daniel 9:26), and that He would rise again to life and come in power to sift the sons of men with eternal judgment (Psalm 22, cf. Zechariah 12:10). But these facts are all a matter of history, which Jesus of Nazareth fulfilled to the letter and which only remain to be consummated at His triumphant return as Judge of the world. Both St. Matthew and St. Luke declare the human fulfillment of God's plan in Mary's conception of the Christchild (Matthew 1:18-25, cf. Luke 1:30-38). Thus the physical existence of Jesus Christ is a biologically established fact. Christian Science vehemently denies this fact and teaches instead that Mary conceived the spiritual idea of God and named *it* Jesus. Denying as she did the reality of the physical universe, this was a strangely logical step for Mrs. Eddy as opposed to her usual contempt for all logical form whatsoever. But be that as it may, all the wanderings of Mrs. Eddy's mind, be they from Dan to Beersheba, can never change the testimony of Old and New Testament Scripture that a demonstrably "real" child was born to Mary, not an "Idea," that this child existed as a concrete physical Being apart from His divine Nature and is now forever, for our sake, both God and Man in Jesus Christ. The virgin birth therefore is a well-supported Biblical doctrine which contradicts most forcibly the false concept Mrs. Eddy has incorporated into the Christian Science religion.

Respecting the miracles performed by Christ during His earthly ministry, Christian Scientists, whether they admit it or not, must logically deny that they were miracles in the first place and discount them as merely "illusions of mortal mind." Mrs. Eddy states that disease, sin, sickness and death are all illusions; they are not "real" since only Mind (God) is real and Mind is spiritual, not material. Therefore following Christian Science theology to its "logical" conclusions — since the "illusion of disease" can exist only in "the illusion called matter," that is itself existent only in the illusion called "mortal mind" which Mrs. Eddy denies exists anyway — there were no miracles at all because there was no corporeal body to be diseased, hence no need of a cure." Mrs. Eddy wrote:

> The sick are not healed merely by declaring there is no sickness, but by *knowing* there is *none* (*Science and Health*, page 447).

This reasoning on the part of Christian Science theology of course presupposes the assumption that there is no evil, since God-Good is *all* that really exists. Unfortunately it places them in the untenable position of having to account for the origin of the *idea* of evil, for even an illusion must have some basis in experience. Notwithstanding the circularity of this Christian Science argument, the Scriptures send a fresh breath of intellectual honesty into their account of Christ's true attitude toward disease, its reality and cure. The Lord Jesus never told the disintegrating leper as Mrs. Eddy's practitioner would, "You have no disease, it cannot exist, only God is good and He is all, etc." Rather He recognized the physical decay and by an act of sovereign grace restored the damaged tissue with one short phrase, "I will, be thou clean." It will be recalled that the leper in question said, "Lord, if thou wilt, thou canst make me clean" (Matthew 8:2, 3). Christ's answer included none of Mrs. Eddy's "Divine Science" or treatments by paid "Quacktitioners" as they are sometimes called. He merely restored the form His power had originally created (Colossians 1:16) and destroyed the bacteria responsible for the disease. Jesus never healed by denying the reality of the disease He intended to cure. Rather, He affirmed its reality and glorified God for its cure. It will be recalled that at the raising of Lazarus (John 11) Christ waited until he was physically dead beyond question (four days) and then restored to the function of life every cell of his decaying body, and glorified God for the victory over man's second oldest enemy.[21] We should note in this connection that Jesus did not deny the reality of death, as do Christian Scientists. He did not consider it "an illusion"; rather He verbally confirmed it: "Lazarus *is dead*" (John 11:14).

Christian Science finds no support for its denial of the physical miracles of Christ; deny the physical though they may, the facts are established. Should further proof be desired, however, the

---

[21]Satan occupies the dubious honor of being the first.

reader is urged to consult the following Biblical references which prove, we believe, that the miracles of Christ were physical realities, the result of supernatural intervention on the part of God in behalf of His erring creatures:

1. Matthew 8:14, 15 — the healing of Peter's mother-in-law.
2. Matthew 8:26, 27 — Christ stills the tempest.
3. Matthew 9:2, 6, 7 — Jesus heals the palsied man.
4. Matthew 9:27-30—Christ restores the sight of two blind men.
5. Mark 1:32-34 — Jesus heals the sick and casts out devils.
6. John 2:1-11 and John 6:10-14 — The miracles of changing water to wine and the feeding of 5,000 people.

Concluding this discussion, it should be noted in reference to John 2:1-11 and 6:10-14 that Christ would hardly have created wine from water or multiplied loaves and fishes to quench the thirst and satisfy the hunger of nonexistent bodies or "illusions of mortal mind," to quote Mrs. Eddy. The nature of all Christ's miracles was that of a divine-human encounter, comprising empirically verified physical events, to meet human needs whether hunger, thirst or suffering — not "illusions" as the theology of Christian Science attempts to make the gullible believe.

The Vicarious Atonement of Christ

There is no doctrine found within the pages of the Bible that is better supported or substantiated than that of the substitutionary death of Christ for the sins of the world. As far back in the Biblical record as Exodus, Moses wrote of God's symbolic use of blood for purification and sacrifice. It will be recalled that Jehovah delivered the Israelites from Egypt by causing all the firstborn of the nation, including Pharaoh's own son, to fall under the shadow of sudden death (Exodus 12). The Jews were instructed in this instance to sprinkle the blood of the young lamb on the doorposts and lintels of their homes, and God promised, "When I see the blood, I will pass over" (Exodus 12:13). The Lord also instituted the animal sacrifices of the Levitical era and expressly stated: ". . . It is the blood that maketh an atonement [covering] for the soul" (Leviticus 17:11). Following this typology through into the New Testament, we find that Jesus was called "the Lamb of God, which taketh away the sin of the world" (John 1:29), and further, that His blood shed upon the cross is our atonement or "covering" for sin, even for the sins of all mankind (Matthew 26:28; Romans 5:6-8; Ephesians 1:7; Colossians 1:20; etc.).

The believer in Christ, therefore, is saved by grace *alone,* through faith in His blood and its efficacy for the cleansing of all sin (Romans 3:25). John, the beloved disciple, reminds us in his powerful epistle, "The blood of Jesus Christ his Son cleanseth us from all sin" (I John 1:7), and Peter no less resoundingly declares, ". . . ye were not redeemed with corruptible things, as silver and gold . . . But with the precious *blood* of Christ, as of a *lamb* without blemish and without spot" (I Peter 1: 18, 19). Indeed, like a crimson cord binding all the Bible into one compact testimony, the trail of blood courses from Genesis to Revelation, testifying from the mouths of unimpeachable witnesses the wondrous story of God's redemptive love. Listen for a moment to the record of Scripture and the picture comes clearly into focus — God loved us and sent His Son to be our Saviour.

"Christ died for the ungodly," Paul triumphantly cries, and "Without shedding of blood there is no remission" (Romans 5:6; Hebrews 9:22); He purchased the church with His own blood (Acts 20:28) Luke informs us, and John adds to the witness by declaring that Christ "washed us from our sins in His own blood" (Revelation 1:5). This was not a pagan sacrifice to placate the wrath of a heathen god's justice as Mrs. Eddy wrote, but a sacrifice offered "through the eternal Spirit" to free the sons of men from the curse of sin, and open the path of salvation by which now we can have "boldness to enter into the holiest by the *blood* of Jesus — a new and living way" to the very throne room of God our Father (Hebrews 10:19, 20).

Contrasting this picture of concrete Biblical theology with the views of Christian Science, no better illustration of Mrs. Eddy's repudiation of this doctrine can be shown than that which comes from her own pen. Said Mrs. Eddy in speaking of the atonement:

> The material blood of Jesus was no more efficacious to cleanse from sin when it was shed upon the accursed tree than when it was flowing in his veins . . . (*Science and Health,* page 330).

According to Mrs. Eddy, then, Jesus, the disciples and apostles, and the early Christian theologians did not understand the meaning of the vicarious atonement, but *she* did and so she wrote:

> . . . He atoned for the terrible unreality of a supposed existence apart from God (*No and Yes,* pages 44-45).
> The efficacy of the crucifixion lies in the practical affection and goodness it demonstrated for mankind (*Science and Health,* page 329).

This is, of course, the opposite of anything the Bible teaches, and when Jesus said, "This is my flesh which I shall give for the life of the world," and "This is my blood shed for many for the remission of sin," Mrs. Eddy would have us believe that He anticipated no sacrifice for man's sin at all but merely martyrdom for "the terrible unreality of a supposed existence apart from God." Further comment on this problem is not deemed necessary in the light of the obvious denial by Christian Science of this historically-accepted Biblical doctrine, so strongly supported by the Scriptures of both Testaments.

The Death, Resurrection and Ascension of Christ

In our age of advanced medicine we read of many miracles ascribed to the labors of medical science; but all these advancements, marvelous though they may be, have only delayed the inevitable decay and death of the body and have yet to guarantee us physical immortality. The Scriptures clearly teach us that there is given to all men first death, and then the judgment (Hebrews 9:27) even as they tell us that our Lord Himself physically died at Calvary (Philippians 2:8). In fact the death of Jesus upon the cross is more thoroughly substantiated from Biblical and secular history than is His birth, which makes it even more difficult to believe that rational persons would deny it; however, Mrs. Eddy and Christian Science do deny it, hence the necessity of refuting their illogical contentions.

Joseph of Arimathaea, it will be remembered, requested the dead body of Jesus from Pontius Pilate (Matthew 27:58) and properly prepared it for burial (verses 59-60) as was the custom of the Jews. One thing that Joseph knew above anything else in the gathering shadows of the Sabbath that marked a solemn hour rent by bitterness, sorrow and fear, was that the body of the Galilean Prophet he buried was physically incapable of life; Jesus of Nazareth was dead. The absolute terror and doubt that gripped the immediate followers of Jesus could have come only from the personal knowledge that He had perished under the Judaeo-Roman conspiracy and that their cause was without a visible leader and apparently doomed to failure. The Apostle Paul tells us repeatedly "Christ died" (Romans 5:6); Peter recounts that He "bare our sins in his own body on the tree" (1 Peter 2:24), and John testifies that the soldiers "saw" . . . when they came to Jesus . . . "that he was dead already" (John 19:33). Certainly such intimate accounts cannot be lightly dismissed, yet Mrs. Eddy and Christian Science boldly assert "His disciples believed Jesus dead while he was hidden in the sepulchre; whereas he was alive . . ." (*Science and Health,* page 349), and once again she states:

> Jesus' students . . . did not perform any wonderful works until they saw him after his crucifixion and learned that he had *not* died (*Science and Health,* pages 350-351).

The issue therefore is a clean-cut one. The Bible says Christ died upon the cross; Mrs. Eddy and Christian Science say He did not. For those who call themselves Christians the choice is not a difficult one to make, and for those who are not Christians we are certain they will accept the words of the Scripture in preference to Mrs. Eddy anyhow, if only on general principles and the testimony of history.

The Resurrection of Christ is treated on a similar basis by the Christian Science religion, which affirms that He never rose from the dead physically any more than He died physically, Mrs. Eddy deliberately perverting numerous texts of Scripture to glean support for her wobbly propositions. Mrs. Eddy wrote with complete lack of concern for Biblical doctrine:

> To accommodate himself to immature ideas of spiritual power . . . Jesus *called* the body which by this power he raised from the grave ,"flesh and bones" (*Science and Health,* page 209).

So it is that we learn how Christian Science often attempts to change the obvious meaning of texts. In the twentieth chapter of John's gospel, the resurrected Jesus, to prove to the doubting Thomas that He was not a Spirit but genuine "flesh and bones," presented His body bearing the imprint of nails and spear for the disciples' examination. To His disciples at another time Jesus also said, "Handle me, . . . for a spirit

hath not flesh and bones, as ye see me have" (Luke 24:39). The Resurrection of Christ and its startling revelation — namely, that He was who He claimed to be, the Son of God — is the one factor which most probably accounts for the rapid rise of Christianity's power over the lives of men. Here was a genuine opportunity to believe in a Saviour who proved His Divinity by vanquishing death, and who promised the same victory to those who believe and preach His Gospel. It is no wonder Satan has so strenuously opposed this doctrine of Scripture, for upon it hangs the verity of our Gospel. As St. Paul puts it, "If Christ be not raised, your faith is vain; ye are yet in your sins" (I Corinthians 15:17). Mrs. Eddy and Christian Science may oppose this truth vigorously, as indeed they do — but the Gospel of Christ will not be hindered by mere denials, and their unbelief does not in any sense nullify the truth of God as the Scriptures so powerfully declare it:

> But now is Christ risen from the dead, and become the firstfruits of them that slept. For since by man came death, by man came also the resurrection of the dead. For as in Adam all die, even so in Christ shall all be made alive[22] (I Corinthians 15:20-22).

As to the doctrine of the ascension of Christ into heaven, physically, another denial is vouchsafed from the pen of Mrs. Eddy. By the same method she uses to spiritualize the Resurrection of Christ, Mrs. Eddy also spiritualizes His Ascension. She describes it thusly:

> . . . (the disciples') . . . dear Master would rise again in the *spiritual scale* of existence and fly beyond their apprehension . . . He would disappear to material sense, in that *change* which has since been called the ascension (*Science and Health,* page 339).

Now to any alert Bible student the Ascension of Christ was a physical one; the disciples *saw* Him carried into the heavenlies visibly; it was not merely an

---

[22]Or to more properly grasp the sense of the Greek, "As in Adam all die, so then through

Christ shall all be resurrected."

upward stroke on the "spiritual scale" of existence as Mrs. Eddy put it, but a change of position from one sphere to another visible in part to the human eye. In connection with this, one need only remember the testimony of the angels who escorted their Lord to His throne:

Ye men of Galilee, why stand ye gazing up into heaven? this same Jesus, which is taken up from you into heaven, shall so come in like manner as ye have seen him go into heaven (Acts 1:11).

Beside these great declarations of Scripture the confused writing of Mrs. Eddy is conspicuously immature and inadequate, since, as always, the Bible, which is the supreme Christian authority, confirms the truth as it really happened, not as Christian Science has imagined it happened.

The Existence of Satan, Evil and Sin

Probably one of the most obvious doctrines of Biblical theology is that of the origin, existence and final disposition of evil. From Genesis to Revelation one can distinguish the powers set in array against God and His people, powers whose ultimate end is spiritual judgment of the most terrible order. We are told in the Scripture that Satan or Lucifer, the "god of this world," was once a mighty and perfect angelic son of God whose dazzling and wondrous countenance earned for him the titles, "Son of the Morning" and "Covering Cherub" (Isaiah 14:12 and Ezekiel 28:14). The Scriptures also tell us that this powerful angel secretly cherished the desire to usurp the throne of his Maker (Isaiah 14:13, 14) and upon gathering numerous supporters he rebelled against the sovereignty of Jehovah. The outcome of this wicked rebellion was the driving from heaven of Satan and the fallen angels that followed him, and he was subsequently allowed dominion over the celestial universe for reasons best known to God and himself, hence his title

"prince of the power of the air" (Ephesians 2:2).

With this rebellion commenced the beginning of all evil or sin, i.e., that which is opposed to the will of God. After his rout in the heavenly encounter, Satan extended his kingdom over the heavenlies and earth, determined to disrupt, if possible, the plans of God. In the Garden of Eden Satan's desires reached fruition and he succeeded in spiritually corrupting the future parents of the human race, Adam and Eve (Genesis 3). As punishment for this sin against the Lord, Satan was sentenced to a humiliating defeat by the "Seed" of the very creatures he had so willfully wronged (Genesis 3:15.) This promised Seed who would bruise the head of Satan was to be the Messiah of Israel, who we have already seen is the Lord Jesus Christ. The final judgment of Satan will come after his complete and utter defeat at Armageddon, when he and all his followers from the ancient days of his heavenly citizenship will then be cast into the lake of fire (Revelation 20:10), there to suffer eternally the righteous judgment of God (Revelation 20:10).

Despite this graphic Biblical portrayal of Satan available for all to see, Mrs. Eddy and Christian Science energetically deny his existence and refer to him as ". . . another elusive personification named Satan" (*Science and Health*, page 81). Further establishing her contention that evil is non-existent, Mrs. Eddy flatly states:

Evil has no reality. It is neither person, place nor thing but is simply a belief, an illusion of material sense (*Science and Health*, page 237).

There never was a moment in which evil was real (*No and Yes*, page 33).

Since Christian Science denies the origin of evil or Satan, it is only logical that it should deny evil, and sin as the result of evil. Concerning sin Mrs. Eddy wrote:

The belief of sin . . . is an unconscious error in the beginning (*Science and Health,* page 81).

There is no sin. . . . Man is incapable of sin . . . (*Science and Health,* Edition of 1917, pages 447-475).

Placing this declaration on a level plane with the Biblical definition and development of the doctrine of sin, it is seen to be at complete odds with the Biblical record. John reminds us that sin, far from being an "illusion" or a non-existent force, is in reality a very potent enemy of man. "Sin," writes John, "is the transgression of the law," and further, "All unrighteousness is sin" (I John 3:4 and I John 5:17). Paul also admonishes "for the wages of sin is death" (Romans 6:23). One can hardly be expected to believe that the Christian Science teaching about sin is truthful when both John and Paul, inspired spokesmen of God, so clearly contradict it. The Bible innumerable times declares: "All have sinned, and come short of the glory of God" (Romans 3:23), and "if we say that we have not sinned, we make him [God] a liar, and his word is not in us" (I John 1:10). As to the personality and power of a personal force of evil (Satan), the Bible equally establishes his existence as opposed to Mrs. Eddy's denials. Jesus, it will be remembered, spoke with Satan, who tempted Him (Luke 4:3-6). This could hardly have been an illusion even of the Christian Science variety, and the Lord also announced that He had come "to destroy the works of the devil" whom He described as a liar and a murderer from the beginning who abode not in the truth, a liar and the father of it (John 8:44). "Mrs. Eddy's devil," as Mr. Wiggin so aptly put it, was Malicious Animal Magnetism, which she invented to explain away the rather obvious fact that evil and sin existed despite her affirmations to the contrary. This doctrine eventually became a mania with Mrs. Eddy and drove her to irrational behavior and fantastically absurd demonstrations of temper, illness and rapid excursions to different communities, "when she felt the Fiend closing in."

The Scriptures, therefore, give more than convincing proof "that God will judge sin" and that it is not an illusion but an ever-present enemy which all men and even Christian Scientists must reap the wages of in the end. It is comforting to know from a Biblical standpoint that though "the wages of sin is death . . . the gift of God is eternal life through Jesus Christ our Lord" (Romans 6:23).

The Doctrines of Prayer and Eternal Salvation

A. The doctrines of prayer and salvation are inseparably joined in the Scripture with the decree and plan of God to redeem the fallen race of men. The Bible, in places too numerous to recount, encourages, instructs and even commands us to "pray without ceasing" (I Thessalonians 5:17) that God may reward our faith in His righteous judgments. The Lord Jesus often prayed to His Father for strength to meet the physical and spiritual rigors of daily life and finally the cross itself (Matthew 26:36). We remember also at the raising of Lazarus, pictured so vividly in the eleventh chapter of John's gospel, Jesus prayed:

Father, I thank thee that thou hast heard me. And I knew that thou hearest me always . . . (John 11:41, 42).

and that He further instructed us to "pray to thy Father which is in secret; and thy Father which seeth in secret shall reward thee openly" (Matthew 6:6). Above and beyond these elementary examples of Christ's attitude toward prayer, it is a well-established Biblical fact that prayer by definition is a direct personal request to God for His intervention, whether it be for the purpose of healing the sick, raising the dead or simply asking for grace and strength to live our separate lives (Philippians 4:6, 7). The entire context of John's seventeenth chapter, for example, is devoted to recording the prayer of Christ for *all* His disciples present and future, that they might be protected from Satan and the powers of darkness during their ministry of gospel truth. Jesus understood only too well the need for personal prayer to God in order to maintain close fellowship with our Father, and it is of this that He reminds us when He said:

Men ought always to pray, and not to faint (Luke 18:1).

Prayer, to Christian Scientists, however, carries none of the meaning that the Bible so clearly portrays because, as Mrs. Eddy wrote:

Prayer to a personal God hinders spiritual growth.[23]

We have seen, of course, that the God of the Bible is a Personal Being, not a mere "Principle" as Christian Science contends; therefore it is easy to see why the meaning of prayer to a Christian and to a Christian Scientist differs markedly. Mrs. Eddy also wrote concerning prayer:

. . . the danger from audible prayer is that it might lead us into temptation . . . (*Science and Health*, pages 312-313).

The mere habit of pleading with the Divine Mind as one pleads with a human being, perpetuates the belief in God as humanly circumscribed, an error that impedes spiritual growth. (*Science and Health*, Edition of 1917, page 2).

It is singularly peculiar, in view of these contradictory claims of Mrs. Eddy, that Jesus addressed His Father as a *personal* Being and commanded us to pray a *personal* prayer, "Our Father which art in heaven, Hallowed by *thy* name. *Thy* kingdom come. *Thy* will be done in earth, as it is in heaven" (Matthew 6:9, 10).

If "Give us this day our daily bread, and forgive us our debts, as we forgive our debtors," etc., is not a plea to God, then, perhaps, Mrs. Eddy's followers can tell us what in the name of reason

it is. Mrs. Eddy says, further:

Don't plead with God. God is not influenced by man (*Science and Health*, Edition of 1917, page 7).

What is more evident from this bold negation of Scripture than the fact that Christian Scientists cannot even logically claim that they pray in the Biblical sense at all, disbelieving as they do the clear definitions the Bible gives of what prayer and communion with God really mean. It was written of the Lord Jesus that prayer was His constant habit, His unceasing attitude and unwearied occupation; it is difficult, therefore, to believe that He would urge us to pray in the sure knowledge that it "might lead us into temptation" as Mrs. Eddy implied it did. Moreover, the Lord Jesus prayed audibly, and commanded His disciples to emulate Him "Lead us *not* into temptation." But Mrs. Eddy says audible prayer itself may lead us into temptation (*Science and Health*, pages 312, 313). One need look no further for evidence of where she obtained her inspiration — it was obviously supplied by the great Counterfeiter (Genesis 3:4; 5). Paul, that noble apostle of personal prayer, instructs us to ". . . let your requests be made known unto God" and to pursue "everything by prayer and supplication with thanksgiving" (Philippians 4:6). Once again the inspired apostle flatly contradicts Mrs. Eddy's unscriptural teachings and those of Christian Science, a fact hardly necessitating further comment upon the subject here. Prayer is the life blood of the Christian's spiritual existence, and personal communion with *the* personal God our ever-present help in trouble, a relationship no Christian Scientist can ever enjoy since they have never known the God of the Bible, or Jesus Christ, both of whom Biblically speaking they and Mrs. Eddy, their "leader," unreservedly deny.

B. The doctrine of eternal salvation

[23] I. M. Haldeman, *Christian Science in the Light of Holy Scripture*, page 268.

is so well documented in the Scripture that I feel sure no major comment at this stage of study is necessary; however, to clarify the doctrine as opposed to Christian Science perversions of it, I shall briefly summarize it here.

Eternal life, the Bible reveals to us, is to be found only in the cross of Christ, that supreme symbol of God's immeasurable love toward a lost and dying world. This life, the Scripture tells us, resides in the Person of His Son, Jesus, "the true God and eternal life" (I John 5:20, and John 17:3; 3:16; 5:24; 6:47; 10:28; 14:6, etc.). The Scriptures further testify that God sent His Son to be the "Saviour of all men, specially of those that believe" (I Timothy 4:10). The Lord Jesus Christ by His sacrifice on Calvary has purchased "eternal redemption" for us promising that if we trust Him fully we shall at length be with Him where He is (John 17:24). God's Word assures us that our Saviour is now at the "right hand of the Majesty on high" (Hebrews 1:3), and that some day by His matchless grace, we, too, shall leave this vale of tears, forever free of earthly shackles, to "dwell in the house of the Lord for ever" (Psalm 23:6).

> For by grace are ye saved through faith, and that not of yourselves: it is the gift of God: Not of works, lest any man should boast (Ephesians 2:8, 9).

This, then, is the true, the Christian meaning of salvation, not only freedom from fear, judgment and the uncertainties of this earthly life, but the knowledge of peace *with* God "through the blood of His cross," and justification *before* God by "the power of His resurrection." All these things, according to both John and Peter, are the result of the operation of God's Holy Spirit in the hearts of men, regenerating, renewing, recreating, until eventually, in His redeemed own, the perfect reflection of Christ, God's "express image" (Hebrews 1:3), shall shine forth triumphant over Satan, the flesh and death itself.

"Ye must be born again," said our Lord to Nicodemus (John 3:3); "having been born again of incorruptible seed," writes Peter; and Paul adds, "Therefore if any man be in Christ, he is a new creature: old things are passed away; behold, all things are become new" (II Corinthians 5:17). Thus it is seen that God's salvation is not a reformation of man, but a regeneration, not just a reorganization of his social habits, but a literal saving of his spiritual life — a complete deliverance of the completely lost.

Christian Science, unfortunately, does not hold this view but teaches instead, as Mrs. Eddy put it, that salvation is *not* a personal deliverance from *real* sin and wickedness, but ". . . boundless freedom and sinless sense," or, as she further stated, "Man as God's idea is *already* saved with an everlasting salvation" (*Science and Health,* page 327).

Christian Science does away altogether with the necessity of Christ's death on the cross for sin. Mrs. Eddy declared that:

> Final deliverance from error . . . is neither reached through paths of flowers, nor by pinning one's faith to another's vicarious effort (op. cit).

These are strange words in contrast to what Christ said, "I am not come to call the righteous, but sinners to repentance" (Matthew 9:13), and to Peter's immortal sentence, "Christ died for *our* sins, the just for the *unjust,* to reconcile *us* to God" (I Peter 3:18). Christian Science offers no eternal life and no salvation for the soul, denying as it does, sin, and hence the necessity of redemption from it. But God's Word stands sure, in powerful opposition to the falsehoods of Mrs. Eddy and Christian Science: "All have sinned, and come short of the glory of God," and "There is none righteous, no, not one" (Romans 3:23 and 3:10); but, "Believe on the Lord Jesus Christ, and thou shalt be saved" (Acts 16:31). This is God's salvation; this is the central message of the Bible; this is eternal life.

Man, His Spiritual and Material Natures

Without fear of contradiction all rational persons will admit the reality of their physical existence. There are three principal reasons for this admission, which, briefly stated, are these:

1. Man is capable of perceiving his corporeal form.
2. The demands of the body, such as food, clothing, etc., prove that it has a material existence.
3. The human mind is capable of discerning the difference between concrete and abstract ideas, the body being easily discerned as a concrete proposition.[24]

In view of these three facts, it is worthwhile to note that Christian Science denies without reservation all physical existence, as Mrs. Eddy wrote:

> Man is not matter, . . . made up of brains, blood, bones and other material elements . . . man is spiritual and perfect, and because of this he must be so understood to Christian Science . . . (*Science and Health,* page 471).

Not only did Mrs. Eddy deny the materially verifiable fact that the body exists, but she even went so far as to correct God in His creative office by asserting that "man originated not from dust, materially, but from spirit, spiritually" (*Miscellaneous Writings,* page 357). At this point in her incoherent ramblings and deplorable mental condition, Mrs. Eddy did the one thing which, by itself devoid of any theological speculation whatsoever, characterizes her system of reasoning as that of a gross philosophic perversion. To deny the reality of matter, philosophically speaking, is to predicate the worst type of absurdity, and Mrs. Eddy was not above such a perpetration. Genesis 2:7 plainly states that "God formed man of the dust

of the ground, and breathed into his nostrils the breath of life; and man became a living soul." Moses further tells us that God created the material Eve, using a part of the material Adam, and David said, "It is he that hath made us, and not we ourselves" (Psalm 100:3). The Scriptures irrefutably declare that God created matter (Genesis 1:1), all forms of living organisms, and finally man himself in the spiritual image and likeness of his immaterial Father. There is therefore no conceivable ground, logically speaking, for denying that man exists physically as well as spiritually, and Mrs. Eddy's repeated attempts to do away with the human body, and for that matter the material universe itself, is only one more evidence of her unsound reasoning processes.

In regard to the spiritual nature of man, Christian Science takes a peculiar attitude, but for once an attitude that is logically consistent when followed through. Since man is totally spiritual ("the reflection of God" as Christian Science would have it), and God is perfect and incapable of sin, therefore man must also be perfect as His reflection and hence incapable of sin. This is exactly what Mrs. Eddy taught. Witness her own words:

> . . . man is incapable of sin . . . (*Science and Health,* page 471).
> . . . man is the ultimate of perfection and by no means the medium of imperfection . . . If God is upright and eternal, man as His likeness is erect in goodness and perpetual in Life, Truth and Love . . . The spiritual man is that *perfect* and *unfallen* likeness co-existent and co-eternal with God (*Miscellaneous Writings,* page 79).
> In Science there is no fallen state of being for there is no inverted image of God . . . (*No and Yes,* page 26).

The logical mind can only deduce from these statements that the Biblical account of man's fall from perfection (Genesis 3:6, 7) and his definition as a finite being (Psalm 89:48 and I Co-

---

[24]Capable of empirical verification in this case.

rinthians 15:47) are totally in error and that man *is* God, because if he coexists with an eternal being (*Miscellaneous Writings,* page 79), he himself is eternal. The weakness of this position can easily be demonstrated by the fact that all material things, including the human body, eventually return to the basic elements of existence, and since God is said to have created all that exists, both material and spiritual (John 1:3), therefore man in both his physical and spiritual forms is a creature, a creation not of a coexistent or inherently eternal character.

In conclusion, it is obvious that the identification of man and God by Christian Science on the basis of a spiritual nature is completely erroneous, if the Judaeo-Christian viewpoint be accepted as to the identity of the true God. Christian Science, it should be noted, claims that it holds the Christian position, and Christian Scientists violently repudiate any attempts to show that their teachings are the opposite of what Jesus taught; yet in every possible sense of the Biblical record, all things having been considered, there is not the slightest possibility that the theology of Christian Science resembles even vaguely the revelation of the Bible concerning the teachings of Jesus Christ. The soul of man, it is true, is immaterial and was created in the image of God, but the body of man is purely physical in every sense of the word. To deny its reality as does Christian Science and attempt to prove that man is totally spiritual, and spiritually perfect at that, is, to say the least, a flagrant perversion of what Biblical theology plainly portrays. The soul of man wilfully sinned against God in the person of Adam (Isaiah 43:27; Romans 5); the souls of all men have forever been in rebellion against Almighty God from that day forward. It is only through the Gospel of Jesus Christ that this rebellion is brought into submission and that the sins of man's evil soul are cleansed, and the soul regenerated to eternal life. To deny these facts on a Biblical basis is dangerous: they are far too obvious. To explain them away as does Christian Science is fruitless; for the "word of the Lord endureth forever," and "it is this Word which through the gospel we preach unto you" (I Peter 1:25).

CHRISTIAN SCIENCE AND HEALING

The central claim of Mrs. Eddy and Christian Science is that she has "restored" to Christendom the power of healing "lost" since the days of the early church. It is continually reiterated in the literature of the cult that their "leader" healed as Jesus did and demonstrated, through Divine Science. Not only this, but Mrs. Eddy herself boldly asserted that she healed all types of diseases including cancer, tuberculosis and diphtheria. Mrs. Eddy wrote to the *New York Sun,* December 19, 1898:

> I challenge the world to disprove what I hereby declare. After my discovery of Christian Science I healed consumption in the last stages that the M.D.'s by verdict of a stethoscope and the schools declared incurable, the lungs being mostly consumed. I healed malignant tubercular diphtheria and carious bones that could be dented by the finger, saving them when the surgeon's instruments were lying on the table ready for their amputation. I have healed at one visit a cancer that had so eaten the flesh of the neck as to expose the jugular vein so that it stood out like a cord.

Notice here Mrs. Eddy gives no particulars, names of patients, localities, dates or witnesses. Indeed the only persons who ever witnessed her "miraculous" cures were either hypnotized lackeys of Mrs. Eddy's without medical training to justify their diagnosis of disease, or Christian Scientists of another era who unfortunately believed as God-breathed truth any claim that either Mrs. Eddy or her contemporary worshipers have conjured up. And so this key phase of the Eddy myth — Mrs. Eddy's power to heal — presents itself as a unique challenge. For if it be true that she healed with such power, then

Mrs. Eddy stands vindicated of any evil. If it is false, she is unmasked as a deceiver of unparalleled cruelty, preying upon the sick and maimed for personal remuneration, prestige and cheap sensational publicity. Briefly then, let us consider this phase of "Mother" Eddy's[25] long career.

To begin with, it should be realized in the process of investigating Mrs. Eddy's healing claims that she refused outright to treat identical cases of diseases she claimed to have cured. Even when a prominent Cincinnati physician offered her every such opportunity, Mrs. Eddy remained strangely silent; indeed she never mentioned the issue again.[26] This is hardly the attitude one would expect from the alleged "successor to Jesus Christ." The foregoing is only one fact of a large number which proved beyond doubt that Mrs. Eddy did not heal as she claimed. During her long life Mrs. Eddy allowed her own little granddaughter, her beloved brother Samuel's wife, and her close friend, Joseph Armstrong, all to die painful deaths of cancer, pneumonia and pleurisy, and never, to any known evidence of the contrary, did she ever lift her "healing" hand to save them.[27] Instead she recommended "absent treatment" in all three cases, which consisted of reading her book, Science and Health, and concentrating upon mentally repulsing the organic deterioration. Mrs. Eddy could have at least paid a call on them, and if her claims were true, healed them "at one visit," but she did not because she could not, and no one knew it better than Mary Baker Eddy. There is an overwhelming mass of evidence from sources unchallengeable that this fact is absolute truth, and no better authority can be quoted than the sworn

testimony of Mr. Alfred Farlow, then chairman of the Publications Committee of the Christian Science Church and President of the Mother Church in Boston. Mr. Farlow's testimony, that of a Christian Scientist in excellent standing with his church and certainly in a position to know the facts about Mrs. Eddy, clearly stated that he did not know of any healing ever having been made by Mrs. Eddy of any organic disease in her entire life but that of stiff leg — hardly a major illness by any reasonable diagnosis (The Religio-Medical Masquerade, F. W. Peabody, page 113). Much more material could be introduced to further verify this contention of history against the Eddy healing legend, but it is sufficient to say that the issue needs no further support. She who professed to "succeed Jesus Christ" as the great healer of our age could not heal even her closest emotional contacts; and to conceal this great threat to her system which was based squarely on her alleged failure to heal, Mrs. Eddy and her contemporaries have masqueraded to the world and to her gullible followers the legend of her miraculous curative power. This power, so widely trumpeted by Christian Science propaganda, history tells us she never exercised or demonstrated openly, for the obvious reason that it was a complete illusion, a phantom of Christian Science publicity and the delusions of Mary Baker Eddy.

Mrs. Eddy however was not above attaching a price-tag to the miraculous healings she claimed for her religion, and so she wrote:

"Christian Science demonstrates that the patient who pays whatever he is able to pay for healing is more apt to recover than he who withholds the slightest equivalent for health." (The Faith,

[25]A self-conferred title of Mrs. Eddy; see the Christian Science Sentinel, December 21, 1899 and Christian Science, Mark Twain, pages 334-336.

[26]New York Sun, January 1, 1899, by Dr. Charles A. L. Reed.

[27]She did, however, send her personal check to defray the cost of her sister-in-law's operation, but by the time the surgeon operated, the time taken in useless Christian Science treatments had taken a fatal toll and she died.

Falsity and Failures of Christian Science, page 267).

But though Mrs. Eddy made many claims, she herself avoided demonstrating the miraculous properties of Christian Science by the careful insertion of a footnote in her book *Science and Health* which read:

"The author takes no patients into clients' medical consultation." (*The Faith, Falsity and Failure of Christian Science,* page 337).

One could hardly picture our Saviour turning away a repentant leper or even allowing Lazarus to remain in the grave, yet Mrs. Eddy herself proclaims having "abruptly closed the door for a chamber of miracles to the faithful."

What testimony this is to the reputedly tender-hearted priestess of the Christian Science history books.

But that was Mrs. Eddy, clever to the last and beyond the comprehension and understanding of even her most intimate friends. It must never be forgotten that Mrs. Eddy once wrote:

"A patient hears the doctor's verdict as the criminal hears the death sentence." (*Science and Health,* page 198).

Yet she made very rare, but real use of doctors for her spasmodic attacks of hysteria, and toward the end of her life even allowed Christian Scientists the right to use anesthetics, surgery, and the services of orthopedists for breaks and fractures, etc. This although she stoutly opposed such practices at the outset of her career!

However, no one can ever accuse Mrs. Eddy of being foolish, since she seemingly made allowance for some situations, but while she provided in a measure for the bodies of her followers she left their souls poverty stricken, barren and destitute, robbed of the true Christ and His Gospel of life.

The chief attraction of Christian Science then lies in its seeming power over disease and mental conflict, but to quote Psychologist David S. Davis: "What has been induced by suggestion can be cured by suggestion."[28]

Most illnesses "cured" by Christian Scientists are imagined illnesses which lack medical documentation and are seldom thoroughly verified by anyone other than the Scientists or their sympathizers. The physical world to most Christian Scientists is an "illusion of mortal mind," but they are quick to seize every opportunity to avail themselves of all the comforts this same "mortal mind" conjures up.[29]

With this philosophy it is easy to see how even sin, with all its hideousness, is reduced to a state of mind, and death to a flighty "illusion."

Since the central doctrine of almost all cults is the denial of both the Deity and Saviourhood of the Lord Jesus, we must exert renewed effort in preaching and teaching these major doctrines of our Christian heritage. We must be quick to expose error and even still quicker to extend to all cultists the love of God and the assurance of forgiveness through His Eternal Son, if they will but come to the Christ of Calvary.

Let us not forget, however, that Christian Science can temporarily induce peace of mind, and this cannot be doubted; but, that it is able to cure "diagnosed diseases," give peace of soul, or most of all, peace with God, is a question to which the Bible emphatically says — No! The Bible clearly teaches that salvation is effected solely through the Grace of God as revealed in Jesus Christ and His substitutionary atonement on the cross. The Christ of Christianity is a Personality — God Incarnate (John 1:1-14) — not the "Divine Idea" of a pantheistic nonentity, as Mrs. Eddy has portrayed Him to be.

---

[28]Prof. David S. Davis, "A Psychologist Views the Cults," from *The Examiner,* Vol. I, January-February No. 1, page 11.

[29]Scripture, however, does cite evidence that

Satan can counterfeit the miracles of God (Exodus 7:22ff) and whatever "cures" Christian Science can present are not the work of our Christ.

It is therefore important to remember that Mrs. Eddy never believed in a Personal God nor does any true Christian Scientist today. Mrs. Eddy's last words, which she scrawled with a trembling hand on a scrap of paper shortly before her death, "God is my life," might just as well have read, "Principle, Love, Spirit or Intelligence is my life." To her utterly confused mind the God of the Bible did not exist; for her, God was not personal in any sense, since her limited theology only permitted an "It" which was "all in all." Aside from adoring this pantheistic, impersonal deity, Mrs. Eddy, and consequently all Christian Scientist practitioners today, expound this principle as the Master Key to all human misery. Paradoxically, however, they deny misery exists in the first place but never tire of trying to convince anyone who will listen, for a handsome fee, that Christian Science can remove this "error of mortal mind" through "prayer." The great byword of Christian Science, incidentally, is "prayer," and they never cease reminding their audience that they always pray to "God" for healing. But is it really prayer? The Scriptures teach that prayer is one's petition to a personal God who sees our needs and answers them (Philippians 4:6, 7). Not so in Christian Science. Mrs. Eddy many times reaffirmed her conviction that prayer to a personal God is a hindrance, not a help. To her and Christian Science the only true prayer is "the affirmation of Principle Allness" and the identification of one's self with this pantheistic Principle. From this basic misconception stems the illusion of man's inherent goodness and the denial of the "erroneous" idea that evil, or for that matter, sin, suffering, disease, or even death, is real. With this view of life it is easy to see how Christian Scientists can appear so apparently happy and so oblivious to everyday worries. Whenever they encounter evil they deny its reality; whenever they behold misery, they affirm its nonexistence; and even when death comes to a loved one, they simply assert that it is an "illusion" since Principle (God) is All, and "It" is *good*.

It would be possible to go on indefinitely with the many strange interpretations which Mrs. Eddy gave to the Scriptures. Suffice it to say, that she never believed in them as God's Word, nor worshiped the Saviour within its pages. The Christian's most holy and sacred doctrine of love, which is Christ crucified for us and His sacrificial blood our atonement with God, Mrs. Eddy abruptly dismissed as unnecessary. She equally ignored the existence of hell, Satan, or, for that matter, a literal heaven. (For her it was a "state of mind.") Nowhere in the annals of cultism is there to be found a person who camouflaged so expertly the "broad way of destruction" under a canopy of apparent serenity as did Mary Baker Eddy. Nevertheless, beneath this "serenity" lies a denial of almost all orthodox Christianity.

In concluding this survey of Mrs. Eddy's religion, it is extremely important that the implications of Christian Science be thoroughly understood by Christians and non-Christians alike. It is important for Christians because ignorance of Christian Science has been one of the main contributing factors to the success of its rapid development. For non-Christians it is important because it is an imitation of the true Gospel which bears no resemblance whatsoever to the historic Christian faith.

Christian Science must be understood and its teachings refuted from the Scriptures which it perverts and wrests to the destruction of many misled souls. But Christian Scientists must be loved and evangelized for the cause of the Gospel and because this is God's command to His church. Here lies the greater challenge by far.

BIBLICAL TEXTS HELPFUL IN REFUTING CHRISTIAN SCIENCE THEOLOGY

1. *The Authority of the Bible*: Psalm 119:140; Isaiah 40:8; Matthew 24:35; John 10:35; 17:17; II Timothy 3:16.
2. *The Trinity and Deity of Christ*: Genesis 1:26; 11:7; 18:1-33; Exodus 3:14; Isaiah 6:8; 9:6; John 1: 1, 14; 8:58; Colossians 1:15; 2:9; Hebrews 1:3; Revelation 1:7, 8, 16.
3. *The Personality of the Holy Spirit*: Luke 12:12; John 16:7, 8; Acts 13:2.
4. *The Virgin Birth and Miracles of Jesus*: Isaiah 7:14; 9:6; Micah 5:2; Matthew 1:18-25; Luke 1:30-38. *Miracles:* Matthew 8:14, 15, 26, 27; 9:2, 6, 7, 27-30; Mark 1:32-34; John 2:1-11; 6:10-14.
5. *The Atonement, Death and Resurrection of Christ*: Exodus 12:13; Leviticus 17:11; Psalm 22; Isaiah 53; Daniel 9:26; Matthew 26:28; 28:5-7; Luke 24:39; John 1:29; 19:33; Romans 5:6-8; Ephesians 1:7; Colossians 1:20.
6. *The Doctrine of Eternal Retribution*: Matthew 13:42, 50; 22:13; Mark 9:44, 46, 48; Luke 3:17; Revelation 20:10.
7. *The Doctrine of Christian Prayer*: Matthew 6:5-15; 7:7-11; Luke 18: 1; Philippians 4:6; I Thessalonians 5:17; James 5:16.
8. *The Doctrine of Sin*: Romans 3:23; 6:23; I John 1:10; 3:4; 5:17.

THE CULT OF NEW THOUGHT

As we have just observed Christian Science came from Francis Lieber and P. P. Quimby, but *New Thought*, which claims a membership of more than 50,000 persons, is strictly an off-shoot of Quimby's system of mental healing.

The Rev. Warren Felt Evans and Julius Dresser, both disciples of Quimby, brought the cult of *New Thought* into existence shortly after Mrs. Eddy's cult began to thrive in the early 1880's,

and it was through their writing that Charles and Myrtle Fillmore (founders of "Unity") gained their initial interest in gnosticism.

The theology of *New Thought* is remarkably similar to that of Christian Science, as would be expected, and can therefore be refuted from a Biblical viewpoint much as we have refuted Christian Science theology.

The following excerpts from *New Thought* writers reveal the close parallel between Christian Science, Unity and New Thought, a fact not generally known by the average Christian, but one interesting enough to merit a brief comparison.

REPRESENTATIVE TEACHINGS FROM NEW THOUGHT

INSPIRATION OF THE BIBLE

"As the Bible is an Oriental Book, in which truth is cast in terms of symbolism, metaphor, hyperbole, allegory, parable, and general poetic expression, literalism has largely stripped it of its power. Emphasis upon special forms of words has an unspiritual and restrictive influence. We want the fruit rather than the shell. . . . Each will translate the text in the light of his own life, experience, and deeper consciousness, and get just that strength and inspiration for which he is fitted. The Bible does not claim any monopoly of truth. It does not originate in its pages. . . . It is not the fault of the Book that it has been abused through superficial interpretation. . . . New Thought teaches that in the last analysis spiritual authority must be within, — the divine element in man." (Henry Wood, *New Thought Simplified*, pages 141-143).

"Indeed the word revelation is illusory if we mean wisdom put into our minds apart from spiritual growth which discloses and proves it." (Horatio W. Dresser, *Spiritual Health and Healing*, page 16ff).

The Bible: "It is really a record of the divine intimacies of gifted and developed souls. It gives an account of their lofty thoughts and experiences, and suggests the way in which we may cultivate similar states of consciousness." (Ibid., page 140).

"Other opinions and standpoints are good as aids and suggestions, but final *authority* should be within." (Italics are the author's) (*Ibid.*, page 14).

THE NATURE OF GOD

"In essence the life of God and the life of man are identically the same, and so are one. They differ not in essence, in quality, they differ in degree." (Ralph Waldo Trine, *In Tune with the Infinite,* page 13).

"This gospel involved the idea that Christianity is not a person in the same sense in which orthodox believers associate the Son with the Father in the Trinity. The leading idea was that Christianity was divine wisdom taught and exemplified by the historic personality Jesus of Nazareth . . . (Horatio W. Dresser, *Spiritual Health and Healing,* page 7).

"Man's thought of God has been mostly as a magnified image of himself. God has been called Lord, King, Ruler, Potentate, Sovereign, and Judge. . . . Such ideals of divine manifestation as we call Order, Law, Harmony, Peace, Wholesomeness, Truth, Beauty, and Happiness are also useful aids in perfecting our conception of the All-Good. But we need not give up the use of the term, God, because it is possible to purify it from its lowering associations." (Wood, op. cit., page 75).

THE DEITY OF CHRIST

"Thus we have the figure of the vine as the symbol of all effective life in the Spirit, all true discipleship and service. The Christ is here a principle such that it can abide in all who are faithful to the precepts and the love set before the disciples as an ideal." (Dresser, op. cit., page 19).

" 'He that hath seen me hath seen the Father,' with understanding the two are absolutely one. But this passage in John, chapter 14, is followed by the explanatory statement, '. . . . the Father is in me, and I in him.' In the sense of this surpassing truth Jesus prays that all may be one, 'as thou, Father, art in me, and I in thee, that they also may be one in us.' Plainly the oneness refers to unity of spirit in universal wisdom." (Dresser, op. cit., page 33).

"Christ is the name of sonship — God, in us. Jesus personally expressed that relation, supremely, ideally. But he was not a "scapegoat," substitute, nor an interposition." (Wood, op. cit., page 182).

"The Christ represents the universal and eternal divine sonship, — the highest possible inner consciousness. In most men it is latent or but feebly developed. It was locally and historically expressed in full degree through the personality of Jesus, but by no means limited to him." (Wood, op. cit., page 182).

"The 'Christ mind' is the full-orbited consciousness of divinity within. It grows in me. I have it. I feel it." (Wood, op. cit., pages 194-195).

THE DIVINITY OF MAN WITH CHRIST

"I hereby recognize every human brother as son of God. I know his divinity, and will help him to uncover and express it." (Wood, op. cit., page 186).

"I send everyone a God-speed and an awakening call to the divine self, or Christ within." (Wood, op. cit., page 187).

"In some guise there must be outward visible saviors because the inmost faith, divinity or Christ does not appeal to the sensuous nature. Hence the worship of physical personality of Jesus which he himself vainly tried to transfer and spiritualize." (Wood, op. cit., page 71).

"To teach . . . the Divinity of Man and his infinite possibilities through the creative power of constructive thinking and obedience to the voice of the Indwelling Presence which is our source of Inspiration, Power, Health, Prosperity." (International New Thought Alliance, A constitution and by-laws, 1916 in Charles W. Ferguson, *The New Books of Revelation,* page 168).

"I am an expression of Divine Life, and in vitality, body, and affairs I show forth the limitless love, power, and wisdom of my Father." (Paul Ellsworth, *The Gist of the New Thought,* quoted in Charles W. Ferguson, *The New Books of Revelation,* page 170).

THE ATONEMENT

"Nothing has been so lightly regarded as a thought, and yet we are thinking outwardly to the world and inwardly into a safe depository. The 'every idle word' for which men shall be judged, when rightly interpreted, is both a startling and a scientific truth. The judgment is not a great arbitrary formality, but an inherent and closefitting reality. Heavenly and hellish conditions are veritable products, and there is no way of escape through proxy or by means of a 'Scapegoat.' " (Wood, op. cit., page 47).

"Christ is the name of sonship — God, in us . . . But he was not a 'scapegoat,' substitute, nor an interposition." (Wood, op. cit., page 144).

THE HOLY SPIRIT

"We may relax all tension and make the whole attitude passive and receptive. If we invite spiritual influences they will flow in as naturally as air inclines to a vacuum. What a glorious experience! The 'still small voice' may become audible to our inner hearing. Can we have the 'Holy Spirit' upon such easy terms every day? (Wood, op. cit., page 36).

"Higher than all else, the conscious mind must learn to pour in a continual sense of the presence of the Universal Spirit of Wholeness (Theologically called the Holy Spirit), and this will surely quicken, cleanse, and level up the hidden and lagging power selfhood." (Wood, op. cit., page 52).

SALVATION

"We can keep closed to this divine inflow, to these higher forces and powers, through ignorance, most of us do, and thus hinder or even prevent their manifesting through us. . . . In the degree that we open ourselves to this divine inflow are we changed from mere men into God-men." (Trine, op. cit., pages 17, 18).

"God is in His heaven within you. You are His perfect son in a perfect world *now.* Let go the outer world and *know* Him within. *Let* go and let God work in you, through you, blessing all the world. . . . Spend your time *blessing* all the world, actively. Get busy *actively blessing* everybody." Elizabeth Towne, "Nautilus," as quoted in Charles W. Furguson, *The New Books of Revelation,* page 175).

THE RESURRECTION

". . . the resurrection takes place when the stone of the lower self-consciousness is rolled away. Here is the divine affinity which feels its oneness with God." (Wood, op. cit., page 182).

SIN

"People do not like to have their diseases connected with their life as a whole. They approve of the artificial separation which Christians have made for centuries between sin and sickness." (Dresser, op. cit., page 71).

"I continually suggest the good to myself. Day by day I extract it from seeming evil." (Wood, op. cit., page 175).

"God never made illness, disorder, nor discord any more than he created sin. They are not normal nor in the highest sense natural. They are man-made perversions." (Wood, op. cit., page 192).

"All those manifestations in mind or body which we call disorderly . . . Whether they occur consciously or through ignorance . . . We call them evil . . ." (Wood, op. cit., pages 54-55).

"Man is made in the image of the God, and evil and pain are but tests and cor-rectives that appear when his thoughts do not reflect the full glory of the image." (International New Thought Alliance, statement in convention, 1917, as quoted in Charles W. Ferguson, *The New Books of Revelation,* page 159).

THE REALITY OF MATTER: MATTER CAN BE CONTROLLED BY MIND

"I affirm spiritual freedom. . . I deny the slavery of sense, I repudiate the bondage of matter." (Wood, op. cit., page 178).

"I assert my freedom from the rule of the seen and temporary. . . . How has thou timidly groped thy way through material fogs and mists. . . . How thy whole horizon has been black with clouds which were only the shadows of thy dark thought and imaginations! . . . I — the real — am impervious to illness and to so-called death. Nothing in the universe can injure *me* but my own false and mistaken thinking." (Wood, op. cit., pages 174-175).

"The law of correspondence between spiritual and material things is wonderfully exact in its workings. People ruled by the mood of gloom attract to them gloomy things. . . . Rags, tatters, and dirt are always in the mind before being on the body." (Trine, op. cit., page 33).

FAITH

"Do you carry a chestnut or a potato in your pocket, or wear a special ring upon your finger to ward off rheumatism? Thousands of people — vastly more than are willing to admit it — do these and similar things, having a greater or less belief in their efficacy. And no matter how absurd, they have just as much power for good as belief bestows upon them." (Wood, op. cit., page 119).

"Believe *something,* for faithlessness is the most negative and hopeless of all the states of the soul." (Wood, op. cit., page 125).

HELL

"We cannot get out of or away from love. Omnipresent! . . . Man can shut it out of his own consciousness. The Bible calls this condition 'outer darkness.' It cannot exist unless one ignorantly makes it for himself." (Wood, op. cit., page 74).

PRAYER

"Every self-treatment for more life, health, and goodness is a prayer. It is not a begging for special bestowment, but rather a recognition that on the divine part everything already is perfect, and that we only need conformity." (Wood, op. cit., page 107).

Chapter 6

MORMONISM — THE LATTER DAY SAINTS

HISTORICAL PERSPECTIVE

The Church of Jesus Christ of Latter Day Saints is unique among all the religious cults and sects active in the United States in that is has by far the most fascinating history, and one worthy of consideration by all students of religions originating on the American continent.

The Mormons, as they are most commonly referred to, are divided into two major groups, The Church of Jesus Christ of Latter Day Saints, with headquarters in Salt Lake City, Utah, and The Reorganized Church of Jesus Christ of Latter Day Saints with headquarters in Independence, Missouri. Today, 134 years after its founding, the Mormons number more than 2,600,000 adherents, own considerable stock in the agricultural and industrial wealth of America, and circle the earth in missionary activities, energetically rivaling evangelical Christianity. The former group, which is the larger of the two, and which is the main concern of this volume, makes its headquarters in Salt Lake City, Utah, and claims a membership in excess of 2,000,000 as of January, 1964. The smaller group is rapidly approaching the half million mark and has won acceptance in some quarters as a "sect of fundamentalists." The Reorganized Church is briefly reviewed in this chapter, but there can be little doubt that it has gained ground in the last 25 years and is composed of a zealous group of dedicated people. They irritate the Utah Church consistently by pointing out that court decisions have established their claim that they are

the true church and Utah the schismatic. From its founding 134 years ago the Morman church has been characterized by thriftiness, zeal and an admirable missionary spirit, and even before the advent of World War Two, it had more than 2,000 missionaries active on all the mission fields of the world. Since the close of World War Two, however, and in keeping with the acceleration of cult propaganda everywhere, the Mormons have more than 15,000 "missionaries" active today, according to a statement published in 1964.

One interesting fact, however, accounts for this large missionary force and that is the practice of the Mormon Church to encourage its most promising young people, boys aged 20 and girls aged 23, to dedicate two years of their lives to missionary work on a self-supporting basis. In some cases the parents support the young people during this two-year tour of duty, but it is significant to note that approximately every two weeks some seventy to ninety young men and women begin such missionary activities.

Membership in the Mormon Church now increases each year at an average rate of 25,000 "conversions"; and the Mormons have a birth rate of 36.6 per thousand, in contrast to the average 24.9 birth rate of our nation.[1] According to the teaching of the Mormon Church, Mormons are to preserve their bodies always in the best of health and are cautioned against the use of tobacco and alcohol, and even the drinking of tea, coffee, and Coca-Cola. Strongly in-

---

[1] The growth of the Mormons since 1900 is an outstanding story. 1900—268,331; 1910—393,437; 1920—526,032; 1930—672,488; 1940—862,664; 1950—1,111,314; 1960—1,693,180; 1962—1,965,786; 1964—2,000,-000.

sistent upon the Old Testament principle of tithing, the Mormon Church requires all members to meet the Biblical one-tenth, with the result that in 1960 the church budget exceeded $20,000,-000, a tremendous figure for a comparatively small organization. The reader should bear in mind that the Mormons put this money to good use in the expansion of their church, a truth borne out by the fact that the church real estate holdings is in excess of 990 buildings, with 600-odd new ward halls contemplated in the near future. Three new Mormon chapels have been dedicated each week since the year 1950, the Mormons claim, and two new temples (England and New Zealand) are currently on the program. The "Saints" have a total of ten temples constructed or under construction throughout the world, and with their heavy emphasis upon education (Brigham Young University alone boasts more than 15,000 students), the Mormons are moving ahead in their battle to out-evangelize evangelical Christianity.

Promulgated as it is by determined, zealous, missionary-minded people who have a practical religion of "good works" and tolerance, the Mormons each year spend millions of dollars in the circulation of the teachings of their chief prophets, Joseph Smith and Brigham Young, while proselyting any and all listeners regardless of church affiliation. In addition to their regular tithing fund, the Mormon Church also encourages what it terms "fast offerings." This unusual practice involves the giving up of two meals on the first Sunday of each month, the price of which is turned over to the church as a voluntary contribution to support and feed the poor. On an annual basis, approximately 200,000 Mormons contribute to this fund, which averages between 700,-000 to a million dollars a year as a charity supplement for the poor.[2]

Since education ranks high in Mormon circles, the existence of their 240 "seminaries," for senior and junior high school students, staffed by 373,000 officers and teachers, is what could be expected of such systematic growth.

Mormonism, then, is not one of the cults tending to appeal merely to the uneducated, as for the most part Jehovah's Witnesses do, but instead it exalts education, which results in huge amounts of printed propaganda flowing from its presses in the millions of copies annually. The Mormons are also great chapel and temple builders, temples being reserved for the solemnization of marriage, proxy baptisms for the dead, and secret rites. Such temples are forbidden to "Gentiles" (a Mormon term for all non-Mormons) and are truly beautiful buildings, usually extremely costly both in construction and furnishings. Along with their strong emphasis on education, the Mormons believe in sports, hobbies, dramatics, music, homemaking courses for prospective brides, dances and dramatic festivals. The Mormon organization which sponsors a good deal of this is known as the Mutual Improvement Association and has sponsored over 16,000 dances, 600 dance festivals and 10,000 dramatic efforts. Each Mormon dance is begun with prayer and closed with the singing of a hymn. Mormonism does all that is humanly possible to make its church organization a home away from home for Mormon children and young people, and the absence of juvenile delinquency is in a marked proportion among Mormons, testifying to the success of their church-centered program.

Emphasizing as they do the importance of missions, the Mormon Tabernacle Choir has become famous and is well known to all radio listeners. The choir contains more than 375 singers and has a repertoire of 810 anthems. It

---

[2]The yearly income of the Mormon church on its business investments is 365 million dollars (*Newsweek* magazine, January 22, 1962, page 67).

is currently entering its thirty-first year of network broadcasting. Those who would tend to write off the Mormons as an influential force in the United States would do well to remember that Mormons have more adherents listed in *Who's Who in America* than any other one religion, and this also holds true for the scientific honor societies of our nation. Mormon leaders have become powerful in almost all branches of American government, headed by former Secretary of Agriculture, Ezra Taft Benson, one of the Twelve Apostles who govern the Mormon Church, U. S. Treasurer Ivy Baker Priest, former president of the U. S. Chamber of Commerce, Mariner S. Eccles, and Michigan Governor George Romney.

The Mormon Church also claims E. Lamar Buckner, president of Standard Oil of California. Far from being an organization with minor influence, the Mormons are indeed a potent force to be reckoned with, and few informed persons would be foolish enough to doubt this sphere of influence.

Church Organization

The organization and general administration of the Mormon Church is directed by the First Presidency (currently filled by 90-year-old David O. McKay), assisted by a Council of Twelve and a First Council of Seventy, consisting of seven men and a presiding bishop with two counselors. All authority resides in the Mormon "priesthood," established under the titles "Aaronic" (lesser) or "Melchizedek" (higher), to either one of which every male Mormon twelve years of age or over, belongs. The Mormon Church administration is divided into territories made up of "wards" and "stakes," the former consisting of from five hundred to a thousand people. Each ward is composed of districts known as "blocks" presided over by a bishop with two teachers as assistants.

The wards are all consolidated into stakes, supervised by a president and two counselors, aided in turn by twelve men known as "The Stake High Council." Today there are approximately 1950 wards, 175 stakes, 130 branches, and 42 missions functioning in the Mormon Church. These various auxiliary groups form a powerful coalition for mutual assistance among Mormons, and it is noteworthy that during the depression of 1929, the Mormon "storehouse" saw to it faithfully that none were in want for the necessities of life.

In their missionary program the Mormons continue to manifest great zeal. Missionaries are well trained in their dogmas and quote the Bible profusely. Thus it is that many true Christians have often unfortunately been literally quoted into silence by the clever disciples of Joseph Smith and Brigham Young, who flourish a pseudo-mastery of Scripture before the uninformed Christian's dazzled eyes and confuse him, sometimes beyond description.

In common with most cults, Mormonism has had its siege of persecutions and slander, but unlike many of the other cults who prefer to "let sleeping dogs lie" the Mormons have attempted at times to defend their "prophets." This has led them into more than one precarious historical dilemma.[3]

The average Mormon is usually marked by many sound moral traits. He is generally amiable, almost always hospitable, and extremely devoted to his family and to the teachings of his church. Sad to say, however, the great majority of Mormons are in almost total ignorance of the shady historical and theological sources of their religion. They are openly shocked at times when the unglamorous and definitely unchristian background of the Mormon Church is revealed to them. This little known facet of Mormonism is "a side of the coin" which innumerable Mormon historians

[3]See *The Mythmakers* by Hugh Nibley. This is a classic example of Mormon apologetics that requires a strong imagination as well as a strong stomach to digest.

have for years either hidden from their people or glossed over in an attempt to suppress certain verifiable and damaging historical evidences. Such evidence the author has elected to review in the interest of obtaining a full picture of Joseph Smith's religion.

Early Mormon History

The seeds of what was later to become the Mormon religion were incubated in the mind of one Joseph Smith, Jr., "The Prophet," better known to residents of Palmyra, New York, in 1816, as just plain "Joe Smith."

Born in Sharon, Vermont, December 23, 1805, fourth child of Lucy and Joseph Smith, the future Mormon prophet entered the world with the proverbial "two strikes" against him in the person of his father and his environment.

Joseph Smith, Sr., was a mystic, a man who spent most of his time digging for imaginary buried treasure (he was particularly addicted to Captain Kidd's legendary hoard!). Besides this failing he sometimes attempted to mint his own money, which at least once brought him into decided conflict with the local constabulary. This fact is, of course, well known to any informed student of Mormonism, and is bolstered by the testimony of the late Judge Daniel Woodward of the County Court of Windsor, Vermont, a former neighbor of the Smith family. Judge Woodward went on record in the Historical Magazine in 1870 with a statement to the effect that the elder Smith definitely was a treasure hunter and that "he also became implicated with one Jack Downing, in counterfeiting money, but turned state's evidence and escaped the penalty."

The mother of the future prophet was as much as her husband the product of the era and her environment, given as she was to extreme religious views and belief in the most trivial of superstitions. Lucy Smith later in her life "authored" a book entitled *Biographical Sketches of*

Joseph Smith and His Progenitors for Many Generations. When published by the Mormon Church in Liverpool, England, however, it incurred the enduring wrath of Brigham Young, the first successor to Smith, who brought about the suppression of the book on the grounds that it contained "many mistakes" and that "should it ever be deemed best to publish these sketches, it will not be done until they are carefully corrected" (*Millennial Star,* Volume XVII, page 298, personal letter dated January 31, 1858).

Mrs. Smith, of course, was totally incapable of writing such a work, the "ghost writing" being done by a Mrs. Carey, who faithfully recorded what came to be known as "Mother Smith's History." This work will be discussed as we progress, as also will the personal history of Joseph Smith, Jr. It is merely mentioned now to indicate the contradictory views held by the Mormon Church and by Smith's mother concerning the prophet's home life, background and religious habits.

I return now to the central character of our survey, Joseph Smith, Jr. The year 1820 proved to be the real beginning of the prophet's call, for in that year he was allegedly the recipient of a marvelous vision in which God the Father and God the Son materialized and spoke to young Smith as he piously prayed in a neighboring wood. The prophet records the incident in great detail in his book, *Pearl of Great Price* (page 2, verses 1 through 25), where he reveals that the two "personages" took a rather dim view of the Christian church, and for that matter of the world at large, and announced that a restoration of true Christianity was needed, and that he, Joseph Smith, Jr., had been chosen to launch the new dispensation.

It is interesting to observe that Smith could not have been too much moved by the heavenly vision, for he shortly took up once again the habit of digging for treasure along with his father and brother, who were determined to unearth Captain Kidd's plunder by means of "peep stones," "divining rods," or just plain digging.[4]

History informs us that the Smith clan never succeeded at these multitudinous attempts at treasure hunting, but innumerable craters in the Vermont and New York countryside testify to their apparent zeal without knowledge.

In later years, the "prophet" greatly regretted these superstitious expeditions of his youth and even went on record as denying that he had ever been a money-digger. Said Prophet Smith on one such occasion: "In the month of October, 1825, I hired with an old gentleman by the name of Josiah Stoal who lived in Chenango County in the State of New York. He had heard something of a silver mine having been opened by the Spaniards in Harmony, Susquehanna County, State of Pennsylvania, and had, previous to my hiring with him, been digging in order, if possible, to discover the mine. After I went to live with him, he took me among the rest of his hands to dig for the silver mine, for which I continued to work for nearly a month without success in our undertaking. Finally I prevailed with the old gentleman to cease digging for it. Hence arose the very prevalent story of my having been a money-digger."[5]

This explanation may suffice to explain the prophet's treasure hunting fiascos to the faithful and to the historically inept; but to those who have access to the facts, it is at once evident that Smith played recklessly, if not fast and loose, with the truth. In fact, it often appeared to be a perfect stranger to him. The main source for promoting skepticism where the veracity of the Prophet's explanation is concerned, however, is from no less an authority than Lucy Smith, his own mother, who, in her account of the very same incident, wrote

that "one, Mr. Stoal, came for Joseph on account of having heard that he possessed certain keys by which he could discern things invisible to the natural eye" (Linn, *The Story of the Mormons,* page 16).

Further evidence, in addition to Mrs. Smith's statement (and prima facie evidence, at that), proves beyond a reasonable doubt that the prophet was a confirmed "Peek Stone" addict, that he took part in and personally supervised numerous treasure-digging expeditions, and further that he claimed supernatural powers which allegedly aided him in these searches. To remove all doubt the reader may have as to Smith's early treasure hunting and "Peek Stone" practices, we shall quote three of the best authenticated sources which we feel will sustain our contention that Smith was regarded as a fraud by those who knew him best. It should also be remembered that Joseph Smith, Sr., in an interview, later published in the *Historical Magazine* of May, 1870, clearly stated that the prophet had been a Peek Stone enthusiast and treasure-digger in his youth, and, further, that he had also told fortunes and located lost objects by means of a "Peek Stone" and the alleged supernatural powers therein. Substantiating Joseph's father's account of his rather odd activities is the testimony of the Reverend Dr. John A. Clark after "exhaustive research" in the Smith family's own neighborhood.

"Long before the idea of a Golden Bible entered the Smith's minds, in their excursions for money-digging . . . Joe used to be usually their guide, putting into a hat a peculiar stone he had through which he looked to decide where they should begin to dig" (*Gleanings by the Way,* page 225, 1842).

Joseph Smith, Jr., in 1820, claimed a heavenly vision which, he said, sin-

---

[4]Peep Stones, or Peek Stones: supposedly magical rocks which when placed in a hat and partially darkened allegedly reveal lost items and buried treasure. Divining rods were sticks supposed to lead to treasure or water, etc.

[5]*Millennial Star,* Vol. XIV, Supplement, page 6.

gled him out as the Lord's anointed prophet for this dispensation, though it was not until 1823, with the appearance of the angel Moroni at the quaking Smith's bedside, that Joe began his relationship to the fabulous "golden plates," or what was to become the *Book of Mormon.*

According to Smith's account of this extraordinary revelation, which is recorded in *The Pearl of Great Price* (Chapter 2, verses 29-54), the angel Moroni, the glorified son of one Mormon, the man for whom the famous book of the same name is entitled, appeared beside Joseph's bedside and thrice repeated his commission to the allegedly awe-struck treasure hunter. Smith did not write this account down until some years later, but even that fails to excuse the blunder he made in transmitting the angelic proclamation. This confusion appears chiefly in the earlier editions of *Doctrine and Covenants* and *The Pearl of Great Price* wherein the former Moroni is named as messenger; yet in the latter Joseph, with equal prophetic authority, identifies the messenger as Nephi, an entirely different character found in the Book of Mormon! This unfortunate crossing up of the divine communication system was later remedied by thoughtful Mormon scribes who have exercised great care to ferret out all the historical and factual blunders not readily explainable in the writings of Smith, Young and other early Mormon writers. In current editions, therefore, both the "revelations" agree by identifying Moroni as the midnight visitor. However, whether Nephi or Moroni carried the message to Smith apparently makes little difference to the faithful.

In 1827 Smith claimed to receive the golden plates upon which the *Book of Mormon* is alleged to have been written. Shortly after this historic find, unearthed in the hill Cumorah near Palmyra, New York, Smith began to "translate" the "reformed Egyptian"[6] hieroglyphics inscribed thereupon by means of the "Urim and Thummin," a type of miraculous spectacles which the always-thoughtful angel Moroni had the foresight to provide for the budding seer. The account of how Smith went about "translating" the plates and of the attendant difficulties with one Martin Harris, his wife, and Professor Charles Anthon, a noted scholar, will be dealt with more fully later in this chapter. However, the plot is obvious to anyone who is even basically informed concerning the real character of Joseph Smith; so we will continue with the prophet's history.

During the period when Joseph was translating the plates (1827-29) one Oliver Cowdery, an itinerant school teacher, visited Smith at the home of his father-in-law (who after some months, for the sake of his daughter, had received Joseph into his home) where he was duly "converted" to the prophet's religion and soon after became the "scribe" who wrote down what Joseph said the plates read, in spite of the fact that he never actually saw them. In the course of time, Smith and Cowdery became fast friends; and the progression of their "translation" and spiritual zeal allegedly attained such heights that, on May 15, 1829, heaven could no longer restrain its joy; and so John the Baptist in person was speedily dispatched by Peter, James, and John to the humble state of Pennsylvania with orders to confer the "Aaronic Priesthood" on Joe and Oliver.

This amazing event is recorded in *The Pearl of Great Price* (Chapter 2, verses 68-73), following which Oliver baptized Joe and vice versa; and they apparently had a real time blessing one another and prophesying future events "which

---

[6]Reformed Egyptian is a non-existent language, according to every leading Egyptologist and philologist ever consulted on the problem. However, the Mormons still maintain their claim with the full knowledge that these are the facts.

should shortly come to pass." Smith was careful not to be too specific in recording these prophecies, because of the fact that more often than not, Mormon prophecies did not come in on schedule, which no doubt accounted for Smith's hesitancy in alluding to details.

From the now hallowed state of Pennsylvania, immortalized by Smith's initiation into the priesthood of Aaron by John the Baptist, Joe repaired shortly to the home of Peter Whitmer in Fayette, New York, where he remained until the "translation" from the plates was completed and the *Book of Mormon* published and copyrighted in the year 1830. On April 6th of this same year, the prophet, in company with his brothers, Hyrum and Samuel, Oliver Cowdery, and David and Peter Whitmer, Jr., officially founded a "New Religious Society" entitled The Church of Jesus Christ Latter Day Saints. Thus it was that one of the more virulent strains of American cults came into existence — Mormonism had begun in earnest.

Following this "momentous" occasion, a conference consisting of thirty men was called by the "prophet" on June 1, 1830, at which time missionary efforts were decided upon and some of the newly ordained elders were set aside to become missionaries to the Indians. In August of 1830 a zealous preacher, one Parley P. Pratt, was "converted" to Mormonism, and allegedly in September Sidney Rigdon, a powerful Campbellite preacher from Ohio, "saw the light" and "converted" his congregation to Smith's religion, which had begun to take root outside of New York State and Pennsylvania, for reasons which we shall view a little later on.

Sidney Rigdon and Parley Pratt, it should be noted, were almost from the day of their "conversions" slated for greatness in the Mormon hierarchy, as was Orson Pratt; and it is their writings, along with those of Young, Orson Pratt, Charles Penrose and James Talmage, which best argue in favor of the

Mormon cause, even to this very day. The role Sidney Rigdon played in the Mormon saga will be discussed in a later chapter, but it must be remembered that Rigdon was later accused of apostasy and excommunicated from the Mormon Church, largely because of his famous "Salt Sermon," which was delivered in 1833 in Jackson County, Missouri. In the course of its presentation, Rigdon soared to the heights of inflammatory rhetoric against the citizens of Jackson County, virtually challenging the whole state to do pitched battle with the "saints," who were subsequently terribly persecuted and expelled in November of 1833.

This volatile bit of rabble-rousing did Sidney no good with his fellow Mormons; and it became known rather bitterly as "Sidney's Salt Sermon." due to the fact that his text was drawn from Matthew and dealt with salt having lost its savor. Rigdon's devastating evaluation of "Prophet" Smith from the "inside" is a masterful piece of factual dissection and should be read by anyone tempted to deify the questionable character of the first Mormon prophet.

Shortly after the Fayette meeting, which officially began the Latter Day Saints, the nucleus of the Mormon Church moved to Kirtland, Ohio, where in a period of six years they increased to almost 1,600 souls. It was from Kirtland that Smith and Rigdon made their initial thrust into Jackson County, Missouri, which ended in the previously recounted disaster. Joe and Sidney were no strangers to persecution and suffered the indignity of an old fashioned "tar-and-feathering" accompanied by a trip out of town on the proverbial rail. While in Missouri, Smith purchased sixty-three acres which he deemed "holy ground" and there marked the exact spot on which he declared that the temple of Zion, the earthly headquarters of the kingdom of Jesus Christ, was eventually to be built. It is an interesting fact of history that one small branch of the

Mormon Church (Church of Temple Lot) today owns that temple site and claims that it once refused five million dollars from the Utah church for the "hallowed ground."

In Kirtland also the First Stake of Zion was established and a quorum of twelve apostles was chosen, presided over by a First Presidency of three, supervised by the president, Joseph Smith, the Seer. Chief reason for the Mormons moving to Kirtland, Ohio, however, was the extreme unpopularity of Smith and his revelations among the people who knew him best and who regarded his new religion as a sham and a hoax, thus hardly recommending them as prospective converts. Smith, of course, conjured up a revelation from God as authorization for the move. In fact, between the years 1831 to 1844, the "prophet" allegedly received 135 direct revelations from God, revelations which helped build the Mormon metropolis of Nauvoo, where the infamous practice of polygamy was instituted by Joseph Smith and confirmed by "divine revelation." Some misinformed persons have declared that Smith was not a polygamist, but one needs only to search the famous Berrian collection in the New York Public Library for volumes of primary information to the contrary, written by Mormon men and women who lived through many of these experiences and testified to the outright immorality of Smith and the leaders of the Mormon Church. Gradually, of course, polygamy filtered down through the entire Mormon Church so that it was necessary for the United States government to threaten to confiscate all Mormon property and to threaten them with complete dissolution in order to stamp out the then widely accepted practice.

In 1890, President Wilfrid Woodruff officially abolished polygamy as a practice of the Mormon Church, one concrete instance at least of the fact that the religious convictions of the Mormons were sacrificed for their political and economic survival, something seldom discussed in Mormon circles today. The facts still remain that in Kirtland, Nauvoo, Jackson County, etc., the Mormons had a chance to win converts to Smith's religion because they were strangers and the character of the prophet was unknown in those areas. But in New York, Smith was known by the most uncomplimentary terms, some of which have a direct bearing upon a proper understanding of his character. Pomeroy Tucker, in his classic work, *The Origin, Rise and Progress of Mormonism* (New York, 1867), collected a number of duly sworn statements by neighbors of the Smith family and by acquaintances of Joseph Smith, Jr., particularly. According to the unanimous consensus, Joseph, Jr., was known for "his habits of exaggeration and untruthfulness . . . by reason of the extravagancies of his statements, his word was received with the least confidence by those who knew him best. He could edit a most palpable exaggeration or marvelous absurdity with the utmost apparent gravity" (page 16).

One of the most interesting statements concerning the early life of the Smith family and of Joseph, Jr., was obtained by E. D. Howe, a contemporary of Smith's, who did tremendous research during the lifetime of Joseph which has never been successfully impugned by any Mormon historians. Smith himself never dared to answer Howe's charges, though they were well known to him, so great was the weight of contemporary evidence.

Mr. Howe obtained a statement signed by sixty-two residents of Palmyra, New York, one that cannot be ignored by any serious student of Mormonism:

"We, the undersigned, have been acquainted with the Smith family for a number of years while they resided near this place. We have no hesitation in saying that we consider them destitute of that moral character which ought to entitle them to the confidence of any community. They were particularly famous for visionary projects; spent much of their time in digging for money which they pretended was hidden in the earth, and a large excavation may be seen in the earth not far from their residence where they used to spend their time in digging for hidden treasure. Joseph Smith, Sr., and his son, Joseph, were particularly considered entirely destitute of moral character and addicted to vicious habits" (*Mormonism Unveiled,* Zanesville, Ohio, 1834, page 261).

Some persons reading this may feel that it is unfair to quote only one side of the story; what about those who are favorable to the Mormons, they will ask. In answer to this, the amazing fact is that *there exists no contemporary pro-Mormon statements from reliable and informed sources who knew the Smith family and Joseph intimately.* It has only been the over-wise Mormon historians, utilizing hindsight over a hundred-year period, who have been able to even seriously challenge the evidence of the neighbors, Joseph's father-in-law, and many ex-Mormons who knew what was going on and went on record with the evidence not even Mormon historians have bothered seriously to dispute.

As the Mormons grew and prospered in Nauvoo, Illinois, and as the practice of polygamy began to be known outside of the Mormon population, increasing distrust of Prophet Smith multiplied, so much so that one John C. Bennett, in 1842 boldly exposed the practice of polygamy at Nauvoo. When the prophet (or "general," as he liked to be known in this phase of his career) learned of this mounting criticism and destroyed its visible mouthpiece, an anti-Mormon publication entitled *The Nauvoo Expositor,* the State of Illinois intervened. The "prophet" and his brother, Hyrum, were placed in a jail in Carthage, Illinois, to await trial for their part in the wrecking of the *Expositor.* However, on June 27, 1844, a mob comprised of some two hundred persons stormed the Carthage jail and brutally murdered

Smith and his brother, Hyrum, thus forcing upon the vigorously unwilling prophet's head the unwanted crown of early martyrdom, thus insuring his perpetual enshrinement in Mormon history as a "true seer."

With the assassination of Joseph Smith, the large majority of Mormons accepted the leadership of Brigham Young, then forty-three years of age and the man who had previously led the Mormons to safety from the wrath of the Missouri citizenry.

In 1846, Young announced that the "saints" would abandon Nauvoo. In 1847, after a brutal trek through the wilderness of the Southwest, Young brought the Mormons to the valley of the great Salt Lake and with the exclamation, "This is the place!" sealed the destiny of the "saints" — they were in what was to become the state of Utah.

For more than thirty years, Brigham Young ruled the Mormon church, and as is still the case, he inherited the divinely appointed prophetic mantle of the first prophet. So it is that each succeeding president of the Mormon church claims the same authority as Joseph Smith and Brigham Young — an infallible prophetic succession.

The "spiritual deed" which the Mormons felt entitled them to possession of the valley of the great Salt Lake was "granted" in June of 1848 when the first Mormon crops were largely saved from a plague of locusts by a vast armada of sea gulls; thus, according to Mormon teaching, God gave visible evidence of His blessing upon the Latter Day Saints' Church.

We cannot, of course, discuss the history of the Mormons under Brigham Young in great detail because that would easily necessitate a full volume by itself, but suffice it to say that Smith gave the movement its initial thrust and Brigham Young supplied the needed momentum necessary to establish it as a bona fide religion. Young himself was a character of many facets, and one cannot understand the theology of Mormonism without understanding the tremendous influence exercised upon it by the person of "Prophet" Young and his teachings. Smith and Young, in company with the pronouncements of the succeeding presidents, have made Mormon theology what it is, and apart from Brigham Young, Mormonism cannot be thoroughly understood.

Young was a man of indomitable courage, possessed of a canny nature, but given to fits of ruthlessness now conveniently forgotten by Mormon historians. One such evidence of his determination to control Utah was the order which he gave to massacre 150 non-Mormon immigrants in what has now become known as the infamous Mountain Meadows massacre. In this particular instance, for reasons known only to himself, Young entrusted to Bishop John D. Lee in 1857 the task of annihilating a wagon train of virtually helpless immigrants. This Bishop Lee did faithfully, and 20 years later he was imprisoned, tried, convicted and executed by the government of the United States for this vicious, totalitarian action.

In his memorable book, *The Confessions of John D. Lee,* a consistent sore spot in the Mormon scheme of historical "reconstruction," Lee confessed to his part in the infamous doings, but he charged that he acted upon the orders of Brigham Young. However, the testimony of Lee and of some of his lieutenants and others connected with the massacre indicates beyond question that Young ordered and sanctioned the action. As we further study Mormon theology, it will become apparent that this was not at all beyond the limits of Young's character; he was the law in Utah; and as it has been so wisely observed, "Power corrupts and absolute power corrupts absolutely."

Mormonism today, then, is a far cry from quite a number of the principles and practices of its early founders. To be sure, it remains faithful to their basic tenets, but, as in the case of polygamy, when those tenets come in conflict with government statutes or political influence, the Latter Day Saints have wisely chosen to ignore (the word commonly used is "re-interpret") the counsels of their two chief prophets. The history of the Mormons is a vast and complex subject; it is a veritable labyrinth of books, testimonies, affidavits, photographs, hearsay and opinions, and it is only after the most careful analysis of the contemporary evidence that a picture emerges consistent with verifiable facts. For the average Mormon, one can but have sympathy and regard. He is, by and large, honest, industrious, thrifty and zealous in both the proclamation and promulgation of his beliefs. One only regrets that he has accepted at face value a carefully edited "history" of the origin and doctrinal development of his religion instead of examining the excellent sources which not only contradict but irrefutably prove the falsity of what is most certainly a magnificent reconstructed history. It is to be hoped that as we further study the unfolding drama of Mormon doctrine, and the basis of such doctrine, the reader will come to appreciate the evolution of Mormonism and the pitfalls which most certainly exist in taking at face value the gospel according to Joseph Smith and Brigham Young. The verdict of history, then, is overwhelmingly against the Mormon version, particularly where Smith and Young are concerned; and there is a vast amount of documentation the Mormons seem content to ignore, but the facts themselves remain too well verified to be ignored.

A NEW REVELATION — THE MORMON BIBLE

Aside from the King James Version of the Bible, which the Mormons accept as part of the Word of God "insofar as it is correctly translated," they have added *Doctrine and Covenants, The Pearl of Great Price* and the Primary volume, the *Book of Mormon,* to the canon of what they would call authorized Scripture. The last mentioned is a subject of this chapter since it occupies a primary place in Mormon theology and therefore must be carefully examined. A great deal of research on the part of a number of able scholars and organizations has already been published concerning the *Book of Mormon,* and I have drawn heavily upon whatever documented and verifiable information was available. The task of validating the material was enormous, and so I have selected that information which has been verified beyond refutation and is available today in some of our leading institutions of learning (Stanford University, Union Theological Seminary, the Research Departments of the Library of Congress, the New York Public Library, and others).

It is a difficult task to evaluate the complex structure of the *Book of Mormon,* and the reader is urged to consider the bibliography at the end of this volume if he should desire further and more exhaustive studies.

The Story of the Ancient People

The *Book of Mormon* purports to be a history of two ancient civilizations which were located on the American continent. According to the Mormon version, the first of these great civilizations left the tower of Babel (about 2,250 B.C. by Mormon reckoning), crossed over into Europe and emigrated to the eastern coast of what we know as Central America.

The second group allegedly left Jerusalem somewhere in the neighborhood of 600 B.C. before the destruction of the city and the Babylonian captivity of Israel. That group is alleged to have crossed the Pacific Ocean, landing on the continent of South America in what

is now known as the country of Peru. According to the Mormons, the *Book of Mormon* is a condensation of the high points of these civilizations. The author of the book was a prophet named Mormon. The book is "the translation of the abridgment of the record of these civilizations" and "includes a brief outline of the history of the earlier Jaredite people, an abridgment made by Moroni, son of Mormon, taken from the Jaredite record found during the period of the second civilization."

The Jaredites were destroyed as the result of "corruption" and were punished for their apostasy, their civilization undergoing total destruction.

The second group, who came to America about 600 B.C., were righteous Jews, the leader of which group was named Nephi. This group eventually met a fate similar to the Jaredites' and were divided into two warring camps, the Nephites and the Lamanites (Indians). The Lamanites received a curse because of their evil deeds, and the curse took the form of dark skins.

The Mormon's record claims that Christ visited the American continent, revealed Himself to the Nephites, preached to them the Gospel, instituted baptism, the communion service, the priesthood and other mystical ceremonies.

The Nephites, unfortunately, proved to be no match for the Lamanites; and they were defeated by them and annihilated in a great battle near the hill Cumorah in Palmyra, New York, approximately A.D. 428.

Some fourteen hundred years later, the Mormons claim, Joseph Smith, Jr., unearthed Mormon's abridgment which was written in reformed Egyptian hieroglyphics upon plates of gold, and with the aid of Urim and Thummin (supernatural spectacles) translated the reformed Egyptian into English. It thus became the *Book of Mormon* which was published in 1829, bearing the name of Joseph Smith, Jr., as translator.

Lest there be any confusion, there are three classes of record plates which were allegedly revealed to Smith: (1) the plates of Nephi, (2) the plates of Mormon, and (3) the plates of Ether; and a fourth set of plates mentioned throughout the *Book of Mormon* known as the brass plates of Laban.

The plates of Nephi recorded mostly the secular history, although the smaller plates of Nephi allegedly recorded sacred events. The second group is an abridgment from the plates of Nephi which was made by Mormon and which included his commentaries and additional historical notes by his son, Moroni. The third set of plates recorded the history of the Jaredites, also abridged by Moroni, who added his own comments. It is now known as the *Book of Ether.*

The fourth set of plates are alleged to have come from Jerusalem and appear in the form of extracts in Nephite records. They are given over to quotations from the Hebrew Scriptures and genealogies.

Joseph Smith is alleged to have received the plates from the hand of Moroni, "a resurrected personage," in the year 1827.

Purpose of the Book

The purpose of the *Book of Mormon* and its mission generally eludes Christian theologians, archaeologists, and students of Anthropology because of the many difficulties which the book introduces in the light of already established facts. But a Mormon explanation of the purpose of the book ought to be considered:

> It is a principle of divine and civil law that, "In the mouth of two or three witnesses every word shall be established" (II Corinthians 13:1). The Bible, its history of the dealings and providences of God with man upon the eastern continent, is one witness for the truth. The Book of Mormon is another witness to the same effect. It recites that providences of God in the basic and vastly important matter of redemption,

as also in general in the laws of nature, and indicates that such provisions were not limited, not confined to the Eastern world. ' God so loved the *world"* (John 3:16), not a mere portion of it, that he likewise ministered in behalf of the race in the great western continent. Being the seat of mighty civilizations, it was entitled to and partook of the ministrations of the Father of the race.

The stated purpose of the *Book of Mormon* (in its introduction) is universal: to witness to the world the truth and divinity of Jesus Christ, and his mission of salvation through the gospel He taught. Its witness is for Jew and Gentile. The house of Israel rejected its Messiah, and in consequence was rejected, scattered, and the government overthrown. The gospel refused by them was then preached to the Gentiles. Israel has ever since remained in unbelief in Christ and without the ministration of inspired men. Bible prophecy frequently declares their restoration in the latter days to divine favor, the gathering of Israel and their permanent establishment in their ancient homeland of Palestine. The sealed book, the *Book of Mormon,* is predicted by Bible prophecy and by its own declarations to be a confirming, additional revelation from God of the Messiahship of Jesus Christ, and of the covenants made with their fathers. It repeatedly predicts regathering, restoration, and other manifold blessings to Israel. The God of Israel is to make a "new covenant" with that people — not the old Mosaic covenant, but another and later one, by which they are to be reinstated as a nation in their holy land. (See also Jeremiah 31:34; Ezekiel 20:33-38, etc., Bible predictions to the same effect.) The *Book of Mormon* interprets Old Testament prophecy to that effect, as it recites predictions of its inspired men. It claims to be part of the new covenant to Israel.

It claims to be the sealed book of Isaiah, chapter 29, which it quotes and interprets. It recites that as a result of its revealment, Israel would come to understanding of the Christ message of salvation; that they would no longer fear but be secured and greatly blessed by divine favor; that the coming forth of its record would be followed by physical blessing upon Palestine to its redemption from sterility to fertility, and thus made capable of maintaining that nation as in ancient times. It is a fact that since the appearance of the book that land has been favored. It produces abundantly. The Jews are now permitted to return and establish cities and industrial and agricultural units. Many Jews, according to predictions of the book, are beginning to believe in Christ. Proponents of the book state that with such predictions fulfilled it is now too late for any similar fulfillment by another record.

The book declares also that the remnants of the former inhabitants of Ancient America, scattered throughout North, Central, and South America — the Indian populations — will by means of the coming to light of the record of their fathers, be converted to the faith and share in the covenants made with their progenitors. It indicates their emergence from primitive conditions to enlightenment. It declares that the Gentile nations occupying their lands would favor their emancipation from degenerate conditions. This is part of the purpose of the book.

The Gospel of Saint John 10:16 contains a statement of Jesus Christ quoted by believers in the divinity of the *Book of Mormon*. It reads: "And *other sheep I have, which are not of this fold*: them also I must bring, and *they shall hear my voice*: and there shall be one fold, and one shepherd." Citing also that Christ declared these words: "I am not sent but unto the lost sheep of the house of Israel" (Matthew 15:24), they believe that since Jesus Christ, according to the record, never appeared to the Gentiles, and "salvation is of the Jews," or Israel (John 4:22), the promise concerning "other sheep" was realized by the appearance of Christ to the Nephites.[7]

For the Mormons, then, the Bible predicts the *Book of Mormon;* the *Book of Mormon* interprets Old Testament prophecy and it claims to be part of the new covenant to Israel. It is also supposed to be "another witness" to the truth of the Christian Gospel. It is unfortunate for the Mormons that this witness is so often found in conflict with the Biblical revelation, as we shall see. It is at the very least a gross assumption

unjustified by any of the internal evidence of the book or the testimony of science and history, that the *Book of Mormon* should be considered "part of the new covenant" in any sense.

Scientific Evidence Against the Book of Mormon

In an attempt to validate and justify the claims of the *Book of Mormon,* the highest authority in Mormonism, Joseph Smith, Jr., the Mormon prophet, related an event which, if true, would add significant weight to some of the Mormon claims for their Bible. Fortunately, it is a fact on which a good deal of evidence can be brought to bear.

Smith put forth his claim in the book, *The Pearl of Great Price;* and it is worthwhile to examine it:

> . . . I commenced copying the characters off the plates. I copied a considerable number of them, and by the means of the Urim and Thummin I translated some of them . . . Martin Harris came to our place, got the characters which I had drawn off the plates, and started with them to the city of New York. For what took place relative to him and the characters, I refer to his own account of the circumstances, as he related them to me after his return, which was as follows: "I went to the city of New York, and presented the characters which had been translated, with the translation thereof, to Professor Charles Anthon, a gentleman celebrated for his literary attainments. Professor Anthon stated that the translation was correct, more so than any he had before seen translated from the Egyptian. I then showed him those which were not yet translated, and he said that they were Egyptian, Chaldaic, Assyriac and Arabic; and he said they were true characters." (Chapter 2, verses 62, 63, 64.)

According to Joseph Smith then, Martin Harris, his colleague, obtained from the learned Professor Charles Anthon of Columbia University a validation of Smith's translation of the

[7]*The Book of Mormon* by R. S. Salyards, Sr., Herald House, Independence, Missouri, pages 13-16.

reformed Egyptian hieroglyphic characters found on the plates which Moroni made available to him. The difficulty with Smith's statement is that Professor Anthon never said any such thing, and fortunately he went on record in a lengthy letter to Mr. E. D. Howe, a contemporary of Joseph Smith who did one of the most thorough jobs of research on the Mormon prophet and the origins of Mormonism extant. Howe has never been refuted, and because of this he is feared and hated by Mormon historians and not a few contemporary Mormons.

Upon learning of Smith's claim concerning Professor Anthon, Mr. Howe wrote him at Columbia. Professor Anthon's letter reproduced here from Howe's own collection is a classic piece of evidence the Mormons would like very much to see forgotten.

New York, N. Y., Feb. 17, 1834
Mr. E. D. Howe
Painseville, Ohio
Dear Sir:

I received this morning your favor of the 9th instant, and lose no time in making a reply. The whole story about my having pronounced the Mormonite inscription to be "reformed Egyptian hieroglyphics" *is perfectly false.*[8] Some years ago, a plain, and apparently simplehearted farmer, called upon me with a note from Dr. Mitchell of our city, now deceased, requesting me to decipher, if possible, a paper, which the farmer would hand me, and which Dr. Mitchell confessed he had been unable to understand. Upon examining the paper in question, I soon came to the conclusion that *it was all a trick, perhaps a hoax.* When I asked the person, who brought it, how he obtained the writing, he gave me, as far I can now recollect, the following account: A "gold book," consisting of a number of plates of gold, fastened together in the shape of a book by wires of the same metal, had been dug up in the northern part of the state of New York, and along with the book an enormous pair of "gold spectacles"! These spectacles were so large, that, if a person attempted to look through them, his two

eyes would have to be turned towards one of the glasses merely, the spectacles in question being altogether too large for the breadth of the human face. Whoever examined the plates through the spectacles, was enabled not only to read them, but fully to understand their meaning. All this knowledge, however, was confined at that time to a young man, who had the trunk containing the book and spectacles in his sole possession. This young man was placed behind a curtain, in the garret of a farm house, and, being thus concealed from view, put on the spectacles occasionally, or rather, looked through one of the glasses, deciphered the characters in the book, and, having committed some of them to paper, handed copies from behind the curtain, to those who stood on the outside. Not a word, however, was said about the plates having been deciphered "by the gift of God." Everything, in this way, was effected by the large pair of spectacles. The farmer added, that he had been requested to contribute a sum of money towards the publication of the "golden book," the contents of which would, as he had been assured, produce an entire change in the world and save it from ruin. So urgent had been these solicitations, that he intended selling his farm and handing over the amount received to those who wished to publish the plates. As a last precautionary step, however, he had resolved to come to New York, and obtain the opinion of the learned about the meaning of the paper which he brought with him, and which had been given him as a part of the contents of the book, although no translation had been furnished at the time by the young man with the spectacles. *On hearing this odd story, I changed my opinion about the paper, and, instead of viewing it any longer as a hoax upon the learned, I began to regard it as part of a scheme to cheat the farmer of his money, and I communicated my suspicions to him, warning him to beware of rogues.* He requested an opinion from me in writing, which of course I declined giving, and he then took his leave carrying the paper with him. *This paper was in fact a singular scrawl. It consisted of all kinds of crooked characters disposed in columns, and had evidently*

[8]Italics are the author's for emphasis.

been prepared by some person who had before him at the time a book containing various alphabets. Greek and Hebrew letters, crosses and flourishes, Roman letters inverted or placed sideways, were arranged in perpendicular columns, and the whole ended in a rude delineation of a circle, divided into various compartments, decked with various strange marks, and evidently copied after the Mexican Calendar given by Humboldt, but copied in such a way as not to betray the source whence it was derived. I am thus particular as to the contents of the paper, inasmuch as I have frequently conversed with my friends on the subject, since the Mormonite excitement began, and well remember that *the paper contained anything else but "Egyptian Hieroglyphics."* Some time after, the same farmer paid me a second visit. He brought with him the golden book in print, and offered it to me for sale. I declined purchasing. He then asked permission to leave the book with me for examination. I declined receiving it, although his manner was strangely urgent. I adverted once more to the roguery which had been in my opinion practiced upon him, and asked him what had become of the gold plates. He informed me that they were in a trunk with the large pair of spectacles. I advised him to go to a magistrate and have the trunk examined. He said the "curse of God" would come upon him should he do this. On my pressing him, however, to pursue the course which I had recommended, he told me that he would open the trunk, if I would take the "curse of God" upon myself. I replied that I would do so with the greatest willingness, and would incur every risk of that nature, provided I could only extricate him from the grasp of rogues. He then left me.

I have thus given you a full statement of all that I know respecting the origin of Mormonism, and must beg you, as a personal favor, to publish this letter immediately, should you find my name mentioned again by these wretched fanatics.

Yours respectfully,
Charles Anthon, LL.D.
Columbia University.

Professor Anthon's letter is both revealing and devastating where Smith's and Harris' veracity are concerned. We might also raise the question as to how Professor Anthon could say that the characters shown to him by Martin Harris and authorized by Joseph Smith as part of the material copied from the revelation of the *Book of Mormon* were "Egyptian, Chaldaic, Assyriac, and Arabic" when the *Book of Mormon* itself declares that the characters were "reformed Egyptian," the language of the Nephites. Since the language of the *Book of Mormon* was known to "none other people," how would it be conceivably possible for Professor Anthon to have testified as to the accuracy of Smith's translation? To this date, no one has ever been able to find even the slightest trace of the language known as "reformed Egyptian"; and all reputable linguists who have examined the evidence put forth by the Mormons have rejected them as mythical.

Archeological Evidence

The *Book of Mormon* purports to portray the rise and development of two great civilizations. As to just how great these civilizations were, some excerpts from the book itself adequately illustrate:

"The whole face of the land had become covered with buildings, and the people were as numerous almost, as it were the sands of the sea" (Mormon 1:7).

". . . fine workmanship of wood, in buildings, and in machinery, and also in iron and copper, and brass, and steel, making all manners of tools . . ." (Jarom 1:8 and 2 Nephi 5:15).

". . . grain, silks . . . cattle, oxen, cows . . . sheep . . . swine . . . goats . . . horses . . . asses . . . elephants . . ." (See Ether 9:17-19).

". . . did multiply and spread — began to cover the face of the whole earth, from the sea south to the sea north, from the sea west to the sea east" (Helaman 3:8).

". . . two million Jaredites slain . . ." (See Ether 15:2).

". . . their shipping and their building of ships, and their building of temples, and of synagogues and their sanctuaries . . ." (Heleman 3:14. See also 2 Nephi 5:15, 16 and Alma 16:13).

". . . tens of thousands of the Nephites slain" (See Mormon 6:10-15).

". . . swords . . . cimeters . . . breastplates . . . arm-shields . . . shields . . . head-plates . . . armor" (See Alma 43: 18, 19; 16:13 and Ether 15:15).

". . . multiplied exceedingly, and spread upon the face of the land, and became exceeding rich . . ." (Jarom 1:8).

". . . cities and inhabitants sunk in the depths of the sea . . ." and "cities and inhabitants sunk in depths of the earth . . ." (See 3 Nephi 8:9, 10, 14 and 9:4, 5, 6, 8).

In addition to the foregoing statements from the *Book of Mormon* which indicate the tremendous spread of the culture of these races, there are some thirty-eight cities catalogued in the *Book of Mormon,* evidence that these were indeed mighty civilizations which should, by all the laws of archeological research into the culture of antiquity, have left vast amounts of "finds" to be evaluated. But such is not the case as we shall show. The Mormons have yet to explain the fact that leading archeological researchers not only have repudiated the claims of the *Book of Mormon* as to the existence of these civilizations, but have adduced considerable evidence to show the impossibility of the accounts given in the Mormon Bible.

The following letter was addressed to the Rev. R. Odell Brown, pastor of the Hillcrest Methodist Church, Fredericksburg, Virginia, an ardent student of Mormonism and its claims. Dr. Brown, in the course of his research, wrote to the Department of Anthropology at Columbia University in New York City. The answer he received is of great importance in establishing the fact that the *Book of Mormon* is neither accurate nor truthful where the sciences of archeology and anthropology are concerned.

Dear Sir:

Pardon my delay in answering your letter of January 14, 1957. The question which you ask concerning the *Book of Mormon* is one that comes up quite frequently. . . . However, . . . I may say that I do not believe that there is a single thing of value concerning the prehistory of the American Indian in the *Book of Mormon* and I believe that the great majority of American archeologists would agree with me. The book is untrue Biblically, historically and scientifically,

Concerning Dr. Charles Anthon of Columbia University, I do not know who he is and would certainly differ with his viewpoint, as the Latter Day Saints (Mormons) tell it. What possible bearing Egyptian hieroglyphics would have on either the *Book of Mormon* or the prehistory of the American Indian I do not know . . . I am,

Very sincerely yours,
Wm. Duncan Strong (Signed).

The Smithsonian Institution in Washington has also added its voice against the archeological claims of the *Book of Mormon.* Such a highly regarded scientific source the Mormons can ill afford to ignore.

There is no correspondence whatever between archeological sites and cultures as revealed by scientific investigations, and as recorded in the *Book of Mormon.* Interpretations of archeological and ethnographic data, moreover, are quite unlike the American prehistory which the *Book of Mormon* describes . . . It can be stated definitely that there is no connection between the archeology of the New World and the subject matter of the *Book of Mormon* . . . The Smithsonian Institution has never used the *Book of Mormon* in any way as a scientific guide. Smithsonian archeologists see no connection between the archeology of the New World and the subject matter of the book . . . We know of no authentic cases of ancient Egyptian or Hebrew writings having been found in the New World. Reports of findings of Egyptian influence in the Mexican and Central America areas have been published in newspaper and magazines from time to time, but thus far no reputable Egyptologist has been able to discover any relationship between Mexican remains and those in Egypt.

With respect to some of the questions which you have raised pertaining to the story in the *Book of Mormon* relating to aboriginal occupation in the New World, I may say that thus far no iron, steel, brass, gold and silver coins, metal, swords, breast-plates, arm shields, armor, horses and chariots, or silk *have ever been found* in pre-colonial archeological sites. It is not until *after* the conquest of the New World by Europeans that materials in those categories appear in association with aboriginal artifacts. As a matter of fact, there are not many such objects occurring in historic sites. Furthermore, cattle, sheep, swine, horses and asses, such as we know them, *were introduced in the Americas by Europeans in post-Columbian times.* No actual elephants have been found in *any* archeological site . . . I do not know of any case where an archeological site has been identified with any of the names of the cities mentioned in the *Book of Mormon.* The most likely ruined cities would be those in the Maya area, and they all have native names which do not correspond to those in your list. It is possible that some of the anthropologists at Brigham Young University who have done some work in the Maya area may have attempted such a correlation, but if so I have not seen it reported. None of the main workers in the field have made any reference to the possibility of one of the well-known ruins being those of a city mentioned in the *Book of Mormon.*

(Letters from the Smithsonian Institution as recorded in *The Book of Mormon Examined* by Arthur Budvarson, Utah Christian Tract Society, 1959, pages 35 and 36).

From this evidence, it is clear that the cities mentioned in the *Book of Mormon* are imaginary, that elephants never existed on this continent, and that the metals described in the *Book of Mormon* have never been found in any of the areas of contemporary civilizations of the New World. Here is not a theologian attempting to discredit the Mormons on the basis of their theology, but recognized archeological experts challenging

the *Book of Mormon* on the basis of the fact that its accounts are not in keeping with the findings of science. Mormon missionaries are generally reluctant to discuss these areas when the evidence is well known, but evidence it is and from most authoritative sources.

The Mongoloid Factor

It is one of the main contentions of Mormon theology that the American Indians are the descendants of the Lamanites and that they were of the Semitic race, in fact of Jewish origin. As we have seen, this claim is extensive in Mormon literature; and if evidence could be adduced to show that the American Indian could not possibly be of Semitic extraction, the entire story of Nephi and his trip to America in 600 B.C. would be proven false.

It is, therefore, of considerable value to learn that in the findings compiled by anthropologists and those who specialize in genetics, the various physical factors of the Mediterranean races from which the Jewish or Semitic race spring bear little or no resemblance to those of the American Indian! Genotypically, there is therefore little if any correlation, and phenotypically speaking the American Indians are considered to be *Mongoloid* in extraction, not Mediterranean Caucasoids.

Now, if the Lamanites, as the *Book of Mormon* tells it, were the descendants of Nephi, who was a Jew of the Mediterranean Caucasoid type, then their descendants, the American Indians, would by necessity have the same blood factor genotypically; and phenotypic, or apparent characteristics, would be the same. But this is not at all the case. Instead, the American Indian, so say anthropologists, is not of Semitic extraction and has the definite phenotypical characteristic of a Mongoloid. A thorough study of anthropology and such writers as W. C. Boyd (The Contributions of Genetics to Anthropology) and Bentley Glass, the gifted geneticist of Johns Hopkins University, reveals that the Mormon claims based upon the *Book of Mormon* are out of harmony with the findings of geneticists and anthropologists. There simply is no foundation for the claims that the American Indian (Lamanites according to the Mormons) is in any way related to the race to which Nephi (a Semite) allegedly belonged.

Corrections, Contradictions and Errors

There is a great wealth of information concerning the material contained in the *Book of Mormon* and the various plagiarisms, anachronisms, false prophecies and other unfortunate practices connected with it. At best then we can give but a condensation of that which has been most thoroughly documented.

Since the publication of the *Book of Mormon* in 1830, the first edition has undergone extensive "correction" in order to present it in its present form. Some of these "corrections" should be noted.

1. In the book of Mosiah, chapter 21, verse 28, it is declared that "King Mosiah had a gift from God"; but in the original edition of the book, the name of the king was Benjamin — an oversight which thoughtful Mormon scribes corrected. This is, of course, no typographical error as there is little resemblance between the names Benjamin and Mosiah; so it appears that either God made a mistake when He inspired the record or Joseph made a mistake when he translated it. But the Mormons will admit to neither, so they are stuck, so to speak, with the contradiction.

2. I Nephi 19:16-20:1, when compared with the edition of 1830, reveals more than fifty changes in the "inspired *Book of Mormon*," words having been dropped, spelling corrected, and words and phraseology added and turned about. This is a strange way to treat an inspired revelation from God!

3. In the book of Alma 28:14-29:1-11, more than thirty changes may be counted from the original edition, and

on page 303 of the original edition the statement, "Yea, decree unto them that decrees which are unalterable," has been expurged. (See Alma 29:4)

4. On page 25 of the edition of 1830, the *Book of Mormon* declares:

"And the angel said unto me, Behold the Lamb of God, yea, even the eternal Father."

Yet in I Nephi 11:21, the later editions of the book read:

"And the angel said unto me: Behold the Lamb of God, yea even the son of the eternal Father!"

5. The Roman Catholic Church should be delighted with page 25 of the original edition of the *Book of Mormon* which confirms one of their dogmas, namely, that Mary is the mother of God.

"Behold, the virgin which thou seest, is the mother of God."

Noting this unfortunate lapse into Romanistic theology, considerate Mormon editors have changed I Nephi 11:18 so that it now reads:

"Behold, the virgin whom thou seest, is the mother of the son of God."

From the foregoing which are only a handful of examples of the more than two thousand changes to be found in the *Book of Mormon* over a period of 131 years, the reader can see that it is in no sense to be accepted as the Word of God. The Scripture says: "The word of the Lord endureth for ever" (I Peter 1:25); and our Saviour declared:

"Sanctify them through thy truth: thy word is truth" (John 17:17).

The record of the Scripture rings true. The *Book of Mormon,* on the other hand, is patently false in far too many places to be considered coincidence.

Added to the evidence of various revisions, the *Book of Mormon* also contains plagarisms from the King James Bible, anachronisms, false prophecies and errors of fact which cannot be dismissed. Some of these bear repetition, though they are well known to students of Mormonism.

The testimony of the three witnesses which appear at the front of the *Book of Mormon* (Oliver Cowdery, David Whitmer, and Martin Harris) declares that "an angel of God came down from heaven, and he brought and laid before our eyes, that we beheld and saw the plates, with the engraving thereon."

It is quite noteworthy that Martin Harris, in his conversation with Professor Anthon relative to the material "translated" from these miraculous plates, denied that he had actually seen them. In fact, when pressed, he stated that he only saw them "with the eye of faith," which is vastly different from a revelation by an angelic messenger.

The Mormons are loath to admit that all three of these witnesses later apostatized from the Mormon faith and were described in most unflattering terms ("thieves and counterfeiters") by their Mormon contemporaries.

A careful check of early Mormon literature also reveals that Joseph Smith and his brother Hyrum wrote three articles against the character of the witnesses of the *Book of Mormon*, which, in itself, renders their testimony suspect if not totally worthless.

Plagiarisms—The King James Version

According to a careful survey of the *Book of Mormon*, it contains at least 25,000 words from the King James Bible. In fact, verbatim quotations, some of considerable length, have caused the Mormons no end of embarrassment for many years.

The comparison of Moroni chapter 10 with I Corinthians 12:1-11, II Nephi 14 with Isaiah 4, and II Nephi 12 with Isaiah 2 reveals that Joseph Smith made free use of his Bible to supplement the alleged revelation of the golden plates. The book of Mosiah, chapter 14 in the *Book of Mormon*, is a reproduction of the fifty-third chapter of Isaiah the prophet; and III Nephi 13:1-18 copies Matthew 6:1-23.

The Mormons naively suggest that when Christ allegedly appeared on the American continent after His resurrection and preached to the Nephites he quite naturally used the same language as recorded in the Bible. They also maintain that when Nephi came to America he brought copies of the Hebrew Scriptures, which account for quotations from the Old Testament. The only difficulty with these excuses is that the miraculous plates upon which they were all inscribed, somehow or another, under translation, came out in perfect King James English without variation approximately a thousand years before this 1611 version was written. Such reasoning on the part of the Mormons strains at the limits of credulity and only they are willing to believe it.

There are other instances of plagiarisms from the King James Bible including paraphrases of certain verses. One of these verses (I John 5:7) is reproduced in III Nephi 11:27, 36. The only difficulty with the paraphrase here is that the text is considered by scholars to be an interpolation missing from all the major manuscripts of the New Testament but present in the King James Bible from which Smith paraphrased it not knowing the difference.

Another example of this type of error is found in III Nephi 11:33-34, and is almost a direct quotation from Mark 16:16, a passage now known to be an addition to that gospel by an overzealous scribe. But Joseph Smith was not aware of this either, so he even copied in translational errors, another proof that neither he nor the alleged golden plates were inspired of God.

Two further instances of plagiarisms from the King James Bible which have backfired on the Mormons are worth noting.

In the third chapter of the book of Acts, Peter's classic sermon at Pentecost paraphrases Deuteronomy 18:15-19. While in the process of writing III Nephi, Joseph Smith puts Peter's paraphrase in the mouth of Christ when the

Saviour was allegedly preaching to the Nephites. The prophet overlooked the fact that at the time that Christ was allegedly preaching his sermon, the sermon itself had not yet been preached by Peter.

In addition to this, III Nephi makes Christ out to be a liar, when in verse 23 of chapter 20 Christ attributes Peter's words to Moses as a direct quotation when, as we have pointed out, Peter paraphrased the quotation from Moses; and the wording is quite different. But Joseph did not check far enough, hence this glaring error.

Secondly, the *Book of Mormon* follows the error of the King James translation which renders Isaiah 4:5: "For upon all the glory shall be a defence" (See II Nephi 14:5).

Modern translations of Isaiah point out that it should read "For over all the glory there will be a canopy," not a defence. The Hebrew word, "chuppah," does not mean defence but a protective curtain or canopy, Smith, of course, did not know this nor did the King James translators from whose work he copied.

There are quite a number of other places where such errors appear, including Smith's insistence in Abraham 1:20 that "Pharaoh signifies king by royal blood," when in reality the dictionary defines the meaning of the term Pharaoh as "a great house or palace."

The Revised Standard Version of the Bible renders Isaiah 5:25: "And their corpses were as refuse in the midst of the streets," correctly rendering the Hebrew *suchah* as refuse, not as "torn." The King James Bible renders the passage: "And their carcases were torn in the midst of the streets." The *Book of Mormon* (II Nephi 15:25) repeats the King James' text word for word, including the error of mistranslating *suchah,* removing any claim that the *Book of Mormon* is to be taken seriously as reliable material.

Anachronisms and Contradictions

Not only does the *Book of Mormon* plagiarize heavily from the King James Bible, but it betrays a great lack of information and background on the subject of world history and the history of the Jewish people. The Jaredites enjoyed "glass" windows in the miraculous barges in which they crossed the ocean; and "steel" and a "compass" were known to Nephi despite the fact that neither had been invented, demonstrating once again that Joseph Smith was a poor student of history and of Hebrew customs.

Laban, one of the characters of the *Book of Mormon* (I Nephi 4:9), makes use of a steel sword; and Nephi himself claims to have had a steel bow (the Mormons justify this by quoting Psalm 18:34 as a footnote in the *Book of Mormon*), but modern translations of the Scripture indicate that the word translated steel in the Old Testament (since steel was non-existent) is more properly rendered bronze.

Mormons sometimes attempt to defend Nephi's possession of a compass (not in existence in his time) by the fact that Acts 28:13 states: "And from thence we fetched a compass." Modern translations of the Scripture, however, refute this subterfuge by correctly rendering the passage: "And from there we made a circle."

Added to the preceding anachronisms is the fact that the *Book of Mormon* not only contradicts the Bible, but contradicts other revelations purporting to come from the same God who inspired the *Book of Mormon.* The Bible declares that the Messiah of Israel was to be born in Bethlehem (Micah 5:2), and the gospel of Matthew (chapter 2, verse 1) records the fulfillment of this prophecy. But the *Book of Mormon* (Alma 7:9, 10) states:

". . . the son of God cometh upon the face of the earth. And behold, he shall be born of Mary, at Jerusalem, which is the land of our forefathers . . ."

The *Book of Mormon* describes Jerusalem as a city (I Nephi 1:4) as was Bethlehem, so the contradiction is irreconcilable.

There are also a number of instances where God did not agree with Himself, if indeed it is supposed that He had anything to do with the inspiration of the *Book of Mormon, The Pearl of Great Price, Doctrine and Covenants,* or the other recorded utterances of Joseph Smith.

In the *Book of Mormon,* for instance, (III Nephi 12:2 and Moroni 8:11) the remission of sins is the result of baptism:

"Yea, blessed are they who shall . . . be baptized, for they shall . . . receive the remission of their sin . . . Behold baptism is unto repentance to the fulfilling of the commandments unto the remission of sin."

But in the book, *Doctrine and Covenants.* (Chapter 20, verse 37) the direct opposite is stated:

"All who humble themselves . . . and truly manifest by their works that they have received of the spirit of Christ unto the remission of their sins, shall be received by baptism into his church."

This particular message from the heavenlies almost provoked a riot in the Mormon Church, and Mormon theologians conspicuously omit any serious discussion of the contradiction.

Joseph Smith did not limit his contradictions to baptism; indeed polygamy is a classic example of some of his maneuvers.

"God commanded Abraham, and Sarah gave Hagar to Abraham to wife. And why did she do it? Because this was the law; and from Hagar sprang many people . . . Go ye, therefore, and do the works of Abraham; enter ye into my law and ye shall be saved" (*Doctrine and Covenants,* Section 132, Verses 34 and 32).

The *Book of Mormon,* on the other hand, categorically states:

"Wherefore, I the Lord God will not suffer that this people should do like unto them of old . . . for there shall not any man among you have save it be one wife; and concubines he shall have none; for I, the Lord God, delight in the chastity of woman" (Jacob 2:26-28).

It appears that Joseph could manufacture revelations at will, depending upon his desires. In the last instance, his reputation and subsequent actions indicate that sex was the motivating factor.

A final example of the confusion generated between the *Book of Mormon* and the other "inspired" revelations is found in the conflict between the book of Moses and the book of Abraham.

"I am the beginning and the end, the Almighty God; by mine only begotten I created these things; yea, in the beginning I created the heaven and the earth upon which thou standest" (Moses 2:1).

The book of Abraham, on the other hand, repudiates this monotheistic view and states:

"And when the Lord said: Let us go down. And they went down at the beginning, and they, that is the gods, organized and formed the heavens and the earth" (Abraham 4:1).

Just how it is possible to reconcile these two allegedly equal pronouncements from Mormon revelation escapes this author, and the Mormons themselves appear reluctant to furnish any concrete explanation.

The question of false prophecies in Mormonism has been handled adequately in a number of excellent volumes, but it should be pointed out that Joseph Smith drew heavily upon published articles both in newspapers and magazines. In fact, one of his famous prophecies concerning the Civil War is drawn chiefly from material published in New York State at the time..

Smith declared in *Doctrine and Covenants,* Section 87:

"At the rebellion of South Carolina . . . the Southern states would call on other nations, even the nation of Great Britain . . . and then war shall be poured out upon all nations . . . And slaves shall rise up against their masters . . . And . . . the remnants . . . shall vex the Gentiles with the sword of fixation."

Though the Civil War did break out some years after Smith's death (1844), England did not become involved in war against the United States. "All nations" were not involved in war as prophesied. The slaves did not rise up against "their masters," and the "remnants" who were Indians were themselves vexed by the Gentiles, being defeated in war and confined to reservations.

Prophet Smith was an extremely ineffective prophet here, as he was when in *Doctrine and Covenants* he also prophesied that he would possess the house he built at Nauvoo "for ever and ever" (Section 124, verses 22, 23, and 59).

The fact of the matter is that neither Joseph nor his seed "after him" lived from "generation to generation" in Nauvoo house, which was destroyed after Smith's death, and the Mormons moved on to Utah.

These, and other instances, indicate that Smith was not only a poor scribe but a false prophet, and his prophecy concerning the restoration of Israel to Palestine clearly reveals that he anticipated the millennium in his own lifetime, whereas in reality the prophecy of Ezekiel 37 began to be fulfilled in 1948, more than a hundred years after Smith's death.

The question quite naturally arises in summing up the background of the *Book of Mormon* — Where did the book come from, since it obviously did not come from God? The answer to this had been propounded at great length by numerous students of Mormonism, particularly E. D. Howe, Pomeroy Tucker and William A. Linn.

All concur that the *Book of Mormon* is probably an expansion upon the writings of one Solomon Spaulding, a retired minister who was known to have written a number of "romances" with Biblical backgrounds similar to those of the *Book of Mormon.* The Mormons delight to point out that one of Spaulding's manuscripts, entitled "Manuscript Story," was discovered in Hawaii some seventy-seven years ago, and it differed in many respects from the *Book of Mormon.*

But in his excellent volume (*The Book of Mormon?*), Dr. James D. Bales makes the following observation, which is of great importance and agrees in every detail with my research over the last decade:

It has long been contended that there is a connection between the *Book of Mormon* and one of Solomon Spaulding's historical romances. The Latter Day Saints, of course, deny such a connection.

What if the Latter Day Saints are right and there is no relationship between the *Book of Mormon* and Spaulding's writings? It simply means that those who so contend are wrong, but it proves nothing with reference to the question as to whether or not the *Book of Mormon* is of divine origin. One could be wrong as to what man, or men, wrote the *Book of Mormon,* and still know that it was not written by men inspired of God. One can easily prove that the *Book of Mormon* is of human origin. And, after all, this is the main issue. The fundamental issue is not *what* man or men wrote it, but whether it was written by men who were guided by God. We know that men wrote it, and that these men, whoever they were, did not have God's guidance.

This may be illustrated by *Science and Health With Key to the Scriptures* — the textbook of Christian Science churches. Mrs. Eddy claims to have been its author, under God's direction. There are others who claim she reworked and enlarged manuscripts by Mr. Quimby and Francis Lieber. The evidence seems to prove that such is the case. But what if those who so maintained failed to prove their case? Would that prove that *Science and Health* was inspired of God? It would prove only that Quimby's manuscript had nothing to do with it. But it would not prove that some other uninspired being did not write it. Regardless of what human being or beings wrote *Science and Health*, it is of human, not divine origin. Just so the *Book of Mormon* is of human origin and uninspired, even though it were impossible to prove what particular man wrote it.

It has not been maintained that the *Book of Mormon* was written by Spaulding. Thus, it has not been claimed that the theological portions were put in by him. Those portions bear the imprint of Smith, Cowdery and Sidney Rigdon (see the proof offered in Shook's *The True Origin of the Book of Mormon*, pages 126-). It is maintained, however, that some things, including a great deal of Scripture, were added to one of Spaulding's manuscripts and that his work was thus transferred into the *Book of Mormon* (see the testimony of John Spaulding, Solomon's brother; Martha Spaulding, John's wife: They maintained that the historical portion was Spaulding's. (E. D. Howe, *Mormonism Unveiled*, 1834, pages 278-; Shook, *The True Origin of the Book of Mormon*, pages 94-).

The Mormons contend that the discovery of one of Spaulding's manuscripts demonstrates that it was not the basis of the Book of Mormon.

"I will here state that the Spaulding manuscript was discovered in 1884, and is at present in the Library of Oberlin College, Ohio. On examination it was found to bear no resemblance whatever to the *Book of Mormon*. The theory that Solomon Spaulding was the author of the *Book of Mormon* should never be mentioned again—outside a museum." (William A. Morton, *op. cit.*, page 6.)

There are three errors in the above paragraph: viz, that Spaulding wrote but one manuscript; that the manuscript discovered in 1884 is the one which non-Mormons have claimed constituted the basis of the *Book of Mormon;* that the manuscript in Oberlin bears no resemblance whatever to the *Book of Mormon*.

(a) *Spaulding wrote more than one manuscript.* This was maintained by D. P. Harlburt and Clark Braden before

the Honolulu manuscript was found (Charles A. Shook, *op. cit.*, page 77). Spaulding's daughter also testified that her father had written "other romances." (Elder George Reynolds, *The Myth of the "Manuscript Found."* Utah, 1833, page 104). The present manuscript story looks like a rough, unfinished, first draft.

(b) *The manuscript found in Honolulu was called a "Manuscript Story" and not the "Manuscript Found."* This Honolulu manuscript, *The Manuscript Story*, was in the hands of anti-Mormons in 1834. However, they did not claim that it was the manuscript which was the basis of the *Book of Mormon*. It was claimed that another manuscript of Spaulding was the basis of the *Book of Mormon*, (Charles A. Shook, *op. cit.*, pages 77, 15, 185. The *"Manuscript Found or Manuscript Story"* of the late Rev. Solomon Spaulding. Lamoni, Iowa: Printed and Published by the Reorganized Church of Jesus Christ of Latter-day Saints, 1885, page 10.)

(c) Although the *Manuscript Story* has not been regarded as the *Manuscript Found* which constituted the basis of the *Book of Mormon* there is a great deal of resemblance between the *Manuscript* and the *Book of Mormon*. These points of similarity can be accounted for upon the basis that the *Manuscript Story* was the first, and rough draft of one of Spaulding's works which he reworked into the *Manuscript Found*.

"Howe, in 1834, published a fair synopsis of the Oberlin manuscript now at Oberlin (Howe's *Mormonism Unveiled*, 288) and submitted the original to the witnesses who testified to the many points of identity between Spaulding's *Manuscript Found* and the *Book of Mormon*. These witnesses then (in 1834) recognized the manuscript secured by Harlburt and now at Oberlin, as being one of Spaulding's, but not the one which they asserted was similar to the *Book of Mormon*. They further said that Spaulding had told them that he had altered his original plan of writing by going farther back with his dates and writing in the old scripture style, in order that his story might appear more ancient." (Howe's *Mormonism Unveiled*, page 288). (Theodore Schroeder, *The Origin of the Book of Mormon, Re-Examined in Its Relation to Spaulding's "Manuscript Found,"* page 5.)

This testimony is borne out by the fact that there are many points of similarity between the manuscript in Oberlin College and the Book of Mormon.[9]

It is then fairly well established, historically, that the Mormons have attempted to use a manuscript admittedly *not* the one from which Smith later copied and amplified the text of what is now known as the *Book of Mormon* as the basis for denying what eye witnesses have affirmed, namely that it was another Spaulding Manuscript (*Manuscript Found*) which Smith drew upon to fabricate the Mormon Bible.

Dr. Bales is right when he states:

There are too many points of similarity for them to be without significance. Thus, the internal evidence, combined with the testimony of witnesses, as presented in Howe's book and reproduced in Shook's, show that Spaulding revised the Manuscript Story. The revision was known as the *Manuscript Found*, and it became the basis of the *Book of Mormon* in at least its historical parts. Also its religious references furnished in part the germs of the religious portions of the *Book of Mormon*.

However, in ordinary conversation, and in public debate on the *Book of Mormon*, it is unnecessary to go into the question of who wrote the *Book of Mormon*. The really important issue is whether or not the *Book of Mormon* is of divine origin. There are some Mormons who seem to think that if they can prove that Spaulding's manuscript had nothing to do with the *Book of Mormon*, they have made great progress toward proving its divine origin. Such, however, is not the case. And one should show, from an appeal to the Bible, and to the *Book of Mormon* itself, that the *Book of Mormon* is not of divine origin.[10]

Let us not forget that the *Manuscript Story* itself contains at least 75 similarities to what is now the *Book of Mormon* and this is not to be easily explained away.

Finally, students of Mormonism

must, in the last analysis, measure its content by that of Scripture, and when this is done it will be found that it does not "speak according to the law and the testimony" (Isaiah 8:20) and it is to be rejected as a counterfeit revelation doubly condemned by God Himself (Galatians 1:8, 9).

Joseph Smith, the author of this "revelation," was perfectly described (as was his reward) in the Word of God almost thirty-three hundred years before he appeared. It would pay the Mormons to remember its message:

If there arise among you a prophet, or a dreamer of dreams, and giveth thee a sign or a wonder,

And the sign or the wonder come to pass, whereof he spake unto thee, saying, Let us go after other gods, which thou hast not known, and let us serve them;

Thou shalt not hearken unto the words of that prophet, or that dreamer of dreams: for the LORD your God proveth you, to know whether ye love the LORD your God with all your heart and with all your soul.

Ye shall walk after the LORD your God, and fear him, and keep his commandments, and obey his voice, and ye shall serve him, and cleave unto him.

And that prophet, or that dreamer of dreams, shall be put to death; because he hath spoken to turn you away from the LORD your God, which brought you out of the land of Egypt, and redeemed you out of the house of bondage, to thrust thee out of the way which the LORD thy God commanded thee to walk in. So shalt thou put the evil away from the midst of thee.

If thy brother, the son of thy mother, or thy son, or thy daughter, or the wife of thy bosom, or thy friend, which is as thine own soul, entice thee secretly, saying, Let us go and serve other gods, which thou has not known, thou, nor thy fathers;

Namely, of the gods of the people which are round about you, nigh unto thee, or far off from thee, from the one end of the earth even unto the other end of the earth;

Thou shalt not consent unto him, nor

---

[9]*The Book of Mormon?* by James D. Bales, Ph.D., The Manney Company, Fort Worth 14, Texas, pages 138-142.

[10]*The Book of Mormon?* by James D. Bales, Ph.D., pages 146-7.

hearken unto him; neither shall thine eye pity him, neither shalt thou spare, neither shalt thou conceal him:

But thou shalt surely kill him; thine hand shall be first upon him to put him to death, and afterwards the hand of all the people.

And thou shalt stone him with stones, that he die; because he hath sought to thrust thee away from the LORD thy God, which brought thee out of the land of Egypt, from the house of bondage (Deuteronomy 13:1-10).

The *Book of Mormon*, then, stands as a challenge to the Bible because it adds to the Word of God and to His one revelation, and the penalty for such action is as sobering as it is awesome:

For I testify unto every man that heareth the words of the prophecy of this book, If any man shall add unto these things, God shall add unto him the plagues that are written in this book:

And if any man shall take away from the words of the book of this prophecy, God shall take away his part out of the book of life, and out of the holy city, and from the things which are written in this book.

He which testifieth these things saith, Surely I come quickly. Amen. Even so, come, Lord Jesus (Revelation 22:18-20).

We need not make this a personal issue with the Mormons but a historical and theological issue which, for all the politeness and tact demonstrably possible, cannot conceal the depth of our disagreement. Even the famous "witnesses" to the veracity of the *Book of Mormon* are impugned by history, since Prophet Smith wrote two articles against them and Hyrum, his brother, wrote one. This does not speak well for the characters of those concerned, nor for their reliability as witnesses.

It was Joseph Smith who declared theological war on Christianity when he ascribed to God the statement that branded all Christian sects as "all wrong," their creeds as "abominations,"

and all Christians as "corrupt . . . having a form of godliness but denying the power thereof" (Writings of Joseph Smith 2:1-25).

The onus of hostility rests upon the Mormons, and their history of persecution (largely the result of their mouthing of Smith's abusive accusations and their practice of polygamy) may be properly laid at their own doorstep. They were the initial antagonists, *not* the Christian Church. We do not excuse those who persecuted the early Mormons, but they were in a great many instances provoked to action by Mormon excesses. (Note: An example of this would be the Mormon expulsion from Jackson County, Missouri.)

We may, then, safely leave the Mormon Bible to the judgment of history and Mormon theology to the pronouncements of God's immutable Word. But we must speak the truth about these things and keep foremost in our minds the fact that the sincerity of the Mormons in their faith is no justification for withholding just criticism of that faith or of its refuted source, the *Book of Mormon* and the "revelations" of Joseph Smith. The truth must be spoken in love, but it must be spoken.

THE THEOLOGY OF MORMONISM

The Mormon church almost from its inception has claimed what no other church today claims to possess, namely, the priesthoods of Aaron and Melchizedek.

The Mormons maintain that Joseph Smith and Oliver Cowdery received the Aaronic priesthood from the hand of John the Baptist on May 15, 1829, and that "the Melchizedek priesthood was conferred upon Joseph Smith and Oliver Cowdery through the ministration of Peter, James and John shortly after the conferring of the Aaronic order."[11]

In the theology of Mormonism, both

---

[11]*Priesthood and Church Government*, John A. Widtsoe, *Deseret* Book Company, 1939, page 107.

the Melchizedek and Aaronic orders are considered to be but one priesthood (*Doctrine and Covenants,* Section 84, Verse 17), and through the authority of this priesthood alone, they maintain "lay men speak and act in the name of the Lord for the salvation of humanity." In order that this may be clearly understood, the following quotation from the leading Mormon volume on the subject of the priesthood must be considered:

"This authoritative priesthood is designed to assist men in all of life's endeavors, both temporal and spiritual. Consequently, there are divisions or offices of the priesthood, each charged with definite duties, fitting especially in the need.

"The Prophet Joseph Smith once said that all priesthood is Melchizedek. That is to say that the Melchizedek priesthood embraces all offices and authorities in the priesthood. This is clearly stated in the *Doctrine and Covenants,* Section 107, Verse 5: 'All other authorities or offices in the church are appendages to this priesthood.'

There are two priesthoods spoken of in the Scriptures, the Melchizedek and the Aaronic or Levitical. Although there are two priesthoods, yet the Melchizedek priesthood comprehends the Aaronic or Levitical priesthood; and as the grand head holds the highest authority which pertains to the priesthood, and the keys of the kingdom of God in all ages of the world to the latest prosperity on the earth; it is the channel through which all knowledge, doctrine, the plan of salvation, and every important matter are revealed from heaven."[12]

The Mormon concept of the priesthood, then, holds that God has placed in that church presidents, apostles, high priests, seventies, elders; and that the various offices all share specific authorities.

The president of the church, they maintain, "may hold and dispense the powers of the administrative responsibilities of that office, the power of the priesthood is decentralized; first according to offices in the jurisdiction of those respective offices; second according to individual priesthoods — theirs. This means that while the church as a whole is delicately responsive to central authority for church-wide purposes, the central, local relationships in the organization do not restrict the full initiative and free development of either territorial divisions of the church, individual quorums, groups of quorums, or the member as an individual . . . The priesthood provides a functional instrumentality for church government which is at once efficient in responsiveness and centralization, but flexible and decentralized in actual administration."[13]

It is apparent, then, that in Mormon theology the priesthood occupies a position of great importance and comprehends every male member of the church above the age of twelve in one capacity or another; and therefore by necessity the refutation of the Mormon claims to its possession undercuts the very foundations of Mormonism.[14]

With the foregoing in mind, let us examine the Scriptures which most thoroughly refute the Mormon contentions, and the Scripture indeed provides a wealth of information.

In the seventh chapter of the epistle to the Hebrews, Melchizedek, who was the king of Salem and priest of the Most High God is mentioned briefly in connection with Abraham. The author of Hebrews points out that the priesthood of Melchizedek is superior to the Aaronic priesthood and the administrations of the Levites because Abraham,

---

12*Ibid.,* page 103.

13*Ibid.,* page 103.

14Negroes, however, are denied the priest-

hood because of a curse upon their race (their skin color) and no Negro can attain to exaltation (godhood) or celestial marriage.

who was the father of the sons of Levi paid tithe to Melchizedek. This establishes the fact that Melchizedek was superior to Abraham. The writer of Hebrews puts it this way: "And without all contradiction the less is blessed of the better. And here men that die receive tithes; but there he receiveth them, of whom it is witnessed that he liveth. And as I may so say, Levi also, who receiveth tithes, paid tithes in Abraham. For he was yet in the loins of his father, when Melchizedek met him" (Verses 7-10).

The establishment of the fact that the Melchizedek priesthood is superior to the Aaronic would be virtually meaningless unless the writer of Hebrews had gone on to say:

"If therefore perfection were by the Levitical priesthood, (for under it the people received the law,) what further need was there that another priest should rise after the order of Melchizedek, and not be called after the order of Aaron? For the priesthood being *changed*, there is made of necessity a change also of the law."

The whole point of the seventh chapter of Hebrews, as any careful exegesis will reveal, is the fact that Jesus Christ who is "a priest forever after the order of Melchizedek" (verse 17) has, by virtue of His sacrifice upon the cross, changed the priesthood of Aaron (verse 12), instituting in its place His own priesthood of the Melchizedek order.

Christ was not of the tribe of Levi and not of the priesthood of Aaron; He was of the tribe of Judah, yet His priesthood is infinitely superior to that of Aaron. It is quite evident that the Levitical priesthood could not evolve into the Melchizedek priesthood, but that it passed away as symbolized by the tearing of the veil leading to the Holy of Holies at the crucifixion (Matthew 27:51).

The writer of Hebrews further states that Christ is our great High Priest and that He has "passed through the heavenlies" to "appear in the presence of God for us." In addition to this, it is declared that "Christ is not entered into the holy places made with hands, which are the figures of the true; but into heaven itself . . . Nor yet that he should offer himself often, as the high priest entereth into the holy place every year with blood of others; for then must he often have suffered since the foundation of the world: but now once at the end of the ages hath he appeared to put away sin by the sacrifice of himself" (Hebrews 9:24-26).

The previous reference is clearly to the truth that the old priesthood, which enabled the priests to enter into the temple apartment once every year on the day of atonement, had come to a close because Christ has once offered an eternal atonement for the sins of all the world (I John 2:2).

How significant indeed are these facts when placed beside the Mormon claim to possession of the Aaronic priesthood which God's Word says has been "changed" and completely consummated in that Priest whose order is after Melchizedek, Jesus Christ Himself.

Our Lord's priesthood is not dependent upon its continuation from father to son, as the Aaronic was through the Levitical order, something which was necessitated by virtue of the fact that all men die; hence its transference. But the writer of Hebrews tells us that the Lord Jesus Christ "arose after the similitude of Melchizedek." He is "another priest" who is made "not after the law of carnal commandment," (which is temporary by nature,) but after the power of imperishable life. The Greek word, *akatalutou,* is rightly translated "imperishable, indestructible and indissoluble"; and in this context it refers to His life. He was not consecrated a priest as were the Levites from father to son, but His priesthood is after the order of endless Being. His is an infinite priesthood because He is eternal.

All this background is of vital importance in refuting the Mormon claims to the perpetuity of the Aaronic priesthood, but even more so in refuting their concept of the Melchizedek priesthood which they also claim to have received.

In the same seventh chapter of Hebrews, this second Mormon claim is tersely dispensed with by the Holy Spirit in an emphatic and irrevocable manner.

"By so much was Jesus made a surety of a better testament. And they truly were many priests, because they were not suffered to continue by reason of death: But this man, because he continues forever, has an unchangeable priesthood. Wherefore he is able to save them to the uttermost that come unto God by him, seeing he ever lives to make intercession for them. For such an high priest became us, who is holy, harmless, undefiled, separate from sinners, and made higher than the heavens; who need not daily, as those high priests, to offer up sacrifice, first for his own sins and then for the people's: for this he did once, when he offered up himself. For the law makes men high priests which have infirmity, but the word of the oath, which was since the law, makes the Son, who is consecrated for evermore" (verses 22-28).

Particular attention should be paid to verse 24, which, in the Greek, is devastating to the Mormon claim. Verse 24, in Greek, literally reads:

"But he continues forever, so his priesthood is untransferable"[15] (Goodspeed).

The Greek word, *aparabatos,* literally rendered as *untransferable,* carries the note of finality. Thayer's Greek-English Lexicon puts it this way:

"Priesthood unchangeable and therefore not liable to pass to a successor, Hebrews 7:24" (Page 54).

Since the word appears but once in New Testament Greek, there is not even the appeal to possible contextual renderings. Here is one instance where no amount of semantic juggling can escape the force of the context and grammar.

The writer of Hebrews, under the inspiration of the Holy Spirit, declares that the priesthood of Melchizedek is the peculiar possession of Jesus Christ, not only by virtue of the fact that He is God, and possessed of imperishable life, but because it cannot be transferred to another. It consummated the Aaronic priesthood; it terminated the Levitical order; it resides in the Son of God, and by the will of His Father, it cannot be transferred. There is no escape from the force of these revelations of Scripture, and no exegetical theologian or commentator has ever held otherwise. It is all well and good for the Mormons to claim the priesthoods of Aaron and Melchizedek, but it should be pointed out that they do so by contradicting the expressed teaching of the Word of God which they claim to respect. And this discrepancy no Mormon theologian has ever attempted to explain.

In his interesting and informative booklet, *Gods, Sex, and Saints,* Dr. George Arbaugh makes the following observation. "The Mormons are advised that the harvest is ripe and that the sickle should be thrust into the Christian churches. The bold proselyting usually includes certain stereotyped challenges, questions and arguments."

Dr. Arbaugh then goes on to point out that the priesthood is one of the areas the Mormons emphasize. They never tire of stating to any and all who will listen, particularly to those who are likely proselytes, "You do not have the priesthood!"

To answer this, the alert Christian should point out that the Mormons

---

[15]The Mormon claim that Melchizedek conferred his priesthood on Abraham when the latter paid tithe to him (Genesis 18) finds no support in Scripture. (*Priesthood and Church Government,* John A. Widtsoe, page 109). Mormons should be pressed at this juncture for the Biblical evidence, the absence of which affords further opportunity to undercut their already weakened position.

themselves do not have any priesthood but that the Church of Jesus Christ has always had a priesthood, a priesthood very clearly taught in the New Testament. This priesthood was emphasized by the great Reformation theologian, Martin Luther, who described it as "the priesthood of all believers."

Dr. Arbaugh rightly observes:

"There are many millions more priests in the Lutheran Church than in the Latter Day Saint organization, for this reason that every believer is a priest. There is a universal priesthood of believers. This means that each believer can come to God in prayer, in his own right, and that he can speak about his Lord to his fellow men. He need not wait for some priest to do the essential Christian things for him. For that matter how could any priest do the essential Christian thing for you, namely, to love God and your fellow man also?

"In the original Mormon Church the only officers were elders, but subsequently many additional offices were established. For this reason *Doctrine and Covenant,* Section 20, Paragraphs 65 through 67, was 'corrected' from the original form in the Book of Commandments. Mormonism even stoops to falsifying its scriptures in order to pretend that there have been the same priestly offices in all ages" (Page 44).

The True Priesthood

In the opening sentences of the book of the Revelation, John the Apostle makes an astounding statement when he declares:

"Blessing and peace to you from him who is, and was, and is coming, and from the seven spirits before his throne and from Jesus Christ, the trustworthy witness, the first born of the dead, the sovereign of the kings of the earth. To him who loves us and has released us from our sins by his own blood — he has made us a kingdom of priests for his God and Father — to him be glory and power forever" (Goodspeed, verses 4-6).

How incisive is this plain declaration by apostolic authority. Jesus Christ who is the sovereign of the kings of the earth, the one who continues to love us and who has released us from our sins through His own blood, has also made us "a kingdom of priests for His God and Father." Here is the true priesthood indeed.

The Christian does not need any temples, secret services, rituals, and mysteries. His priesthood knows no special offices and power to communicate with the dead, something which the Mormon priesthood most definitely claims (See *Leaves from the Tree,* a catechism for young people by the president, Charles Penrose, page 38). The Christian priesthood embraces all those who have been loosed from their sins by the blood of Jesus Christ, and who enjoy the perpetual love of the Lamb of God who takes away the sins of the world.

This concept is further developed in the writings of Peter, who affirms that:

"You are the chosen race, the *royal priesthood,* the consecrated nation, his own people, so that you may declare the virtues of him who has called you out of darkness into his wonderful light; you who were once no people, but are now God's people; once unpitied, but now pitied indeed . . ." (I Peter 2:9 and 10, Goodspeed).

In this context, the words of the apostle establish that long before there were any mythological Mormon priesthoods, there was a priesthood embracing all the redeemed, a "royal priesthood," neither Aaronic nor Melchizedekian. This priesthood is composed of all consecrated "ambassadors for Christ," to quote the Apostle Paul, whose task it is to exhort men to "be reconciled to God," "knowing the terror of the Lord" (II Corinthians 5:20 and 11).

As has been observed, Mormonism places great stress upon the priesthood. But as we have also seen, it is not the priesthood described in the Scriptures.

Instead they have substituted the revelation of "Prophet" Smith concerning a priesthood which has been changed (Hebrews 7:12) and a priesthood which by its nature is "untransferable" (7:24). The resulting dilemma is that they have no priesthood at all since their denial of the true deity of Jesus Christ and the nature of God rules out the possibility that they could share in the priesthood of all believers. In order for one to be one of the "kingdom of priests to God His Father" (Revelation 1:4-6) and a member of the "royal priesthood" (I Peter 2:9, 10), one must first have undergone personal regeneration in a saving encounter or experience with the God-man of Scripture — Jesus Christ. Mormon theology with its pantheon of gods, its perverted view of the Virgin Birth, and its outright condemnation of all churches as "abominations" (*The Writings of Joseph Smith*, Section 2, Verses 1-25) removes itself from serious consideration as a form of Christianity. There is more to Christianity than the application of the Christian ethic. There is a great deal more to the Gospel than the similarity of terms, albeit re-defined. Christianity is not just a system of doctrinal pronouncements (though they are of vast importance). It is a living vital experience with the God of the Bible as He was incarnate in the man from Nazareth. Mormonism, with its many doctrinal vagaries and outright denials of historic Christian teachings, disqualifies itself. And its priesthood, on which it places so much emphasis, is shown to be the antithesis of the divine revelation.

It is to be earnestly hoped that more Christians will acquaint themselves with the Biblical evidence concerning the true priesthood in which we all participate. It is only when a thorough understanding of the fundamentals of Christian theology is obtained that it is possible to successfully encounter and refute the Mormon doctrine of the priesthood.

THE MORMON DOCTRINE OF GOD

It will be conceded by most informed students of Christianity that one cannot deny the existence of the one true God of Scripture and at the same time lay claim to being a Christian. The New Testament writers, as well as our Lord Himself, taught that there was but one God, and all church theologians from the earliest days of church history have affirmed that Christianity is monotheistic in the strictest sense of the term. Indeed it was this fact that so radically differentiated it and the parental Judaism from the pagan, polytheistic societies of Rome and Greece. The Bible is particularly adamant in its declaration that God recognizes the existence of no other "deities." In fact, on a number of occasions the Lord summed up His uniqueness in the following revelation:

> Ye are my witnesses, saith the Lord, and my servant whom I have chosen: that ye may know and believe me, and understand that I am he: before me there was no God formed, neither shall there be after me. I, even I, am the Lord; and beside me there is no saviour . . . Thus saith the Lord the King of Israel, and his redeemer the Lord of hosts: I am the first, and I am the last; and *beside me there is no God* . . . Ye are even my witnesses. Is there a God beside me? *yea, there is no God; I know not any* . . . I am the Lord, and there is none else, *there is no God beside me:* I girded thee, though thou hast not known me: . . . *There is no God else beside me;* a just God and a Saviour; *there is none beside me.* Look unto me and be ye saved, all the ends of the earth: *for I am God, and there is none else* (Isaiah 43:10, 11; 44:6; 8; 45:5, 21, 22).

Throughout the Old Testament, God is known by many titles. He is Elohim, Jehovah, Adonai, El Gebor, and He is also spoken of by combinations of names, such as Jehovah-Elohim, Jehovah-Sabaoth, etc. If the Hebrew Old Testament tells us anything, it is the fact that there is but one God: "Hear, O hear, Israel, the Lord our God, the Lord is one" (Deuteronomy 6:4).

And Jewish monotheism, as all know, at length gave birth to Christian monotheism, the one developing from the other by progressive revelation from God the Holy Spirit. It is not necessary to belabor the point; it is common knowledge that the facts as they have been stated are true. But as we approach our study of the Mormon concept of God, a subtle yet radical change takes place in the usage of the vocabulary of Scripture as we shall shortly see.

It must also be admitted at the outset that the Bible does designate certain individuals as "gods," such as Satan who is described by Christ as "the prince of this world" and elsewhere in Scripture as "the god of this world." It must be clearly understood, however, that whenever this term is assigned to individuals, to spirit personalities, and the like, metaphorical and contextual usage must be carefully analyzed so that a clear picture emerges. For instance, the Lord declared to Moses: "See, I have made thee a god to Pharaoh: and Aaron thy brother shall be thy prophet" (Exodus 7:1). The Hebrew indicates here, when cross-referenced with Exodus 4:16 ("And he shall be even to thee in place of a mouth, and thou shalt be to him in place of God") that a definite relationship was involved. The context also reveals that Moses, by virtue of the power invested in him by God, became in the eyes of Pharoah "a god." Aaron in turn became a prophet of the "god" (Moses) that Pharaoh beheld, since he was the spokesman for Moses. So metaphorical usage is obviously intended, from the very usage of the language and its contextual analysis. On this point all Old Testament scholars are agreed. But this should never cloud the issue, that there is only one true and living God as the previous quotations readily attest.

Another instance of similar usage is the application of the term "Elohim," the plural usage of the term often translated God in the Old Testament. In some contexts the judges of Israel are referred to as "gods," not that they themselves possessed the intrinsic Nature of Deity but that they became in the eyes of the people as gods, or more literally "mighty ones" (Psalm 82 cf. John 10) representing, as they did, the Lord of Hosts. In the New Testament usage, the Apostle Paul is quite explicit when he declares that in the world, i.e., as far as the world is concerned, "there are lords many and gods many, but to us there is one God the Father and one Lord Jesus Christ" (I Corinthians 8:5), a statement emphasized by our Lord when He stated: "I am the first and I am the last, I am He that liveth and became dead, and behold I am alive forever more" (Revelation 1:17, 18). We conclude, then, that polytheism is totally foreign to the Judeo-Christian tradition of theology. In fact, it is the antithesis of the extreme monotheism portrayed in Judaism and Christianity. The God of the Old Testament and the God and Father of our Lord Jesus Christ are one and the same Person; this the Christian Church has always held. In addition to this, God's Nature has always been declared to be that of pure spirit. Our Lord declared that "God is spirit, and they that worship Him must worship Him in spirit and in truth" (John 4:24 — Greek). In numerous other places within the pages of the inspired Word of God, the Holy Spirit has been pleased to reveal God's spiritual nature and "oneness." The Apostle Paul reminds us that "a mediator is not a mediator of one, but God is one" (Galatians 3:20), the Psalmist reminds us of His unchangeable Nature, "From everlasting to everlasting thou art God" (Psalm 90:2), and Moses records in the initial act of creation that "the Spirit of God brooded over the face of the waters" (Genesis 1: 2). The "gods" mentioned in Scripture, then, are never gods by either identity or nature, they are "gods" by human creation or acclamation, and as we have seen. This, then, is a far cry from comparison with the one true and living

God described by the writer of the epistle to the Hebrews as "the Father of spirits" (Hebrews 12:9; Galatians 4:8, 9).

The Truth About the god of the Mormons

In sharp contrast to the revelations of Scripture are the "revelations" of Joseph Smith, Brigham Young, and the succeeding Mormon "prophets." So that the reader will have no difficulty in understanding what the true Mormon position is concerning the Nature of God, the following set of quotations in the context, derived from recognized Mormon sources fully portray what the Mormons mean when they speak of "God."

I. "In the beginning the head of the *Gods* called a council of the Gods and they came together and concocted a plan to create the world and people it" (*The Journal of Discourses,* Volume VI, Sermon by Prophet Joseph Smith).

II. "God himself was once as we are now and is an exalted man. . . ." (The Teachings of the Prophet Joseph Smith by Joseph Fielding Smith, page 345 cf., *The Journal of Discourses,* Volume VI, page 3).

III. "The Father has a body of flesh and bone as tangible as man's; the Son also, but the Holy Ghost has not a body of flesh and bones but is a personage of spirit . . ." (*Doctrine and Covenants,* Sec. 130:22).

IV. "When our father Adam came into the Garden of Eden, he came into it with a celestial body and brought Eve, *one* of his celestial wives, with him. . . . He is our father and our God and the only God with whom we have to do" (Brigham Young, in *The Journal of Discourses,* Volume I, page 50)

V. *"Gods"* exist, and we had better strive to prepare to be one with them" (*Discourses of Brigham Young,* page 351).

VI. "As man is, God once was; as God is, man may become" (Lorenzo Snow, former president of the Mormon Church, *Millennial Star,* Volume 54, also *The Gospel Through the Ages* by Milton R. Hunter, pp. 105, 106).

VII. "Each of these gods, including Jesus Christ and His Father, being in possession of not merely an organized spirit but a glorious body of flesh and bone. . . ." (*Key to the Science of Theology,* page 42, by Parley Pratt).

VIII. "And then the Lord said: Let us go down. And they went down at the beginning, and they (i.e., the *gods*) organized and formed the heavens and the earth" (*Book of Abraham,* Chapter 4, verse 1).

IX. "Remember that God our Heavenly Father was perhaps once a child and mortal like we are and rose step by step in the scale of progress, in the school of advancement: has moved forward and overcome until He has arrived at the point where He now is" (Orson Hyde, *Journal of Discourses,* Volume I, page 123).

X. "Mormon prophets have continuously taught the sublime truth that God the eternal father was once a mortal man who passed through the school of earth-life similar to that through which we are now passing. He became God — an exalted being, through obedience to the same eternal gospel truth that we are given opportunity today to obey" (*The Gospel Through the Ages,* Milton R. Hunter, chapter 16, pages 104, 105).

XI. "Christ was the God, the father of all things . . . behold, I am Jesus Christ. I am the Father and the Son" (Mosiah 7:27 and Ether 3:14).

XII. "Many men say there is one God; the Father, the Son, and the Holy Ghost are only one God! I say this is a strange God anyhow . . . all are to be crammed into one God . . ." (Joseph Smith as recorded in E. F. Parry's *Joseph Smith's Teachings,* page 55, ff.).

It would be quite possible to continue quoting sources for many volumes and other official Mormon publications, but the fact is well established.

The Reorganized Church of Jesus Christ of Latter Day Saints which disagrees with the Utah church on the subject of polytheism, steadfastly maintains that Joseph Smith, Jr. never taught or practiced either polygamy or polytheism, but the following direct quotation from Smith relative to the plurality of gods and the doctrine that Mormon males may attain to godhood vexes the Reorganized Church to no end. But, it is fact, nonetheless.

The following quotations are excerpted from the Mormon publication, *Times and Seasons* (August 1, 1844) published four months after Smith delivered it at the funeral of Elder King Follet and only two months before Smith's assassination in Carthage, Illinois.

This discourse was heard by more than 18,000 people and recorded by four Mormon scribes. It is significant that the split in Mormonism did not take place for more than three and one-half years. So apparently their ancestors did not disagree with Smith's theology, as they themselves do today. Nor did they deny that Smith preached the sermon and taught polytheism, as does the Reorganized Church today. But the facts must speak for themselves:

"I am going to inquire after God, for I want you all to know Him and to be familiar with Him. . . I will go back before the beginning, before the world was, to show you what kind of a being God is.

"God was once as we are now, an exalted man, and sits enthroned in yonder heavens . . . I say, if you were to see Him today, you would see Him like a man in form — like yourselves and all the person, image and very form of man.

"I'm going to tell you how God came to be God. We have imagined and supposed that God was God from all eternity. I will refute that idea, and take away the veil, so that you may see.

"It is the first principle of the Gospel to know for certainty the character of God, to know that we may converse with Him as one man converses with another, and that he was once a man like us, yea, that God Himself, the Father of us all, dwelt on an earth the same as Jesus Christ did.

"What did Jesus say . . . the Scripture informs us that Jesus said, 'As the Father has power to himself, even so hath the Son power! . . to do what? Why, what the Father did.

"The answer is obvious — in a manner, to lay down His body and to take it up again.

"Here then is eternal life — to know the only wise and true God, and you have got to learn how to be gods yourselves, and to be kings and priests, the same as all gods before you, namely by going from one small degree to another, and from a small capacity to a great one, from grace to grace, from exaltation to exaltation, until you attain to the resurrection of the dead and are able to dwell in the everlasting burnings, and to sit in glory, as do those who sit enthroned in everlasting power."

Mormon theology then is polytheistic, teaching in effect that the universe is inhabited by different gods who procreate spirit children which are in turn clothed with bodies on different planets, Adam-god being the god of this planet, as Brigham Young graphically put it. In addition to this, the "inspired" utterances of Joseph Smith reveal that he began as a Unitarian, progressed to tritheism and graduated into full fledged polytheism, in direct contradiction to the revelations of the Old and New Testaments as we have observed. The Mormon doctrine of the Trinity is a gross misrepresentation of the Biblical position, though they attempt to veil their evil doctrine in semi-orthodox terminology. We have already dealt with this problem, but it bears constant repetition lest the Mormon terminology go unchallenged.

On the surface, they appear to be

orthodox; but in the light of unimpeachable Mormon sources, Mormons are clearly evading the issue. The truth of the matter is that Mormonism has never historically accepted the Christian doctrine of the Trinity; in fact, they deny it by completely perverting the meaning of the term. This is one of the chief reasons why they have never been accepted by any Christian council of churches (National Association of Evangelicals, National Council of Christian Churches, World Council of Churches, American & International Council of Churches, etc.). The Adam-God doctrine of Mormon Church theology is the outgrowth of their polytheism, and forces Mormons to deny not only the Trinity of God as revealed in Scripture but the immaterial nature of God as pure spirit. The Mormons, in *Look* magazine, stated that they accepted the Trinity but as we have seen it is *not* the Christian Trinity. God the Father does not have a body of flesh and bones, a fact clearly taught by our Lord (John 4:24, cf. Luke 24:39). Talmage in *The Articles of Faith* describes the Mormon teaching in this manner:

> We affirm that to deny the materiality of God's person is to deny God; for a thing without parts has no whole, and an immaterial body cannot exist. The Church of Jesus Christ of Latter Day Saints proclaims against the incomprehensible God devoid of "body, parts or passions" as a thing impossible of existence, and asserts its belief in and allegiance to the true and living God of Scripture and Revelation . . . Jesus Christ is the son of Elohim, "the spiritual and bodily offspring"; that is to say, Elohim is literally the father of the spirit of Jesus Christ and also the body in which Jesus Christ performed his mission in the flesh . . . Jehovah, who is Jesus Christ the Son of Elohim, is called "the father" . . . that Jesus Christ whom we also know as Jehovah, was the executive of the father, Elohim, in the work of creation set forth in the book *Jesus the Christ*, chapter IV (pages 48, 466, 467).

In these revealing statements, Talmage lapses into the error of making Elohim and Jehovah two separate gods, apparently in complete ignorance of the fact that Elohim "the greater god" and Jehovah — Jesus the lesser god, begotten by Elohim, are compounded in the Hebrew as "Jehovah the Mighty One," or simply "Jehovah God" as any concordance of Hebrew usage in the Old Testament readily reveals (Lord—Yahweh; God—Elohim). This error is akin to that of Mary Baker Eddy, who, in her glossary to *Science and Health With Key to the Scriptures* made exactly the same error, she too being in complete ignorance of the Hebrew language. In this grammatical error, Christian Science and the Mormons are in unique agreement, though it is virtually certain that they are unaware of it.

Talmage's argument that "to deny the materiality of God's person is to deny God; for a thing without parts has no whole and an immaterial body cannot exist" is both logically and theologically an absurdity. To illustrate this, one need only point to the angels whom the Scriptures describe as "ministering spirits" (Hebrews 1:7), beings who have immaterial "bodies" of spiritual substance and yet exist. The Mormons involve themselves further in a hopeless contradiction when, in their doctrine of the pre-existence of the soul, they are forced to redefine the meaning of soul as used in both the Old and the New Testaments to teach that the soul is not immaterial, while the Bible clearly teaches that it is. Our Lord upon the cross spoke the words, "Father, into thy hands I commend my spirit." Certainly this was immaterial. And Paul, preparing to depart from this world for the celestial realms, indicated that his real spiritual self (certainly immaterial, since his body died) was yearning to depart and to be with Christ, which is far better (Philippians 1:21-23). The martyr Stephen also committed his spirit (or immaterial nature) into the hands of the Father, crying, "Lord Jesus, receive my spirit" (Acts 7:59). And there are numerous passages in both the Old and New Testaments which indicate that an "immaterial body" can exist, provided that form is of a spiritual substance as is God the Father and the Holy Spirit, and as was Jesus Christ as the pre-incarnate Logos (John 1:1, cf., John 1: 14). Far from asserting their "belief and allegiance to the true and living God of Scripture and revelation," as Talmage represents Mormonism, Mormons indeed have sworn allegiance to a polytheistic pantheon of gods which they are striving to join, there to enjoy a polygamous eternity of progression toward godhood. One can search the corridors of pagan mythology and never equal the complex structure which the Mormons have erected and masked under the terminology and misnomer of orthodox Christianity, as previously demonstrated. That the Mormons reject the historic Christian doctrine of the Trinity no student of the movement can deny, for after quoting the Nicene creed and early church theology on the Trinity, Talmage, in the Articles of Faith, declares: "It would be difficult to conceive of a greater number of inconsistencies and contradictions expressed in words as here . . . the immateriality of God as asserted in these declarations of sectarian faith is entirely at variance with the Scripture, and absolutely contradicted by the revelations of God's person and attributes . . ." (page 48).

After carefully perusing hundreds of volumes on Mormon theology and scores of pamphlets dealing with this subject, the author can quite candidly state that never in over a decade of research in the field of cults has he ever seen such misappropriation of terminology, disregard of context, and utter abandon of scholastic principles demonstrated on the part of non-Christian cultists than is evidenced in the attempts of Mormon theologians to appear orthodox and at the same time undermine the foundations of historic Christianity. The intricacies of their complex system of polytheism causes the careful researcher to ponder again and again the ethical standard which these Mormon writers practice and the blatant attempts to rewrite history, Biblical theology, and the laws of scriptural interpretation that they might support the theologies of Joseph Smith and Brigham Young. Without fear of contradiction, I am certain that Mormonism cannot stand investigation and wants no part of it unless the results can be controlled under the guise of "broadmindedness" and "tolerance."

On one occasion when the Mormon doctrine of God was under discussion with a young woman leaning in the direction of Mormon conversion, I offered in the presence of witnesses to retract this chapter and one previous effort (*Mormonism*, Zondervan Publishing House, 1958), if the Mormon elders advising this young lady would put in writing that they and their church rejected polytheism for monotheism in the tradition of the Judaeo-Christian religion. It was a bona fide offer; the same offer has been made from hundreds of platforms to tens of thousands of people over a ten-year period. The Church of Jesus Christ of Latter Day Saints is well aware of the offer. To the unwary, however, they imply that they are monotheists, to the informed they defend their polytheism, and like the veritable chameleon they change color to accommodate the surface upon which they find themselves.

G. B. Arbaugh, in his classic volume, *Revelation in Mormonism* (1932), has documented in exhaustive detail the progress of Mormon theology from Unitarianism to Polytheism. His research has been invaluable and available to interested scholars for thirty years, with the full knowledge of the Mormon church. To this date they have never refuted Arbaugh's evidence or conclusions: in fact, they are significantly on the defensive where the peculiar origins of their "sacred writings" are involved or when verifiable evidence exists which reveals their polytheistic perversions of the Gospel of Jesus Christ. It is extremely difficult to write kindly of Mormon theology when they are so obviously deceptive in their presentation of data, so adamant in their condemnation of all religions in favor of the "restored gospel" allegedly vouchsafed to the prophet Joseph Smith. We must not, however, confuse the theology with the person as is too often the case, for while hostility toward the former is scriptural, it is never so with the latter.

Continuing with our study, Apostle Orson Pratt, writing in *The Seer,* declared: "In the heaven where our spirits were born, there are many gods, each of whom has his own wife or wives which were given to him previous to his redemption while yet in his mortal state" (Volume 1, page 37). In this terse sentence, Pratt summed up the whole hierarchy of Mormon polytheism, and quotations previously adduced from a reputable Mormon source support Pratt's summation beyond reasonable doubt. The Mormon teaching that God was seen "face to face" in the Old Testament (Exodus 33:9, 11, 23; Exodus 24:9-11; Isaiah 6:1, 5; Genesis 5:24; Genesis 6:5-9, etc.) is refuted on two counts, that of language and the science of comparative textual analysis (hermeneutics).

From the standpoint of linguistics, all the references cited by the Mormons to prove "that God has a physical body that could be observed" melt away in the light of God's expressed declaration, "Thou canst not see my face: for there shall no man see me and live" (Exodus 33:20).

Exodus 33:11 (face to face) in the Hebrew is rendered "intimate" and in no sense is it opposed to verse 20. Similar expressions are utilized in Deuteronomy 5:4, while in Genesis 32:30 it is the angel of the Lord who speaks, *not* Jehovah Himself. The Old Testament is filled with theophanies (literally, God-forms), instances where God spoke or

revealed Himself in angelic manifestations, and it is accepted by all Old Testament scholars almost without qualification that anthropomorphisms (ascribing human characteristics to God) are the logical explanation of many of the encounters of God with man. To argue, as the Mormons do, that such occurrences indicate that God has a body of flesh and bone, as Prophet Smith taught, is on the face of the matter untenable and another strenuous attempt to force polytheism on a rigidly monotheistic religion. Progressing beyond this, another cardinal Mormon point of argument is the fact that because expressions such as "the arm of the Lord," "the eye of the Lord," "the hand of the Lord," "nostrils," "mouth," etc., are used, all tend to show that God possesses a physical form. However, they have overlooked one important factor. This factor is that of literary metaphor, extremely common in Old Testament usage. If the Mormons are to be consistent in their interpretation, they should find great difficulty in the Psalm where God is spoken of as "covering with his feathers," and man "trusting under his wings." If God has eyes, ears, arms, hands, nostrils, mouth etc., why then does He not have feathers and wings? The Mormons have never given a satisfactory answer to this, because it is obvious that the anthropomorphic and metaphorical usage of terms relative to God are literary devices to convey His concern and association with man. In like manner, metaphors such as feathers and wings indicate His tender concern for the protection of those who "dwell in the secret place of the Most High and abide under the shadow of the Almighty." The Mormons would do well to comb the Old Testament and the New Testament for the numerous metaphorical usages readily available for observation, and they must admit, if they are at all logically consistent, that Jesus was not a door (John 10:9), a shepherd (John 10:11), a vine (John

15:1), a roadway (John 14:6), a loaf of bread (John 6:51), and other metaphorical expressions any more than "our God is a consuming fire" means that Jehovah should be construed as a blast furnace or a volcanic cone.

The Mormons themselves are apparently unsure of the intricacies of their own polytheistic structure, as revealed in the previously cited references from Joseph Smith, who made Christ both the Father and the Son in one instance, and further on indicated that there was a mystery connected with it and that only the Son could reveal how He was both the Father and the Son. Then to compound the difficulty, Smith later separated them completely into "separate personages," eventually populating the entire universe with his polytheistic and polygamous deities. If one peruses carefully the books of Abraham and Moses as contained in *The Pearl of Great Price* (allegedly "translated" by Smith), as well as sections of Ether in the *Book of Mormon, Doctrine and Covenants,* and *Discourses of Brigham Young,* the entire Mormon dogma of the pre-existence of the soul, the polygamous nature of the gods, the brotherhood of Jesus and Lucifer, and the hierarchy of heaven (telestial, terrestrial, and celestial — corresponding to the basement, 50th floor, and observation tower of the Empire State Building respectively), and the doctrines of universal salvation, millennium, resurrection, judgment and final punishment, will unfold in a panorama climaxing in a polygamous paradise of eternal duration. Such is the Mormon doctrine of God, or, more properly, of the gods, which rivals anything pagan mythology ever produced.

The Holy Spirit in Mormonism

Having discussed the nature and attributes of God in contrast to Mormon mythology and its pantheon of polygamus deities, it remains for us to understand what the Mormon teaching concerning the third person of the Christian Trinity is, since they do deign to describe Him as "a personage of spirit."

It is interesting to observe that in their desire to emulate orthodoxy where possible, the Mormons describe the Holy Ghost in the following terms:

"The term Holy Ghost and its common synonyms, Spirit of God, Spirit of the Lord, or simply Spirit, Comforter, and Spirit of Truth occur in the Scriptures with plainly different meanings, referring in some cases to the person of God the Holy Ghost, and in other instances to the power and authority of this great personage, or to the agency through which He ministers . . . The Holy Ghost undoubtedly possesses personal powers and affections; these attributes exist in Him in perfection. Thus He teaches and guides, testifies of the Father and the Son, reproves, rebukes, speaks, commands, commissions . . . These are not figurative expressions but plain statements of the attributes and characteristics of the Holy Ghost" (*Articles of Faith,* page 115).

It is interesting to recall that, according to Talmage, who wrote the *Articles of Faith* (as we previously mentioned): "It has been said, therefore, that God is everywhere; this does not mean that the actual person of any one member of the godhead can be *physically* present in more than one place at one time . . . Admitting the personality of God, we are compelled to accept the fact of His materiality; indeed an immaterial being, under which meaningless name some have sought to designate the condition of God, cannot exist; for the very expression is a contradiction of terms. If God possesses a form, that form is of necessity of definite proportions, and therefore of limited extension and space. It is impossible for him to occupy at one time more than one space of such limits" (pages 42, 43).

Here exists a contradiction in Mormon theology if ever there was one. Talmage declares that the Holy Spirit is a personage of spirit, obviously "an immaterial being" and obviously God (compare *Doctrine and Covenants,* chapter 20, verse 28), and yet not possessing a form of material nature; hence, not limited to extension and space, and therefore rendering it possible for Him to occupy at one time more than one space of such limits, in direct contradiction to Talmage's earlier statements in the same volume. For the Mormon then, "a thing without parts has no whole and an immaterial body cannot exist" (*Articles of Faith,* page 48), and yet the Holy Spirit is a "personage of Spirit," one of the Mormon gods, according to *Doctrine and Covenants.* To cap it all, "He is an immaterial being possessed of a spiritual form and definite proportions!" Mormon theology here appears to have really become confused at the roots, so to speak; but Talmage does not agree with Talmage, nor does *Doctrine and Covenants;* they are forced into the logical position of affirming the materiality of God in one instance, and denying that materiality in the next instance where the Holy Spirit is concerned. It would be enlightening to see how Mormon theologians reconcile this logical and theological contradiction.

Parley P. Pratt, the eminent Mormon theologian, further complicated the doctrine of the Holy Spirit in Mormon theology when he wrote: "Jesus Christ . . . was filled with the divine substance or fluid called the Holy Spirit, by which He comprehended and spake the truth in power and authority, and by which He controlled the elements and imparted health and life to those who were prepared to partake of the same . . . The purest, most refined and subtle of all these substances and the one least understood or even recognized by the less informed among mankind is that sub-

stance called the Holy Spirit" (*Key to Theology,* pages 38, 46).[16]

In the thinking of Pratt, then, certainly an official source of Mormon theology and a man whose writings are still circulated today by his church as authoritative and representative, the Holy Spirit is both a substance, a fluid, and a person, but this is not the teaching of Scripture, which consistently portrays God the Holy Spirit, Third Person of the Trinity, as an eternal, omnipotent, omnipresent, and omniscient Being, sharing all the attributes of deity and one with the Father and the Son, in unity of substance. Mormons are, to say the least, divided in their theology on this issue, although Talmage bravely attempts to synthesize the mass of conflicting information and "revelations" found within the writings of Smith and Young and the early Mormon writers. Try as he will, however, Talmage cannot explain the Mormon confusion on the subject, as evidenced by the following facts.

In the book, *Doctrine and Covenants,* section 20, verse 37, the following statement appears:

"All who humble themselves . . . and truly manifest by their works that they have received of the Spirit of Christ unto the remission of their sins, shall be received by baptism into His church."

Joseph Smith the prophet was the recipient of this alleged revelation from the throneroom of the "gods," and he is to be believed at all costs; yet the same Joseph Smith translated the *Book of Mormon,* which unreservedly declared:

"Yea, blessed are they who shall . . . be baptized, for they shall . . . receive remission of their sins . . . Behold, baptism is unto repentance to the fulfilling of the commandments unto the remission of sins (III Nephi 12:2; Moroni 8:11)."

---

[16]Some Mormons quoting early Mormon writers have attempted to differentiate between the Holy Spirit and the Holy Ghost!

This is linguistically impossible in New Testament Greek as any lexicon reveals.

In one instance, Smith taught that baptism follows the initial act — remission of sins — and in the second instance, the initial act — remission of sins — reverses its position and follows baptism. According to Talmage, "God grants the gift of the Holy Ghost unto the obedient; the bestowal of this gift follows faith, repentance, and baptism by water . . . the apostles of old promised the ministration of the Holy Ghost unto those who had received baptism by water for the remission of sins (*Articles of Faith,* page 163)."

The question naturally arises—When, then, is the Holy Spirit bestowed? Or indeed, can He be bestowed in Mormon theology when it is not determined whether the remission of sins precedes baptism or follows it? Here again, confusion on the doctrine of the Holy Spirit is evidenced in Mormon thinking.

It would be possible to explore further the Mormon doctrine of the Holy Spirit, especially the interesting chapter in President Charles Penrose's book, *Mormon Doctrine* (Salt Lake City, 1888), in which over twenty times he refers to the Holy Spirit as an "it" devoid of personality, although, in the usual polytheistic Mormon scheme, endowed with deity. Penrose closes his comment by stating, "As baptism is the birth of water, so confirmation is the birth or baptism of the Spirit. Both are necessary to entrance into the Kingdom of God . . . The possessor of the Holy Ghost is infinitely rich; those who receive it can lose it, and are of all men the poorest, but there are various degrees of its possession. Many who obtain it walk, but measurably, in its light. But there are few who live by its whisperings and approach by its mediumship into close communion with heavenly beings of the highest order. To them, its light grows brighter every day" (pages 18, 19).

Mormonism then, for all its complexities and want of conformity to the revelation of God's Word, indeed contradicts the Word of God repeatedly, teaching in place of the God of pure spiritual substance (John 4:24), a flesh-and-bone deity and a pantheon of gods in infinite stages of progression. For Mormons, God is restricted to a narrow, rationalistic and materialistic mould. He cannot be incomprehensible, though Scripture indicates that in many ways He most certainly is. "My thoughts are not your thoughts, neither are your ways my ways, saith the Lord. For as the heavens are higher than the earth, so are my ways higher than your ways, and my thoughts than your thoughts" (Isaiah 55:8, 9). Mormon theology complicates and confounds the simple declarations of Scripture in order to support the polytheistic pantheon of Joseph Smith and Brigham Young. It is obvious, therefore, that the God of the Bible and the "god" of the Mormons, the "Adam-god" of Brigham Young and the flesh-and-bone deity of Joseph Smith, are not one and the same; by their nature all monotheistic and theistic religions stand in opposition to Mormon polytheism. Christianity in particular repudiates as false and deceptive the multiplicity of Mormon efforts to masquerade as "ministers of light" (II Corinthians 11).

THE VIRGIN BIRTH OF CHRIST

One of the great doctrines of the Bible, which is uniquely related to the supreme earthly manifestation of the Eternal God, is the doctrine of the Virgin Birth of Jesus Christ. In one very real sense, this doctrine is indissolubly linked with that of the Incarnation, being, so to speak, the agency or instrument whereby God chose to manifest Himself. Time and again the Bible reminds us that Deity was clothed with humanity in the manger of Bethlehem, and Christians of all generations have revered the mystery prefigured by the cryptic words of Isaiah the prophet:

Behold, a virgin shall conceive, and bring forth a son, and shall call his name Immanuel . . . For unto us a child is born, unto us a son is given: and the government shall rest upon his shoulder: and his name shall be called Wonderful, Counsellor, The Mighty God, The Everlasting Father, The Prince of Peace (Isaiah 7:14 and 9:6).

The Apostle Paul numerous times refers to the Deity of our Lord, declaring that "In Him dwells all the fulness of the Deity in the flesh" (Colossians 2:9).

Attempts to minimize the virgin birth of Christ, or to do away with it altogether, as some liberal theologians have energetically tried to do, have consistently met with disaster. This was true because the simple narratives of this momentous event recorded in Matthew and Luke refuse to surrender to the hindsight reconstruction theories of second-guessing critics.

Some persons have, on the other hand, decided upon a middle course where this doctrine is concerned. They affirm its biological necessity. In a word, Matthew and Luke, who had access to eyewitness testimonies (Mary, Joseph, Elizabeth, etc.), never really believed the teaching as recorded; rather it was a pious attempt to endow Christ with a supernatural conception in order to add glory to His Personality. Regardless of how distasteful the unbiblical concepts of liberal and so-called Neo-orthodox theologians may be concerning the virgin birth of our Saviour, no group has framed a concept of the virgin birth doctrine in the terms employed by the Mormon prophet Brigham Young, whose words and teachings among Mormons remain unchallenged to this day. Mormon doctrine concerning the virgin birth of Christ is derived directly from the pronouncements of Brigham Young and as we have previously pointed out, no higher authorities can be quoted in Mormonism than Joseph Smith and Brigham Young. Theirs then is representative Mormon theology. This fact the Mormons have never denied.

Relative to the doctrine of the virgin birth of Christ, Brigham Young has unequivocally stated: "When the virgin Mary conceived the child Jesus, the father had begotten him in his own likeness. He was *not* begotten by the Holy Ghost. And who was the father? He was the first of the human family . . . Jesus our elder brother was begotten in the flesh by the same character that was in the Garden of Eden and who is our father in heaven" (*Journal of Discourses*, Vol. I, pages 50 and 51).

Now, in order to understand what "Prophet" Young was saying, another of his pronouncements found in the same context should be considered:

"When our father Adam came into the Garden of Eden, he came into it with a celestial body and brought Eve, *one* of his celestial wives, with him . . . He is our father and our God and the only God with whom we have to do."

As we have seen in Chapter 4, where the Mormon doctrine of God was considered, Mormon theology teaches that polytheism is the divine order. Belief in many gods is the cornerstone of their theology, and polygamous gods they are, one of which entered the Garden of Eden in a celestial body and brought one of his wives with him. Parley Pratt, a leading Mormon writer whose books are recommended by Mormon publishing houses as representing their theological views, also writes concerning this doctrine:

"Each of these gods, including Jesus Christ and his Father, being in possession of not merely an organized spirit but a glorious body of flesh and bones . . ." (*Key to the Science of Theology*, page 42).

Added to this polytheistic picture are other official Mormon sources, many of whom confirm the sexual Adam-god conception of Jesus enunciated by Young. Wrote James Talmage in the 1925 edition of *Articles of Faith:*

"His [Christ's][17] unique stature in the flesh as the offspring of a mortal mother (Mary) and of an immortal, or resurrected and glorified Father (Adam-god)" (pages 472-473).

Brigham Young, therefore, taught this anti-Biblical doctrine of which he spoke openly more than once as recorded by Mormon historian John Widtsoe, in the *Discourses of Brigham Young* (1925):

"When the time came that his first-born, the Saviour, should come into the world and take a tabernacle (body) the Father came himself and favored that Spirit with a tabernacle instead of letting any *other* man do it" (page 77).

The crass polytheism of Mormonism was never more clearly dissembled than in the foregoing statements, and Young's classification of Adam-god as a glorified, resurrected or immortal Father but the same "man" who originally occupied the Garden of Eden cannot be misunderstood. The phrase "any *other* man" rules out the efforts of Mormon apologists to defend Young and unmasks the entire anti-Christian teaching.

We see, then, the Mormon teaching concerning our Lord's birth is a revolting distortion of the Biblical revelation and one which is in keeping with the Mormon dogma of a flesh-and-bone god. In Mormon thinking, as reflected in the authoritative declarations of one of their prophets, our Saviour was produced, not by a direct act of the Holy Spirit but by actual sexual relations between Adam-god, "an immortal or resurrected and glorified Father," and Mary — a blasphemous view which takes its place beside the infamous mythology of Greece, wherein the gods fathered human sons through physical union with certain chosen women.

Brigham Young further declared: "He (Christ) was *not* begotten by the Holy Ghost . . . Jesus our elder brother was begotten in the flesh by the same character who was in the Garden of Eden, who is our father in heaven." There can be no mistaking the fact that Adam-god is here meant. The language is too clear, the cross reference easily demonstrable, and the denial of His conception by the Holy Spirit evident for all to see.

Mormon leaders, however, while accepting the doctrine as Young declared it, are extremely careful not to allow "the Gentiles" (all non-Mormons) to understand the full impact of the teaching until they have come under extremely favorable Mormon influences. This is understood by the fact that in *Look* magazine,[18] later reproduced in Leo Rosten's *A Guide to the Religions of America* (1955, pages 91-100), the Mormons employed the subterfuge of semantics to escape declaring this position to the general public.

In the *Look* article, the question was asked, "Do Mormons believe in the Virgin Birth?" (page 94). To which the Mormon spokesman, a high-ranking member of the Mormon hierarchy, replied, "Yes, the Latter Day Saints accept the miraculous conception of Jesus the Christ."

Now, it is obvious that if Mr. Evans, the Mormon spokesman, had set forth the doctrine of Brigham Young, a doctrine which has been taught by his church and which appears in authoritative publications, even nominal Christians would have been shocked and goaded to some comments, and the one thing the Mormon Church does not desire is adverse publicity. Indeed they maintain a public relations staff in order to avoid such embarrassments, so Mr. Evans resorted to semantic vagaries in an attempt to make his religion appear "orthodox," which it is not!

According to the revelation of the virgin birth as recorded within the Scrip-

---

[17]Brackets are ours for emphasis.

[18]October 5, 1954.

ture, our Lord was conceived by a direct act of God the Holy Spirit, wholly apart from human agency. The Scripture is explicit in declaring that this conception took place while Mary was "espoused to Joseph, *before* they came together." Matthew, therefore, flatly contradicts Brigham Young in no uncertain terms, declaring: "She was found with child by the Holy Spirit" (Matthew 1:18). And the angel Gabriel, who appeared to Joseph to reassure him concerning the divine origin of Christ's conception, reiterated this fact by declaring, "That which is conceived in her is *by* the Holy Spirit" (verse 20).

Luke, the beloved physician, in his narrative of the virgin birth, describes the revelation of our Lord's conception in unmistakable terms: "The Holy Spirit shall come upon thee, and the power of the highest shall overshadow thee, therefore also that holy thing which shall be born of thee shall be called the Son of God" (Luke 1:35).

Some Mormon apologists have attempted to prove from this verse, however, that the phrase "the power of the highest shall overshadow thee" in fact refers to Adam-god's impregnation of Mary, thus proving "the truthfulness" of Brigham Young's assertion. But as we shall see from Matthew's account, this is an impossible contention and is unworthy of further refutation.

It is true that many debates have been instigated over the nature of the virgin birth of Christ, but the Christian position has always been based upon a literal acceptance of the event as recorded in the first chapters of Matthew and Luke. It might be noted that even liberal and Neo-orthodox scholars have repudiated the grossly polytheistic and pagan concept enunciated by Brigham Young and handed down through Mormon theology.

We would do well to remember "Prophet" Young's denials: "He (Jesus) was not begotten by the Holy Ghost ... Jesus, our elder brother, was begot-

ten in the flesh by the same character that was in the Garden of Eden and who is our father in heaven," and contrast it with the reliable testimony of the Word of God:

"When as his mother Mary was espoused to Joseph, before they came together, she was found with child of the Holy Ghost ... The angel of the Lord appeared unto him in a dream, saying, Joseph, thou son of David, fear not to take unto thee Mary thy wife: for that which is conceived in her is of the Holy Ghost" (Matthew 1:18-20).

The Mormon church today finds itself, no doubt, in a very difficult position where this heinous teaching concerning our Lord's conception is concerned. Some Mormons with whom the author has spoken repudiate violently Brigham Young's doctrine of the virgin birth, maintaining that he never really taught such a thing; but upon being faced with statements from Young's *Journal of Discourses* and quotations from Mormon periodicals and magazines between the years 1854 and 1878, particularly, they are forced to admit that such was the teaching of their church under Brigham Young. Then, not wanting to appear before a Mormon "court" for failure to uphold the prophetic office of Young, they lapse into silence or reluctantly affirm it.

One Mormon writer and historian, B. H. Roberts, writing in the *Deseret News* (July 23, 1921) went so far as to deny that the Mormon church taught the Adam-god doctrine or the doctrine of the virgin birth as pronounced by Young. Wrote Mr. Roberts in answer to the charge of the Presbyterian Church that "the Mormon church teaches that Adam is God . . . and that Jesus is His Son by natural generation":

"As a matter of fact, *the Mormon church does not teach that doctrine.* A few men in the Mormon church have held such views and several of them quite prominent in the councils of the church . . . Brigham Young and others *may* have taught that doctrine but *it has never been accepted by the church as her doctrine."*

The unfortunate thing about Mr. Roberts' statement is that (1) he was not empowered to speak for the church and (2) he is in direct conflict with the teachings of his church on the subject of prophetic authority, not to mention Talmage's *Articles of Faith* previously cited. He also used a carefully qualified term when he said that "Brigham Young and others *may* have taught that doctrine." As we have seen, Brigham Young *did* teach that doctrine; and according to the Mormon faith, Brigham Young was a prophet of God as was Joseph Smith, in the same category as Jeremiah, Ezekiel or Daniel. So, if Brigham taught it, it *is* the doctrine of the Mormon church, by definition, a fact challenged only by uninformed students of Mormonism. That the Mormon Church accepts as her doctrine whatever Joseph Smith and Brigham Young taught must, we feel, be documented beyond reasonable doubt so that the reader will become familiar with the unfortunate Mormon habit of re-defining terms and qualifying statements to elude detection of their true teachings. The following quotation is taken from *The Latter Day Saints Biographical Encyclopedia* (January 5, 1901, No. 1, Vol. I), an official publication of the Mormon church, and clearly reveals the authority of Brigham Young and his high position in the church. In the light of this statement and numerous others, it is hard to see how his doctrines can be denied by the Mormons, which in fact *they have never been.*

In a revelation given to the Prophet, Joseph Smith, January 19, 1841, the Lord says: "I give unto you my servant, Brigham Young, to be a president over the Twelve Travelling Council, which Twelve hold the keys to open up the authority of my kingdom upon the four corners of the earth and after that to send my word to every creature."

The Quorum of the Twelve stands next in authority to the presidency of the church, and in the case of the decease of the prophet, the Twelve preside over the church with their president at the head, and thus was brought to the front Brigham Young, the man whom God designed should succeed the prophet Joseph Smith . . . When the Twelve were sustained as the presiding authority of the church, Brigham Young arose to speak and in the presence of the multitude was transfigured by the spirit and power of God so that his form, size, countenance and voice appeared as those of the martyred prophet. Even non-members were struck with amazement and expected to see and hear the departed Seer. From that moment doubt and uncertainty were banished from the hearts of the faithful; they were fully assured that the mantle of Joseph Smith had fallen upon Brigham Young. After the martyrdom of Joseph and Hyrum, persecution did not cease; the prophets were slain but truth did not die. The man who stood at the earthly head was taken away, but the authority he held had been conferred upon others . . . During his administration of thirty years as president of the church, he made frequent tours accompanied by his associates in the priesthood . . . Though he did not utter so many distinct prophecies, he builded faith fully upon the foundation laid through the prophet Joseph Smith, and all his movements and counsels were prophetic, as fully demonstrated by subsequent events. He was a prophet, statesman, pioneer and colonizer (pages 11, 13, 14).

Supplementing this detailed account of Brigham Young's authority and position as a source of doctrinal reliability, the reader will find innumerable statements concerning the government of the Mormon church in their circulated literature, all of which indicate that every succeeding first president of the church wears the "prophetic mantle" of Joseph Smith and Brigham Young; they, too, are considered prophets of God as were Joseph and Brigham.

When all the facts are considered, two things emerge from the mass of evidence available, which no Mormon writer has yet attempted to explain away — that is, the fact that the Mormon church teaches the absolute authority of its prophetic office and that Brigham Young is regarded as *second* greatest in lineage. When one reads, therefore, Young's statements concerning the nature of God and the virgin birth of our Lord in particular, and duly notes the circuitous tactics of the Mormons and their pointed lack of official denial where the teachings of Young and other prominent Mormons are involved, there is very little left to the imagination as to their true teachings. The Christian, who reverences the revelation God has given concerning the nature of His Son's birth, cannot find fellowship with the Mormons, who subscribe to the teachings of their prophet. Henceforth, when Mormons speak of "the miraculous conception of Jesus the Christ," let it be well remembered what they mean by these terms, for in no way can they be equated with the teaching of the New Testament wherein God has so effectively spoken: "That which is conceived in her is *of* the Holy Spirit" (Matthew 1:20).

SALVATION AND JUDGMENT IN MORMONISM

Personal salvation in Mormonism is one of the doctrines most heavily emphasized, and since Christianity is the Gospel or "Good News" of God's redemption in Christ, it is inevitable that the two should come into conflict.

The Mormon doctrine of salvation involves not only faith in Christ, but baptism by immersion, obedience to the teaching of the Mormon church, good works, and "keeping the commandments of God (which) will cleanse away the stain of sin" (Brigham Young, *Journal of Discourses,* page 159.) Apparently Brigham was ignorant of the Biblical pronouncement that "without the shedding of blood there is no remission (of sin)" Hebrews 9:22.

The Mormon teaching concerning salvation is, therefore, quite the opposite of the New Testament revelation of justification by faith and redemption solely by grace through faith in Christ (Ephesians 2:8-10).

Brigham Young, an authoritative Mormon source by any standards, was quite opposed to the Christian doctrine of salvation which teaches that a person may at any time sincerely repent of his sins, even at the eleventh hour, and receive forgiveness and eternal life. Wrote Brigham:

"Some of our old traditions teach us that a man guilty of atrocious and murderous acts may savingly repent on the scaffold and upon his execution will hear the expression, 'Bless God, he has gone to heaven to be crowned in glory through the all-redeeming merits of Christ the Lord!' This is all nonsense. Such a character will never see heaven" (*Journal of Discourses,* page 157).

Prophet Young never did explain the words of the Lord Jesus Christ addressed to the thief on the cross who had repented of his sins at the last moment, so to speak, crying: "Jesus, Lord, remember me when thou comest into thy kingdom" (Luke 23:42). The answer of our Saviour was unequivocal: "Today shalt thou be with me in paradise" (Luke 23:43).

The parable of the laborer (Matthew 20:1-16) which presents Christ's teaching that God agrees to give to all who will serve Him the same inheritance, i.e., eternal life, was also ignored by Brigham Young, who would most likely have been numbered among the voices which "murmured against the good man of the house, saying: these last have worked but one hour and you have made them equal with us, who have borne the burden and the heat of the day" (verses 11 and 12).

The answer of the Lord is, however, crystal clear: "Friend, I do thee no wrong: did you not agree with me for a penny? Take what is thine, and go thy way: I will give unto the last workers, even as unto thee. Is it not lawful for me to do what I will with mine own? Is thine eye evil, because I am good? . . ." (verses 13-15).

Our Lord was obviously teaching, to use a modern illustration, that the "base pay" given to all laborers in the Kingdom is the same; namely, eternal redemption. But the rewards are different for length and content of the services rendered, so whoever comes to Christ for salvation receives it, whether at the first hour or the eleventh hour. The "gift of God," the Scripture tells us, is "eternal life," and although rewards for services may be earned as the believer surrenders himself to the power of the Holy Spirit and bears fruit for the Lord, God is no respector of persons. His salvation is equally dispensed without favor to all who will come.

According to the Mormon scheme of salvation the gods who created this earth actually planned that Adam, who was to become ruler of this domain, and one of his celestial wives, Eve, were predestined to sin so that the race of man who now inhabit this earth might come into being and eventually reach godhood. The fall in the Garden of Eden was actually the means "by which Adam and Eve became mortal, and could beget mortal children" (J. Widtsoe, *A Rational Theology,* Deseret Publishing Company, page 47).

Since Mormons believe in the pre-existence of the human soul, it is part of their theology that these pre-existent souls must take human forms since it is necessary, in order to enjoy both power and joy, that bodies be provided. This was the early Mormon justification for polygamy which accelerated the creation of bodies for these pre-existent off-springs of Joseph Smith's galaxy of gods. A careful reading of the *Book of Abraham* will reveal that life on this earth was designed by the gods to discipline their spirit children and at the same time provide them with the opportunities to reproduce and eventually inherit godhood and individual

kingdoms as their personal possessions.

According to Mormon revelation, the great star Kolob was the site for the conception of these plans, and it will come as no surprise to students of Mormonism to learn that Lucifer, who was a spirit brother of Jesus prior to His incarnation, fell from heaven because of his jealousy of Christ. Christ was appointed by the gods to become the redeemer of the race that would fall as a result of Adam's sin, and it was this office to which Lucifer aspired, hence his antipathy.

Lucifer is even quoted as saying: "Behold, here am I, send me. I will be thy son, and I will redeem all mankind, that one soul shall not be lost and surely I will do it; wherefore give me thy honor" (Chapter 4 of the *Book of Moses,* found in *The Pearl of Great Price,* catalogs all of these events, including the fall of Satan and the establishment of the Garden of Eden [Chapter 6], which students of the Scripture will be surprised to learn was really located in Missouri and not the Mesopotamian area!)

The Book of Moses also records the fact that Cain, the first murderer, was the progenitor of the Negro race, his black skin being the result of a curse by the gods. On this basis, the Mormons do not stress too much the evangelization of Negroes, believing as they do that pre-existent souls which were considered evil entered Negro bodies; and to this day the Mormons refuse Negroes their priesthood.

The Indians also are accursed because of their allegedly evil activities; so Mormonism is clearly a religion of white supremacy.

These and many other interesting factors comprise the background of the Mormon doctrine of salvation, but it is also important to understand the Mormons' teaching concerning their redeemer, one of the main areas of their controversy with historic Christianity.

The Mormon Saviour

The record of the Bible concerning the Saviour of the world, the Lord Jesus Christ, is well known to students of the Scriptures. In Christian theology, there is but one God (Deuteronomy 6:4, I Corinthians 8:4-6) and Jesus Christ is His eternal Word made flesh (John 1:1 and 1:14). It was the function of the Second Person of the Trinity, upon His reception by the sons of men, to empower them to be the sons of God (John 1:12); and this the Scripture teaches came about as a result of God's unmerited favor and His great love toward a lost race.

The Lord Jesus offered one eternal sacrifice for all sins and His salvation comes not by the works of the law or any human works whatever(Galatians 2:16 and Ephesians 2:9) but solely by grace through faith (Ephesians 2:8). The Saviour of the New Testament revelation existed eternally as God; lived a holy, harmless and undefiled life, separate from sinners, and "knew no sin." He was "a man of sorrows and acquainted with grief," "the Lamb of God that takes away the sin of the world" (John 1:29).

The Saviour of Mormonism, however, is an entirely different person, as their official publications clearly reveal. The Mormon Saviour is not the second person of the Christian Trinity since, as we have seen previously, Mormons reject the Christian doctrine of the Trinity and he is not even a careful replica of the New Testament Redeemer. In Mormon theology, Christ as a pre-existent spirit was not only the brother of the devil (*Pearl of Great Price,* Book of Moses, Chapter 4, Verses 1-4) but celebrated his own marriage to "both the Marys and to Martha, whereby he could see his seed before he was crucified" (Apostle Orson Hide, See J. W. Gunnison, *The Mormons,* page 68, and J. H. Snowden, *The Truth About Mormonism,* 1926, page 130). As we have seen previously the Mor-

mon concept of the virgin birth, alone, distinguishes their "Christ" from the Christ of the Bible.

In addition to this revolting concept, Brigham Young categorically stated that the sacrifice made upon the cross by Jesus Christ in the form of His own blood was ineffective for the cleansing of *some* sins. Brigham went on to teach the now suppressed but never officially repudiated doctrine of "blood atonement."

To better understand Young's limitation of the cleansing power of Christ's blood, we shall refer to his own words:

"There is not a man or woman who violates covenants made with their God that will not be required to pay their debt. The blood of Christ will never wipe that out. Your own blood must atone for it; the judgments of the Almighty will come sooner or later, and every man and woman will have to atone for their covenants . . . All mankind love themselves: and let those principles be known by an individual who will be glad to have his blood shed . . . I could refer you to plenty of instances where men have been righteously slain in order to atone for their sins . . . This is loving our neighbor as ourselves; if he needs help, help him; if he wants salvation and it is necessary to spill his blood on earth in order to be saved, spill it" (*Journal of Discourses,* Volume III, page 247, and Volume IV, pages 219-20). So clearcut was Brigham's denial of the all sufficiency and efficiency of the atoning sacrifice of Christ in the foregoing quotation that Mormons have had to develop an argument "to explain" what the prophet really meant. It is their contention that a criminal is "executed to atone for his crimes and this is all Brigham Young meant."

However, they completely omit any discussion of the fact that Young's statement is not dealing with this subject at all. Young's statement declared that what Christ's blood could *not* cleanse, a man's own blood atonement could. This teaches that in some instances human sacrifice, which Brigham states took place and which he sanctioned, were efficacious where Christ's blood was not!

The Mormons want no part of the Biblical doctrine of the all-sufficiency of Christ's atonement, in the words of John, "The blood of Jesus Christ, His Son, cleanses us from *all* sin" (I John 1:7), for this both contradicts Young and reveals the true Biblical teaching.

There can be no doubt from the Biblical record that it is in Jesus Christ that we have redemption and that His blood is the means of the cleansing of the conscience (Hebrews 9:14) and of the loosening from sin (Revelation 1:5). It is the very basis of our justification (Romans 5:9).

The Christ of the Mormons cannot save, for he is as the Apostle Paul describes him, "another Jesus," the subject of "another gospel," and the originator of a "different spirit," whose forerunner (the angelic messenger, Moroni) was anticipated by the Apostle (Galatians 1:8 and 9) and who along with the entire revelation is to be considered "anathema" or more literally from the Greek, "cursed" by God.

It may be difficult for some to grasp what is in fact an incredible concept, but Mormonism fits perfectly into the descriptions given by the Word of God. The greatest of the apostles, in his second letter to the Corinthian church, after mentioning a counterfeit Jesus, gospel and spirit, goes on to state that such occurrences should not come as a surprise to the Christian church:

"For such are false apostles, deceitful workmen, transforming themselves into apostles of Christ, and it is not surprising, for Satan himself transforms himself into an angel of light. It is therefore no great marvel if his servants also transform themselves as servants of righteousness whose end will be according to' their works" (II Corinthians 11:13-15, Greek).

This is harsh language indeed, but it is the language of God's choosing and it cannot be ignored by anyone who takes seriously the revelations of Scripture and apostolic authority.

Mormonism, with the apostles, priesthood, temples, secret signs, symbols, hand shakes and mysteries, quite literally masquerades as "the church of the restoration"; but at its heart, in its doctrine of the Messiah, it is found to be contrary to every major Biblical pronouncement.

Salvation by Grace?

It is common to find in Mormon literature the statement that "all men are saved by grace alone without any act on their part." Although this appears to be perfectly orthodox, it is necessary to study *all* the Mormon statements relative to this doctrine in order to know precisely what they mean by what they appear to say.

In one such official Mormon publication (*What The Mormons Think of Christ* by B. R. McConkie), the Mormons give their own interpretation:

Grace is simply the mercy, the love and the condescension God has for His children as a result of which He has ordained the plan of salvation so that they may have power to progress and become like Him . . . All men are saved by grace alone without any act on their part, meaning that they are resurrected and become immortal because of the atoning sacrifice of Christ . . . In addition to this redemption from death, all men by the grace of God have the power to gain eternal life. This is called salvation by grace coupled with obedience to the laws and ordinances of the gospel . . . Hence Nephi was led to write: "We labor diligently to write to persuade our children and also our brethren to believe in Christ and to be reconciled to God; for we know it is by grace that we are saved *after all we can do.*"

Christians speak often of the blood of Christ and its cleansing power. Much that is believed and taught on this subject, however, is such utter nonsense and so palpably false that to believe it is to lose one's salvation. Many go so far, for instance, as to pretend and at least to believe that if we confess Christ with our lips and avow that we accept Him as our personal Saviour, we are thereby saved. His blood without other act than mere belief, they say, makes us clean . . . Finally in our day, He has said plainly: "My blood shall not cleanse them if they hear me not." . . . Salvation in the kingdom of God is available because of the atoning blood of Christ. But it is received only on condition of faith, repentance, baptism, and *endurance to the end* in *keeping the commandments of God.* (Pages 24, 25, 27 and 28).

The foregoing is a typical example of what might be termed theological double talk which in one breath affirms grace as a saving principle and in the next declares that it is "coupled with obedience to the laws and ordinances of the gospel" and ends by declaring that confession of Christ and acceptance of Him as "personal Saviour" is "utter nonsense" and "palpably false." McConkie decries the fact that Christ's blood "without other act that mere belief . . . makes us clean" (page 27).

The Biblical position is, however, quite clear in this area; we are saved by grace alone, as previously mentioned, but it in no way enables us to "have power to progress and become like Him." As we have seen, in the Mormon sense such a progression refers to becoming a god, not to the Christian doctrine of sanctification, or of life of the believer being brought into conformity to the Holy Spirit as clearly enunciated in the epistle to the Romans (chapters 8 and 12).

Mr. McConkie's assertion, that "salvation by grace" must be "coupled with obedience with the laws and ordinances of the gospel" in order for a person to be saved, introduces immediately the whole Mormon collection of legalistic observances and requirements. In the end, salvation is not by grace at all, but it is in reality connected with human efforts: "baptism, and enduring to the end in keeping the commandments of God" (page 28).

This is not the Christian doctrine of redemption which the Apostle Peter described graphically when he wrote:

"Forasmuch as ye know that ye were not redeemed with corruptible things, as silver and gold, from your vain conversation received by tradition from your fathers; but with the precious blood of Christ, as of a lamb without blemish and without spot . . . Being born again, not of corruptible seed, but of incorruptible, by the word of God, which liveth and abideth for ever" (I Peter 1:18, 19, 23).

In diametric opposition to the Mormon concept, the confession of Christ with the lips and the acceptance of Him as "our personal Saviour" is indeed the very means of personal salvation. It is the Biblical record which states that "with the heart man believeth unto righteousness and with the mouth confession is made unto salvation" (Romans 10:10). The Gospel's command is "believe on the Lord Jesus Christ and thou shalt be saved" (Acts 16:31). This is, of course, totally foreign to what the Mormons would have us believe. Jesus Christ did not die merely to insure our resurrection, as Mr. McConkie declares (page 24), but He died to reconcile us to God, to save us by grace, to redeem us by blood, and to sanctify us by His Spirit. But such Biblical doctrines the Mormons most decidedly reject. It appears that they cannot conceive of a God who could save apart from human effort, and Nephi's statement betrays this: "For we know it is by grace that we are saved *after all we can do*" (page 25).

In Mormonism it is they who must strive for perfection, sanctification, and godhood. Grace is merely incidental.

It was no less an authority than Brigham Young who taught concerning salvation:

"But as many as received Him, to them gave he power to *continue* to be the sons of God" (*Journal of Discourses,* Vol. IV, page 7).

In Brigham's theology, "instead of receiving the gospel to become the sons of God, my language would be — to receive the gospel that we may *continue* to be the sons of God. Are we not all sons of God when we were born into this world? Old Pharaoh, king of Egypt, was just as much a son of God as Moses and Aaron were His sons, with this difference — he rejected the word of the Lord, the true light, and they received it."

In agreement with their doctrine of the pre-existence of souls, the Mormons believe that they are already the sons of God and that the acceptance of God merely enables them to "continue to be the sons of God," a direct contradiction of the Biblical record which states:

"But as many as received him, to them gave he power to become the sons of God, even to them that believe on his name" (John 1:12).

The Apostle Paul points out, with devastating force, the fact that: "They which are the children of the flesh, these are *not* the children of God: but the children of the promise are counted for the seed" (Romans 9:8).

The Apostle, with equal certainty, affirms that only those who are led by God's Spirit can be called the sons of God (Romans 8:14). It is difficult to see how in any sense of the term, "Old Pharaoh, king of Egypt, was just as much a son of God as Moses and Aaron were His sons," as Brigham Young declared.

The Biblical teaching is that "Ye are all the children of God *by faith* in Christ Jesus" (Galatians 3:26), a fact Brigham obviously overlooked.

It is one of the great and true statements of the Word of God that salvation is not "of him that wills or of him that strives, but of God who shows the mercy" (Romans 9) and that Jesus Christ has redeemed us from the curse of the law, having become a curse for us (Galatians 3:13).

It was the teaching of our Lord that:

"All that the Father giveth me shall come to me; and him that cometh to me I will in no wise cast out" (John 6:37), and the salvation which He still offers to lost men is "not by any works of righteousness which we have done, but according to his mercy he saved us" (Titus 3:5).

In the Mormon religion, they boldly teach universal salvation, for as Mr. Evans, a leading Mormon spokesman, put it: "Mormons believe in universal salvation that all men will be saved, but each one in his own order" (*Look* magazine, Oct. 5, 1954).

It is the teaching of the Scripture, however, that not all men will be saved and that at the end of the ages some shall "go away into everlasting punishment, but the righteous unto life eternal" (Matthew 25:41, 46).

The somber warnings of the Apostle John stand arrayed against the Mormon doctrine of universal salvation:

And I saw the beast, and the kings of the earth, and their armies, gathered together to make war against him that sat on the horse, and against his army. And the beast was taken, and with him the false prophet that wrought miracles before him, with which he deceived them that had received the mark of the beast, and them that worshipped his image. These both were cast alive into a lake of fire burning with brimstone . . . And the devil that deceived them was cast into the lake of fire and brimstone, where the beast and the false prophet are, and shall be tormented day and night for ever and ever . . . And whosoever was not found written in the book of life was cast into the lake of fire . . . But the fearful, and unbelieving, and the abominable, and murderers, and whoremongers, and sorcerers, and idolators, and all liars, shall have their part in the lake which burneth with fire and brimstone: which is the second death . . . The same shall drink of the wine of the wrath of God, which is poured out without mixture into the cup of his indignation: and he shall be tormented with fire and brimstone in the presence of the holy angels, and in the presence of the Lamb: And the smoke of their torment ascendeth up for ever and ever: and they have no rest day nor night, who worship the beast and his image, and whosoever receiveth the mark of his name (Revelation 19:19, 20; 20:10, 15; 21:8; 14: 10, 11).

By no conceivable stretch of the imagination is universal salvation to be found in these passages where the Greek words in their strongest form indicate torment, judgment, and eternal fire that defies human chemical analysis.

The Mormon doctrine of "celestial marriage" derived from their original concept of polygamy and substituted for it in 1890, when they were forced to abandon this immoral conduct under penalty of losing the state of Utah, is tied to their doctrine of salvation. The Mormons believe that the family unit will endure unto the eternal ages, hence their insistence upon the sealing of Mormon men to many women and the sealing of their families, priesthood offices, etc. It was for this reason that there are many special rites and ceremonies instituted in behalf of the dead (particularly relatives); hence, their practice of baptism for the dead and laying on of hands (for the bestowing of the gift of the Holy Ghost), all by proxy.

Mormon Eschatology

Believing as they do in the literal second advent of Christ, the Mormons teach that at His return the Jews will have been gathered to Palestine, the Mormons will be miraculously gathered together in Missouri and the judgment of the Lord will be poured out upon the earth everywhere except on old and new Jerusalem. (See *Doctrine and Covenants,* Section 29, verses 9-11).

The Mormons also have something in common with the cult of Anglo-Israel, believing as they do in the restoration of the ten lost tribes. The difference is that the Anglo-Israelites believe that the ten lost tribes are the English people, whereas the Mormons believe the ten lost tribes are somewhere in the polar region and will be released and trans-ported to Zion (Missouri) where all the riches they have accumulated will be shared with the rest of the "saints" (*Mormonism and the Mormons,* page 91, D. P. Kidder).

Mormons also believe in the bodily resurrection of all men and in salvation in a three-fold heaven. In Mormon theology, there are three heavens: the telestial, the terrestrial and the celestial. The first heaven is designed for heathen people who rejected the Gospel and those who are at that time suffering in hell, pending the last resurrection. The second heaven will be inhabited by Christians who did not accept the Mormon message, along with men of good will of other religions who rejected the revelations of the saints. The final or celestial heaven is itself divided into three kingdoms, the highest of which is godhood or the possession of a kingdom for one's self and one's family. This particular estate has as its prerequisite the candidate's having been sealed by celestial marriage in a Mormon temple while upon the earth. Even in the celestial kingdom godhood is by slow progression, and in the end each who becomes a god will, with his family, rule a separate planet and all these planets inhabited by elevated gods will have the divine communication system of the Holy Spirit, who will be diffused throughout the visible universe (*Doctrine and Covenants,* Section 130, verse 22).

It is almost superfluous to comment that this entire scheme of the consummation of Mormon salvation is the antithesis of the Biblical revelation, which knows nothing of godhood, either constituted or progressive, and which teaches instead that in heaven the destiny of the redeemed will be the special providence of God Himself, which "eye hath not seen, ear hath not heard" and which has "never entered into the mind of men" for these are "the things which God hath prepared for them that love Him." God has revealed many of these things to us by His Spirit; but as Paul so eloquently puts it, we "see through a glass darkly, but *then* face to face" (I Corinthians 13:12).

Let us understand clearly, then, that salvation in the Biblical sense comes as the free gift of God by grace alone through faith in the vicarious sacrifice of Christ upon the cross. The Lord Jesus Christ said: "He that hears my word and believes Him that sent me *has* eternal life, and shall never come into judgment; but has passed out of death into life" (John 5:24; Greek).

The command of the Gospel is to all men everywhere "Repent! for God has appointed a day in which he will judge the world in righteousness by that man whom he has ordained; whereof he has given assurance unto all men, in that he has raised him from among the dead" (Acts 17:31).

The Scriptures disagree with the Mormons in their insistence upon good works as a *means* of salvation. The book of James clearly teaches (chapter 2) that good works are the *outgrowth* of salvation and justify us before men, proving that we have the faith which justifies us before God (Romans 4 and 5).

No Mormon can today claim that he *has* eternal life in Christ. This is the very power of the Gospel which is entrusted to Christ's church (Romans 1:16, 17). Let us therefore use it in an attempt to bring them to redemptive knowledge of the true Christ of Scripture and the costly salvation He purchased for us with His own blood.

John, the beloved apostle, has summed it up thus:

If we receive the witness of men, the witness of God is greater: for this is the witness of God which he hath testified of his Son. He that believeth on the Son of God hath the witness in himself: he that believeth not God hath made him a liar; because he believeth not the record that God gave of his Son. And this is the record, that God hath given to us eternal life, and this life is in

his Son. He that hath the Son hath life; and he that hath not the Son of God hath not life. These things have I written unto you that believe on the name of the Son of God; that ye may know that ye have eternal life, and that ye may believe on the name of the Son of God. And this is the confidence that we have in him, that, if we ask any thing according to his will, he heareth us: And if we know that he hear us, whatsoever we ask, we know that we have the petitions that we desired of him . . . And we know that we are of God, and the whole world lieth in wickedness. And we know that the Son of God is come, and hath given us an understanding, that we may know him that is true, and we are in him that is true, even in his Son, Jesus Christ. This is the true God, and eternal life (I John 5:9-15, 19, 20).

Let us follow in his train "for the hour is coming in which no one can work" and the Mormons too are souls for whom Christ died.

We have seen in the preceding pages how the Mormon religion utilizes Biblical terms and phrases and even adopts Christian doctrines in order to claim allegiance to the Christian faith. Mormons have also come to lay much stress upon public relations and take pains to make certain that they do not use language which might reveal the true nature of their theological deviations. We have also seen that the Mormon church considers itself alone the true church of Christ in our age, and further that they consider all other groups to be Gentiles and apostates from the true Christian religion.

We further read into the words of Joseph Smith himself, whom all Mormons are bound to recognize as the prophet of God, equal if not superior, to any of the Old Testament prophets.

Wrote prophet Smith concerning an alleged interview with the deity:

"My object in going to inquire of the Lord which of all the sects was right, that I might know which to join. No sooner therefore, did I get possession of myself so as to be able to speak, then

I asked the Personages who stood above me in the light, which of all the sects was right and which I should join.

"I was answered that I must join none of them, for they were all wrong, and the personage who addressed me said that all their creeds were an abomination in His sight; those professors were all corrupt; they draw near to Me with their lips but their hearts are far from Me; they teach the doctrines and commandments of men having a form of godliness but they deny the power thereof.

"He again forbade me to join any of them; and many other things did he say unto me which I cannot write at this time."[19]

In addition to this statement of Smith's, Samuel W. Taylor, noted Mormon author, wrote in answer to the question, "Are Mormons Christians?" the following reply:

"Yes, indeed, but neither Protestant nor Catholic. Mormons believe that there was a breaking away of the other churches from true Christianity and that their religion is the restored gospel."[20]

From these facts it is evident for all to see that Mormonism strives with great effort to masquerade as the Christian church complete with an exclusive message, infallible prophets, higher revelations for new dispensation which the Mormons would have us believe began with Joseph Smith, Jr.

But it is the verdict of both history and Biblical theology that Joseph Smith's religion is a polytheistic nightmare of garbled doctrines draped with the garment of Christian terminology. This fact, if nothing else, brands it as a non-Christian cult system.

Those who would consider Mormonism would be greatly profited by a thoughtful consideration of the facts and evidence previously discussed, lest they be misled into the spiritual maze that is Mormonism.

---

[19]*Pearl of Great Price,* Joseph Smith, Chapter 2, verses 1 through 25.

[20]*The American Weekly,* April 3, 1955.

Chapter 7

SPIRITISM — THE CULT OF ANTIQUITY

By far the oldest form of religious cult extant today, and certainly one of the deadliest where the certainty of divine judgment is concerned, is that of Spiritism, often erroneously referred to as "Spiritualism." However, in speaking of this cult, it is sometimes necessary to use that term in order to communicate in the vernacular of our day.

Dr. Charles Braden informs us that in America today Spiritist leaders "estimate of from 500 thousand to 700 thousand spiritualists in the United States; and of one million five hundred thousand to two million in the world" (*These Also Believe,* page 356).

It is the opinion of this writer that this estimate, as far as the United States is concerned, is inaccurate. For, as of 1963, the International General Assembly of Spiritualists, the Nationalist Spiritualist Alliance of the United States and the National Spiritualist Association of Churches reported 441 churches, with a total membership of less than 200,000. This does not take into account Spiritualism in Europe, which is reputed to have twice as many members as in the United States. In South America, there are more than 4,000,000 practicing spiritists, 3,000,000 of these being in Brazil alone. The Brazilian government is seriously considering, in honor of the recognition of Spiritism as a bona fide religion, the publication of a postage stamp bearing one of the spiritistic voodoo goddesses of one of Brazil's growing spiritistic cults. This is evidence indeed that Spiritism is finding new life, even in what is referred to as the scientific age of the Atom!

Dr. Marcus Bach, the noted liberal scholar, who has examined a great deal of spiritistic phenomena, states that, in his opinion, "The *raison d'etre* of Spiritualism is . . . demonstration and proof of the continuity of life, coupled with the comforting assurance that the life is good."

Dr. Bach went on in the same context to explain that in a seance, he saw the apparent reunion of a family, "a son telling his mother that life over there was just a continuation of life on earth. There were not two worlds at all; there was but one interblended, interrelated world, closely interwoven by memory and the love of life. Consciousness could not die. Personality could not be destroyed. The spirit of man was indeed eternal."

Dr. Bach concluded his observation with the statement:

> I left the room overpowered by a strange onrush of comfort about life and death. If this is all true, I thought, it will be difficult to speak of it without emotion. I have always believed in life after death. The traditional church has believed it too. Spiritism went a step further. It asked us to believe that the spirits were interested and active in human affairs; that they could be reached, seen and communicated with. The sense of assurance and comfort lingered. The feeling of genuineness persisted. I walked past the Chesterfield grotto. Someone was praying within the shrine. For those who believe, Spiritualism leads to God. (*They Have Found a Faith,* Marcus Bach, pages 116, 121).

We cannot agree with Dr. Bach that "for those that believe, Spiritualism leads to God," for it is the direct testimony of Holy Scripture that Spiritualism is the masquerade of demonic forces, who pretend to be departed spirits with the intent of deceiving through the power of Satan those foolish enough to believe the testimony of demons in

199

preference to the authority of the Word of God Himself. One need only to read I Samuel, chapter 28, to learn that King Saul's encounter with the medium of Endor brought divine condemnation and Saul's death; for God interrupted the seance, shocked the medium (verse 12) who was expecting the usual counterfeiting of personalities by her own familiar spirit, and allowed Samuel to speak to Saul of God's displeasure and coming wrath.

Spiritists repeatedly attempt to prove that the Bible endorses Spiritism, in fact, they cite any number of references in an attempt to prove that many Biblical characters, not excepting the apostles and our Lord Himself, were indeed mediums, and encouraged such practices.

Spiritism does indeed have a tremendous appeal to the minds of many persons, because, as Dr. Bach points out, it confirms for them life after death and reunion with their loved ones, something which the Scriptures also teach, and further declares that it is not necessary to confirm such truth through Satanic channels, unless one wishes to court the judgment of God.

SPIRITISM — YESTERDAY AND TODAY

Since the first World War the religious horizons of the globe have seen the rapid rise of various forms of Spiritism, a religion unique in that it offers contact with and information from, beings beyond the grave. The crude seances exposed by Houdini, the famous magician, and nemesis of fraudulent mediums, have given way to the sober testimonies of Sir Arthur Conan Doyle, Dr. William James, Sir Oliver Lodge and Sir William Crookes, all men of great learning and scientific background. They put spiritistic phenomena to the most grueling tests of scientific method, and confirmed its reality beyond doubt. It never occurred to them, however, that the information they derived from such findings

was a direct contradiction of the Word of God and was indeed a spiritual snare from which no empirical methodology could extricate them.

In contemporary American life, so acute and complete is the recognition of supernatural sensitivity of communication and spirit manifestations, that Duke University has set up a special division for the study of extrasensory perception (e.s.p., as it commonly is referred to in discussion). There are other such centers for psychic research and the studies of perception which transcends the normal senses, but all are calibrated to achieve the same end —confirmation of what God has forbidden — the exploration of the dimension of the spirit.

The greatest of all source books on the subject of Spiritism is, of course, the Bible, which gives a historical outline of Spiritism in a most concise and dependable form.

Beginning graphically in the Book of Exodus, Scripture reveals that the ancient Egyptians were practitioners of cultism of magic sorcery and necromancy, which were utilized by the priests of the demon gods of Egypt to duplicate the miracles of Moses when he appeared before Pharaoh with the divine command (Exodus 7:11 and 22; 8:18, etc.).

The attitude of God toward those who practice the forbidden sin is also clearly outlined in Scripture. The Lord ordered the death penalty for all sorcerers as recorded in Exodus 22:18; Leviticus 20:27, to cite two specific instances. The Old Testament also named as those cursed by God, persons consorting with "familiar spirits" and "wizards" (Leviticus 19:31 and 20:6), in our language demons and mediums.

In company with these violators of divine command, Daniel the Prophet often speaks of the magicians, sorcerers, soothsayers and astrologers (Daniel 1: 20; 2:2; 2:27; 4:7 and 5:7), who specialized along with the Chaldeans, in the art of interpreting dreams and visions. The prophet Isaiah also speaks of ancient spiritists as casting sorceries upon Israel (Isaiah 8:19; 19:3; 47:9), and King Saul, before his apostasy, under God's command drove such practitioners from Israel (I Samuel 28:3, 9) as did the righteous King Josiah after him (II Kings 23:24, 25).

The Scriptures likewise bear record that Manassah's downfall came about as the result of his delving into Spiritism (II Kings 21:6; II Chronicles 33:6) and his ensuing practice of idolatry in defiance of the command of God. The Bible then presents a devastating resumé of man's forbidden desire to uncover the hidden spiritual mysteries of the universe, even if witchcraft, divination, or enchantments must be employed to further his unholy quest. Egyptians, Babylonians, Chaldeans and the Canaanites the Scriptures tell us, all practiced Spiritism, which practice, in one form or another, continued through the ages. In 1848 Spiritism received its modern rebirth at Hydesville, New York, in the persons of Kate and Margaret Fox, two of the best known of the nineteenth century promulgators of Spiritism (see II Kings 9:22; Micah 5:12; Nahum 3:4; I Samuel 15:23; II Chronicles 33:6; Exodus 8:18; Daniel 2:2; Leviticus 19:31).

THE REVIVAL OF MODERN SPIRITISM

March 31, 1848, then marked, as far as most church historians are concerned, the rise of modern Spiritism. On that date Mrs. John Fox, of Hydesville, New York, heard peculiar noises in the upstairs rooms and cellar of her home. Margaret and Katie Fox seemed to be peculiarly sensitive to these noises, and through this sensitivity they developed into mediums, and their communications became known as "The Rochester Rappings."

Some time afterward, the Fox sisters allegedly stated that the noises originated from their cracking the joints of their toes, but modern day spiritists scorn this explanation, and today in Lilydale, New York, the Fox sisters' cottage has become a spiritualistic shrine, with a large marker, "There Is No Death," reaffirming the ancient practices of those whom God condemned as practitioners of abominations (Deuteronomy 18:9-12).

The roster of those interested in Spiritism is not inconsiderable. Dr. Bach lists a number of "great names" interested in psychic phenomena and research, names such as James Fenimore Cooper, William Cullen Bryant, Robert Dale Owen, Daniel Webster, Harriet Beecher Stowe, Elizabeth Barrett Browning, Horace Greeley, Elisha Cane, Sir Oliver Lodge, English physicist and author; E. Lee Howard, former pastor of the historic Congregational Church at Painesville, Ohio; Sherwood Eddy, world traveler and writer; Arthur Conan Doyle and Sir William Crookes, the last of whom was honored with degrees from at least five English universities and was inventor of the Crookes tube and discoverer of Thallium. According to Bach, "Crookes reported that he had seen manifestations of levitation, and heard accordions play without being touched by human hands; had seen a luminous hand write upon the wall, and a medium handle live coals with bare hands.' All of this he had subjected to scientific tests to prove there were forces at work which could not be explained by any known physical law."

While some of these names might be readily challenged, we are concerned only with the judgments of the Bible, in which we are admonished to "prove (test) all things; hold fast that which is good" (I Thessalonians 5:21).

It is interesting to note that Spiritism has made its strongest appeal to those who have suffered great loss, and after each great war, Spiritism always seems to be on the upgrade following the death of a beloved husband, brother or son.

One of the great early prophets of

modern-day Spiritualism was Andrew Jackson Davis, a poorly educated, but extremely earnest disciple of spirit communication.

In 1847 Davis published his *Principles of Nature, a Divine Revelation* and his, *The Voice of Mankind,* which is reputed to have gone through over fifty editions in the United States. To this day Davis is revered by modern spiritualists as one of the great prophets of the movement. In 1852 Spiritualism was re-introduced into England, and in Germany in 1856, there were exhibitions of so-called "Spiritistic or Automatic Writings."

Other famous mediums were Daniel Dungláss Home, William Stainton Moses and Leonora Kuiper. Chiefly through the works of these people the famous British scientist Sir William Crookes accepted Spiritualism as genuine, and his testimony in no small way influenced Dr. William James, the noted philosopher and psychologist of Harvard.

The *American Mercury* (May, 1950) carried in detail one of James' exhaustive verifications of spiritistic phenomena which stands today as a scientific confirmation of supernatural activity and empirical evidence of an existence that transcends the death of the body.

The Housewife Who Confounded Two Countries

In the city of Boston in 1885, Mrs. Leonora E. Piper, wife of a Boston merchant, and possessed of but limited education, began what was to be a forty-year career as a spiritistic medium, a career which was to confound the best minds in psychical research in both the United States and Europe with scientifically validated evidence which has never been refuted. Mrs. Piper became interested in Spiritism after visiting a clairvoyant for the relief of severe pain after the birth of her first child. It was during sessions with him that she lapsed into trances during which period she could answer with amazing accuracy questions concerning persons who had died.

For some 26 years she continued under the various "spirit controls" that possessed her during her trances as a medium and stopped only in 1911 when "the spirits" suggested that her health would not bear the strain of their manifestation.

In 1924 Mrs. Piper conducted a special series of seances and the records of these seances run more than 3,000 pages in length with a fantastic score for accuracy.

Mrs. Piper gave some 88 sittings, for example, carefully observed at all times by members of the British Society for Psychical Research. Professor Oliver Lodge, later Sir Oliver Lodge, one of England's most brilliant scientists and a careful psychic investigator, compiled a checklist of some 41 specific incidents wherein Mrs. Piper stated facts and general information concerning those who attended her seances, facts which were unknown to those persons at the very time the seances were in session! This was carefully verified and is beyond refutation.

Mrs. Piper also had the amazing capacity to find lost objects and to relate incidents which were taking place many hundreds of miles away from where she was in a trance. Professor William James testified to this when Mrs. Piper informed him that his aunt living over two hundred miles away in New York had died early that very morning. According to James:

"On reaching home an hour later I found a telegram reading as follows: 'Aunt Kate passed away a few minutes after midnight.' "

Dr. James, undaunted by Mrs. Piper's capabilities, went so far as to bring visiting professors from foreign universities with whom Mrs. Piper was not acquainted only to have her give the correct names of the professors, some of their parents, and the illnesses from which they died. James once wrote of her:

"I now believe her to be in possession

of a power as yet unexplained."

The British Society for Psychical Research enlisted the aid of detectives and investigators who observed Mrs. Piper under all conditions while she was in England, and Dr. Richard Hodgson, who had dedicated his life to exposing "psychic wonders," threw up his hands in complete capitulation when without any previous encounter with him, she informed him of his real name, members of his family which were still living and two who had died.

Hodgson brought her to England only to have her go under the control of a spirit named Dr. Phinuit who communicated through her to Dr. Hodgson during the course of three months of exhaustive investigation. During the course of that investigation she told him the exact movements of persons in distant cities, and at another time under the control of a spirit who identified himself as "George Pellew," Mrs. Piper informed Dr. Hodgson of events and facts which were subsequently verified by more than thirty of Pellew's friends. Pellew correctly rejected more than a hundred persons claiming to have known him in life and showed only those whom he had known!

Under the control of Pellew, Mrs. Piper translated perfectly a Greek phrase composed on the spur of the moment by a classical Greek scholar. Mrs. Piper knew no Greek whatever, but George Pellew did. She also reported under Pellew's control with complete accuracy what Pellew's father, who lived in another city, was doing at that moment.

Professor James Hyslop of Columbia University was totally bewildered by Mrs. Piper when with the cooperation of Dr. Hodgson, he interviewed Mrs. Piper in Sion seventeen times, only to be told by her his correct name and perfect answers to the questions which he addressed to her though she could not possibly have an access to the answers. Dr. Hyslop ended up believing that through Mrs. Piper he had actually communicated with the spirit of his departed father!

Mrs. Piper herself believed that the powers which she possessed were not supernatural. In fact, she stated:

"I never heard of anything being said by myself during the trance which might not have been latent in my own mind or in the mind of the sitters or in the mind of some absent person alive somewhere else in the world. The theory of telepathy strongly appeals to me as the most plausible solution of the problem."

Despite this modest statement Mrs. Piper convinced Sir Oliver Lodge, Sir William Crookes, Dr. William James, Dr. Hodgson and Dr. Hyslop (after more than $150,000 was spent on "the most prolonged investigation in the history of psychical research"), that she was indeed possessed of supernatural capacities and as the *American Mercury* pointed out, "Mrs. Piper is the only famous medium against whom no charge of fraud was ever brought."

Evidence such as this cannot be dismissed but must indeed be studied carefully and will, I believe, demonstrate beyond a question of a doubt not only the existence of a spiritual dimension of reality of which the Bible speaks consistently but of the capacity of some to penetrate this dimension. In the terms of Scripture such a penetration can only culminate in a liaison with the forces of darkness of whom, in the light of Scripture, Mrs. Piper was the vehicle of communication.

The National Spiritualist Association with offices in Washington, D. C., has much evidence akin to Mrs. Piper's case and welcomes investigations, as well as sponsoring missionaries, maintaining free libraries, and organizing and arranging for lectures and camp meetings which are held throughout the United States and Canada as well as in other lands. The Spiritualist Institute, named after Morris Pratt, in Whitewater, Wisconsin, offers a two-year course for instruction to those qualified to undertake advanced training in spirit communication. There are various spiritualistic headquarters in the United States, Lilydale, New York being one of the best known and most-widely visited.

The history of Spiritism literally spans the ages, but throughout it all, two things remain constant. The first is that Spiritism is to be found everywhere posing as a universal, common denominator for all religious groups, not excepting Judaism and Christianity. It teaches the continuity of life and the eternal progression of man toward perfection in the spirit realm. Second, the Eternal God has condemned its practice in the sternest possible terms, maintaining that the interpretation of the supernatural realms belong solely to Him (Genesis 40:8), and that those who practice intrusion into these realms are worthy of death (Exodus 22:18).

We are repeatedly warned in the strongest terms, not to seek after mediums, and not to dabble in the realms of divine dominion (Leviticus 19:31). Only the deluded prefer the doctrines of demons to faith in the Word of God, and, as we shall see, the doctrines of Spiritism are precisely of such a nature.

VERIFIED INSTANCES OF SPIRITISTIC PHENOMENA

No discussion of the history of Spiritism would be complete without pointing out that there are specific instances reliably tested and documented that attest to the reality of some spiritistic manifestations. There are many Christians, unfortunately, who suffer from the illusion that all Spiritism, or spiritistic evidence, is fraudulent, and prefer to rest comfortably in the belief that Spiritism is not an indication of demonic power in our age. But an overwhelming amount of evidence can be produced, evidence that has been empirically verified by observers whose reputations are

beyond reproach, as we have seen, which render such a position untenable.

We must either maintain that the witnesses were prejudiced, or deceived; or we must allow that there was a supernatural manifestation experienced by them, a manifestation which the Bible clearly teaches, could come from no other source than the prince of darkness. To best illustrate some irrefutable instances of spiritistic manifestations, I have included the following two cases, which cannot be explained on any other basis than that of supernatural knowledge and/or ability.

Case I

The first of these was experienced by Dr. Marcus Bach, whose painstaking research and spirit of fairness and integrity in examining Spiritism data places his observations above reproach. Dr. Bach recorded the following instance of extra-sensory phenomena.

> On August 26 I drove into Chesterfield, Indiana, and proceeded immediately to the spiritualist camp adjoining the town. It is called a city of peace, a New Jerusalem, a Great Mecca. Expecting a morbid cloister for communication with the dead, I found to my surprise a bucolic vacationland. Two large hotels and twenty cottages look out upon a grass-carpeted amphitheater and a grotto in a "garden of prayer."
>
> Symbolizing the unbroken tradition of spiritualism, there is a "Trail of Religions." Spiritualists say there is nothing like it in the world. Life-sized busts of Abraham, Buddha, Zoroaster, Mohammed, Lao-tse, Confucius, Vardhamana, Zeus, Osiris, and Jesus suggest that spiritualism is universal in appeal and application. Overlooking the scene, an Indian stands with face uplifted to the invisible heavens of the spirit world.[1]

After arriving at this Mecca of modern American Spiritism, Dr. Bach visited two seances. He records this for us as a skeptic who became a believer in the phenomena of Spiritism:

---

[1] *They Have Found a Faith* by Marcus Bach, Bobbs-Merrill, 1946, page 99.

The moments passed. My eyes became accustomed to the dark and I could make out the vague outline of Pressing next to me. He leaned over and whispered somberly, "Well, when's something going to happen?"

Before I could answer —

"How do you do, Dr. Bach! How do you do, Mr. Pressing!" came to us out of the darkness. It was a tantalizing, childish voice with a slightly roguish touch. It might have been a winsome little prodigy stepping out in debut. It might have been a tiny actress in a puppet show.

"Good afternoon," responded Mr. Pressing.

"Who are you?" I asked.

With a friendly lilt the answer came, "I'm Sylvia. . . . We are glad you are here, Dr. Bach," she said with a neat curtsy in her voice. "This is going to be a good seance. There are good vibrations. Look!"

The small trumpet was slowly rising from the floor. It stopped slightly above the larger one and hovered uncertainly. . . .

"But who are you?" I insisted.

"Sylvia!" said the voice emphatically. "Didn't I tell you I am Sylvia? . . . I can get other spirits for you, if you want me to."

"How?" I demanded. "With millions of spirits in the spirit world, how do you get them? Call Bob Whitehand for me."

"Bob Whitehand?" The voice seemed to drift from us for a moment. "Bob Whitehand?" it returned reflectively. "I'll try. It is done by vibrations. . . . I'll try to get Bob Whitehand afterwhile. But look at the trumpet now, Dr. Bach!"

It had risen to five or six feet above the floor and was slowly floating in space. . . .

"Where would you like the trumpet to go?" asked Sylvia.

"Bring it close to me," I told her.

Outlined by the luminous bands, the trumpet floated toward me. It stopped close to my right ear.

"Put it in my hands, Sylvia," I said.

"Hold them out!"

I extended my hands and the trumpet came to rest in them. Now, I thought, here's my chance to find those strings. Balancing the feather-light tube in my left hand, I passed my right hand completely around it. No strings.

"Put your hands on each end of the trumpet," Sylvia directed.

I did, holding the trumpet about elbow's length from my body.

"Now I'll talk to you from inside the trumpet."

A whispered voice—Sylvia's—came from within the trumpet. I put it to my right ear — the voice was there; to my left ear — Sylvia speaking.

"Well," I admitted, "that's interesting." Then I withdrew both hands quickly. Unaided, the trumpet remained fixed in space.

A conversation between Sylvia and Pressing was lost in my amazement upon seeing the other trumpet begin a slow take-off. Without stopping, it ascended to a point near the ceiling. It hung there, then started a slow swinging motion, round and round, like the retarded movement of a helicopter.[2]

Dr. Bach continued the discussion of the seance to point out that Dr. William James then addressed him for perhaps fifteen or twenty minutes. The trumpet continued its levitating motion and, after Dr. James stopped speaking, Sylvia, the capricious spirit creature, took the trumpet which seemed suspended from the air, and caused it to crash with a bang against the wall behind Dr. Bach. Dr. Bach records Mr. Pressing asking, "What the devil was that?"

Sylvia's impish laugh was the answer. "I wanted to show you how poltergeists work! Well, that's the way!" The room was quiet for a few moments. Nothing could be seen save the luminous bands of the small trumpet. Then Sylvia's voice said, "I think I have Bob Whitehand for you."

"Good!" I said, in a tone of co-operation. "Bob? Bob? Can you hear me?"

A luminous head appeared levitated about four feet from the floor. It was not materialized in the way that materialization is usually described. It simply appeared out of nothingness. It was like a blurred flashlight reflected on a human face. I made out the unmistakable features of my friend who had been killed in France. This apparition hovered in the room for only a few seconds and then blacked out. How

[2]Ibid., pages 104-106.

should I explain it? If it were actually a human face illuminated by a flashlight, it must have been shrouded in a curtain in the center of the room. But I knew there had been no curtain. Besides, why would the flashlight diffuse over no other single part of the room, curtain or apparatus — if apparatus were used? And if it were someone impersonating Bob Whitehand, how could he make up such a marked resemblance of Bob, inasmuch as no one knew that I would request Bob's appearance? It was an inexplicable happening and remained the most vivid of the afternoon's demonstration.

Sylvia was now bidding us good-by. The little trumpet returned to its original position.[3]

Dr. Bach records one more confrontation in seance which certainly bears close study and analysis because it was of a closely personal nature. He described it this way:

I was making minute mental notations of all that was happening — the hovering, swaying motion of the "spirits," the rhythm of life, like the rise and fall of a tide, as many as four speaking simultaneously in whispered voices, excited, hurried persuasive. Suddenly the galaxy of spirits melted away. For a long still moment nothing happened. Then the swirling ectoplasmic effluvia glowed from the floor and quickly took on the form of a girl. Before the figure was complete, it spoke.

"Marc, dear — Marc, dear — Marc, dear."

Those who know me well call me Marc; those who know me better call me Marc, dear, so I knew this must be a "familiar spirit!" I got up and walked over until there was a space of less than four feet between us. "Yes?" I said. "Who are you?"

The answer was fraught with disappointment. "Don't you know me?"

I did not. I had no idea who this might be. I had really been too absorbed to think very much about personal contact with the spirits. . . . Nor did I propose to offer any hint of whom I thought she *might represent*. No leads, I determined.

"I do not know you. Who are you?"

"Paula," came the answer.

The name and soft manner in which it was uttered brought the sudden un-

folding of a forgotten drama. Twenty years ago my sister Paula had died at the age of twenty-three. Her child Janette had died shortly before. These deaths had been among the deep sorrows of our family, but time and travel reduce the past into forgetfulness. No medium or spirit had plucked this name out of my mind because I wasn't thinking of Paula. I had not thought of her even once during the seance.

I looked at the presence before me closely.

"How do I look?" she asked.

"You look fine," I replied.

"The right height?" she whispered. "Do you think I should be taller?"

"No. You are about the height I remember."

"I wanted to do a good job," she told me earnestly. "Do I look all right?"

"Yes," I assured her, recalling that one theory of materialization is that the spirit "takes" the ectoplasm and fashions according to its memory the human form which clothed it on earth. . . . Did this form and these features resemble Paula? I must admit they did. Very much. The outline of the figure was recognizable and convincing. It was like a "false front," a flat, two-dimensional body with the semblance of arms clothed in a shadowy gray-white film. The face, though typically masklike, was strikingly reminiscent. There was an illusion of long blond hair. I cannot say whether the voice was Paula's or not. After twenty years I would not remember. Just now, however, it was Paula returned.

But why shouldn't it be? I asked myself as I stood there. The spiritualists at Chesterfield knew I was coming. If, as some people say, they have a well-laid system of espionage they could easily have traced my family and got Paula's description. If this was someone "dressed up," play-acting, if this was a marionette using the voice of a ventriloquist, naturally it would be constructed as to represent Paula. This thought haunted me more than the presence. I wished I could convince myself some way. The impulse to reach out and touch the figure became stronger. I moved closer. I moved slightly to one side so that the red light would strike the spirit's face more directly. We were about three feet apart now. Paula was talking about life in the spirit world.

I was asking hasty questions: Have you seen Jesus? What is heaven like? What about the element of time? Can you be everywhere at once? Are terms like Methodist, Reformed, Presbyterian, Catholic ever used where you are?

Her voice seemed to laugh. She answered, "No, no," to all questions save the one about heaven. It was like speaking to a living person secretly, clandestinely, knowing that time was running out. Her features seemed to become clearer. Perhaps it was my mind playing tricks.

And then a thought came to me. "Paula," I said, "do you remember the catechism we learned at home?"

"Of course!"

"Paula, do you remember the first question in that catechism?"

"I remember."

"What was it?" I asked almost fearfully.

The answer came at once. " 'What is your chief comfort in life and in death?' "

"Go on," I urged.

" 'That I, with body and soul, both in life and in death am not my own—' " She interrupted herself. "Here where we are the words have a greater meaning!"

Then quickly, breathlessly, she told me that serving God means personal development. Life on the spirit plane is an evolvement. Like the breaking of a chrysalis. Like the ascent in a spiral. Like the growth of moral affection to higher and higher "heavens." Several times she interrupted herself with "Do you understand? Is that clear?" as if she felt her message was vital, all-absorbing. Death, she insisted, was not a violent result of sin. It had no sting. It was neither friend nor enemy. It was part of the divine purpose, a purpose without beginning or end.

The whispering grew fainter. "I can stay no longer. I must go now."

"Paula, one more thing. Can you put your arms around me?"

"I'll give you a kiss," she said. "Come closer."

"You come close to me." I wanted her to come nearer the red light. She did. There was now scarcely a foot between us. Her face was luminous, seemingly transparent, and without depth.

I leaned forward and lowered my head. The weblike texture of ectoplas-

mic arms encircled my neck. Something soft and flaxen brushed my forehead. Then Paula vanished — into the floor, it seemed.

I walked back to my chair and sat down. . . . The seance was ended.[4]

Case II

An example of spiritistic demonstration is recorded by J. Arthur Hill in his book, *Spiritualism, Its History, Phenomena and Doctrine*, pages 74 and 75, wherein Mr. Hill cites the case of Daniel D. Home, medium extraordinary, who practiced communication and levitation:

In 1855, Daniel D. Home, a young man of Scottish-American descent, arrived in the British Isles, and it is in the case of Home and his claims of spiritistic mediumship, that the objective observer finds evidence of supernatural manifestations that has been challenged by no one who has thoroughly investigated the life of Mr. Home.

There are many instances recorded of Home's ability to communicate with forces beyond this earth, but the physical phenomena or manifestations of spirit influence which reveal themselves in Home's fantastic ability, are the best testimonies to his possession by supernatural powers.

Sir Wm. Crookes, famed British scientist and acknowledged authority on the phenomena of spiritualism, testified that beyond a shadow of a doubt in the case of Mr. Home, there was "definitely the operation of some agency unknown to science."

In the presence of Sir William and Home, "an accordion placed under the table and untouched by the medium, played tunes, and could manage a few notes, though no tune, when it was held by Mr. Crookes himself. A lath of wood on a table, three feet from Home, rose 10 inches and floated about in the air for more than a minute, moving gently up and down as if it were on rippling water, the medium's hands, meanwhile, being held by Mrs. Walter Crookes and Mrs. William Crookes. A pencil on the table stood up on its point and tried to write, but fell down; the lath then slid across to it and buttressed the pencil, while it tried again. Tables slid

4*Ibid.*, pages 117-121.

about, untouched. Luminous clouds were seen and materialized hands, which carried flowers about. And Home himself was lifted into the air, thus paralleling the levitations of many saints. All this in a fair light, usually one gas burner.

The most famous of the levitations, however, occurred in 1868, at 5, Buckingham Gate, London, in the presence of Lords Lindsay and Adare, and Captain Wynne. Home floated or appeared to float out of one window and in at another. The windows were 76 inches apart, 85 feet above the ground, and there was no ledge or foothold between them. . . . It is difficult to believe that the whole of Home's phenomena were due to fraud or hallucination. As we so often have to say, certainty concerning matters of history, which are vouched for only by a few people, most or all of whom are now dead, is not attainable, and when the alleged events are of a kind to which our own experience supplies no parallel, it is easiest to suppose that the things were done fraudulently somehow. But we must admit that this conclusion is due to prejudice, for in any other matter we should unhesitatingly accept as final the word of so distinguished a man of science as Sir William Crookes, especially when supported by such massive testimony.

There are many other instances which we could cite to demonstrate the claims of spiritists, that they do indeed make contact with powers beyond this earth, and such claims are doubtless quite valid. The question is, are such contacts approved of in the Word of God, and if not, then is not the practice of such contacts disobedience to the expressed will of God, and harmful to the soul of man?

As we have noted, the Bible speaks emphatically on this very point, and as we move on to discuss doctrinal content and contrasts of spiritistic teachings with those of Christianity, we shall be better able to understand the divine viewpoint where Spiritism and the practices of spiritists are concerned.

In this connection, let us note at least two specific things in the account given

us by Dr. Bach and Mr. Hill. In the case of Dr. Bach, it will be remembered that the apparition which purported to be his departed sister, Paula, completely contradicted the New Testament, particularly the fifteenth chapter of I Corinthians, where death is described as an enemy (verse 26). Death does indeed have a sting for mankind that can only be removed by faith in the resurrection of Jesus Christ, which makes possible the resurrection of those who believe in Him (verses 55-57).

It might also be profitably recalled that in his epistle to the Romans, the Apostle Paul spoke quite markedly of the reality of sin, evil, and spiritual death or separation from fellowship with God. Chapters five and six particularly point out that Christ alone restores man to fellowship, and this He did by ruining Satan's power. (See Hebrews 2: 14.) In the revelation of the New Testament, death is indeed the result of sin. (See also Genesis chapter three.) It is a part of the divine purpose which God has permitted to take place and has provided a solution for: i.e., its eventual destruction by resurrection, in Christ. Although it is a part of the divine purpose, it is not neutral; it is indeed the "last enemy" to be destroyed (I Corinthians 15:26).

Though we may also find ourselves in agreement with the statement of Mr. Hill concerning Daniel Home and his supernatural powers, we ought not to forget that Home was a true spiritist-medium who denied the deity of Jesus Christ, the atonement and the bodily resurrection of our Lord. Hence the powers which indeed possessed him, not the reverse as is supposed by spiritists, were not powers that could, in any sense, have proceeded from the God and Father of Jesus Christ, who is the Father of Spirits, and the eventual judge of him who is known to us as the prince of the powers of the air.

THE THEOLOGY OF SPIRITISM

Its "Seven Principles" have been set forth as follows:[5]

I. The Fatherhood of God
II. The Brotherhood of Man
III. Continuous Existence
IV. Communion of Spirits and Ministry of Angels
V. Personal Responsibility
VI. Compensation and Retribution Hereafter for Good or Evil Done on Earth
VII. A Path of Endless Progression
1. Spiritualism is the Science, Philosophy and Religion of continuous life, based upon the demonstrated fact of communication, by means of mediumship, with those who live in the Spirit world.
2. A Spiritualist is one who believes, as the basis of his or her religion, in the communication between this and the spirit world by means of mediumship, and who endeavors to mould his or her character and conduct in accordance with the highest teachings derived from such communion.

Definitions adopted by the
National Spiritualist Association
October 9, 1914, and October 24, 1919

Infinite Intelligence pervades and controls the universe, is without shape or form and is impersonal, omnipresent and omnipotent.
It teaches that the spark of divinity dwells in all.
That every soul will progress through the ages to heights, sublime and glorious, where God is Love and Love is God.

What Spiritualism Is and Does
Spiritualist Manual Revision of 1940

Man is a spiritual being, evolved from the lower forms of life, up through the period of consciousness, to the state of the higher moral and spiritual faculties, which survive, unaffected, the decomposition of the physical body.
Good deeds, springing from a good heart, have a creative force in building pleasant abodes in spirit life, and conversely the sinful create their own unhappy habitations. The wicked must compensate for their evil deeds, here or hereafter, and attain a state of justice before they are prepared to enter upon the path which leads to spiritual happiness and progression.

Philosophy of Spiritualism
Spiritualist Manual Revision of 1940

[5]The pamphlet with the title, "The Seven Principles of Spiritualism," by the Secretary of the Spiritualists' National Union, is quoted by

Spiritualism is an outpouring of the spirit upon humanity, a divine revelation from the spheres of light. It is the highest message of truth which we have, as yet, grown to grasp; and one whose depth, beauty and mighty significance we still imperfectly realize.
Spiritualism is the broad educator, the great redeemer, the emancipator which releases human souls from the bondage of superstition and ignorance, lifts the clouds of error that have so long enshrouded the world, and illumines the darkness of the world's materiality.

What Is Spiritualism?
Spiritualist Manual Revision of 1940

The Spiritualistic Hymnal indicates changes made on well-known hymns and we have listed two to demonstrate their theological position in so doing. One on the Trinity and the other concerning the atonement of Christ.

Just As I Am

Just as I am, without one plea,
But that, O God, Thou madest me,
And that my life is found in Thee
O God of Love, I come, I come.

Just as I am, nor poor, nor blind,
Nor bound by chains in soul or mind;
For all of Thee within I find
O God of Love, I come, I come.

Just as I am, Thou wilt receive,
Tho' dogmas I may ne'er believe,
Nor heights of holiness achieve
O God of Love, I come, I come.

*Holy, Holy, Holy**

Holy, Holy, Holy, Lord God Almighty!
Early in the morning our song shall rise to Thee;
Holy, Holy, Holy! Merciful and Mighty!
God in Three Persons, Blessed Trinity!

Holy, holy, holy! Lord God Almighty!
Early in the morning our song shall rise to Thee;
Holy, holy, holy! Merciful and Mighty!
Who wert, and art, and evermore shalt be.

Holy, Holy, Holy! Lord God Almighty!
All Thy works shall praise Thy name, in earth, and sky, and sea;
Holy, Holy, Holy! Merciful and Mighty!
God in Three Persons, blessed Trinity!

Mr. Hiil in *Spiritualism*, page 144.

*Indented verses are spiritist version.

Holy, holy, holy! Lord God Almighty!
All Thy works shall praise The name in
earth, and sky, and sea;
Holy, holy, holy! Merciful and Mighty!
Who wert, and art, and evermore shalt
be.
From *Hymnal*
Copyright 1936 by
The Board of Directors of the
General Assembly of Spiritualists
New York

It is an absurd idea that Jesus was any
more divine than any other man.—*Weisse*

Tom Paine is in the seventh sphere, one
above our Lord, though he was so many
centuries behind him in entering into the
spirit life. — *Weisse*

The miraculous conception of Christ is
merely a fabulous tale. — *Haweis*

Advanced spirits do not teach the atonement of Christ — nothing of the kind. —
Nocholas

Your doctrine of the atonement is the
very climax of a deranged imagination,
and one that is of the unrighteous and
immoral tendency. — *Hall*

We regret and condemn the practice of
Spiritualists sending their children to be
instructed at the various religious denominations in the teaching of a vicarious
atonement, or salvation by faith and not
of works. — A resolution passed at the
Spiritualistic Convention in Bradford,
England.

All advanced Spiritualists—though few
have the courage to confess it — repudiate
marriage in its legal sense, and believe in
the doctrine of affinities. — The Founder
of the Free Love Society, a Spiritualist, in
a letter to the *New York World* in 1856.
Quotations from the writings of noted
Spiritualists, *Spiritualism* by
Wm. Edward Biederwolf, D.D., page 32

I am here tonight as one of the founders
of Spiritualism to denounce it as an abso-
lute falsehood from beginning to end, as
the flimsiest of superstitions, the most
wicked blasphemy known to the world. —
R. B. Davenport, *The Deathblow to Spir-
itualism*, 1888, page 76; cf. *The New York
Daily Tribune*, for Oct. 22. See also *New
York World*, Oct. 21, 1888.
Spiritualism Today by LeRoy Edwin Froom,
Copyright 1963 by the
Review and Herald Publishing Association.
Offset in U.S.A.

Lord Dowding, a strong advocate of
Spiritualism, says in his book, *Many Mansions* (page 107): "The first thing which
the orthodox Christian has to face is that

the doctrine of the Trinity seems to have
no adherents in advanced circles of the
spirit world. The Divinity of Christ as a
co-equal partner with the Father is universally denied. Jesus Christ was indeed
the Son of God, as also are we sons of
God. . . . We (i.e., orthodox Christians)
are taught to believe in the remission of
sins to the penitent, through the virtue of
Christ's sacrifice and atonement. This doctrine Imperator (the pseudonym of one
of these advanced spirits) vigorously com-
bats in a score of passages."
Spiritualism by
The Rev. J. Stafford Wright, M.A.
Principal of Tyndale Hall, Bristol, 1959,
page 11

Sir Arthur Conan Doyle: "Spiritualism
is the greatest revelation the world has
ever known."

I have seen spirits walk around the room
and join in the talk of the company.

We are continually conscious of protection around us.

General experience shows that a facile
acceptance of these claims of spirit is very
rare among earnest thinkers and that
there is hardly any prominent Spiritualist
whose course of study and reflection has
not involved a novitiate of many years.
The History of Spiritualism
Spiritualist Manual, Revision of 1940,
page 131

Every Human Soul born into life is a
child of GOD and the opportunity for development will at some time be realized
and taken advantage of by each one. Spiritualism proclaims "THE DOORWAY TO
REFORMATION IS NEVER CLOSED AGAINST
ANY SOUL HERE OR HEREAFTER." (Page
181)

We do not believe in "fairies," "demons," "elementals," "astral shells," nor
any such imaginary beings, whose existence cannot be proven. We know no
reason why such creatures should exist.
Such beliefs are neither scientific, nor do
they follow the Laws of Nature, as these
are disclosed by our science and philosophy or by the other natural sciences. We
impress upon you once more that our belief contains nothing but what is in accord
with Natural Law, and which can be con-
cretely proven. (Page 181)

We believe in intelligent and ignorant
spirits. No being is naturally "bad" — evil
always originates in ignorance. Merely
leaving the physical body does not change
the condition of the spirit, which is the
actual personality. It must learn to desire,
and to progress to higher and better con-

ditions, just as we do on earth.

"Miracle" means something done in defiance of Natural Law, therefore there are no Miracles. The demonstrations you speak of can be manifested today by our Sensitives (often called mediums) by the application of perfectly natural forces, when necessary conditions for such manifestations are provided. (Page 182)

We do not believe in such places as Purgatory and Hell. Communicating spirits have merely graduated from this form of life into another. That life can be heaven or hell-like, just as each spirit chooses to make it; the same applies to our life here. (Page 183)

Even the most degraded personality can in time attain to the greatest heights. It is easier, however, to begin progression in earth life.

Each must work out his own salvation; each has an equal opportunity to do this when he shall have atoned for the wrongs and overcome the temptations and allurements to the sense gratifications of earth life. (Page 184)

Spiritualist Manual, Revision of 1940

THE VERDICT OF THE HOLY SPIRIT

The previously cited quotations show most clearly some of the basic teachings of Spiritism. Such quotations from their representative literature, when contrasted with familiar Christian truths, reveal that Spiritism cannot in any sense qualify as Christianity. In fact, it is a particularly virile form of cultism, opposed in almost every specific to the historic doctrines of the Christian faith. It is hardly necessary therefore to refute Spiritism since its own statements are of such an anti-Christian nature as to be self-convicting.

Perhaps the most striking example in the New Testament of the immutable attitude of God toward Spiritism and mediums, is recorded in the thirteenth chapter of the Book of Acts and which merits careful scrutiny:

Now there were in the church that was at Antioch certain prophets and teachers; as Barnabas, and Simeon that was called Niger, and Lucius of Cyrene, and Manaen, which had been brought up with Herod the tetrarch, and Saul. As they ministered to the Lord, and fasted, the Holy Ghost said, Separate

me Barnabas and Saul for the work whereunto I have called them. And when they had fasted and prayed, and laid their hands on them, they sent them away. So they, being sent forth by the Holy Ghost, departed unto Seleucia; and from thence they sailed to Cyprus. . . . And when they had gone through the isle unto Paphos, they found a certain sorcerer, a false prophet, a Jew, whose name was Barjesus; which was with the deputy of the country, Sergius Paulus, a prudent man; who called for Barnabas and Saul, and desired to hear the Word of God.

But Elymas the sorcerer (for so is his name by interpretation) withstood them, seeking to turn away the deputy from the faith. Then Saul (who also is called Paul) filled with the Holy Ghost, set his eyes on him, And said, O full of all subtility and all mischief, thou child of the devil, thou enemy of all righteousness, wilt thou not cease to pervert the right ways of the Lord? And now, behold, the hand of the Lord is upon thee, and thou shalt be blind, not seeing the sun for a season. And immediately there fell on him a mist and a darkness; and he went about seeking some to lead him by the hand (Acts 13: 1-11).

The context of this chapter indicates that Paul and Barnabas were set apart specifically by the Holy Spirit (verses 2,4) to preach the Word of God as the Spirit directed.

In the course of discharging the duties assigned to them by the Holy Spirit, they found a certain magician or medium, a false prophet, a Jew, whose name was Barjesus (verse 6).

We learn from the account that this man deliberately obstructed the preaching of the Gospel to the deputy of the country, Sergius Paulus, a man of integrity who desired to hear the Word of God (verse 7). The judgment of God fell upon this man (verse 11). But it is not significant until it is noted that in verses 9 and 10 the judgment was preceded by the announcement that Paul, was "filled with the Holy Spirit," when he set his eyes upon him. Paul's scathing denunciation of the medium identifies him as a destructive, mischievous son of Satan, the enemy of all divine righteousness, and the perverter or twister or the right pathway of the Lord.

The Scripture reminds us that we are the temple of the Holy Spirit (I Corinthians 6:19). The Spirit of God dwells within each Christian, and Scripture assures us that "greater is he that is in you, than he that is in the world" (I John 4:4). The Christian then can never be possessed by demonic forces; he is constantly shielded and protected by the power of the indwelling Spirit. There is no demonic force that can withstand the presence and power of the Holy Spirit. This is why in the thirteenth chapter of Acts, the Scripture reminds us that Paul dealt with the forces of darkness in his capacity as a believer filled with the Holy Spirit, and with complete assurance and confidence that God's power, grace and all-pervading presence would give him the victory over any medium, false prophet or "son of Satan" (as the Holy Spirit, through Paul, so graphically describes Barjesus.

As we close our study of Spiritism, three important factors can be gleaned from the comparison of Spiritism historically and theologically with the Gospel of Jesus Christ.

First, Spiritism as a cult has been from its beginning in opposition to the Judaeo-Christian religions. In order for one to embrace its teachings, every major doctrine of the Christian faith must be rejected, including the inspiration and final authority of the Bible, the doctrines of the Trinity, the Deity of Christ, the Virgin Birth, Vicarious Atonement, and Bodily Resurrection of our Lord from the grave. The Biblical doctrine of salvation by grace alone, through faith in Christ, apart from the works of the Law, is anathema to spiritist theology which relies on progressive evolution or growth in the "spirit world," to attain final perfection.

No informed student of Spiritism for a moment denies these things, and the previously noted quotations taken from bonafide spiritist publications more than substantiate the validity of this contention.

Second, it cannot be forgotten that there are supernatural manifestations in the practice of Spiritism. Many noted authorities have validated them beyond reasonable doubt. All of these persons and scores more have sworn to the scientific credibility of spiritistic manifestations, and their testimony cannot be fairly impugned. True Spiritism, then, can produce supernatural manifestations, which the Bible describes as originating in demonic forces, and thus under the judgment of God (Leviticus 19:31; 20:6; Deuteronomy 18:9-11; I Samuel 28:3-9; II Kings 21:6; II Chronicles 33:6; Isaiah 47:9).

Third, Christians must realize that Spiritism is practiced by persons who willfully ignore the God of the Bible and His declared means of making men holy, i.e., the sending of His Son into the world that the world through Him might be saved (John 3:16, 36).

In the spirit of Christian love, we are committed to bear witness to Spiritists, refute their teachings, and confront them with the Christ of Calvary, who alone can "take away the sins of the world" (John 1:29). Spiritism properly understood, is indeed a cult of antiquity, but its motivating force comes from him who said long ago, in pristine Eden, "You shall not surely die," and of whom Jesus Christ said, "He is a liar" and "a murderer from the beginning and obeyed not the truth" (John 8:44).

Chapter 8

THE REIGN OF FATHER DIVINE

In the words of Charles W. Ferguson, that humorous chronicler of America's religious horizon, "It is obvious that the land is overrun with messiahs," and although Ferguson penned this more than thirty years ago, his utterance was, in a real sense, prophetic of our own time.

The Peace Mission Movement, headed by the Rev. M. J. Divine (better known as Father Divine), is a phenomena unique to the United States, which as we have seen, has formed many cults over the last 135 years. The kingdom of Father Divine, for in a very real sense, this is precisely what he presides over, is a growing sect of zealots, comfortably ensconced in luxurious hotels and homes, which Divine refers to as "heavens," and devoted to propagating the concept that "Father Divine is God."

Father Divine is the only flesh and blood god now available for observation, and his age has been calculated as anywhere between eighty-three and ninety-one years, the truth probably falling somewhere in between. The Peace Mission Movement became prominent during the depression-ridden 1930's, where particularly in New York's Harlem, Father Divine fed scores of thousands of persons, and provided shelter and jobs, thus winning the allegiance of many who were willing to trade their souls, apparently, for daily sustenance. Perhaps such a movement could have only come into existence in the religious melting pot of the world that is America. But whether this be true or not, over a million persons worship, adore and venerate a Negro octogenarian with a white "virgin bride" as the incarnation of deity and the visible representation of infinite perfection.

There can be no doubt that to the followers of Father Divine, he is God Almighty. And let no one think he does not teach this, for he has openly said numerous times that it was he who created the universe as recorded in the first chapter of Genesis.

> . . . these blessings to you and all humanity I have extended, not just today or yesterday, but I have extended these blessings to humanity since the time when in spirit and in spirit alone I, or spirit, moved out upon the face of the water and said, "Let there be light, and there was light!"

Further than these statements, Father Divine has never ceased claiming eternal titles. He has openly said, "I am God," in terms few persons could fail to understand.

On April 29, 1948, Father Divine took unto himself a white bride and proclaimed that this nuptial event was the marriage feast of the Lamb and the church recorded in chapter nineteen of the book of Revelation. On this fantastic occasion Divine said:

> I do hereby this day make this proclamation that from now henceforth, the 29th day of April shall be a national, universal, inter-racial holiday, commemorating the marriage of Christ to His creation, yea, God, his spotless church, his virgin bride. . . .

Literature from the Father Divine cult is filled with literally scores of thousands of quotations, prayers, poems and articles hailing their leader as God Incarnate, and ascribing to him titles of worship, adoration and praise such as alone belong to the one true and living God.

The followers of Father Divine will not believe in the invisible God and Father of our Lord Jesus Christ, whom they refer to as a "sky god." For them,

Father Divine is all the deity they need or want, and the Father has encouraged this concept from the very beginning. The faithful in the Divine movement all say with one accord what their god has taught them so well:

Bless your holy heart, father dear. Your children are happy knowing you are a god at hand, and not a sky god, afar off.

Corroborating this statement, Father Divine once said:

Why believe in something that they claim can save you after passing from this existence to keep you living in poverty, debauchery, lacks, wants and limitations, while on this earth you are tabernacling. I will not only lift you as my true believers, but I shall lift humanity from all superstition, and cause them to forget all about that imaginary God I am now eradicating and dispelling from the consciousness of the people. Aren't you glad?

Father Divine has also described himself as "the holy spirit," third person of the Trinity, when he said:

I shall fulfill the Scriptures to the letter, and you may tell all the critics and accusers and blasphemers when they speak maliciously and antagonistically concerning me, that I am the holy ghost personified! Whether they believe it or not, is immaterial to me, for all shall feel the results of the thoughts they think and speak concerning me (*The New Day,* July 16, 1949).

Unfortunately for Father Divine, he has made far too many mistakes Biblically, historically and politically to be for a moment considered seriously as deity, as we shall see. However, one clear fact emerges from the theology of his movement, and that is, that to his followers, he is indeed a god. In a July, 1949 edition of *The New Day,* Divine declared:

So it is the same spirit, the same one you have been praying to. But I am in the body now, and I am summed up and recognized in this body to reach them and to save them from every undesirable condition. . . . It is such a glorious privilege! Even as you see it in my office now, you would not, or

could not have thought, that such an expression as being termed different races and colors could be united together in the unity of the spirit, of mind, of aim and of purpose, until I came personally! But I came to let you and all mankind know that "out of one blood God created all nations of men for to dwell upon the face of the whole earth!"

Divine then went on to say,

If the prejudiced and antagonistic employers refuse to have you in their service just because of your belief in me and your conviction of my deity, they will suffer, even as Sodom and Gomorrah did, in whom righteousness was not found sufficient to save them.

The Scripture is clear that in "the last days perilous times shall come. For men shall be lovers of their own selves, covetous, boasters, proud, blasphemers, disobedient to parents, unthankful, unholy . . . having a form of godliness, but denying the power thereof" (II Timothy 3:1-5). In this frame of reference, Father Divine certainly qualifies, for through the proclamation of his Peace Mission Movement, he has usurped the name of God, displaying almost unimaginable pride, and has, as the Apostle Paul prophesied, become one of the teachers who "shall turn away their ears from the truth, and shall be turned into fables" (II Timothy 4:4).

The terms utilized by Divine's followers to describe him, might be said at the very least to be blasphemy, especially their association of Divine with Jesus Christ.

This is the mission for which I came. It is written, "the government shall be upon his shoulders, and he shall be called wonderful, counselor, the mighty god, the everlasting father." Why do you call me Father? "God Almighty!" thunders the response from thousands. Now isn't that wonderful! And prince of peace! Why do you say peace around here? Because the Prince of Peace has been recognized (*Spoken Word,* June 16, 1936).

Added to such statements are ecstatic utterances mirrored in the early days of the movement, and current till this day:

> Down through Christendom many have sung, *Steal Away to Jesus.* Tuesday morning, in the small hours just before dawn, Jesus himself in a beautiful body known to over twenty-two millions as Father Divine, God Almighty, stole quietly down the stairs of his New York headquarters . . . quickly stepping into a waiting car, the very same Jesus stole away to Saville, Long Island (*The Spoken Word,* March 14, 1936).

In a personal letter directed to Mr. Kenneth Daire, dated March 16, 1949, Father Divine stated: "Thus the greater the opposition, the more I advance and the more my deity is observed and the more I prove my omnipotence, omniscience and omnipresence. And I proved my mastery over all flesh; for if I were not God, I would have long since failed!"

Divine's usage of the term omniscience is interesting, for it means all knowledge of all things. But if Father Divine were God, and did know all things, certainly he would have known that the previously cited quotation from the seventeenth chapter of Acts concerning God making all men of one blood is inaccurately rendered in the King James Bible, since the word "blood" does not appear in the Greek manuscripts. What the Apostle Paul was declaring, contrary to the Athenian position that they were a special race, created out of the soil of grace, was the fact that God had made from one man (Adam) all people, so that they shared a common ancestry with the rest of the nations of the earth and were alike unto the condemnation of sin.

The attribute of omniscience would also have revealed to Father Divine the true nature of the communist conspiracy, which he in no small sense aided during the 1930's among the colored people of Harlem, and particularly among his followers. This, however, we will discuss in detail later in the chapter.

In considering the phenomenon of Father Divine, the question logically arises, where did all this begin, and who really is this peculiar little man who claims the allegiance of over one million followers and boldly asserts that he is God? It should be carefully noted that Divine did not always claim to be God, except in the sense of the theology of Unity and Christian Science, i.e., an impersonal presence indwelling all men. In fact, an interesting conversation ensued between Father Divine and a judge in a court of law, during the early days of the movement, which ought to be pointed out. Divine was asked by the judge, "Father Divine, are you God . . . do you claim you are God?" Father Divine answered, "No, I am not God, but millions think I am and I would like them to believe it" (*An Exposure of Father Divine,* E. J. Daniels, page 25).

Father Divine has come a long way from that position as the evidence indicates. But it is significant to note that in a court of law where he had to tell the truth under oath Father Divine's deity was denied by Father Divine himself!

Historical Roots of the Peace Mission Movement

The Rev. M. J. Divine, M.S.D., D.D., better known as Father Divine, was born some eighty-odd years ago on a plantation on Hutchinson Island, on the Savannah River in the State of Georgia of a poor Negro family of sharecroppers, and was given the name George Baker. This is all that is known of his origin, at least all that he has ever revealed or all that could be found out about him. Little is known publicly about George Baker until 1899, when he made the acquaintance of the Rev. St. John the Divine Hickerson, a dynamic Negro mystic, the only known living person who knew George Baker before he became "God."

At the time of this meeting both Baker and Hickerson were living in Baltimore, Maryland, the former working as a gardener, and the latter working as pastor of a church. George Baker was a Baptist then, and attended a colored Baptist church whose pastor was a Mr. Henderson. During his stay at Mr. Henderson's church, Baker met Samuel Morris, a mulatto itinerant preacher of great personal magnetism. Unlearned as he was and uninstructed in the Word of God, Morris had deduced from I Corinthians 3:16, which refers to believers being "the temple of God," that since God dwelt in him, he was God, and entitled to divine authority. With this odd bit of exegesis, Morris persuaded George Baker that it was absolute truth, and conferred upon him the name of "The Messenger," with the exalted title "God and the Sonship Degree," while he appropriated the name "Father Jehovia." This team lasted until 1908, when St. John the Divine Hickerson threw in his lot with them, and for four years they were the most colorful trio ever to have graced the unfortunate city of Baltimore. In the year 1912 however, dissension split the ranks of the group, Hickerson insisting that he was as much God as Morris, although at the time Baker was perfectly content to retain his "God and the Sonship Degree." With the departure of Hickerson, Baker apparently decided he was entitled to be God if Hickerson and Morris were, so he shortly thereafter left Morris and headed South, where in 1914 in Valdosta, Georgia, he was arrested and jailed as a "public menace." Since Baker refused to give his right name, the court writ stated "The people versus John Doe, alias God."

The final outcome of this action was that the jury found Baker guilty and "not crazy enough to be sent to the state sanitarium, but crazy enough to be ordered to leave the state of Georgia at once."

Thus it was that the future God made a hurried exodus from the ungrateful state of Georgia.

From Valdosta, George Baker led his little band of followers to New York city, where he arrived in 1915 and promptly sought out Hickerson, then pastor of a successful work "The Church of the Living God" on Forty-first Street. During the month that followed, Baker learned methods of organization from Hickerson, and though terribly lacking in formal education, Baker was an apt pupil in the art of "God-hood."

Shortly after his arrival in New York, Baker married one of his faithful Valdosta followers, Penniah, or "Sister Penny," as she was called. In keeping with his ban on sex, Baker and she slept in separate rooms all the days of their married life together. By this time the faithful numbered nearly two dozen, and Baker began to feel crowded. So after much deliberation, he bought, for $2,-500, a two-story frame house at 72 Macon street, in the all-white community of Sayville, Long Island, and proceeded to move in. The deed to this house carried the names of Major J. Devine, and his wife Penniah. Here it was that history tells us that George Baker took the second step toward the title "Father Divine."

During Major Devine's stay in Sayville things were anything but tranquil. Not only did the neighbors object to colored persons living next to them, but they strenuously objected to the bus loads of Harlemites the Major transported each weekend to Sayville for his lavish banquets.

To the credit of George Baker, it should be mentioned in all fairness, that between the late twenties and middle thirties, when the great depression rocked the underprivileged, ill-fed and poorly housed inhabitants of Harlem, his various "heavens," the first being located at 20 West 115th Street, fed and clothed thousands of starving Negroes and gave shelter to many who otherwise might have died on the streets.

Naturally, the efforts of bona fide ministers, priests, social workers and the like, accomplished greater and more lasting effects than did Father Divine's. But one cannot fairly minimize his actions in that terrible hour of the Negroes' need.

Many persons have wisely observed that the drawing card in Father Divine's kingdom is his emphasis upon material needs. He is most willing to garner converts by supplying their needs and then to bask in the grateful praise which rightly belongs to the Lord, "the giver of every good and perfect gift."

So it was that Baker wooed with food and shelter and an employment service, tens of thousands of starving, dissatisfied Negroes, who in turn gave him all their earnings, their unrestrained worship, adoration and praise. The converts, however, were not restricted to Negroes alone, but included whites, as well as Orientals, and he prides himself on his "interracial heavens."

As the clock of time ticked on, the years found Major Devine riding the crest of a Harlem popularity wave, for in the midst of the great depression resulting from the stock market crash of 1929 there were many empty stomachs which, when filled, prompted their owners to hail the benefactor as Divine. In keeping with this trend in thinking, George Baker, alias Major Devine, took the final step up the ladder of success, and named himself Father Divine, Saviour of the Negro race and of the world at large.

In the wake of these astounding developments the Sayville neighbors of Father Divine could stand no more of his swelling followers, who they charged, chanted, long into the night, songs of adoration to Father Divine. On Sunday, November 15, 1931, Father Divine's Sayville home was raided, and Divine, along with eighty of his followers, arrested on the charge of "disturbing the peace."

On May 24, 1932, George Baker, alias Father Divine, went on trial before Supreme Court Justice Lewis J. Smith

in Mineola, Long Island, charged with being a public nuisance. Judge Smith showed Divine no mercy whatever, and certainly no respect for his deity. The Judge cancelled his bail and confined him to the county jail for the period of the trial. After many pages of testimony in this trial, Father Divine was found guilty as charged, but a recommendation of leniency was made. Judge Smith, however, ignored this and sentenced him to one year in jail and a five-hundred dollar fine. For Father Divine and his movement this might have spelled sudden disaster, had not a most peculiar event occurred which transformed defeat into victory and proved the turning point in the career of Father Divine.

On the Wednesday following the Saturday that Judge Smith pronounced sentence on Divine, his Honor was stricken with a fatal heart attack and died. He was only fifty years old and apparently in perfect health.

This tragic occurrence was trumpeted abroad by the followers of Divine as the result of Judge Smith's disobedience to the Divine commands, and his prejudice against "Father." That Judge Smith was prejudiced, there can be no doubt, for Divine's conviction was reversed by a higher court, and "Father" freed, to the unbounded joy of the faithful, on June 24, 1932. From this time forward Father Divine rose in prominence, wealth and power, until today he controls millions of dollars in property and cash in the New York and Philadelphia metropolitan areas alone. And his properties and holdings extend throughout the world, aided and abetted by the adoration of approximately one million persons who continue to worship him as God Incarnate.

Father Divine has had other skirmishes with legal authorities throughout the years, but no one, including the Bureau of Internal Revenue, has ever been able to prove that Divine owns anything, or that he has profited personally from the contributions made to his movement.

Father Divine, however, lives like the God his followers contend he is, and possesses many expensive automobiles, homes, apartments and clothes, those things befitting his position. The depth of devotion the faithful feel for Divine was demonstrated on one occasion when process servers attempting to reach "Father" were attacked by Divinites who resisted their invasion of Father's "heaven" by stabbing one and assaulting another. Father Divine was also caught in a Milford, Connecticut coal bin in the middle thirties, where he was attempting to hide from legal representatives bent on discussing his activities. The comment of Viola Wilson, better known as "Faithful Mary," Divine's loyal confidant for many years, and later an apostate from the movement, is most apropos at this time. Said Faithful: "God should have been able to hide without being found." Further comment at this juncture is needless.

A few years ago Father Divine made headlines by cursing the New Jersey turnpike which had been inconsiderate enough to ticket him for riding in a private limousine well over the prescribed speed limit. As a result of this curse, none of Divine's followers can travel the turnpike, and every time an accident happens, they point to it as evidence of "Father's justice." Before drawing this summary of Father Divine's kingdom to a close, we find it necessary to mention two of the relationships this peculiar man is most anxious to forget, since they so formidably demonstrate the fact that he is not deity at all. At best, Father Divine is a confused, poorly informed ex-gardener, either possessed by dark powers, or suffering from a pitiful form of mental degeneration, now beyond his power to control or alter. For the sake of his soul, one can only pray that it is the latter. But, unfortunately, the former choice is closer to the truth in view of Baker's apparent sanity on other topics.

The first of these two embarrassing relationships concerns one Viola Wilson, the former prostitute and alcoholic now deceased, whom Father Divine rehabilitated and elevated to the position of his First Lieutenant under the promising new name of "Faithful Mary." Viola Wilson never ceased to praise her benefactor for his many kindnesses to her throughout their happy relationship, but as the years passed, "Faithful Mary" began to have a following of her own in the very ranks of Divine's most ardent worshipers. This, coupled with her effervescent personality, eventually led her to defy "Father's" commands, which resulted in her forsaking the movement and exposing, among other things, the sex life of Divine.

The most shocking of these inside views of the Father's private life rocked the journalistic world back in the thirties, and is here reproduced exactly as it was transcribed by Faithful Mary:

> Up in the chambers of Divine at night with the lights low, Divine can be seen going through strange movements while upon the floor lay several angels, moving their bodies in sexual, spasmodic jerks, disrobing themselves, and some completely nude. They are hysterically crying out to him and you can see that they are burning up, and that the evangelical life is not in them. Many parents would be shocked whose daughters have deserted them and gone into Father Divine's kingdom, if they could see their daughters lying in the bedroom of this beast under the spell of hypnotism, their breasts rising and falling, while the hands of Divine are caressing every curve of their bodies, and in this act of seduction he whispers, "Your body belongs to God, and now you are being blessed by giving your body to God."
>
> On leaving the corridors of Divine, these angels can be heard saying, "Thank you, Father," and he replies, "It's truly wonderful." In telling this story, I am not saying that this is true among all his angels. There are, I believe, the majority leading the evangelical life. Many of these angels who are claimed in body as well as in spirit, dropped out of the kingdom when they

found out how Divine actually was.

Though Faithful later retracted these statements when misfortune plagued her, it is quite clear that at the time, she meant them. There is no reason to believe that they did not contain some measure of truth relative to Divine's activities at that time, for she was certainly in a position to know, if anyone ever was.

The second unfortunate relationship Father Divine would like to have forgotten, was his eight-year "on again, off again" flirtation with the Communist Party and its propaganda paper, *The Daily Worker,* which used Divine and his Negro followers as a sounding board in their exploitation of class and racial inequalities in the United States. So completely did the communists deceive Father Divine that he described them as champions of racial equality and freedom with the following glowing terms:

> I stand for anything that will deal justly between man and man. The communists stand for social equality and for justice in every issue and this is the principle for which I stand. I am not especially representing religion. I am representing God on earth and among men, and I will co-operate with an organization that will stand for the right and will deal justly.

This statement shows, if any one statement can fully show, the logical contradiction that is so apparent in the Divine movement. If Father Divine were God, which he most certainly is not, he would have known that international communism never "stands for social equality and for justice in every issue," nor has it ever stood for the right or dealt justly with anyone except to gain political advantage in time in order to enslave the wills of others. As "God," Father Divine should have remembered the slaughter of almost four million Kulaks in the Ukraine in the early days of the Stalin reign, when they refused to be collectivized by the communists. He should have known of the awful terror of the Siberian labor camps, not to mention the murder of millions of clergymen and religious laymen by the Communist Party's numerous purges. A tour of the Soviet concentration camp of Vorkuta near the Arctic circle, from which only a few have escaped alive, would have convinced Father Divine that the communists are anything but the friend of the Negro, or for that matter, of freedom, anywhere in the world.

These things Father Divine either did not know and was duped, or he did know and cooperated anyhow to gain his own ends, in which case his condemnation as an opportunist is justly deserved.

In 1933, *The New Day,* Divine's propaganda newspaper, in an open editorial further stated Father's endorsement of the communists and their aims. Said the *New Day:*

> It is plain to see the extent to which Father Divine has co-operated with the communists insofar as their actions have been in harmony with his teachings, and it is gratifying to see to what extent communists co-operate with him; yet they do not participate or co-operate in the activities of any other religious movement. They recognize Father Divine and his principles as absolutely honest, sincere, and of constructive benefit to the people, and even write constructive editorials concerning the movement.

Climaxing this idyl between the Divine movement and the communists was the appearance of Father Divine and thousands of his followers in the communist-sponsored "Anti-Facism Parade," which was staged in 1934 in New York City. Amidst a literal sea of placards proclaiming in one breath such devotional phrases as "every knee shall bow, and every tongue confess that Father Divine is God, God, God," and such communist slogans as "Workers of the world unite, down with capitalistic imperialism!" Father Divine rode through the admiring throng in his bourgeois Packard touring car, down Madison Avenue from 115th Street to

23rd Street, ending at the Madison Square park. At this and many other communist-sponsored affairs Father Divine lauded the communists for their common desire to "bring peace on earth," and in general, became a type of glorified stooge whom the *Daily Worker* pictured as "the representative of the underprivileged black folk, and as such, must be worked with."

By 1941 Father Divine's admiration for the communists had worn rather thin however, and with the great depression over, the communists needed new fronts, and Father Divine was of the vintage of 1933. Their relationship came to an abrupt end. In that year Father Divine described the communists as "un-American and ungodly," and with the outbreak of the Korean war in 1950, he declared himself "a righteous fighter against the forces of communism."

Thus ended the saga of Father Divine's romance with the Communist Party, an affair in which he was not alone, as a careful perusal of the lists of the House Committee on un-American Activities and the Attorney General reveal so decisively.

The interested reader cannot help but see from this that Father Divine was a much-deceived god, one who mistook the outspoken enemies of freedom, the Communist Party, as the champions of what they were irrevocably committed to destroy. It is indeed a wonder that such a man is acclaimed as a deity.

In drawing our portrait of Father Divine, the reader will note that we have not bothered to erect a refutation of Father Divine's theology, since we believe it totally unnecessary in the light of the clear teaching of Biblical Christianity that "God is spirit; and they that worship him must worship him in spirit and in truth" (John 4:24).

The educational background of Father Divine rules out any possibility that he is capable of formulating a systematic theology which in any way bears a resemblance to that which is revealed in the Scriptures. Father Divine has claimed that he is Christ; He has claimed that he is God the Father, and he has claimed that he is the Holy Spirit. He applies all Biblical texts referring to the Deity to himself, and it is perfectly valid to deduce that he considers himself Saviour of men and God in the fullest sense of the term. It is claimed by the followers of Father Divine that he died almost 2,000 years ago in the form of Jesus of Nazareth, who died on Calvary's cross. And further, he believes that all miraculous events in the Scriptures are the result of his presence.

In direct opposition to this portrait of human egotism and subtle blasphemy, the Scriptures declare most pointedly the invisible nature of Almighty God and the fact that He took the form of man once and for all time in Jesus Christ (John 1:14) for the redemption of the sins of man. We are distinctly enjoined countless times to beware of "false christs" and "false prophets" who shall come in sheep's clothing, but inwardly, as our Lord indicated, "they are savage wolves," who seal their apostasy from Christianity with the denial of "the only Lord God and our Lord Jesus Christ."

Father Divine, or George Baker, has irrevocably committed the sin of blasphemy against the only true God. Moreover, he has claimed to be what his own soul knows he is not, and it is as certain as the rising of the sun that he must some day answer for the terrible delusions he has foisted on the minds of over a million persons.

One of the most common objections raised by many erstwhile do-gooders, who are almost totally ignorant of Biblical theology, is that Father Divine, while certainly in error, or mentally unbalanced regarding his obsession of his "deity," has apparently done many wonderful works for others. Therefore these persons maintain that he is doing, in a sense, the works of God, ignorant though he may be of their origin and operation.

To this apparently reasonable objection the Scriptures offer a complete refutation, for it was the Lord Jesus Himself who, when asked by the Jews, "What shall we do, that we might work the works of God?" (John 6:28), replied, "This is the work of God, that you believe on him whom he hath sent" (verse 29). All of Father Divine's good works are not *the* work of God, which is believing in and living for Jesus Christ as Saviour and Lord. This work in turn results in works that *God* reckons good, because they are done through Him, and not through the selfish motive of self-justification or personal glory.

The Scriptures plainly tell us that "all our righteousnesses are as filthy rags" (Isaiah 64:6) in the sight of a holy God, and further, that works adjudged "good" by human standards do not accurately portray the relationship of a man to the Lord. Those who measure Father Divine therefore on the basis of his "wonderful works" might give ear to the words of our Lord Jesus Christ, who solemnly warned that:

> Many will say to me in that day, Lord, Lord, have we not prophesied in thy name? and in thy name cast out devils? and in thy name done many *wonderful works?* And then will I confess unto them, I never knew you: Depart from me, ye that work iniquity (Matthew 7:22, 23).

Thus we see that, although "being evil," many "know how to give good gifts" to their own (Matthew 7:11), even as the Lord said. Father Divine knows how to give good gifts to his children who are in reality through their denial of the Lord Jesus Christ, and their espousal of Father Divine of "their Father the Devil," preferring to "worship the creature (Father Divine) more than the Creator, who is blessed for ever" (Romans 1:25). In the words of Paul, "the things which are seen are temporal, but the things which are not seen are eternal" (II Corinthians 4:18); thus it is that, for Christians, the "eternal God is thy refuge, and underneath are the everlasting arms" (Deuteronomy 33:27). A sound refutation indeed for the temporal and finite god George Baker has become.

The words of the Lord "I will not give my glory unto another . . . I am he: I am the first, I also am the last and beside me there is no God" (Isaiah 48:11, 12) are Father Divine's sentence, for he has usurped the glory which belongs only to God. And upon the death of his mortal form, which he claims will never die, the world and all his followers will know that he was a deceiver, spoken of centuries before in the Scriptures in the twentieth century (Matthew 24:5).

Chapter 9

THE THEOSOPHICAL SOCIETY

Theosophy as a cult system derives its name from the Greek term *theosophia*, literally, divine wisdom. And, in the words of J. H. Fussell its teachings are,

> at the same time religious, philosophic and scientific, postulating one eternal, immutable, all-pervading principle, the root of all manifestation. From that one existant comes forth periodically the whole universe, manifesting the two aspects of spirit and matter, life and form, positive and negative, the two poles of nature between which the universe is woven. Those two aspects are inseparably united; therefore all matter is ensouled by life, while all life seeks expression through forms. All life being fundamentally one with the life of the supreme existence which contains in germs all the characteristics of its source, evolution is only the unfolding of those divine potentialities brought about by the conditions afforded in the various kingdoms of nature. The visible universe is only a small part of this field of evolution.[1]

Theosophy then, may be recognized at the outset as a pantheistic form of ancient Gnosticism, which attempts to embrace religious, philosophic and scientific truth as it is found in all religio-philosophic sources.

According to the views of Theosophists, their Society aims at becoming "a unifier and peace-maker in religion," and further it purposes to "form a nucleus of the universal brotherhood of humanity, without distinction of race, creed, sex, caste or color."[2]

This enobling ideal dreams of a brotherhood of all faiths, or, if we may use the term, a type of homogenized religion, in which all men will agree to the cardinal tenets of Theosophy, in one degree or another. In this respect, it is related to Spiritism, Rosicrucianism, Bahaism and the Great I Am cults.

In theory of course, and quite apart from the Christian Scriptures, this idea is most appealing. But even a cursory perusal of man's demonstrably depraved nature, as revealed in history and in the Bible, renders this Utopian concept an absurd theological farce.

Theosophy as a religion is opposed to virtually every cardinal doctrine of the Christian faith, and finds no support from Judaism, little from Islam, and certainly none from the majority of world religions, with the exception of Buddhism and Hinduism. Christianity, Judaism and Islam all confess a personal God; all believe in a resurrection of the body, and in the authority of the Old Testament. Theosophy, on the other hand, rejects *all* these doctrines. Yet it continues to qualify for the role as a "unifier and peace-maker in religion."

It is an interesting fact that Theosophy speaks in glowing terms of the ancient cult of Gnosticism, which thrived in the first three centuries of the Christian era, and which almost succeeded in doing irreparable damage to historic Christian faith. Paul's epistle to the Colossians, and the epistle of I John are recognized by all Biblical scholars to be direct apologetic thrusts against this cult which spiritualized the Old Testament, redefined contemporary Christian terminology, substituted an impersonal God for the God of revelation, and reduced Jesus Christ to a demi-god, or a pantheistic emanation

---

[1] *The New Schaff-Herzog Religious Encyclopaedia*, Article on Theosophy, page 407.

[2] I. C. Cooper, *Theosophy Simplified*, page 1.

222

from the unknowable divine essence. The well-known Theosophical writer L. W. Rogers however, disdains the counsel of the Holy Spirit, not to mention the warnings of the apostles Paul and John when he states:

> The antagonism between scientific and religious thought was the cause of the great controversy that occurred in the intellectual world in the nineteenth century. If the early teaching of the Christian Church had not been lost, the conflict could not have arisen. The gnostic philosophers who were the intellect and heart of the Church, had a knowledge of nature so true that it could not possibly come into collision with any fact of science; but unfortunately, they were enormously outnumbered by the ignorant, and the authority passed wholly into the hands of the latter. It was inevitable that misunderstanding should follow.[3]

Theosophists then are great admirers of the Gnostics, and this is not at all surprising, since they have adopted much of the terminology and vocabulary of ancient Gnosticism, which looked with disdain upon the material properties of both the world and man, depersonalized God and created various planes of spiritual progression culminating in universal salvation and reconciliation through reincarnation and the wheel concept of progression borrowed unblushingly from Buddhism.

Theosophy does not hesitate to declare that:

> God and man are the two phases of the one eternal life and consciousness that constitutes our universe! The idea of immanence of God is that He is the universe; although He is also more than it is; that the solar system is an emanation of the supreme being as clouds are an emanation of the sea. This conception makes man a part of God, having potentially within him all the attributes and powers of the supreme being. It is the idea that nothing exists except God, and that humanity is one portion of Him — one phase of His being.[4]

In the theology of Theosophy there are seven distinct planes in the universe.

The Physical is the most dense of these planes; that which is next in the order is called the Astral Plane, and above it, the Mental. There are four higher spiritual planes, but to all except initiates and adepts they are as yet "mere names." Man of course has a physical body, a mental body and an astral body. But at this particular stage of cosmic evolution, with but few exceptions, the so-called higher spiritual bodies are still awaiting organization.

A little further on in the chapter, we shall see what relationship this has to the basic doctrines of Christianity. But there can be little doubt that such hypothetical fancies, saturated with gnostic terminology and concepts, cannot help but generate conflict where Biblical theology is concerned.

HISTORICAL SOURCES

It is one of the strange historical peculiarities of the saga of cultism that at least six cults were either started by women or were influenced in a major way by the allegedly weaker sex, (Christian Science, Mary Baker Eddy; Unity, Myrtle Fillmore; Spiritism, the Fox sisters; Jehovah's Witnesses, Marie Russell; Theosophy, Helena Blavatsky and Annie Besant; The Peace Mission Movement, [Father Divine] Sister Penny and Faithful Mary [Viola Wilson].

There is little surprise then, as we consider the cult of Theosophy, that a woman also founded this modern form of Hindu and Buddhistic philosophy, popularized in our age as The Theosophical Society.

The term "theosophy" was introduced, to the best knowledge of reputable scholars, in the third century by a noted philosopher, Ammonius Saccas, the teacher of Plotinus, the great Roman philosopher. Theosophy, however, has a long history traceable directly to the Orient, particularly India, where the Hupanashads and Vedas or Hindu Scriptures form the basis for no small

---

[3]*Elementary Theosophy*, page 22.   [4]*Ibid.*, page 23.

part of the doctrines. The writings of Gautama Buddha and the early Christian Gnostics also heavily influenced the formulation of Theosophical doctrines.

Theosophy claims to be a universal world religion of a distinct nature all its own. But any careful study of its eclectic background readily reveals that much of its "original theology" is borrowed from easily recognizable sources. The modern American history of Theosophy began with the activities of the young and mystically inclined Russian lady Madam Helena Blavatsky in the year 1875 in New York City. Helena Petrovna was born in Ekaterinoslav, Russia, in 1831, the daughter of Peter Hahn, the son of the noble Von Hahn family of Germany. At the age of seventeen, Helena married the Czarist general Blavatsky, a cultured gentleman many years her senior, whom she promptly left after only three months of marriage. It is a known fact that Madam was notoriously short of the virtue of patience and had a violent temper. It is asserted by at least one of her biographers that she married General Blavatsky merely to spite her acid-tongued governess, who, in a moment of sarcasm, declared that even the noble old gentleman would not marry a shrew like Helena. To her credit, Madam Blavatsky repented quite hastily of her revenge upon the governess, but she had already beguiled the General and was forced into a position of compliance with matrimony.[5]

Shortly after her separation from General Blavatsky, Helena embarked upon a long career of travel which eventually led her into the field of mystical religion, which she studied from Tibet, India, Egypt to Texas, Louisiana, Cuba and Canada, landing eventually in New York long enough to found, in the year 1875, The Theosophical Society, in conjunction with Colonel H. S. Olcott and W. Q. Judge, two ardent devotees.

In 1879, Madam Blavatsky left the United States for India, and later died in London, England in 1891. W. Q. Judge split the Society in 1895 and then saw his organization also divided into the "Universal Brotherhood and Theosophical Society" and "The Theosophical Society in America."

Mrs. Blavatsky held Judge in the highest esteem, and Judge wore her mantle of leadership to all intents and purposes as head of the Aryan Theosophical Society of which he was president until 1896 when he died. Madam Blavatsky also founded the Esoteric School of Theosophy in London in 1888, and during her travels in India and England, influenced profoundly one Annie Wood Besant, who took over the reins of leadership after the deaths of Madam Blavatsky, Judge and his successor, Catherine Tingley.

Helena Blavatsky was a woman of tremendous physical proportions with piercing, almost hypnotic eyes, and she ruled the Theosophists during her life and in many areas, even after her death, through her literary works—principally, *The Secret Doctrine*—which is still regarded as divinely inspired interpretations or oracular instructions by most loyal Theosophists.

Annie Besant (1847-1933) was the most prominent of all the British Theosophical luminaries, and one destined to become a bright star in the political fortunes of India. Among her many accomplishments, Mrs. Besant founded the Central Hindu College at Benares, India, in 1898, and also the Indian Home Rule League in 1916. In the year 1917 she was elected president of the Indian National Congress, and was almost always regarded as a powerful figure in Indian politics.

[5]G. B. Butt, *Madam Blavatsky*, London, 1936, page 13.

In 1889, Mrs. Besant, a native of London, became enthralled by the personality and teachings of Madam Blavatsky and forthwith became a devout pupil and disciple. Mrs. Besant believed firmly in the teachings of Madam Blavatsky, and her writings best represent the true doctrines of the cult and are always laudatory of the departed Russian seer.

Mrs. Besant herself had not a few idiosyncrasies, and was highly mystical in her approach to both life and religion, as evidenced in 1925, when she claimed for her adopted son Krishnamurti, an Indian mystic, the title of "Messianic Leader and Reincarnation of the World Teacher."

Such grandeur, however, was renounced by the new Messiah on November 20, 1931, at Krotana, California, then headquarters of the American branch of Theosophy. Mrs. Besant died in 1933, since which time George Arundale and C. Jinara Jodosa have succeeded to the presidency of the Society.[6]

The history of Theosophy then, is marked indelibly by the imprint of the female minds, which, ever since Eve, has apparently been vulnerable to forbidden fruit and the tantalizing tones of various varieties of serpents.

It should be remembered that the Apostle Paul strictly enjoined the Christian Church to forbid women the teaching ministry, especially when men were available to meet this need:

> Let the woman learn in silence with all subjection. But I suffer not a woman to teach, nor to usurp authority over the man, but to be in silence. For Adam was first formed, then Eve. And Adam was not deceived, but the woman being deceived was in the transgression (I Timothy 2:11-14).

It can be clearly seen from the study of non-Christian cults, ancient and modern, that the female teaching ministry

has graphically fulfilled what Paul anticipated in his day by divine revelation, and brought in its wake, as history tells us, confusion, division and strife. This is true from Johanna Southcutt to Mary Baker Eddy to Helena Blavatsky and the Fox sisters, all of whom were living proof of the validity of our Lord's declaration that "if the blind lead the blind, both shall fall into the ditch" (Matthew 15:14b).

THEOSOPHY AND CHRISTIAN THEOLOGY

According to the literature of the Theosophical cult as represented chiefly by Madam Blavatsky, Mrs. Besant, I. C. Cooper, A. P. Sinnett, L. W. Rogers and C. W. Leadbeater, there is a great fraternity of "Mahatmas" or "Masters," who are highly evolved examples of advanced reincarnations whose dwelling place is somewhere in the far reaches of remote Tibet.[7] These divine beings possessed Madam Blavatsky, and utilized her services to reach the generations now living upon the earth with the restored truths of the great religions of the world, which have been perverted by mankind. In this highly imaginative picture the Theosophists add seven planes of progression previously noted, through which the souls of men must progress, on their way to the Theosophist's "heaven" or Devachan.

In keeping with the Theosophists' concept of heaven in the final analysis, is the Nirvana of Buddhism, where the absorption of the personality or the soul into a type of world soul eventually extinguishes personal cognizance — the Theosophists also have their "hell," which, oddly enough, resembles the Roman Catholic purgatory, with indescribable tortures and degrees of degradation. The name for this intermediate state of existence where the departed souls suffer for their past sins while awaiting

[6]See the *New Books of Revelation*, C. W. Ferguson, pages 133-134; Van Baalen, *The Chaos of Cults*, and Horton Davies, *Christian Deviations*, page 21.

[7]See *The Mahatma Letters*, A. P. Sinnett, from the Mahatmas, A. and K. H., London, 1923, page 7.

reincarnation, or the chance to start living in a new body, is Kamaloka, where the atmosphere is ". . . gloomy, heavy, dreary. Men here show out all their passions in all their naked hideousness. . . . They are full of fierce, unsatiated appetites, seething with revenge, hatred. . . ."[8]

Contrary to the Christian doctrines of redemption and punishment, Theosophy offers no forgiveness for sin except through myriads of reincarnations ever progressing toward Devachan, and no eternal retribution for man's rebellion or sin, only the evolutionary terrors of Kamaloka.

> "The Theosophical Society maintains that it has three primary objectives which are: 1) to form a nucleus of the brotherhood of humanity, without distinction of race, creed, sex, caste or color; 2) to encourage the study of comparative religions through philosophy and science; 3) to investigate the unexplained laws of nature, and the powers latent in man. Assent to the first of these objectives is required of membership; the remaining two are optional. The Society has no dogmas or creed, is entirely non-sectarian and includes in its membership adherents of all faiths and of none, exacting from each member only his tolerance for the beliefs of others that he would wish them to exhibit toward his own" (*Schaff-Herzog*, pages 408, 409).

Theosophy then, makes no demands of absolute allegiance to any religion or religious leader, and is resolutely opposed to any form of dogmatism, particularly that type manifested by the Son of God, who said: "I am the Way, the Truth and the Life: no man cometh unto the Father but by me" (John 14:6).

GOD AND MAN IN THEOSOPHY

In common with Christian Science, Unity and other pantheistic theologies, Theosophy conceives of God in strictly impersonal terms, while asserting that man is in a spiritual sense, part of God. L. W. Rogers put it this way, when he wrote:

In divine essence, latent power and potential spirituality, man is an image of God, because he is part of Him. The same idea is more directly put in the Psalms, with the assertion "ye are gods." If the idea of the immanence of God is sound, then man is a literal fragment of the consciousness of the Supreme Being, is an embryo-god, being destined to ultimately evolve his latent powers into perfect expression. The oneness of life was explicitly asserted by Jesus. . . . It is an unqualified assertion that humanity is a part of God as leaves are part of the tree, not something a tree has created, in the sense that a man creates a machine, but something that is an emanation of the tree and is a living part of it. Thus only has God made man. Humanity is a growth, a development, an emanation, an evolutionary expression of the Supreme Being. . . . It is simplicity itself when we think of the solar system as just an emanation of the Supreme Being, as something generated from a central life, an expression of that life which gives rise to the poles within it that we know as consciousness and matter. The human soul is an individualized fragment of that divine life . . . is literally a spark of the divine fire, and latent within it are the characteristics of that central light from which it originated. The theosophical conception of the soul is that it is literally an emanation from God, and since it is therefore of its own essence, it becomes clear why Theosophists assert that man is a god in the making.[9]

In keeping with this position, Mrs. Besant once declared, "Man is a spiritual intelligence, a fragment of divinity clothed in matter" (*Man's Life in Three Worlds*, page 3). As Mrs. Besant's adopted son Krishnamurti once stated, ". . . you are God and you will only what God wills; but you must dig deep down into yourself to find the God within you, and listen to His voice, which is your voice. . . ."

These pantheistic views of the Deity are drawn from the deadly trinity of Hinduism, Buddhism and Gnosticism. And one wonders why Theosophy even

---

[8] Annie Besant, *Ancient Wisdom*, London, 1897, page 93.

[9] *Elementary Theosophy*, pages 23-25; 19, 20.

attempts to use Christian terms at all, except when it is realized that it is easier to reach the Western mind in terms of the Christian religion, than in the language of Hinduism, Buddhism and Gnosticism! So this is the obvious reason for the utilization of redefined Christian terminology by Theosophists.

Concerning the Deity of Jesus Christ and His unique place as *the* Saviour of the world, Theosophy declares that "all men are innate divinity . . . so that in time all men become christs" (Annie Besant, *Is Theosophy Anti-Christian?* page 16).

The clearest position on this subject however, is declared by Rogers, who summed up the position of Theosophy where our Lord and His mission are concerned, when he wrote:

> Most readers will probably agree that a world teacher known as the Christ did come, and that he founded a religion nearly 2,000 years ago. Why do they think so? They reply that God so loved the world that he sent his son the Christ to bring it light and life. If that is true, how can we avoid the conclusion that he or his predecessors, must have come many times before. The belief that he came but once is consistent only with the erroneous notion that Genesis is history, instead of allegory . . . when a new era in human evolution begins, a world teacher comes in a voluntary incarnation and founds a religion that is suited to the requirements of the new age. Humanity is never left to grope along alone. All that it can comprehend and utilize is taught in the various religions. World teachers, the christs and saviours of the age, have been appearing at propitious times since humanity began existence. . . . In the face of such facts, what becomes of the assertion that God so loved the world that he sent his son to help ignorant humanity about 2,000 years ago — but never before? What about the hundreds of millions of human beings who lived and died before that time? Did he care nothing for them? Did he give his attention to humanity for a period of only 2,000 years and neglect it for millions of years? Has anybody believed that God in his great compassion sent just *one* world teacher for that brief period. . . . If God so loved the world that he sent his son 2,000 years ago, he sent him, or some predecessor very many times before.

> Supermen are not myths, or figments of the imagination. They are as natural and comprehensive as humans beings. In the regular order of evolution, we shall ourselves reach their level, and join their ranks, while younger humanity shall attain our present state. As they rose, we too shall rise. Our past has been evolution's night. Our present is its dawn. Our future shall be its perfect day. . . . That is the magnificent future the Theosophist sees for the human race.[10]

The refutation of these non-Christian concepts concerning God and the Lord Jesus Christ, are clearly found in various places in the Bible. The personality of God and the Deity of Christ are forcefully set forth, along with many of the other things that Theosophists deny. The God of the Bible created man, and is separate and distinct from him (Genesis 1:27). He is a cognizant ego, or personality (Exodus 3:14; Isaiah 48:12; John 8:58), and He is triune, three separate persons, Father, Son and Holy Spirit, yet one in essence, or nature (Deuteronomy 6:4; Galatians 3:20). The God of the Bible cannot be equated with the God of Theosophy, nor can Jesus Christ be redefined so that Christ becomes the "innate divinity . . . so that in time all men become christs." Neither the laws of language, logic, nor Biblical theology can permit such extravagances as the Theosophists must insist upon to arrive at such inconceivable equations.

The Theosophist, in his de-personalization of God, however, fails to recognize that man is a cognizant, reflective ego, and that he is a creation of God, in the divine spiritual image, debased though he may be by sin. How is it possible to claim for the creation what is not possessed by the Creator, namely, personality? Are we to assume that the creation, even though part of the divine.

[10]*Elementary Theosophy*, pages 260-263.

is greater in that part, i.e., the possession of ego and personality than the divine itself? To use the analogy of Mr. Rogers, is the spark greater than the flame, the ray greater than the source from which it emanated? Of course not! So then, neither is man greater than God. If man possesses personality and ego, and the Theosophists grant this, then God, by definition, must be personality and ego — a disconcerting fact, but a fact, nonetheless!

The Bible gives much evidence to this effect by underscoring the personality of God in terms of attributes which only a personality can manifest. These traits forever separate Him from the pantheistic God of Theosophy, which is incapable, by definition, of performing these things.

1. *God remembers* — "I, even I, am he that blots out thy transgressions for mine own sake, and I will not remember thy sins" (Isaiah 43:25). 2. *God creates* — "In the beginning God created the heavens and the earth" (Genesis 1: 1). 3. *God knows* — i.e., He has a mind — "The Lord knoweth them that are his" (II Timothy 2:19). "For I know the thoughts that I think toward you, saith the LORD" (Jeremiah 29: 11a). 4. *God is a Personal Spirit* — "I am the Almighty God; walk before me, and be thou perfect" (Genesis 17: 1b). 5. *God has will* — "Lo, I come . . . to do thy will, O God" (Hebrews 10:7, 9).

From this brief resumé of some of God's attributes, the interested reader can doubtless see the vast difference between the God and Father of our Lord Jesus Christ, and the impersonal God of Theosophy. Theosophy's God is not a personal being. He cannot remember, He cannot create, He cannot will, He cannot know, because He is not a personality, but an impersonal "it," an abstract, pantheistic principle, not the God of divine revelation.

Theosophy makes the grave error of all gnostic cults; it divides Jesus and Christ, making Jesus only the outer man, and Christ a divine consciousness immanent within Him, and within all men, to a greater or lesser degree. For Theosophists, Jesus is not *the* Christ of divine revelation, as distinct from the Christ who is immanent within all men. They do not understand that the word *Christ* (*Christos* in the Greek) is a title corresponding to the Hebrew *Messiah*. It is not a force, essence, or divine spark, as any careful reading of a good Greek lexicon will speedily reveal. In the sixteenth chapter of Matthew's gospel, the Apostle Peter affirmed this truth by pointing out in his confession of faith, "Thou art the Christ, the son of the living God" (Matthew 16:16). And John reminds us that, "Who is a liar but he that denies that Jesus is the Christ? He is antichrist, that denieth the Father and the Son" (I John 2:22).

It is unnecessary to pursue this point any further since Christian theology has always maintained that Jesus of Nazareth was the Christ, or the Anointed Redeemer of God; that in some mysterious sense He is God (Isaiah 9:6; Micah 5:2; John 1:1, 14, 18; Colossians 2:9; Revelation 1:16, 17; Isaiah 44:6, etc.). He is the second person of the Trinity, not the theosophical emanation from the impersonal essence they acknowledge as God. And this is why Theosophy is not Christian, and is indeed the very antithesis of historic Christian theology.

In regard to the lengthy statement previously quoted from Rogers, the argument that God must have sent other "world teachers" to meet the requirements for humanity's redemption prior to Christ, is the purest speculation, and directly contradicts the statement of our Lord who affirmed:

> He that entereth not by the door into the sheepfold, but climbeth up some other way, the same is a thief and a robber. . . . All that ever came before me are thieves and robbers: but the sheep did not hear them. . . . I am come that they might have life, and

that they might have it more abundantly. I am the good shepherd: the good shepherd giveth his life for the sheep" (John 10:1, 8, 10b, 11).

The epistle to the Romans points out that God has revealed Himself to the hundreds of millions of human beings about whom Mr. Rogers is so concerned, and that in the face of His revelation, they ". . . changed the glory of the uncorruptible God into an image made like to corruptible man . . . and worshiped and served the creature more than the Creator, who is blessed for ever. . . . Professing themselves to be wise, they became fools" (Romans 1: 23, 25, 22). And as a direct result of this, the Apostle Paul informs us, God abandoned them to themselves so that ". . . when they knew God, they glorified him not as God . . . but became vain in their imaginations, and their foolish heart was darkened" (Romans 1:21).

So it is apparent that mankind has never been without a witness of God's grace and love, but that every time it has been manifested, in His law, His prophets, and finally, in His Son, men have responded with violence, evil and sin of every proportionate degree, so that they are without excuse, and deserving of eternal condemnation.

Quite to the contrary, the idea is not preposterous, as Mr. Rogers suggests, but quite consistent with the character of God and His judgment upon depraved human nature (Romans 3:23). It is a fact that Theosophists refuse to face despite the Dachaus, the Belsens, Auschwitzes and the Buchenwalds and the horrors of contemporary communism. They apparently think that when Adam sinned (an allegory) the race fell spiritually upward, a condition controverted by all the facts of history!

It is true that God so loved the world that He gave His only begotten Son, but it is not true that He has many sons, that they came many times, and that Christ was only one among them. This He Himself denied, and on far better au-

thority than any Mr. Rogers or Theosophy can muster (John 12:44-50).

THE VICARIOUS ATONEMENT

Theosophy is opposed to not only the true Biblical teaching of God's personality and nature, as well as the deity of His Son, but it also vigorously denies Christ's substitutionary sacrifice for all sin (I John 2:2).

One of the most concise statements concerning the views of Theosophy in this area, comes from the pen of L. W. Rogers, who wrote:

Back of the ancient doctrine of the vicarious atonement is a profound and beautiful truth, but it has been degraded into a teaching that is as selfish as it is false. That natural truth is the sacrifice of the Solar Logos, the Deity of our system. Sacrifice consists of limiting himself in the manner of manifested worlds, and it is reflected in the sacrifice of the Christ and other great teachers. Not the sacrifice of life, but a voluntary returning to live in the confinement of material body. Nobody more than the Theosophist pays to the Christ the tribute of the most reverent gratitude; we also hold with St. Paul that each must work out his own salvation. Were it not for such sacrifice, the race would be very, very far below its present evolutionary level. The help that such great spiritual beings have given mankind is incalculable, and is undoubtedly altogether beyond what we were able to comprehend. But to assume that such sacrifice has relieved man from the necessity of developing his spiritual nature, or in any degree nullify his personal responsibility for any evil he has done, is false and dangerous doctrine. . . . And true too, we know that any belief that is not in harmony with the facts of life is a wrong belief . . . the vital point against this plan of salvation is that it ignores the soul's personal responsibility, and teaches that whatever the offenses against God and man have been, they may be cancelled by the simple process of believing that another suffered and died in order that those sins might be forgiven. It is the pernicious doctrine that wrongdoing by one can be set right by the sacrifice of another. It is simply astounding that such a belief could have survived the middle ages and should continue to find millions who accept it in these days of clearer thinking.

The man who is willing to purchase bliss by the agony of another is unfit for heaven, and could not recognize it if he were there.

A heaven that is populated with those who see in the vicarious atonement the happy arrangement letting them in pleasantly and easily, would not be worth having. It would be a realm of selfishness, and that would be no heaven at all. . . . The hypothesis of reincarnation shows our inherent divinity, and the method by which the latent becomes the actual. Instead of the ignoble belief that we can fling our sins upon another, it makes personal responsibility the keynote of life. It is the ethics of self-help. It is the moral code of self-reliance. It is the religion of self-respect![11]

The inconsistency of Theosophists is eclipsed only by their apparent lack of concern for the validity of established terms in both philosophy and theology. Here is a classic example of what we mean. Rogers wants Christians to believe that "nobody more than the Theosophist pays to the Christ the tribute of the most reverent gratitude." But he denies categorically the expressions of that very Christ and the prophecies concerning Him, which state that He came for the express purpose of paying the penalty for all sin.

The Theosophist wants no part of the vicarious sacrifice of Jesus; in fact, it is personally repugnant to him. By his own admission, he considers it "an ignoble belief" that we can fling our sins upon another. But this is exactly what we are called upon to do in the New Testament!

The Scriptures bear incontrovertible witness to the truth that, "Christ died for the ungoldly" (Romans 5:6), and that "The blood of Jesus Christ . . . cleanses us from all sin" (I John 1:7). There is no doctrine found within the pages of the Bible that is better supported or substantiated than that of the substitutionary death of Christ for the sins of the world. As far back in the

Biblical record as Exodus, Moses wrote of God's symbolic use of blood for purification and sacrifice. It will be recalled that Jehovah delivered the Israelites from Egypt by causing all the first-born of the nation, including Pharaoh's own son, to fall under the shadow of sudden death (Exodus 12). The Jews were instructed in this instance to sprinkle the blood of the young lamb on the doorpost and lintels of their homes, and God promised "When I see the blood, I will pass over" (Exodus 12:13). The Lord also instituted the animal sacrifices of the Levitical era and expressly stated, "It is the blood that maketh an atonement for the soul" (Leviticus 17:11).

Following this typology through into the New Testament, we find that Jesus was called the Lamb of God, who takes away the sin of the world (John 1:29), and further, that His blood, shed upon the cross, is our atonement or covering for sin, even for the sins of all mankind (Matthew 26:28; Romans 5:6-8; Ephesians 1:7; Colossians 1:20).

The believer in Christ therefore is saved by grace alone through faith in His blood, and its efficacy for the cleansing of all sin (Romans 3:25). John, the beloved disciple, reminds us in his powerful epistle of this fact (I John 1:7) and Peter declares, ". . . we were not redeemed with corruptible things, such as silver and gold . . . but with the precious blood of Christ, as a lamb without blemish and without spot (I Peter 1:18, 19).

The pages of the New Testament bear incontrovertible testimony that Jesus Christ on Calvary "purchased the church with his own blood" (Acts 20:28), and in the great message of Christ to John recorded in the book of Revelation, we are told that He "washed us from our sins in his own blood" (Revelation 1:5). This was not a pagan sacrifice to placate the wrath of a heathen god's justice. The sacrifice was offered

[11]*Elementary Theosophy*, pages 201-206.

through the Eternal Spirit, to free the sons of men from the curse of sin and to open the path to salvation, through which we now can have boldness to enter into the holiest by the blood of Jesus — a new and living way to the very throne of God our Father (Hebrews 10:19, 20).

Contrasting this picture of concrete Biblical theology with the views of Theosophy, the facts speak for themselves, and they cannot honestly be ignored.

Theosophy, on the other hand, refuses to accept the vicarious atonement for personal sin; it holds instead the Karma (Action and Reaction are equal and opposite) or the "law of causation . . . bidding man . . . surrender all the fallacious ideas of forgiveness, vicarious atonement, divine mercy and the rest of the opiates which superstition offers to the sinner."[12]

Through the application of Karma then, the Biblical doctrine of atonement is neatly supplanted and the authority of Scripture circumvented or negated. Mrs. Besant once wrote that "The atonement wrought by Christ lies not in the substitution of one individual for another. . . ."[13]

As the daughter of an Anglican clergyman, and the former wife of another, Mrs. Besant must have known better. But despite this, she never does satisfactorily explain what the Biblical doctrine of the Atonement *does* mean, if it does not mean what the Christian Church has always maintained.

For Theosophists then, the redemptive love of a personal God as revealed in the substitutionary sacrifice of His most precious possession, His Son, Jesus Christ, is totally unnecessary, and is not the way of salvation. This fact alone would remove Theosophy from any serious consideration of compatibility with Christianity, and we can be grateful that the cult today numbers less than 25,000

world-wide, although its "chapters" or centers can be found in many major cities of the United States and throughout the world. Its rate of growth seems considerably slower than it was in the 1920's, and we can hope that the very fact of its complexity and the involved vocabulary utilized to describe its maze-like theology may yet render it more ineffective, in an age in which precision of definition is at last coming into its own.

In order to be Christian, one must conform to the Scriptures. Theosophy fails to meet this requirement, and must be considered as anti-Christian.

SIN, SALVATION AND PRAYER

The Christian concepts of sin, salvation and prayer need but passing mention relative to the reinterpretation they receive at the hands of Theosophical writers. The teaching of Theosophy on these principal Christian doctrines is very definite and important, and should be understood.

The Bible plainly states that all men have come under the divine indictment of sin (Romans 3:23). The divine remedy for sin, as we have seen, is the redemptive work of Jesus Christ who, "died, the just for the unjust, to bring us to God" (I Peter 3:18). So hideous and degrading was human sin in the eyes of the Holy God, that it required the God-man's death to satisfy the righteous judgment of His Father. Salvation from sin then, is full and complete by faith in Jesus Christ "once for all" (Hebrews 10:10); for the wages of sin is death (Romans 6:23). Since the Theosophist wants no part of the redeeming sacrifice of the cross, and since he denies that personal sin must be atoned for by a power outside himself, like Petra of old, he is deceived by the pride of his heart (Obadiah 3). There can be little doubt that Theosophists, like Unitarians, make salvation by character and progression. Theirs must be a God of love, who al-

---

[12]Annie Besant, *Karma.*

[13]*Is Theosophy Anti-Christian?*, Annie Besant, page 11.

lows the penalty of sin to be worked out on the wheel of reincarnation, and by infinite progression. He does not judge; He cannot, for the spectacle of an impersonal principle judging the actions of a personal being is too much for any serious student of the philosophy of religion, not excepting Theosophists!

The Biblical doctrine of prayer also suffers at the hand of Theosophy. For in the Biblical vocabulary, prayer is personal communion with a personal God; not an abstract force or a cosmic consciousness. Jesus Christ Himself encouraged us to pray many times. (See Matthew 5:44; 6:6, 7, 9; 9:38). He repeatedly emphasized its virtues and benefits. For the Christian then, prayer is the link with the Eternal by which man can come to "the throne of grace," in the power of the Holy Spirit and find "grace to help in time of need" (Hebrews 4:16).

Salvation for the Christian is by grace and true faith in God's only method for making men holy, and through the only "name under heaven given among men, whereby we must be saved" (Acts 4:12). Human sin makes it necessary for this grand redemption, and since Theosophy denies it, it follows of a necessity that redemption would also be negated. Since Theosophy rejects the God of the Bible, or any concept of a personal God, prayer in the Biblical sense becomes impossible, and the sinner's most desperate need, which is to "call upon the name of the Lord" that he might be saved, not from a wheel of incarnations, but from eternal, spiritual and conscious separation from the life and fellowship of God Himself, is ignored or denied.

Contrasted to this Biblical picture of sin, salvation and prayer, Theosophy equates God the Father with the pagan gods, Buddha and Vishnu,[14] and defines prayer, not as personal supplica-

tion for divine mercy and grace (Philippians 4:6, 7), but as "concentrated thought" (*The Changing World,* page 68, Annie Besant). Theosophists also believe that personal sin is removed only by suffering in Kamaloka, and personal salvation is obtained through various reincarnations, ending in absorption of the individual ego. These cannot be viewed as pleasant alternatives to Biblical revelation, but they are all that Theosophy offers.

RESURRECTION VERSUS REINCARNATION

In bringing to a conclusion this chapter on Theosophy, it is necessary for the Christian to understand the one great doctrine which forever removes any possibility of realizing fellowship with Theosophists.

The Apostle Paul, in his great and grand chapter on the resurrection of the body (I Corinthians 15), cites the Resurrection of Christ and its subsequent effect upon the bodies of all mankind as *the* proof that God exists, that Christ is His Son and that the redemption of all believers is assured by His personal triumph over the grave.

Paul goes to great lengths in this chapter to show that "if Christ be not risen, your faith is vain, ye are yet in your sins" (verse 17). For the great apostle, our hope for physical immortality lies alone in the triumphant physical Resurrection of Christ (verse 14), who visibly and tangibly presented Himself alive "with many infallible proofs" (Acts 1:3) to over 500 persons, who knew that it was indeed Jesus, who had conquered the grave in their behalf.

Our risen Lord also promised that one day we should be physically and morally as He is, and that God the Father, through Him, would raise the believing dead and clothe them with immortality at His second advent (I Thessalonians 4).

[14]*Seven Principles of Man,* page 58, Annie Besant.

The condition of the Christian in death, however, is not one of suffering, or repeated reincarnations while atoning for sin, as Theosophy would have it, but one of cognizant personal joy, literally the state of being "at home with the Lord" (II Corinthians 5:8).

The Resurrection of Jesus Christ then, and for that matter, the resurrection of all mankind, leaves no room for the Theosophical dogma of concurrent reincarnations.[15] We indeed concur with the Apostle Paul that, "If in this life only we have hope in Christ, we are of all men most miserable" (I Corinthians 15:19). The souls of the dead do not pass through various reincarnations as Theosophy contends; rather, these souls are either experiencing happiness in Christ's presence (Philippians 1:21), in which case, to die is gain; or they are suffering conscious separation from His presence (Luke 16:19-31). In any case, Scripture clearly shows that reincarnation is not man's destiny, nor is it God's revealed plan for perfecting the souls of men. The Bible tells us that Christ died to fully redeem (Romans 5:6; Hebrews 9:26; 10:12).

OUT OF THE LABYRINTH, INTO THE LIGHT

To wend our way completely out of the maze-like labyrinth of Theosophy and its anti-Christian doctrines into the light of Biblical reality, would probably take many volumes of exacting systematic analysis of this cult, but suffice it to note that Theosophy offers to the sinner no hope of full redemption from sin, only endless reincarnations; it guarantees no personal relationship with a loving, personal heavenly Father, and it ignores completely the true nature, person and work of the Lord Jesus Christ.

The entire system is Eastern in its origin; it is Hinduistic and Buddhistic in its theology, Gnostic in its vocabulary and Christian only in its key terminology, which is specifically designed to imitate the true content of the Gospel.

The Theosophist proudly rejects the atonement on the cross, preferring to trust in his own righteousness (and Karma) and is willing to brave the terrors of Kamaloka itself, rather than to bow the knee to Jesus Christ (Philippians 2).

Let us not then be deceived by the veneer of the intellectual and metaphysical jargon the Theosophist has mastered, nor retreat before his attempt to belittle the preaching of the Cross as "foolishness." We need not defer to his alleged "deeper revelation," to his claims that Theosophy is a higher form of revelation for our age. We are informed in Scripture repeatedly that, "The preaching of the Cross is to them that perish foolishness; but unto us which are saved, it is the power of God" (I Corinthians 1:18). Theosophy is just one more attempt to supplant the authority of Christ and Scripture with "the philosophy and empty deceit" of the world (Colossians 2:8).

Theosophy, in common with the religions of the world, offers no living Redeemer, no freedom from the power of sin, and in the end, no hope for the world to come. Jesus Christ, on the other hand, offers promises by the mouths of prophets and the God who cannot lie, that those who trust in and serve Him shall "receive (for their faith) an hundredfold, and shall inherit everlasting life" (Matthew 19:29).

We must seek to win Theosophists to a saving knowledge of the Gospel, but we must not forget that its theology has many labyrinths, for "there is a way which seemeth right unto a man," in the words of Solomon, "but the end thereof are the ways of death" (Proverbs 14:12).

---

[15]Extensive reference is made to this in Blavatsky, Besant, Cooper, Leadbeater, Rogers, etc.

Chapter 10

ZEN BUDDHISM

The second oldest of all the cult systems considered in this book is a form of Buddhism, one of the major world religions, with a following of more than 153,000,000 persons.

"Zen," as it is known in America, is derived from the Japanese branch of the "meditation" school of Buddhist philosophy, introduced into Japan from China in the seventh century A.D.

The two great pioneers of Zen in Japan were Eisai, who originated the Rinzai sect in A.D. 1191 and Dogen, who founded the Soto sect in A.D. 1227. The Rinzai emphasized the protection of the Japanese nation, and the Dogen emphasized the centralization of power in the Emperor, thus fusing Zen with the very life of the Japanese people and their government.

Today, Zen claims better than 5,000,-000 followers in Japan, and in America there are in excess of 80,000 Buddhists, a good segment of whom are devotees of Zen.

Zealous followers of Zen trace their origin to Buddha, who, they claim, imparted to one of his disciples, Mahakasyapa, what has become known as "the doctrine of the Buddha mind." Buddha, as the legend goes, merely picked the flower in silence, and thus communicated the mystical fragment of his mind, hence the emphasis upon the "Buddha mind" in Zen.

This school of Buddhism, the forerunner of Zen, was formerly established in China about the fifth century A.D., although it had been known and practiced since A.D. 150.

In the United States, Zen has not been taken too seriously by Christians, or Christian theologians, primarily because it has been associated with the so-called beatnik element, as popularized in the writings of such off-beatniks as Jack Kerouac (Dharma Bums).

But Zen cannot be taken lightly, especially when it receives favorable attention from magazines of the standing of *Time, Newsweek, Life* and *The Saturday Review of Literature*. While it is true that Zen has become associated in the minds of some people with bearded beatniks sipping Espresso in Greenwich Village-type Bohemian clubs and garrets, theirs is but a superficial mastery of the Zen terminology, and an almost pathetic attempt to identify their lack of moral and social responsibility with a religio-philosophic system of thought which impresses the Western mind with its virtually irrational and pantheistic approach to religion, and, for that matter, reality. Zen itself is far more complex than the garbled jargon of pseudo-intellectual beatniks who desperately want "a place in the sun" not by virtue of their capacity to earn it, but on the singularly selfish principle that they are entitled to it, because of their own imagined intellectual and philosophical superiority to their fellow man. This is no exaggeration, and anyone acquainted with beatnik adherents to Zen will readily testify to it. They literally believe that the world owes them a living. So, ceaselessly mouthing fragmented sentences, liberally sprinkled with symbolic language, Zen terminology and fractured logic, they urge the clean-shaven and showered populace to embrace what they claim has emancipated them. As one well known comedian stated, "Man! If this is emancipation, we ought to export it to Castro! At least, he has the beard and the plumbing to appreciate it."

THE THEOLOGICAL IMPLICATIONS OF ZEN

Gautama Buddha, who founded the Buddhist religion, was the son of the famous chief of the Kaya tribe of North India, and was born and brought up within a hundred miles of Benares. At an early age, Siddhartha Gautama, his true name, observed the many contradictions and problems of life; he abandoned his wife and son when he felt he could no longer endure the life of a rich nobleman, and became a wandering ascetic in search of the truth about life. Buddhist historians tell us that after almost seven years of wandering, inquiring, meditating and searching, he found "the true path," and "great enlightenment," under the legendary bo tree (tree of wisdom), and thus attained Nirvana, that most desirable of all states, which Zen Buddhism says can be the experience of any member of the meditation school. In this they differ with classical Buddhist thought, which maintains that cycles of reincarnations are necessary in order to attain Nirvana. Zen maintains that it is a here-and-now possibility.

The teachings of Buddha are embodied in his "Four Noble Truths": 1) The truth of suffering; 2) The truth of the cause of suffering; 3) The truth of the cessation of suffering; and 4) The Truth of the Way to remove suffering.

According to Buddhism:

Existence is pain . . . because it is irrevocably bound to the cycle of births and deaths. In this connection, suffering is an undeniable fact of existence.

The cause of suffering is craving, which is in turn due to ignorance, as explained by the twelve-fold chain of causation . . . this chain bears a striking resemblance to the Sankhya categories of Hinduism. . . . At any rate the Buddha was not interested in the deduction of categories; he was wholly concerned with the practical problem of removing the cause of suffering. To this end he put forth the doctrines of impermanence and non-ego. The Buddha declared that things as compounds are always in the process of productions, stagnation, deterioration and extinction and are, therefore, impermanent. Neither is the self permanent, because it is but an aggregate of elements. This does not mean . . . a denial of the empirical self, but a refutation of the permanent, abiding personal identity. These doctrines suggest no nihilism; they were intended to reveal the true nature of existence, which to the Buddha was dynamic becoming, instead of static being or non-being. . . . When suffering is destroyed, Nirvana (negatively, the extinction of passions and positively, the state of bliss) is attained. One then becomes an Arhat or a worthy one, either in this life or after death.

The fourth noble truth is the truth of the Way to remove suffering. This involves a comprehensive system of moral cultivation, but the fundamental Way is a noble, eight-fold path. . . . Right views, right intentions, right speech, right livelihood, right effort, right mindfulness, right concentration and right action. . . . The most important element of these teachings is the middle path, between the extremes of passions and asceticism, the way to realize the four noble truths which the Buddha stated in his first sermon at Benares. Throughout the entire history of Buddhism, the middle path has remained the central concept, although its interpretation varies with the different schools. To the Buddha it was a way of life, a sensible, moderate, comprehensive, practical system of ethics. He called the truths noble, because he regarded nobility as a moral and not a racial quality. His order was established on moral principles, a brotherhood without distinction of castes.[1]

With the true Zenist, teachings of the Buddha places man within the tension of the eternal "now." Reality becomes timeless, and "man will only find his integrity if he can react with an instinctive act to 'now.'" Zen is hence revolutionary, holding that enlightenment comes with clarification and simplification through acting out of old values of time and experience, and depending upon only the supreme experience, "now." One state of consciousness and the next cannot be measured by hours or miles, as the Master tries to say, in a *koan* . . . the standard advice of Zen, using one of the 1700 traditional questions to highlight it. The snap of a finger can be a lesson . . . indicating that this very moment is the immediate experience of reality, past time and embracing all dimensions.

Zen is brusque in its teachings, aimed at the roots of inconsistency. It demands action of a curious sort. This can only be achieved when it is simple, natural and totally correct. It finds truth through shrinking away from error, not discovering a way to truth.

Such a mystic philosophy, oddly enough, bears a kinship to primitive Christianity. Like the ardent fundamentalist awaiting the second coming which will bring heaven to earth, the Zen ideal is to achieve a Nirvanic state and a saintly condition on this earth. . . . The *koan*, which goes back to the twelfth century, when it was devised to test the students' understanding of the Zen spirit and shake his mind from conventional thinking, leaves most professed Zen followers in Japan uninterested today. And, of course, one can never achieve *satori* — the nonrational and intuitive understanding of reality — until he understands the exercises of *koan*. . . . Zen is a paradox within a paradox, a mystical doctrine which laughs at all doctrines and dogma, and becomes a doctrine and dogma in the doing (*Faiths, Cults and Sects of America*, Richard Mathison, pages 364-368).

With a philosophy such as this, it is easy to understand how Zenists can sit cross-legged (zazen — Japanese) meditating upon a flower petal, or a rock thrown haphazard over a floor or on a garden path. For them, reality is not objective correlative truth, but subjective, egocentric reflection, which becomes reality if they deign to participate in its manifestation. The following quotations deal with the theology of Zen Buddhism in a general way, for if ever a system was devoid of a theology, except by implication and interpretation, it is Zen.

SOME AFFIRMATIONS OF ZEN

1. *Revelation*

"Neither logic nor metaphysics is to be relied upon for insight. Theoretical instruction may be positively harmful. The truest of books can be at best but a 'finger pointing at the moon.' If we fix our gaze on the finger, we miss the heavenly glory." Compare this with: Pratt, *The Pilgrimage of Buddhism*, page 264.

"It is an experience of Reality beyond doctrine" — Watts, A. W., *The Way of Liberation in Zen Buddhism*, pages 28, 38.

"Zen is the science of the Real, and the nature of the Real forbids all mental representation of attribution. Reality transcends the dualistic intellectual analysis" — C. F. Linssen, *Living Zen*, pages 76, 79, 81, 131.

2. *Authority*

"Zen is the most irrational and inconceivable thing in the world. Zen was not subject to logical analysis or to intellectual treatment. It must be directly and personally experienced by each of us in his inner spirit" (Barrett, (ed.), *Zen Buddhism*, pages 7-13).

"Zen is ex-hypothesi, beyond the intellect and chains of intellectual usage" (Humphreys, *Zen Buddhism*, pages 2, 3).

"Zen teaches nothing. Whatever teachings there are in Zen, they come out of one's own mind. Zen merely points the way. There is nothing in Zen purposely set up as its cardinal doctrine or as its fundamental philosophy" (Suzuki, *Introduction to Zen Buddhism*, page 38).

"Zen purposes to discipline the Mind itself, to make it its own master through an insight into its proper nature. Anything that has the resemblance of an external authority is rejected by Zen. Absolute faith is placed in man's own inner being . . . Zen wants to live from within, not to be bound by rules, but to be creating one's own rules" (cf. Suzuki, *Introduction to Zen Buddhism*, page 40, 44, 45, 64, 131).

3. *The Nature of God (Pantheism) and Morality*

"I see much common ground in Zen and the mysticism of Meister Eckhart, as he wrote, 'The eye by which I see God is the same eye by which God sees me. My eye and God's eye are one and same — one in seeing, one in knowing and one in loving'. . . . When I have shut the doors of my five senses, earnestly desiring God, I find him in my soul as clearly and as joyful as he is in eternity. . . ." (Ogata, *Zen for the West,* pages 17-19).

"Immaculate Yogins do not enter Nirvana and the precept-violating monks do not go to hell. To avoid sin and evil by obedience to any moral law is only an idle attempt. Every being must act according to the Nature. . . . There is no need of rules of morality" (Humphreys, *Zen Buddhism,* pages 178-179).

"The finite is infinite and vice versa. There are not two separate things, though we are compelled to conceive them so intellectually. The mistake consists in our splitting into two what is really and absolutely one" (Barrett, (ed.), *Zen Buddhism,* page 15).

"Since Zen does not affirm the existence of God, it is not only absolutely destitute to the special revelations of God in His Word, but it is also alien to the God of revelation" (Lit-Sen Chang, *A Christian Challenge to Zen Buddhism and Existentialism,* page 38).

"To quote Meister Eckhart again, 'Simple people conceive that we are to see God as if He stood on that side and we on this. It is not so; God and I are one in the act of my perceiving Him.' In this absolute oneness of things, Zen establishes the foundations of its philosophy" (Barrett (ed.), *Zen Buddhism,* page 245, 270).

4. *Self-Salvation*

"There is no supernatural intervention, way or refuge. We bear the whole responsibility of our actions and no sage whosoever he be has the right to encroach on our free will. . . . Only ignorance, laziness and cowardice can lead us to seek outside aid. One thing seems fundamentally necessary: 'To know ourselves.' If we attain the perfectly clear vision of what we are, we no longer need 'to go elsewhere.' The exterior ways become to us ways of perdition. Just as all men and women of all the people of the earth have said and will say at the moment of their Awakening, so do we say simply, 'I am the way' " (Linssen, *Living Zen,* pages 73-75).

"Smash whatever you come across, smash Buddha, smash your parents and relations. You will be in real emancipation!" (*The Sayings of Master Linchi,* cf. Ogata, *Zen for the West,* page 12).

"The attainment of cosmic consciousness (Satori) does not touch the deepest levels of human life. It does not generally reach down to the depths of conscience in its relation to God. Although a 'cosmic awakening' may bring a certain clarity and peace of mind to a man . . . his life of faith has not been kindled at all, because the object of faith is vague and unhistorical, it is all veiled in the mist of pantheism" (Reichelt, *Meditation and Piety in the Far East,* pages 16, 17).

"Zen takes us to an absolute realm wherein there is no antithesis of any sort."

"Unless we break through the antithesis of 'yes' and 'no,' we can never hope to live a real life of freedom."

"To be free, life must be an absolute affirmation" (Suzuki, *Introduction to Zen Buddhism,* pages 66, 68).

5. *The Holy Spirit (In Zen this is "Satori," which is Enlightenment).*

Example of the Phenomena:

"After his master Matsu abruptly took hold of his nose, he gave it a twist. This made his back wet with cold perspiration. He was said to have 'Satori' " (Barrett (ed.), *Zen Buddhism,* Selected Writings of D. T. Suzuki, page 92).

"When he (Yun-men) was pushed out of the gate by his master, one of his legs was caught and broken. It is said the intense pain resulting from this awakened him, and he had 'Satori' " (Barrett (ed.), *Zen Buddhism,* page 12).

6. *Sin*

"The real human tragedy began when nature was to be dominated by man, for when the idea of power, which is domination, comes in, all kinds of struggles arise" (Barrett (ed.), *Zen Buddhism,* pages 232-234).

"As long as there is a dualistic way of looking at things, there is no emancipation. Light stands against darkness, the passions stand against enlightenment. The Buddha nature knows neither decrease nor increase. The Buddha nature is above birth and death" (Teaching of Hui-Neng, Barrett (ed.), *Zen Buddhism,* pages 169-170).

7. *The Nature of Reality*

"The Unconscious is thus the Ultimate Reality, the true form" (Barrett (ed.), *Zen Buddhism,* page 193).

"Reality transcends the duality. Reality is in itself entirety, it is beyond the traditional opposition of mobility and immobility. The experience of Satori is a result of emancipation from the arbitrary practice of partitioning our mind" (Linssen, *Living Zen,* pages 76, 79, 81, 131).

From the foregoing, the deep-seated philosophical mysticism of the Zen school of meditation of Buddhism is accurately reflected, revealing Zen to be a philosophy that negates a personal God. Secondly, it denies the reality of sin due to the absence of an absolute standard of revealed law and holiness. Thirdly, it rejects the necessity of personal redemption from the penalty of sin revealed in the Person of Jesus Christ, who is *the* Way.

It was the Apostle John who declared, "If we say that we have no sin, we deceive ourselves, and the truth is not in us" (I John 1:8), and this is the curse of Zen, with which its adherents are forced to live and from which they can never fully escape, psychologically or spiritually. The transgression of the law of God does produce guilt in the soul and mind of men which no amount of meditation, cross-legged or head-standing can obliterate. Adherents of the Zen cult dislike intensely the Christian doctrine of personal responsibility for sin. They quite naturally revolt against any form of authority, particularly if it be a revealed authority outside of their own subjective criterions of morality, reality and truth. In dealing with the Zenist, it is wise to concentrate upon the fact of human depravity, and the truth of their famous eternal *now* that, "the heart (cf man) is deceitful above all things and desperately wicked" (Jeremiah 17:9).

Zenists have no antidote for the piercing analytical pronouncements of Scripture "All have sinned, and come short of the glory of God. There is none righteous, no not one" (Romans 3:23; 3:10). And the reality of divine judgment can be brought to bear upon them through proper use of the Scriptures and logic. As we have mentioned previously, one trip through the gas ovens of Dauchau, Belsen, Auschwitz and Buchenwald is worth a thousand theological propositions, and Zenists ought to be reminded of this fact — the fact that those crimes were crimes against an absolute standard which is not subjective, but objective and universal, i.e., "Thou shalt not kill" (Exodus 20:13).

The true nature of Zen is, in reality, that of ego-absorption, to the extent that one becomes obsessed with himself, not with his sins and the desperate need for their erasure. The Zenist is a stranger to social responsibility also, which leaves little to justify his existence.

The finest work from a Christian standpoint on the subject of Zen Buddhism was written by Lit-Sen-Chang, a Christian convert from Zen, and a graduate of Gordon Divinity School in Boston. Mr. Chang has performed a real service for evangelical Christianity by analyzing Zen from the inside, so to speak, in his illuminating book entitled, *A Christian Challenge to Zen Buddhism and Existentialism.*

Excerpts from this book were printed in a symposium entitled *The Challenge of the Cults* (Zondervan, 1961) and with the author's permission, I have quoted some of his telling criticisms from both a philosophical and an experiential viewpoint:

> . . . While, however, Zen gains plausibility from some of its teachings, it is nevertheless objectionable because of its serious inadequacy and sheer futility. 1. *It supersedes the doctrine of a real Creator.* Zen is a peculiar and subtle form of atheism. By identifying deity with nature, it denies the infinity and transcendence of a living personal God. *All visible objects thus become but modifications of self-existence, of an unconscious and impersonal essence which is called God,* Nature, the Absolute, Oneness, Suchness or Tathagata, and so on. This robs God of sovereignty by denuding Him of His power of self-determination in relation to the world. God is reduced to the hidden ground. Since Zen does not affirm the existence of the living God, it is not only absolutely destitute of the special revelation of God in His Word, but is wholly alien to the God of revelation. Since Zen contends that it does not deny the existence of God, it is more plausible in its pretension, more fascinating to the imagination, and less revolting to the reason than those colder and coarser theories which ascribe the origin of the world to mere mechanical laws of matter and motion. Besides, Zen adopts the very language of theism, and may even generate a certain mystic piety; statements are often embellished with the charms of seductive eloquence, and become the formidable rival of Christian theism. . . . Charles Hodge reminds us that "there is a sense in which the Spirit is given to every man. He is present with every human mind exciting to good, restraining from evil. Without this common grace, or general influence of the Spirit, there would be no difference between our world and hell." But, he stresses, "the fact that the Spirit is present with every human mind, and constantly enforces the truth to that mind, is no proof that He makes immediate supernatural revelations to every human being. *The fact is, we cannot see without light. It is vain to say that every man has an inward light sufficient to guide him without the sun. Facts are against the theory. . . . To tell men, therefore, to look within for an authoritative guide and to trust to their irresistible convictions, is to give them a guide which will lead them to destruction!"* (*Systematic Theology*, 1, pages 101, 102).

In "seeing into one's own nature" Zen fails to recognize that self-knowledge is rather twofold: first, the condition in which man was at first created; and second, his condition since Adam's fall. Ever since Adam revolted from the fountain of righteousness, all the parts of the soul have been possessed by sin. The nature of man, in both intellect and will, requires regeneration of the Spirit. Romans 3:10-18 depicts our human nature as vicious not simply by custom (or as some modern Zen scholars put it in terms of so-called "force of habit," Linssen, *op. cit.,* pages 103-106, but rather perpetually corrupted. Therefore, instead of "seeing into one's own nature," our need is for a new nature and for the Spirit of God to form in us anew the image of God which was marred by the transgression of Adam.

In the attainment of Enlightenment, Zen ignores the Pauline declaration in I Corinthians 2:5 that "your faith should not stand in the wisdom of man, but in the power of God." . . . Although Zen asserts that without "Satori" (Enlightenment), "Zen is a sealed book" (Barrett, *op. cit.,* page 135), the actual fact is that apart from divine revelation, "Satori" can never be genuine. Even a psychologist as sympathetic to Zen as Dr. Carl G. Jung says, "We can never decide definitely whether a person is really enlightened, or whether he merely imagines it; we have no criterion of this." These words of Jung actually appear in the foreword of *An Introduction to Zen Buddhism,* by Suzuki, greatest living authority of Zen Buddhism.

Although Zen professes to open a "third eye" (Barrett, *op. cit.,* page 3), we recall Augustine's statement that "the mental eye remains shut until it is opened by the Lord" (*De Peccat. Merit. et Remiss.,* II, v). Because "the god of this world hath blinded the minds of them which believe not" (II Corinthians 4:4), Zen in fact is truly "a sealed book."

Since Zen is a revolt against any authority and it does not affirm the existence of God nor the need of a Saviour, it has no object of faith. It purposes to discipline the mind and make it its own master, through seeing into one's own nature. Although Zen masters claim "certain similarities between Satori and the sudden conversion of Christianity" (Watts, op. cit., page 76), there is in fact no ground for comparison. In their own words they say, "conversion is held to come to essentially depraved man from an external God, while Satori is the realization of one's own inmost nature. . . . It is one's own spiritual realization that makes the difference and the mind is its own place, and of itself can make a heaven of hell, a hell of heaven" (Ibid., pages 79, 80).

"Zen thus distorts the Biblical truth by ignoring the gravest factor in the history of mankind, namely, the fall of Adam, by which the ground is cursed and our sorrows are multiplied (cf. Genesis 3:16-19). It is true, Adam's spiritual life was originally united and bound to his Maker, but his estrangement and his revolt against God perverted the whole order of nature in heaven and earth and deteriorated his race. Zen masters, like other philosophers, only tell us to live in harmony with nature, but the Bible enjoins us to regulate our lives with a view to God to whom nature belongs (*The Challenge of the Cults*, Zondervan, A *Christianity Today* Symposium, 1961, pages 66-72).

THE CORE OF ZEN

Zen Buddhism is one of the more philosophic and orientally flavored imports of cultism, peculiarly adapted to the Western mind in that it decidedly shuns outright supernaturalism, but encourages a "Satori" (enlightenment) experience, "an awakening of our original inseparability with the universe."

The ultimate goal of Zen Buddhism is "the freeing of the will," so that "all things bubble along in one interrelated continual." Those who would be disciples of Zen must allow their ego to be detached until "one's real self calmly floats over the world's confusion" like a ping-pong ball skimming over the turbulent rapids of life. In a world faced with deprivation, hunger, disease, death and the ever-present shadow of nuclear warfare, the denial of such reality borders on the criminal. Zen Buddhism, in our opinion, is the most self-centered, selfish system of philosophy that the depraved soul of man can embrace, for it negates the two basic principles upon which all spiritual reality exists, "Thou shalt love the Lord thy God with all thy heart, with all thy soul and with all thy mind . . . and thy neighbor as thyself" (Matthew 22:37, 39).

For Zenists, it is love of self first, last and always. This is the core of Zen, which releases one from spiritual responsibility and substitutes intellectual enlightenment for conversion, and the absence of concern for one's fellow man for peace with God. Historically, Buddhism has produced nothing but indescribable conditions under which its subjects live. For in almost every area of the world where Buddhism of any form holds sway, there stalks the spectre of disease, hunger, and moral and spiritual decay. The peoples of the Orient are the slaves of their religions, and Buddhism, with its egocentricity, inherently selfish concept of life and of responsibility to society is by all odds one of the greatest offenders. Let those who consider Zen as a superior form of religious philosophy look well at its history and its fruit, for "by their fruits ye shall know them" (Matthew 7:20).

Chapter 11

THE CHURCH OF THE NEW JERUSALEM — SWEDENBORGIANISM

It is virtually impossible to study the field of cult systems without coming to grips with the theology of the Church of the New Jerusalem, which, although small in number in America (46 churches and 6,000 members), wields a considerable influence in intellectual church circles. This is true both in the United States and abroad. In foreign countries, particularly in England and in the Scandanavian nations, this particular cult has had a steady growth and today numbers more than a hundred thousand members throughout the world.

Whereas most if not all of the major cult systems are the products of individuals who could scarcely be called intellectuals, the Church of the New Jerusalem had as its founder, one of the most gifted and reṣpected intellectuals of any age — Emanuel Swedenborg.

Swedenborg was born in Stockholm, Sweden, on January 29, 1688. He died in London on March 29, 1772, in his eighty-fifth year. The son of the Reverend Jasper Swedborg, noted Lutheran minister and court chaplain to the king of Sweden, he was later to become a professor and dean of the University of Upsala. Swedenborg indeed sprang from noble roots, and at an early age, distinguished himself as a mathematician, mining expert, engineer and inventor. So enormous were his contributions to his homeland, particularly in the area of high finance and in mining, that in 1808, thirty-six years after his death, his remains were removed from their crypt in the Lutheran church in Princes Square, Radcliffe Highway, London, and transported by the Swedish navy to their final resting place in a cathedral in Upsala. Some two years after this,

the king of Sweden and his family, in the presence of numerous dignitaries and churchmen, dedicated a memorial to him, which action had been unanimously voted by the Swedish parliament.

Swedenborg received his education at Upsala and then traveled for the next four years in Germany, Holland, England and France. He occupied his spare time between studies with various inventions.

William White, in his life story of Swedenborg, stated that, as a result of his inventive genius, Swedenborg produced "a new stove, a magazine air gun, methods of salt manufacture . . . and drew plans for a flying machine and the construction of docks" (page 29, also see *Transactions of the International Swedenborg Congress,* 1910, page 5).

To add to his achievements during this particular period of inventive genius, Swedenborg was working on what he called, "a sort of ship in which a man can go below the surface of the sea and do great damage to the fleet of an enemy."

At the close of his journeys abroad, Swedenborg wrote various books and attracted the attention of his sovereign, King Charles XII, who recognized his genius and appointed him a professor in the Swedish College of Mines. Following the death of the king in 1718, Swedenborg became a member of the Swedish Diet. In his capacity as Royal Assessor of Mines, he traveled extensively throughout Europe, broadening his background and already-tremendous grasp of philosophy, art, theology and metaphysics. This he dutifully recorded in his *Diary of Travel,* a type of John Gunther approach to the Europe of the eighteenth century.

Swedenborg was the associate of kings, princes, scholars, mathematicians, engineers, astronomers and theologians. Few men have ever attained the degree of acceptance and prominence which he enjoyed during his long life, a recognition which extended to multiple fields of interest, and was a lasting tribute to his intellectual breadth and brilliance.

The year 1745 marks the turning point in Swedenborg's career as a world figure in many fields of endeavor, for it was then that he maintained that he received a divine summons to become "both a seer and a revelator of the things of the spiritual world, and simultaneously of the spiritual truth and doctrine which underlies the literal and symbolic sense of the sacred Scriptures." Between the years 1743 and 1749 Swedenborg maintained that he experienced heavenly visions and periods of great temptation, which culminated in a prodigious writing program, containing such works as *Arcana Coelestia; The Earths in the Universe; The White Horse of the Apocalypse; The Apocalypse Explained; The Last Judgment; The New Jerusalem and Its Heavenly Doctrines* and *The Apocalypse Revealed.*

Swedenborg went on to publish *The Angelic Wisdom Respecting the Divine Love and Wisdom,* 1763; *The Angelic Wisdom Respecting the Divine Providence,* 1764; *The Delights of Wisdom Concerning Conjugial Love,* 1768; *A Re-fixed Position Concerning the Doctrine of the New Church, Signified by the New Jerusalem in Revelation,* 1769; and his final work, *The True Christian Religion Containing the Universal Theology of the New Church, or Universal Theology and the New Church,* 1771. This was, quite literally, a compendium of his entire theological structure.

One authority on Swedenborg also points out that,

He wrote books on algebra, giving the first account in Swedish of the differential in integral calculus; on a mode of finding the longitude at sea by the moon; on decimal money and measures; on the motion and position of the earth and planets; on the depth of the sea and the greater force of the tides in the ancient world; on docks, sluices and salt works; on chemistry and on atomic geometry. . . . After some philosophical writing, dissatisfied with his results, he studied anatomy and physiology and wrote books thereon. . . . At the age of fifty-four, Swedenborg was probably one of the most learned men alive, taking learning as meaning acquaintance with the universe as then known. One small indication of this is the fact that the then president of our royal society, Sir Hans Sloan, invited him to become a corresponding member.

Then a curious thing happened. In 1743 he had spiritual illumination, with tremblings, voices, lights, etc. and began to have access to the spiritual world, or to think that he had. During the years 1749 to 1756 he published in London his *Arcana Coelestia,* in four volumes quarto, and later, other books containing the exposition of his doctrines, which were mainly concerned with the spiritual interpretation of the Scriptures, and particularly, of Genesis and Exodus. Much of this seems fanciful, but the thought is always systematic, and no one can reasonably say that Swedenborg was insane. Moreover, he was shrewd in worldly affairs, affable in society, and discussed politics and finance in the Swedish Diet like a man of the world. For a score of years after, he began to write and publish his theological works, which number about forty volumes.

But this exposition of Scripture, received, as he believed, direct from the Lord, and considered by him to be the important part of his work, is less interesting to us than his spiritual experiences, which are mostly described in his spiritual diary, from whence he copied extracts occasionally into his theological works. These experiences were admittedly of such a character, that in an ordinary man they would have sufficed to qualify him for an asylum. Swedenborg talked, or thought he talked, with Luther, Calvin, St. Augustine, St. Paul — arguing theological questions with them and disagreeing violently with the last-named, and many others including "one who, it was given me to understand, was Cicero."

All this, although probably not hallucinatory, is at least perilous stuff, and the Swedenborgians have done wisely not to base much on it. He wrote automatically, heard clairaudiently, and saw writings and the very words of the writings, even with the eyes shut. But there are a few incidents on record which are evidential, and these may reasonably give us pause before deciding for a subjective explanation of this seer's experiences.[1]

I shall allude in a few moments to the evidence just mentioned. But enough has been shown to establish beyond reasonable doubt, that Swedenborg was a unique individual, whose mind and influence reached into many quarters in the age in which he lived. Frank Sewall has best summed it up when he wrote:

> Like many leaders of the world's thought, Swedenborg has required the vista of the years by which to be seen in his real significance. Immanuel Kant concealed his indebtedness to him under the persiflage of the "Dreams of the Spirit Seer"; Goethe is more outspoken in his gratitude and his Faust is full of the Swedenborg world view. Swedenborg's trinal monism, the doctrine that the one embraces in itself three essential degrees, end, cause, effect: the grand man, or the human form of society; the spiritual, as being the real, world; the spiritual meaning as being the true and essential meaning of the Scriptures; God as divine man, visible and adorable in the glorified humanity of Jesus Christ; the doctrine of the world as a vast system of tremulations, set in motion by its center, the infinite, divine love, and transmitted through successive spiritual and natural spheres and atmospheres; of the kingdom of heaven as a kingdom of uses — these ideas are permeating all the new developments of philosophic and religious thought.

> Early theological prejudice is giving way to profound respect; the time seems near when Swedenborg's own prophecy from the words of Seneca will be realized, "There will come those

who will judge without offense or favor."[2]

I cannot agree with Mr. Sewall relative to any idea of accepting Swedenborg's basic theological system, which I shall review shortly. But that his place in the intellectual hall of man is secure, no objective person can deny. Swedenborg's theological position, however, in the realms of non-Christian cultism, constitutes quite another area of concern. For genius though he was, his concept of the Bible, the writings of the Apostle Paul and numerous other books of the Old and New Testaments, places him well outside the pale of Christian theology. This is true not only concerning the Canon, but concerning such doctrines as the nature of God, the holy Trinity, the Atonement of Jesus Christ, and the doctrines of Salvation and Resurrection. We cannot ignore the person of Emanuel Swedenborg; in fact, as the years pass, through the church which he inspired and the reputation which he earned, he is becoming a growing influence to be reckoned with and carefully examined in the light of historic Christianity.

No less an authority than the noted scholar Conrad J. Bergendoff, writing in the *Encyclopedia of Religion* edited by Virgilius Ferm, declared of Swedenborg's theology and background:

> Swedenborg's student days included impressions from Rudbeck at Upsala, Newton Boyle Halley, Locke in England, Polhem in Sweden, the Cartesian philosophy and the Cambridge neoplatonists.

> The Principia, 1734, explained the universe in mechanistic terms. A mystical view pervaded the Oeconomia Regni Animalis (1736); the world was now less a machine, more an organism. The anima receives illumination from the central source of life and light when the mense controls man's physical nature. Between the physical and spiritual worlds there is a close correspondence, each natural phenomena shadowing a spiritual reality. . . . This idea was ex-

---

[1]*Spiritualism, Its History, Phenomena and Doctrine*, J. Arthur Hill, pages 42-44.

[2]*The New Schaff-Herzog Religious Encyclopaedia*, page 188.

tended to the mystical correspondence between words and their inner meanings — a basis for his later spiritual interpretation on Scripture, which was a means whereby the divine was communicated to the mind of man.

In Amsterdam, in 1736, Swedenborg had an experience in photism; in Amsterdam in 1744 and in London in 1745, he experienced visions, which he interpreted as revelations of the Creator-Redeemer. Henceforth he proclaimed the truth received by direct vision, though the Biblical imagery of *De Cultet Amore Dei,* 1745, concealed much the same cosmology and psychology as the earlier works. Even his visions were more confirmation than a source of speculation.

The theology of Swedenborg is systematically presented in *The True Christian Religion,* 1771. The orthodox doctrines of the Trinity and the Atonement were repudiated. Redemption consists of the Incarnate God overcoming the increasing powers of hell. Man's freedom enables him to choose and follow the good. On death he enters the realm of the spirits, when he either ascends to the heavenly sphere, becoming an angel, or descends to hell, becoming an evil spirit. Following a spiritual mode of interpreting Scripture which he held to be inspired, Swedenborg considered the Judgment to have come in 1757, and Christ's second coming as a victory over rebellious spirits. The heavenly world corresponds to the human, and even marriage finds transcendent meaning in the heavenly marriage of kindred souls. The orthodox churches must give way to the new church (which dates from the completion of *The True Christian Religion,* 1771) when men will be correctly instructed in the truth of God (page 752).

The organization of The Church of the New Jerusalem took place in London, in 1788, although it is generally traced back by its membership to the Second Coming of Christ, which, according to Swedenborg, took place when he received "the key to the interpretation of Scripture." There can be little doubt that Swedenborg's revelation of what he termed the spiritual meaning of Scripture did indeed become the doctrinal basis of the church formed in his honor.

The first general conference of the church met in 1789. It was organized in 1821 the "General Conference of the Ministers and Other Members of the New Church Signified by the New Jerusalem in the Apocalypse, or Revelation of John."

This particularly British convention in 1926 numbered seventy societies, with 7,100 members.

The Swedenborg Society since the year 1810 has published a voluminous amount of literature, specializing in translations of Swedenborg's works. Branches of the church are today to be found in Africa, South America, Russia, Italy, Sweden and many other countries.

In the United States, the church was organized in Baltimore, Maryland, in 1792. Its name is "The General Convention of the New Jerusalem in the United States," the name taken in 1817. The churches are essentially autonomous, but are bound together in a cooperative type of association governed by a general convention, which meets annually. Under the powers of the convention, the education and ordination of pastors for the establishment of missions, orders of worship and church government, etc., are carried out. In 1876 a form of worship was adopted for the United States, for in the church structure, Swedenborgian ministers may serve any place throughout their convention, but the pastors are restricted to local societies.

The Church of the New Jerusalem has had its internal controversies, however, particularly in 1890, when the Pennsylvania association, which might be termed "fundamentalist Swedenborgians" insisted upon the virtual canonization of Swedenborg's writings, and withdrew when they could not force this upon the convention. In 1897, this group became known as "The General Church of the New Jerusalem," which has a presiding bishop, a cathedral and an educational institution, located in

Bryn Athyn, Pennsylvania.

The Church of the New Jerusalem is therefore inextricably bound to teachings of Swedenborg and his interpretations of the Bible. Women may join the church at the age of eighteen and men at the age of twenty-one, but only after studying the writings of Swedenborg for some six months. The Christian sacraments of baptism and communion are maintained in the church, as are the marriage and burial services. The official litrugy (resembling in practically every detail the Anglican *Book of Prayer*) and the church government are Episcopal, with but minor alterations.

Such is the background of Swedenborgianism, seen in the perspective of history. In the realm of theology, however, a somewhat different picture emerges.

THE OCCULT THEOLOGY OF SWEDENBORG

As has been noted in the preceding history, Swedenborg considered himself, from 1745 until his death, the seer of a new revelation from God, which superseded the interpretational powers of the apostles, church fathers and the reformers. This is a singular fact which emphasizes that modesty was not one of his strong points. Mr. Hill has already mentioned a point which can be easily documented, namely Swedenborg's preoccupation with dreams, visions and alleged messages and conversations with spirits and the spirit world. It is of no small significance that Sir Arthur Conan Doyle, the great advocate of Spiritism, and every Spiritist, historian and theologian of note, claim Swedenborg as a medium who practiced clairvoyance and other phenomena associated with Spiritism. Swedenborg never denied such practices, and therefore, whether his followers wish to concede it or not,

he was most certainly, in a large area of his theological and metaphysical practices and thought, a thorough-going Spiritist. One instance of Swedenborg's clairvoyance should be noted, in order to underscore this fact:

In September, 1759, Swedenborg was one of a party of sixteen guests at the home of Mr. William Castel at Gottenburg, three hundred miles from Stockholm. He had arrived from England at four o'clock P.M.

About six o'clock Swedenborg went out and returned to the company, quite pale and alarmed. He said a dangerous fire had just broken out in Stockholm at the Sodermalm (Gottenburg is about fifty German miles from Stockholm), and that it was spreading very fast. He said that the house of one of his friends, whom he named, was already in ashes, and that his own was in danger. At eight o'clock, after he had been out again, he joyfully exclaimed, "Thank God! The fire is extinguished the third door from my house!" This news occasioned great commotion throughout the whole city. . . . It was announced to the governor that same evening. Sunday morning, Swedenborg was summoned to the governor, who questioned him concerning the disaster. Swedenborg described the fire precisely, how it had begun and in what manner it ceased, and how long it had continued. On the same day the news spread throughout the city, and as the governor thought it worthy of attention, the consternation was considerably increased; because many were troubled because of their friends and property. . . . On Monday evening a messenger arrived at Gottenburg, who was dispatched by the Board of Trade during the term of the fire. In the letters brought by him the fire was described in precisely the manner stated by Swedenborg. On Tuesday morning a royal courier arrived at the governor's with a melancholy intelligence of the fire, of the losses it had occasioned, and of the houses which had been damaged and ruined, not in the least differing from that which Swedenborg had given at the very time when it happened; for the fire was extinguished at eight o'clock.[3]

---

[3]See Borowsky's, *Darstellung Des Lebens und Charakters*, Immanuel Kant, Konigsberg. 1804, pages 211-225. Trans. in *Dreams of A Spirit Seer*, pages 158, 159, appen. Letter from Kant to Charlotte Von Knobloch. See also Tafels, *Documents Concerning Swedenborg*, Vol. II, Part One, page 628.

This remarkable piece of clairvoyance is in company with Swedenborg's actual communication with a deceased Dutch ambassador. This "ghost" had informed Swedenborg that his wife should not pay for a silver service as demanded by a goldsmith, for he declared he had paid the smith several months earlier. The receipt of the transaction was in a bureau in a room upstairs in the house which the widow then occupied. The lady insisted that the bureau had been thoroughly searched, but Swedenborg informed her that her husband had a secret drawer behind the left drawer of the bureau, where the receipt would be found. Upon complying with Swedenborg's instructions, the widow found the receipt, precisely as he had described it. Jung Stilling in his *Theory of Pneumotology,* page 92, recounts this, as does Kant in *Dreams of a Spirit Seer,* appendix, pages 157 and 158. The gentleman who "received the proof from Swedenborg" was an intimate friend of Stilling.

Such evidence of Swedenborg's communication with the spirit world in direct violation of the express commands of Scripture (Leviticus 19:31; 20:6) would be sufficient to make any thoughtful Christian suspicious of his theological system, even before examining it thoroughly. But happily, an exhaustive analysis of his voluminous works is not necessary to reveal the fact that Swedenborg was far from being a Christian, and certainly was not a Christian theologian.

The following quotations drawn from his basic writings reveal his thinking in certain key areas of Christian theology, and are reproduced for the purpose of contrast with the teachings of Scripture.

DOCTRINES

I. *The Holy Scriptures — the Word of God*

"Which are books of the Word? That the books of the Word are all those which have the internal sense; but that those books which have not the internal sense are not the Word. The books of the Word in the Old Testament are: The five books of Moses, the book of Joshua, the book of the Judges, the two books of Samuel, the two books of the Kings, the Psalms of David, the prophets Isaiah and Jeremiah, Ezekiel, Daniel, Hosea, Joel, Amos, Obadiah, Jonah, Micah, Nahum, Habakkuk, Zephaniah, Haggai, Zechariah and Malachi. In the New Testament, the four evangelists, Matthew, Mark, Luke and John and The Apocalypse. The rest have not the internal sense . . . The book of Job is an ancient book, which indeed contains internal sense, but not in series . . ." *Miscellaneous Theological Works* of Emanuel Swedenborg, page 312, No. 16.

II. *The Trinity of God*

1. "That many of the false tenets . . . as likewise concerning the person of Christ, together with all the heresy from the first ages down to the present day, have flowed from no other source than from a doctrine founded upon the idea of three Gods. We have not room to demonstrate within the limits of this epitomy, but shall be shown and proved at large in the work itself. . . ."

2. "From the Nicene Trinity and the Athanasian Trinity together a faith arose by which the whole Christian Church has been perverted. That both the Nicene and Athanasian trinities are a Trinity of Gods can be seen from the creeds. . . ." *(The Swedenborg Epic* by C. O. Sigstedt, page 177).

3. "After this they proceeded to deliberate about the Holy Spirit; and previous thereto they laid open the idea generally received concerning God the Father, the Son and the Holy Spirit which is, that God the Father is seated on high with the Son at His right hand, that by them is sent forth the Holy Spirit to enlighten and instruct mankind. But instantly a voice was heard from heaven saying, "We cannot endure an

idea formed on such a conception. . . . There is not a mediating God distinct from Him (Jehovah); much less is there a third God distinct from two others, as one person is distinct from another person; wherefore, let the former idea which is vexing and frivolous be removed, and let this which is just and right be received, then you will see clearly. . . . One God cannot come forth and proceed from another, by another, but what is divine may come forth and proceed from one God? Is not the Divine Essence one and indivisible, and inasmuch as the Divine Essence or the Divine Esse is God, is not God therefore one indivisible? On hearing these words, they that sat on the seats unanimously agreed in this conclusion, that the Holy Spirit is not a distinct person of Himself, consequently not a distinct God of Himself; but that by the Holy Spirit is meant the divine sanctity, coming forth and proceeding from the one and only omnipresent God, who is the Lord. . . . Lastly this decree was passed: that from what has been deliberated, in this council clearly sees and of consequence acknowledges the only truth, that in the Lord God of the Saviour Jesus Christ, there is a divine Trinity, consisting of the all-begetting divinity which is called Father, the Divine Humanity, which is the Son, the Divine Proceeding, which is the Holy Spirit: and they lifted up their voices together saying, "In Jesus Christ dwells all the fullness of the Godhead bodily" (Colossians 2:9). Thus there is one God of the Church" (*Miscellaneous Theological Works* of Emanuel Swedenborg, pages 249, 250 and 251).

III. *Vicarious Atonement*

1. "Who does not know that God is essential compassion and mercy . . . and who does not hereby see that it is a contradiction to assert that mercy itself or goodness itself can heal man from anger, become his enemy, turn himself away from him and determine on his damnation, and still continue to be the same, divine being or God? Such things can scarcely be attributed to a good man, but only to a wicked man, thus not to an angel of heaven, but only to an angel of hell; wherefore, it is abominable to ascribe them to God. That they have been ascribed to Him appears evident from the declaration of many fathers, churches and councils from the first ages unto the present day; also from the inferences which have necessarily followed from first principles and to their derivatives, or from causes and to their effects, as from a head into the members; such as, that He required to be reconciled; that He is reconciled through the love He bears toward the Son, and by His intercession and mediation; that He required to be appeased by the view of the extreme sufferings of His Son; so to be brought back to mercy and constrained as it were, to show it, and thus from an enemy to be made a friend, and to adopt those who were the children of wrath, as the children of grace. That the notion that God can impute the righteousness and merits of His Son to an unrighteous man, who supplicates it from faith alone, is also a mere human invention, as will be seen in the last analysis of this work" *(Miscellaneous Theological Works,* page 202-203).

2. "This I can affirm, that whenever the angels hear anyone say, that God determined in anger on the damnation of the human race, and as an enemy was reconciled by His Son, as by another God begotten from Himself, they are affected in a manner similar to those who from an uneasiness in their bowels and stomach are excited to vomiting; on which occasion they say, What can be more insane than to affirm such things to God?" (ibid., page 203).

3. "That no other salvation is believed this day than such as is instantaneous, from an immediate act of mercy is evident from hence . . . for if the cooperation is taken away which

is effective through the exercise of charity by man as of himself, the spontaneous cooperation which is said to follow faith of itself, becomes passive action, which is nonsense, and a contradiction of terms; for supposing this to be the case, what need would there be of anything more than such momentary and immediate prayer as this: 'Save me, O God, for the sake of the sufferings of Thy Son, who has washed me from my sins in His own blood, and presents me pure, righteous and holy before thy throne?' . . . And this ejaculation of the mouth might avail even at the hour of death, if not sooner, as a seed of justification. But nevertheless, instantaneous salvation, by an immediate act of mercy, is to this day a fiery, flying serpent in the church, and that thereby religion is abolished, security introduced and damnation imputed to the Lord, may be seen . . . in the work concerning Divine Providence, published at Amsterdam in the year 1764" (ibid., page 204, 205).

4. "Hence may be seen the import of the Lord's words in Mark, 'He that believeth and is baptized shall be saved, but he that believeth not shall be damned' (Mark 16:16).

"Here, to believe, signifies to acknowledge the Lord and to receive divine truths from him by means of the Word, and to be baptized, is to be regenerated by the Lord by means of those truths . . . hence it is evident what is signified by these words of the Lord, 'Except a man begotten of water and of the spirit, he cannot enter into the kingdom of God'; namely, that unless man is regenerated by the truths of faith, and by a life according to them, he cannot be saved . . . that all regeneration is effected by the truths of faith and by a life according to them . . . Let those therefore

who are baptized remember that baptism itself confers upon its subjects neither faith nor salvation, but testifies that they will receive faith and that they will be saved if they are regenerated" (ibid., page 110, 111).[4]

IV. *The Destiny of Man*

1. "Man is so created that, as to his internal, he cannot die . . . . this internal exists in every man who is born: his external is that by which he brings into effect the things which belong to his faith and love. The internal of man is the spirit, and the external is the body. The external, or the body, is suited to the performance of uses in the natural world, and is rejected or put off, at death, but the internal, which is called the spirit, and which is suited to the performance of uses in the spiritual world, never dies. After death, this internal exists as a good spirit and an angel, if the man has been good during his abode in his world, but if during that time he has lived in evil, he is, after death, an evil spirit. . . . The spirit of man after the dissolution of the body appears in the spiritual world in a human form in every respect, as in the natural world . . . except that he is not encompassed with the gross body which he had in the world. This he leaves when he dies, nor does he ever resume it. This continuation of life is meant by the Resurrection. The reason why men believe that they shall not rise again before the Last Judgment, when, as they suppose, the whole creation will be destroyed, is that they do not understand the Word, and because sensual men place all their life in the body and imagine that unless the body be re-animated, the man be no more" (ibid., page 117, 118).

---

[4]Apparently Swedenborg's line of communication broke down with the celestial plane at this juncture, because in the light of the best contemporary Biblical scholarship, it is now conceded that Mark 16:9-20 are spurious, and were not written by Mark at all, since they are missing from the best manuscripts of the New Testament, Codex Vaticanus and Siniaticus. This is only one more proof that it is unsafe to impute to God one's own theological interpretations, since the Deity has the disconcerting habit of acquitting Himself at the expense of would-be seers, in this case, Swedenborg.

SOME ANSWERS TO SWEDENBORG

Swedenborg is consistently and energetically refuted by the epistles of Paul, particularly, the Book of Romans, chapters five through eight, which Swedenborg detested with abject horror. By attempting to circumscribe the New Testament revelation of Christianity to the gospels and the Book of Revelation, Swedenborg revealed the essential weakness of his theological system. He was apparently well aware of the fact that Pauline theology, if accepted at face value, would vitiate almost en toto his own. So he began with the basic assumption that *he* was right, and that the Apostle Paul was wrong! In some of his visions and dreams, he stated that he actually argued with Paul, Luther, Calvin and others. And, as ego triumphed, these great thinkers all retreated before Swedenborg's new revelations.

However, one factor must never be forgotten, and that is the statement that the New Testament is the criterion for measuring all subsequent revelations, and whatever is found to be contrary to it, must be and always has been, rejected by the Christian Church.

Swedenborg would have done well to remember that the interpretations of dreams and visions, and the things of the dimension of the spirit "belong to God" (Genesis 40:8), and that we are constantly admonished to accept no other gospel, even if it be revealed by an "angel from heaven" (Galatians 1:8, 9), two points he apparently overlooked. The Apostle Peter, ever consistent with Paul, urges the Christian Church to always remember that "prophecy came not in old time by the will of man, but holy men of God spoke as they were moved by the Holy Ghost" (II Peter 1:21). But since Swedenborg did not believe in the person of the Holy Spirit, it is easy to understand how he could reject such divine counsel.

True to the pattern of most non-Christian cults and cult leaders, Swedenborg vigorously attacked the Christian doctrine of the Trinity. Apparently he was unaware of the fact that he was involved in contradiction when he asserted that Jesus Christ was Jehovah, while at the same time he denied the tri-unity of Jehovah, so clearly taught in both the Old and New Testaments (see Genesis 1:26; Isaiah 6:8; Zechariah 12:10; Luke 1:35; Matthew 3:16, 17; Matthew 28:19, etc.).

Dr. Charles Hodge, the great Princeton theologian, recognized the dangers of Swedenborg's theology and summed them up in his own terse manner when he wrote:

> Concerning God, Swedenborg taught that He was not only essence, but form, and that that form was human. He called God "the eternal God-Man." There are two kinds of bodies, natural and spiritual. Every man, besides his external, material body, has another, which is internal and spiritual. The latter has all the organs of the former, so that it can see, hear and feel. At death the outer body is laid aside, and the soul thereafter acts through the ethereal spiritual vestment. This is the only resurrection which Swedenborg admitted. There is no rising again of the bodies laid in the grave. As, however, the spiritual corresponds to the material, those who know each other in this world will enjoy mutual recognition in the world to come. This feature of his anthropology is connected with his doctrine concerning God. For as the soul from its nature forms for itself a body for action . . . so the essence of God forms for itself a spiritual body for external manifestation.
>
> As there is but one divine essence Swedenborg maintained that there can be but one divine person. The church doctrine of the Trinity he regarded as tri-theistic. He admitted trinity of principle, but not of persons. As soul and body in man are one person, and from them proceeds the activity which operates without, so in God the divine and human are the Father and the Son as one person, and the Holy Spirit is their efficiency, or sanctifying influence.
>
> Concerning man, Swedenborg taught that he was created in the image of God, and was created with a very exalted nature. The scriptural account of

the fall he understood allegorically as the apostasy of the church. Men, however, he admits are sinful, and are even born with a bias to evil, but they have not lost their ability to do good. They consequently need redemption. They are susceptible of being delivered from evil, not only because they retain their moral liberty, but also because in virtue of the inward spiritual body they are capable of intercourse with spiritual beings. . . . Swedenborg reports many instances in which he conversed with God and angels, good and bad. By angels, he meant men who had departed this life. He did not admit the existence of any created intelligence other than man.

Christ he held to be Jehovah, the only living and true God, the creator, preserver and ruler of the world. As the divine person was God and man from eternity, his incarnation, or manifestation in the flesh, consisted in his assuming a material body with its cyclical life in the womb of the Virgin Mary. This was the body which grew, suffered and died. In the case of ordinary men, the material body is left forever in the grave, but in the case of Christ, the outward body was gradually refined and glorified, until it was lost in that which is spiritual and eternal. This idea of a two-fold body in Christ is not by any means peculiar to Swedenborg. . . . Christ's redemptive work does not consist in his bearing our sins upon the tree, or making satisfaction to the justice of God for our offenses. All idea of such satisfaction, Swedenborg rejects. The work of salvation is entirely subjective. Justification is pardon granted on repentance. The people of God are made inwardly righteous and being thus holy, are admitted to the Presence of God as holy spirits in heaven (*Systematic Theology*, Vol. II, pages 421-423).

Dr. Hodge's evaluation is of course accurate, and Swedenborg's denial of the person of the Holy Spirit, as previously mentioned, places him and his followers not only outside historic Christian theology, but in diametric opposition to the express declaration of the Word of God.

The Apostle Peter, in dealing with the sin of Ananias and Sapphira, most explicitly declared that the Holy Spirit was a person to whom men could lie, as did they, and that in perpetrating this sin, its magnitude could only be realized when it was understood that "thou hast not lied unto men, but unto God" (Acts 5:4, 5).

Numerous other incidents in the New Testament can be used to document the person of the Holy Spirit, and Swedenborg's denial of the vicarious nature of the atonement needs no serious refutation in the light of such passages as Isaiah 53, Matthew 20:28, Mark 10:45 and I Peter 2:24.

In his epistle to the Romans, chapter five, the Apostle Paul underscores the role of our Lord as the "second Adam," who died for us when we were "yet sinners," and his entire fifteenth chapter of his first epistle to the Corinthians is devoted to proving the resurrection of the body, citing Christ as the archetype of that resurrection (see also Colossians 1:15-18; I Thessalonians 4:13-17; II Thessalonians 1). Far from Swedenborg's concept that Christ's body was not raised in mortal flesh and bones, and that man will not participate in this resurrection, the redeemed to immortality and the unregenerate to eternal judgment, the Bible is replete with references to just such a historical and still future event. The Book of Revelation, of which he was so fond, refutes his position entirely by teaching the very thing Swedenborg denied, namely, that there will be a resurrection of both the just and the unjust (Revelation 20:1-14), an event declared to be in conjunction with "the appearing of the glory of the great God and our Saviour, Jesus Christ" (Titus 2:13).

Quite to the contrary then where Swedenborg's theology is involved, Jesus Christ's Second Coming did not take place in the eighteenth century. The New Jerusalem has not descended out of heaven from God. Our resurrection has not taken place, and judgment has neither begun, nor consummated. Swedenborg, despite his acknowledged brilliance and abilities, is found in far too many places to be in opposition to the teachings of the Word of God, and demonstrates in a most unique way an analysis of this type of mind. Oddly enough, this type was described by the Apostle Paul, whom Swedenborg could not abide:

> For Christ sent me not to baptize, but to preach the gospel: not with wisdom of words, lest the cross of Christ should be made of none effect. For the preaching of the cross is to them that perish foolishness; but unto us which are saved it is the power of God. For it is written, I will destroy the wisdom of the wise, and will bring to nothing the understanding of the prudent. Where is the wise? where is the scribe? where is the disputer of this world? hath not God made foolish the wisdom of this world? For after that in the wisdom of God the world by wisdom knew not God, it pleased God by the foolishness of preaching to save them that believe. For the Jews require a sign, and the Greeks seek after wisdom: But we preach Christ crucified, unto the Jews a stumblingblock, and unto the Greeks foolishness; But unto them which are called, both Jews and Greeks, Christ the power of God, and the wisdom of God. Because the foolishness of God is wiser than men; and the weakness of God is stronger than men. For ye see your calling, brethren, how that not many wise men after the flesh, not many mighty, not many noble, are called: But God hath chosen the foolish things of the world to confound the wise; and God hath chosen the weak things of the world to confound the things which are mighty; And base things of the world, and things which are despised, hath God chosen, yea, and things which are not, to bring to nought things that are: That no flesh should glory in his presence. But of him are ye in Christ Jesus, who of God is made unto us wisdom, and righteousness, and sanctification, and redemption: That, according as it is written, He that glorieth, let him glory in the Lord (I Corinthians 1:17-31).

It would be possible to go on at some length in a refutation of Swedenborg's theology, but the issues, we believe, are clearly discernible, as is the verdict of Scripture. Swedenborg was a rationalist, and paradoxically, a mystic. He was one who absorbed the introspective and subjective philosophy of René Descartes, and the empiricism of John Locke, which he combined with the transcendentalism of Immanuel Kant, thus forming a mold into which Christian theology was poured, and what would not go into the mold (selected Old Testament works, the Pauline epistles, Acts, James, Peter, Jude, etc.), he simply discarded. What emerged was a deeply speculative philosophical system of theology, couched in a redefined Christian terminology, and buttressed with mystical visions, trances and dreams, which, when apparently confirmed by clairvoyant experiences, such as the Stockholm fire episode, previously narrated, gave some credence to his claims, and still continues to deceive many so-called intelligent persons today.

In his counsel to the church at Colosse, the Apostle Paul uttered a warning which the followers of Swedenborg in particular might well take cognizance of:

> Beware lest any man spoil you through philosophy and vain deceit, after the tradition of men, after the rudiments of the world, and not after Christ. For in him dwelleth all the fulness of the Godhead bodily (Colossians 2:8, 9).

The great tragedy of Emanuel Swedenborg is that he would not submit himself and his great mind to the discipline of the Holy Spirit and the Scriptures, and because of this, and because of his deliberate preoccupation with spiritism and the occult, in direct disobedience to the express teachings of God, he was despoiled, even as Paul had warned. He was deceived by dreams and visions and the machinations of him whom the Scriptures describe as the "spirit that now worketh in the children of disobedience" (Ephesians 2:2b).

Chapter 12

THE BAHAI FAITH

The Bahai Faith is a non-Christian cult of distinctly foreign origin, and began in Persia in the nineteenth century with a young religious Persian business man known as Mirza Ali Muhammed, who came to believe himself to be a divine manifestation projected into the world of time and space as a Bab or Gate, leading to a new era for mankind.

As Christianity almost since its inception has had heretics and heresies within its fold, so Islam was destined to experience the same fragmenting forces. Mirza Ali Muhammed, alias the "Bab," thus became one of the sorest thorns in the flesh of Islamic orthodoxy, so much so, that he was murdered by Mohammedan fanatics in 1850, at the age of thirty-one. He had derived much of his early encouragement and support from the Shaykahis sect in Persia, and was a prominent teacher among them for six years prior to his death. Though Christians have not been known historically for putting to death those who disagreed with them, (notable exceptions are the Reformation and Counter-Reformation, the Inquisition and certain phases of the Crusades), violence may generally be said to follow in the wake of "new" revelations in most other religions, and unfortunately, in the case of Mirza the pattern held true.

The history of Bahai then, began with the stupendous claims of a young Persian to the effect that "the religious leaders of the world had forgotten their common origin . . . Moses, Jesus and Mohammed were equal prophets, mirroring God's glory, messengers bearing the imprint of the Great Creator . . ."[1]

Today this still remains the basic tenet of the Bahai faith, albeit with the addition of Zoroaster, Buddha, Confucius, Krishna, Lao and Baha'u'llah, the last great manifestation of the Divine Being, whose name transliterated means, "the glory of God."

As Bahai history records it, the Bab was sentenced to death and was executed July 8, 1850, at Tabriz. In the view of thousands, as the Bahais tell it, 750 Armenian soldiers raised their rifles and fired at the figure of the prophet. Alas, all this was to no avail, for, when the smoke cleared, the Bab had not only emerged unscathed from the fusilade of bullets, but the bullets had burned through the ropes which held him, and he stood unfettered.

The story goes on to relate that he then disappeared from their vision, but upon returning to his cell, the guards found him lecturing his disciples. After he had finished his speaking with them, he is reported to have said, "I have finished my conversation. Now you may fulfil your intention."

He was then led out before the same firing squad and this time they did not miss.

All of these events were accompanied by the cries of "Miracle! Miracle!" from the assembled populace, who, though they outnumbered the luckless Armenian soldiers, failed to rescue the Bab from his appointment with the Dark Angel.

The Bahai history of the event also records that a fierce black whirlwind swept the city immediately after the execution of the Bab, somewhat remi-

[1]*Faiths, Cults and Sects in America,* Richard Mathison, page 105.

niscent of the earthquake and darkness which fell over the earth upon the death of Jesus Christ on Golgotha, eighteen centuries before.

The death of the Bab however, did not dim the rising star of the new faith. Instead, he had, according to his followers, prophesied that "The oneness of all mankind" was an inevitability, and that in time there would come, "a Promised One" who would unify all the followers and would himself be a manifestation of the only true and living God.

Modern Bahaism considers that the Bab's great prophecy has been fulfilled by one Mirza Husayn Ali, better known to the initiated as "Baha'u'llah," who succeeded the Messianic throne of Bahaism upon the death of his unfortunate predecessor, the Bab.

In the year 1863 this same Baha'u'llah declared himself as that one prophesied by the Bab thirteen years previously, the One who was "chosen of God, and the promised one of all the prophets."[2]

Apparently Baha'u'llah's conviction that he was to play Christ to the Bab's John the Baptist, convinced the majority of "Babis," as they were then known. However, his brother, Mirza Yahya apparently did not receive the message clearly, for he forthwith renounced Baha'u'llah and allied himself with the enemies of the new-found religion, the Ski'ihs.

His nefarious plot however, miserably failed, and the Bahai movement gradually evolved into what is known today as the Bahai Faith, a worldwide religious organization which continues to teach in the tradition of Baha'u'llah, who, despite his claims to immortality, was rather unceremoniously deprived of his earthly existence by the Angel of Death who overtook him in 1892 in Bahji in Palestine. He was seventy-five at the time.

The Bahais have had their share of persecution, and more than nine thousand were killed between 1850 and 1860. But in their emigration to America, in the person of Abdul Baha, son of Baha'u'llah, who arrived in the United States in 1912, Bahaism truly received "a new birth of freedom," and today carries on its work in more than 50 countries, claiming a world membership in the millions. This figure, however, is quite suspect, since in 1963 they reported only 204 "centers" in the United States, with a membership a shade less than 10,000. Since the Bahais are not overly strong in publication of statistics, and the information must literally be ferreted out, it is hard to estimate their rate of growth. However they have gained some notable converts in the past, and no less a figure than Count Leo Tolstoy spoke warmly of their "spirit of brotherhood," and Woodrow Wilson's daughter became one of the first converts to Bahaism through the work of Baha'u'llah in the United States.

The world headquarters of the Bahai Faith is in Haifa, Israel, from whence are circulated the writings of Baha'u'llah and Abdul Baha. Baha'u'llah reputedly left behind him 200 books and tablets, which, along with the writings of his son, constitute the final authority for religious faith and conduct where members of the cult are concerned.

The writer had the opportunity to visit the famous nonagon structure, or Temple, as it is known, in Wilmette, Illinois, a building which utilizes the symbolic number nine, sacred to Bahais. Its architecture is a combination of synagogue, mosque and cathedral, in which

[2]J. E. Esslemont, *Baha'u'llah and the New Era,* Bahai Publishing Company, Wilmette, Illinois, 1951, page 38.

there are nine concrete piers, nine pillars representing the nine living world religions, and nine arches. The building is beautifully centered in a park having nine sides, nine avenues and nine gateways, and containing nine fountains. The worship service consists of readings from Baha'u'llah, Abdul Baha, and whatever sources from the major religions are thought to be meaningful for the worshipers that day. Around the central dome of the building are various quotations both inside and out, all of which emphasize the unity of all the great religions of the world.

The Bahai Faith utilizes the calendar for observances designed by the Bab, which consists of nineteen months, each having nineteen days. New Year's Day falls on March 21st. There are no ministers, and no ecclesiastical machinery or organization. The Bahais employ only teachers, who conduct discussion groups in homes, or Bahai Centers, and who are willing to discuss with anyone the unity of all religion under Baha'u'llah.

The Bahai cult also maintains schools for study in Colorado Springs, Colorado; Geyserville, California; Eliot, Maine and Davison, Michigan.

Bahaism then, is a Persian transplant to the United States, a syncretistic religion which aims at the unity of all faiths into a common world brotherhood, in effect, giving men a right to agree to disagree on what the Bahais consider peripheral issues, but unifying all on the great central truths of the world religions, with Baha'u'llah as the messiah for our age. Abdul Baha did his work well, and when he died at the age of seventy-seven in Palestine (1921), he bequeathed a budding missionary arm of his father's faith to Shoghi Effendi (Guardian of the Faith), whose influence continues in and through the teaching hierarchy of the Bahai movement in America.

An Interview with a Bahai Teacher

In the course of researching the history and theology of Bahaism the author had many interviews with adherents of the cult during which direct questions were asked concerning Bahaism in its relationship to Christianity. The following are excerpts in question and answer form from a number of these interviews with recognized Bahai teachers and leaders. The quotations are direct in all instances and were compared with my notes after each dialogue.

QUESTION: Do you in Bahaism believe in the Holy Trinity?

Answer: If by the Trinity you mean the Christian concept that the three persons, Father, Son and Holy Spirit, are all the one God, the answer is No.

We believe that God is one person in agreement with Judaism and Islam. We cannot accept the idea that God is both three and one and find this foreign to the Bible which Christianity claims as its source. Not a few Jewish scholars are in complete agreement with us on this point as is the Koran.

QUESTION: Is Jesus Christ the only manifestation of Deity, that is, is He to be believed when He said, "I am the Way, the Truth and the Life, no one comes to the Father but by Me?"

Answer: No, we believe that Jesus was only one of nine manifestations of the divine being and appeared in His era of time to illumine those who lived at that time. Today Baha'u'llah is the source of revelation.

Jesus was the way, the truth and the life for His time but certainly not for all time.

Abdul Baha points out that we are to honor all the major prophetic voices, not just one of them. He said:

"Christ was the prophet of the Christians, Moses of the Jews — why should not the followers of each prophet recognize and honor the other prophets?"[3]

[3]*Wisdom of Abdul Baha,* page 43.

Abdul Baha also occupied an exalted place in the thinking of Bahais. It was he who said:

"The revelation of Jesus was for His own dispensation, that of the Son, and now it is no longer the point of guidance to the world. Bahais must be severed from all and everything that is past — things both good and bad — everything . . . Now all is changed. All the teachings of the past are past. Abdel Bahai is now supplying all the world." Ref. Star of the West, official Bahai publication, December 31, 1913.

QUESTION: Since you believe that Jesus spoke to His own dispensation, how do you account for the fact that in numerous places in the New Testament both He and His apostles and disciples asserted that He was the same "yesterday, today and forever" (Hebrews 13: 8), and that His words were binding and "would never pass away"?

Answer: You must realize that many of the things written in the New Testament were written long after Jesus died, hence it is impossible to have absolute accuracy in everything. It would be natural for His followers to assert such things, but the revelation of Baha'u'llah supersedes such claims.

QUESTION: Resurrection of Jesus Christ from the dead is the true foundation of Christian experience. Does Bahaism accept His bodily resurrection and ascension into heaven, and do you believe that He is indeed a high priest after Melchizedec's order as intercessor before the throne of God for all men?

Answer: The alleged Resurrection of Jesus and His Ascension into heaven may or may not be true depending upon your point of view. As I said before, we are concerned with Baha'u'llah and the new era or age, and while we reverence Jesus as we do the great prophets of other religions, we do not believe that it is necessarily important that the Bahai faith recognize every tenet of a specific religion. We believe that Jesus conquered death, that He triumphed over

the grave, but these are things which are in the realm of the spirit and must receive spiritual interpretation.

QUESTION: Then you do not actually believe in the bodily resurrection of Christ?

Answer: Personally, No. But we do believe that resurrection is the destiny of all flesh.

QUESTION: In Jewish theology and Christian theology much stress is laid upon sacrificial atonement for sin. The theology of Christianity in particular emphasizes that Jesus Christ is the Lamb of God who takes away the sin of the world. It was John the Baptist who so identified Him, and the New Testament gives ample testimony to His substitutionary atonement for the sins of the world. If, as Christianity maintains, "He is the satisfaction for all our sins, not for ours only, but for the sins of the whole world" (I John 2:2), why, then, is Abdul Baha, or for that matter, Baha-'u'llah important? If God has revealed Himself finally and fully as the New Testament teaches in Jesus Christ (Colossians 2:9), why should further manifestation be necessary?

Answer: But you see that is precisely our position. God has not finally and fully revealed Himself in any of the great manifestations but through all of them culminating in Baha'u'llah. A Christian may find spiritual peace in believing in a substitutionary atonement. In Bahaism this is unnecessary. That age is past. The new age of spiritual maturity has dawned through Baha'u'llah, and we are to listen to his words.

QUESTION: If, as you say, Moses, Buddha, Zoroaster, Confucius, Christ, Mohammed, Krishna, Lowe and Baha-'u'llah are all equal manifestations of the divine mind, how do you account for the fact that they contradict each other, for we know that God is not the author of confusion, or is He?

Answer: While it is true that there are discrepancies between the teachings of the great prophets, all held to basic moral and spiritual values. So we would expect unity here, and in the light of man's perverse nature, variety of expression in the writings and teachings of their disciples.

QUESTION: Do you accept all of the sacred books of the world religions, that is, do you consider them all to be of equal authority with the writings of Bahai Ali?

Answer: The writings of Baha'u'llah, since they are the last manifestation, are to be considered the final authority in matters of religion so far as the Bahai faith is concerned.

QUESTION: Jesus Christ taught that salvation from sin could be effected only by acceptance of Him as the sin-bearer mentioned so prominently in the 53rd chapter of the Prophet Isaiah. Just how in Bahaism do you deal with the problem of your own personal sin?

Answer: We accept the fact that no one is perfect, but by the practice of principles laid down by Baha'u'llah and by making every effort through prayer and personal sacrifice to live in accord with the character of the divine being revealed in him, we can arrive at eventual salvation as you like to term it.

QUESTION: What you mean then is that you, yourself, are cooperating with God in working for your salvation?

Answer: Yes, in a sense I suppose you could say this is true, though God in the end must be merciful to us or no one would be fit to escape the divine judgment.

QUESTION: Then you do believe in final judgment and the existence of paradise and hell?

Answer: Yes, the Bahai faith recognizes divine judgment though not in the graphic terms which Christians portray it. We know nothing of eternal flames where sinners will be confined forever without respite. We do believe in the paradise of God which will be the abode of the righteous and in the resurrection and the final writing of all things.

QUESTION: Putting this on a per-

sonal basis without meaning to be offensive, might I ask you if you personally this moment believe that you are a good practicing disciple of Baha'u'llah, and, this being true, do you at this moment know with certainty that your sins have all been forgiven you, and that if you were to be called to accounting tonight before the throne of God, you would be adjudged fit and worthy to enter His kingdom?

Answer: I don't believe any person can make that statement, for no one is perfect or holy enough to merit the paradise of God, and those who so claim to have attained this exalted position are in the eyes of the Bahai faith presumptuous, to say the very least. I could not at the moment say this for myself, but I hope that this will be the case when I die.

QUESTION: Does the Bahai faith recognize the personality and deity of the Holy Spirit of God as revealed in the New Testament?

Answer: I believe it is in your Gospel of John that Jesus promised another Comforter who would abide always. We understand this to be the coming of Baha'u'llah, a direct fulfillment of the words of Jesus.

QUESTION: Is it not true that a great deal of your theology is borrowed from Islam and that Mohammedans have made the same claim for Mohammed where Christ's prophecy in John 14 is recorded as you have for Baha'u'llah?

Answer: There is no doubt that we reverence the Koran as one of the divine manifestations of illumination and Mohammed as one of the nine revelators, but Islam historically has persecuted us, in fact, it was followers of Islam who killed the Bab and persecuted Baha'u'llah.

With reference to the Mohammedan claim in John 14, I believe it is true they also make this claim.

The foregoing interview is better than a hundred statements of a nonmember of the cult and most clearly expresses what separates Bahaism from historic Christianity. No true follower of Baha'u'llah, by his own admission, can claim this moment peace with God and the joy of sins forgiven, an experience which belongs only to those who have put their faith and trust in the grace and sacrifice of the Son of God (John 5:26; 6:47; Ephesians 2:8-10).

The fact that the major prophets of Bahaism contradict each other is paradoxically overlooked by Bahaism, which in its quest for an ecumenical syncretism prefers to avoid rather than explain the great contradictions between the major faiths.

As do most cults, the Bahai faith will pick and choose out of the Bible that which will best benefit the advancement of their own theology, irrespective of context or theological authority. The author was impressed during this interview with the fact that the Bahai teacher who granted it had been a disciple for more than fifty years and was certainly in a position to understand the historic views of Bahaism. Throughout the course of the interview which was held at a Bahai meeting in her home, we had the opportunity time and time again to present the claims of Jesus Christ, and it became apparent that her god was Baha'u'llah. The Bahai plan of salvation is faith in him plus their own good works. Their concept of hell is largely remedial not punitive. Their eschatology, a combination of Islam, Judaism and Christianity, and their authority the writings of Baha'u'llah and Abdul Baha.

All of the some thirty persons present took extreme pride in the fact that they had arrived at a faith which was progressively superior to all other religions and which magnanimously was willing to embrace the truth that was in every one of them to bring about the new era of which their leader had prophesied.

There was no virgin born Son, there was only a Persian student; there was no miraculous ministry, there was only the loneliness of exile; there was no power over demons, there were only demons of Islam; there was no redeeming Saviour, there was only a dying old man; there was no risen Saviour, there was only Abdul Baha; there was no Holy Spirit, there was only the memory of the prophet; there was no ascended High Priest, there were only the works of the flesh; and there was no coming King, there was only the promise of a new era. In that room the words of the Lord of hosts were fulfilled with frightening accuracy:

"This people honor me with their lips but their heart is far from me; in vain do they worship me, teaching for doctrines the commandments of men" (Matthew 15:8, 9).

All the Bahai temples in the world and all the quotations from sacred books cannot alter the fact that the heart of man is deceitful above everything and desperately wicked. Who can understand it? Baha'u'llah could not, but could his disciples today? Penned in the words of our Lord:

If ye were blind ye should have no sin: but now ye say, We see; therefore, your sin remaineth. . . . Ye are from beneath, I am from above: ye are of this world; I am not of this world. I said therefore unto you, that ye shall die in your sins: for if ye believe not that I am he, ye will die in your sins. . . . When ye have lifted up the Son of man, then shall ye know that I am he, and that I do nothing of myself; but as my Father hath taught me, I speak these things. . . . He that believeth on me, believeth not on me, but on him that sent me. . . . if any man hear my words, and believe not, I judge him not: for I came not to judge the world, but to save the world. He that rejecteth me, and receiveth not my words, hath one that judgeth him: the word that I have spoken, the same shall judge him in the last day. For I have not spoken of myself; but the Father which sent me, he gave me a commandment, what I should say, and what I should speak. And I know that his commandment is life everlasting: whatsoever I speak therefore, even as the Father said unto me, so I speak (John 9:41; 8:23, 24, 28; 12:44, 47, 48-50).

CONCLUSION

Looking back over our survey of Bahaism, we can learn a number of things about this strange cult. First, we can discern that, although it is Oriental in its origin, Bahaism has carefully cloaked itself in Western terminology, and has imitated Christianity in forms and ceremonies wherever possible in order to become appealing to the Western mind.

Second, Bahaism is eager *not* to come into conflict with the basic principles of the Gospel, and so, Bahais are perfectly willing that the Christians should maintain their faith in a nominal sense, just so long as they acknowledge Baha'u'llah and the general principles of the Bahai Faith.

Third, Bahaism deliberately undercuts the foundational doctrines of the Christian faith, by either denying them outright, or by carefully manipulating terminology so as to "tone down" the doctrinal dogmatism which characterizes orthodox Christianity.

Bahaism has few of the credentials necessary to authenticate its claims to religious supremacy. An honest Bahai will freely admit that in not a few respects, their system was patterned after many of the practices of Islam and Christianity.

Bahais will quickly draw upon the scriptures of any religion of their sacred nine to defend the teachings of Baha'u'llah and Abdul Baha. In this they have a distinct advantage, because not a few of them are well informed concerning the Scriptures of the religions of the world, particularly, the Old and New Testaments and the Koran.

Thus, it is possible for a well-trained Bahai cultist literally to run the gamut of theological quotations in an eclectic Mosaic design to establish their basic thesis, i.e., that all men are part of a great brotherhood revealed in this new era by the manifestation of Baha'u'llah.

The cardinal doctrines of the Christian faith, including the absolute authority of the Bible, the doctrines of the Trinity, the Deity of Jesus Christ, His Virgin Birth, Vicarious Atonement, Bodily Resurrection and Second Advent are all categorically rejected by Bahaism. They maintain that Christ was *a* manifestation of God, but not the *"only* manifestation" of the Divine Being.

There is very little indeed that a true Christian can have in common with the faith of Bahai. There is simply no common ground on which to meet, or to talk once the affirmations have been made on both sides of Jesus Christ, as opposed to Baha'u'llah. Of course, there is the common ground of Scripture upon which we can meet all men to proclaim to them the indescribable gift of God in the Person of Christ, but there can be no ground for fellowship with the Bahai Faith, which is, at its very core, anti-Christian theology.

Finally, as is always the case with non-Christian cults, the refutation of Bahaism must come from a sound knowledge of doctrinal theology as it appears in the Scriptures. No Christian can refute the perversions of the Bahai Faith unless he is first aware of their existence and of their conflict with the doctrines of the Bible. We must therefore be prepared to understand the scope of the teachings of the Bahais, their basic conflict with the Gospel and the means by which we may refute them as we witness for Christ. The United States has become a great battleground where the cults are concerned. More and more new varieties are springing up each year, many of them drawing heavily upon Oriental sources to convert the naive and the uninformed. It is for these people that we must have a deep compassion, and we must not only be actively engaged in refuting that which is false in their teachings, but we must also be giving ourselves constantly to the cause of evangelizing them, that they may find the truth of God as it is in Scripture.

Chapter 13

THE BLACK MUSLIM CULT

In the furor of racial tensions in Africa and the United States, so characteristic of our times, a new force is stirring throughout the Negro world, and it is one to be reckoned with by responsible persons of all races. Designated The Black Muslim Movement, its membership is conservatively estimated at more than a hundred thousand persons, all of them Negro, although there is good evidence that the hard core of the Muslim movement does not exceed 15,000 in the United States. The Movement owns sixty-nine temples and has set a membership goal of 5,000,000 by the close of 1964. Muslim real estate holdings and investments are scattered across America and they are sufficiently solvent to propose the erection of an Islamic Center in Chicago, Illinois, at a cost of $20,000,000.

There can be little doubt that the Black Muslim Movement is propelled by a fervent nationalistic spirit on the part of Negroes, and the most disconcerting feature of its growth is the fact that it has capitalized upon the Christian church's apparent reticence in some quarters to support vigorously the rights of Negroes guaranteed under the Constitution. In addition to this the Black Muslims make the consistent charge that Christianity is "the white man's religion," ignoring totally the fact that Jesus Christ was an Asiatic, a Semite, a descendant of Isaac, half-brother of the Arabs through Ishmael (Genesis 16:1-12). Thus Christianity claims closer ties to any supposed Islamic brotherhood than any Negro Muslim movement ever could. Christianity is certainly not the white man's religion; it is the religion of the Jew and the Arab through Judaism. And any national connection with the Negro race of either a black Judaism or a black Islam is totally foreign to the Bible, the Koran and all the available evidence of anthropology and genetics. Yet despite these facts, the Black Muslims move forward with a militant, vitriolic and denunciatory spirit against all white people, merely because they *are* white, not because they belong to a religion other than Islam. The official view of the Muslim religion concerning Elijah Muhammad, prophet of the Black Muslim Movement, is one of outright disdain, since the Koran forbids anyone to discriminate against another on the basis of his skin. And it is an open fact that there are millions of Moslems who are neither black nor brown, and who are indeed, yellow and white, in many quarters of the earth.

The Black Muslim Movement is characterized by a vigorous racism, which describes all white men as "devils," and enemies by nature of the black race. They vigorously reject any form of integration under the Constitution of the United States or of any other country, preferring an all-black state. They have not hesitated to suggest that seven or eight of the states of the United States be allotted to them for the creation of their own separate nation. The Black Muslims are also vigorously opposed to intermarriage between the black race and the white race, and are segregationists par-excellence, surpassing even the white extremists of certain sections of our country. In the Black Muslim Movement one can see emerging the outlines of what is most certainly a black Ku Klux Klan, which wants not equality with the white race, but which maintains instead, the intrinsic superiority of the black race. It is a swing of the historical and anthropological pendulum, liberally seasoned with a hatred that defies description. It is a movement born of many centuries of slavery and degradation, and unfortunately, in the United States, a hatred not totally unjustified. This is seen in the light of the exploitation of the Negro by unscrupulous and unprincipled white men, who have nodded to the Emancipation Proclamation, but have subtly disobeyed each of its precepts and those of the Supreme Court in favor of a segregation of the black man, both racial and social. We are reaping the fruit of this today. Black Islam presents the awesome spectacle of a growing black funnel engulfing potentially millions of Negroes in the United States who, though they have no sympathy for its religious fervor, know that in a number of areas it speaks with truth concerning the exploitation of the colored man. Many Negroes support the Black Muslim Movement because it is a voice in defense of their rights. This voice speaks with increasing frequency and intensity throughout the major Negro population centers of America (New York, Washington, Detroit, Chicago, etc.), and the Black Muslim Movement sweeps into its fold daily by the enunciation of a militant nationalism those underprivileged and exploited Negroes who are promised the eschatological dream of a Pan-Negro brotherhood, in which at last the white man will have to recognize their independence, and if the Black Muslims have their way, their superiority.

Many Negroes, though non-Muslims, give aid, comfort and support to Elijah Muhammad's growing kingdom, as a type of protest vote against race-shy politicians and segregationalists of all varieties, Christian as well as non-Christian. It is sad to have to admit that such occurrences as Little Rock and Birmingham have only served to pour

fuel upon the fires so zealously fanned by the Black Muslim Movement. Every instance where they can legitimately show persecution of the colored man, violation of his constitutional rights and privileges as an American citizen only serves to demonstrate the validity of their basic charge that the white man intends to always be the "slave-master" of the Negro race. And though this is of course false and demonstrably refutable from numerous sources, it still serves the propaganda purposes of Elijah Muhammad. There is a new spirit abroad among the Negro in America today, aided and abetted by the ignorant, the uninformed and the law breaker, whatever his apparently legal maneuvers may be. It is forging a solid wedge of discontent, unrest and antagonism toward the white man and even in some instances, toward Negro leaders who have attempted a moderate approach, fully aware of the grave dangers inherent in any Negro insurrection. The Black Muslim Movement is the fuse that could ignite racial, cultural, political and economic explosions that could do irreparable damage to our country and its image abroad — an image which has been marred and scarred by the excesses of a few on both sides of the racial controversy. These seem willing to sacrifice the future welfare of our nation for a continuance of something we fought one of the bloodiest wars in all human history to eradicate, a war in which white brother faced white brother as enemies, in order to free black slaves, that they might become black brothers, and citizens of a truly United States of America, free from bigotry, slavery, exploitation and oppression — a just government, in the words of the Great Emancipator "with malice toward none, with charity for all." The Black Muslim Movement, by its insistence upon a separate black state within the United States, would divide the Federal Union, and is therefore untenable and un-American. If the black race were given its own state, what then of the yellow race, and the brown race? Would they too not have a just claim, and if these be granted, then what of the Union? The answer to all this is, of course, that the Black Muslims will never get their state, for the cornerstone of American government is as Lincoln once put it, "The Federal Union — it must be preserved." There can be no doubt that it will be. The danger however has not been removed, and will not be until the general public and Christians in particular become aware of the challenge of the Black Muslim Movement.

The Black Muslim Movement then, is not an insignificant cult that the Christian church can afford to become complacent about, or ignore. Instead, it directly challenges the very foundations of historic Christianity and paradoxically, it attempts to do this in terms taken from Scripture itself.

To better evaluate the Black Muslims, some understanding of the historical and theological roots from which the cult sprung, is necessary. Such an evaluation, we believe, is necessary to gain an understanding of the psychological and spiritual motivations and drives which seemingly compel these zealous and sincere people upon a course even they cannot fully understand. That neither they, nor those who oppose them can accurately predict what the outcome will be, gives pause for thought in the light of the growing tensions of racial conflict so apparent in America today.

HISTORICAL, PSYCHOLOGICAL AND THEOLOGICAL INSIGHTS

There can be little doubt that the American Negro has been exploited, oppressed and suppressed by the white man in not a few states of our country, in the North, as well as in the South. Emerging as they have, from slavery, and denied their civil rights in far too many instances, the American Negro has by and large, been forced into a ghetto-like existence. This is evidenced by his concentration in such places as New York's Harlem and its equivalents in Detroit, Chicago and Washington, D. C.

Elijah Muhammad has capitalized upon this, emphasizing what he calls "the knowledge of self," and stimulates pride in the black men, pride in his race, his heritage and his abilities. Riding the crest of this wave of racial pride, the Black Muslims have made enormous strides.

According to Louis Lomax, distinguished Negro journalist who made an intensive survey of the Black Muslim Movement:

> The same general approach teaching race pride as knowledge of self, accounts for the success the Black Muslims have among low-income Negroes. For these people are in something of a prison too; they see themselves as failures and need some accounting for why they are what they are, why they are not what they are not. These needs are met when a wave of the downtrodden sit at the feet of Malcolm X and hear him proclaim the divinity of the black man, hear him blame the white man for his sin and lawlessness, and then go on to herald the impending destruction of the "white devil."

Thus it is that a growing segment of the American Negro population, beset with economic, psychological pressures, and remembering only too well, a history of slavery, limited emancipation and Jim Crow discrimination in the realms of education, economics and civil rights, is beginning to listen, if not to follow, the exhortations of Elijah Muhammad and Malcolm X. Goaded by a ground swell of nationalism prevalent throughout the world, and badgered by cries of "Brotherhood within the black race, to the exclusion of all others," the American Negro finds himself at the crossroads, in an era when crises have become the commonplace. Should he trust the United States government, dominated by white legislators, in which he feels he has little voice to guarantee him the rights and privileges legally accorded him a hundred years ago, but never fulfilled? Or shall he cast his lot with the nationalistic movement, founded in racial pride and promising him dignity and a life of equality, coupled with the respect of all races? This is the dilemma in which many Negroes find themselves today, and the psychological appeal cannot be underestimated, especially among a Negro populace which has suffered much and is today striving for recognition and justice.

Mr. Lomax has performed a great service for those interested in studying the Black Muslim Movement, for he, in company with C. P. Eric Lincoln, whose classic volume, *The Black Muslim Movement in America,* is by all odds the finest objective evaluation of the work of Elijah Muhammad and Malcom X now in print.

THE BLACK GOD

The history of the Black Muslim Movement began with one Wallace Fard, an Islamic Negro, who in 1930 appeared among the Detroit Negro community.

Fard spoke softly and intelligently to the Negro mind about their living conditions, lack of civil rights, the all-too-prevalent discrimination of the era. He utilized the Bible as an introductory primer to the study of the Koran and projected the teachings of Jesus Christ concerning the "turning of the other cheek" to one's enemies. He built a following, and eventually, a temple, in 1934. It was Fard who coined the phrase, "Blue-eyed devils," as a description of the white man, and in a country gripped by great depression, in the Negro slums of Detroit filled to the brim with the starving and the jobless, "Prophet" Fard's description seemed quite apropos.

Fard selected a corps of intelligent young Negroes, surrounded himself with these disciples and personally trained them. He was not adverse to using the literature of the Watch Tower Bible and Tract Society, the Koran and the Bible, for the basis of his instructions. He eventually wrote two manuals, *The Secret Ritual of the Nation of Islam* and *Teachings for the Lost-Found Nation of Islam in a Mathematical Way.* The first of these works was, and still is, orally transmitted. The second is written in "symbolic language," requiring translation and interpretation by the Prophet.

Fard founded the University of Islam, the Muslim Girls' Training Class and a military organization for the protection of Muslims known as "The Fruit of Islam."

At the end of 1933, this organization was progressing so well that Fard was able to withdraw from active leadership and supervise through his picked disciples the burgeoning cult.

One of these disciples was Elijah Poole, a Georgian Negro, who, after the disappearance of Fard in 1934, broke with the organization and founded what he considers to be the continuation of Prophet Fard's revelation.

The whereabouts of Wallace Fard has never been learned. In an interview given to the *New York Herald Tribune,* the attitude of Elijah Muhammad and the Black Muslim cult toward him was clearly spelled out:

"I asked Mr. Muhammad about this. Is there, I asked, a mystery about what happened to him?"

"No, sir, there is no mystery about what happened to him," he answered.

"Did Mr. Muhammad say what happened?"

"He is just waiting for the proper time to deliver speeches."

"Did Mr. Muhammad consider Mr. Fard, whose name he pronounces, 'Farad,' to be not only a holy man, but actually a divine person?"

"He is God Himself. He is the One that we have been looking for for the last 2,000 years to come. He is the One, and His Word bears witness to the fact that He is the One."

"And you know him?" I asked.

"I do know him."

"Is Mr. Muhammad in touch with him now?"

"Yes. Spiritually."

"I asked him about a successor. Did

he have in mind the identity of his own successor, since he himself is known as the inspired messenger of Allah?"

"His answer to this was a swift one. 'No. That is not my job, to do anything like that. This work has been put upon me to do by the will of almighty Allah, who has appointed me; there will be no such thing as a successor, because everything will be guided according to the will of Allah. And whatever He reveals will be carried on. It is like today we have the sun and moon and stars up there, and they are not changed for others."

"I asked him about the membership figures in his approximately eighty temples around the country, saying that law enforcement officers seemed agreed that the hard-core membership of the Black Muslims is between 5,000 and 6,000 members, with a less attached number of followers between 150,000 and 300,000."

"I don't even know that, because we don't have a record showing that figure," he said. "That figure is only known with Allah" (*New York Herald Tribune,* Tuesday, April 3, 1963).

In the theology of the Black Muslim Movement, Wallace Fard was God Himself, and it is no exaggeration to state that the Black Muslims worship a black God whom, they say, is awaiting the proper time to return, and proclaim the triumph of Black Islam.

Should a death certificate, and the discovery of a grave identifying Wallace Fard's remains ever be found, this would doubtless embarrass the Black Muslim Movement considerably, though the wily Mr. Poole would no doubt explain the resurrection was imminent!

It was Mr. Fard who taught the Black Muslims that they did not owe any allegiance to America or the American Flag. After Elijah Muhammad's break with the Movement following Fard's disappearance, he abandoned this phi-

losophy, at least, outwardly. Eric Lincoln has described the conditions which followed the split.

. . . the Muslims soon lost their aggressiveness; the Movement to which Fard had drawn 8,000 adherents, began to decline in size and in power. Strife broke to the surface and the relatively lethargic moderates drove Elijah Muhammad from Detroit to the Temple No. 2 in Chicago, which had been established at the southside mosque two years earlier. Here he set up new headquarters, and began to reshape the Movement under his own highly militant leadership. Fard became identified with the god, Allah; being thus deified, he was worshiped with prayer and sacrifice. Muhammad, who had served Allah, naturally assumed the mantle of Prophet, which Allah had worn during his mission in Detroit. Today Muhammad is referred to both as a Prophet and more often, as the Messenger of Allah.

The Black Muslims have come far under Muhammad. He has given them temples and schools, apartment houses and grocery stores, restaurants and farms. Most important of all, he has given them a new sense of dignity, a conviction that they are more than equals of the white man, and destined to rule the earth.

"The Messenger," the faithful say reverently, "has taught us knowledge of ourselves; and this is the knowledge that makes it possible for us to obtain justice, freedom and equality in the world, no matter what the white man thinks, no matter what the white man does. This is not a passive belief: Muhammad has promised to do something for my beautiful black nation. The Muslims are certain that he will. That's right, that's right, they say fervently, and swear to lay down their lives, if it should be his will."[1]

BLACK MUSLIM ATTITUDES AND TEACHINGS

The following quotations were taken from a tape-recorded exclusive interview with Malcolm X, who at the time of the interview was Elijah Muhammad's right-hand man. He later broke from this group and started his own

---

[1]See Eric Lincoln, *Black Muslims in America,* pages 16, 17.

organization. In 1965 he was shot and killed, presumably by supporters of Elijah Muhammad. Although this interview took place several years ago, it is indicative of the current philosophy and intent of the Black Muslims.

Question: What is the ambition of the Black Muslims?

MALCOLM X: Freedom, justice and equality are our principal ambitions, and to faithfully serve and follow the Honorable Elijah Muhammad is the guiding goal of every Muslim. Mr. Muhammad teaches us the knowledge of our own selves and of our own people. He cleans us up — morally, mentally and spiritually — and he reforms us to the vices that have blinded us here in the Western society.

I don't know when Armageddon is supposed to be. But I know that the time is near when the white man will be finished. The signs are all around us.

Christ wasn't white. Christ was black. The poor, brainwashed Negro has been made to believe Christ was white, to maneuver him into worshiping white men.

Verwoerd is an honest white man. So are the Barnetts, Eastlands and Rockwells. They want to keep white people white; we want to keep black people black. But to do this, we must have land of our own. The brainwashed black man can never learn to stand on his own two feet until he is on his own. We must learn to become our own producers, manufacturers and traders; we must have industry of our own, to employ our own. The white man resists this, because he wants to keep the black man under his thumb and jurisdiction in white society . . . the black man always dependent and begging—for jobs, food, clothes, shelter, education. The white man doesn't want to lose somebody to be supreme over. He wants to keep the black man where he can be watched and retarded. Mr. Muhammad teaches that as soon as we separate from the white man, we will learn that we can do

without the white man, just as he can do without us. The white man knows that once the black men get off to themselves and learn, they can do for themselves, the black man's full potential will explode, and he will *surpass* the white man.

There are 20,000,000 dormant Muslims in America . . . all of them will be Muslims when they wake up; that's what's meant by the Resurrection. But Mr. Muhammad says that Allah is going to wake up all black men to see white man as he really is, and see what Christianity has done to them. The black masses that are waking up don't believe in Christianity any more. All it's done for black men is help to keep them slaves. Mr. Muhammad is teaching that Christianity, as white people see it, means that whites can have their heaven on earth, but the black man is supposed to catch his hell here. The black man is supposed to keep believing that when he dies, he'll float up to some city with golden streets and milk and honey on a cloud somewhere. Every black man in North America has heard black Christian preachers shouting about "tomorrow in good old Beulah's land," but the thinking black masses today are interested in *Muhammad's land*. The promised land that the Honorable Elijah Muhammad talks about is right here on this earth . . . You must understand that the Honorable Elijah Muhammad represents the fulfillment of Biblical prophecy to us. In the Old Testament, Moses lived to see his enemy, Pharaoh, drowned in the Red Sea — which in essence means that Mr. Muhammad will see the completion of his work in his lifetime, that he will live to see victory gained over his enemy.

The British lion's tail has been snatched off in black Africa. The Indonesians have booted out such would-be imperialists as the Dutch. The French, who felt for a century that Algeria was theirs, have had to run for their lives back to France. Sir, the point

I make is that all over the world, the old days of standing in fear and trembling before the almighty white man is gone!

Question: Are you anti-white?

MALCOLM X: As soon as the white man hears a black man say that he's through loving white people, then the white man accuses the black man of hating him. The Honorable Elijah Muhammad doesn't teach hate. The white man isn't *important* enough for the Honorable Elijah Muhammad and his followers to spend any time hating him. . . . What I want to know is how the white man, with the blood of black people dripping off his fingers, can have the audacity to be asking black people do they hate him. That takes a lot of nerve.

Question: How do you reconcile your disavowal of hatred with the announcement you made last year that Allah had brought you the "good news" that 120 white Atlantans had just been killed in an air crash en route to America from Paris?

MALCOLM X: Sir, as I see the law of justice, it says as you sow, so shall you reap . . . the black man's true God, Allah, to defend us — and for us to be joyous because our God manifests his ability to inflict pain on our enemies. We Muslims believe that the white race, which is guilty of having oppressed and exploited and enslaved our people here in America, should and will be the victims of God's divine wrath. All civilized societies in their courts of justice, set a sentence of execution against those deemed to be enemies of society, such as murderers and kidnapers. The presence of 20,000,000 black people here in America is proof that Uncle Sam is guilty of kidnaping — because we didn't come here voluntarily on the *Mayflower*. And 400 years of lynchings condemn Uncle Sam as a murderer.

Dr. Bunche serves the white man well — he represents, speaks for and defends the white man. He does none of this for the black man. Dr. Bunche has functioned as a white man's tool, designed to influence international opinion on the Negro. The white man has Negro tools, national tools, and Dr. Bunche is an international tool.

Islam is a religion that teaches us never to attack, never to be the aggressor — but you can paste somebody if he attacks you. These Negro leaders have become aware that whenever the Honorable Elijah Muhammad is caused by their attacks to level his guns against them, they always come out on the losing end. Many have experienced this.

Another thing to think of — in the 20th century, the Christian Church has given us two heresies: fascism and communism.

Question: On what ground do you attribute these "isms" to the Christian Church?

MALCOLM X: Where did fascism start? Where's the second-largest Communist Party outside of Russia? The answer to both is Italy. Where is the Vatican? But let's not forget the Jew. Anybody that gives even a just criticism of the Jew is instantly labeled anti-Semite. The Jew cries louder than anybody else if anybody criticizes him. You can tell the truth about any minority in America, but make a true observation about the Jew, and if it doesn't pat him on the back, then he uses his grip on the news media to label you anti-Semite. Let me say just a word about the Jew and the black man. The Jew is always anxious to *advise* the black man. But they never advise him how to solve his problem the way the Jews solved their problem. The Jew never went sitting in and crawling in and sliding in and freedom riding, like he teaches and helps Negroes to do. The Jews stood up, and stood together, and they used their ultimate power, the economic weapon. That's exactly what the Honorable Elijah Muhammad is trying to teach black men to do. The Jews pooled their money and *bought* the hotels that barred them. They bought Atlantic City and

Miami Beach and anything else they wanted. Who owns Hollywood? Who runs the garment industry, the largest industry in New York City? But the Jew that's advising the Negro joins the NAACP, CORE, the Urban League and others. With money donations, the Jew gains control, then he sends the black man doing all this wading in, boring in, even burying in, everything but buying in. Never shows him how to set up factories and hotels. Never advises him how to own what he wants. No, when there's something worth owning, the Jew's got it.

A man who tosses worms in the river isn't necessarily a friend of the fish. All the fish who take him for a friend, who think the worm's got no hook in it, usually end up in the frying pan. All these things dangled before us by the white liberal posing as a friend and benefactor have turned out to be nothing but bait to make us think we're making progress. The Supreme Court decision has never been enforced. Desegregation has never taken place. The promises have never been fulfilled. We have received only tokens, substitutes, trickery and deceit. . . . I've never seen a sincere white man, not when it comes to helping black people. Usually things like this are done by white people to benefit themselves. . . . The white man is interested in the black man only to the extent that the black man is of use to him. The white man's interest is to make money, to exploit . . . no evidence will be found that justifies any confidence or faith that the black man might have in the white man today. . . . White people are born devils by nature. They don't become so by deeds. If you never put popcorn in a skillet, it would still be popcorn. Put the heat to it, it will pop.

Question: You seem to have based your thesis on the premise that all non-white races are necessarily black.

Malcolm X: Mr. Muhammad says that the red, the brown and the yellow are indeed all part of the black nation.

Which means that black, brown, red yellow, all are brothers, all are one family. The white one is a stranger. He's the odd fellow. . . . And white people who also are seeing the pendulum of time catching up with them are now trying to join with blacks, or even find traces of black blood in their own veins, hoping that it will save them from the catastrophe they see ahead. But no devil can fool God. Muslims have a little poem about them. It goes, "One drop will make you black, and will also in days to come save your soul."

Thoughtful white people *know* they are inferior to black people. Even Eastland knows it. Anyone who has studied the genetic phase of biology knows that white is considered recessive and black is considered dominant. When you want strong coffee, you ask for black coffee. If you want it light, you want it weak, integrated with white milk. Just like these Negroes who weaken themselves and their race by this integrating and intermixing with whites.

Question: If all whites are devilish by nature, as you have alleged, and if black and white are essentially opposite, as you have just stated, do you view all black men — with the exception of their non-Muslim leaders—as fundamentally angelic?

Malcolm X: No, there is plenty wrong with Negroes. They have no society. They're robots, automatons. No minds of their own. I hate to say that about us, but it's the truth. They are a black body with a white brain like the monster Frankenstein. The top part is your bourgeois Negro. He's your integrator. He's not interested in his poor black brothers. He's usually so deep in debt from trying to copy the white man's social habits that he doesn't have time to worry about nothing else. They buy the most expensive clothes and cars and eat the cheapest food. They act more like the white man than the white man does himself. These are the ones that hide their sympathy for Mr. Muhammad's teachings. It conflicts with the sources from which they get their white-man's crumbs. This class to us are the fence-sitters. They have one eye on the white man and the other eye on the Muslims. They'll jump whichever way they see the wind blowing. Then there's the middle class of the Negro masses, the ones not in the ghetto, who realize that life is a struggle, who are conscious of all the injustices being done and of the constant state of insecurity in which they live. They're ready to take some stand against everything that's against them. Now, when this group hears Mr. Muhammad's teachings, they are the ones who come forth faster and identify themselves, and take immediate steps toward trying to bring into existence what Mr. Muhammad advocates. At the bottom of the social heap is the black man in the big-city ghetto. He lives night and day with the rats and cockroaches and drowns himself with alcohol, and anesthetizes himself with dope, to try and forget where and what he is. That Negro has given up all hope. He's the hardest one for us to reach, because he's the deepest in the mud. But when you get him, you've got the best kind of Muslim. Because he makes the most drastic change. He's the most fearless. He will stand the longest. He has nothing to lose, even his life, because he didn't have that in the first place. I look upon myself, sir, as a prime example of this category — and as graphic an example as you could find of the salvation of the black man.

Question: Could you give us a brief review of the early life that led to your own "salvation?"

MALCOLM X: Gladly. I was born in Omaha on May 19, 1925. My light color is the result of my mother's mother having been raped by a white man. I hate every drop of white blood in me. Before I am indicted for hate again, sir, is it wrong to hate the blood of a rapist? But to continue: My father was a militant follower of Marcus Garvey's "Back to Africa" movement. The Lansing, Michigan equivalent of the Ku Klux Klan warned him to stop preaching Garvey's message, but he kept on and one of my earliest memories is of being snatched awake one night with a lot of screaming going on because our home was afire. But my father got louder about Garvey, and the next time he was found bludgeoned in the head, lying across streetcar tracks. He died soon and our family was in a bad way.

I happened to become the ward of a white couple who ran a correctional school for white boys. This family liked me in the way they liked their house pets. They got me enrolled in an all-white school. I was popular. I played sports and everything, and studied hard, and I stayed at the head of my class through the eighth grade. That summer I was 14, but I was big enough and looked old enough to get away with telling a lie that I was 21, so I got a job working in the dining car of a train that ran between Boston and New York City.

On my layovers in New York, I'd go to Harlem. That's where I saw in the bars all these men and women with what looked like the easiest life in the world. Plenty of money, big cars, all of it. I could tell they were in the rackets and vice. I hung around those bars whenever I came in town, and I kept my ears and eyes open, and my mouth shut. And they kept their eyes on me too. Finally, one day a numbers man told me that he needed a runner, and I never caught the night train back to Boston. Right there was when I started my life in crime. I was in all of it that the white police and the gangsters left open to the black criminal, sir. I was in numbers, bootleg liquor, "hot goods," women. I sold the bodies of black women to white men. I was in dope, I was in everything evil you could name. The only thing I could say for myself, sir, was that I did not indulge in hitting anybody over the head.

It was here that I learned that vice and crime can only exist, at least the kind and level that I was in, to the degree that the police cooperate with it. I had several men working and I was a steerer myself. I steered white people with money from downtown to whatever kind of sin they wanted in Harlem. I didn't care what they wanted, I knew where to take them to it. And I tell you what I noticed here — that my best customers were always the officials, the top police people, businessmen, politicians and clergymen. I never forgot that. I met all levels of these white people, supplied them with everything they wanted, and I saw that they were just a filthy race of devils. But despite the fact that my own father was murdered by whites, and I had seen my people all my life brutalized by whites, I was still blind enough to mix with them and socialize with them. I thought they were gods and goddesses — until Mr. Muhammad's powerful spiritual message opened my eyes and enabled me to see them as a race of devils. . . . Elijah Muhammad's statement, "The white man is the devil," it just clicked. I am a good example of why Islam is spreading so rapidly across the land . . . Mr. Muhammad's teachings . . . brought me from behind prison walls and placed me on the podiums of some of the leading colleges and universities in the country. I often think, sir, that in 1946, I was sentenced to 8 to 10 years in Cambridge, Massachusetts, as a common thief who had never passed the eighth grade. And the next time I went back to Cambridge was in March 1961, as a guest speaker at the Harvard Law School Forum. This is the best example of Mr. Muhammad's ability to take nothing and make something, to take nobody and make somebody. . . . No man on earth today is his equal. Whatever I am that is good, it is through what I have been taught by Mr. Muhammad.

They don't stand for anything different in Africa than America stands for.

The only difference is over there they *preach* as well as practice apartheid. America preaches freedom and practices slavery. America preaches integration and practices segregation. . . . Any white man is against blacks. The entire American economy is based on white supremacy. Even the religious philosophy is, in essence, white supremacy. A white Jesus. A white Virgin. White angels. White everything. But a black devil, of course. The "Uncle Sam" political foundation is based on white supremacy, relegating non-whites to second-class citizenship. It goes without saying that the social philosophy is strictly white supremacist, and the educational system perpetuates white supremacy.

Kennedy doesn't have to fight; he's the President. He didn't have any fight replacing Ribicoff with Celebreeze. He didn't have any trouble putting Goldberg on the Supreme Court. He hasn't had any trouble getting anybody in but Weaver and Thurgood Marshall. He wasn't worried about Congressional objection . . . but when it comes to the rights of the Negro, who helped to put him in office, then he's afraid of little pockets of white resistance.

Question: Has *any* American President, in your opinion — Lincoln, FDR, Truman, Eisenhower, Kennedy — accomplished anything for the Negro?

MALCOLM X: None of them have ever done anything for Negroes. All of them have tricked the Negro, and made false promises to him at election times which they never fulfilled. Lincoln's concern wasn't for freedom for the blacks, but to save the Union.

Question: Wasn't the Civil War fought to decide whether this nation could, in the words of Lincoln, "endure permanently, half slave and half free?"

MALCOLM X: Lincoln said that if he could save the Union without freeing the slaves, he would. But after two years of killing and carnage he found out he would have to free the slaves. He wasn't interested in the slaves, but in the Union.

As for the Emancipation Proclamation, sir, it was an empty document. If it freed the slaves, why a century later, are we still battling for civil rights? . . . You talk about the progress of the Negro. I'll tell you, mister, it's just because the Negro has been in America while *America* has gone forward that the Negro appears to have gone forward. . . . The white man must finally realize that *he's* the one who has committed the crimes that have produced the miserable condition that our people are in. He can't hide this guilt by reviling us today because we answer his criminal acts — past and present — with extreme and uncompromising resentment. He cannot hide his guilt by accusing us, his victims, of being racists, extremists and black supremacists. The white man must realize that the sins of the fathers are about to be visited upon the heads of the children who have continued those sins, only in more sophisticated ways.

Mr. Muhammad is warning this generation of white people that they, too, are facing a time of harvest in which they will have to pay for the crime committed when their grandfathers made slaves out of us. But there is something the white man can do to avert this fate. He must atone—and this can be done by allowing black men, those who choose, to leave this land of bondage and go to a land of our own. . . . He should give us several states here on American soil, where those of us who wish to, can go and set up our own government, our own economic system, our own civilization. Since we have given over 300 years of our slave labor to the white man's America, helped to build it up for him, it's only right that white America should give us everything we need in finance and materials for the next 25 years, until our own nation is able to stand on its feet. Then, if the Western Hemisphere is attacked by outside enemies, we would have both the capability and the motivation to join in defending the hemisphere, in which we would then have a sovereign stake. . . . The Honorable Elijah Muhammad . . . teaches that it is now God's intention to put the black man back at the top of civilization, where he was in the beginning — before Adam, the white man, was created. The world since Adam has been white — and corrupt. The world of tomorrow will be black — and righteous. In the white world there has been nothing but slavery, suffering, death and colonialism. In the black world of tomorrow, there will be true freedom, justice and equality for all. And that day is coming — sooner than you think. . . . It's not a case of what would we do, it's a case of what would God do with whites. What does a judge do with the guilty? Either the guilty atone, or God executes judgment.

The Black Muslim Movement speaks more eloquently for itself than any of its interpreters or critics. The above quotations accurately mirror their true attitudes and designs.

INSIDE THE BLACK MUSLIM MOVEMENT

As we previously stated, Louis Lomax has done a masterful job of describing Black Islam from the inside as an interested Negro observer. The following are excerpts from his lengthy article:

> The life of the Black Muslim centers around his temple — sometimes called a mosque — and the temple restaurant. They are usually located close together, in the heart of the Negro ghetto, and are the nerve centers of work and worship. Temple services are held two or three times a week and are generally preceded by family and group meals at the restaurant. Families — most of them former Methodists and Baptists — come in groups, the men dressed in white, and the children wearing pins or buttons to let the world know of their commitment to the Honorable Elijah Muhammad.
>
> The restaurant—like the Black Muslims homes—strictly adhere to Moslem dietary laws. Muslim sisters glory in their ability to prepare dishes that satisfy the traditional eating habits of the

American Negro without violating these laws. The best example of imaginative Black Muslim cooking is their famous bean pie, something of a gourmet's delight in the Negro community. Negroes in New York have been known to come to Harlem from miles around just to buy a bean pie for the family table. The restaurants also serve as business headquarters for the movement; they are the distribution centers for Black Muslim newspapers and other periodicals, the place where one is invited to have a talk with a Black Muslim leader.

Throughout the nation the Muslims generally meet in rented halls—a Masonic Temple in one town, over a pool room in another. Men and women enter the temple together, but once in the vestibule the families are separated. Everybody is searched thoroughly and all sharp objects, to say nothing of weapons, are taken away. The search is carried out by well-trained sisters and brothers who work with the efficiency of jail guards. They assign a small paper bag to each worshiper, and such objects as nail files, pocket-knives, scissors — any sharp objects that might conceivably be used as weapons — are put into the bag for safe keeping until the parishioner leaves the temple. Even the ordeal of being searched is made palatable by a pleasant brother or sister who explains that the visitor must be relieved of all weapons, because once the truth about the white man is explained, the visitor might run out and start his private Armageddon before the "word" comes.

The men and women are ushered into the temple through separate doors and are ordered to sit on opposite sides. The auditorium is generally a drab room, one used by many groups in the course of a week. In Birmingham, Alabama, for example, the Black Muslims use the Masonic Hall auditorium. The Sunday I visited the services there one could see posters, fans, and other material left by groups who had used the same hall earlier in the week. The chairs of the auditorium are arranged in rows, a wide gulf between the "brothers side" and that of the "sisters." Dark-suited young men, members of the Fruit of Islam, patrol the floor incessantly. They dart about, nudging children to silence, awakening a slumbering brother or sister, and performing whatever duties might come to hand, all the while keep-

ing up a rapid-fire "That's right," "You tell it like it is," in response to what the minister is saying.

The visitor finds himself inside a strange new world at a Black Muslim service. Many religions separate men and women during their services, but few Negroes are members of such faiths, and so they are intrigued from the outset. Their sense of being in on something exotic, thus meaningful, is increased when one of the lesser ministers takes the platform and says a few words in Arabic. The Negro is told that this was his language before the white man kidnaped his father and truncated his culture.

As-Salaam-Alaikum! the minister says — "Peace be unto you." *Wa-Alaikum-Salaam,* the visitor is taught to reply. "Peace be also unto you." The Black Muslims have little or no liturgy. They do not sing in the temple, for they have not yet developed hymns that enunciate their faith. The nearest thing I have heard to a Black Muslim hymn is a plaintive and moving song written by Minister Louis X of Boston, "The White Man's Heaven is the Black Man's Hell." It is often sung in the temples, but only as a solo by some gifted member of the congregation.

Then the stage is set for the "teaching." In lieu of the cross, the focus of the Black Muslim's religious service is a huge blackboard divided into two sections. On one side is a drawing of the American flag with the Christian cross superimposed on it. Under this flag is written, "Slavery, Suffering and Death." On the other side of the blackboard is the half-crescent symbol of Islam, and under it is written, "Freedom, Justice and Equality." Under both flags, running the full length of the blackboard, is the somber warning: "Which one will survive the war of Armageddon?"

And it is against this backdrop that the minister gets up to "teach." Each temple has its own minister, who is extremely well trained in what he is to say and do. And he does it well.

The Black Muslims have but one message: The white man is by nature evil, a snake who is incapable of doing right, a devil who is soon to be destroyed. Therefore, the black man, who is by nature divine and good, must separate from the white man as soon as possible, lest he share the white man's hour of total destruction.

This sermon, or "teaching," is the high point of the service, what everybody has come to hear. An air of expectancy runs through the crowd as the moment to begin the teaching approaches. This is stock drama for the Black Muslims whether the meeting be a national affair where Elijah himself is to speak or a local meeting where the temple minister is to teach.

This air of expectancy is set stirring by the second-in-command, who keeps up a running promise that something good is about to happen. As a warm-up man for Elijah's Washington, D.C. speech, Malcolm X electrified a crowd of some five thousand in Uline Arena with this:

"You are here to get some good news!"

"Make it plain, Mr. Minister. Make it plain."

"But you must remember that what is good news for some is bound to be bad news for others."

"All praise to Allah," the people shouted back.

"What is good news for the sheep," Malcolm continued, "is bad news for the wolf!"

"Make it plain, Mr. Minister. Make it plain."

The good news, as everybody knew, was that Elijah would be there soon with a message of freedom for the "sheep" (the black man) and a message of destruction for the "wolf" (the white man).

Broadsides at Christianity delivered by Malcolm X and other ministers seem to make the strongest impression on the audience. The minister explains that the Negro was introduced to Christianity while a slave, a bondsman to the man who taught him about Jesus. Employing any history text, he reads at length, using "the white man's own writings to show that Christianity is a white man's religion." This strikes home, because the average Negro has read enough to know there is a good deal of historical soundness in what the minister says. Then the minister goes on to point out that the Christian church (and they quote Adam Clayton Powell on this) "is the most segregated institution in America," and the Negro does not need a history book to know that this statement has total validity.

Then the minister goes on to attack Christianity on the grounds that its practitioners are immoral. He calls the roll of criminals and public failures, making much of the fact that they are "all Christians." The minister uses clippings from the newspapers showing white clergymen and churchgoers either sanctioning segregation or being neutral about it. During the Birmingham crisis I attended the Black Muslim service and saw Minister James X deliver a devastating indictment of Christianity simply by showing pictures of Birmingham Negroes being turned away from white churches. One picture showed the rebuffed Negroes praying on the church steps while white bullies, their fists balled up, stood nearby.

Black Christians are also indicted for immorality; the minister points out that "All of us were once in the church and we did everything evil." I have watched this argument at work and come away amazed at the way the Black Muslims take the Christian ethic as a measuring stick; they arouse the guilt complex of the wayward Christians in the audience and then go on to blame Christianity for the individual's moral failure. This, to be sure, is a contorted argument. But it works. Christians sit in the temple audience and confess their Christian failing, then they repent themselves right out of the Christian church.

After the sermon the visitors are asked to raise any questions that may trouble them. The ministers deal with each question in detail, but the Black Muslim ushers (The Fruit of Islam) make certain the questioner is not an "agitator," someone who has come into the temple just to start a philosophical or theological argument.

"You are here to be taught, brother," I heard one Black Muslim say to a visitor, "not to argue." And when the visitor frankly says he does not understand what the Black Muslims are up to, or that, after honestly trying, he is unable to agree, the minister explains that this is not to be held against the visitor. "You are among the deaf, dumb and blind," the minister explains to him kindly. Then he assures the visitor that further study and estrangement from "the teaching of the devil" will open his eyes and ears.

The climax of each temple service comes when visitors are invited to join the movement. There is great rejoicing when converts come forth. Dr. Eric Lincoln, author of *The Black Muslims in America,* who has attended more of these services than I have, says that the larger temples average a dozen or so converts at each meeting.

Once the visitor decides to join the temple, he is given a letter he must copy by hand:

Address
City and State
Date

Mr. W. F. Muhammad
4807 South Woodlawn Avenue
Chicago 15, Illinois

Dear Savior Allah, Our Deliverer:

I have been attending the teachings of Islam by one of your Ministers, two or three times. I believe in it, and I bear witness that there is no God but Thee, and that Muhammad is Thy Servant and Apostle. I desire to reclaim my Own. Please give me my Original name. My slave name is as follows:

Name
Address
City and State

This letter of application is dispatched to Chicago, and if the copy contains no errors, the visitor is sent a detailed questionnaire that inquires into his family and employment status. This completed, the applicant is given a thorough investigation by local members of the "Fruit." If the applicant stands muster, he is admitted to membership in the Black Muslim movement.

Then, and only then, is the convert allowed to drop his "slave" name. If his name is, say, John King, he becomes John X. If there are other Johns in the local temple, his "X" will denote that he is the third, fourth, or whatever number John to join that particular temple. Thus it is very common to find John 2X or John 7X. Eric Lincoln discovered a midwestern Muslim whose name was John 17X. The "X" is the Black Muslim's way of saying that his own origins — before the white man — and name are a mystery; it is also the Muslim's shout that he is an "ex," and "no longer what I was when the white man had me deaf, dumb and blind."

I have sat with Black Muslims during temple meetings and have seen the people, particularly the young children, come alive with a new sense of identity; they seem to have a new reason to go out and do battle with the rats and roaches in the slums that are their homes. A feeling of unity and love for one another grips the entire room as they silently stand to be dismissed.

They stretch forth their hands, palms upward, and in the name of Allah, the most powerful and all-merciful God, they vow to go in peace. But every Black Muslim temple meeting is saturated with expectation. It reaches its peak when the minister makes the promise that the war of Armageddon is drawing closer and closer. No one ever really says it, but there is an intense feeling that one day soon, at just such a meeting, the "word" will be given. Just what the word is, nobody says; just what will happen when the word is given, nobody seems to know. Yet everybody — man, woman and child — is determined to be on hand when the "word" comes.

Such meetings as these have been going on all over the nation for several years. Most of us heard talk about the "temple people" as the Black Muslims were called, but there was very little real information about them. Nobody seemed to know just how many temple people there were, how they were organized, what they were really about. The consensus was that they were just another offbeat sect, one of the scores of "Islamic" movements that have sought to convert American Negroes during the past century. We had no idea of the power of the Black Muslims as a religious and political organization capable of rallying mass support, but early in 1957 we got the message.

THE POWER OF ISLAM

Shortly after dark on the night of April 26, 1957, police at Harlem's 28th Precinct received what had all the appearances of a routine call — a fight between two Negroes at the corner of 125th Street and Seventh Avenue. The dispatch officer barked into his microphone, and his orders squawked out in a dozen radio cars patrolling the area. The cars, their revolving red lights glaring, sped to the scene of the incident. Police poured out of the cars, their clubs at the ready, and began to batter their way through the mob that had gathered.

One Johnson Hinton, a man nobody knew and who had nothing to do with the fight, was one of the spectators who had stopped to watch the melee. The police shoved and knocked aside several Negroes and finally came upon Hinton. What happened then is still a matter of argument, but one fact is agreed upon by all concerned: Hinton and the police entered into a verbal exchange and a policeman knocked Hinton to the ground, his head split open. A police ambulance was called and police took the position that another Negro agitator had been subdued. But they were in for a major surprise, and the city was on the brink of a race riot. Hinton, it turned out, was a Black Muslim, Johnson X, a member of Malcolm's Temple Number Seven in Harlem.

Within minutes after Hinton hit the ground, the word spread that a Black Muslim had been assaulted by the police. An hour later some five hundred sullen, angry Black Muslim men put a cordon around the 28th Precinct Station house where Hinton was being held. This meant trouble, and plenty of it. Precinct Captain McGowan realized he had the makings of a riot on his hands and sent out an urgent call for responsible Negroes to rush to the scene and intervene. One of the first to arrive was James Hicks editor of *The Amsterdam News,* a Harlem newspaper. Hicks accurately sized up the situation and told Captain McGowan that only one man, Minister Malcolm X, could manage the crowd and get them to disperse.

The police captain asked, in essence, "Who's he?"

Shortly afterward, Captain Mc-Gowan found out just who Malcolm X was. Flanked by several strapping, angry Muslim brothers, Malcolm walked into the station house. As he entered the door, he gave a sign, and the hundreds of Muslim brothers surrounding the area knew their stand was affirmed. The call went out for still more Muslim brothers to converge upon the area.

Once inside the station, Malcolm X sat down for hard bargaining. First, there was the matter of Brother Johnson Hinton lying on the floor of a jail cell with his head split open. Malcolm demanded that Hinton be given immediate hospital treatment. This was "agreed to." Then Malcolm went on to place on record the facts of the affair. Johnson was standing on the street, he was not involved in the fight, he at no time disobeyed a police order, and the police struck him out of sheer flailing frustration.

As Johnson Hinton was carried out of the station to an ambulance, Malcolm walked out the door and paused at the top of the steps. The dimly lit night was filled with Black Muslims and onlookers. Malcolm made a slight gesture, and, according to both police and editor Hicks, in exactly three minutes the streets were empty. The hundreds of Muslims simply vanished — at least the police thought they had vanished. In actuality they shifted their cordon to the hospital, where Hinton was being treated. And it was only after Malcolm emerged from the hospital and gave another sign, that the Black Muslims finally dispersed to their various homes.

"No man," Police Captain McGowan said to James Hicks, "should have that much power over that many people. We cannot control this town if one man can wield that kind of power."

Johnson Hinton now walks around with a silver plate in his head. An all-white jury awarded him $75,000 in damages against the City of New York. Those knowledgeable about the case and the Black Muslims feel that $75,-000 is a small fee to pay for the service Malcolm X rendered the city that night. As the jury found, the police were absolutely wrong, and as Negroes know, Hinton's was only one of the Negro heads that are cracked open without reason by the New York police each year.

But there is a difference between Johnson Hinton and all the other Negroes who got their heads split open in Harlem: Hinton had black brothers and sisters who cared for him; he was a member of a tightly knit congregation of believers whose basic tenet is "fight in defense of your life" and whose main social ethic is "be ready to exact justice when one of your brothers is abused."

The Muslims will deny it, but they have a "crisis system" that moves into action whenever a Muslim is abused. It involves a telephone pyramid — one man calls 10 people and each of them call 10 — that in one hour can produce upward of a thousand Muslims at any given point in New York.

And the night Johnson Hinton's head was split open was the night New York police officials went into a huddle and named the Black Muslims, particularly Malcolm X, as people to watch.[2]

The Black Muslim movement and the cult of Black Islam, whichever one prefers to call it, will at length be seen, we

[2]Louis Lomax, "A Phony Islam's Unveiled Threat," *True* Magazine, December, 1963.

believe, by the American Negro as an organization founded upon racial hatred, not brotherhood, and which will only succeed in begetting more hatred. The American Negro must continue to trust the influential friends he has among white legislators, whose sincerity cannot be questioned in the light of past elections. President Kennedy pushed the civil rights bill, although he knew it would cost him many votes, far more than he would gain from the Negroes, which indicates good faith on the part of white men. And President Johnson has followed in his footsteps. In the end, civil rights legislation and true equality for the Negro will be realized.

As to the establishment of a black state, the isolation of the Negro from the cultural and racial complex of our times in the American republic, is not the answer, but instead his full and complete integration as intended by the founding fathers and the Great Emancipator. Such responsible leaders, such as Martin Luther King and others who invoke Christian ethics in resistance to evil within the boundaries of the law, will in the end, lead the black man through love, patience and faith, into his rightful heritage.

In the light of Holy Scripture, we can expect the testimony of history to say that the Black Islam cult and all movements based upon hate and revenge have disappeared under the sands of time, as has Wallace Fard and Malcolm X, and as will Elijah Poole, to whom the words of Hosea were fittingly applied when he said:

"If you sow to the wind, you shall reap the whirlwind" (Hosea 8:7).

Apostle Paul's fitting comment upon this statement was, "Be not deceived; God is not mocked, for whatsoever a man soweth, that shall he also reap" (Galatians 6:7).

This speaks of divine judgment for the Black Muslim movement and its misguided followers, who are willing to love their neighbors if their neighbors are black, and to hate their enemies, i.e., those who are not black.

The Christian attitude in the midst of all this, must be one of patience, love and firm resolve. We must turn the other cheek to their abuses, and strive to guarantee for them and for all Americans, regardless of race, their just rights under the laws of our land. In this way, we shall indeed demonstrate to them the love and teachings of Jesus Christ.

In stark contrast to the teachings of their black Allah must be the words of the Son of God, who warned us that many would come in His name claiming to be the Christ, and would deceive many (Mark 13:6), and who wrote of one's neighbors:

> Ye have heard that it hath been said, Thou shalt love thy neighbor, and hate thine enemy. But I say unto you, Love your enemies, bless them that curse you, do good to them that hate you, and pray for them which despitefully use you, and persecute you; That ye may be the children of your Father which is in heaven: for he maketh his sun to rise on the evil and on the good, and sendeth rain on the just and on the unjust. For if ye love them which love you, what reward have ye? do not even the publicans the same? Matthew 5:43-46.

Chapter 14

THE UNITY SCHOOL OF CHRISTIANITY

The Unity School of Christianity, with a reputed world membership of 1,200,000, is the largest Gnostic cult in Christendom. It is also by far the best advertised, through the printed page, correspondence courses, and multiple publications which have made it the largest mail-order religious concern in the world. After a careful study of its history and present day methods of doing business with the United States mails, this writer is convinced that Unity supplies salvation as Sears-Roebuck supplies overalls, cut to size and delivered parcel post. The direct-mail approach of Unity has catapulted it to a phenomenal rate of growth, especially when one realizes that it has grown from two people in a rented hall in Kansas City in 1889, to an entire city (Unity City) in Lee's Summit, Missouri. The United States government has had to supply this city with its own post office, in order to process the correspondence of America's largest mail-order religion. From the presses of Unity each year flow literally hundreds of tons of printed matter, dutifully shipped to the faithful in Uncle Sam's mail sacks. For a nominal fee, the prospective convert may purchase magazines, newspapers, pamphlets and numerous books, all telling of the marvelous benefits to be derived from accepting the philosophy of Unity, and filling the mind with "happy thoughts," and "kind ideas," thereby banishing for ever the awful concept that man is essentially an unregenerate rebel against the laws of the Holy God, and desperately in need of personal redemption through Jesus Christ.

Unity, as it is known to millions of persons, is probably the most inoffensive of all the cults, since its adherents usually retain their membership in the church of their choice, while at the same time subscribing to the Unity publications, thus giving them a direct access to many churches and many congregations where the Unity cult teachings are subtly disseminated under the guise of a higher plane of Christian experience. As we shall see in the pages to follow, Unity has not been judged as a non-Christian cult solely on this basis. But it is non-Christian on the basis that it violates virtually every cardinal doctrine of the Christian faith necessary to salvation, as outlined within the pages of Scripture. It is for this reason that it comes under our scrutiny as we obey the command of the Holy Spirit to "prove all things; hold fast that which is good" (I Thessalonians 5:21).

As we have seen in our study of Christian Science, Mary Baker Eddy was definitely not its originator. And in studying the Unity cult, careful historical examination will readily reveal that Charles and Myrtle Fillmore, who began the operation of the Unity School of Christianity, were no more *its* theological parents than was Mrs. Eddy of Christian Science. Both of these cult systems, Christian Science and Unity, are the twin sisters of American Gnosticism, and were fathered by the writings of Phineas Parkhurst Quimby, an old time Maine mental healer, whom Mrs. Eddy credited with restoring her to perfect health when she was on the verge of despair.[1]

[1]*Portland Evening Courier,* November 7, 1862.

275

Both Mrs. Eddy and the Fillmores merely played Trilby to Quimby's theological Svengali, and the result was the birth of two variations of Quimby's pantheistic metaphysical system, neither of which is willing to own Quimby as its legitimate parent. But a careful perusal of the *Metaphysical Bible Dictionary* published by the Unity School, will quickly show that Christian Science, Unity and New Thought (which *does* recognize Quimby) have an almost interchangeable vocabulary, a fact denied by only the uninformed and those who are unwilling to study the facts of history and semantics.

Literature of the Unity School is published in the best taste. The paper is good and the bindings are excellent. Style of writing is also very appealing since its makes much of Biblical references and illustrations. Unfortunately, the average person either listening to a Unity broadcast, or reading from its numerous publications, doubtless believes Unity to be a form of Christian theology. It is not, however, in any sane use of the word, as we shall see. For, like other non-Christian cults, the Unity School adopts Biblical language to portray its essentially anti-Christian theological propositions. But when its true theological teachings are projected against the backdrop of Biblical revelation, and stripped of their protective terminology camouflage, the entire system is revealed to be a Gnostic masquerade and a clever counterfeit of the genuine Gospel of Jesus Christ.

Openly rivaling the propaganda activities of Jehovah's Witnesses, Mormonism and Herbert W. Armstrong, Unity continues to grow in power and prestige throughout America, especially in the Midwest and the Eastern seaboard. The activities of Unity are not restricted however to "air mail or special delivery" salvation, since over its own and numerous other radio stations across the United States and Canada, the movement broadcasts its metaphysical remedies for everything from sin, sickness and death to domestic troubles and the incessant demands of the local finance companies. Unity teaches that there is no problem insoluble, if one practices its tenets faithfully, and offers not only health and happiness but financial security as well. Couple if you will these material benefits with an extremely palatable theology (palatable, that is, to those uninstructed in the Word of God), and one can easily see why Unity is a certain prospect for popularity and expansion in the Kingdom of the Cults.

Unity City, which is the central headquarters of the cult, is located in Lee's Summit, Missouri and houses a huge printing operation, including a Sunday School quarterly, *Wee Wisdom,* for children; *Good Business,* for the working man; and *Weekly Unity,* a devotional magazine. Since one of the major tenets of the theology of Unity is reincarnation, which frowns upon the consumption of flesh foods, Unity maintains a large vegetarian cafeteria, which has no equal, either for variety or quality, anywhere.

With the advent of such non-Christian cults as Theosophy, Rosicrucianism, Spiritism, etc., all emanating from Oriental sources in greater or lesser degrees, reincarnation has taken on a new look, especially in Europe and America, and, from all appearances, an eminently successful one.

This new look has been specifically designed for consumption by the occidental mind and frowns upon the thought of passing from a human form to that of a snail or a chimpanzee. It is, however, receptive to the thought of reincarnation or rebirth in another human form. It comes as no surprise, then, that the most vocal proponent of this modern schoool of transmigrational thought should be the Unity School of Christianity, which is in agreement in many areas with the before-mentioned cults, primarily where reincarnation is involved.

We deal more thoroughly with this when we come to Unity's concept of reincarnation, but it is one of the most effective doctrines of the cult from an evangelical standpoint, since it becomes a substitute for hell, and eternal punishment, unpleasant subjects which the human mind, experience teaches us, seeks to avoid contact with, at all costs.

THE BEGINNINGS OF UNITY

Though Phineas P. Quimby was the father of Christian Science, New Thought and Unity, Myrtle Fillmore was the theological mother and grand interpreter of Quimby, New Thought and Christian Science. She formed Unity into a system which today resembles all three, but which clings to the special designation, "School."

Myrtle Fillmore was raised a Methodist, and earned her living as a school teacher. Her early New England background was reflected in the naming of her sons, Lowell and Waldo after James Russell Lowell and Waldo Emerson. There is no doubt that she became interested in transcendental philosophy at an early age.

Mrs. Fillmore moved to Kansas City, Missouri, in 1884, and became a convert to Christian Science in 1887.

Her conversion to Mrs. Eddy's version of Quimby's theology came about when she realized that "I am a child of God; therefore I do not inherit sickness."

Thus inspired and allegedly healed of divers diseases, including tuberculosis, Mrs. Fillmore converted her husband, Charles, a former real-estate salesman who had built a considerable fortune, only to lose both it and his health.

Charles Fillmore dabbled in Spiritualism, and later became interested in Hinduism, from which the Fillmores derived a concept of reincarnation, properly modified, of course, so as to appeal to the Western mind.

Burning with zeal for their new religious discovery, Myrtle and Charles Fillmore rented a small hall in Kansas City. Thus began the great religious cult which today girdles the globe.

In April of 1889, the Fillmores published their first magazine, *Modern Thought,* which they changed in 1890 to *Christian Science Thought.* Mary Baker Eddy, however, strongly objected to the Fillmores apparently capitalizing upon her copyrighted titles and terminology. Therefore, in 1891, the title of the publication was changed to *Thought.*

The name Unity was adopted in 1895, "devoted" as Charles Fillmore stated, "to the spiritualization of humanity from an independent standpoint. . . ." a religion which ". . . took the best from all religions."

Unity was a member for many years of the International New Thought Alliance, from which they withdrew in 1922, having far outstripped in membership both New Thought and Christian Science.

During this period, notably, at the Columbian exposition in Chicago in 1893, the Fillmores became intensely interested in the philosophy of Hinduism and Yogaism as later popularized by Swami Vivekananda of India. Charles Fillmore, who was no stranger to the writings of Spiritualists and Theosophists, drew heavily upon this encounter, and became an admirer of Vivekananda, incorporating many of the concepts of Yogaism, reincarnation, diet (vegetarianism), etc., into the theology of the emerging Unity School.

Unity differs primarily from Christian Science in that it admits that God is expressed in matter, as well as in mind or spirit, whereas, Christian Science maintains that matter is illusory and has no real existence.

Myrtle Fillmore, as a result of her experience with Christian Science and Swami Vivekananda, went on to found, with her husband, such publications as *Unity* Magazine, *Good Business, Wee*

Wisdom, Progress, Weekly Unity and *Daily Word*. Unity also set about establishing centers throughout the South and Middle West, and constructing a publishing house from which poured multiple millions of copies of tracts, pamphlets, books and magazines, all propagating the theology of the Fillmores.

In 1903, Unity established its own ordination machinery. In 1918, Unity Field Department was established, and, in 1921, the Unity Statement of Faith was adopted.

Three years after the adoption of the Statement, the Fillmores established the Unity Church Universal, which became the Unity annual conference, which ordains ministers, approves their standings on a yearly basis and supervises the operation of Unity centers, radio and television broadcasts, literature and lecturers.

Upon the death of Myrtle Fillmore in 1931, Charles took over the operation and later married Cora Dedrick, who, in company with his sons, continued the operation successfully.

Charles Fillmore had little or no contact with orthodox Christianity, for, as he put it himself:

> I was not biased on the God question by orthodox education. Born and raised in the wilderness of the West, my religious education was quite limited. God was an unknown factor in my conscious mind, and always has been, until the past few years (*Modern Thought*, Vol. 5, February 1894, page 454, editorial).

From this unusual union then, a Methodist turned Christian Scientist and a religious agnostic turned reincarnationist, came the Unity School of Christianity, in which many well-meaning persons are today imprisoned, totally unaware of the great debt that Unity owes to Phineas Quimby, Warren Evans and Mary Baker Eddy. In fact, they are unlikely to uncover this, since those who at the helm of the Unity barque are most careful never to discuss in detail the various origins of the cult, doubtless because they wish to continue representing it as an original "higher form" of Christianity.

Through Myrtle Fillmore's conviction and drive came the Unity School of Christianity, with its Society of Silent Help, now known as "Silent Unity." Of Mrs. Fillmore's abilities and accomplishments, Dr. James Teener, whose outstanding research of the history and theology of this cult must be considered by any serious student of Fillmore's religion, has declared:

> This silent and absent healing agency became most important in Unity, and also the most productive financially. Through it wealth has come. As need arose, other organizations were set up, the Unity Tract Society, the Unity Correspondence School, the Silent Seventy and the Unity Pure Food Company. All were consolidated into corporation as the Unity School of Christianity in 1914. The founders and their two living sons became the trustees with power to operate the business and determine their own compensation and to appoint their successors. The Fillmores did not start out to develop a sect or denomination. They have insisted that they merely had "an independent educational institution, teaching the use of the Jesus Christ doctrine in every day life."
>
> Nevertheless, their activity has been an increasing annunciation of this avowed purpose. Very early they developed their own Sunday school and worship services, putting them at the same time as the established denominational meetings. How then could their students be faithful to their individual churches? . . . Unity's strength does not lie in its theology. It is more effective than most of the mental cure agencies, because it has added religious motivation and warmth to mental and emotional guidance. Added to this is the personal interest of authors to those who approach it. People are assured that Silent Unity operates twenty-four hours a day. There is always someone in the prayer room. Letters, telegrams asking for help, are promptly answered. . . . God is always successful. "God is your highest self, and is constantly waiting upon you." This is also a weakness of Unity, for in experience, we discover that our "highest self" is still

far short of the glory of God, the Father of our Lord Jesus Christ.[2]

The history of Unity then, is one of unbounded success from humble beginnings, springing from a relatively small gathering of persons under the tutelage of Myrtle Fillmore, who held twice-weekly meetings, setting forth a redefinition of the theology of Phineas P. Quimby and the "love principle, as taught by Christ" (*Modern Thought,* Vol. I, October, 1889, No. 80).

Leaving the historical picture of Unity, we shall now allow the doctrinal teachings to speak for themselves and then examine them in the light of the Word of God.

SOME OF THE DOCTRINES OF UNITY

1. The Authority of the Bible.

". . . spiritual principle is embodied in the sacred books of the world's living religions. Christians hold to the Bible as the supreme exponent of spiritual principle. They believe that the Bible is the greatest and most deeply spiritual of all the Scriptures, though they realize that other Scriptures, such as the Zend-Avesta, and the Upanishads, as well as the teachings of Buddha, the Koran, and the Tao of Lao-tse and the writings of Confucious, contain expressions of eminent spiritual truths. . . ." (*What Unity Teaches,* Unity School of Christianity, page 4).

". . . Scripture may be a satisfactory authority for those who are not themselves in direct communion with the Lord" (*Unity,* VII, October 1896, page 400).

2. The Triune God (the Trinity).

"The Father is Principle, the Son is that Principle revealed in the creative plan, the Holy Spirit is the executive power of both the Father and Son, carrying out the plan" (*Metaphysical Bible Dictionary,* Unity School of Christianity, page 629).

"God is loving, God does not love anybody . . . God is the love in everybody and everything . . . God is love . . . God exercises none of His attributes except through the inner consciousness of the universe and man" (Fillmore, *Jesus Christ Heals,* Unity School of Christianity, 1944, pages 31, 32).

"God is not a . . . person, having life, intelligence, love, power. God is that invisible, intangible, but very real, something we call life. God is perfect love and infinite power. God is the total of these, the total of all good, whether manifested or unexpressed" (H. Emily Cady, Kansas City, Unity School of Christianity, *Lessons in Truth,* 1925, page 6).

"We all have direct access through the Father in us — the central 'I' of our being — to the great whole of life, wisdom, power, which is God. What we now want to know is how to receive more from the fountainhead, and to make more and more of God [who is but another name for All-good] manifest in our daily life" (*ibid.,* page 11).

"I believe the Hottentot, or the truest heathen that ever lived, he who worships the golden calf as his highest conception of God, worships God" (*ibid.,* page 126).

"Many good people think that God is a person located in a place in the skies called heaven. They pray to Him for what they want and are satisfied. This is the prayer of the primitive, personal man, and it meets his needs; but this is not direct communion of the Father and

[2]"The Challenge of Unity," James W. Teener, *Crossroads* Magazine, July 6, 1952, pages 9-11. The author has drawn heavily upon this article and the original sources from which it was printed, the *Unity School of Christianity, A Partial Dissertation of Doctrinal Thesis,* University of Chicago, Library of Chicago, Illinois, 1942 by James W. Teener. The author wishes to express his indebtedness to Dr. Teener for the excellent research which made possible the condensation of the history of Unity found in this chapter.

Son. . . ." (Fillmore, Charles and Cora, *Teach Us to Pray,* page 13).

3. *The Deity of Jesus Christ.*

"The Bible says that God so loved the world that He gave His only begotten Son, *but the Bible does not here refer to Jesus of Nazareth the outer man; it refers to the Christ, the Spiritual identity of Jesus,* whom he acknowledged in all his ways, and brought forth into his outer, until even the flesh of his body was lifted up, purified, spiritualized and redeemed. Thus he became Jesus Christ, the Word made flesh. And we are to follow in this perfect state and become like him, *in each of us is the Christ, the only begotten Son. We can through Jesus Christ, our Redeemer and example, bring forth the Christ within us, the true self of all men,* to be made perfect even as our Father in heaven is perfect as Jesus Christ commandeth His followers to be" (*Unity* Magazine, Vol. 57, No. 5, page 464; Vol. 72, No. 2, page 8).

"Jesus Christ Himself was a parable, and his life an allegory of the experiences that man passes through in development from natural to spiritual consciousness" (Fillmore, *Christian Healing,* page 68).

"Christ is the only begotten Son of God, the one complete idea of perfect man and divine Mind. This Christ or perfect-man idea existing eternally in divine Mind is the true, spiritual, higher-self of every individual" (*Metaphysical Bible Dictionary,* Unity School of Christianity, page 150).

"The difference between Jesus and us is not one of inherent spiritual capacity, but in difference of demonstration of it. Jesus was potentially perfect, and He expressed that perfection; we are potentially perfect, and we have not yet expressed it" (*What Unity Teaches,* Unity School of Christianity, page 3).

"By Christ is not meant the man Jesus" (*Unity* Magazine, No. 2, page 146).

"The Christ is the perfect-idea man, whom God created, the real self of all men. Jesus Christ is the Christ-self brought into perfect expression and manifestation" (*Weekly Unity,* December 19, 1954).

"It is not difficult to see in Elisha an incarnation of the Christ, and he was in a certain degree Christ manifest. Jesus was a fuller manifestation of the same Christ" (Fillmore, Charles and Cora, *Teach Us to Pray,* page 150).

4. *The Atonement of Jesus Christ.*

"The atonement is the union of man with God the Father in Christ. Stating it in terms of mind, we should say that the atonement is the At-one-ment or agreement or reconciliation of man's mind with divine Mind, through the superconsciousness of Christ-mind" (Fillmore, *What Unity Christianity Stands For,* page 5).

"Jesus Christ became the way by which all who accept Him may 'pass over' to the higher consciousness" (*Unity,* April, 1954, Vol. 120, No. 4; page 4).

"These theories of the sin offering of Jesus are conceived with the personal God idea. They carry out the pagan concept of a big god who becomes very angry with his disobedient children and can be mollified only with a human sacrifice. A correct understanding by man of God as the supreme creative Mind creating under laws that must be observed by both Creator and creation, reveals how broken law may be mended by one who is willing to make certain sacrifices" (Fillmore, *Teach Us to Pray*).

"Atonement means reconciliation between God and man through Christ. It means a reuniting of our consciousness with the God consciousness" (*Unity,* April, 1954, Vol. 120, No. 4; page 4).

5. *Salvation.*

"The Christ in man never changes; it always has been and always will be the perfection that God created" (Turner, Elizabeth S., *What Unity Teaches,* page 8).

"Being 'born-again' or 'born from above' is not a miraculous change that takes place in man; it is the establishment of that which has always existed as the perfect man idea of divine Mind" (Fillmore, *Christian Healing,* page 24).

"In man a wonderful being is in process of creation. This being is spiritual man, who will be equal with God, when he overcomes or handles with wisdom and power, the faculties of the body" (*Twelve Powers of Man,* page 163).

"It is not only a privilege, but an absolute necessity to bring forth that perfection of character and form which was originally imaged in soul by the Godmind" (*Teach Us to Pray,* page 72).

6. *The Holy Spirit.*

Definition: "The very spirit of truth lying latent within us, each and every one" (*Lessons in Truth,* page 8).

7. *The Resurrection.*

"We believe that the dissolution of spirit, soul and body caused by death, is annulled by rebirth of the same spirit and soul in another body here on earth. We believe the repeated incarnations of man to be a merciful provision of our loving Father to the end that all may have opportunity to obtain immortality through regeneration as did Jesus. . . ." (*Unity Statement of Faith,* Art. 22).

"Eventually all souls reincarnate on the earth as babes and in due time take up their problems where they left off at death" (Fillmore, Charles and Cora, *Teach Us to Pray,* page 50).

". . . the soul leaves the body to mortal dissolution, yet it does not fail to return in due time to take up a body — as long as it believes in the limitations of sense. . . . If his life has been according to the Golden Rule . . . his soul basks in the sunshine of a world Elysian and his hope of heaven is for a season fulfilled" (*Talks on Truth,* pages 47, 48).

"Jesus demands of the Pharisees,

'What think ye of Christ? whose son is he?' They answered, not as one might ordinarily expect, 'the son of Joseph,' but 'the son of David.' In other words, He was the reincarnation of David" (Wilson, Ernest C., *Have We Lived Before?,* page 41).

8. *Sin.*

"Pain, sickness, poverty, old age and death are not real, and they have no power over me. There is nothing in all the universe for me to fear" (*Lessons in Truth,* page 35).

"1. I deny that I have inherited disease, sickness, ignorance or any mental limitation whatsoever. 2. I deny that I am a child of the flesh. I deny all belief in evil, for God made all that really is and pronounced it good. 3. Therefore no such deception as a belief in evil can darken my clear understanding of Truth. 4. I deny that the sins and omissions of my ancestors can reflect upon me in any way. Selfishness, envy, malice, jealousy, pride, avarice, arrogance, cruelty, hypocrisy, obstinancy and revenge are not part of my present understanding and I deny all such beliefs" (Fillmore, *Christian Healing,* pages 150, 250, 251).

9. *The Reality of Matter.*

"God, then, is the substance (from *sub* — under and *state* — to stand), or the real thing standing under every visible form of life, love, intelligence or power. Each rock, tree, animal, everything visible, is a manifestation of the one Spirit — God — differing only in degree of manifestation, and each of the numberless manifestations, or individualities, however insignificant, contains the whole. . . ." (Cady, *Lessons in Truth,* pages 8, 9).

REFUTING THE TEACHINGS OF UNITY

The theology of the Unity cult, as revealed in the previously quoted extracts from some of its standard publications, is far removed indeed from the Gospel of Jesus Christ as preached by the early apostles and as transmitted through the centuries by faithful witnesses of God in each age.

We cannot, of course, in the space allotted for a publication of this type cover in any extensive detail the various perversions so apparent in the teachings of Unity, but we shall for the remainder of this chapter concern ourselves with the dogmas of Unity as they affect some well-known Biblical doctrines, which are, in order: (1) The Bible; (2) The Trinity; (3) The Deity of Christ; (4) The Atonement of Christ; (5) The Doctrine of Salvation; (6) The Resurrection of Christ; (7) The Second Coming of Christ.

It is hoped, by contrasting the clear, historical teachings of Christianity which the Bible forthrightly states with the teachings of Unity, that the reader may be able to discern the vast difference which exists between the doctrines of the Unity cult and those of orthodox Christianity.

1. The Bible.

We have seen in our study of the Unity cult that the use of the Scriptures is an integral part of their entire system of teachings. By this we do not mean that teachings of Unity conform to the Scriptures, but rather that the Unity adherents use the Scriptures in a vain attempt to bolster up the unscriptural doctrines of the Fillmores.

Dr. James Teener, in his thorough analysis of Unity, has stated that for Unity ". . . the Bible is one of many sacred books, all of which are to be treated with reverence as 'records of men as to what their experiences have been communing with the omnipresent God.' The general tendency of Unity, however, is not to criticize statements of the Bible but to reinterpret them by the process of allegorization. The Fillmores belong in the lineage of Origen, Swedenborg and Mrs. Eddy in this respect. Thus they are able to unite the Metaphysical-mystical East and the practical-ethical West, but the East is always regent" (page 13, *Unity School of Christianity,* University of Chicago Library, 1942).

With Dr. Teener's analysis this writer is in wholehearted agreement, having studied numerous publications of the Unity School. In his *The Twelve Powers of Man (Unity School of Christianity,* 1930, page 114; also *Unity,* Vol. 7, October, 1896, page 400), Charles Fillmore stated, "Scripture may be satisfactory authority for those who are not themselves in direct communion with the Lord" (see also "The Scripture," *Unity,* Vol. 7, July, 1902, No. 19). From this it is at once obvious that Scripture is for those dwelling on a lower plane of spiritual development, whereas personal experience with God transcends the authority of Scripture!

Proof that the Unity School continues to spiritualize and allegorize all passages of the Bible which are in direct contradiction to their jumbled theological structure, can be found in any edition of *Unity* Magazine, where the International Sunday School Lessons (a Biblical presentation) are reinterpreted in the framework of Unity theology. This writer challenges anyone to read the parallel columns therein contained and by any conceivable stretch of the imagination or rational exercise of the mind in the light of the plain declarations of Scripture, to reconcile them as Unity claims it has done.

In company with Mrs. Eddy and most other gnostic religious thinkers, Unity wants no truck with the historic exegetical positions of the Bible, and deliberately shuns any controversy with informed Bible scholars, lest their shallow pretentions and fraudulent scholarship be exposed to the glaring light of Biblical truth. The Christian faith is founded upon belief in the Bible as the Word of God, or, as Paul put it, "All Scripture is given by inspiration of God (God-breathed), and is profitable for doctrine, for reproof, for correction, for instruction in righteousness that the man of God may be perfect, throughly furnished unto all good works" (II Timothy 3:16, 17).

The Lord Jesus Christ, in referring to the Word of His Father said, "Sanctify them through thy truth, thy word is truth" (John 17:17); and it was the Psalmist who stated, "For ever, O Lord, thy word is settled in heaven" and "Thy word is very pure" (Psalm 119:89, 140).

It is a well-known fact that Christ, during His lifetime, recognized the three-fold division of the Old Testament — the law, the prophets and the writings — and referred to them in their proper order at various times during the course of His ministry. Therefore, it is inconceivable that the early church should not have held in great esteem the record of the Old Testament, as well as the then-forming record of the new covenant, for which many of them eventually were to pay with their very life's blood.

Christians of all denominations who confess the cardinal doctrines of Scripture (The Trinity, The Deity of Christ, The Virgin Birth, The Sinless Nature of Christ, The Vicarious Atonement, The Physical Resurrection, The Second Coming of Christ, etc.), recognize the importance of accepting the Bible in its historic and linguistic framework, and only those with no concern for the testimony of history and the facts of sound exegesis, allegorize and spiritualize texts which they know reinforce the foundational doctrines of historic Christianity.

The adherents of the Unity cult are guilty of allegorization and spiritualization of all the cardinal doctrines of the Christian faith, and rather than to criticize outright the statements of Scripture, they subtly undercut the great pronouncements of the Word of God by reinterpreting them, allegorizing them and spiritualizing them, until they have sapped all of the revealed power of the Word of God, twisted it into the mold of the Fillmore religion and, in effect, "wrested the Scriptures to their own destruction" (II Peter 3:16).

Let us keep in mind then, that the members of the Unity cult speak devotedly of the Bible, but they utilize the Bible *only* insofar as it can be wielded as a successful tool to lure the unwary soul into the meshes of the Fillmore cult. But for the true Christian, the Bible in its proper context and framework of history, must ever remain the Word of God, inviolate, the final authority for the Church of Jesus Christ and the individual Christian life.

2. *The Trinity.*

It is the clear teaching of the Word of God that the nature of God is spirit (John 4:24), and further, that He has manifested Himself in the Old Testament in different ways (the Angel of Jehovah — Exodus 23:20; Judges 6:12 and 13; Judges 13, etc.; the Son of God — Daniel 3:25; as Emmanuel, *God with us* — Isaiah 7:14, etc.). In the eighteenth chapter of Genesis, for instance, it is recorded that Abraham entertained three visitors on the plains of Mamre, two of whom were angels (Genesis 19:1), the other whom Abraham addressed fourteen times as Jehovah God! To further clarify the picture where an understanding of the true nature of God is concerned, the Bible in the creation account (Genesis 1:26, 27) quotes the Lord as saying, "Let *us* make man in *our* image after *our* likeness . . . so God created man in his own image, in the image of God created he him, male and female created he them," utilizing the Hebrew plural "us" and "our" while at the same time returning to the singular "his" in verse 27, clearly a Trinitarian indication.

As we approach the New Testament revelation of God we also find something far beyond the Jewish interpretation of solitary unity (Deuteronomy

6:4) for both at the baptism of the Lord Jesus Christ and His last resurrection appearance (Matthew 3:16, 17; cf. Matthew 28:19) three distinct Persons are viewed as the one God, and nothing could be clearer than Christ's command to baptize in this threefold name of the Deity, Jehovah!

The God of the Bible and Father of our Lord Jesus Christ is a personal Being, a personal Spirit. This Almighty Person performs acts that only a personality is capable of: God hears (Exodus 2:24), God sees (Genesis 1:4); God creates (Genesis 1:1), God knows (II Timothy 2:19, Jeremiah 29:11), God has a will (I John 2:17); God is a cognizant reflectable ego, i.e. a personal being "I AM that I AM" (Exodus 3:14; Genesis 17:11). This is the God of Christianity, an omnipotent, omniscient, and omnipresent Personality, who manifests every attribute of a personality. He is therefore definitely not the God of Unity theology for Unity teaches that "belief" in a personal God has retarded the progress of the race![3]

According to the theology of Unity, "The Father is principle, the Son is that principle revealed in a creative plan, the Holy Spirit is the executive power of both Father and Son, carrying out the creative plan" (*Metaphysical Bible Dictionary,* page 629). However, this description does not coincide with the Biblical revelation of the character of God, for Unity is at its very core a pantheistic form of religion, maintaining that man is in effect, part of God, whereas the Scriptures clearly teach that man is the result of God's creative power and separate from Him, as every creation is by its very nature, separate from its creator.

Bear in mind that, whenever the adherents of Unity speak of "God," they do not speak of the God of Christianity

or of the Judaeo — Christian heritage. They speak, instead, of an abstract Principle, a divine Mind, which in no sense has a personality, neither can "it" be addressed as a personal being.

Unity perverts the doctrine of the Trinity, spiritualizing the very terms used to describe the relationship between the members of the godhead (Father, Son, Holy Spirit), and this dishonest practice should be unmasked at every opportunity by those interested enough in the truth concerning the character of God, as we find it within the pages of Scripture.

3. *The Deity of Christ.*

One needs only to peruse superficially the literature of the Unity cult to realize quickly that in the theology of Unity, Jesus Christ is not the God-man of the New Testament doctrine.

The New Testament, which is in reality the continuation or the unfolding of the expression of God's will under the old covenant, categorically teaches that Jesus Christ is the Eternal Word of God (John 1:1), that He took upon Himself the form of a man (John 1:14; Philippians 2:6, 7), and further, that He is the Redeemer of Israel and the Saviour of the world (Matthew 1:21-24; Acts 4:12).

Unity, in company with Christian Science, New Thought, Religious Science, etc., divides Jesus and Christ, reducing the God-man of Scripture to a perfect man indwelt by the Christ-consciousness, a consciousness present in *every* human being and which only needs to be cultivated and developed. Or, as the *Metaphysical Bible Dictionary* states it, page 150, ". . . Christ is the only begotten son of God with one complete idea of perfect man and divine Mind. This Christ, or perfect-man idea, existing eternally in divine Mind is the true spirit and higher self of every individual." We see, then, that all men are

[3]*The True Character of God,* Sarah B. Scott page 3, Unity School of Christianity, etc.

miniature "christs" so to speak, and in no sense whatsoever does Unity teach the intrinsic deity and uniqueness of the incarnate Word of God.

By subtly making a differentiation between the man Jesus and "the Christ, the spiritual identity of Jesus," Unity attempts to divest the Lord Jesus Christ of His true identity, which the Scriptures reveal to be that of incarnate Deity (see Isaiah 9:6; John 5:18; Colossians 1:15-18; 2:9; Revelation 1:7, 8, 17, 18).

Charles Fillmore, in his book, *Christian Healing* (Unity School of Christianity 1928, pages 106, 107), counsels the adherents of Unity when in doubt to "claim your Christ understanding at all times. . . ." which in one short phrase, sums up the position of Unity regarding the Lord Jesus Christ. For Mr. Fillmore taught that "Christ" is in reality "the superconscious mind, Christ-conscious, or spiritual-consciousness. . . ." (*Metaphysical Bible Dictionary,* page 155), a position which is directly opposed to the teaching of Scripture; for there has been but one Christ, of whom Peter spoke when he said, "Neither is there salvation in any other, for there is none other name under heaven given among men, whereby we must be saved," and "this same Jesus, God hath made Lord and Christ" (Acts 4:12; 2:36).

Jesus Christ then, was not Jesus and Christ as the Unity cultists would have us believe; rather, He was the God-man — two natures in one being, "Jesus Christ the same, yesterday, today and for ever" (Hebrews 13:8). In the eighth chapter of John's gospel, verse 58, the Lord Jesus Christ unmistakably identified Himself with Jehovah when He stated that "Before Abraham was, I AM" (cf. Exodus 3:14). And it is this one fact that establishes the unity of Christ with the Eternal Trinity, Father, Son and Holy Spirit, and establishes beyond question in the mind of any intelligent exegetical student of Scripture the identity and deity of Jesus Christ. "This

is the true God, and eternal life" (I John 5:20).

4. *The Atonement of Christ.*

The verdict of the Scriptures on the state of unregenerate mankind is most explicit: "All have sinned and come short of the glory of God" (Romans 3:23). Punishment for this is declared to be "everlasting" (Matthew 25:46), unless one accepts the death of Jesus Christ upon Calvary's cross in his stead, for then, and then alone, the Scriptures teach, can a man find peace with God (Romans 5). The Bible declares in unmistakable terms that the atonement (reconciliation) of Christ was the fulfillment of the Old Testament sacrifice of the lamb for the sins of the people (Exodus 12:5-14) and further, that Jesus Christ as the Lamb of God (John 1:29) made atonement for all sin forever upon the cross of Calvary "once," then seated Himself on the right hand of the "Majesty on High" (Hebrews 1:3 and 9:26). Through His substitutionary sacrifice then we "have peace with God" (Colossians 1:20) and "the blood of Jesus Christ his Son, cleanseth us from all sin" (I John 1:7). In his book, *What Practical Christianity Stands For* (page 5), Charles Fillmore made the following statement: "The atonement is the unity of man with God the Father, in Christ. Stating it in terms of mind, we should say that the atonement is the At-one-ment or agreement or reconciliation of man's mind with divine Mind through the superconsciousness of Christ Mind."

It is hardly necessary to expand upon the direct contradiction which exists between these two positions. The atonement of the cross is a great deal more than the "reconciliation of man's mind with divine Mind through the superconsciousness of Christ Mind," as Mr. Fillmore would have us believe.

According to the testimony of Scripture, Christ "bore in his own body our sins upon the tree" (I Peter 2:24), and the Scriptures irrevocably state that, "Without the shedding of blood there is no remission" (Hebrews 9:22), a vastly different position from that of Mr. Fillmore and the Unity cult.

Peter, in his first epistle, states the doctrine of the atonement in a nutshell, when he writes

> Forasmuch as ye know that ye were not redeemed with corruptible things as silver and gold, from your vain conversation received by tradition from your fathers; but with the precious blood of Christ as of a lamb without blemish and without spot . . . being born again, not of corruptible seed, but of incorruptible, by the word of God which liveth and abideth forever . . . but the word of the Lord endureth forever. And this is the word which by the gospel is preached unto you (I Peter 1:18, 19, 23, 25).

Christ therefore, upon Calvary's cross, ransomed the souls of all who will believe, from the power of eternal death, and as John so beautifully puts it in the Apocalypse, "From Jesus Christ, who is the faithful witness and the first begotten of the dead, and the prince of the kings of the earth. Unto him that loved us and washed (loosed) us from our sins in his own blood" (Revelation 1:5).

The theology of the Unity School, then, is directly opposed to the clear revelation of Scripture which teaches that it is through the blood of the Lord Jesus Christ shed in a vicarious effort that man has peace with God (Colossians 1:20; cf. Romans 5), and with Moses of old we can rest in the sure Word of God which states, ". . . for the blood through the life in it serves for expiation" (Leviticus 17:11, Berkeley Version).

5. *The Doctrine of Salvation.*

There are many who will ask, "Since Unity denies practically every cardinal doctrine of the Christian faith, how then

can they claim any kind of salvation; and if so, what type of salvation is it?"[4]

To answer these questions, we must understand that Unity denies the existence of a literal heaven or hell (Luke 16). Indeed, all the heaven or hell a man is likely to get, according to the Fillmores, he will get here upon this earth, either in this incarnation or in future incarnations, dependent upon his behavior during each incarnation. In Vol. 58 of *Unity* Magazine, July, 1922, No. 49, Charles Fillmore summed up the Unity teaching on salvation when he wrote, "Unity teaches that the eternal life taught and demonstrated by Jesus is not gained by dying, but by purifying the body until it becomes the undying habitation of the soul."

The Unity cult today continues to hold this teaching, and knows nothing of the "eternal life" offered to mankind by the Lord Jesus when He said, "Come unto me all ye that labor and are heavy laden and I will give you rest" (Matthew 11:28) and "Ye must be born again" (John 3:5). Let us then beware of Unity's perversions of Scripture and cling to the Gospel of the Son of God, "who loved us and gave Himself for us" (Ephesians 5:2), for He alone is the "author of eternal salvation to all them that obey Him" (Hebrews 5:9).

6. *The Resurrection of Christ.*

Unity, through its various publications and especially its *Statement of Faith,* Article 22, has gone on record as stating the following things relative to the Resurrection.

"We believe the dissolution of spirit, soul and body, caused by death, is annulled by rebirth of the same spirit and soul in another body here on earth. We believe the repeated reincarnations of man are the merciful provision of our loving Father to the end that all may

---

[4]The fact that Unity adherents deny every cardinal teaching of the Christian faith fails to deter them from calling themselves Christians, and this is true of every non-Christian cult.

come to obtain immortality through re-generation, as did Jesus."

In lieu of the great doctrine of the bodily resurrection as taught in both the Old and the New Testaments the Unity cult teaches cycles of reincarnation until eventual perfection is reached. The true Christian position concerning death however, is taught in numerous places in Scripture as, for example in II Corinthians 5:8, where Paul emphatically states that "to be absent from the body is to be present with the Lord (or at home with the Lord)." And again, in Philippians 1:21-23, the great apostle anticipates his departure from this life to be with Christ, and certainly not to go through repeated incarnations until he was found worthy to share the glory of the Lord.

To refute the Unity position, reincarnation vs. resurrection, the reader is referred to the fifteenth chapter of I Corinthians, where the doctrine of the physical resurrection of the body to immortality is clearly stated. After reading this, the writer feels, the observant reader will immediately note the difference between the theology of Paul under the inspiration of the Holy Spirit, and the theology of the Fillmores and Unity, via the medium of the "great deceiver!"

In *Unity* Magazine for May of 1927, Charles Fillmore wrote: "When we finally understand the facts of life and rid our mind of the delusion that we shall find immortal life after we die, then we shall seek more diligently to awaken the spiritual man within us. . . ." The Unity cult has not departed from this teaching of Fillmore, which directly contradicts the testimony of the Lord Jesus Christ in the fourteenth chapter of John, when He said, "Let not your heart be troubled, ye believe in God, believe also in me. In my Father's house are many mansions: if it were not so I would have told you. I go to prepare a place for you. And if I go and prepare a place for you, I will come again and receive you unto myself; that where I am, there ye may be also" (verses 1-3). Contrary to the teachings of Unity then, "it is appointed unto men once to die, but after this the judgment" (Hebrews 9:27); and "It is a fearful thing to fall into the hands of the living God" (Hebrews 10:31), pronouncements which, while they held no terror for the Fillmores during their long lives, doubtless are most meaningful today, since both the first Mrs. Fillmore and her patriarchal husband, Charles, have departed this life to face the judgment of the God of the Bible and not the god that they fashioned with deceptive words and metaphysical speculations. The God who is not a respecter of persons (II Samuel 14:14), and who is the Judge of all the earth has commanded that all men honor His Son, even as they honor Him (John 5:23) and He has especially stated His intention of eventually raising the dead (I Corinthians 15) not subjecting them to repeated reincarnations in the traditions of the Fillmores and the Unity cult.

7. *The Second Coming of Christ.*

It is quite unnecessary to go into detail relative to the teaching of Unity on the Second Coming of the Lord Jesus Christ, except to note as has already been mentioned in the preceding chapter, that *Unity* recognizes no personal return of Jesus Christ to judge the world (see I Thessalonians 4:13-18).

In direct contradiction to this unscriptural teaching, the Bible clearly prophesies the return of the Messiah of Israel and the Saviour of mankind to execute righteous judgment upon the earth (Zechariah 12:10; cf. Revelation 1:7; also Matthew 25:31-46; and II Thessalonians 1:7-10).

The great expectation of the Church of Christ has been the imminent return of her blessed Lord, which Paul describes in his letter to Titus as "looking for that blessed hope and the glorious appearing of the great God and our

Saviour Jesus Christ, who gave himself for us, that he might redeem us from all iniquity, and purify unto himself a peculiar people, zealous of good works" (2:13-15).

When we consider these objective facts of Scripture and carefully compare them with the mangled jargon of the Unity School, it becomes increasingly apparent that our faith must rest as always, upon the sure revelations of Scripture. We must be prepared for the "scoffers" who the Holy Spirit through Peter said, would come toward the end of the age (II Peter 3:3), and whom we are to "reprove, rebuke and exhort with all longsuffering and doctrine" (II Timothy 4:2), that we may be faithful to Christ, "who is over all, God blessed for ever. Amen" (Romans 9:5).

Before closing our study of the Unity School, we believe it is necessary to examine one of the major tenets of Unity, which makes it so attractive to so many persons in our day. We have reference to the doctrine of reincarnation which the Unity School propagates, in company with other reincarnationists, and which should be analyzed and answered from the Bible.

THE REINCARNATION THEORY OF UNITY

The theory of reincarnation, transmigration or rebirth, is best described briefly as a process whereby at the death of the body, the soul passes into the bodies of lower animals, or other human beings in an ever-rotating cycle (from body to body) until purification from sin is accomplished. When this sinless state has been attained, the soul passes thence to Nirvana (Buddhism), or the dwelling place of Brahma (Hinduism). These places consist of nothing more than "the eternal peace," reached by absorption of the soul and all vestiges of individual personality into the world soul, or whatever philosophical abstraction it may constitute.

In the case of the Unity School, as we have previously observed, reincarnation has been given a new facade, and a good deal of "evidence," has been introduced to show that the Unity concept of reincarnation is not only logical and rational, but that it is the only "reasonable" solution to many so-called insoluble problems that orthodox Christianity cannot solve.

We shall consider at this time, only those evidences most frequently submitted, the remainder being largely peripheral in character.

The Evidence

1) There are persons, places and experiences with which we do not have to become acquainted. Somehow we feel we already know them. Have you ever felt that you have been to a place, or known a person before you experienced the meeting? This is evidence of reincarnation.

2) All men are not born equal in regard to either station in life, opportunity or condition of health. Some babies are born blind, deaf or diseased, many persons are cut down in the flower of youth. If God is just, He cannot allow such things to happen to the apparently innocent. Therefore, He must be punishing them for their previous sins while in another form, and this will continue on until all are purified of past mistakes. Reincarnation, then, is the only fair evidence of God's being perfectly just to all men.

3) Unfinished thoughts and unfinished work abound in everyone's experience, and God could not justly waste these undeveloped talents. Rather, He gives us countless opportunities to utilize them by supplying concurrent rebirths in which to bring our thoughts and works to fruition.

4) Many documented and verified cases of persons who have been able to recount their previous lives in detail are recorded in the files of reputable professional hypnotists, psychologists and research organizations; these establish

the fact of reincarnation beyond reasonable doubt, and are available for evaluation.

These four points in one form or another make up the basic premises upon which the theory of reincarnation is based; abundant "evidence" is also submitted from the "inspired" writings of numerous Eastern Religions and Western Cults, but the pattern is always uniformly the same. The Unity School, however, differs slightly from the more "orthodox" systems of transmigration in that Unity claims that reincarnation is a "Christian doctrine" (*Have We Lived Before?* E. C. Wilson, page 26) and that the Bible fully teaches and supports it as such. Some of the common texts cited are: Matthew 16:17; 17:11; 22:42; John 9:2; Revelation 5:5 and 22:16.) We shall discuss these, and their contextual meanings contrasted with the interpretation of Reincarnationists a little later on, but the fact remains, that not a few have dared to claim support from the Scriptures for this pagan dogma.

The Biblical Position

Reincarnation can easily be refuted from the Bible by at least ten Old and New Testament doctrines, but for the sake of brevity, we have elected to list only four, all of which those believing in reincarnation, including the Unity School, deny automatically, by accepting their transmigration hypothesis. These Biblical doctrines are: (1) The Personality of God; (2) The Atonement of Christ; (3) The Physical Resurrection and (4) Divine Retribution.

1. For some unknown reason, all Reincarnationists reject the Personality of God, that He is a personal cognizant Spirit, a divine Ego, (Exodus 3:14), capable of a subject-object relationship with man and within the Godhead.

All Reincarnationists, then, are committed to a pantheistic concept of Deity, that is, God is conceived of as being the fountain of all existence from the tiniest atom to the most gigantic forms of matter, and further, these things are all part of His Substance, which permeates every particle of existence.

This position, that God is all, and all is God, or a manifestation of Him, is thoroughly refuted by the following verses of Scripture, which teach incontrovertibly that God is a Personal Spirit possessed of attributes which only a personality has, immanent in creation, but apart from it as Creator. Transcendent in that He does not share His spiritual substance (John 4:24; Hebrews 1:3) with the products of His creative will.

A. God remembers. Isaiah 43:25; Jeremiah 31:20; Hosea 8:13.
B. God speaks (Subject, object relationship). Exodus 3:12; Matthew 3:17; Luke 17:6.
C. God sees, hears and creates. Genesis 6:5; Exodus 2:24; Genesis 1:1.
D. God knows (has a mind). Jeremiah 29:11; II Timothy 2:19; I John 3:20.
E. God is a personal spirit. John 4:24; Hebrews 1:3.
F. God has a will. Matthew 6:10; Hebrews 10:7, 9; I John 2:17.
G. God will judge. Ezekiel 18:30; 34:20; II Corinthians 5:10.

2. Reincarnation is refuted most decisively by the atonement of Jesus Christ, since the doctrine of the atonement teaches that God, through Christ's sacrifice on the cross, has "purged" believers from all their sins (Hebrews 1:3) and counted them righteous for the sake of His Son (II Corinthians 5:21). Reincarnationists, on the other hand, claim that successive "rebirths" are the instrument of cleansing for the soul and thereby do away with not only the efficacy of the atonement, but the very necessity itself of Christ's dying at all for the sins of the world.

The Bible, however, clearly teaches that "without the shedding of blood is no remission" (Hebrews 9:22) of sin, and Christ purchased the church with His own blood which is not corruptible as silver or gold are (I Peter 1:18, 19) but which is precious, and the price of the soul's redemption.

For the Unity adherent of the reincarnation theory, then, almost endless cycles of rebirth are necessary to cleanse the soul from sin, but for the Christian the blood of Jesus Christ God's Son cleanses us from all sin (I John 1:9). This is the message of the Bible from Genesis to Revelation, redemption by blood through the sacrifice of "him that loved us and washed us from our sins in his own blood" (Revelation 1:5). (For further Scriptures see Matthew 26:28; Romans 5:6-8; Ephesians 1:7; Colossians 1:20, etc.)

3. The doctrine of the physical resurrection of Jesus Christ (and all men, for that matter!) is the foundation stone upon which the validity of Christianity stands, for in the words of the Apostle Paul — "If Christ be not raised, your faith is vain; ye are yet in your sins" (I Corinthians 15:17). The Bible plainly states that Jesus arose from the grave in a physical form (John 20:27), that He was not raised a spirit (Luke 24:39-44) and that Christ Himself after He had risen, rebuked His disciples for their unbelief in His physical Resurrection (Mark 16:14). It is evident, therefore, that though Jesus Christ was raised physically, He had what the Bible terms a "spiritual body" (I Corinthians 15: 44-49), not a spirit form, but an immortal, incorruptible physical body possessed of spiritual characteristics forever exempt from death (Romans 6:9), a body the like of which all believers shall one day possess at His glorious return and our resurrection (I John 3:2; I Corinthians 15:52-54).

The Unity School, however, does away altogether with physical resurrection, and even claims that Christ rose spiritually, not physically, pointing to the facts that Mary Magdalene (John 20:14, 15) and the Emmaus disciples did not recognize their risen Lord until He revealed Himself (Luke 24:16, 31).

Whereas, it is claimed, they would have known Him immediately, if His body had seen a physical resurrection. Further than this, such persons often refer to I Peter 3:18, where it states that Christ was "made alive in the spirit," the inference being that His was a spiritual resurrection. These objections, though apparently valid, crumble under the relentless pressure of sound exegesis, for in no way does Christ's veiling His identity from some persons after His Resurrection prove that He was not physically raised, as any cursory study of the Greek at the respective texts clearly indicates. The key to understanding these veiled appearances is found in Luke 24: 16 and 31, two texts Reincarnationists religiously avoid commenting upon for the obvious reason that a correct exegesis of them destroys their spiritual resurrection claims.

Luke 24:16 in the Greek states simply that the eyes of the disciples "were kept from recognizing Him" (Greek—ekratounto) which proves conclusively that Christ willed that they should behold His features yet be incapable of knowing that it was He, not because His form had changed, but because His will had dictated otherwise!

The other text, Luke 24:31, fully substantiates the Greek of 24:16 by showing that, although the disciples had been conversing with Christ, *the eyes of their understanding were closed* by His will, so that they could not comprehend until He chose to reveal it, that the risen Christ was their companion (Greek — dienoichthesan — opened).

In regard to I Peter 3:18, a word study of the Greek completely corroborates the testimony of Scripture that Christ was raised in a physical form by God the Father but *through* the agency of the Holy Spirit (Romans 8:11). Thus, when Peter says "put to death in the flesh," he quickly announces the triumph of God the Father, who raised His Son Jesus from the dead (Acts 17: 31) "by the spirit" (I Peter 3:18). Going beyond this, we further see that Jesus Christ was not raised *a* Spirit (John 20:28) and that in the Bible a spiritual resurrection is never taught at all, for His body did not know corruption (Acts 2:31; 13:37) and on the third day His Spirit and soul returned to that *same* body and brought it to life (Matthew 28:9). Henceforth, it was a glorified body (Philippians 3:21), model of all the bodies of the saints (I John 3:2). It could pass through walls (John 20:19), but it could be handled and felt (Luke 24:36-39). It could ascend into heaven (Acts 1:9), but before it did so, it could eat fish and honey (Luke 24:41-43). What is unmistakably asserted, then, is that while Christ died on Calvary, He was "made alive" in a spiritual body; thus we see that the eternal Word made flesh for the suffering of death ceased living a mortal, fleshly existence, and began to live a resurrection life in a spiritual body. As Luther so succinctly stated it:

> . . . Christ by His suffering was taken from the life which is flesh and blood . . . and is now placed in another life and made alive according to the Spirit . . . He has now passed into a spiritual and supernatural life.

The great doctrine of the physical resurrection of all men, saved and unsaved, (John 5:28, 29), therefore eliminates the necessity of concurrent reincarnations and proves once more the fallacy of the entire system.

4. Reincarnation is further refuted by the Biblical doctrine of divine retribution for sin, a doctrine inseparably connected with the nature of man and the state of the dead.

The Bible unmistakably teaches that at the death of the physical form, the soul leaves the body (Genesis 35:18) and if saved, is instantly transported to the Presence of God (II Corinthians 5:8; Philippians 1:21-23). Those who have rejected Jesus Christ, on the other hand, go instantaneously to hell, a place of conscious separation from God and spiritual torment of a terrible nature (Luke 16:19-31). In addition to this, the Bible further warns that at the last judgment (Matthew 25:31-46) the unsaved dead will be cast into "outer darkness," there to be forever in conscious separation and the indescribable retribution of eternal fire, for the endless ages of eternity (Matthew 8:12; 25:41, 46; II Peter 2:17; Jude 13; Revelation 20:15).

Such is the divine Will, Scripture tells us, for those who have committed the infinite transgression of rejecting God's love as expressed in Jesus Christ (John 3:16, 36). To this eternal pronouncement, Reincarnationists can offer no refutation, only a denial, and the pretended mysticism which dictates cycles of reincarnations in a clever attempt to accomplish what the Lord in His Word has already ordained, perfect justice at the hands of God's Son, the perfect righteous Judge (John 5:22).

Explanation of the Texts Misapplied to Prove Reincarnation*

1. Matthew 16:17; 22:42. "Jesus calls Simon Peter, Bar-Jonah, or literally, 'Son of Jonah.' The use of son here is figurative, implying that the present incarnation is the 'son' or offspring of the previous life. This explains the passage Matthew 22:42 in which Jesus demands of the Pharisees, 'What think ye of Christ, whose son is he?' They answered, not as one might ordinarily expect, 'The son of Joseph,' but 'The son of David.' In other words, He was 'the reincarnation of David'" (page 39).

Comment — These texts hardly need to be explained, since the context in which they appear explains them perfectly, and rules out any such attempts as Mr. Wilson makes to read into them reincarnation.

*These are found on pages 38-40, *Have We Lived Before?* E. C. Wilson, Unity, 1953.

In both cases the usage of common Hebrew expressions is indicated in the Greek. Jesus called Simon "Son of Jonah" as a means of contrasting Peter's background with the character of the revelation Peter had declared (Matthew 16:16-18), thus revealing that the source of Peter's knowledge of His true identity — "the Christ, the Son of the Living God," — was God the Father, Himself. Neither the Greek grammar nor the context allows such a fanciful interpretation as Reincarnationists read into the text at Matthew 16:17.

Regarding Matthew 22:42 and the weird interpretation there read into the text by Mr. Wilson, the context is decidedly one of Judaistic theology and history. The Pharisees and Sadducees, it can be seen from the preceding narrative, had tried to trap Christ with trick questions, but having failed in this, they were in turn asked a searching question by Christ Himself (verse 21), regarding David's relationship to his coming son, the Messiah. The answer of the Pharisees, "the son of David" (verse 42) merely expressed their common acceptance of the fact that Messiah was to be of David's lineage, no more, no less. Certainly, they never meant that Messiah was to be the reincarnation of David, as Mr. Wilson states, since the idea of reincarnation was as totally foreign to Old Testament theology as it is to that of the New; therefore, that argument cannot stand.

2. Matthew 11:14. "Jesus . . . when speaking of John the Baptist (Matthew 11:14) . . . said, 'And if you are willing to receive it, this is Elijah that is to come' " (page 40).

Comment — Jesus was here commenting on Malachi 4:5, and applying to John the Baptist the mantle of prophecy in the tradition of Elijah. So Christ, in answering the Jews, merely gave the prophecy its true meaning. Neither the context nor the prophecy refers in any way to John being a reincarnation of Elijah, as Mr. Wilson so vainly strives

to establish, and no exegetical Bible scholar has ever supported Reincarnationists on this point.

3. Revelation 5:5; 22:16. "In Revelation 5:5 Jesus is called 'the lion that is of the tribe of Judah, the root of David' . . . In Revelation 22:16 Jesus says, 'I, Jesus . . . am the root (as Joshua) and the offspring (as Jesus) of David' " (page 39).

Comment — These texts have been so sorely tortured out of their historical and contextual meanings that it seems almost unbelievable that supposedly honest people would stoop to such depths. The argument that since the Hebrew form of Jesus is Joshua, and since Jesus was of David's line, therefore Joshua and David were previous incarnations of the man later called Jesus of Nazareth, is completely without Biblical foundation!

4. John 9:12ff. These particular texts are favorites of Reincarnationists, because it is claimed that the man born blind was suffering for sins he committed in a previous incarnation (pages 43-46).

As is the case with most text-lifting cultists, the Unity School never looks beyond the passages it contextually abuses, and where, in many cases, the explanation usually lies.

In verse 3 of John 9, Christ explained that the man was born blind, not as a result of the sins of his parents, or his own sins for that matter, but "that in him works of God should be displayed" (Berkeley Version). Following this thought out, in verses 6 and 7 of the same chapter, Jesus restored the man's sight to the glory of His Father, and once again testified to His intrinsic Deity.

The thought of reincarnation then, never once enters the context of John 9 in any form, as even Mr. Wilson could learn by *reading* it thoroughly, instead of trying to *read into it* his preconceived theory of reincarnation.

The Son of God warns in the closing verses of the Revelation (22:18, 19) that the plagues there recorded will be the certain destiny of those who tamper with His Word, and that their very names will be *subtracted* from the Book of Life if they *subtract* from His Word.

Evaluation of the Evidences for Reincarnation

1. The familiarity with persons, places and things never consciously traceable to experienced events is one of the strongest pillars on which the faith of the Unity cultist rests. It must therefore, be duly examined. The question is: Do such occurrences prove that one has lived before in similar circumstances? The opinions of leading scientists, psychologists, psychiatrists and hypnotists are almost all to the contrary. It is quite possible, they tell us, to connect subconscious memories of "forgotten" stories and facts with religious beliefs. Through hypnotic regression, it is possible to weave strange tales, many of which dwarf "Bridey Murphy," and are also recorded in the files of reputable, competent evaluators (see *Life,* March 19, 1956). Such feelings then, are largely the result of pure subjectivism, and as empirical evidence are therefore valueless.

2. The argument from equality. This particular argument attempts to show that the evils and inequalities that beset mankind are the result of sins committed in previous incarnations. This argument is weak, however, in that it does not recognize the prerogative of God to discipline His creatures or His children for His own purposes (Romans 8:28) that He might refine us in the fires of testing (I Peter 4:12). While it is true, however, that there are inequalities in the world, the Scriptures never indicate that sins committed in a previous life are their logical antecedents, and no Reincarnationist, living or dead, has ever been able to prove that any connection exists at all between divine judgment and alleged pre-birth existences. On the contrary, the Bible formally and flatly states that sin is in this world as the result of the sin of Adam (Romans 5:12). We must never forget that God is Sovereign, and that He orders all things after the good pleasure of His will. It is man who is accountable to God, and *never* is God accountable to man. Let us not forget, though, as do the pantheists, that the God of the Bible is not just a set of cold, abstract attributes. He is a Personality, for there is a Person behind the decrees of God and His attributes, who is definitely perfect, loving, just and good — a Person whose fullness has been seen for all time in the face of Jesus Christ, as it is written, "He that hath seen me hath seen the Father" (John 14:9).

3. Unfinished thought and unfinished work. This "evidence" for the necessity of reincarnation is totally worthless, since God, in order to be just, does not "have" to allow man to finish all his thoughts or works, or, for that matter, any of them! In fact, it was Solomon, the wisest man who ever lived, who stated that the wisdom of man and his works perish in the grave, a hard pill indeed for Reincarnationists to swallow (Ecclesiastes 9:10; see also Psalm 146:4).

4. The final "evidence" for reincarnation is that of various cases (Bridey Murphy, etc.), which are adduced as incontestable proof of the theory. With reference to many of such occurrences *Life* magazine has presented logical, scientific explanations which largely answer the questions raised. In many cases, however, for purposes of deception, Satan has in the past and most certainly still does, exercise demonic forces to lead the unwary soul from God's truth into the dark passages of occultism (Exodus 7:11, 12).

Were not the New Testament doctrine of the new birth or regeneration tied to the "Bridey Murphy" and similar so-called reincarnationist cases, then Christians might well write the whole affair off as a hoax, or as the pranks which our human mental processes sometimes play on us. The attempt, however, to reinterpret the new birth as reincarnation, by both Unity and the "Bridey Murphy" believers (see *The Search for Bridey Murphy,* page 215), stamps the entire subject as demonic in origin and purpose, to be avoided by the Christian.

The Christian doctrine of the new birth plainly teaches that when one receives Jesus Christ as Lord and Saviour, the Holy Spirit of God regenerates his soul (John 3:3; I Peter 1:23), restores his relationship to God, lost because of Adam's sin, and creates a sinless nature within (II Corinthians 5:17). This nature will eventually through progressive sanctification, enable us to reach perfection, either at the death of the body and the reunion of the soul with Christ (II Corinthians 5:8); or, if we survive to the Second Coming of Christ, at our translation or resurrection to immortality (I Thessalonians 4:14-17 and I Corinthians 15:51-54).

This great Biblical truth, then, can never be logically, rationally, or exegetically connected to or compared with the rebirth or new birth of reincarnation, and it is best that the Christian public be alerted to the "new" menace which Unity advocates, and which "tickles the ears" and the vanity of many deluded souls today, and leads them away from the Prince of life (Acts 3:15) and into the chasm of spiritual death.

In order to join the Unity School of Christianity, it must be understood that one would have to renounce every basic doctrine of the Christian faith; deny the deity of, physical resurrection and personal Second Coming of our Lord and believe in the reincarnation of the soul, as opposed to the doctrine of the physical resurrection of the body.

Let us not forget, then, that under the apparent sugar-coated shell of tolerance and pseudo-love which characterizes the Unity School of Christianity, there lies a subtle, but firm denial of the basic principles of the Gospel of Jesus Christ.

To those who would drink at this well of supposed spiritual refreshment, our warning must be clear and definite:

> Try the spirits whether they are of God: because many false prophets are gone out into the world. . . . I John 4:1.

Even in this brief study of the Unity cult, no objective student of Scripture can deny that Unity is distinctly within the boundaries of this warning, and we would be bereft of wisdom not to listen to this counsel from the Word of God.

Charles W. Ferguson, the great liberal critic of cultism, writing in his revealing book, *The New Books of Revelation,* has summed up the Unity School in a masterful way, and we close our study with his succinct appraisal (with which, the facts of both history and theology force us to agree):

> Thus it is that, with much wind and high sales pressure, the Unity School of Christianity serves the multitudes. It gets results. It offers a philosophicism that sounds well and works better. It has demonstrated its success for the millions of adherents who have been swept into the paper fold. Underpinning its vast machinery are of course, the cases in which it has cured diseases of every sort and its glib promise of physical immortality to its followers. The machinery is not to be despised.
>
> We have in Unity an enormous mail order concern dispensing health and happiness on the large scale of modern business enterprise. It is mass production in religion, and its work is carried on shrewdly and systematically with infinite pains to capitalize upon the old demand and extend the market. It is the work of a retired realtor, and his inspired wife, and with its tedious array of tabulated facts and its insufferable efficiency, it suggests pretty well what Americans want in the realm of the spirit.[5]

[5]Doubleday-Doran and Company, Garden City, 1929, page 250.

Chapter 15
HERBERT W. ARMSTRONG AND THE RADIO CHURCH OF GOD

The Radio Church of God (the official name of Herbert Armstrong's cult) could more properly be designated "The New Galatianism" because of its emphasis on legalism. Since this group is gaining momentum throughout the entire world, it is essential that its theological system be analyzed in the light of the Word of God, to see whether or not it is, as advertised, "The Plain Truth."

To facilitate a clearer understanding of this relatively new cult system, some historical background is necessary.

THE RISE OF HERBERT ARMSTRONG

Mr. Armstrong's organization does not have a lengthy history; in fact, what is purported to be "the inside story of The World Tomorrow broadcast" published by Armstrong is sketchy and points out that he began his professional life as an advertising and promotional man who wrote copy for the Merchants Trade Journal in Des Moines, Iowa, 1912-15[1]. His whole advertising business, however, was wiped out in 1920, in what was described as "a flash depression."[2] In 1924, Armstrong moved to the Pacific Northwest where twice[3] his business enterprises were destroyed by "forces beyond Mr. Armstrong's control."

Mr. Armstrong was "converted" chiefly through the influence of Mrs. Armstrong[4] who made a great discovery: "obedience to God's spiritual laws summed up in the Ten Command-

ments is necessary for salvation. Not that our works of keeping the commandments save us, but rather that sin is the transgression of God's spiritual law. Christ does not save us in our sins but from our sins. We must repent of sin, repent of transgressing God's law which means turning from disobedience as a prior condition to receiving God's free gift."

Mr. Armstrong's Sunday school days had taught him that there are no works to salvation . . . God's law was done away. To him religion had not been a way of life but a mere belief, an acceptance of the fact of God's existence, Christ's virgin birth, the efficacy of Christ's shed blood. Controversy arose between Mr. and Mrs. Armstrong. She refused to give up the truths she had found. He was angered into his first real study of the Bible undertaken for the avowed purpose of proving to his wife that "all these churches can't be wrong." He believed then just as *fundamentalist persecutors* do today. He would have said that "anyone proclaiming what Christ and the Apostles actually proclaimed was a false prophet."[5]

Armstrong concluded that "his wife had found the truth after all. It was a bitter pill to swallow. A furious interstruggle ensued within him."[6]

After the study of his Bible and much prayer, we are informed, Mr. Armstrong began writing and doing evangelical work. It was in June of 1931 that Armstrong conducted an evangelistic campaign in Eugene, Oregon, and at

---

[1]Armstrong, Herbert W.: *The Autobiography of Herbert W. Armstrong.* Pasadena: Ambassador College Press, 1967, Vol. I., pp. 68, 72, 78 f., 88 ff.

[2]*Ibid.,* p. 234.

[3]e. q., *Ibid,* p. 284, etc.

[4]*Ibid.,* pp. 281-84, 286 ff.

[5]*The Inside Story of the World Tomorrow Broadcast*, page 47

[6]*Ibid.,* page 48.

that time was "ordained as a minister of Jesus Christ."

His tremendous zeal, tireless energy, writing, speaking and promotional ability stood Armstrong in good stead through the years and culminated in the founding of the Ambassador College, located in Pasadena, California, *Plain Truth Magazine* which was started in February, 1934, and *The World Tomorrow Program* which originated in Eugene, Oregon, January, 1934.

Today Armstrong has branch headquarters in Vancouver, British Columbia; Johannesburg, South Africa; New South Wales, Australia; Manila in the Philippine Islands; Dusseldorf, West Germany; Geneva, Switzerland; and another college now so named Ambassador in St. Albans, Hertfordshire, England.

THE ECLECTICISM OF
HERBERT ARMSTRONG

Armstrong's biographer, Roderick Meredith, goes to great pains to point out that "there was never any association in any way with Jehovah's Witnesses, Seventh-day Adventists, Mormons, or any such sects as some accusers have falsely claimed."[7]

1. SEVENTH-DAY ADVENTISM
    AND HERBERT ARMSTRONG.

Unfortunately for Mr. Meredith, the Seventh-day Adventist denomination has done a complete historical resume of Herbert W. Armstrong and his association with them. Writing for the Ministerial Association and his church, George Burnside states concerning Mr. Armstrong:

". . . Mr. Armstrong is an off-shoot of an off-shoot of an off-shoot of the Seventh-day Adventist church."

In 1866 Elders B. F. Snook and W. H.

Brinkerhoff, two ministers of the small and newly organized Iowa Conference of Seventh-day Adventists apostatized, and with a few members formed a group of their own. They directed their work from Marion, Iowa. In 1889 they centered their work in Stanbury, Missouri, calling their company "the Church of God (Adventist)."

Mr. Armstrong joined this church and after a stormy experience with them, he reported that Mr. Duggar, in a dispute over leadership, led off a sizable part of the membership and called their group "the Church of God (Seventh-day)." Mr. Armstrong joined this off-shoot movement. Sometime later because of Mr. Armstrong's acceptance of the British Israelism theory and other subjects, he went out on his own and formed his own church calling it "The Radio Church of God."[8]

Having checked the Adventists' documentation on this thoroughly, and finding it to be accurate, what Mr. Meredith glosses over lightly now takes on significance. The neighbor lady who revealed the great discovery to Mrs. Armstrong about the law of God was a former member of the Seventh-day Adventist Church and a member of the splinter group. Mr. Armstrong's theology in many areas paralleled Seventh-day Adventism, such as, his insistence upon observance of the Seventh-day Sabbath, abstinence from certain articles of food as unclean, a general Adventist system of prophetic interpretation (albeit with his own peculiar modifications), his extreme legalism and the observance of feasts, and new moons, and his denunciation of the doctrines of hell and eternal punishment for which he has substituted the Adventist doctrine of the annihilation of the wicked. Mr. Armstrong owes a consid-

---

[7]*Ibid.*, pp. 48 F.; Cf. *Autobiography, Vol. I,* p. 302 Where he denies having attended any Seventh-day Church Services, although he admits becoming familiar with their literature. He also denies being a member of that denomination (e.q. p. 338).

[8]*Bulletin* for the Ministerial Association of Seventh-day Adventists Ministers. George Burnside, Ministerial Association Secretary. Austral Asian Division, part III of the series on Herbert W. Armstrong.

erable debt to Seventh-day Adventism as he does to Jehovah's Witnesses (with whom he agrees in his denial of the doctrine of the Trinity and the bodily resurrection of Christ) and the Mormon Church, whose teaching that man may become as God was appropriated by Armstrong without even the slightest acknowledgment to Joseph Smith and Brigham Young.

Mr. Meredith seems overly eager to pass by these facts, but facts they are. His blanket dismissal "there was never any association in any way with Jehovah's Witnesses, Seventh-day Adventism and Mormons" is a clear misrepresentation of historical fact.

2. ANGLO-ISRAELISM

Anglo-Israelism is, properly speaking, neither a sect nor a cult since it transcends denominational and sectarian lines and because it does not set up an ecclesiastical organization. It has existed for more than a century in the United States, having come to this hemisphere from England. Apparently it originated there shortly after the close of the Elizabethan era, its "first apostle," being Richard Brothers (1757-1824).

The most vocal proponents of the Anglo-Israelic system of Biblical interpretation in North America are James Lovell of Fort Worth, Texas, and Howard Rand of Destiny Publishers.

The former has spoken on as many as sixty radio stations in the United States and Canada, edits the Kingdom Digest, a monthly magazine that distributes more than 50,000 tracts, pamphlets and magazines a year.

The latter heads up "Destiny Publishers," and was one of the organizers of The Anglo-Saxon Federation, founded in 1930. Rand's headquarters

is in Haverhill, Massachusetts, where he maintains a publishing house and circulates a magazine of more than 23,000 copies each month.

The teachings of these men and their followers are comparatively innocuous and free from serious doctrinal error. The chief harm results from the appeal to nationalism with its accompanying vanity and the two-fold way of salvation which some advocates have implied (see below).

a. Herbert Armstrong and Anglo-Israelism.

In addition to the two groups headed by James Lovell and Howard Rand, there are several other groups which also teach some of the doctrines of Anglo-Israelism. The largest of all these groups is headed by Herbert W. Armstrong, founder of the Radio Church of God and the World Tomorrow radio program. This is a half-hour coast-to-coast broadcast heard over 101 domestic stations and 48 foreign stations via short wave.

Armstrong is also the founder of Ambassador College in Pasadena, and is by far the most well known and widely heard and read of all Anglo-Israelite cultists. Mr. Armstrong is editor of *The Plain Truth,* a monthly magazine with a circulation of 1,292,000, and is a growing influence in the burgeoning field of non-Christian cults.

The Radio Church of God is outside the historic Christian Church because it denies foundational Christian truth. All other forms of Anglo-Israelism (or at least the vast majority of them) maintain a guarded orthodoxy at least in the areas of the Nature of God, personal redemption, and the Person and Work of Jesus Christ.[9] THIS IS NOT THE SITUATION WITH ARMSTRONG'S GROUP; it

[9]A few of them have taught, by implication at least, a form of salvation by physical birth into the nation Israel (i.e., Great Britain or the United States, for example) along with the usual Christian teachings of individual personal salvation. Some also have suggest-

ed some rather naive ideas, e.g., that the Jerusalem of the Bible is really Edinburgh, Scotland. (See, for example, Beaumont, Comyns: Britain — *The Key to World History.* London: Rider & Co., 1948 ?. 291 pp.)

plainly advocates HERETICAL teachings, as we shall see.

To sum up the theories of the Anglo-Israel cult in a concise manner is not difficult, and to refute them from the Scriptures as noted scholars and Biblical expositors have done many times, is essentially an elementary task. But with the advent of Herbert Armstrong's version of the old error, and his utilization of it as a cloak for his own confusion on Biblical theology, the problem is no longer elementary, in fact, it is quite complex and deserves the careful consideration of responsible Christian ministers and laymen. For it is certain that they will be affected, sooner or later, by the plausible propaganda which flows from the Armstrong presses and out over the air waves.

We shall deal with Anglo-Israelism then, only as a prelude to dealing with the theology of Herbert Armstrong, with which it has now become identified in the minds of most people — in England, Canada and the United States.

The basic premise of the Anglo-Israelite theory is that ten tribes were lost (Israelites) when the Jews were captured by the Assyrians under King Sargon and that these so-called "lost" tribes[10] are, in reality, the Saxae, or Scythians, who surged westward through Northern Europe and eventually became the ancestors of the Saxons, who later invaded England. The theory maintains that the Anglo-Saxons are the "lost" ten tribes of Israel, and are substituted, in Anglo-Israel interpretation and exegesis, for the Israel of the Bible.[11]

In the heyday of the British Empire, when their colonies spanned the globe under Victoria, Anglo-Israelites were in

their glory, maintaining that, since the British were the lost tribes and therefore, inheritors of the covenants and blessings of God, it was obvious that God was honoring His promises and exalting His children in the latter days.

In light of recent history, however, and the loss by Britain of virtually all her colonial possessions, Anglo-Israelites are content to transfer the blessings of the Covenant to the United States, maintaining as they do that Ephraim is Great Britain and Manasseh, the United States. The fact that Ephraim is called "the exalted one" in Scripture and that Manasseh is designated as the inferior of the two, creates both historical and exegetical problems for the Anglo-Israelites. This is particularly true because the United States, the inferior (Manasseh), has now far surpassed the allegedly superior Ephraim, a minor problem that will not for long forestall the cogitations and prophetic conjectures of the Anglo-Israelites school of Biblical interpretation.

Relative to the relationship of Israel to Judah in Scripture, Anglo-Israelism maintains that Judah represents the Jews who are still under the divine curse, and are not to be identified with Israel at all. In this line of reasoning, all the promises recorded in the Scripture are applied, not to the Church, which is Christ's body, but to a nation (Israel), which, as we have seen, is, in their system of thought, to be identified with Great Britain and the United States!

Herbert Armstrong, in dealing with this subject, enunciates the basic idea of Anglo-Israelism that Israel is to be distinguished from the Jews[12] (Judah) in these words:

[10]Allen, J. H.: *Judah's Sceptre and Joseph's Birthright.* 6th ed., Boston: A. A. Beauchamp, Pub., 1918, pp. 124-145.

[11]Roberts, L.G.A., Rev. Commander, *Commentary on the Book of the Prophet Isaiah.* London: The Covenant Publishing Co., Ltd., 1931, p. 159.

[12]"There is not a particle of evidence to show that the Jews of to-day are other than the house of Judah, or that they represent the Twelve Tribes. The evidence is clear that Israel did not rejoin the Jews." Thomas, J. Llewellyn: *God and My Birthright.* London: The Covenant Publishing Co., Ltd., n.d. 2nd ed. rev., p. 21. The Covenant Publishing Company is in no way associated

We want to impress here that Israel and Judah are not two names for the same nation.[13] They were and still are, and shall be until the Second Coming of Christ, two separate nations. The House of Judah always means Jew. This distinction is vital if we are to understand prophecy. Because most so-called Bible students are ignorant of this basic distinction; they are unable rightly to understand prophecy!

The next place where the term "Jew" is mentioned in the Bible, the House of Israel had been driven out in captivity, lost from view, and the term only applies to those of the House of Judah. There are no exceptions in the Bible.[14]

It is further maintained by Anglo-Israelites that in their migration of the Mediterranean area across Europe to the British Isles, the "lost" tribes left behind them landmarks, bearing names of the tribes. Thus, the Danube River and Danzig are clear indications to them of the Tribe of Dan.[15] The term Saxon is obviously derived from the Hebrew and means Isaac-son, or "the son of Isaac!"[16]

Another Anglo-Israel exercise in semantics is their insistence that the Hebrew term for covenant berith, and for man, ish, is to be interpreted as meaning "the man of the covenant,"[17] a fact that would be amusing, if it were not for the unpleasant truth that the Hebrew and Anglo-Saxon tongues have as much in common as do Chinese and Pig-Latin!

Herbert Armstrong, however, who can read neither Hebrew, Aramaic or Greek, states with dogmatic authority:

The House of Israel is the covenant people. The Hebrew word for covenant is beriyth, or berith. . . . The Hebrew word for man is iysh, or ish. In the original Hebrew language, vowels were never given in the spellings, so omitting the vowel e from berith, but retaining the i in its Anglicized form to preserve the y sound, and you have the Anglicized Hebrew word for covenant, brith. The Hebrews, however, never pronounced their h's. The Jew, even today, in pronouncing the name Shem will call it Sem. Incidentally, this ancient Hebrew trait is also a modern British trait, so the Hebrew word for covenant would be pronounced, in its Anglicized form as Brit.

And the word for covenant man or covenant people would therefore be Brit-ish. So the true covenant people today are called the British. And they reside in the British Isles. . . .

To Abraham God said, "In Isaac shall thy seed be called," and this name is repeated in Romans 9:7, Hebrews 11:18. In Amos 7:16 they are called the "house of Isaac."

They are descended from Isaac, and therefore are Isaac's sons. Drop the "i" from Isaac, vowels are not used in Hebrew spelling, and we have the modern name, Saac's sons, or, as we have spelled it in shorter manner, Saxons.[18]

It is sufficient to point out at this stage that the Hebrew words berith and ish, lierally mean "covenant and man," not, "men of the covenant," as Armstrong and Anglo-Israelites maintain. When this is added to the fact that both the *Oxford Dictionary of the English Language, Webster's Dictionary* and every major work on the subject of English derivatives reveal a total absence for support for the Anglo-Israelite contention that there is a connection between

---

with Herbert W. Armstrong or his teaching, does not subscribe to his beliefs, does not believe he has the correct interpretation of prophecy, and does not think he has rightly drawn conclusions concerning modern Israel in the Latter Days.

[13]Thomas (*ibid.,* p. 5) states: "All Jews and Levites were Israelites, but all Israelites were not Jews or Levites."

[14]*Where Are the Ten Lost Tribes?* Herbert W. Armstrong, page 8.

[15]Rutherford, Adam: *Israel-Britain or Anglo-Saxon Israel.* London: publ. by author, 1936. 3rd. ed. p. 36.

[16]The Roadbuilder: *God's Commonwealths: British and American.* Toronto: Common-Wealth Pubs. Ltd., 1930, pp. 161 F.; Rutherford, *op. cit.,* p. 9.

[17]Cf. Rutherford, *op. cit.,* p. 30.

[18]The United States and British Commonwealth in Prophecy, pages 17, 18.

the Anglo-Saxon tongue and the Hebrew language, the paucity of their claims becomes all too apparent.

Moreover, it should be noted that the Anglo-Israelite theory and the Radio Church of God both maintain that the throne of England is the throne of David. In the June 1953 issue of *The Plain Truth* appears the statement:

Herman L. Hoeh now reveals the astonishing fact that Elizabeth II actually sits on the throne of King David of ISRAEL—that she is a direct descendent, continuing David's dynasty[19] — the VERY THRONE on which Christ shall sit after His return . . . Elizabeth II was crowned "Queen of thy people Israel."[20] Turning to the article by Hoeh,[21] it clearly states that the throne upon which she was crowned (i.e., the "Stone of Scone," lodged in Westminster Abbey) is really the stone which Jacob used for a pillow, which he took with him when he departed from Bethel, and which later came under the care of Jeremiah the Prophet, who took it with him to England, where it became the Coronation Stone for the British (Davidic) dynasty.

The disturbing scientific fact that the Stone of Scone has been examined and analyzed, and found to be . . . "calcareous, a sandstone of a reddish or purplish color, with heterogeneous pebbles and of Scottish origin"[22] does not deaden the enthusiasm of Anglo-Israelites,[23] who must make Jacob a native of Scotland, and Bethel,[24] a suburb of London, if they are to maintain the fiction that the Stone of Scone is of Asiatic origin.[25]

The Anglo-Israelites school of interpretation claims more than 3,000,000 adherents, in England, Canada, the British Commonwealth and throughout the world, including the United States. They are found in many already-established denominations in Christian churches, and so do not constitute a separate denomination, preferring as does the Unity School, to work through all groups, instilling its propaganda and its fierce emphasis upon racial pride as a type of nationalistic leaven grounded in what is known to be a totally discredited method of scholarship and linguistic analysis.

Were it not for the fact that Herbert Armstrong has capitalized so successfully upon it as a means of inculcating his own peculiar interpretation of the Bible for almost a half-million readers and millions of listeners, we might well ignore Anglo-Israelism. But Armstrong has, in a very real sense, resuscitated what was a gradually dying theological body, and its death throes have now given way to militant life, with which the church of Jesus Christ must come to grips.

[19]Dr. Henry Hedyt of the American Board of Mission to the Jews has a letter from the Office of the Lord Chamberlain which states that no known reason exists why any assertion should be made that Her Majesty Queen Elizabeth was crowned Queen of Israel. It goes on to say that she is demonstrably not the Queen of Israel and cites a portion of the Coronation Service in which the Queen took the oath. He also has a letter from Brigadier Wieler, the Resident Governor of the Tower of London, which states clearly that in the Tower of London and in the Public Records Office no ancestral chart is known which substantiates the claim, "Yes, on the throne of England reigns a daughter of David, . . . a dynasty that has ruled Ireland, Scotland and England for over 2500 years!" Hoeh, "The Coronation Stone," *Plain Truth*, June 1953, p. 640.

[20]Richard D. Armstrong (one of Herbert Armstrong's sons), "Why was Elizabeth II crowned Queen of Israel?", *Plain Truth*, June, 1953, p. 8; cf. Allen, op. cit., pp. 309 ff.

[21]Herman L. Hoeh, "The Coronation Stone," *Plain Truth*, June 1953, p. 640. cf. Rutherford, *op. cit.*, pp. 74 ff.

[22]*The Ten Tribes of Israel Never Lost*, W. H. Smith, page 91. Enthusiasts like Beaumont (op. cit., pp. 128 ff), have no difficulty since they identify Bethel with Glastonburg and Jerusalem with Edinburgh, Scotland (*ibid.*, pp. 259 ff.).

[23]Vid. Beaumont (*op. cit.*, p. 64) who identifies Jacob's Mispah with Avebury Circle.

[24]See footnote 2 above.

[25]Beaumont, *et. al.*, maintain the fiction that the British Isles contain the Biblical Holy Land cites.

b. *The Biblical Answer to Anglo-Israelism*

There are two principal areas in which the Anglo-Israel theory must either stand or fall. They are, first, the question whether any tribes *were* lost, and therefore later reappeared as the British and American nations; second, there is the question of whether or not it is possible, in either the Old or New Testaments, to teach that

> Israel and Judah are not two names for the same nation. They were, and still are, and shall be until the second coming of Christ, two separate nations. The House of Judah always means Jew . . . the term applies only to those of the House of Judah. There are no exceptions in the Bible![26]

Rather than become bogged down in an attempt to interpret Anglo-Israel chronology and methodology in the Old Testament, we have elected to let one of the greatest Hebrew scholars of the Christian Church, Dr. David Baron,[27] an Englishman, answer the first question. It should be remembered that Dr. Baron's answer is substantiated in every detail by scholars of the Old Testament, whether or not they are Christian.

> The Anglo-Israelite theory . . . I cannot help regarding as one of the saddest symptoms of the mental and spiritual shallowness of the present day. . . . I believe that you . . . like many other simple-minded Christians are perplexed and imposed upon by the plausibilities of the supposed identifications (of British Israelism), and are not able to detect the fallacies and perversions of Scripture and history upon which the whole theory is based.
>
> Let us glance at the question of the so-called "lost" ten tribes in the light of Scripture history and prophecy. Anglo-Israelism first of all loses the ten tribes, claiming for them a different

destiny from the Jews, whom it supposes to be descendants of the two tribes only and then it identifies this "lost" Israel with the British race. But there is as little historical reason for the supposition that the ten tribes are lost, in the sense in which Anglo-Israelism uses the term, as there is Scriptural basis for a separate destiny for "Israel" apart from "Judah."

The most superficial reader of the Old Testament knows the origin and cause of the unfortunate schism which took place in the history of the elect nation after the death of Solomon. But this evil was to last only for . . . a limited time; for the very commencement of this it was announced by God that He would in this way afflict the seed of David, but *not for ever* (I Kings 11:39).

The final overthrow of the northern kingdom took place, as we have seen, in the year 721 B.C., but when we read that the "king of Assyria took Samaria and carried Israel away into Assyria," we are not to understand that he cleared the whole land of all the people, but that he took the strength of the nation with him.

Jerusalem was finally taken in 588 B.C., by Nebuchadnezzar — just 133 years after the capture of Samaria by the Assyrians. Meanwhile the Babylonian Empire succeeded the Assyrian; but although dynasties had changed, and Babylon, which had sometimes, even under the Assyrian *régime*, been one of the capitals of the Empire, now took the place of Nineveh; the region over which Nebuchadnezzar now bore rule was the very same over which Shalmaneser and Sargon reigned before him, only somewhat extended.

With the captivity (Assyrian and Babylonian) the divisions and rivalry between "Judah" and "Israel" were ended, and the members of all the tribes who looked forward to a national future were conscious not only of one common destiny, but that that destiny was bound up with the promises to the house of David, and with Zion or Jerusalem as its center, in accordance with

---

[26]*Where Are the Ten Lost Tribes?* Herbert W. Armstrong, page 8.

[27]An important but often neglected work is: Godbey, Allen H.: *The Lost Tribes: A Myth — Suggestions Towards Rewriting Hebrew History.* (Durham, N.C.: Duke University Press, 1930). xxii, 802 pp. This work is

written from a liberal scholarly viewpoint; the chief merit lies in its vast amount of historical material (including reports from missionaries), anthropological reports, and archaeological data — coupled with its rather extensive, annotated bibliography. It, like the work of Baron, needs to be brought up to date with recently discovered data.

the prophecies of Joel, Amos, and Hosea, and of the other inspired messengers who ministered and testified more especially among them until the fall of Samaria. This conviction of a common and united future, no doubt, facilitated the merging process, which cannot be said to have begun with the captivity, for it commenced almost immediately after the rebellion under Jeroboam, but which was certainly strengthened by it.

Glimpses into the feeling of the members of the two kingdoms for one another, and their hopes and aspirations for unity, we get in the writings of Jeremiah, Ezekiel, and Daniel, who prophesied during the period of exile. The most striking prophecy in relation to this subject is Ezekiel 37:15-17: "The word of the Lord came again unto me, saying, Moreover, thou son of man, take thee one stick, and write upon it, For Judah, and for the children of Israel his companions (that is, those of Israel who before the captivity fell away from the ten tribes and joined the southern kingdom): then take another stick, and write upon it, For Joseph, the stick of Ephraim, and for all the house of Israel his companions: and join them one to another into one stick; and they shall become one in thine hand."

Then follows the Divine interpretation of this symbol: Behold, I will take the stick of Joseph, which is in the hand of Ephraim, and the tribes of Israel his fellows, and will put them with him (or literally, I will add them upon, or to him), even with the stick of Judah, and make them one stick, and they shall be one in mine hand. And the sticks whereon thou writest shall be in thine hand before their eyes. And say unto them, Thus saith the Lord God; Behold, I will take the children of Israel from among the heathen, whither they be gone, and will gather them on every side, and bring them into their own land; and I will make them one nation in the land upon the mountains of Israel; and one king shall be king to them all: and they shall be no more two nations, neither shall they be divided into two kingdoms any more at all: neither shall they defile themselves any more with their idols, nor with their detestable things, nor with any of their transgressions: but I will save them out of all their dwelling-places, wherein they have sinned, and will cleanse them; so shall they be my people, and I will

be their God. And David my servant shall be king over them; and they all shall have one shepherd; they shall also walk in my judgments, and observe my statutes, and do them. And they shall dwell in the land that I have given unto Jacob my servant, wherein your fathers dwelt; and they shall dwell therein, even they, and their children, and their children's children for ever: and my servant David shall be their prince for ever (Ezekiel 37:19-25).

In 458 B.C. Ezra, "the scribe of the law of the God of heaven," in accordance with the decree of Artaxerxes Longimanus, organized another large caravan of those whose hearts were made willing to return to the land of their fathers. Part of this most favorable royal proclamation, was as follows: "I make a decree that all they of the people of Israel, and of his priests and Levites in my realm, which are minded of their own free will to go up to Jerusalem, go with thee"; and in response to it "this Ezra went up from Babylon . . . and there went up (with him) of the children of Israel, and of the priests, and the Levites, and the singers and the porters, and the Nethinims, unto Jerusalem in the seventh year of Artaxerxes the king" (Ezra 7:13, 6, 7).

This party consisted of about one thousand eight hundred families, and apart from the priests, Levites, and Nethinims, was made up of "the children of Israel," irrespective of tribal distinctions, from all parts of the realm of "Babylon," or Assyria, now under the sway of the Medo-Persians.

The narratives contained in the books of Ezra and Nehemiah, under whose administration the position of the restored remnant became consolidated, covers a period of about 115 years, and brings us down to about 420 B.C.

Anyhow it is a fact that the remnant in the land grew and grew until, about a century and a half later, in the time of the Maccabees, and again about a century and a half later still, in the time of our Lord, we find "the Jews" in Palestine a comparatively large nation, numbering millions, while from the time of the downfall of the Persian Empire, we hear but very little more of the Israelite exiles in ancient Assyria or Babylon. By the conquest of Alexander, who to this day is a great favorite among the scattered nation, the regions of ancient Babylonia and Media were brought comparatively near and a highway opened between East and West. From about this time settlements of "Jews" began to multiply in Asia Minor, Cyprus, Crete, on the coasts of the Aegean, in Macedonia and other parts of Southern Europe, in Egypt and the whole northern coast of Africa, whilst some made their way further and further eastward as far as India and China. There is not the least possibility of doubt that many of the settlements of the Diaspora in the time of our Lord, north, south, and west, as well as east of Palestine, were made up of those who had never returned to the land of their fathers since the time of the Assyrian and Babylonian exiles, and who were not only descendants of Judah, as Anglo-Israelism ignorantly presupposes, but of all the *twelve tribes scattered abroad* (James 1:1).

As a matter of fact, long before the destruction of the second Temple by Titus, we read of currents and countercurrents in the dispersion of the "Jewish" people.

To summarize the state of things in connection with the Hebrew race at the time of Christ, it was briefly this:

I. For some six centuries before, ever since the partial restoration in the days of Cyrus and his successors, the descendants of Abraham were no longer known as divided into tribes, *but as one people,* although up to the time of the destruction of the second Temple tribal and family genealogies were for the most part preserved, especially among those who were settled in the land.

II. Part of the nation was in Palestine, but by far the larger number were scattered far and wide, and formed innumerable communities in many different lands, north and south, east and west. But wherever dispersed and to whatever tribe they may have belonged, they all looked to Palestine and Jerusalem as their national center. "They felt they were of the same stock, stood on the same ground, cherished the same memories, grew up under the same institutions, and anticipated the same future. They had one common center of worship in Jerusalem, which they upheld by their offerings; and they made pilgrimages thither annually in great numbers at high festivals."

The name of "Jew" and "Israelite" became synonymous terms from about the time of the Captivity. It is one of the absurd fallacies of Anglo-Israelism

to presuppose that the term "Jew" stands for a bodily descendant of "Judah." It stands for all those from among the sons of Jacob who acknowledged themselves, or were considered, subjects of the theocratic kingdom of Judah, which they expected to be established by the promised "Son of David" — the Lion of the tribe of Judah — whose reign is to extend not only over *"all the tribes of the land,"* but also "from sea to sea, and from the river unto the ends of the earth."

"That the name 'Jews,' " writes a Continental Bible scholar, "became general for all Israelites who were anxious to preserve their theocratic nationality, was the more natural, since the political independence of the ten tribes was destroyed." Yes, and without any hope of a restoration to a separate national existence! What hopes and promises they had were, as we have seen, linked with the Kingdom of Judah and the House of David.

Anglo-Israelism teaches that members of the ten tribes are never called "Jews," and that "Jews" are not "Israelites," but both assertions are false. Who were they that came back to the land after the "Babylonian" exile? Anglo-Israelites say they were only the exiles from the southern kingdom of Judah, and call them "Jews."

It is clear from the prophecies of Amos and Hosea, which were primarily addressed to the ten tribes, that if they were in the first instance "cast out" by force from their own land, as the word in the Hebrew means, it was with a view that they should be "tossed about" and "wander" among "all nations."

Now note, Anglo-Israelism tells you to identify the ten tribes with one nation, but if you are on the line of Scripture and true history, you will seek for them "among all nations." He that scattered Israel will gather him, and by His own Divine power and omniscience separate them again into their tribes and families.

My last words on this subject must be those of warning and entreaty. Do not think, as so many do, that Anglo-Israelism, even if not true, is only a harmless speculation. I consider it nothing short of one of the latter-day delusions by which the Evil One seeks to divert the attention of men from things spiritual and eternal.

Summing up his judgments on the Anglo-Israel question relative to their methods of interpretation, Dr. Baron stated:

> One of its foundation fallacies is that it anticipates the millennium and interprets promises which will only be fulfilled in that blessed period. After Israel as a nation is converted, the British nation at the present time. By this process, it makes all prophetic Scripture meaningless. It fosters national pride, and nationalizes God's blessings in this dispensation which is individual and elective in its character. It diverts man's attention from the one thing needful, and from the only means by which he can find acceptance with God . . . after all, in this dispensation, it is a question only as to whether men are in Christ, or not. If they are Christians, whether Jew or Gentile, their destiny is not linked either with Palestine or with England, but with that inheritance which is incorruptible and undefiled, and which fades not away; and if they are not Christians, then instead of occupying their thoughts with vain speculations as to a supposed identity of the British race with the lost ten tribes, it is their duty to seek the One and only Saviour, whom we must learn to know, not after the flesh, but after the Spirit, without whom a man, either an Israelite or not, is undone.
>
> And finally, it not only robs the Jewish nation, the true Israel, of many promises in relation to their future by applying them to the British race in the present time, but it diverts attention from them as the people in whom is bound up the purpose of God in relation to the nations, and whose receiving again to the heart of God after the long centuries of unbelief, will be as life from the dead to the whole world.[28]

Dr. Baron's brilliant and thorough refutation cannot be improved upon. And excerpts from this personal letter which he addressed to a Christian, perplexed by Anglo-Israelite perversions of history and Biblical interpretation remain a classic, and has never been refuted by Anglo-Israelites.

The second barrier is that of the identification of Israel and Judah as separate nations, as seen by Mr. Armstrong's previously quoted statement. This matter can be summarily dismissed by careful consideration of the following facts.

First, after the Babylonian captivity, from which the Jews returned, Ezra records that the remnant were called by the name Jews (eight times), and by the name Israel, forty times. Nehemiah records eleven times that they were Jews, and proceeds to describe them as Israel, twenty-two times. The Book of Esther records their partial restoration, calling them Jews forty-five times, but never Israel. Are we to conclude that only Judah (the Jews), and not Israel, were restored under Zerubbabel and Joshua? History, archaeology and a study of Hebrew, refute this possibility completely.

The sixth chapter of Ezra describes the sin offering, mentioning specifically that ". . . twelve he goats, according to the number of the tribes of Israel" were offered for all Israel (v. 17), a fact attested to by Ezra 8:35.

While it is true that in the post-exilic period, we no longer have two kingdoms, but one nation, the prophet Zechariah describes them in comprehensive terms as "Judah, Israel and Jerusalem" (Zechariah 1:19), literally, the House of Judah, and the House of Joseph" (Zechariah 10:6). Zechariah 8:13 identifies Judah and the House of Israel as one nation, and Malachi called the Jews Israel, or Jacob, in contrast to Esau.

The coup de grace to Anglo-Israelism's fragmented exegesis is given by the prophet Amos of Judah, a man specifically set apart by God to prophesy to the ten-tribed kingdom of the North. Dr. Baron points out that he "abode in Bethel, which was a center of the idolatrous worship set up by Jereboam . . . there his duty was to announce the coming judgment of God on the Israel of the

---

[28] *A Letter to An Inquirer,* pages 36-38.

ten tribes on account of their apostasy" (David Baron, *ibid.*, p. 34).

In the last chapter of his book, Amos in approximately 728 B.C. declares:

> Behold, the eyes of the Lord GOD are upon the sinful kingdom, and I will destroy it from off the face of the earth; saving that I will not utterly destroy the house of Jacob, saith the LORD. For, lo, I will command, and I will sift the house of Israel among all nations, like as corn is sifted in a sieve, yet shall not the least grain fall upon the earth. All the sinners of my people shall die by the sword, which say, The evil shall not overtake nor prevent us (9:8-10).

We learn from this prophecy that as a kingdom, the ten tribes were to suffer destruction and their restoration would never be realized. How then is it possible for them to be "lost" for almost three millenniums, and then reappear as the British Kingdom, when the kingdom was never to be restored?

The Prophet Jeremiah informs us that Israel and Judah are both declared to be "an outcast," (chapter 30), which, in combination with Isaiah 11, proves that they are considered to be one nation in both the eyes of the prophets and in the eyes of God.

Anglo-Israelism would do well to consider these facts, as would Mr. Armstrong in particular, who speaks perpetually with breath-taking dogmatism on subjects about which he apparently knows very little historically, theologically or linguistically. He therefore pours forth interpretations which can only be construed to have progressed out of the abundance of his ignorance.

Second and finally, the New Testament speaks on the subject of the equation of Israel and Judah as one nation, described alternately and interchangeably as "the Jews," and "Israel."

Peter at Pentecost, proclaims the message of redemption to "all the house of Israel." Paul in Acts 26:6 and 7 apparently took Zechariah's statement:

> And it shall come to pass, that as ye were a curse among the heathen, O house of Judah, and house of Israel, so will I save you, that ye shall be a bless-

ing . . . (Zechariah 8:13).

In this context, Israel shall indeed be scattered among the nations, and so will Judah, and they shall be redeemed again together, to bring forth a blessing in the Person of the Messiah, whose Gospel is to the Jew first, (not just to the house of Israel but as a separate nation), and also to the Gentiles (Romans 1:16b).

A cursory reading of the tenth chapter of Matthew indicates that Jesus Christ Himself considered "the lost sheep of the house of Israel," to include "the Jews," since the missionary journeys of the twelve were limited to the environs of Palestine.

It should be recalled also that Pauline theology especially in the Book of Romans (chapters 9-11), deals specifically with Israel, not as a lost nation, in the sense of geography, but in the sense of spiritual transgression. He refers to them as God's people who have not been cast away.

If Israel and Judah are separate nations, why then does the Apostle describe the Jews as "his brethren," and as "kinsmen according to the flesh," and then identify them as "Israelites, heirs to the promises of God" as they are provided in the Messiah?

The New Testament uses the word "Jew" one hundred and seventy-four times and the term "Israel" seventy-five times. It is quite obvious then, to an impartial scholar of the language and context of the passages, that they are interchangeable.

The Apostle Paul made this clear by declaring "I am a man which am a Jew . . . for I am also an Israelite . . . are they Israelites? So am I?" (Acts 21:39; 22:3; Romans 11:1; II Corinthians 11:22; Philippians 3:5).

Jesus Christ sprang from Judah "a Jew," in Anglo-Israelite reckoning, and the Apostle Paul declares in Romans that it was in Israel that "Christ came, who is God over all, blessed for ever" (9:5 Greek).

Let it not be forgotten that Anna the Prophetess was "of the tribe of Aser"

(Israel), but she is called "a Jewess" of Jerusalem, facts which forever decimate the concept of Armstrong and the British Israelites that England is the throne of David and is Ephraim, while America is Manasseh.

The words of Jeremiah the Prophet conclude our observations, where he states:

> In those days, and at that time, saith the LORD, the children of Israel shall come, they and the children of Judah together (50:4).

This is proof positive that both the house of Israel and the house of Judah would return from the captivity, and that, as the New Testament amply demonstrates, it would be considered as one nation, no longer a kingdom in the historic meaning of that term.

Anglo-Israelism stands refuted by the facts of Scripture and history, and it would be unworthy of attention, if it were not being utilized as a tool by the Armstrong cult, which opens a Pandora's box of multiple and destructive heresies, some of which we shall consider.

c. Other Eclectic Sources and Traits of Herbert Armstrong

Like so many other non-Christian cultists, Herbert Armstrong claims for himself a divine mandate and nowhere is this more clearly exemplified than in his own writing:

> Yet, is there anything so shocking and so hard to believe as this statement that the whole world is religiously deceived?
>
> Thirty-seven years ago I simply couldn't believe it until I found it proved! And even then, my head was swimming. I found myself all mixed up. To see with my own eyes in the Bible precisely the opposite of what I had been taught from boyhood in Sunday school, well this was pretty hard to take, yet there it was in plain type before my eyes!
>
> If this were the year A.D. 30 and you took a trip to Jerusalem and there

speaking to a throng around him you should see an ordinary looking young man about the age of 33 teaching the same things you hear me and Garner Ted Armstrong say over the radio today, it would have been just as astonishing to you then as it is today — and it was to those who heard Him then. . . . You would have been truly astonished! His doctrine was so different! And He spoke dogmatically with assurance, with power and authority. . . . Yet He had foretold a prophecy. He had foretold wolves coming in sheep's clothing to deceive the world. He had said they would enter in professing to come in His name claiming to be Christian, yet deceiving the whole world. That happened!

> For two 19-year time cycles the original apostles did proclaim this Gospel, the Gospel of the Kingdom of God, but in A.D. 69 they fled. In A.D. 70 came the military siege against Jerusalem. The ministers of Satan had wormed their way in, had gained such power that by persecution of political influence they were able to brand the true people of God as heretics and prevent further organized proclaiming of the same Gospel Christ brought from God. For eighteen and one-half centuries that Gospel was not preached. The world was deceived into accepting a false gospel. Today Christ has raised up His work and once again allotted two 19-year time cycles for proclaiming His same Gospel, preparatory to His Second Coming. . . . The World Tomorrow and The Plain Truth are Christ's instruments which He is powerfully using. Yes, His message is shocking today. Once again it is the voice in the wilderness of religious confusion![29]

Mr. Armstrong's son, Garner Ted, heir apparent to the 19-cycle throne, carries the same theme through:

> No man ever spoke like this man reported their offices of the Pharisees regarding Jesus. The multitudes were astonished at His doctrine.
>
> It is the same today, the same living Christ through The World Tomorrow Broadcast, The Plain Truth Magazine, and this work proclaims in mighty power around the world the same Gospel preached by Peter, Paul and all the original apostles.[30]

---

[29]The Inside Story of the World Tomorrow Broadcast, pages 7-11.

[30]Ibid., page 2.

As did Joseph Smith, "Pastor" Russell, and Mary Baker Eddy, before him, so does Mr. Armstrong pose his efforts as the only work which is accurately representing Christianity today. But a tree is known by its fruit, and fruits are not only manifested in a life which is lived, but also in doctrines which are believed and taught. And so it is to the doctrines and teachings of The Radio Church of God that we shall now turn for a closer look at what Mr. Armstrong calls The Plain Truth.

THE THEOLOGY OF THE RADIO CHURCH OF GOD

I. THE DIVINE ORIGIN OF THE RADIO CHURCH OF GOD

I'm going to give you the frank and straightforward answer. You have a right to know all about this great work of God, and about me. First, let me say — this may sound incredible, but it's true — *Jesus Christ foretold this very work — it is, itself, the fulfillment of his prophecy* (Matthew 24:14 and Mark 13:10).

Astounding as it may seem, there is no other work on earth proclaiming to the whole world *this very same gospel* that Jesus taught and proclaimed!

He went on to insist:

And *listen again!* Read this twice! Realize this, incredible though it may seem — *no other work on earth is proclaiming this true Gospel of Christ to the whole world.* As Jesus foretold in Matthew 24:14 and Mark 13:10! This is the most important activity on earth today![31]

The prophecies bring this Church into concrete focus in the 12th chapter of Revelation. There she is shown spiritually, in the glory and splendor of the Spirit of God, but visibly in the world as a persecuted, commandment-keeping Church driven into the wilderness, for 1,260 years, through the middle ages!

In New Testament prophecy *two churches* are described.

One, the great and powerful and universal church, a part of the world, actually ruling in its politics over many nations, and united with "Holy Roman Empire," brought to a concrete focus in Revelation 17.

. . . She is a *mother* Church! Her daughters are also churches who have come out of her, even in protest, calling themselves Protestant — but they are fundamentally of her family in pagan doctrines and practices! They, too, make themselves a part of this world, taking active part in its politics — the very act which made a "whore" out of their Mother!

The entire apostate family—Mother, and more than 500 daughter denominations, all divided against each other and in *confusion* of doctrines, yet all united in the chief pagan doctrines and festivals — has a family *name!* They call themselves "Christian," but God calls them something else—"Mystery, Babylon the Great!"

But the true Church of God is pictured in prophecy as the "Little Flock!" It has kept God's festivals . . .

That Church always has existed, and it exists today![32]

II. THE TRINITY OF GOD AND THE DIVINITY OF MAN

The *purpose of life is that in us* God is really re-creating his *own kind — reproducing himself* after his own kind — for we are, upon real conversion, actually *begotten* as sons (yet unborn) of *God;* then, through study of God's revelation in His Word, living by His very Word, constant prayer, daily experience with trials and testings , we grow spiritually more and more like God, until, at the time of the resurrection we shall be instantaneously *changed* from mortal into *immortal* — we shall then be *born of God* — We *shall then be God!*

Do you really grasp it? The *purpose* of your being alive is that finally you be *born* into the Kingdom of God, when you will actually *be God,* even as Jesus was and is God, and His Father, a different Person, also is God!

You are setting out on a training to become *creator* — to become *God!* [33]

. . . When we are *born of God, we shall be* of His *very family* — we shall be *spirit* as He is Spirit — immortal as He is immortal — divine as He is Divine!

Christ was born a *Son* of God by a resurrection from the dead (Romans 1:4).

. . . the *only human* so far *born of* God, though many have already been *begotten.*

---

[31] Personal letter to Robert Sumner, November 27, 1958.

[32] *Easter is Pagan,* pages 8, 9.

[33] *Why Were You Born?* pages 21, 22.

. . . Yes, just the first of many *brethren*, in the very image of bright shining *glory* of the *invisible God*. And we are to be conformed to the *same image* (Romans 8:29).

. . . Yes, and as a *born son of God*, Christ is God! God Almighty His Father is God. They are two separate and individual Persons (see Revelation 5:1, 6, 7).

. . . I suppose most people think of God as one single individual Person. Or, as a *"trinity." This is not true.*

Now, remember, the true Christian is an *heir* of God (Galatians 3:29) and a joint-heir with Christ (Romans 8:17). We are to be *glorified together with him* (same verse). Christ is now an inheritor — a possessor. We are still only *heirs* — not yet inheritors — not until we are *born again!*

Yes, the name "God" as God revealed it in the Hebrew language, is a name like *family, church, or team.*

. . . only, *we see not yet* this entire universe put under the dominion of mankind!

. . . But the theologians and "Higher Critics" have blindly accepted the heretical and false doctrine introduced by *pagan* false prophets who crept in, that the Holy Spirit is a third person — the heresy of the *"trinity."* This *limits* God to "Three Persons." This *denies* that Christ, through His Holy Spirit, actually comes now into the converted Christian and does His saving work on the *inside* — "Christ in you the Hope of Glory" (Colossians 1:27).[34]

Christ is our Maker and a member of the Godhead — the God Family. Therefore, His life which He gave for us is of greater value than the total of all human beings.[35]

God came in the flesh as Jesus Christ, lived without sin, and thus was able to die and pay the full penalty of sin in our stead.

So Jesus took human nature upon Himself and was made subject to death in order to be our Saviour. "He also likewise (as the children are partakers of flesh and blood) took part of the same" — took on *human nature* — became flesh and blood — that through death he might destroy him that had the power of death, that is, the devil" (Hebrews 2:14).

Jesus was really *dead* during the three days and nights His body was in the grave. He who had been one of the personalities of God — was changed into flesh so *He could die* for our sins.

Christ, one of the beings in the Godhead, had now been changed into flesh — still having the *personality* and *will* to do right which distinguished Him as an entity . . ."[36]

That is, He who had existed from eternity — He by whom God created the worlds and all things therein — He who was and is *life* — He who was *God* — He was made flesh — converted *into* flesh, until He became flesh — and then He was flesh!

Yes, Jesus was a fleshly *Man*. He was God come in human flesh. And, when converted into human flesh the *life* that kept Him alive resided in the blood, as in all who are flesh (Leviticus 17:11).

But He was not *God* inside of, yet separate from the body of flesh — He, God, was *made flesh*, until He, still *God* — God with us — became God *in* (not inside of) the human flesh — God manifest in the *flesh* (I Timothy 3:16).

What happened is that the Logos — the *Word* — the Eternal — was *made flesh*. He was converted into—*changed into* flesh. Now He was *flesh and blood*, exactly as you and I.

His life was in His blood, and He gave His *life* by the fact His blood poured out while He was on the cross! He had taken on *human* nature. He was God — but now God changed *into* flesh and blood — God *with us* — Emmanuel!

Yes, the Word was *made flesh*, and He *was flesh* and blood, not just an immortal Spirit in a body of flesh and blood.[37]

III. THE NATURE OF CHRIST

Jesus, *alone*, of all humans, has so far been *saved!* By the resurrective power of *God!* When Jesus comes, at the time of the resurrection of those *in Christ*, He then brings His reward with Him![38]

— *He was the first human ever to*

[34]*Just What Do You Mean — Born Again?* pages 17, 19.

[35]*The Plain Truth* Magazine, November, 1963, page 10.

[36]*Ibid.*, page 11.

[37]*Op. cit.*, April, 1963, page 10.

[38]*Why Were You Born?* page 11.

achieve it — to be perfected, finished as a *perfect character*.[39]

Christ, one of the beings in the Godhead, had now been *changed* into flesh — still having the *personality* and *will* to do right which distinguished Him as an entity — yet now had become human, having *human nature* with all of its *desires, weaknesses and lusts* — and subject to *death* just like any other human.

This is a truth about which *millions are deceived.*

The Satan-inspired doctrine that Jesus was *not* human, that He did *not* inherit the human nature of Adam, that He did *not* have all the normal human nature of Adam, that He did *not* have all the normal human passions and weaknesses against which all of us have to struggle — in a word, that Jesus did *not* really come "in the flesh" as a normal human being — *This is the doctrine of the anti-Christ.* Notice Romans 8:3: "God sending His own Son in the likeness of sinful flesh."

The idea Satan is trying to put across is that it is *impossible* for man to keep the spiritual law of God, and so Jesus came as our Saviour—not "in the flesh" with normal human nature — but through "special process" so that He could keep the law of God *in our stead* to *die* for us! But His *obedience* was our example!

. . . that Jesus taught, *"If thou wilt enter into life, keep the commandments"* (Matthew 19:17).

. . . We are not only to keep the letter of the law, but to follow it as it is magnified throughout the Bible in "every word of God" (II Corinthians 3:6).

Satan the Devil, through His *false ministers* who appear as "ministers of righteousness" (II Corinthians 11:13-15), is trying to deceive the world into believing in a *false Christ* — a Christ who *did away* with the Father's spiritual *law* and made it possible for us to inherit eternal life without having to build, with the help of God's Spirit, the kind of holy, righteous *character* which would enable us to obey God's eternal, spiritual *law* both now and forever.[40]

How plain! How abundantly clear! Not having *human nature* with its *passions and lusts*, God *cannot* be tempted with evil. And on the contrary, *every* man is tempted by his own *lust* — because every man does have *human nature.*

So it is not only *possible* — but *obligatory* — that we obey God's spiritual law, the Ten Commandments, as they are, magnified throughout the Bible. Keeping them in the spirit does *not* mean "spiritualizing" them away, but really obeying them as Jesus set us the example, through the power of God's Holy Spirit, which He gives to them that obey Him (Acts 5:32).

The *only difference* between Jesus and any other human is that He was conceived of the Holy Spirit. Therefore He obeyed God's laws *from birth* — and never had to go through the process of *repenting* of going the wrong way, of *unlearning* wrong ideas and habits, and of gradually learning to exercise His will to do right continually.

. . . And, praying for the strength He needed through the Holy Spirit, *He always* did *right.*

Yes, Jesus had *sinful* flesh — human nature. But by exercising the *will* to always obey God, and by receiving the extra help He needed to *master* His fleshly desires, Jesus *repudiated* the sway of sin in the human flesh and showed that the law of God *could be kept.*

. . . They were not worshiping Jesus as just another *Man.*

. . . Christ came *in the flesh* to set us a *perfect example,* then *to die* in payment for our sins and make it possible for us to be reconciled to a holy, righteous God and receive of His Spirit — His very *life and character* implanted within us.[41]

That is, He who had existed from eternity — He by whom God created the worlds and all things therein — He who was and is *Life* — He who was God—He *was made flesh*—converted *into flesh,* until He *became flesh* and then He *was* flesh!

Yes, Jesus was a fleshly *man.* He was God, come in human flesh. And, when converted into human flesh the *life* that kept Him alive resided *in the blood,* as in all who are *flesh* (Leviticus 17:11).

. . . But He was not God inside of, yet separate from the body of flesh — He, God, was *made flesh,* until He, still

[39]*Ibid.,* page 14.

[40]*The Plain Truth,* vol. 28, No. 11, November, 1963.

[41]*The Plain Truth* Magazine, November, 1963, pages 11, 12.

God — God, with us — God *in* (*not* inside of) the human flesh — God manifest *in the flesh* (I Timothy 3:16).

If there was no other Person in the Godhead, then the Giver of all Life was dead and all hope was at an end!

If there was no *Father* in heaven while Jesus Christ lay dead — His blood in which resided His *life* shed from *His* veins, given for you and for me — then all life everywhere had come to an end.

. . . That's where His life resided — in His *blood*, not in spirit! He did not shed *a spirit* to save us from our sins— He shed His *blood, and* in so doing *gave His life.*

But, "as the Father hath life *in Himself;* so hath He given to the Son to have life in Himself" (John 5:26). God the Father raised Jesus from the dead. Cf. John 2.

NOT RESURRECTED IN SAME BODY

Now notice carefully, God the Father did not cause Jesus Christ to get back into the body which had died.

Some seem to believe that it was only the *body* which died—that Jesus Christ never died.

. . . What they believe is that a *body* Christ lived in died, but Christ *Himself* never died, Christ was God, and they argue, God could not die!

If they are right, they are lost and doomed to eternal punishment! If Christ did not die for their sins — if it was only a mortal *body which* died — then we have no Saviour, and we are *lost.*

What happened is that the Logos — the *Word* — the Eternal — was *made flesh.* He was converted into—changed into flesh. Now He was flesh and blood, exactly as you and I.

His *life* was in His blood, and He gave His *life* by the fact His blood poured out while He was on the cross! He taken on a *human* nature. He was God — but now God changed *into* flesh and blood — God with us — Emmanuel!

Yes, the Word was *made flesh*, and He was flesh and blood, not just an immortal Spirit *in* a body of flesh and blood.

It was *Christ Himself* who was *dead.* He was *revived.* Nowhere does the Scripture say He was alive and active,

or that God had Him get back into the human *body,* that had died and was now resurrected.

Jesus Christ was *dead.* He was as much "out" as a boxer knocked senseless — much *more,* for the boxer usually is not dead but only unconscious. Jesus was *dead* — but was *revived!*

And the resurrected body was no longer human — it was the Christ resurrected, *immortal,* once again *changed!* As He had been changed, converted *into* mortal human flesh and blood, subject to death, and for the *purpose* of *dying for our sins, now,* by a *resurrection from the dead, He was again changed, converted, into immortality* — and He is alive forevermore! Now a *living* Saviour, not a *dead* Saviour, He *was* dead — but only for three days and three nights.[42]

IV. THE PERSONALITY OF THE HOLY SPIRIT

God's Holy Spirit is His *life.* *It* imparts His *life* to you! *It* imparts more as we shall see!

One thing more, the Holy Spirit is *divine, spiritual love* — the love of God flowing into you from God Almighty — through the living Christ! (Romans 5:5) [43]

But the theologians and "Higher Critics" have blindly accepted the heretical and false doctrine introduced by *pagan* false prophets who crept in, *that the Holy Spirit is a Third Person* — the *heresy of the "trinity."* This limits God to "Three Persons." This *denies* that Christ, through His Holy Spirit actually comes now *into* the converted Christian and does His saving work on the *inside* — "Christ in you, the hope of glory" (Colossians 1:27).

Jesus Christ is *come* in the flesh, as inspired in its original Greek language means, literally, *present tense* — that *Christ is now coming. . . .*

. . . If the Holy Spirit were a third *person* that would be impossible!

. . . That heresy *denies* the *true born-again* experience![44]

V. SALVATION BY GRACE AND LAW

Salvation, then, is a *process!*

But how the god of this world would blind your eyes to that! He tries to deceive you into thinking all there is to it is just "accepting Christ" with *"no*

---

[42]*The Plain Truth,* April, 1963, page 10.

[43]*What Do You Mean . . . Salvation?* page 19.

[44]*Just What Do You Mean Born Again?*

works" — and presto-chango, you are pronounced "Saved."

But the *Bible* reveals that *none* is yet "saved.'[45]

. . . Human mortals, in Christ, living and dead, receive *eternal life* — immortality — the *promises* God made to Abraham at Christ's Second Coming. That is *when* they shall *put on* immortality![46]

People have been taught, falsely, that "Christ *completed* the plan of salvation on the Cross" — when actually it was only *begun* there. The popular denominations have taught, "Just believe — that's all there is to it; believe on the Lord Jesus Christ, and you are that instant *saved!"*

That teaching is false! And because of deception — because the *true Gospel* of Jesus Christ has been blotted out, lo these 1900 years by the preaching of a false gospel *about the person* of Christ — and often a false Christ at that — millions today *worship Christ* — and all in vain!

The *blood* of Christ does not finally save any man. The death of Christ merely paid the penalty of sin in our stead — it wipes the slate clean of past sins—it saves us merely from the *death penalty* — it removes that which separated us from God and reconciles us to God.

But we are *saved* — that is, given immortal life — by Christ's *life,* not by His death (Romans 5:10).

It is *only those* who, during this Christian, Spirit–begotten life, have grown in knowledge and grace, have overcome, have developed spiritually, done the works of Christ, and endured unto the end, who shall finally be given *immortality* — finally changed from mortal to *immortal* at the time of the Second Coming of Christ (I Corinthians 15:53, 54).

So, being, as we say, converted — receiving the Holy Spirit of God — is *merely the beginning!* Then begins a lifelong of *living* under the *government of God* — by God's laws which express His will, instead of by self-will and desire.

A Person is not even begotten of God unless he is Christ's (I John 5:12) *and He is not Christ's unless He has received the Holy Spirit* (Romans 8:9).

One is not even converted — spiritually begotten — not even started on the way to final salvation, unless and until he *receives the Holy Spirit from God!*

No, water baptism is a required *condition* to receiving the Holy Spirit.

But there is no promise that anyone will receive the Holy Spirit until baptized in water.[47]

. . . God *only* has eternal life. *Life* can come only from life — not from death. Christ's *death* paid the penalty of your guilty *past* — it reconciled you to God — gave you access direct to God. But it *did not* give you eternal *life* — did not, yet, *save you!* Now what?

Some religious teachers tell you Christ lived a righteous life *for* you 1930 years ago, and since you *"can't keep the Law,"* as they claim, God *"imputes"* Christ's righteousness of 19 centuries ago to you — by sort of "kidding himself" that you are righteous, while you are given license to still be a spiritual *criminal* breaking His law. God does not impute to you something you do not have.[48]

. . . A Christ who did away with the Father's spiritual law and made it possible for us to inherit eternal life without having to build, with the help of God's Spirit, the kind of holy, righteous character which would enable us to *obey* God's eternal, spiritual *law* both now and forever.

. . . So it is not only *possible* but *obligatory* — that we obey God's spiritual law, the *ten commandments,* as they are magnified throughout the Bible. Keeping them in the spirit does *not mean* "spiritualizing" them away.

. . . But by exercising the *will* to always obey God, and by receiving the extra help He needed to Master His fleshly desires, Jesus *repudiated* the sway of sin of the human flesh and showed that the law of God *could be kept.*[49]

God's *purpose* in salvation is to rescue men from *sin, and* its resulting unhappiness, misery, and death! To *repent* of sin is the first step. Then the blood of Christ, upon acceptance and faith, cleanses of all past sins. And by *faith* we are kept from sin in the future. Thus the resulting righteousness is of *faith* — the righteousness imparted from God.

We are not justified *by the law* — we

[45]*Why Were You Born?* page 11.

[46]*Lazarus and the Rich Man,* page 6.

[47]*All About Water Baptism,* pages 1, 2, 3, 8.

[48]*What Do You Mean . . . Salvation?* pages 18, 21.

[49]*The Plain Truth Magazine,* November, 1963, pages 11, 12.

are justified by the Blood of Jesus Christ! But this justification will be given only on condition that we *repent* of our transgressions of God's Law — and so it is, after all, only the *doers of the law shall be justified* (Romans 2:13).[50]

VI. THE NEW BIRTH AND THE RESURRECTION

. . . If we overcome, grow in grace and knowledge and endure unto the end, *then* . . .

. . . this flesh and blood body shall *become a spirit* body! Then, and not until then, shall we be *fully born of God.*

We are saved by *grace,* and through *faith* — make no mistake about that; *but* — there are conditions!

It is *only* those who, during this Christian, Spirit–begotten life, have grown in knowledge and grace, have overcome, have developed spiritually, done the works of Christ, and endured unto the end, who shall finally be given *immortality* — finally changed from mortal to *immortal* at the time of the Second Coming of Christ (I Corinthians 15:53-54).[51]

Nearly every error is based on a false assumption, taken carelessly for granted. The universal error, in this case, is the untrue *assumption* that when one is converted — when one has fully repented, accepted Christ in faith, and received God's Spirit — or, as some state it, "been baptized by the Holy Spirit" — that he has then been "born again."

This misapplication of *one word* of religious terminology has deceived a confused world into viewing the matter of being "born again" as some ethereal, mystic "experience" one is supposed to "feel" or, somehow, though he sensed nothing, to have gone through when he professed Christ!

What most religious people — if they use the term — call being "born again" is simply *misnamed.* Actually, the term "born again" does not apply at all, nor refer to, the experience of a true *conversion* — the receiving of God's Holy Spirit — or as some phrase it, the "baptism of the Holy Spirit." Most, however, who use this latter term are as deceived as to what is, as they are about being "born again."

The real *source of this whole stupendous error* is this. In the English language, we have *two different* words to express the *two phases* that occur in the reproductive process of all mammals.

The one, which is the very Start of the new life, we call *conception,* or a *begettal.*

But *no one ever calls this beginning of the process a* birth!

The phase of the process which in the English language we call being *born* is that process by which the foetus is *delivered* from the mother's womb, and out into the world comes a little baby to gasp its own first breath. It has then *been born!*

But if you would try to tell a doctor, or a nurse, that the yet unborn foetus has already been *born,* as soon as you knew it had been *conceived,* or *begotten,* the doctor or nurse would surely think you ignorant, and probably try to explain.

The New Testament of the Holy Bible was originally written in the *Greek* language. And, in this case, the Greeks had *only one word* for the *two* vitally *different* phases of the process!

That Greek word is "gennao" (pronounced ghen-ah-o). The Greek-English dictionary (lexicon) gives this definition of the Greek word; *to procreate* (properly of the father, but by extension of the mother): beget, be born, bring forth, conceive, be delivered of, gender.

Four of those definitions mean to beget or to conceive — but *not* to be *born.* To *procreate means to beget.* To *conceive* has the same meaning. Webster's dictionary defines "gender" as to beget, breed, generate. It does *not refer* to the birth. But three of the Lexicon definitions of "gennao" mean the actual *birth*: "be born," "bring forth" and "be delivered of."

. . . and since the "scholars" of our comparatively recent years who translated the Bible into English did not, themselves, *understand* God's Plan — they often translate the Greek word "gennao" into the English word *"born"* where it actually meant "begotten."

". . . for in Christ Jesus I have *begotten* you through the gospel." There it is correctly translated, showing that Paul's converts at Corinth, as his "spiritual children," had been *begotten* of God, *but not yet born.*

[50]*What Kind of Faith is Required for Salvation?* page 10.

[51]*All About Water Baptism,* pages 1, 3.

The experience of conversion, in this life, is a *begettal*—a "conception—an impregnation" — but *not yet a birth*. This we shall make *plain*.

One more — Hebrews 1:5 — speaking of *Christ's* begettal in the Virgin Mary. This verse shows that Christ, later *born* of God by a resurrection from the dead (Romans 1:4), was an actual *Begotten Son of* God, in a manner that no angel is, or can be. Angels are merely *created* beings. They are not actually *begotten* of God, so that in this sense they become His *born* sons, as Christ now is — and as we may also be. Notice the verse: "For unto which of the angels said He at any time, 'Thou art my Son, this day have I *begotten* thee'?"

If those who are deceived would listen to *Jesus, and* be willing to believe He *meant what He said, they could understand!*

Let's look at all Jesus said! Let's understand *what* it means to be *born of God* — in what respect *one shall be different* after he is *born of God* — let's see *when* this spiritual *birth takes place!*

But the Holy Spirit is the *Spirit that* emanates *from* both the Father, and from Christ, and literally enters *into us, begetting us, so that we may be born as the very sons of God!*

All who *now* are *begotten* sons of God shall then be *born* — elevated from mortal to *immortal*, from decaying *flesh* to *spirit*, from *human to divine!* And that *true born-again experience* will be as incomparably more *glorious* than the fake, vague, meaningless, so-called "born-again experience" that deceived *thousands think* they have had, now, as the present transcending *glory of Christ* is superior to the status of sickly, diseased, sinning, suffering *humanity today!*[52]

. . . After people are actually *born of God*, they, too, shall *be spirit, just* as God is Spirit. They will be invisible to material human sight, just as angels are.

He is now *begotten* of God. The very *life* and *nature* of God has *entered into* him, impregnating him with immortal spirit — life, exactly as the physical sperm cell from the human father enters into the ovum or physical egg-cell when a new *human life* is first *conceived, impregnated, or begotten.* But, just as that tiny ovum, as small as a pin-point, is merely *begotten* of its human father — *not yet born* — so the converted human is, at what we properly call, conversion, merely *begotten* of God the heavenly Father — *not yet born.*

He is *still* material *flesh*, even though God's Spirit has now *entered into* his *mind*. He is *still visible.*

A newly converted human is actually *begotten of* God. Such a person is, already, an actual begotten *son of God*. He can call God "Father." *But He is Not Yet Born of God.*[53]

The New Birth and the Resurrection

All true Christians who shall have died before Christ's coming shall rise first — in a resurrection — and then all Christians *still alive*, in mortal flesh, shall be instantaneously—in the twinkling of an eye — *changed from mortal to immortal* — from material flesh to immaterial spirit — from *human* to *divine*, at last *born of God!*

But, He was then *born of God, how?* By a resurrection from the dead (Romans 1:4). When? *At the time* of His resurrection!

And *that is* the way *you* and I shall look, if and when we are finally *born of God!* These deceived people who talk about having had a "born again experience" certainly don't look like *that!*

That tremendous, glorious event of being *born of God is* to take place *at the resurrection of the just* — at the time of Christ's Second Coming to earth!

We are now *flesh* — vile, corruptible flesh subject to rotting and decay. But at Christ's coming, when we shall be *born of God*, this vile body shall be *changed*, and made exactly like Jesus in His *glorified body.*[54]

VII. The Guilt of God and the Nature of Man

God has *made* man's natural mind so that it wants to do things that are contrary to His laws; "The carnal mind (with which we are all born) is enmity against God" (Romans 8:7). Compare this with Romans 3:9-18. "The flesh (man's natural heart and mind) *lusteth* against the Spirit and the Spirit against the flesh: and these are *contrary* the one to the other" (Galatians 5:17). *All*, as

[52]*Just What Do You Mean Born Again?* pages 6, 18, 19, 20.

[53]*Ibid.*, page 11.

[54]*Ibid.*, pages 13-15.

originally born, have a desire-lust — to go contrary to God's Laws! (James 1: 4 and Psalm 81:11, 12).

It is by man's own carnal mind that God blinds him . . .

God, in love and wisdom, blinds human beings who by nature reject the truth so they will unwittingly *sin all the more often* and thereby *learn their lesson all the more deeply.*[55]

The Soul Is Mortal

The *Bible,* which is God's *message* and *instruction to mankind,* nowhere teaches any such thing as the *pagan* doctrine of an "immortal soul" going to heaven at death. It teaches that the soul is *mortal,* and shall *die* (Ezekiel 18:4, 20).[56]

VIII. The Sabbath, Unclean Foods and Legalism I Timothy 4:4

Passover, the days of unleavened bread, Pentecost, and the holy days God had ordained *forever* were all observed by Jesus . . .

The New Testament reveals that Jesus, the apostles, and the New Testament Church, both Jewish and Gentile-born, observed God's Sabbath, and God's festivals — weekly and annually.[57]

The Theology of Biblical Christianity

In the tradition of Jehovah's Witnesses whom he follows concerning the doctrine of eternal retribution and the Resurrection of Jesus Christ, Herbert Armstrong's theology has no room for the deity or personality of the Holy Spirit. (See Sections 2 and 4 of the preceding theological statement).

For Armstrong, God's Holy Spirit is an impersonal "it," and though he makes a pathetic effort to rescue the divinity of the Spirit, he only succeeds in reducing Him to "the love of God" on abstract principle at best.

In our analysis of the theology of Jehovah's Witnesses we observed how the depersonalization of the Holy Spirit strikes at the very heart of the Christian Gospel, for it is through the agency of the third person of the Trinity that God

regenerates men to eternal life (John 3:5). By denying the personality of the Spirit, i.e., that the Spirit is a personal ego and one of the persons of the Holy Trinity, Armstrong invalidates the only means whereby a man can be saved. All too few listeners to his program are aware of this particular serious deviation from historic Christianity. It is always wise in listening to Armstrong and his alter ego, Garner Ted, to keep in mind that the more vigorously they enunciate what small fragments of truth that somehow manage to escape the multiple strands of error woven into the very fabric of The Radio Church of God, the more carefully one ought to listen for the inevitable overtones of Armstrong's interpretations which nullify the small percentage of truth he does retain.

It is unnecessary to repeat what we have stated before, but even a careful consideration of the thirteenth chapter of Acts reveals that the Holy Spirit uses the personal pronoun "I" denoting ego or personality. He also commands the Church to set apart Paul and Barnabas, then He sends them forth (verses 2 through 4).

The twenty-first chapter of the Book of Acts pictures the Spirit instructing the prophet, Agabus, to speak:

"Thus says the Holy Spirit, So shall the Jews at Jerusalem bind the man that owns this belt, and shall deliver him into the hands of the Gentiles" (verse 11).

Thus Luke reveals that the third person of the Trinity has the capacity to think, command and prophesy. This certainly does not correspond to Mr. Armstrong's caricature of the Spirit as an "it." For even an elementary knowledge of psychology reveals that an "it" is devoid of personality and cannot speak, command or prophesy!

Further analysis of the fifth chapter of Acts underscores the fact vividly

---

[55]*Is This the Only Day of Salvation?* C. P. Meredith, page 2.

[56]*Just What Do You Mean Born Again?* pages 13, 14.

[57]*Easter Is Pagan,* pages 4, 12.

that the Holy Spirit is deity and is so designated by the Apostle Peter (verses 3 and 4). That the Holy Spirit is considered a member of the heavenly Trinity is evident by His presence at the incarnation (Luke 1:35), the baptism of Christ (Matthew 3:16), the Resurrection of Christ (Romans 8:11 and I Peter 3:18), and in the Great Commission (Matthew 28:19).

One cannot read Mr. Armstrong's writings without becoming increasingly aware of the fact that he is radically anti-Trinitarian. A perusal of the quotation from his writings found in the earlier part of this chapter indicates forcefully that he wants no part of Christian theology in this and far too many other areas for the spiritual good of himself or his listeners.

In the theology of Herbert Armstrong:

> Genesis 1:1 gives God's name as in the Hebrew Elohim. This is a uniplural name. It means more than one person, but combined into the one family, which family is God. . . . For the word "God" comes to us from the Hebrew word "Elohim" which means "living, eternal, creating, all-powerful, governing kingdom." Elohim means one God, not many gods. But that one God is a kingdom. There is but one true church — one church but many members! (I Corinthians 12:20). So it is with God.
>
> Do you really grasp it? The purpose of your being alive is that finally you will be born into the kingdom of God when *you will actually be God* even as Jesus was and is God and His Father a different person also is God! . . . You are setting out on a training to become Creator, to become God![58]

The similarity to Mormonism in Armstrong's theology at this point is quite striking, for as previously observed in our chapter on the Mormons, they, too, believe and teach that men may become members of the God-family and become gods. Armstrong, on the other hand, exceeds even the Mormon fantasy boldly teaching what appears to be a pantheistic unity of God in which all the members of the "family" participate. This is certainly a view which is not shared by any of the inspired writers of the Scripture, and his recourse to the Hebrew plural (Elohim) in which he stretches it beyond all proportion and contextual meaning to the forced interpretation of a "family" or "kingdom," is indirectly a pathetic admission of the extremely limited knowledge he possesses of the language.

Armstrong's usage of Elohim is not consistent with any scholarly presentation, in fact, as he uses it, it is simply a perversion tailored to impress those who can be impressed with the ludicrous.

The followers of Armstrong's cult should consult the third chapter of Genesis where they will find that Satan first taught the "God family" doctrine to Adam and Eve. Both Armstrong and the Mormons have received and believed the same perversion which ushered in the reign of sin and death upon the human race, for if Satan lied when he said "you shall be as gods" (verse 5) so does Mr. Armstrong "wrest the Scripture to his own destruction" and sadly to the destruction, spiritually speaking, of those who follow in his training.

The plain truth of this whole matter is that we do indeed grasp what Mr. Armstrong is teaching. His Radio Church of God serves only as a camouflage for his doctrinal deviations which are mixed with orthodox terminology and evangelical cliches and infused with numerous half-truths. This concoction is enunciated with a dogmatism and arrogance akin to that of the late Judge Rutherford of Jehovah's Witnesses. And were it not for Armstrong's dynamic presentation and wide radio coverage coupled with the spiritual vacuum which

---

[58]*Just What Do You Mean Born Again?* pages 16, 17, 19, 20. See also *The Plain Truth,* November, 1963, page 10, and the pamphlet *Why Were You Born?* pages 11, 13, 14, 25, 26.

today pervades many quarters of Christendom, his entire system of interpretation would be the object of humor instead of the serious consideration it now demands.

The Armstrong cult appeals to the Hebrew and Greek languages and is conspicuously devoid of the scholastic background or knowledge of the languages which Armstrong so glibly quotes. The Hebrew plural Elohim, as we have stated, does not refer to any family or kingdom of God; it is one of the divine names utilized in Scripture and is distorted by the Mormons, Jehovah's Witnesses and Mr. Armstrong in a vain attempt to alter the nature of God which, as revealed in the Bible, controverts their respective theologies.

In our study of Jehovah's Witnesses the doctrine of the Trinity has been given full consideration, so it will not be necessary to go into further detail on this subject. But it should not be forgotten that every major non-Christian cult system either perverts subtly, or denies outright, the Christian doctrine of the Trinity and Mr. Armstrong's cult is no exception to the rule even though he mixes the theologies of Jehovah's Witnesses and Mormonism with his own peculiar interpretations. The denial is uniquely his own and should be recognized for what it is.

THE NEW BIRTH — A NEW TWIST

The doctrine of the New Birth or Spiritual Regeneration as it is taught in the New Testament apparently has an effect upon Mr. Armstrong when he either hears or reads it which is little short of hysterical. In his pamphlet, *Just What Do You Mean Born Again* he vigorously criticizes the Christian doctrine of regeneration (See VII), and in its place substitutes by all odds, one of the strangest doctrines in the area of cultism. Through it he has quite literally given the new birth a new twist!

According to the theology of The Radio Church of God the doctrine of the new birth is divided into two segments or areas. In the first or initial area which takes place upon the acceptance of Jesus Christ as the Son of God, the believer is impregnated with the life of God through the Holy Spirit which Armstrong terms "begetting." The second phase is the new birth itself which he informs us takes place not at the moment of faith but at the resurrection of the body![59]

Mr. Armstrong strenuously maintains that it is "a universal error" to believe that when a person is converted and has fully repented and accepted Christ in faith that that person is born again in the Biblical sense. For Herbert Armstrong the original Greek word "Gennao" is the pivot point of the controversy. Armstrong holds that since the word can also be translated "beget" or "conceive" the translators of the Bible erred in not rendering the word consistently as "begotten" instead of "born," and this they did because "they did not themselves understand God's plan . . . the experience of conversion in this life is a begettal, a conception, an impregnation, but not yet a birth" (*Ibid.*, pages 7 and 8).

It is worthwhile to note in studying this particular phase of Mr. Armstrong's theology that his appeal to the Greek which was meant by him to carry the convincing weight of scholastic authority in reality becomes the proverbial albatross around his neck. Mr. Armstrong's contention that "the original Greek in which the New Testament was written has only the one word for both meanings" (Footnote: *Ibid.*, page 7) is a most damaging remark for any good lexicon reveals immediately that the Greek has at least four other terms to describe the idea of conception and birth (*sullabousa, tiktei, apotelestheisa,* and *apokuei*) which are translated variously as "conceive," "bring forth," "delivered," "born," "when finished," and "begat." One need only study Luke 1: 24, 37; 2:21, 36; James 1:15, 18 and not a few others, and he will come to the immediate conclusion that Mr. Armstrong has no concept whatever of New Testament Greek. In fact, the Greek language even has a term which describes pregnancy from conception to delivery!

Mr. Armstrong's blatant statement to the effect that "the Greek had only one word for two vitally different phases of the process . . . since the original Greek in which the New Testament was written had only the one word for both meanings (*gennao*)," is either a product of his own ignorance or a deliberate falsehood. Since he seems to be aware of the existence of lexicons and concordances this writer is convinced that it is the latter.

It is only necessary to look for a moment at Mr. Armstrong's manufactured distinction between the uses of Gennao in the New Testament to see what his attempt to stretch the term beyond all limits of its usage in New Testament Greek, is only done in order to teach that no one is *now* born again of the Holy Spirit, but that instead this can only take place at the resurrection.

The followers of Mr. Armstrong must settle for an impregnation by the Spirit and a gestation period (their entire life!) before they can be born again. This new birth is dependent upon keeping the commandments of God and enduring to the end in Mr. Armstrong's theology, a fact overlooked by some of his more zealous disciples.

The fact that the new birth has nothing to do with the resurrection is demonstrated by the usage of the term by the Apostle Peter who reminds us that through faith in the Lord Jesus Christ we have been "born again (past tense) not of corruptible seed, but of incorruptible, by the Word of God which liveth and abideth forever" (I Peter 1:23).

The new birth in the New Testament is synonymous with spiritual regeneration to eternal life, and the very fact that Jesus Christ and the apostles described the possessors of the new birth as "saved" decimates Mr. Armstrong's contention that one must wait until the resurrection in order to be born again.

In his epistle to the Ephesians the Apostle Paul is adamant in his declaration that "by grace you have been saved through faith; and this is not your own doing, it is the gift of God — not because of works, lest any one should boast" (Ephesians 2:8 Greek). Here is the usage of the past tense in reference to Christians, an instance which is amply supplemented throughout the New Testament by such passages as John 5:24; 3:36; 6:47; Romans 8:1; I Peter 1:18 and I John 5:1, 11-13 and 20.

It is wholly unnecessary to pursue this thought further since Mr. Armstrong has no scholarly precedent for subdividing the new birth and attempting to attach it to the resurrection of the body, something which the Scripture nowhere does. His is a lame attempt to distort the basic meaning of *gennao* which incidentally he, himself, admits is listed in the lexicon as "to be born, to bring forth, to be delivered of." It is only one more indication of the limitations of his resources.

When Jesus Christ addressed Nicodemus (John 3) and spoke of the new birth, He connected this birth to the person of the Holy Spirit whom the disciples received in the Upper Room (John 20) and whose power and presence were manifested at Pentecost (Acts 2). This has always been accepted in Christian theology for just what the Bible says it is, an instantaneous experience of spiritual cleansing and re-creation synonymous with the exercise of saving faith in the person of Jesus Christ and through the agency of the grace of God (Acts 16:31; 2:8-10; Colossians 1:13, 14; Galatians 2:20; I Corinthians 6:11, 19; II Corinthians 5:17).

The Apostle Paul instructs us that our salvation has been accomplished not by any efforts on our part, but by "the kindness and love of God our Saviour" (Titus 3:4-7). It is not something we must wait for until the resurrection; it is our present possession in Christ totally separate from the immortality of the body which is to be bestowed at the return of Christ and the resurrection of the body (I Corinthians 15:49-54; I John 3:2; Romans 6:5).

It is all well and good if Mr. Armstrong's followers wish to make the new birth a process, as indeed they do with the doctrine of salvation, but we must be quick to point out that this is not the Christian doctrine of the new birth and as such is not consistent with the revelation of the Bible. Mr. Armstrong's new twist to the new birth is just that, and the Christian church can ill afford to sit by in silence while The Radio Church of God propagates it as Biblical theology.

THE RESURRECTION OF CHRIST

The Resurrection of Jesus Christ along with the Christian doctrine of the Trinity is assailed most vigorously by the majority of non-Christian religious cultists. Such persons steadfastly maintain that they believe in the Resurrection of Christ but then proceed to redefine the term "resurrection" until it generally comes to mean merely the conquest of death by the spiritual nature of Jesus. Herbert Armstrong is no exception in this category, teaching as he does that Jesus Christ was raised from the dead as a spirit and that the saints will be resurrected as spirits.

Wrote Mr. Armstrong:

"The saints of God now born of the spirit and become spirit at the resurrection will be able to be invisible or visible at will." [60]

The Radio Church of God does not hesitate to state that "the resurrected body was no longer human. . . ." and

that Jesus Christ Himself was spirit in His Resurrection:

Now notice carefully God the Father did not cause Jesus Christ to get back into the body which had died. Nowhere does the Scripture say He was alive and active or that God had Him get back into the human body that had died and was now resurrected . . . and the resurrected body was no longer human . . . He was again changed and converted into immortality . . . [61]

What has been said about Jehovah's Witnesses doctrine of the Resurrection of Christ can also be said about Armstrong's position.

The reader can consult the second chapter of John's gospel (verses 19-21), to ascertain from the lips of the Lord Jesus that He promised to raise His own body from the grave. The Greek word as has been observed (*soma*) refers to a physical form not to an immortal spirit!

Luke goes to great pains to point out that Christ identified the body in which He conquered death as physical in nature (flesh and bone) and further that this body had the marks of the cross in the hands and feet (verses 37-39).

The Apostle Thomas could not doubt that Christ had risen in the physical form after our Lord's appearance in the Upper Room (see John 20), for it was there that the risen Christ invited him to place his fingers into the wounds in His hand and his hand into the spear wound in His side. One thing is certain from all this, Jesus Christ conquered death *as a man not* as a spirit, and at this juncture Mr. Armstrong's theology is in complete opposition to the revelation of the Scripture. At the Second Coming of Christ (I Thessalonians 4) when the dead in Christ rise, they will rise immortal according to the Apostle Paul (I Corinthians 15) and will possess a form like Christ's own form (I John 3:2). This form will be composed of flesh and bone in the structural composition of Christ's resurrected body (Luke 24), for nowhere does the Bible say that either

[60]*The Plain Truth*, October, 1959, page 30.

[61]*The Plain Truth*, April 1963, pages 10 and 40.

Christ or the resurrected bodies of Christians are composed of spirit.

In the 26th chapter of Matthew's gospel, Jesus Christ promised His disciples that they would drink wine with Him in the kingdom of His Father (verse 29), and He reiterated this same promise in Luke's gospel, "you may eat and drink at my table in my kingdom" (Luke 22:30).

It is the hope of Christians that at His glorious appearing Jesus Christ will "change our vile body that it may be fashioned like unto His own glorious body" (Philippians 3:21). And if He is indeed the firstfruits of them that slept (I Corinthians 15:20) then we shall indeed be like Him (I John 3:2), and He is an immortal man not a spirit as Mr. Armstrong's theology so erroneously declares.

SALVATION AND ATONEMENT

As the theology of the Radio Church of God does violence to the true nature of the new birth, so also does it categorically deny the Biblical doctrine of the Atonement.

According to Mr. Armstrong:

> Salvation then is a process but how the god of this world would blind your eyes to that! He tries to deceive you into thinking all there is to it is just accepting Christ with no works, and presto changeover, you are pronounced saved! . . . But the Bible reveals that none is as yet saved . . . people have been taught falsely that Christ completed the plan of salvation on the cross when actually it was only begun there. The popular denominations have taught just believe that that's all there is to it, believe on the Lord Jesus Christ and you are that instant saved. That teaching is false . . . the blood of Christ does not finally save any man, the death of Christ merely paid the penalty of sin in our stead and wipes the slate clean of past sins . . . it is only those who during this Christian spirit-begotten life have grown in knowledge and grace, have overcome, have developed spiritually, done the works of Christ and endured to the end who shall finally be given

immortality, finally changed from mortal to immortal, at the time of the Second Coming of Christ. So being, as we say, converted, receiving the Holy Spirit of God is merely the beginning! Then begins a life long of living under the government of God by God's laws which expresses His will instead of by self-will and desire.[62]

After reading Mr. Armstrong's statements any serious student of the Bible wonders how anyone could take seriously his theological interpretations, for if there is one thing that the Bible does emphatically teach, it is the fact that salvation is *not* a process but an accomplished fact based upon the completed sacrifice of Jesus Christ (Hebrews 1:3, 9:26, 28).

Regarding Mr. Armstrong's shocking statement to the effect that the blood of Christ does not finally save anyone, it is in direct contradiction to the words of the Apostle Peter who taught that persons have not been redeemed by anything corruptible but "by the precious blood of Christ" (I Peter 1:19). It should be noted that this is in the *past tense* as an accomplished fact, a teaching amplified in the Book of Hebrews repeatedly. The writer of Hebrews tells us that "by one offering He has perfected forever them that are sanctified" and that by the will of God "we are sanctified through the offering of the body of Jesus Christ once for all" (Hebrews 10:14, 20).

The Lord Jesus has entered

> not into a sanctuary made with hands, a copy of the true one, but into heaven itself, now to appear in the presence of God on our behalf. . . . But as it is, he has appeared once for all of the end of the age to put away sin by the sacrifice of himself. And just as it is appointed for men to die once, and after that comes judgment, so Christ, having been offered once to bear the sins of many, will appear a second time, not to deal with sin but to save those who are eagerly waiting for him (Hebrews 9:24-28 RSV).

Mr. Armstrong and his Radio Church

[62]*Why Were You Born?* page 11, *Lazarus and The Rich Man*, page 6, *All About Water Baptism*, pages 1, 2, 3, and 8.

of God consistently ignore the fact that

> Christ had offered for all time a single sacrifice for sins. Therefore, brethren since we . . . have confidence to enter the sanctuary by the blood of Jesus, by the new and living way which he opened for us through the curtain, that is, through his flesh, and since we have a greater priest over the house of God, let us draw near with a true heart in full assurance of faith, with our hearts sprinkled clean from an evil conscience and our bodies washed with pure water. Let us hold fast the confession of our hope without wavering, for he who promised is faithful (Hebrews 10:12-23 RSV).

The Apostle Paul reiterates the completed nature of the atonement upon the cross when he deals with the subject in such passages as Ephesians 1:7, Colossians 1:20 and Romans 5:9. The Apostle John's reminder that God has provided for continual cleansing from sin (I John 1:7, 9) should only serve to strengthen Christians in the knowledge that Jesus Christ has indeed by the sacrifice of the cross "loosed us from our sins in His own blood" (Revelation 1:5 Greek). This is a completed act, the benefits of which are shed abroad in the hearts of all true believers by the Holy Spirit. Nowhere does the Bible teach that the atonement of Christ is *yet* to be completed! This particular doctrine is drawn from the early writings of Seventh-day Adventists with whom, as we mentioned, Mr. Armstrong was associated at one time. It is to the credit of the Adventists that their denomination has officially repudiated this position, maintaining that the atonement has already been completed.

Pauline theology makes clear the fact that in Jesus Christ God has determined to redeem men by sovereign grace, and the record still stands:

> For what saith the scripture? Abraham believed God, and it was counted unto him for righteousness. Now to him that worketh is the reward not reckoned of grace, but of debt. But to him that worketh not, but believeth on him that justifieth the ungodly, his faith is counted for righteousness. Even as David also describeth the blessedness

of the man, unto whom God imputeth righteousness without works, Saying, blessed are they whose iniquities are forgiven, and whose sins are covered. Blessed is the man to whom the Lord will not impute sin (Romans 4:3-8).

The theology of the Radio Church of God in regard to the doctrine of salvation is refuted thoroughly by the Apostle Paul in his epistle to the Galatians. Wherein when describing the purpose of the law of God, Paul points out that its primary function was to "lead us to Christ" that we might be justified by faith. The law was a pedagogue, a teacher, but it was finally and completely fulfilled in the person of Jesus Christ, who as incarnate, love as the universal all fulfilling principle which is implemented through grace, first toward God and then toward one's neighbor. (See Romans 13:8-11).

Mr. Armstrong attaches to salvation the requirement of "keeping the law and commandments of God." This can only be described as adding to the gospel of grace the condition of law-keeping, a first century heresy scathingly denounced in the Galatian epistle as "another gospel" by no less an authority on the law than St. Paul (Galatians 2:16, 21; 1:8, 9).

If all law is fulfilled in love as Christ and the apostles taught, then the insistence upon observance of the Ten Commandments (or, for that matter, the over six hundred laws of Moses) on the part of Mr. Armstrong and his followers as a condition of salvation injects into the Christian Church what the apostles so successfully expelled (Matthew 22:36-40; Acts 15:24).

It is certainly true that no informed Christian believes in the destruction or setting aside of the laws of God, but, as we shall see, when dealing with the Seventh-day Adventists' concept of this subject, there is a vast difference between the abolition of law and the fulfillment of law, which fulfillment Christ accomplished once for all on the cross (Romans 3:31, 10:4).

The theology of Herbert Armstrong includes what can only be termed a type of universalism where the redemption of man is concerned:

> As Lord of lords Christ will begin to convert and save the entire world during His reign . . . all peoples will then come to know God. Their blindness and religious confusion will be removed and they will finally be converted. The resurrected saints will teach the people God's way. [63]

The New Testament repeatedly urges men to assume the forgiveness God has provided now, not during some future millennial reign. "Now is the accepted time; behold, now is the day of salvation" (II Corinthians 6:2), is the watchword of New Testament theology. Along with "Pastor" Russell, the founder of Jehovah's Witnesses, Armstrong teaches what amounts to a second chance for unregenerate men.

Jesus Christ urged men to accept Him "for the Son of man is come to seek and to save that which was lost" (Luke 19: 9, 10) and the writer of Hebrews emphasizes "how shall we escape if we neglect so great salvation" (Hebrews 2:3).

The writer of Hebrews also exploded another of Mr. Armstrong's theological fantasies when he wrote that during the millennial kingdom "they shall not teach every man his neighbor, and every man his brother, saying, Know the Lord: for all shall know me, from the least to the greatest" (Hebrews 8:11). The followers of The Radio Church of God would do well to put Mr. Armstrong's theology to the test (I Thessalonians 5:21) for then it would be apparent that what he says is anything but "the plain truth."

Inherent within the theological structure of The Radio Church of God and stemming from Mr. Armstrong's perversion of the Biblical doctrine of salvation, is his insistence (also borrowed from the Seventh-day Adventists) that Christians abstain from specific types of food

which he claims are "unclean."

No devoted follower of The Radio Church of God will therefore eat pork, lobster, clams, shrimp or oysters or any of the prohibitions of the Mosaic system. They are in effect Orthodox Jews in this particular area of theology!

In his first epistle to Timothy the Apostle Paul recognized among the Gentiles the problem of so-called unclean foods and dealt with it in the following manner:

> Now the Spirit expressly says that in later times some will depart from the faith by giving heed to deceitful spirits and doctrines of demons, through the pretensions of liars whose consciences are seared, who forbid marriage and enjoin abstinence from foods which God created to be received with thanksgiving by those who believe and know the truth. For everything created by God is good, and nothing is to be rejected if it is received with thanksgiving; for then it is consecrated by the word of God and prayer (I Timothy 4:1-5 RSV).

Further comment on this particular subject is unnecessary in the light of the Apostle's clear statement, but a reading of the fourteenth chapter of Romans reveals instantly that Christians are not to sit in judgment upon one another relative to days of worship or foods to be consumed. We are not to judge spirituality on the basis of diet or the observance of days. But in The Radio Church of God this is not true for Mr. Armstrong does indeed sit in judgment upon all those who do not subscribe to his particular interpretation of dietary laws allegedly enforced in this era of history.

Relative to the problem of Sabbath-keeping, Mr. Armstrong also derived this from the Seventh-day Adventist denomination, but he has gone further than the Adventists have ever even intimated.

The literature of The Radio Church of God is literally filled with insistence

[63]*The Plain Truth*, October, 1959, page 30.

upon the observance of the Jewish feast days, new moons, festivals and sabbaths, all of which were dealt with fully and finally by the Apostle Paul in his Colossian epistle.

And you who were dead in trespasses and the uncircumcision of your flesh, God made alive together with him, having forgiven all our trespasses, having canceled the bond which stood against us with its legal demands; this he set aside, nailing it to the cross. He disarmed the principalities and powers and made a public example of them, triumphing over them in him. Therefore, let no one pass judgment on you in question of food and drink or with regard to a festival, a new moon or a sabbath. These are only a shadow of what is to come; but the substance belongs to Christ (2:13-17 RSV).

When the preceding quotation from Paul is placed beside his counsel in Romans 14 the picture is transparently clear:

Let not him who eats despise him who abstains, and let not him who abstains pass judgment on him who eats; for God has welcomed him. Who are you to pass judgment on the servant of another? It is before his own master that he stands or falls. And he will be upheld for the Master is able to make him stand. One man esteems one day as better than another, while another man esteems all days alike. Let everyone be fully convinced in his own mind. He who observes the day, observes it in honor of the Lord. He also who eats, eats in honor of the Lord, since he gives thanks to God; while he who abstains, abstains in honor of the Lord and gives thanks to God. . . . Why do you pass judgment on your brother? Or you, why do you despise your brother? . . . Then let us no more pass judgment on one another, but rather decide never to put a stumbling-block or hindrance in the way of a brother. I know and am persuaded in the Lord Jesus that nothing is unclean in itself; but it is unclean for anyone who thinks it unclean. . . . Do not, for the sake of food, destroy the work of God. Everything is indeed clean, but it is wrong for anyone to make others fall by what he eats; it is right not to eat meat or drink wine or do anything that makes your brother stumble (14:3-21 RSV).

There is a memorable passage in the Book of Acts where when the Council of Jerusalem was in session concerning the problem of Jewish prohibitions on diet and practice as it affected the Gentile converts, the Apostle James once for all time dealt with the issue, a fact Mr. Armstrong seems content to ignore:

Therefore my sentence is, that we trouble not them, which from among the Gentiles are turned to God; But that we write unto them, that they abstain from pollutions of idols, and from fornication, and from things strangled, and from blood . . . Forasmuch as we have heard, that certain which went out from us have troubled you with words, subverting your souls, saying, Ye must be circumcised and keep the law: to whom we gave no such commandment. . . . For it seemed good to the Holy Ghost, and to us, to lay upon you no greater burden than these necessary things; that you abstain from meats offered to idols, and from blood, and from things strangled, and from fornication: from which if ye keep yourselves, ye shall do well (Acts 15: 19, 20, 24-29).

It is evident that law keeping, dietary prohibitions, the Mosaic ordinances which were binding upon Israel, and the Jewish customs of observances of feasts, etc., were abrogated by the Holy Spirit (verse 28), and it is certainly not amiss to comment that what the Spirit of God saw fit to lift as restrictions upon the Church of Jesus Christ the so-called Radio Church of God has no right to reimpose! Mr. Armstrong, however, has done precisely this and his action stands condemned not only by the Council at Jerusalem and the Apostle James but by the clear words of the Apostle Paul and the pronouncement of the Holy Spirit Himself.

THE INDICTMENT OF GOD

We close our observations on the theology of the Armstrong cult by pointing out that he has not hesitated to indict God for the guilt of man.

God has made man's natural mind so that it wants to do things that are contrary to His laws . . . it is by man's own carnal mind that God blinds him . . . God in love and wisdom blinds human beings who by nature reject the truth so they will unwittingly sin all the more often and thereby learn their lessons all the more deeply . . .[64]

While it is certainly true that the carnal mind "is enmity against God" (Romans 8:7) and that "the natural man does not receive the things of the Spirit" and by nature rebels against the decrees of the Creator, nowhere in Scripture does it state that God "made man's natural mind so that it wants to do things that are contrary to His laws," as Mr. Armstrong's theology teaches. Rather, it is the clear testimony of Scripture that both Satan and his followers and the human race in Adam voluntarily and freely chose to rebel against the Lord, thereby, coming into possession of carnal or fleshly natures which are at enmity with God.

The fifth chapter of Romans informs us that the spiritual attributes of rebellion are in all men because of Adam and that only in Christ can these be controlled by creation of a new nature, thus restoring man to fellowship with God.

In the theology of Mr. Armstrong's cult then, God is ultimately responsible for the evil nature of man, and he has not even hesitated to state concerning the human nature and character of the Lord Jesus Christ:

> Christ now had become human having human nature with all of its desires, weaknesses and lusts . . . and subject to death just like any other human. This is a truth about which millions are deceived.[65]

When dealing with the sinless nature and character of Christ Mr. Armstrong states:

> . . . He was the first human ever to achieve it — to be perfected, finished as a perfect character.[66]

In the fifteenth chapter of I Corinthians the Apostle Paul contradicts Mr.

Armstrong in the strongest possible terms by referring to Jesus Christ as "the last Adam," (verse 45) thereby teaching incontrovertibly that Jesus Christ had a perfect human nature and character and was never under obligation to achieve it or "to be perfected, finished as a perfect character." He was perfect as the last Adam and as the eternal Word made flesh (John 1:1, 14).

It is perfectly true that the Scriptures speak of Christ as "learning obedience as a faithful son." It is also true that He was made "complete" (Hebrews 2:10; 5:9; 7:28). The Greek word translated "perfect" in the passages from Hebrews basically means "completion," a fact demonstrated by Jesus Christ Himself when in speaking of Herod, He said:

"And He said unto them, go ye and tell that fox, Behold, I cast out devils, and I do cures today and tomorrow, and the third day I shall be perfected" (Luke 13:32).

The Revised Standard Version correctly renders the word "finish," carrying with it the meaning of the completion of a plan, literally "I finish my course." Far from being imperfect and in need of suffering and death to perfect His character and human nature as Armstrong maintains, these terms only describe the completion of the divine plan of the ages whereby God brought to completion or fulfillment the foreordained consummation of His majestic design for human redemption. The attempt by Mr. Armstrong to imbue Jesus Christ with a tainted human nature and to seize upon the word "perfect" as the means to accomplish this cannot alter the plain declarations of Scripture which describe our Lord in His human nature and character in far different terms than does Mr. Armstrong. When applied to our Lord, the term "perfect" or "perfected" refers only to Christ's completion of His human life and sacrifice for

[64]*Is This the Only Day of Salvation?*, page 2.

[65]*The Plain Truth*, November, 1963, pages

11 and 12.

[66]*Why Were You Born?* page 14.

our sins. He became complete only in the sense of perfect obedience and submission to the Father's will. He was always "holy" and without sin in His human nature and character.

In the gospel of Luke which describes the annunciation to the virgin Mary by the angel Gabriel, the child to be born is designated as "the son of the Highest," by the angelic messenger who does not hesitate to emphasize "that holy thing which shall be born of thee shall be called the Son of God" (1:32, 35).

The Apostle Peter in the course of one of his great sermons in the Book of Acts quotes David in his description of the Messiah as God's "Holy One" (2: 27) and reiterates this title in the third chapter as "the Holy One and the Just" (verse 14).

The Apostle John preaching with Peter further on in the Book of Acts states in a stirring prayer to God: "For of a truth against thy holy child Jesus, whom thou hast anointed, both Herod, and Pontius Pilate, with the Gentiles, and the people of Israel, were gathered together" (4:27).

The word translated "child" can also be rendered "servant" in Greek, but regardless of which way one takes it, it is qualified by the word "holy" which any lexicon or dictionary defines as "without sin — pure." Our Lord made this claim for Himself when, in conflict with the Jews, He challenged them to dare to accuse Him of sin (John 8:46), and the writer of the epistle to the Hebrews declares Him to be "holy, harmless and undefiled, separate from sinners" (7: 26). None of these pronouncements of the Scripture are in agreement with Mr. Armstrong's contention that Jesus Christ had a sinful nature and a character that needed to be perfected due to defects which he implies existed, thereby necessitating a "perfecting" process.

The Radio Church of God does indeed honor Christ with its lips, but in the cold analytical dawn of Biblical examination and analysis there can be little doubt that its heart is far from Him.

There are many other errors in the theology of Mr. Armstrong which could easily fill a small volume, but space does not allow us to deal with it in the confines of a chapter. Let it be said, however, that the theology of Herbert Armstrong and his Radio Church of God contains just enough truth to make it attractive to the listener who is unaware of the multiple sources of heretical doctrine he has drawn upon for the balance of his theological system, enough of which permeates both his radio programs and his publications to insure the uninformed listener a gospel of confusion unparalleled in the history of American cultism. The Radio Church of God is all the more dangerous as it makes profuse use of the Bible and professes to swear allegiance to only "the plain truth of the Scripture," while, in reality, its allegiance is to the interpretations of the Scripture propagated by Herbert W. Armstrong whom one magazine has aptly described as "Mr. Confusion." Since "God is not the author of confusion," and this "plain truth" no student of the Scripture will deny, there is one sure remedy to the problem of the spread of Mr. Armstrong's radio religion. Turn off the set and open your Bible, for within its pages God is always broadcasting the eternal message of the Gospel of Grace impregnated by the Spirit of God in every essential necessary to the redemption of the soul and re-creation and living of the Christian life. When this is supplemented by attendance in a truly Christian Church where that Gospel is preached there is no need to listen to the Herbert Armstrongs of our day for as the Psalmist so beautifully described it, "the entrance of thy Word giveth light."

Chapter 16

THE CULTS ON THE
WORLD MISSION FIELDS

We have observed in our study of the various cults in the preceding chapters the fact that the cults are particularly effective amongst those in whom the early seeds of Christianity have previously been planted. It is much easier for them, therefore, to promulgate their doctrines among young Christians, nominal Christians, and those who have only a passing acquaintance with the Scriptures. Throughout the United States, the various non-Christian cults are in evidence everywhere; they boldly advertise themselves and eagerly covet the one great prize that all of them desperately seek—prestige and recognition as "Christians." This, however, is not always the case, especially on the foreign mission field, and it is with this area that we shall now briefly concern ourselves.

In the summer of 1958 it was the privilege of the author to be a part of the Pastor's Conference Team of World Vision Incorporated, headed by Dr. Bob Pierce. These conferences were specifically designed to meet the needs of pastors, missionaries, and Christian workers on the various foreign mission fields of Asia and Africa, and in the course of this tour of some 25,000 miles, I had opportunity to meet and speak to over 5,000 dedicated Christian workers and students on the problem of non-Christian cults on those mission fields. Beginning in Japan with the largest pastors' conference in Japanese church history (1560 persons), we journeyed through Formosa, Hong Kong, Singapore, Thailand, Burma, India and Ghana, Africa. At the conclusion of the African meetings I had the opportunity to travel throughout Europe, meeting and interviewing Christian workers there, so it was possible for me to get a fairly well-rounded picture of what the various cults were doing in these specific locales. I returned to Europe again in 1961 to lecture on the cults, and then interviewed missionaries whose work ranged from Scandanavia through Germany, Switzerland, Italy, Belgium, Holland and France. I traveled in most of these countries and gathered first-hand impressions which gave me the theological pulse of cultism in Europe.

A few things emerged very clearly from this unprecedented opportunity, which Dr. Pierce made possible, as well as my subsequent European trip three years later. I say unprecedented, because never before in the history of Christian missions has any researcher in the field of cults been able to visit so many mission fields in so short a time (two and one-half months), delivering lectures and gathering information on a subject about which very little is known. In the course of my travels I learned much about cult methodology on the mission fields, and in contrast to our previous statements concerning their activities in the United States, the cults generally are happy to remain virtually anonymous, until they have established a bridgehead. This is important in an area where a work has already begun or has been functioning for many years. One missionary explained to me that young converts in particular, were the prey of such cults as Jehovah's Witnesses and Mormonism, two of the most virulent strains of non-Christian cults, and a duo which are found on practically every major mission area throughout Asia and Europe. In Hawaii, for instance, the Mormons already have erected a $75,000 temple; Jehovah's Witnesses have well established works in those islands. In Japan both the Witnesses and the Mormons constitute a real problem and threat to the mission·ary efforts of many Christian workers. In addition to their evangelical endeavors the cults specialize in reaching people in their own language and it is here that the printing establishments of Jehovah's Witnesses, the Mormons and the Unity School of Christianity are revealed at their effective best. The average missionary who encounters a Jehovah's Witness in Japan, for instance, can expect to find copies of *The Watch Tower* and *Awake* Magazines dutifully mailed from Brooklyn, New York, the cult headquarters, and translated into the language of the people. There is also the very real problem of literature to combat these movements; literature which itself must, by the very nature of cult propaganda, also be in the language of the country in question and such literature today is virtually unobtainable. At the Japanese conference many hours were consumed, both in the lecture period and in private counseling sessions with missionaries and native pastors, explaining the vulnerable areas of cult theology and in turn, gleaning much valuable information on the tactics of cults abroad.

We learned that Jehovah's Witnesses were making an attempt to convince people that their own translation of the Bible (*The New World Translation*) is "the latest American translation," and should be accepted in questionable areas of theology as "the best and most recent rendering of the original languages."

The informed person, of course, knows that the Watch Tower's translation is accepted as sound *only* by the Watch Tower and those who have not carefully checked its many perverted renderings. But when one is 15,000 miles from home, laboring among people of a foreign tongue, and generally beset by the pressing problems of hostile indigenous religions (Buddhism, Islam, Shintoism, Taoism, Confucianism, Hinduism, etc.), it is difficult to check these things, and the Watch Tower eagerly supplies *their* Bible to all interested persons — converts and pagans alike — something the Christian church has found it difficult to accomplish, even in the twentieth century.

The startling growth of Jehovah's Witnesses, and the astronomical figures in publishing and distribution that the Watch Tower yearly accomplishes, can only be appreciated when one sees a mission field, literally inundated by tracts, pamphlets, Bibles, books and magazines, all stamped Brooklyn, New York, U.S.A.! The world today is hungry to read, and the underdeveloped countries of Asia and Africa will read — anything, even Watch Tower propaganda, which appears as a torrent, in comparison with the trickle of Christian literature currently in circulation.

It also became apparent in the course of questioning missionaries, that many of them are disturbed by the fact that Watch Tower people always seemingly have enough literature to proselytize Christian converts, but the missionary has little, if any, literature which will answer such cultists, much less evangelize them or their converts.

Perhaps one of the most graphic illustrations of cultic growth can be shown in the following chart of the missionary activities of Jehovah's Witnesses, spanning a twenty-five-year period.

This information has been compiled from the Watch Tower's own publications and one cannot but be astounded at their ability to produce and distribute such enormous quantities of material in such a relatively short time.

SOME MISSIONARY ACTIVITIES OF JEHOVAH'S WITNESSES
*The Growth of the Jehovah's Witnesses**

	1949	1953	1962
MEXICO			
Congregations	306	380	923
Ministers	6,733	9,759	27,054
PHILIPPINES			
Congregations	315	487	1,032
Ministers	6,601	18,053	36,829
BRAZIL			
Congregations	72	148	695
Ministers	2,187	5,774	26,390
BRITISH ISLES			
Congregations	613	729	935
Ministers	18,692	26,104	49,924
NIGERIA			
Congregations	304	442	640
Ministers	8,103	13,056	31,923
NORTHERN RHODESIA			
Congregations	248	327	575
Ministers	14,650	20,373	28,426
SOUTH AFRICA			
Congregations	276	496	469
Ministers	6,288	10,492	17,657
UNITED STATES OF AMERICA			
Congregations	2,905	3,195	4,564
Ministers	91,463	139,966	286,908

From the above chart, Christian Missions can draw little comfort, and Christian Bible Colleges, Institutes and Seminaries would do well to consider the ramifications of such rapid growth, since very little, if anything, is being done to prepare missionaries and ministers to meet these problems, either at home or on the field of world missions.

When we remember that approximately 33 per cent of the membership of Jehovah's Witnesses reside in the United States, and almost 67 per cent on the mission field, the gravity of the problem which confronts the Christian Church is apparent to all but the most adamantly obtuse.

Since the close of World War II, Jehovah's Witnesses have grown to over 70,000 in West Germany; almost 48,-000 in Great Britain; 39,000 in Canada; 60,000 in Africa; 31,000 in the Philippines; 24,000 in Mexico and 26,000 in Brazil.

The Witnesses in 1962, at their world-wide communion service known as their Memorial, numbered 1,639,681 persons, as over against 1,553,909 persons in 1961, a total increase of almost 88,000 persons!

It is no wonder that on the mission field, many missionaries are discouraged, and, in the United States, an increasing number of pastors are beginning to share that discouragement. This stems from the fact that a cult so obviously non-Christian as Jehovah's Witnesses, is becoming increasing successful in its missionary outreach, particularly in the field of literature, when

*Any perusal of the statistical Yearbook issued by the Jehovah's Witnesses indicates a steady rise & growth of their number worldwide. In the above chart we have endeavored to show their most phenomenal growth in significant areas around the world.

both clergy and missionary representing the historic Gospel of Jesus Christ finds little or no support in this vital area of literary mass evangelism.

The Watch Tower Society has not restricted itself, however, to just the publication of literature on the mission field. They have better than 30,000 full-time workers, only 1,000 of which are on the mission field. And their two-by-two doorstep evangelism has become the plague of the British Commonwealth, most of the countries of Europe, Asia and Africa. The number of hours that Jehovah's Witnesses put in such personal evangelism pursuits in 1961 was 132,695,540, of which over 90,-000,000 hours were devoted to work in foreign countries. During such calls, Witnesses left better than 8,000,000 pieces of literature, and 70,000,000 copies of their magazines, *Watch Tower* and *Awake!* The Witnesses made better than 30,000,000 back-calls and established more than 400,000 Bible studies in these same foreign lands. Figures released by the *Watch Tower* in 1962 indicate that almost 4,000,000 of the *Watch Tower* are printed annually in more than sixty languages, and that their publication, *Awake!*, is close upon the heels of the *Watch Tower* in circulation, being distributed in twenty-five languages and in a number of 3,800,000 copies per issue. When it is noted that a large percentage of this is earmarked for foreign distribution and personal delivery by *Watch Tower* representatives, full and part-time, in over 214 countries, the missionary activities of the Watch Tower come into the proper perspective.

The World-wide growth of the Watchtower Bible & Tract Society

Total output of all literature including magazines

United States of America
1935   1962
14,416,857   54,989,532

Cost of shipping literature outside of the United States
1935   1962
$110,000 $875,249.69

Language translation of Watchtower publications
1935   1962
37 languages 158 languages

Shipment of foreign literature to foreign lands
(excluding magazines)
1935   1962
2,347,161   16,345,996

Number of countries reporting work of Society
1935   1962
77 countries 158 countries

Branch offices and homes in all parts of the world
1935   1962
42   87

Number of "ordained ministers" known also as publishers

1918	1928	1938
746	6,040	25,596
1948	1949	1962
72,945	82,958	285,908

Watch Tower missionaries also have made it extremely difficult for Christian missions throughout the various trouble spots of the world, such as East Germany, Africa, Japan, Indonesia, Viet Nam and Cuba, by emphasizing their rigid anti-government stand, based upon their theological presupposition that all governments are under the direct supervision of Satan, and are opposed to the theocracy rule of Jehovah. It is unnecessary to observe that since they identify themselves as Christian, utilize the Bible and vocabulary of Christianity, those who are by nature hostile to the Christian message, and who are seeking only the opportunity to persecute it and restrict its activities, seize upon the Watch Tower organization's many statements that to them, at least, seem to incite disloyalty to governmental authority, as well as a militant pacifism and allegiance to a theocracy, in place of the individual nation.

The Watch Tower Society seems totally oblivious to the thirteenth chapter of Romans, and its demand that "every soul be subject unto the higher powers, for the powers that be are ordained of God." And for the average Jehovah's Witness, all governments, and all forms of supposed Christianity, except his own, are enemies, to be harassed, vilified and condemned as tools of Satan. This hardly makes for good public relations, and in the fervent spirit of emerging nationalism, particularly in the so-called underdeveloped countries of the world, those in authority have taken a rather dim view of the Watch Tower's activities, resulting in their persecution and unfortunately, the persecution of true disciples of the Cross, who suffer because of the Watch Tower's identification, albeit mistaken, with Biblical Christianity.

All in all, Jehovah's Witnesses are a growing concern everywhere, and a challenge to evangelical Christianity, which desires to win them to a redemptive knowledge of Jesus Christ, and in the process, to give every man an answer, "a reason for the hope that is in us — Christ in you, the hope of glory" (I Peter 3:15; Colossians 1:27).

The Growth of The Watch Tower Bible & Tract Society from 1935 to the Present

Number of persons employed full time at the Brooklyn Headquarters

1935	1962
195	571
	105 part time

Number of Bibles printed

1935	1962
21,109	1,782,602

Number of *Watch Tower* Magazines published

1950	1962
23,190,737	64,397,141

Number of *Awake* Magazines published

1950	1962
16,136,389	55,751,824

Grand total of miscellaneous printing

1935	1962
23,053,126	380,676,862

Ink used in the production of printing

1935	1962
34,997 lbs.	257,282 lbs.

Amount of paper used in printing

1935	1962
1,948 tons	8,907 tons

MORMON MISSIONARY EFFORTS

Second only to the Jehovah's Witnesses is the rapidly-burgeoning missionary effort of the Church of Jesus Christ of Latter Day Saints (Mormon).

Boasting a missionary force approaching 15,000 full-time workers, and bolstered by a church whose gross income last year was $365,000,000, the Mormon cult is moving at a rapid pace, particularly in Europe and Asia. The growth of the Mormons in Africa has been somewhat limited by the fact that they consider, as we have noted, the Negro to be an inferior race, unworthy of their priesthood, a type of religious, second-class citizen. However, in Europe and Asia, not to mention the United States, the Mormons are surging forward with great vigor.

The following chart demonstrates the growth of Mormon missions over the last few years, and should suffice to remind us that Jehovah's Witnesses are not the only cult which competes with Christianity on a large scale on most of the large mission fields.

The Growth of the Mormon Church

1900	268,331
1910	393,437
1920	526,032
1930	672,488
1940	862,664
1950	1,111,314
1960	1,693,180
1962	1,965,786

While it is obvious that the Mormon growth, from the standpoint of foreign missionaries, workers and literature distribution, is nowhere near that of the Watch Tower organization, it is significant that the Mormons do have fifteen thousand full-time foreign missionaries. This does compare favorably on the over-all with Jehovah's Witnesses, considering the fact that the Witnesses have greater facilities for mass distribution of their propaganda, which aids immeasurably in the expansion of their activities on the foreign field.

The methodology of Mormon missionaries is similar in many respects to that of Jehovah's Witnesses, in that they, too, are door-to-door canvassers, and tireless, round-the-clock "backcallers," on contacts previously made either by themselves, or by those missionaries who preceded them. Mormon missionaries, unlike those of the Jehovah's Witnesses, come fully equipped quite often, with flannelgraph illustrations and free copies of the *Book of Mormon, Doctrine and Covenants* and *Pearl of Great Price,* the sacred books which they believe "properly interpret" the Bible. Whereas the Jehovah's Witnesses will emphasize the absolute authority of the Scriptures as a supreme criterion for truth, the Mormons will hedge at this juncture, maintaining that the Bible is the Word of God insofar as it is "correctly translated," and will insist gently, but firmly, that the *Book of Mormon* and the other two sacred books "throw light upon the Bible, and explain the Bible in the light of restored Christianity and the ministry of the prophet, Joseph Smith." In England, where the Latter Day Saints have recently doubled their membership, they are particularly proud to point out that Brigham Young came from English background, and did missionary work in England himself, prior to the assassination of Joseph Smith in 1844. Young returned from England to assume the leadership of the Mormon church, and some of his wives were English girls whom Brigham Young recruited on his missionary journey. It is not unusual to find second generation Mormons returning to the same country where their parents did missionary work, to carry on the family tradition. An example of this would be the return to England in 1963 of a son of George Romney, Governor of Michigan and presidential hopeful of the Republican Party, a prospect which delights the Mormon hierachy no end. The election of Romney would do more to increase the prestige of Mormonism than anything since the building of the Salt Lake City Temple and the establishment of the internationally famous Mormon Tabernacle Choir.

Another aspect of Mormon missionary activity is their preoccupation with the anthropological background of the *Book of Mormon,* which leads them to declare that the American Indian and the Central and South American Indian races, have similar origins, and are mentioned in the *Book of Mormon.* They do not hesitate to suggest the linkage of the Inca civilization, the Aztec civilization and other such archaeologically verified Indian groups as giving credence to the teachings of the *Book of Mormon.* The fact that no reputable archaeologist has ever verified their hypothetical and unsupported propositions, (in fact, others have gone on record as repudiating them outright, [see chapter on Mormonism]), apparently does not hinder the zeal of Mormon missionaries one whit.

Such archaeological and anthropological razzle-dazzle, however, does have quite an effect on the untutored and uninformed mind outside the United States, where verifications or contradictions of the Mormon claims would be difficult, if not impossible, to obtain. Thus we see that in Mexico and South America particularly, Mormon missionaries appealing to the nationalistic pride of both Indians and Latins, are telling them that they are the heirs of great civilizations which the *Book of Mormon* reveals are connected with the origins of Christianity and its nineteenth-century "restoration," through the establishment of the Mormon Church. By utilizing the *Book of Mormon* as a prophetic volume, and "new light on the Bible," the Mormons have succeeded to an amazing degree, in Mexico and in South America, to the great dismay of many mission agencies, and a large company of missionaries. As we previously observed however, the Mormons are careful not to point out their discrimination against the black race, for it simply would not do for the "Restored Church of Jesus Christ" to be on the one hand, busily engaged in promoting the archaeological myth of the *Book of Mormon* and the races of the Americas, while virtually ignoring the black race, purely on the ground of their skin color and imagined curse! Wherever possible, it is good for missionaries to point out this glaring inconsistency, which is well-known in Africa, where the Mormons in force are conspicuously absent. Apparently, Mormon missionary zeal is confined to those races which qualify in the theology of Joseph Smith and Brigham Young, but one could hardly seriously consider, on the basis of such racial discrimination, the claims of the Mormons to being the restored church of Christ.

The Mormon missionary approach also differs from that of other cults, particularly Jehovah's Witnesses, in that it emphasizes the need for education, preferring to reach a higher strata of intellect, generally speaking, than the Jehovah's Witnesses have been able to attain. From a standpoint of educational background, social graces and personal habits which include a quiet, tolerant regard for evangelical Christianity (something lacking most pointedly in the methods of Jehovah's Witnesses), the Mormons make a good impression on the prospective converts, and many ex-members of Christian denominations are now the disciples of Joseph Smith and Brigham Young because of

this distinctive Mormon emphasis.

The foreign missionary staff of the Mormons also include young ladies, who sometimes gain access where their male counterparts would be denied an opportunity. The Jehovah's Witnesses lag behind them in this respect, as do other cult systems.

A typical Mormon missionary approach is oriented around three prime factors:

1. The Mormon Church alone has the marks of true Christianity. It is called the Church of Jesus Christ; it has apostles and prophets; it has a priesthood (Melchizedek and Aaronic) as well as elders, seventies and other New Testament practices.

The Mormons claim the unique ability to baptize for the dead (I Corinthians 15:29) and sacred extra-Biblical literature which interprets the Bible.

2. The Mormons maintain that Christianity is an open apostasy, as evidenced by the rise of Roman Catholicism during the dark ages and the various and multiple divisions in Christendom since the Reformation.

3. The outward success of the Mormon Church, its enormous prosperity and growth since 1830, in the face of persecutions and ostracism (due to their own immoral practices of polygamy one should note) proves conclusively say the Mormon missionaries, that the Church of Jesus Christ of Latter Day Saints is the restoration of true, Biblical Christianity, and should be embraced as such.

Since the average person knows very little of church history, and even less of the backgrounds of Joseph Smith, Brigham Young and the early "Mormon saints," some of these things will go unchallenged. But if even a general knowledge of the massive contradictions and historical myth-making about the origins of Mormonism is known to a prospective convert, not to mention the Mormon's polytheistic theology, which by definition is not Christian, then the "saints" have a difficult time indeed defending the maze that is their history and theology. Pretty generally, when this occurs, they will depart, never to return.

The Reverend Gordon Fraser, who has spent some thirty years working as a missionary among the Navaho Indians in Arizona and Mexico, has had numerous encounters with Mormon missionaries, and his judgment in this realm is most relevant.

The Mormons have striven for years to gain recognition as a Christian body. Until within a decade or so, their claim has been denied by even the most liberal groups of professing Christians. Lately, however, with the general lowering of Christian standards of thought and with the remarkable build-up in the public press and on the radio, the Mormons have achieved their goal in the thinking of the general public. But are the Mormons Christians? If the term covers all who use the name of Christ in their titles or in their teaching, we would have to allow the Mormons their claim, but we would have to include with them the Jehovah's Witnesses, Christian Scientists and most of the other metaphysical cults, as well as Unitarians, Universalists, Bahais and a host of socalled liberal adherents to the various Christian denominations, which were originally, completely orthodox.

All of these refer freely to Jesus Christ and use quotations from the Bible to support their views, but these, along with Mormons, deny what we consider to be the indispensable tenets of true . . . Christianity.

The Mormons are well trained in their methods, and nominal Christians are an easy prey to their arguments. We have yet to see, however, an intelligent and regenerate person who knows the Bible and its doctrines, succumb to Mormonism.

The Mormon missionaries who come to your door will be well-mannered, attractive young people. They will introduce themselves as "Christian missionaries," or will use some other innocuous term.

One team which has recently returned from Honduras announced themselves as members of the Central American Mission. Another team encountered recently merely asked:

"Could we step in and have a Christian word with you?"

They will avoid identifying themselves as Mormons or Latter Day Saints until they have gained an audience.

These young missionaries are given very careful training, both in the fine points of good sales approach and in the best methods of appealing to the members of the various churches. It is part of their training to attend services of the various churches, so as to be informed on matters of phraseology and doctrine.

We should insist that such visitors identify themselves. . . .

What Mr. Fraser says is, of course, a sound evaluation of Mormon practices, and we are forced to his conclusion when he says,

Many Christians, uninformed as to the true nature of the Mormon teachings, will defend their Mormon neighbors as good, clean-living, pious and honest folks. They will point to the wonderful relief practices of the Mormon Church. They will extoll the thrift and industry of the Mormons as a whole. All these things we recognize and appreciate as valuable contributions to society. We cannot criticize these things. These virtues do not make one a Christian. Satan is delighted when his followers put up a good appearance. We insist that these virtues have nothing to do with one's acceptance before God, if one has never yielded to God's claims concerning His Son, Jesus Christ. When Christians fail to demonstrate the above virtues, they are coming short of God's purpose, but these are the by-products of the Christian life (*Is Mormonism Christian?*, pages 7, 8 and 117).

We must look then, beyond the appearances of Mormonism and its missionaries; we must consider the fruit of its tree, not just its social benefits and moral reform, but its doctrine, which, as has been noted, is as much fruit from the tree of religion as is the practice of that religion.

In the case of the Mormons, their doctrinal fruit is corrupt, denying as they do, the Christian doctrine of the Trinity, the Deity of our Lord and salvation only by grace through justifying faith in Jesus

Christ (Ephesians 2:8-10). The Jehovah's Witnesses and the Mormons share one thing in common. Both are dedicated opponents of historic Christianity, and although they utilize the name of Christ and the methods of Christianity, where witnessing and evangelism are concerned, the content of Christianity which by necessity revolves about the Person of Jesus Christ, is either ignored or redefined by them, so that in the end, it is the gospel of "another Jesus, another spirit," and the product of that supreme architect of religious deviltry, who delights in arraying himself and his ministers as angels of light. Of him Jesus Christ said, "He is a liar and a murderer from the beginning,"—Satan, the god of this age.

There is scarcely a mission field of the world that has not felt the impact of these two major cult systems, and we would be foolish indeed, in discussing the problem of missionary activities of the cults, to ignore their methodology and their already-fantastic accomplishments in a relatively short space of time.

Much more could be written on this subject, but everything that needs to be said could hardly be included in a chapter of this length. It might be observed however, that the cults do share some traits in common when it comes to missionary methodology, and the primary ones are worth noting.

1. The cults do not generally identify themselves by their popular names (Jehovah's Witnesses, Mormons, Swedenborgians, etc.). They prefer such titles as Latter Day Saints, Bible Students, or The Church of the New Jerusalem, and generally reveal themselves in their historic connections only when the prospect is on the way to indoctrination.

2. The literature of many cult systems is unmarked, so that it is difficult to identify them because of the similarity of terminology employed in the setting forth of their teachings.

3. Most cultists utilize terminology of historic Christianity, and are masters of evangelical cliches, as Mr. Fraser has pointed out.

4. Their public meetings are seldom identified with the official name of the sponsoring group. The Seventh-day Adventists in particular, have been guilty of this, although they are not a non-Christian cult. But the fact that many are reluctant to identify themselves underscores some of their divisive methods of proselyting, which though regretted by some quarters of Adventist leadership, still continue on many mission fields around the world.

5. All major cult systems will use the Bible, quoting profusely from it, mostly out of context. In the case of Jehovah's Witnesses, they will even proffer copies of their own translation (the Mormons have an "inspired version" also) to "aid a deeper understanding of the Scriptures."

6. Missionaries of the cults will also, when pressed, deny the historic doctrines of the Trinity, Deity of Jesus Christ and salvation by grace alone, and the bodily resurrection of our Lord, (with the exception of the Mormons).

7. Cult missionaries will follow up major evangelistic campaigns, such as Billy Graham, as they did in England and elsewhere. Mormons and Jehovah's Witnesses specialize in this, and have even been found in counseling rooms after altar calls, attempting to proselytize the young converts. This was particularly true after Graham's campaign in Britain.

These are some of the marks of the methods and content of some of the major cults on the world mission fields. There can be no doubt that they are effective, and that the Church must rise to meet this challenge while there is yet time.

Chapter 17

THE JESUS OF THE CULTS

Since the earliest days of Christianity, both apostle and disciple alike have been confronted with the perversion of the revelation God has given us in the Person of Jesus Christ. This perversion has extended historically, not just to the teachings of our Lord, but more important, to the Person of Christ; for it is axiomatic that if the doctrine of Christ Himself, i.e., His Person, nature and work are perverted, so the identity of the life-giver is altered, then the life which He came to give is correspondingly negated. And it is at precisely this juncture that in this day and age, we come face to face with the phenomenon which the Apostle Paul described in II Corinthians chapter eleven as "the other Jesus."

The problem, then, is twofold, in that we must understand the nature of the "other Jesus," and then give the Biblical reasons why it is the obligation of Christians to identify him as a counterfeit, and refute his other gospel.

There can be little doubt that the Christian of today then, can expect to encounter the very same, or at least, similar errors and perversions of the Gospel message that his ancestors before him did. He should not be discouraged when they appear to have more success in twisting the truth of God, than the Christian has in presenting it.

The epistle to the Galatians reminds us that there are those who would "pervert the Gospel of Christ," and who represent "another gospel," which in reality, is not another, but a counterfeit of the original, designed by the master craftsman of all evils, our adversary, the devil.

It may seem like over-simplification and naiveté to some people to suggest that Satan is the prime mover and architect of the major cult systems, but a careful consideration of the Biblical evidence will allow no other conclusion.

In his Second Corinthian epistle, Paul penned one of the most solemn warnings recorded anywhere in the Bible, to which we have made previous reference. He addressed this warning to Christians who were in great danger of having their minds (not their soul's salvation) corrupted from the simplicity that is in Christ Jesus. He was afraid, he said, that if someone should come to Corinth preaching "another Jesus, another Spirit and another gospel," the Corinthians might well be swept along with it to the sterilization of their Christian life and witness for Christ. Paul went on to underscore this point by drawing a deadly parallel between true Christianity and pseudo-Christianity, that he likened to a carefully designed copy of the original revelation of God in Christ.

After revealing the existence of a counterfeit Jesus, Holy Spirit and gospel, Paul completed the parallel by showing that there are also counterfeit "apostles," and counterfeit "disciples," (workers), who transform themselves in appearance and demeanor to appear as ministers of Christ, but in reality, Paul states, they are representatives of Satan (II Corinthians 11:13). He further informs us that this is not to be considered fantastic, unbelievable and incredible, for Satan himself is often manifested as "an angel of light." So we are not to be surprised when his ministers emulate their master and disguise themselves as ministers of righteousness (II Corinthians 11:14, 15).

Now of course, Paul was speaking of those who could be readily identified as spiritual wolves in sheep's clothing the moment their teachings were compared with the true Gospel (Galatians 1:8, 9), not just anyone with whom we have a disagreement in the realm of theology.

Simply because Christians disagree on certain issues cannot be taken as a valid reason for asserting that such are dissenters and ministers of Satan, unless — that dissent involves the Person and work of our Lord, in which case their unbelief would automatically invoke the apostolic judgment.

THE NATURE OF THE OTHER JESUS

The Person and work of Christ is indeed the very foundation of Christian faith. And if it is redefined and interpreted out of context and therefore contrary to its Biblical content, the whole message of the Gospel is radically altered, and its value correspondingly diminished. The early apostle clearly saw this, as did John and Jude, hence their repeated emphasis upon maintaining the identity and ministry of the historical Jesus, over against the counterfeits of that Person, already beginning to arise in their own era.

The "other" Jesus of the false cults of that day (Gnosticism and Galatianism), threatened the church at Colosse, Ephesus and Crete, and invoked powerful apostolic condemnation and warning in the epistles of I John, Galatians and Colossians.

In order that we may better understand precisely how these Scriptures may be applied in our own day, we need only cite some contemporary illustrations of the "other" Jesus the Bible so graphically warns against, and the entire issue will come into clear perspective.

1. *The Jesus of Christian Science.*

In the. theological structure of the Christian Science religion as we have already seen, Gnosticism was revived, and Mrs. Eddy became its twentieth century exponent. Mrs. Eddy declared concerning *her* Jesus:

The Christian who believes in the first commandment is a monotheist. This virtually unites with the Jews belief in one God and recognizes that Jesus Christ is not God, as Jesus himself declared, but is the son of God (*Science and Health,* page 61, ed. 1914).

Mrs. Eddy spelled out her view so that no one could possibly misinterpret her when she wrote:

The spiritual Christ was infallible; Jesus as material manhood was not Christ (*Misc. Writings,* page 84).

Now a careful study of Matthew, chapter sixteen, will reveal that Jesus Christ acknowledged the confession of Peter to the effect that He *was* the Christ, the Son of the Living God. And it would be foolish to maintain that Jesus was not material manhood, in the light of the New Testament record that He was born of woman, subject to the limitations of our nature apart from sin, and physically expired upon the cross in our place. The Jesus of Mrs. Eddy is a divine ideal or principle, inherent within every man, and Jesus was its supreme manifestation. Since Mrs. Eddy denied the existence of the physical universe, she also denied the reality of human flesh and blood, maintaining that it was an illusion of mortal mind. Hence, neither Christ, nor any man for that matter, possesses a real body of flesh and bones, and for her, Jesus Christ has not come in the flesh.

It seems almost unnecessary to refer to the fact that our Lord acknowledged the reality of flesh and blood when He declared to Peter: "Blessed art thou, Simon Bar-jona, for flesh and blood hath not revealed it unto thee, but my Father which is in heaven" (Matthew 16:17).

At this particular juncture, the words of the Apostle John take on new meaning when he declares:

Every spirit that confesseth not that Jesus Christ is come in the flesh is not of God: and this is that spirit of antichrist, whereof ye have heard that it should come; and even now already is it in the world (I John 4:3).

John's previous words then apply with great force to the Jesus of Christian Science and its prophetess, Mrs. Eddy:

> Who is a liar but he that denieth that Jesus is the Christ? He is antichrist, that denieth the Father and the Son (I John 2:22).

We need not emphasize the point, for it is quite evident that the "other" Jesus of Christian Science is a gnostic Jesus, an idea, a principle — but not God Incarnate, (John 1:14), and because of this, although Mrs. Eddy, her literature and Christian Scientists utilize the name of Jesus, theirs is not the Christ of the Scriptures, but an extremely clever counterfeit, about whom the Holy Spirit graciously saw fit to warn the church.

2. The Jesus of Jehovah's Witnesses.

The next example is quite different from the Jesus of Christian Science, but another Jesus, nonetheless. According to the theology of the Watch Tower, the Jesus they own is

> . . . a mighty God, but not the Almighty God who is Jehovah . . . in other words, he was the first and direct creation of Jehovah God . . . he was the start of God's creative work (*The Truth Shall Make You Free,* page 47; *The Kingdom Is at Hand,* pages 46-49).

The founder of Jehovah's Witnesses, Charles Taze Russell, described *his* Jesus as having been Michael the Archangel prior to his divesting himself of his angelic nature, and appearing in the world as a perfect man (*Studies in the Scriptures,* Vol. 15, page 84); so for Jehovah's Witnesses, their Jesus is an angel, who became a man. He is *a* god, but he is not God the Son, second Person of the Holy Trinity.

As the chapter on Jehovah's Witnesses amply demonstrated, the Scriptures refute this, and flatly controvert the Watch Tower's christology, by teaching that Jesus Christ is the Word, God the only begotten one (John 1:18, Greek), and no less that the great "I Am" of Exodus 3:14 (compare John 8:58) and the First and the Last of the

apocalyptic-Isaiah contrast, well known to any informed student of the Scriptures (compare Revelation 1:16, 17 with Isaiah 44:6).

As Mrs. Eddy's Christ is an abstract idea, and the Christ of Jehovah's Witnesses is a second god, with an angelic background, he, too, qualifies as "another" Jesus in the context of the Pauline prophecy.

3. The Jesus of the Mormons.

The teachings of the Mormon religion, which differs from both Christian Science and from Jehovah's Witnesses, claim that their god is one among many gods, as evidenced by their own literature:

> Each of these gods, including Jesus Christ and his Father being in possession of not merely an organized spirit, but a glorious body of flesh and bone . . . (*Key to the Science of Theology,* page 42, Parley Pratt).

Theologian Pratt held no unique view where Mormonism was concerned; in fact, the Mormons have a full pantheon of gods. Jesus, who before His incarnation was the spirit brother of Lucifer, was also a polygamist, the husband of the Marys and Martha, who was rewarded for his faithfulness by becoming the ruler of this earth (see chapter 6).

The Apostle Paul reminds us in his epistle to the Galatians that "God is one" (Galatians 3:20), and the numerous passages from the Old Testament, previously cited in the chapter on Mormonism, demonstrate the absolute falsity of the idea that there are a multiplicity of gods and an exaltation of godhood to which men can aspire. As for the concept of a polygamist, Jesus who was brother of Lucifer, this need not be dignified by further comment.

The Jesus of the Mormons is quite obviously "another" Jesus, with whom truly redeemed men have no truck, even though he be arrayed as an angel of light, and with all the credentials of the angel Moroni's angelic proclamation to Joseph Smith, the prophet of the restored Christian religion!

It would be possible to go on listing the other cult systems, but it is apparent that other comment would be superfluous; the evidence is overpowering.

The Jesus of the Christian Scientists, the Mormons, the Jehovah's Witnesses, and of all the cult systems, is but a subtle caricature of the Christ of divine revelation. In cult theology, He becomes an abstraction (Christian Science, Unity, Metaphysics, New Thought), a second god, (Jehovah's Witnesses, Mormonism, Theosophy, Rosacrucianism, Baha'ism), or a pantheistic manifestation of deity, (Spiritism, The Great I Am), but He is still incontrovertibly "another Jesus," who represents another gospel, and imparts another spirit, which by no conceivable stretch of the imagination could be called holy.

Herein lies the problem which Christians must face and come to grips with, and there are excellent reasons why it is not only our responsibility, but our duty.

To Every Man an Answer

In the course of delivering numerous lectures on the subject of non-Christian cults and their relationship to the Christian Church, one of the most frequent questions addressed to me has been, "What are the reasons why Christians should oppose and criticize the beliefs of others whether they be cults or other world religions?"

To answer this question we must first recognize that to oppose and criticize is neither unethical, bigoted, or un-Christian; rather it is the epitome of proper Christian conduct where a very vital part of the Christian witness is concerned. There are some good people who feel that it is beneath their dignity to engage in the criticism of the beliefs of others and the society in which we live has done much to foster this belief. "Live and let live" is the motto of our civilization; don't buck the tide of uncritical tolerance, or as the saying goes,

"bend with the wind or be broken." In addition to this type of reasoning there also has been promulgated a distinctly non-controversial spirit mirrored in the fact that leading newspapers and periodicals, not to mention the mass media of communication, radio and TV, refuse to carry advertisements for debates on religious issues for fear of being thought un-American since it is now fashionable to equate criticism of another's religion with an un-American spirit!

We must remember, however, that controversy in itself has always been a stimulus to thought and in our own great country has provoked many needed reforms in numerous instances. We might also observe that there is the easily verifiable fact that the criticism of another's religious beliefs does not necessarily postulate personal antagonism toward those who entertain such beliefs. Hence it is possible for a Protestant to criticize Roman Catholicism or Judaism for example without being in the least antagonistic to members of either faith. Let us not forget that honest criticism, debate, and the exploration of controversial issues involves the basic right of freedom of speech within constitutional limits and the New Testament itself, the very cradle of Christianity, reflects in a startling way the fact that the faith of Jesus Christ was built and nourished upon the controversy which it provoked. It was said of the early Christians that they "turned the world upside down" (Acts 17:6) indeed the message of the Cross itself is offensive and controversial by nature. Robert Ingersoll, the late great agnostic and renowned antagonist of Christianity was wise enough to recognize this fact and stated in his famous lectures "If this religion is true, then there is only one Saviour only one narrow path to life. Christianity cannot live in peace with any other religion."

There are many reasons why books and chapters like this should be written but we shall turn to the Bible itself for the basic reasons believing that in God's

Word, the source of our faith, will be found the evidence that its defense is very much His will.

Let us begin by noting the historical fact that Jesus Christ and His apostles warned repeatedly of false prophets and teachers.

Throughout His entire ministry our Lord was constantly on guard against those who attempted to ensnare Him with trick questions and supposed contradictions between what He taught and the teachings of Moses and the Prophets. Added to this, these professional interrogators masqueraded as religious, pious, and even tolerant zealots and professed that they were the descendants of Abraham, heir to the covenant and servants of God. To these people our Lord addressed His most scathing denunciations calling them among other things "whited sepulchres," "children of the devil," "dishonorers of God," "liars," "murderers" and "wolves." Since our Lord was both God and man, He alone could gaze through the centuries and see those who would arise following in the train of His contemporary antagonists and at least two very graphic prophecies of their characters and objectives are to be found in His discourses.

In the seventh chapter of the gospel according to Matthew, as previously noted in chapter 1, Christ enunciated a very definite warning (verses 15-23).

From this discourse we learn some very important things. We learn that there shall be false prophets; that they shall appear in sheep's clothing and that their inward or spiritual nature is that of wolves (verse 15). We are further told that we shall be able to recognize them by their fruits. We are informed that they will prophesy in His name; in His name cast out devils, and in His name perform miracles (verses 16, 22). With the full knowledge that they would do these things, our Lord then adds "I will profess unto them; I never knew you: . . . ye that work iniquity" (verse

23). There can be little doubt that He intended this as a warning for He prefaces His statements with a very strong Greek term, "beware" literally "be wary of or take care, because of" false prophets. The designation "wolves in sheep's clothing" is therefore not that of some misguided and over zealous Christian apologist, but one that finds its authority in the words of God the Son and this is the reason why Christians are to listen to it.

Our Lord supplemented His discussion of these individuals when in the twenty-fourth chapter of Matthew while speaking of the circumstances surrounding His Second Advent Christ declared: "for there shall arise false christs and false prophets and shall shew great signs and wonders; insomuch that, if it were possible, they shall deceive the very elect" (verse 24).

Further comment on this point is not necessary; He designated them "false christs" and "false prophets"; it was He who prophesied that they would show great signs and wonders, and it was He who warned that if it were possible, the subtlety of their evil would deceive the very elect, or the church. Apparently our Saviour thought it important enough to repeat for in verse twenty-five He says "Behold, I have told you before."

The Apostle Paul, utilizing the identical language of the Lord Jesus Christ, succinctly phrases a divine warning concerning these same people.

For I have not shunned to declare unto you all the counsel of God. Take heed therefore unto yourselves, and to all the flock, over the which the Holy Spirit hath made you overseers, to feed the church of God, which he hath purchased with his own blood. For I know this, that after my departing shall grievous wolves enter in among you, not sparing the flock. Also of your own selves shall men arise, speaking perverse things, to draw away disciples after them. Therefore watch, and remember, that by the space of three years I ceased not to warn every one night and day with tears (Acts 20:27-31).

It appears from this very pointed statement that Paul was not afraid "to declare unto you all the counsel of God." Indeed, the greatest of the apostles warns us to "take heed" and this is to involve not only ourselves but all Christians and though it is addressed principally to pastors, it underlines the existence of "grievous wolves" about whom Paul, in his own words says, "cease not to warn every one night and day with tears." Should not that which was important to him be as important to us for whom he intended it? It is of no small interest and importance that this charge of Paul to the Ephesian elders was taken very seriously by them for in Revelation, chapter 2, Christ commends the church at Ephesus for heeding Paul in that they "tested them who say they are apostles and are not and have found them out to be liars" (verse 2).

Paul of course made much mention of such persons elsewhere, describing them as "enemies of the cross of Christ" (Philippians 3:18), "false apostles and deceitful workers transforming themselves into the apostles of Christ" (II Corinthians 11:13). He does not even hesitate to describe them as "satan's ministers" (II Corinthians 11:14, 15). The first and second epistles to Timothy, also of Pauline authorship, reflect the same attitude: "Now the Spirit speaketh expressly that in the latter times some shall depart from the faith, giving heed to seducing spirits, and doctrines of devils; speaking lies in hypocrisy; having their conscience seared with a hot iron" (I Timothy 4:1-2).

The express speaking of the spirit, of course, underscores the importance of the counsel given, and it is significant to observe that it is to take place in the "latter times" when men shall "depart from the faith," listen to "seducing spirits," and become captives of "the doctrines of demons." This is tremendously strong language in the original Greek and is followed by his counsel in the sec-

ond epistle to, "preach the Word" and to "reprove, rebuke, and exhort with all longsuffering and doctrine" those who in the time to come "will not endure sound doctrine; but after their own lusts shall heap to themselves teachers who shall tickle their ears; and the truth shall be turned into fables" (II Timothy 4:3-4, literal Greek).

It is more than a casual coincidence that the Apostle Peter acknowledges the authority of Christ and Paul by utilizing their very language: "But there were false prophets also among the people, even as there shall be false teachers among you, who privily shall bring in damnable heresies, even denying the Lord that bought them and bring upon themselves swift destruction" (II Peter 2:1).

For Peter, it appears "false prophets" were a distinct reality, "false teachers" not figments of overwrought fundamentalist imaginations, and "destructive heresies" which "denied the Lord that bought them," vivid dangers to be guarded against. As we approach the end of the New Testament we find John, always noted for his doctrine of love, balancing that doctrine magnificently with the teaching of divine judgment upon those whom he describes as "false prophets that are gone out into the world" (I John 4:1) and "deceivers are entered into the world who confess not that Jesus Christ is come in the flesh. This is a deceiver and an antichrist" (II John 7).

The next to the last book in the Bible, the comparatively small epistle of Jude, is likewise in full agreement with the verdict of our Lord and the other apostles:

Certain men crept in unawares, who were before of old ordained to this condemnation, ungodly men, turning the grace of our God into lasciviousness, and denying the only Lord God, and our Lord Jesus Christ . . . These are spots in your feasts of charity . . . clouds without water, carried about of winds; trees whose fruit withereth, without fruit, twice dead, plucked up by the roots; raging waves of the sea, foaming out their own shame; wandering stars, to whom is reserved the blackness of darkness forever (verses 4, 12, 13).

As we have noted, all of the quotations are in context, refer to the same individuals, and characterize them in an identical manner. The description is not pleasant, but it is a Biblical one originating with God the Holy Spirit, not with the so-called interpretational fancies or bigoted intolerances of uninformed extremists. God used these terms for people He describes in His Word; God warns the church of Christ about their existence, their methods, teachings, their subtilties, and their final judgment. The church neglects, at her peril, such divine counsel.

There are naturally some who will not agree with this position; they will quote the advice of Gamaliel which he addressed to the Jews in the book of Acts (5:38, 39); they, too, will say "let them alone; if the work is of man, it will perish; if it is of God we will be found to be opposing him." The only difficulty, as we have noted earlier, is that the context clearly indicates the advice was given by Gamaliel to the Jews and Gamaliel was not an inspired writer, an apostle or even a Christian. If his advice is to be followed and his criterion to be recognized then the thriving growth of the various non-Christian cults, all of which deny the fundamentals of the Christian faith, must be acknowledged as the work of God! No consistent thinker of Christian orientation could long entertain such a warped conclusion without doing violence to a great portion of the New Testament.

There are also others who, in their attempt to excuse themselves from meeting the challenge of the Jesus of the cults, will refer to the ninth verse of Jude

where Michael the archangel, when contending with the devil, refused to argue with him but rather referred him to the Lord for rebuke. Once again, however, the context reveals that Michael did not keep silence by choice but by necessity because as the Greek so clearly reveals "he did not dare bring against Satan a blasphemous judgment" for the simple reason that Satan was his superior in authority. The Greek word translated "durst" in our King James Bible carries the meaning of not doing something for fear of retaliation by a superior power (Greek etolmese) so this line of reasoning also fails.

The reasons why we must answer as well as be prepared to evangelize such people then are quite clear. The Church must do it because Christ and the apostles commanded it to do so, unpopular though it may be, and to this all true Christians should be unequivocally committed for no other reason than out of respect for our Lord. Certainly if our mothers, wives, children or country were attacked and misrepresented, our love for them would compel us to defend them. How much more then should love for our Redeemer so motivate us in the defense of Him and His Gospel.

The Jesus of the cults is a poor substitute for the incarnate God of the New Testament but along with the equally important imperative of cult evangelism stands the very real need to give to everyone that asks of us "a reason for the hope that is within us" (I Peter 3: 15). That hope is the Jesus of Biblical theology and of history and once we understand the true nature of the Jesus of the cults we can discharge out duty faithfully and by contrast unmask him and his creator for all to see. We may sum this up with the thought provoking words of our Lord when with absolute finality He declared: "Behold, I have told you before" (Matthew 24:25).

Chapter 18

CULT EVANGELISM —
MISSION FIELD ON THE DOORSTEP

The last ninety years of American history have seen the evangelization of large segments of the American populace, to a degree never imagined by any evangelist in the history of Christianity.

Beginning with the evangelical emphasis of Charles G. Finney, through the massive impact of D. L. Moody, Gypsy Smith, Billy Sunday, culminating in Billy Graham, American Christianity has enjoyed great spiritual privileges, withheld from the world since the days of the Reformation and the Knox, Wesley and Whitefield revivals, so dear to the memory of church historians.

Yet there are many people today in both the clergy and the ranks of the laity, who are seriously re-evaluating the meaning of evangelism and its importance, if not to the church, at least to themselves. More and more, Christians are beginning to think in terms of *personal* evangelism as opposed to mass evangelism, primarily because all evangelism, since the earliest days of Christianity, that is, all *successful* evangelism of enduring worth, has been of a personal nature. While it is true that great evangelists draw crowds and preach to multitudes of people, they, too, are dependent upon the so-called "personal touch," as evidenced by the fact that Billy Graham has more than once attempted to remove the "tag line" from his Hour of Decision radio program "The Lord bless you real good," only to have such attempts reversed by the constituency that, despite its size, still desires the feeling of a personal relationship.

The follow-up work of every major evangelical crusade must be on a personal basis to be effective. A stamped envelope and a short memory course are no substitute for the personal workers, whose on-the-spot faithfulness, patience and perseverence builds up and edifies young converts after the first warm glow of the conversion experience has begun to abate.

This of course brings us to a consideration of the all-important question: What is evangelism? Is it merely mass rallies, where so-called "wholesale" decisions for Christ are made? Is it on the other hand, just the task of the local church to shoulder the responsibility of having a week or two of meetings for revival and evangelistic purposes each year? By evangelism, do we mean massive emphasis upon radio and television, to communicate the good news of redemption? Or, is evangelism somehow or other, bound up with *all* of these forms of expression, and yet, in essence, none of them? Is it perhaps possible that evangelism was intended, in its primary purpose, to be personal and individualistic to the degree that each Christian feels the responsibility to evangelize his neighbor, and that this is really the root of the whole matter from which the tree of church evangelism and mass evangelism, both in crusades and the mass media are to draw their strength and spiritual stamina? To answer these questions, and to place evangelism in its proper perspective where the challenge of non-Christian cults is concerned, we must consider carefully the pattern laid out for us in the New Testament.

HOLDING FORTH THE WORD
OF LIFE

If anything proceeds from the pages of the New Testament, it is the message that the early Christian church labored under the magnificent obsession of the divine paradox. They were separate as individuals in each congregation, whether it be Ephesus, Corinth, Crete or Philippi. But in some mysterious sense, they were "one body" in Christ (Ephesians 4:4). Through acceptance of the divine Redeemer, God had shattered and broken down the walls of race, color and social status. There were no longer "Barbarian, Scythian, bond or free, but all were one in Christ" (Colossians 3:11).

Each of these New Testament Christians was admonished by the Holy Spirit to be an ambassador, or representative for his Saviour (II Corinthians 5:20). The Apostle Paul set the supreme example of this in the New Testament church, by declaring that the primary responsibility of the Christian was to preach the Gospel (I Corinthians 1), and it is precisely at this juncture, that, if we are willing, we can understand the meaning of New Testament evangelism.

The Greek word translated *gospel,* literally means "good news," as most Christians well know. But what many do not know is that the word translated *preach* comes from the Greek *evangelizomai,* which means "to publish" the Gospel, or declare it abroad, for all the world to hear.

The early Christians considered themselves evangelists in that sense (I Corinthians 1:17), and in the writings of Paul, Peter, John and others, this great unalterable truth shines through. Christianity was not something entrusted to clergymen, pastors, teachers or professional evangelists. It was a personal message, entrusted to those who had experienced the power of its transforming properties in their own lives, and who went literally from house to house and turned the world upside down, because they were not ashamed to proclaim it. The early Christians went forth two-by-two. They went forth in the power of the resurrected Christ. They went forth with a message — a message based upon experience, an experience shared by all — an experience which strengthened and comforted all. These were not people who were preoccupied with the things of the world, with contemporary political intrigues or the reigns of the Caesars, with the show places of Ephesus and the coliseums of Rome. These were people who were possessed by an alien Spirit — a Spirit totally removed from the spirit of the age in which they lived — a Spirit who commanded them to convict the world of sin, because they had been its victims, and because of the Redeemer, they had now become its conquerors.

The incredible zeal with which they proclaimed this message of the living Christ, the Gospel of Resurrection, the certainty of sin forgiven, the present possession of peace with God, exerted an awesome influence and power over the minds of those with whom they came in contact, almost without exception. The Philippian jailer abused Paul and Silas until he experienced the Presence of their Master. Then he, too, with his whole house believed the incredible. Sergius Paulus, beset though he was by a demonic medium who sought to pervert the Gospel and turn him away from the faith of Christ, was stunned by the authority of a man filled with this alien Spirit, Saul, who was also called Paul, and whose amazement turned to faith and life eternal. Even those who resisted the magnificence of New Testament evangelism were frightened by its clarity and power, and felt even as Festus, who raved at the Apostle Paul, "Paul, thou art beside thyself; much learning doth make you mad" (Acts 26:24). Agrippa the king, could not be dissuaded even by the remarks of Festus, but withdrew from the Presence of the Holy Spirit with the trembling admission, "Almost, thou persuadest me to be a Christian" (Acts 26:28).

All of these evangelists had three things in common. They had experienced the Person of the Risen Christ, and had passed out of death, into life. Second, they were dominated by the Holy Spirit, alien to this world because the world does not know Him, and cannot receive Him, because the world is evil, and He is God. Last, they obeyed the injunction of the apostles and fearlessly as ambassadors for Christ, published the Good News that Light had come into the world, and that God had indeed appointed a day in which He would judge the world in righteousness by that man whom He had ordained, and given assurance to all men, by raising Him from among the dead.

It is not difficult to see why the Christians of the first century were able to spread Christianity throughout the earth without the aid of radio, television, traveling caravan, precision crusades or yearly evangelistic and revival meetings. Every day was an evangelistic campaign for them; every service a revival meeting; every road a path to someone who needed Christ; every house a dwelling place for those for whom He died. These were people who were evangelists in the full meaning of the term as God had intended and commanded it. They rose to the challenge with a supreme confidence and conviction born of experience and faith, which, despite their limitations and human frailties, made them worthy of the name, "saints." They could do all this because they had truly found him, "of whom Moses in the law and in the prophets did write, Jesus of Nazareth" (John 1:45) . . . and they had believed Him that "Wherever two or three are gathered together in my name, there am I in the midst of them" (Matthew 18:20).

If we want to have evangelism in the true Biblical sense of the term, we must return to the content of the evangel, and to the methods of the New Testament church. We must utilize every modern method possible, but we must not allow them to overshadow or interfere with the great personal responsibility which rests upon every Christian. For, in that very real and personal sense it is true of us as it was of the Apostle Paul, "For Christ sent me not to baptize, but to preach the gospel" (I Corinthians 1:17).

The Philippian Christians were admonished by the Apostle Paul to "shine as lights in the world, holding forth the word of life" (2:15-16). This they could do only by being willing to shine in contrast to the darkness which surrounded them, and by being willing to stand in the defense of the Gospel as they held forth the Word of Life.

We are told in the simplest terms that the Gospel is God's power unto salvation, but what *is* that Gospel?

The Apostle Paul states it for us in what might be called a capsule version when writing to the Corinthians he said:

> For I delivered unto you first of all that which I also received, how that Christ died for our sins according to the scriptures; And that he was buried, and that he rose again the third day according to the scriptures" (I Corinthians 15:3, 4).

The very usage of the word Christ in the Pauline theology identifies the office of the Anointed One with that of the second Person of the Trinity, He who is God "over all, God blessed for ever. Amen" (Romans 9:5 Greek).

Paul does not however, stop at this, but goes on to point out that Christ died for our sins, that is, in place of our sins, a clear statement of the substitutionary atonement of the Cross. Then he concludes with "He rose again the third day," which in the context of I Corinthians 15 can only refer to a bodily resurrection (Luke 24:39ff).

We can see then, that the content of the Gospel is at its very minimum, the Deity of Christ, the substitutionary atonement of the Cross and His bodily

Resurrection from the grave. This good news, when enunciated and published fearlessly by believers, has the effect of convicting them of their sins, and leading them to true repentance toward God and faith in the Lord Jesus Christ. James Packer in his stimulating book *Evangelism and the Sovereignty of God,* has put it this way:

> What was this Good News Paul preached? It was the news about Jesus of Nazareth. It was the news of the incarnation, the atonement, the kingdom, the cradle, the cross and the crown of the Son of God. It was the news of how God glorified His Servant, Jesus, by making Him Christ, the world's long-awaited Prince and Saviour. It was the news of how God made His Son man, and how as man, God made Him Priest and Prophet and King, and how as Priest, God also made Him a sacrifice for sins, and how as a Prophet, God also made Him a law-giver to His people, and how as King, God has also made Him Judge of all the world, and given Him prerogatives which in the Old Testament are exclusively Jehovah's own — namely to reign until every knee bows before Him, and to save all who call on His Name. In short, the good news was just this, that God has executed His eternal intention of glorifying His Son by exalting Him as the great Saviour for great sinners. Such was the Gospel which Paul was sent to preach; it was a message of some complexity, needing to be learned before it could be lived by, understood before it could be applied and needed therefore to be taught. Hence Paul as a preacher of it, had to become a teacher. He saw this as part of his calling; he speaks of the Gospel whereunto I am appointed a preacher . . . and a teacher (II Timothy 1:10ff).[1]

Evangelism then, has content, as well as zeal, courage and an attitude of constant prayer, distinct methods of propagation.

TECHNIQUES OF CULT EVANGELISM

It is the testimony of the Word of God that He has raised up the Gentile nations and made available to them the Gospel of the Kingdom and its Messi-

anic King, which Israel rejected, because of unbelief. The Scriptures declare that the purpose of God in doing this is to "provoke them to jealousy" (Romans 11:11) that they may perceive what they have lost, and repent, that the natural olive branch may be grafted in again, whereas now, only the wild branch (Gentiles) shares the blessing of Messiah's covenant and coming Kingdom.

In the kingdom of the cults today, however, we are witnessing something akin to this and yet, despite its corrupt purposes, progressing at an alarming rate of speed. We see the various cult systems, specifically Jehovah's Witnesses, Mormonism, Moral Rearmament, Unity, etc., utilizing the methods of Christianity and of New Testament propagation of the Christian message, wooing converts from professing Christian communions, Protestant as well as Roman Catholic! This bewildering proselytizing has caused consternation in many Protestant and Roman Catholic parishes across America and abroad and it is accelerating, not slowing down. We see the strange, but just, judgment of God upon the Christian Church because of its lethargy in that He is allowing the forces of darkness to succeed with the methods of light, while denying the source of light and life, the Gospel of Jesus Christ. In order that we may offset the ever-widening circle of cultic influence, Christians must first of all face the fact that we have been woefully delinquent in the exercise of our responsibility of personal evangelism. Second, many Christians have taken for granted the great doctrines of the Bible which they learned and accepted at their conversion and have not "studied, to show themselves approved by God, workmen who do not need to be ashamed, rightly dividing the word of truth." Third, the average Christian knows *what* he believes, insofar as being able to document the *why* of his belief from the Scripture,

[1]Page 47.

which he finds at times a frustrating and exasperating task. The clergy is largely at fault in this respect, because they do not always emphasize the teaching ministry of the pulpit, but rather, settle for an evangelistic emphasis, with very little doctrinal depth.

Recently, we took a survey in the Department of Biblical Studies at the King's College. Of some three hundred students polled, less than ten had heard a sermon in the last four years in their respective churches on the doctrines of the Trinity, the Deity and Humanity of Jesus Christ, or the relationship of grace and faith to works. We have conducted similar surveys in colleges, seminaries and Bible institutes in many major cities throughout the country. The result has been almost identical. There *must* be something fundamentally wrong when important areas of doctrine such as these are neglected or glossed over lightly.

The various cult systems, particularly Jehovah's Witnesses and the Mormons, capitalize on conditions such as this, and there is many an embarrassed Christian who rushes to the telephone when he has a Jehovah's Witness "minister" or Mormon "elder" in his living room, to get answers from a generally-over-worked and harassed pastor, when a little consistent study of the Scriptures would have given him a tremendous sense of security and more important, provided him an opportunity to preach Christ in the true sense of personal evangelism, to the cultists.

Throughout the world today, Christian missionaries are faced with proclaiming the unsearchable riches of the Gospel. And due to the tremendous amount of funds made available, comparatively speaking, for world missions in the last 100 years in the United States, a good many Christians have become lethargic and apathetic as to their own personal responsibility toward proclaiming the Gospel of Christ. Ministers are constantly discovering that their congregations are dwindling at prayer meetings, that even their Sunday evening services have been winnowed considerably by television and other extra-curricular social activities. Here then, lies part of the problem.

As we have shown in the preceding chapters, the non-Christian cult systems in America have grown tremendously in the last sixty-five years. By a subtle utilization of a redefined terminology, coupled with a surface knowledge of the Bible, and encouraged by the fact that a great many Christians are unable to answer their perversions, (a fact which serves to confirm them even more definitely in those deviations), the zeal and missionary activities of the cults have tremendously increased. There is only one way actively to offset this, and this is by a return to positive Christian evangelism on the fiercely personal basis of door-to-door and neighbor-to-neighbor effort whenever the opportunity presents itself. But over and beyond this, it is time that the Church of Jesus Christ begins to consider the cults themselves as a mission field — a mission field on the doorstep of the church wherever she exists in the world, both at home and abroad.

This is by no means an impossible task, for the last decade of the writer's life, which has been spent largely in this field, confirms his opinion that cultists too can be reached with the Gospel, for they are part of the world that God so loved that He sent His only begotten Son to redeem.

Precisely how we may implement the evangelization of cultists is an important and vital subject about which nothing has been written, comparatively speaking, in the last half century and which today presents an ever-expanding challenge to the Christian who wishes to obey, as did the Apostle Paul and the church at Philippi, the command to publish the Good News and to pick up our credentials as ambassadors for Christ and present them to those who would evangelize *us* with a gospel other than that which the New Testament proclaims.

The following techniques and observations the author feels would be useful in any genuine Christian effort to evangelize cultists, when they are offered, not as a panacea to the problem, but as a tested means toward the end of bringing cultists to personal faith in Jesus Christ. This is the object of all true evangelism, in any century.

1. The Human Element.

One of the first things which confronts a Christian as he attempts to evangelize a cultist, is the psychological barrier which exists in the minds of a great many persons, to the effect that cultists must be a special breed of individuals impervious to standard techniques of evangelism and generally well enough versed in the Bible to confuse, if not convince, the average Christian.

While there is an element of truth in both of these statements, it is generally traceable to experiences the Christian has had personally, either directly or indirectly, with cultists, or to those encounters with cultists in which the Christians did not fare too well. In fact, in not a few instances, they have been routed, frustrated and embarrassed. This generally tends toward reticence, lest there be a repeat performance.

The second explanation for this phenomenon is the seemingly implanted fear that cultists should not be permitted to enter the Christian's home, in the light of II John, verse 10:

> If there come any unto you, and bring not this doctrine, receive him not into your house, neither bid him God speed.

Now in context, this passage is a sentence in a letter to the Elect Lady, in whose home a Christian church quite obviously met, as the early church was prone to do, there being no cathedrals, or modern churches such as we know

them today. In this connection, a very common one (see Philemon 2), John warns her not to allow anyone to preach in church meetings or teach doctrines which do not honor Christ in every aspect of His Person, Nature and Work. It is clear that he is referring to false teachers being given a voice in the church, not to a cultist sitting in your living room! That the passage cannot be taken literally in that connection is quite evident, because if a twentieth century Christian's plumbing froze when the weather was twenty degrees below zero and his cellar was rapidly flooding with water, he would not dream of asking the plumber who came over at 2:00 A.M. to fix the pipes, whether he "brought the doctrine of Christ" to his home. Rather, such a question would never enter his mind. Yet the plumber might be a Unitarian, Mormon or a Jehovah's Witness! Doubtless, Christians have had them in their homes, fixing their plumbing, electricity or oil burner and never once inquired of their views concerning the doctrine of Christ. Yet some Christians who utilize II John 10 as an excuse for not evangelizing cultists, would never dream of using it if the cultist were a plumber!

Many pastors have instructed their flocks on the basis of this passage and other out-of-context quotations, to close the doors in the faces of cultists rather than to invite them in and in the tradition of Christian evangelism confront them with the claims of Christ. There is no authority in the Word of God for neglecting one's responsibility as an ambassador of Christ, and the cults do not constitute a special category of evangelism.

The Christian is probably right in assuming that the average cultist does have a working knowledge of the Bible. Most of them are quite diligent in their study, both of their own literature, and that of the Scriptures. And it may be true that the well-trained cultist may appear to be impervious to the proclamation of the Gospel and its defense (when necessary). But that he is some special species of unbeliever, in whose presence the Christian must remain mute and the Holy Spirit impotent, is a gross misconception, and should be abandoned by all thinking Christians.

We must strive to keep foremost in our minds at all times that cultists are precious souls for whom Jesus Christ offered Himself, and that they are human beings who have homes, families, friends, emotions, needs, ambitions, fears and frustrations which all men have in common. The cultist is special in only one sense, that he is already "deeply religious," and therefore, probably one of the most difficult persons in the world to reach with the Gospel of Christ. He has rejected historic Christianity and entertains in most cases a hostility, if not active antagonism, to its message. The cultist therefore considers evangelical Christians their greatest potential, if not actual, adversaries. Hence, an attitude of tolerance and love should always be manifested by the Christian to relieve, where possible, this tension and the hostile feelings of the cult adherent. The technique of "setting the cultist at ease" does indeed take a great deal of patience, for the individual cultist firmly believes that he has found "the truth," and as such, often considers the Christian message to be inferior to his own revelation. This fact is generally reflected in his attitude of superiority and even genuine resentment when the Gospel is presented. This resentment may take many forms, but always it conforms to the general thrust that since he has found the truth, how can the Christian dare to attempt to convert *him?* Cultists believe they already have progressed far beyond the evangelical Christian stage or station on the "religious railroad track" through their special revelations and superior experiences with God.

According to one psychologist, cultists also transfer their antagonism for the theology of historic Christianity, to those who propagate that message, thus identifying the belief with the individual, and personalizing the controversy. If the Christian who is interested in evangelizing cultists would realize this fact at the outset of his conversation with cult adherents, he could then make a careful distinction between the theology of Christianity, which is the real source of the antagonism, and the personality of the individual Christian, thereby allowing the cultist to see the Christian as a redeemed personality, independent of his theological structure. This would make possible a form of objective discussion of Biblical truth, subject to the categories of analysis, logical consistency, context and exegesis.

While this may not necessarily undercut any portion of the cultist's theological system, it will break down or assist in breaking down the psychological conditioning of the cultist to the attitude that any person who disagrees with *his* interpretation of Christianity is automatically an object of antagonism.

Approaching the problem of cult evangelism, it must be remembered that cultists, in their respective systems of theology, are almost always by nature dependent upon either forms, ceremonies, rituals, good works, right-living or self-sacrifice as a means of pleasing God and obtaining justification. Fundamentally then, cultism is a form of self-salvation, emphasizing deliverance from sin through human effort or merit in cooperation with their concept of the personality of the Deity.

The Christian must therefore, in the light of this fact, point out from Scripture (since most cults recognize it as authoritative, or at least partially binding), the folly of self-justification, righteousness or human effort as a means of obtaining redemption. We should always remember that repentance, atonement, regeneration, resurrection and retribution in the Biblical sense is seldom part of the cultist's vocabulary, and *never* of his personal experience. The Christian must *define, apply* and *defend* the historic meanings of these terms, before it is possible to effectively proclaim the Gospel. In a word, one must begin at the beginning, repeat, emphasize and repeat. This is the sowing of seed that one day, by God's grace alone, will bear fruit to eternal life.

Adherents of the cults are constituted, psychologically speaking, so that they are, almost always, vicitms of what might be termed a mass delusion of grandeur, coupled with a dogged sense of personal pride. The Scripture records that Satan fell from his first estate through measureless pride (Isaiah 14:12-14), so also today, he uses the same weaknesses of the human character as a tool in shaping cult adherents to his own ends. This pride is evident in most cultists, and contributes to the delusion that they are the possessors of the true faith that saves, guardians and defenders of that which is alone holy, and administrators of divine revelation to the mass of mankind who are enmeshed in a Christianity which all cultists agree has been perverted by theologians and philosophers, thus necessitating the true restoration of the Gospel through their efforts. It has been the writer's experience that almost all cultists suffer from the concept that his or her group will at last emerge victorious over all its adversaries, inherit an eternal kingdom and have the pleasure of viewing its enemies being either tormented or destroyed. Such cultists cling to an illusion of impending and imminent majesty or greatness, which, when linked with their intrinsic concepts of human ability and supposed merit before God, leads to mass delusion and spiritual darkness of the most terrible nature imaginable.

The task of the Christian evangelist then, is to reveal tactfully the true nature of man as Scripture portrays it. And in a spirit of deep concern with the practice of earnest prayer, reveal to the cultist God's view of fallen man, and the certain destiny of those who follow in the pride-filled footsteps of Lucifer, "the god of this world" (II Corinthians 4:4).

The nature of cultists is to be on the defensive, for they are acutely aware of the lack of unity and brotherly love clearly evidenced in many reputedly evangelical movements. They know that evangelicals are united, insofar as the cultist is concerned, only in their opposition to *him*. They therefore lay much stress upon the various divisions in orthodox circles, not to mention the lack of clarity where the cardinal doctrines of the Chrisitan faith are concerned. They apparently never tire of stating, "at least we are united; you are divided, even in your own groups." It is this type of accusation which cuts the true Christian deeply. He must answer this charge by admitting differences of opinion on minor issues, but emphasizing solidarity on the fundamentals of the Gospel, which all cultists deny in one form or another.

The Christian must never let it leave his mind for an instant, that a well-trained cultist can be a powerful opponent, adept at text-lifting, term-switching and surprise interpretations of "proof texts." He should be on guard constantly lest he be deceived into admitting something that will later be utilized against him and to the detriment of both the Gospel and his personal witness.

2. *Common Ground.*

Before attempting to evangelize a cultist, the Christian should, whenever possible, find a common ground of understanding (preferably the inspiration and authority of the Scriptures, or the Personality of God), and work from that point onward. Christian workers must, in effect, become all things to all men, that we might by all means, save some (I Corinthians 9:22). The Christian cannot afford to have a superiority complex or reflect the idea that he is redeemed and the cultist is lost. Redemption of the soul is a priceless gift from God, and should be coveted in all humility, not superiority as just that — a gift — unearned and unmerited, and solely the result of Sovereign Grace.

The necessity of a common ground cannot be overemphasized for any sane approach to the problem of cult evangelism. Unless some place of agreement, some starting point be mutually accepted by both parties, the discussion can only lead to argument, charges, countercharges, rank bitterness and, in the end, the loss of opportunity for further witness; and the soul of the cultist will be forfeited! Friendliness then, open and free manifestation of Christian love and a willingness to talk over the points of diversions, will go a long way toward allaying the suspicion of the average cultist and open further vistas for profitable and effective witnessing.

Throughout all of this, the Christian should be governed by increased activity in his prayer life, praying wherever possible in the presence of, and with, cultists, so that through the prayers that are uttered, the cultist may sense the relationship of the Christian to Him who is the Father of spirits, and our Father by faith in Jesus Christ.

3. *Subliminal Seeding.*

The advertising industry of America has pioneered in motivational research and has taught us that ideas may be implanted in our minds beneath the level of consciousness or conscious awareness, and that they are dutifully recorded and do in no small measure influence our thinking and actions. Jingles sung on the radio and the television quite often motivate people to purchase the product about which the jingle chants.

Christians who wish to evangelize cultists can profit from the findings of such motivational research into subliminal suggestion to an amazing degree.

It is the conviction of this writer that the Word of God and prayer, addressed to Him through the Holy Spirit, is the most powerful motivating force in the universe, and can be subliminally utilized in cult evangelism by the implantation of seed thoughts about the Gospel of Christ, as well as the Gospel itself.

How this may be done is best illustrated by examples drawn from the writer's own experiences.

Jehovah's Witnesses are probably the most active and zealous of all the missionaries of cultism in America today. When called upon by a Jehovah's Witness the writer for many years employed the following approach with great success.

I would invite the Watch Tower adherent or adherents into the living room, but before they had opportunity to speak concerning their literature, I would state that I never discussed religion or the Bible unless such a discussion was preceded by prayer, to which all present agreed. I would then quickly bow my head and address the Lord as Jehovah-God. One must be particularly careful in dealing with Jehovah's Witnesses, to always address the Deity by the name, Jehovah, or else the Witnesses may not pray or bow their heads. Instead, they will admire the bric a brac, thumb through their Bibles, reach for their briefcases and generally, keep occupied until you have completed your prayer. Should the reader be interested in knowing how I learned this, I must confess that on occasions — I peeked!

When the name of Jehovah is being used, the average Watch Tower adherent will immediately bow his head, and after you have finished praying and *before* they can pray, begin the conversation by saying, "Now what was it that you wanted to discuss?"

Always keep in mind in dealing with Jehovah's Witnesses, that they come equipped with a portable arsenal in the form of a briefcase which contains the major publications of the Watch Tower Society for their handy reference. At the outset you must insist that they use nothing but the Scriptures, and that it must be a recognized translation (King James, R.S.V., Goodspeed, etc.). You must further insist upon a discussion of cardinal doctrines, particularly concerning the Person, Nature and Work of Jesus Christ. Thus deprived of his Watch Tower material and his Watch Tower translations and circumscribed to the Person of Christ in discussion, even the best trained Jehovah's Witness is at a distinct disadvantage. On the other hand the Christian who is indwelt by the Holy Spirit then has a definite advantage.

After the discussion had gone on for some time, and I had listened to as much of "Pastor" Russell's theology as I could tolerate for one evening, I would remind the Witnesses of the lateness of the hour and asked if we couldn't close with a word of prayer. I would then immediately bow my head and begin praying again.

Now what I have mentioned is, by itself, only an outline of how to conduct one's self in the presence of Jehovah's Witnesses, with one important exception. During my opening and closing prayers I would totally preach the Gospel, emphasizing the Deity of Christ, His death for our sins, the certainty of knowing that we have eternal life *now*, by faith in Him, and that salvation comes by grace alone, independent of human works. I would profusely quote the Scriptures, and in actuality be preaching a three-minute sermonette, subliminally implanting the true Gospel of Jesus Christ and, I might add, blissfully uninterrupted. For no one, not even the most zealous disciple of "Pastor" Russell, Joseph Smith or Brigham Young, can interrupt a prayer. I have seen such a methodology or technique of evangelism make a tremendous impact upon Jehovah's Witnesses and other cultists, because, for six minutes of the evening at least, the Christian has the opportunity to present the true Gospel of Christ without interruption.

We must believe that God's Word "will not return unto Him void, but shall accomplish what He has ordained and prosper in the thing whereunto He has sent it" (Isaiah 55:11).

4. The Vocabulary of Redemption.

Non-Christian cultists of all varieties are prone to one psychological and spiritual insecurity. They are all aware of the fact that they do not *now* possess eternal life *or* peace with God. In fact, it is toward this end that they are vigorously pursuing the theology and practices of their respective systems. There can never be a substitute therefore, for an individual Christian's personal witness to what Christ has done for him. A word of caution, however, must be inserted at this juncture. As we know, cultists have their own vocabulary, so it will be necessary for the Christian to define carefully his terms, when he speaks of conversion, its means and its effect upon his spirit, mind and life. The only really unanswerable argument is the argument of a transformed life, properly grounded in the authority of the Scriptures and motivated by love for God and for one's fellow man. Key terms which must be carefully defined are: the new birth, or "born again"; justification; atonement; Deity and Resurrection of Christ; resurrection; forgiveness, grace and faith. It is inevitable that eternal retribution be discussed, because this is the very thing from which Christ died to save us.

The Scriptures admonish us to be "His witnesses," and in order to do this, we must be willing to endure all things and be governed by patience, temperance, grace and love. Then regardless of how the truth of God be assailed, perverted or distorted, and no matter how much our own characters and motives are attacked, Christ will be honored by our conduct.

The vocabulary of redemption involves personal involvement, testimony to the effect of Christ's power both to redeem the soul and to transform the individual, his morals, his ethics, his life. And most of all it involves the power to impart to him the peace of God, which passes all understanding, the peace which Christ said would come only to those who made peace with God (Philippians 4:7).

5. The Secret of Perseverance.

One of the most important techniques of cult evangelism is that of perseverance with cultists. Anyone who has ever worked extensively in the field of cults will readily testify that this takes a great deal of grace and understanding on the part of the Christian. Many times cultists will deliberately "bait" Christians (particularly Jehovah's Witnesses and the Mormons) in an attempt to provoke the Christian into losing his patience, thus justifying their own teachings. In order to avoid such pitfalls, and to be able to endure the many forms of abuse and persecution which will come about, the moment a Christian penetrates the theology of the cultist with the Sword of the Spirit, one must have discovered a secret which, when prayerfully understood and applied, can make the endurance of *anything,* for the sake of Christ, possible.

If one were attacked, severely assaulted and abused by a frightened blind man, it would be possible not only to forgive him, but even persevere to the end of loving him, despite his actions. For after all, both reason and logic argue, he *is* blind, and in a sense, not responsible for his actions.

We are forever in debt to the Apostle Paul, who pointed out in his second letter to the Corinthians that those who are outside of Christ have indeed been spiritually blinded by the god of this age, Satan, who has caused a cloak of delusion to descend over their minds and understandings, so that Christ's Gospel, which is the light of the world, cannot penetrate to them. The secret of perseverance is to know and to un-

derstand, regardless of what a cultist says or does, that he is doing it out of spiritual blindness. Since our warfare as Christians is not against flesh and blood (the cultist), but against the spiritual forces of darkness which rule this world (Satan and his emissaries) it does become possible to love the cultist, endure his abuses, perversions and recriminations, while at the same time faithfully bearing witness for Christ. This technique of cult evangelism should never be minimized. And once it is properly appreciated, it can become a great asset to the Christian.

There are doubtless many, many more things which could be mentioned in connection with cult evangelism, such as the important fact that when dealing with the Gnostic cults (Christian Science, Unity, New Thought, etc.), distinct emphasis must be placed upon personal sin, which they all negate, or deny; also the certainty of retribution as taught by the Lord Jesus Christ should be emphasized. We might also profitably note that, in dealing with religions which have had their origin outside the United States (Bahaism, Theosophy, Zen, etc.) the Christian ought to have a working knowledge of what the doctrines of these cults are, in relation to the historic Christian revelation. It is foolish to attempt to discuss Christian doctrines with those who do not accept the authority of the Scriptures, which is most certainly the case in regard to the three cults just mentioned.

Finally, evangelism, particularly cult evangelism, must never fail to emphasize that Christ and the disciples taught certain irrevocable doctrines as well as consistent ethics and morality.

It has been the experience of the author, based upon numerous personal contacts with cultists of all varieties, that there has yet to be born a cultist who can confuse, confound or in any way refute a Christian who has made doctrinal theology an integral part of his study of the Scriptures. Cults thrive upon ignorance and confusion where the doctrines of the Scriptures are concerned, but are powerless to shake Christians in their faith or effectively proselytize them when the Christian is well grounded in the basic teachings of the Bible and given over to a study of the great doctrinal truths of the Word of God. These mighty buttresses of Christian theology must no longer be taken for granted by Christian believers nor should pastors and teachers assume that the average Christian has sound knowledge concerning them. The rise of cultism to its present proportions indicates a great dearth of knowledge where doctrine is involved, and is a decided weakness in the battlements of orthodox theology, which the Church ignores, at the risk of innumerable souls.

Accepting then the fact that the poison of cultism can be effectively combated only by the antidote of sound doctrine, the next problem is the immunization of Christians against the teachings of the cults. The answer to this problem lies within the pages of God's Word; it involves study (II Timothy 2:15) on the part of Christians, instruction on the part of the pastor and teacher (I Timothy 4:1), coupled with a willingness to start at the beginning where sound doctrine is concerned, even as the risen Christ did with the doubting disciples, and to re-examine the reasons *why* Christians believe what they believe. Particularly recommended for intensive study are the doctrines of Biblical inspiration, the Trinity, Deity of Christ, Personality and Work of the Holy Spirit, the Atonement, Justification by faith and works and the Bodily Resurrection of Christ and of all mankind.

The great and true Trinitarian doctrine of God and the Deity of Jesus Christ should ceaselessly be inculcated in Christian minds so that the Lord's people may never forget that Jesus Christ is the core of God's plan for the ages. The facts that He vicariously died and bodily arose, thus vindicating His claim to Deity through obedience to the righteous character of both His Father's will and law, both of which He perfectly fulfilled at Calvary, must be perpetually emphasized.

It is a well-known fact that no antidote for poison is effective unless it is administered in time, and in the proper dosage prescribed by a competent physician. In like manner, Christian doctrine should not be taught in a dry, matter-of-fact way, as it so often is, but should be given in small doses over a long period. The treatment should begin at once, from the Sunday school level right through college and seminary where the need is urgent.

Christians must realize while the opportunity is yet ours that the teaching of sound doctrine does not predicate a dead orthodoxy. When properly understood, a living acceptance of and familiarity with doctrine form the giant pillars of truth upon which our faith rests, a familiarity which has always produced great leaders and effective workers for the proclamation of the Gospel of grace.

The evangelization of cultists is the task of the Christian church of which each Christian is a member, literally a part of the Body of Christ. Until this is recognized, and Christians are urged and encouraged by their pastors and leaders to forsake the portals of Hollywood and the domain of the great god, Television, etc., for door-to-door publishing of the Good News of God's love for a lost world in Jesus Christ, the evangelization of cultists will continue to be one of the great tragedies of the Christian church in our day. It is well and good for us to support foreign missions, and to send the light of God's Gospel around the globe, but it is quite another thing for us to begin here, where the demand is personal, challenging and equally rewarding. This challenge is cult evangelism, the mission field on *your* doorstep.

Chapter 19

THE ROAD TO RECOVERY

In the preceding chapters of this volume, we have studied and evaluated in the light of the Word of God the major non-Christian cults or sects which have consistently challenged the missionary outreach of the Church of Jesus Christ. All the groups which were discussed are admitted rivals of historic Christianity. The question then quite logically arises, "What action can the church take, in both the ecumenical and independent wings of Christendom, to meet the challenge of contemporary American cults?" It is the purpose of this chapter to outline, both a methodology and a plan whereby we may not only bring the inroads of the cults under control, but what is more important, to actually take positive steps to evangelize cultists, which of course is the primary task of the Christian church. By traveling what might be called "the road to recovery," the church may once again see the day when, by speaking the truth in love, but by speaking it with clarity, much of the ground lost to unchristian cults in the last century may be regained. It should never be forgotten that whatever a specific cult offers to attract individuals is infinitesimal compared with what Jesus Christ offers to the soul who will cast all his care upon Him. The church has nothing to fear from the cults as long as the church is faithful to her mission of both proclaiming and vigorously contending for, the faith that was once for all delivered unto the saints (Jude 3).

It is the feeling of the writer that if the following suggestions were put into immediate practice, both in the United States and on the foreign mission fields, a constructive approach to the mounting problem of cults would emerge.

PROJECT ONE — RESEARCH

In order to provide information of any type for the pastor, teacher, missionary, student or layman, it is vitally important that there be careful research into the background and theology of the major cult systems. There already exists a considerable amount of data which could be utilized, once it has been validated, codified and carefully weighed by mission agencies and field representatives of the major denominations and independent Christian groups. The average cultist is willing to listen to facts, particularly if they are at variance with what he has been taught, if only those facts, once he checks them, are shown to be accurate and reliable. We have seen more than a few Jehovah's Witnesses and Mormons, for instance, carefully re-evaluate their religion as a result of careful research on the part of interested Christians.

Secondly, a statistical breakdown of the growth and development of the major cult systems at home and abroad must be worked out, so that those areas where they have grown most rapidly may be plotted, and the factors contributing to that growth analyzed, in contrast to their lack of growth in other areas.

Thirdly, questionnaires must be sent out to key personnel in all Christian movements, seeking their reaction to the challenge of the cults in those areas under their jurisdiction. In this way, a broad perspective of cult methodology will be obtained.

Clipping services must also be utilized, for major population centers throughout the world are generally the targets of the major sects, and it is always helpful to know the coming and going of cult missionaries, as well as their planned area meetings (international conventions, missionary report sessions, special lectures, etc.).

Of course a research center dealing with cults is not a new proposal, but one that would collate and disseminate information to all Christian groups, ecumenical as well as independent, would go far beyond any proposals made by anyone to this date.

Through the facilities of what would essentially be a bureau of information on comparative religions, Christian leaders, missionaries and workers throughout the world would have ready access to information which is currently unavailable, except in limited quantity, at the present period. In the Christian Research Institute, and through the facilities of the *Religious Research Digest,* the writer has attempted to do this for the past five years. But the project is far too involved to be merely an independent effort. There must be cooperation, and the free interchange of information between all concerned Christian groups, followed by financial support, in order that any research project of such scope and magnitude succeed in its objective.

PROJECT TWO — SPECIALIZED LITERATURE

Just as the function of project one would be the collecting, sorting and condensing of usable facts and information, so project two would be its logical outgrowth, the publication and distribution and also the translation of such material on an international scale. The value of tracts, pamphlets and books printed and disseminated at cost, both in the United States and on those mission fields where specific cults are rapidly growing, is incalculable, as any foreign missionary will readily testify.

Through the facilities of such organizations as The American Tract Society, The New York Bible Society, The International Missionary Council, The Evan-

gelical Foreign Missions Association and numerous other interested groups, practically all missionaries would have information available for distribution to indigenous churches and to Christian workers on their respective fields, so that no longer would it be possible for such organizations as Jehovah's Witnesses and the Mormons to capitalize upon the absence of literature accurately describing their faith and refuting their claims.

In a survey conducted by the writer in 1958, in which more than 5000 missionaries and mission workers in seventeen countries were questioned about the provision and distribution of such literature, more than ninety-five per cent responded in the affirmative as to the need and wisdom of such an approach.

In South America alone, where the Mormons and the Jehovah's Witnesses, not to mention the indigenous animistic and spiritistic cults, exist in growing numbers and force of influence, preliminary surveys indicate that almost ninety per cent of those questioned not only desire, but earnestly request literature that will assist them in both refuting and evangelizing cults.

In the United States and Canada — where much headway is being made by cult systems — universities, colleges, seminaries, Bible institutes and local churches have consistently requested reliable literature from recognized denominational and independent sources. But very little has been forthcoming, because there has been no organization of research data, and very little funds to insure its publication and distribution. Special commissions should therefore be appointed, similar to that already sponsored by the World Council of Churches, so that independents and ecumenicists may pool their information, and erect a systematic defense against the proselyting of the cults. Though conservatives and liberals may disagree theologically, they suffer from the inroads of the cults individually, and yearly the ranks of American cultism are swelled by former Methodists, Episcopalians, Lutherans, Baptists, Congregationalists, etc., who attended both liberal and conservative churches until they were proselyted by the cults.

That there is a desperate need for literature and that it must be doctrinally oriented, no serious scholar in the field of cults will deny. But that such literature can be made available without the cooperation of interested churchmen, educators and lay readers, is quite dubious, if not impossible. The cults have captalized upon the fact that the Christian church has not made any really significant effort to halt their proselytizing techniques, and to answer their propaganda directed against all forms of Christianity. This has been, in no small measure, a contributing factor to their success. It is true that research will produce and has already produced considerable amounts of useful information, but its printing and distribution is a fundamental concern, if we are to deal effectively with the issues which face us.

PROJECT THREE — EDUCATIONAL RE-EVALUATION

Samuel Johnson, the great educator, once wrote, "The foundation of every state is the education of its youth," and we would do well to paraphrase this in the context of Christianity, "The future of the church is in the education of its leaders."

As a college professor, the writer has been deeply interested in the courses offered in Bible institutes, colleges and seminaries, as well as pre-theological schools, dealing with the subject of Comparative Religions, and particularly with non-Christian cults or sects. In this area, a very real problem exists, and it will do no good to let the matter rest with this observation. Rather, the facts, appalling as they may be, should be aired.

Since the advent of Christian missionary activities on an organized scale some 200 years ago, the proclamation of the Gospel message has faced many problems. Obstacles of language, culture, race, militant nationalism and the competition between missionaries of different doctrinal persuasions, have contributed a stormy atmosphere to world missions.

In addition to these difficulties, major non-Christian religions, such as Islam, Buddhism, Hinduism, Taoism, Shintoism, etc., have actively opposed Christian missionaries, so that progress has been slow in many areas, and in some instances, hardly recognizable.

Beyond this aspect however, looms, as we have mentioned, the formidable obstacle of non-Christian American cults, many of which are now world-wide. Some of these movements have proselytized new converts on already established fields with startling success. Utilizing the methods reminiscent of early Christianity, the cults cater to the culture patterns of those they proselytize, provide literature in the language of the people, and one way or another, keep a certain emphasis on the Bible in the forefront of their work. In many instances they preach a militant "separation" from tobacco, alcohol and other practices classified as worldly and unspiritual. All these activities are bolstered by their so-called revelations (all of 19th Century vintage), with an appeal to which they wage unceasing warfare against all religions, but against Christian denominations in particular. It is significant that they first approach known Christians. Seldom do they attempt to reach the unevangelized, which should be the first step in any genuine missionary program.

We are not to suggest that the activities of these movements be curtailed by law, or that they should become the target of an evangelical barrage of abuse. Full freedom of worship and the right to promulgate one's convictions are historic planks in the platform of Protestant evangelism. Even such terms as "sect" or "cult" seem more appropriate in lands with a State Church than in open religious situations. But Christianity will need to preserve the distinction between truth and heresy if it is to have a future. Some groups, particularly Jehovah's Witnesses, by their demonstrated hostility to governmental authorities, have frequently jeopardized the reputation and efforts of others of genuine Christian persuasion. As a result, there has been great friction between their workers and Christian missionaries. It is difficult indeed for Christian missionaries to compete successfully with such divisive forces in a positive way and to evangelize missionaries of such zealous groups as the Mormons, Jehovah's Witnesses and other virulent indigenous groups.

Now we might ask at this juncture, "What is being done to train Christian missionaries abroad (and, for that matter, pastors, teachers and leaders in the United States) to deal with this growing problem. On the educational level, are Christian institutions taking seriously the needs at home and on the mission fields? Are there mandatory courses for future Christian leaders to aid them in both evangelizing and refuting cultists?"

The cults continually emphasize the Bible, but despite the prominence given the Scriptures, without exception they place themselves in the roles of infallible interpreters of the Word of God, their dogmatism rivaled only by Jesuit scholars. Instead of being the infallible rule of faith and practice, the Bible is relegated to a secondary position. This is accomplished almost subliminally, so that the convert is unaware that his primary authority is not really grounded in Scripture, but rather in the interpretation of Scripture put forth by the respective cult.

Though this fact is well known among missionaries and Christian workers, it

apparently has not filtered back to seminaries, Bible colleges and Bible institutes. It is a fact that at present less than five per cent of all such institutions in the United States require as a prerequisite of graduation that a student take a course on comparative religions, or non-Christian American cults, a fact which staggers the imagination, when one can see the obvious inroads the cults have made both at home and abroad.

In a recent article, Prof. Gilbert Peterson, Chairman of the Department of Religious Education at the Philadelphia College of the Bible, made the following observations concerning the educational curricula of American Bible colleges, institutes and seminaries:

> Preparation is a word which is found to headline some newspapers, on the lips of statesmen, military leaders and educators as well as church leaders and mission board directors. It has taken on a significant meaning in our times as the threats of world leaders, nations and the varied ideologies of men vie for prominence in the world around us. Christian educators need to stop from time to time, and evaluate the preparation men and women are receiving in the various Christian schools of higher learning. . . .
> It is with a sense of great urgency that the graduates of Bible colleges, along with Christian young people from other educational backgrounds, face the task of living and witnessing to the truth of the Gospel in these troubled times. Each spring a new group of young people receive their diplomas or degrees to serve God as missionaries, both at home and on the foreign field.
> In a recent survey conducted, by the author, of over twenty-three Bible colleges in the United States and Canada, representing a total number of graduates in excess of 15,000, it was found that approximately twelve and one-half per cent of this number, or about 1900 individuals are presently serving on the foreign mission fields of the world. Our concern at present is not with the percentage of Bible college graduates going to the mission field, but rather, the preparation they receive in the area of formal cult apologetics before going to

the mission field.

In the past ten years the outreach of cults and isms through the mediums of radio, the printed page and missionary endeavors, has reached enormous proportions. The rapidity of their growth is traceable in large measure to the dearth of information among Christians in regard to what is being promulgated by the various cults on the one hand, and a failure to act upon the Scriptural command to resist them on the other. In the survey, questionnaires were sent to over fifty Bible colleges. In the twenty-three schools replying, there is great diversity of requirements in the section of the curriculum dealing with apologetics, cults and unchristian religions. The course most often required of all graduates was "Cults and Isms." The course usually entailed the study of the history and development of several cults, their doctrinal position and a refutation of their position from the Scriptures. Apologetics was next in order of numbers of requirements. This course covers a systematic presentation of the reasons and evidences of the Christian faith. The course offered most often was Comparative Religions, with nine schools offering it as an elective, three requiring it for all mission majors, and four schools requiring it of all graduates. This course covers a comparative study of the major living religions of the world.

In order to meet the challenge of our day in preparing our young people to face the present religious world situation, we need to realize what is being offered to the students in our Bible colleges, institutes and seminaries by way of preparing them to serve Christ in the midst of the rise of cultism. The following is offered as a suggestion as to how we might structure this one area of the curriculum. This is of course, not a final pronouncement, rather, a recommendation for exploration of this difficult field.

There is no substitute for a thorough knowledge of the Word of God and the truth of God which it reveals. Courses in direct Bible study and doctrine provide one with the necessary foundation. In addition to this, a three-hour course in Apologetics where the needs of men, the Christian answer to these needs, and the reasons for the uniqueness and truth of Christianity are presented.

It is not enough that one know only his own beliefs when faced by the average non-Christian and cultist, and therefore, following Apologetics there should be a three-hour course in Cults and Isms. This course, as previously suggested, would examine the historical and doctrinal development of such non-Christian groups as Jehovah's Witnesses, Christian Science, Mormonism, Unity and the like. The course would include the Christian answer to these systems and an evaluation of their terminologies, and an accurate, consistent method of approaching them with evangelism as the goal.

A course such as comparative religions could be offered on an elective basis, to give the student a broader view of non-Christian religions. When a student goes to the mission field, a far more detailed study of the religion of that particular field must be made by the missionary candidate, and can be made in comparative religions. Therefore, specialized courses should be offered in these fields. Also the training received in apologetics and cults along the lines of definitive terminology and doctrinal evaluation will prove extremely valuable.

At present, of the twenty-three Bible colleges reporting, ten offer a course in Apologetics, with six requiring it of all students; eleven schools offer a course in Cults, with seven requiring it of all students; sixteen schools offer a course in Comparative Religions, with three requiring it of all mission majors and four requiring it of all students.

This means that a little more than one-fourth of the Bible colleges replying already follow the suggested curriculum outlined or one very similar to it, and a little less than one-half of the reporting schools offer all three courses (Apologetics, Cults and Comparative Religions) in their present curriculums.[1]

Mr. Peterson's remarks are very much to the point, for when it is remembered that only eleven schools out of twenty-three offered courses on Cult Apologetics, and only seven out of those eleven required it for graduation, the situation is seen to be acute.

[1]*Religious Research Digest,* December, 1961, pages 8-11.

Now in the case of seminaries and Bible institutes in the United States, a detailed study now in preparation indicates even at this early date that the problem of non-Christian cults is not taken seriously by the majority.

Such information will not paint an encouraging picture to be sure, especially in the light of accelerated cult growth on our major mission fields.

Mission fields have the added problem of dealing with certain indigenous cults with strong nationalistic overtones, particularly in Africa and Asia. These groups amalgamate some of the teachings of Christianity with the older pagan religions, particularly animism and spiritism, and come equipped complete with their own special revelations and messiahs. The situation is particularly true in the Philippine Islands, Japan and Africa, where Christianity is caricatured as a "white man's religion," a Western import super-imposed on native cultural and religious patterns. Such an approach by the cults has been disastrously successful, particularly in South America, where in Brazil we have seen a resurgence of Spiritism on an unprecedented scale. *Time* Magazine recently devoted its religious section to comments by a Roman Catholic missionary deploring the inroads of the Spiritists on the Roman Catholic Church. Unfortunately, the same can be said also in respect to some Protestant agencies; so the problem is universal. In passing, it might be noted that the Roman Catholic Church has recently begun detailed research in the area of non-Christian cults and sects, so effective have been the methods of both American-based and indigenous cults in proselyting Roman Catholic converts.

On the basis of past performance, it is safe to prognosticate that within the next decade, all things remaining constant, the cults will intensify their propaganda activities to three or four times their present rate. The question is, will the Church of Jesus Christ rise to the occasion while time remains? The church must be prepared to defend the claims of Scripture interpreted by the Holy Spirit that it alone is "inspired by God and is profitable for doctrine, for reproof, for correction and for instruction in righteousness" (II Timothy 3:16).

The Christian church must also be ready to remind indigenous nationalistic sects that Christianity is an Eastern religion, that Christ was born, died and was resurrected in Asia, and ascended from the Mount of Olives; so it is anything but "a foreign religion." But if the cults are to be effectively dealt with at home and on the foreign mission fields of the world, then missionaries, pastors and particularly educators, who mold the curricula of Christian institutions, must press for strong curricula in those institutions. Christians must be taught not only what they believe, but why they believe it, that they may be able, as the Scripture admonishes us, "to be ready always to give an answer to every man that asketh you a reason of the hope that is in you with meekness and fear" (I Peter 3:15).

The teachings of the major sects must be codified and indexed, and a running commentary provided for all interested parties in the form of the publication of literature and perhaps a semi-annual journal. It will then be possible to understand the methodology of the cults at home and abroad, to note the areas of their doctrinal emphasis and growth and their use and abuse of Christian terminology. The Church of Jesus Christ, as we have noted, has nothing to fear from the zeal and competition of the cults, but she has much to fear from her own apathy and lethargy in this vital area of missionary concern. The means to evangelize and combat adherents of the cults can be made readily available to all interested parties. It remains for Christians of both ecumenical and independent persuasion to agree to cooperate in the dissemination of pertinent literature on this ever-growing field of mutual concern.

On every front the church is faced with unrelenting and mounting pressures from anti-Christian forces. Our Lord has warned us, "The night cometh when no man can work" (John 9:4), but the publication of literature may yet give us some time to work in the twilight which precedes the sunset.

It will do us little good, however, to sponsor research and to publish and distribute literature, if at the fountainhead of all Christian work, the educational preparation of Christian leadership, we do not revise the curricula of numerous Bible institutes, colleges and seminaries to meet the needs, both in the United States and on the mission field. So it appears that education, as always, is of vital significance.

PROJECT FOUR — CONFERENCES ON CULTS

A final suggestion to help implement support for a unified approach to the challenge of the cults is the sponsoring of specialized conferences or lectures on the local church level, at Bible conferences and in schools and seminaries, by competent students of the major cult systems. Such conferences would stimulate a great deal of interest, showing as they would by contrast, the differences between the teachings of the cults and historic Christianity. If conducted in a dignified, scholarly, and yet popular manner, with question and answer periods following each lecture, such conferences would serve a dual purpose. They would both explain the divergent doctrines of the cults and, at the same time, strengthen the faith of Christians in the great fundamental teachings of

Christianity. The author has been engaged in such a ministry for some years with considerable success, but much more yet remains to be done. For, as the Scripture reminds us, "The fields are white already to harvest, but the labourers are few. Pray ye therefore the Lord of the harvest, that He will send forth labourers" (John 4:35; Matthew 9:37, 38).

If the preceding suggestions were adopted and put into operation, it is the conviction of this writer that the major cult systems would soon feel the impact and receive the benefit of the unified Christian witness to the veracity of the faith which they have chosen to reject.

Through the use of good research material, properly disseminated and translated where possible into the language of the fields where the cults are most active, and aided by clipping services which would keep the research center informed of major cult efforts around the world, Christians of all denominations, as well as pastors, educators and missionaries would be kept abreast of the activities of the larger cult systems.

Concluding our observation then, the road to recovery will not be an easy one to travel, and will be fraught with problems and conflicts, but if we will begin to travel it, we will find at the end of it and along the way, those who have been delivered from the cults, those who have been dissuaded from joining them and those who have been both evangelized and strengthened by a determined effort of the Christian church not only to proclaim the message of redeeming grace, but to defend the claims and the Gospel of her Saviour. We can go a long way toward recovering the ground we have lost, but we must begin now.

APPENDIX:

THE PUZZLE OF SEVENTH-DAY ADVENTISM

PREFACE

In a volume such as this dealing with the problem of non-Christian cults, the question might be logically asked, "Why include Seventh-day Adventism, especially since the writer has classified them in a full-length volume as a Christian denomination?" (See *The Truth About Seventh-day Adventism,* Zondervan, 1960.)

The answer to this is that for over a century Adventism has borne a stigma of being called a non-Christian cult system. Whether or not this was justified in the early development of Adventism, I have already discussed at length in my earlier book, but it should be carefully remembered that the Adventism of 1965 is different in not a few places from the Adventism of 1845, and with that change the necessity of re-evaluation comes naturally.

It is my conviction that one cannot be a true Jehovah's Witness, Mormon, Christian Scientist, Unitarian, Spiritist, etc., and be a Christian in the Biblical sense of the term, but it is perfectly possible to be a Seventh-day Adventist and be a true follower of Jesus Christ despite certain heterodox concepts which will be discussed.

Such Christian leaders as Louis T. Talbot, M. R. DeHaan, John R. Rice, Anthony A. Hoekema, J. K. Van Baalen, Herbert Bird and John R. Gerstner have taken the position that Adventism is in fact a cult system; whereas, the late Donald Grey Barnhouse, myself, E. Schuyler English, and quite a few others have concluded the opposite.

Since the opposing view has had wide circulation over a long period of time, I felt it was necessary to include Seventh-day Adventism as a proper counter-balance — presenting the other side of Adventism and representing the theology of Adventism as the Adventists themselves believe it and not as many critics have caricatured it.

This, of course, is not to be construed in any sense of the term as an endorsement of the entire theological structure of Seventh-day Adventism, a portion of which is definitely out of the main stream of historic Christian theology and which I have taken pains to refute. But I believe it is only fair and ethical to consider both sides of an extremely difficult and provocative controversy which shows very little sign of abating in our day.

It was Dr. Donald Barnhouse who said that simply because a person is a member of a specific denomination there is no reason to suppose that the entire denomination is represented by that person's theology, nor is it proper to assume that because there are heretical Baptists, Presbyterians, Methodists, Episcopalians, etc., that all such denominations are therefore heretical.

To expand upon this we might say that simply because a denomination is Christian in its profession does not guarantee that all members of that denomination are Christian by their confession and experience. Hence, it is our position that Seventh-day Adventism as a denomination is essentially Christian in a sense that all denominations and groups professing Christianity are Christian if they conform to the classical mission of Christianity as given in the Bible and the creeds and counsels of the Christian church. But this does not mean that all Baptists, all Methodists, all Episcopalians, all Lutherans, or all Adventists are necessarily Christians. This is a matter between the individual and God and is to be viewed in the light of the revelation of Scripture and the testimony of the Holy Spirit.

This section on Seventh-day Adventism is an attempt to present for consideration facts which are little known in many areas and often distorted in others. It is an effort to examine, commend and criticize where necessary the theological structure of the Adventist denomination and is submitted with a prayerful hope that honest investigation, even if it does not agree with our preconceived notions, is to be encouraged and profited from, under the guidance of the Spirit of God.

360

THE HISTORICAL BACKGROUND OF SEVENTH-DAY ADVENTISM

Seventh-day Adventism sprang from the "great second advent awakening" which shook the religious world about the middle of the nineteenth century, when a reemphasis about the second advent of Jesus Christ was rampant in Britain and on the continent of Europe. Before long, many of the Old World views of prophetic interpretation crossed the Atlantic and penetrated American theological circles.

Based largely upon the apocalyptic books of Daniel and Revelation, the theology of the Advent Movement was discussed in the newspapers as well as in theological journals. New Testament eschatology competed with stock market quotations for front-page space, and the "seventy weeks," "twenty-three hundred days," and "the abomination of desolation"(Daniel 8, 9) were common subjects of conversation.

Following the chronology of Archbishop Ussher, and interpreting the 2300 days of Daniel as 2300 years, many Bible students of various denominations concluded that Christ would come back about the year 1843. Of this studious number was one William Miller, a Baptist minister and resident of Low Hampton, New York. The great second advent movement which swept the United States in the 1840's stemmed largely from the activities of this William Miller, who confidently taught in the year 1818, that in "about" twenty-five years, i.e., 1843, Jesus Christ would come again. As Miller himself put it, "I was thus brought in 1818 at the close of my two-year study of the Scriptures to the solemn conclusion that in about twenty-five years from that time all the affairs of our present state would be wound up."[1]

Miller further wrote,

I believe the time can be known by all who desire to understand and to be ready for His coming. And I am fully convinced that some time between March 21, 1843 and March 21, 1844, according to the Jewish mode of computation of time, Christ will come and bring all His saints with Him; and that then He will reward every man as His work shall be.[2]

At length his associates set October 22, 1844, as the final date when Jesus Christ would return for His saints, visit judgment upon sin, and establish the Kingdom of God upon earth.

One need only read the words of the Lord Jesus Christ to realize that Miller was teaching in contradiction to the Word of God. Jesus said, "But of that day and hour knoweth no man, no, not the angels of heaven, but my Father only" (Matthew 24:36; also 24:42; 24:44; 25:13).

The gospel of Mark also shows that dates cannot be set, for in verse 33 of chapter 13 our Lord stated, "Take ye heed, watch and pray: for ye know not when the time is." And almost His last words to His disciples are a rebuke to those who set dates: "It is not for you to know the times or the seasons, which the Father hath put in his own power" (Acts 1:7). Certainly this should have been deterrent enough for William Miller and his associates, but sad to say it was not.

Compare the two positions, Miller versus the Scriptures: God declared that no man would know the time; Miller stated that he did know the time. God said the times and seasons were within His own Power; the Millerites declared that they had the prophetic key to them. Jesus Christ stated, "No man knows the day or the hour," but the Millerites set the exact day (October 22, 1844). And history bears a bitter record of their terrible disappointment.

Lest anyone reading the various accounts of the rise of Millerism in the United States come to the conclusion that Miller and his followers were "crackpots" or "uneducated tools of Satan," the following facts should be known:[3] The great advent awakening movement which spanned the Atlantic from Europe was bolstered by a tremendous wave of contemporary Biblical scholarship. Although Miller himself lacked academic theological training, actually scores of prophetic scholars in Europe and the United States had espoused Miller's views before he himself announced it. In reality, his was only one more voice proclaiming the 1843/1844 fulfillment of Daniel 8:14, or the 2300 days period allegedly dating from 457 B.C. and ending in 1843-1844.

---

[1] Francis D. Nichol, *The Midnight Cry* (Washington, D. C.: Review and Herald, 1944), page 35.

[2] *Signs of the Times*, January 25, 1843.

[3] The various charges to the effect that the Millerites were fanatics who waited on rooftops attired in white "ascension robes" anticipating the return of Christ; and further that insanity swept the Millerite ranks in 1843-4 in the wake of the "Great Disappointment" are purely mythological in character and have little basis in verifiable facts. (See F. D. Nichol, *The Midnight Cry*, Review and Herald, Takoma Park, 1944, pages 321-498, for a documented study of the evidence.)

William Miller was born in Pittsfield, Massachusetts, on February 15, 1782, and while still a young child his family moved to Low Hampton, New York, close to the Vermont State borderline. Miller was raised by a deeply religious mother, but despite her zeal for his conversion Miller himself became a deist. Only after a soul-searching experience which culminated in his conversion did he begin his preparation for the ministry in the Baptist church. A great many books have been written about William Miller and the Millerite movement, but to this writer's knowledge none of them has justly accused Miller of being dishonest or deceptive in his prophetic interpretation of Scripture. Indeed, he enjoyed the reputation, among all who knew him, of being an honest, forthright Christian. One does not have to endorse the errors of Millerism, therefore, to respect the historical figure of William Miller. Regardless of his shortcomings, Miller was a deeply religious Christian who, had he had a more extensive understanding of the Scriptures, most probably would never have embarked upon his disastrous date-setting career.

Clearly it may be seen that although Miller popularized the 1843-1844 concept of Christ coming again, he was by no means alone. If we condemn him, we must also condemn a large number of internationally known scholars who were among the most highly educated men of their day. Yet they too had a blind spot in prophetic interpretation and endorsed this fallacious system of date-setting. Regardless of the number of scholars who confirmed his errors, however, the fact remains that Miller and the Millerite movement operated contrary to the express injunctions of Scripture. Both Miller and his followers lived to reap the reward of their foolhardy quest and to suffer crushing humiliation, ridicule and abject despair.

William Miller set the time for the return of the Lord between March 21, 1843, and March 21, 1844, reckoning according to the Jewish calendar.[4] As the first-named date approached, religious frenzy shook the Millerite world — the Lord was coming back!

Zealous and sincere though the followers of Miller were, stark disappointment awaited them as the Jewish year 1843 faded from time and the Lord did not come. When the dream closest to their hearts failed to materialize, they eagerly sought enlightenment from William Miller, who replied with characteristic honesty. Wrote Miller, in the very shadow of spiritual anguish:

Were I to live my life over again, with the same evidence that I then had, to be honest with God and man I should have to do as I have done. Although opposers said it would not come, they produced no weighty arguments. It was evidently guess-work with them; and I then thought, and do now, that their denial was based more on an unwillingness for the Lord to come than on any arguments leading to such conclusion. I confess my error, and acknowledge my disappointment; yet I still believe that the Day of the Lord is near, even at the door; and I exhort you, my brethren, to be watchful and not let that day come upon you unawares.[5]

In the wake of this stunning declaration, the Millerites strove vainly to reconcile their interpretations of the prophetic Scripture with the stark truth that Christ had not returned. With one last gasp, so to speak, Miller reluctantly endorsed "The Seventh-month Movement," or the belief that Christ would come on October 22, 1844, the tenth day of the seventh month according to the Karaite reckoning of the Jewish Sacred Calendar.[6] Once again the Millerites' hopes were lifted, and October 22, 1844, became the watchword for the return of the Lord Jesus Christ. The outcome can best be summed up in the words of Dr. Josiah Litch, a Millerite leader in Philadelphia, who wrote on October 24: "It is a cloudy and dark day here — the sheep are scattered — the Lord has not come yet."[7]

From Litch's statement, it is easy to piece together the psychological framework of the Millerites in the wake of these two disappointments. They were a shattered and disillusioned people — Christ had not come to cleanse the "sanctuary" (the earth), to usher in judgment, and to bring the world into subjugation to the "everlasting gospel." Instead, the sky was cloudy and dark, and the historical horizons were black with the failure of the Millerite movement. There was, of course, terrible confusion, of which God, Scripture tells us, is not the author (I Corinthians 14:33).

The final phase of the movement, then, closed with the *Great Disappointment of 1844*, but as the Millerites disbanded,

[4]*The Midnight Cry*, page 169.
[5]Sylvester Bliss, *Memoirs of William Miller*, page 256.

[6]*The Midnight Cry*, page 243.
[7]*The Midnight Cry*, page 256.

there emerged other groups, such as the First-day Adventists. However, in our study we are concerned primarily with three segments which later fused to produce the Seventh-day Adventist denomination. William Miller, it should be noted, was *never* a Seventh-day Adventist and stated that he had "no confidence" in the "new theories" which emerged from the shambles of the Millerite movement. Dr. LeRoy Froom, professor of prophetic interpretation at the Seventh-day Adventist Theological Seminary, Takoma Park, Washington, D. C., in the fourth volume of his masterful series *The Prophetic Faith of our Fathers*, pages 828-29,[8] succinctly states exactly what Miller's position was:

Miller was outspokenly opposed to the various new theories that had developed following October 22, 1844, in an endeavor to explain the disappointment. He deplored the call to come out to the churches that had been given, and he never accepted the distinctive positions of the Sabbatarians. The doctrine of the unconscious sleep of the dead and the final destruction of the wicked was not, he maintained, part of the original Millerite position, but was introduced personally by George Storrs and Charles Fitch. He even came to deny the application of the parable in *The Midnight Cry* to the Seventh-month Movement and eventually went so far as to declare unequivocally that the movement was not "a fulfillment of prophecy in any sense."

Aside from chronological speculation, therefore, the theology of William Miller differed from Seventh-day Adventist theology in three distinct points: he denied the Seventh-day Sabbath, the doctrine of the sleep of the soul, and the final, utter destruction of the wicked — all doctrines held by the Seventh-day Adventist denomination. And he never embraced the "sanctuary" and "investigative judgment" theories developed by Seventh-day Adventists. For William Miller the era of chronological speculation was over, and he died shortly after the fiasco, a broken and disillusioned man who was, nevertheless, honest and forthright when in error or when repudiating error. I believe he now enjoys the presence of the Lord whose appearing he so anxiously awaited.

In order to understand the background of Seventh-day Adventist history and theology, let us look at the three segments of

Millerism which eventually united to form the Seventh-day Adventist denomination. Each of these groups held a distinctive doctrine. The group headed by Hiram Edson in western New York proclaimed the doctrine of the sanctuary "as embracing a special or final ministry of Christ in the Holy of Holies in the *heavenly* sanctuary," thus giving new meaning to the message, "The Hour of God's Judgment has come." The second group, headed by Joseph Bates, whose main following was in Massachusetts and New Hampshire, advocated the observance of the Seventh-day "as involved in the keeping of the commandments of God." The third group, in Maine, emphasized the "spirit of prophecy" or "the testimony of Jesus," which they believed was to be manifest in the "remnant" (Revelation 14:6-12; also Revelation 12:17, 19:10), or "the last segment of God's church of the centuries." Between the years of 1844 and 1847 the thinking of these groups crystallized and was actively declared and promulgated in the writings of their respective leaders, Hiram Edson, O. R. L. Crosier, Joseph Bates, James White and Ellen G. White.

At this point in our historical analysis of Seventh-day Adventism, we believe it will be profitable to briefly review *The Great Disappointment of 1844* and its relationship to the Seventh-day Adventist doctrines of the heavenly sanctuary and the investigative judgment. The entire superstructure of the Millerites' prophetic interpretation was based upon their view of the book of Daniel, chapters eight and nine, with particular emphasis upon Daniel 8:14 and 9:24-27. The Millerites believed that the prophecy of the seventy weeks of Daniel nine must date from the year 457 B.C., which, as recent archaeological evidence confirms,[9] was the exact date of the decree of King Artaxerxes to rebuild Jerusalem (Daniel 9:25). Tracing the seventy weeks of Daniel on the theory that, as the Hebrew indicated, it should be rendered "seventy weeks of years" or 490 years, the Millerites arrived at the date A.D. 33; that is from 457 B.C. to A.D. 33. Since this date reliably refers to Christ's crucifixion, Millerites then linked it to Daniel 8:14, "Unto two thousand and three hundred days; then shall the sanctuary be cleansed" with the seventy weeks of years prophecy, and the 2300 days became 2300 years. Thus if you subtract 490 years (adding of course, A.D. 1 to 33)

8Review and Herald Pubishing Association, Takoma Park, Washington, D. C., 1950.

9*The Chronology of Ezra 7,* Siegfried H. Horn and Lynn H. Wood, Review and Herald Publishing Association, Takoma Park, Washington, D. C., 1953.

the figure 1843 is arrived at. Many Biblical scholars have historically shown that in Scripture a day frequently symbolizes a year; further, that the seventy weeks and 2300 days of Daniel could have begun on the same date. And that date, according to the Millerites, was 457 B.C. In *The Prophetic Faith of Our Fathers*, Dr. LeRoy Froom shows that many expositors had embraced the same method of interpretation, which is no argument for accepting it, but a strong argument for the *right* of the Millerites to do so.

As we have seen, when the Millerite calculations failed, all appeared to be lost; but a singular event took place the very next day in a cornfield near Port Gibson, New York, which changed the face of Adventist history and brought about a reinterpretation of the eighth and ninth chapters in the book of Daniel, an interpretation which is a keystone in the arch of the Seventh-day Adventist view of prophecy.

On October 23, 1844, the morning following the *Great Disappointment*, Hiram Edson, a devout Adventist and follower of William Miller, was wending his way homeward with his friend, O. R. L. Crosier. In order to avoid the mocking gazes and taunts of their neighbors, they cut across a cornfield.

As they walked through the cornfield in deep silence and meditation, Hiram Edson stopped, became more deeply immersed in meditation, and then with upturned face indicative of a heartfelt prayer for spiritual light, he suddenly received a great spiritual "revelation." In the words of Dr. Froom,

> Suddenly there burst upon his mind the thought that there were two phases to Christ's ministry in the Heaven of Heavens, just as in the earthly sanctuary of old. In his own words, an overwhelming conviction came over him "that instead of our high priest coming out of the most holy of the heavenly sanctuary to come to this earth on the tenth day of the seventh month at the end of the twenty-three hundred days, He for the first time entered on that day the second apartment of that sanctuary, and that He had a work to perform in the most holy before coming to this earth."[10]

In that instant, according to Seventh-day Adventist history, Hiram Edson found the reason why the Millerites had been disappointed the day before. They had expected Christ to come to earth to cleanse the sanctuary, but the sanctuary was not the earth but was located in Heaven! Instead of coming to earth, therefore, Christ had passed from one "apartment" of the sanctuary into the other "apartment" to perform a closing work now known as the "investigative judgment." In the year 1846 this new interpretation of Daniel was convincingly put forth by O. R. L. Crosier,[11] who outlined and defended Hiram Edson's concept in a lengthy article in a special number of *The Day Star*, a Millerite publication in Cincinnati, Ohio. F. D. Nichol in *The Midnight Cry* refers to "a fragment" which Edson wrote about his experience in the cornfield. But as Dr. Froom has pointed out, Edson himself really believed that Christ had passed from the "holy place" to the "most holy" place in the heavenly sanctuary. The Old Testament tabernacle was divided by a veil into two apartments, the holy place, and the most holy place. In the most holy place was the Ark of the Covenant. Into this apartment the high priest went once a year to sprinkle blood upon the mercy seat to make atonement for the sins of the people. In Christian theology, this blood symbolized prophetically the death of the Lord Jesus Christ, the Lamb of God, for the sins of all the world.

Transferring this Old Testament ceremonial to the New Testament, and making an extremely literalistic interpretation of the book of Hebrews, Edson and Crosier formulated the doctrine of "the heavenly sanctuary and investigative judgment." This concept, now understood to mean that in 1844 Christ entered the "second phase" of His ministry in the heavenly sanctuary, and ever since has been reviewing the cases of believers to determine their worthiness for eternal life (a rather literalistic Arminian interpretation). Further, He will come forth from the "second apartment," or finish the "second phase" of His ministry in the sanctuary, to usher in judgment upon the world at His great second advent. This in essence was the interpretation which shaped the later concept of the "heavenly sanctuary" and the "investiga-

---

[10]*The Prophetic Faith of Our Fathers*, Vol. IV, page 881. An extremely literalistic concept, which is refuted by Hebrews 9:12, 24 and Acts 1, which show that at His ascension Christ entered into the "holy places" not the "second apartment" of the heavenly sanctuary in 1844. Seventh-day Adventists have re-defined their teaching in terms of "phases." See *Questions on Doctrine*, page 381.

[11]Crosier later rejected this concept though it was endorsed by Ellen G. White and other prominent Adventist leaders. (See D. M. Canright, *Life of Mrs. E. G. White*, page 107; also, *A Word to the Little Flock* (pamphlet), pages 11-12.)

tive judgment" in Seventh-day Adventist theology. Thus, good Millerite-Adventists were justified in endorsing the work of William Miller. They even maintained that God had allowed Miller to make mistakes for the greater blessing of the "little flock." In her *Early Writings* Ellen G. White made this assertion:

I have seen that the 1843 chart was directed by the hand of the Lord, and that it should not be altered; that the figures were as He wanted them, that His hand was over and hid a mistake in some of the figures so that none could see it until His hand was removed (page 74).

In this context Mrs. White was distinctly referring to Fitch's prophetic chart utilized by the Millerites, which led them to the year 1843 instead of the date which she considered to be correct—October 22, 1844.

F. D. Nichol in *Ellen G. White and Her Critics* (pages 332-34), attempts to explain Mrs. White's statement in the light of Acts 24, Mark 16, Exodus 8:15 and Exodus 10. Of course any are at liberty to accept his interpretation of the problem, which I do not. The fact remains, however, that the Millerites erred in their prophetic, chronological interpretation of the book of Daniel, and only the concept of Hiram Edson in the cornfield and the explanatory writings of O. R. L. Crosier buttressed by the "revelations" of Ellen G. White saved the day.

Although I do not accept Ellen White's explanation, or the interpretations of Edson, Crosier, Froom or Nichol, I would be at a loss to account for the growth and development of Seventh-day Adventism apart from the psychological framework of the *Great Disappointment of 1844*. Therefore, I have carefully reviewed the doctrines which evolved from the Edson-Crosier-White pronouncements and set forth the results in chapter six of my book, *The Truth About Seventh-day Adventism*. Suffice it to say here that the psychological factor is very important in Seventh-day Adventist history.

The second of the three Millerite-Adventist groups mentioned, is also of great historical import. In Fairhaven, Massachusetts, following the *Great Disappointment of 1844*, one Joseph Bates, a retired sea captain, issued a 48-page pamphlet entitled *The Seventh-day Sabbath a Per-*

petual Sign (1846). In it he argued for the Sabbath as a divine institution ordained in Eden, prefigured in Creation, and buttressed at Mt. Sinai. Some three years later Bates wrote a second pamphlet entitled, *A Seal of the Living God*, based largely upon Revelation 14:9-12. Bates' Sabbatarianism exerted a great influence upon what later became the Seventh-day Adventist denomination.

In Volume IV of *The Prophetic Faith of Our Fathers* (pages 957-58), Dr. Froom sums it up:

This became henceforth a characteristic and separating feature of Sabbatarian Adventist preaching. Bates here held that the message of Revelation 14 is the foundation of the full Advent message "Fear God and give glory to Him, for the hour of His judgment is come." This, he maintained, began to be fulfilled in the preaching of the Millerite movement. And the second angel's message on the fall of Babylon, with its climax in the call "Come out of her my people" was likewise initially sounded in 1843-1844 . . . They must not stop with the first two messages. There is a third inseparable in the series to be received and obeyed — namely, full obedience to God's holy commandments, including the observance of the Seventh day as a Sabbath. But that obedience is by faith. The Sabbath was next set forth as the "seal of God" as based on the sealing work of Revelation 7. On January 8, 1849, Bates issued his tract, "A Seal of the Living God." From the fact of John's declaration that the number of sealed was 144,000, Bates drew the conclusion that the "remnant" who keeps the commandments of God and have the testimony of Jesus Christ would number 144,-000.[12] So, to the concept of Christ entering the most holy place in the heavenly sanctuary on October 22, 1844, for the final work of judgment and the receiving of His kingdom, was added the Sabbath as involved in the third of this commission series of special "latter-day" messages. This concept of the "seal" was likewise built into the message of the Sabbath, as an added prophetic element. And this thought was similarly attested by Ellen White who wrote: "This seal is the Sabbath," and described the "most holy place" in which was the ark (Revelation 11:9).

---

[12]A position held by Uriah Smith and certain earlier Adventists, long since repudiated by the denominational leadership and majority of members.

containing the Ten Commandments with a halo of light surrounding the fourth! Thus the Sabbath and the sanctuary became inseparably tied together.

The third group, which fused with the other two to form the Seventh-day Adventist church, emphasized "the spirit of prophecy" (Revelation 19:10). This body of former Millerites accepted the interpretations of one Ellen G. Harmon of Portland, Maine. Ellen Harmon, later Mrs. James White, was recognized by this group as the possessor of the "Spirit of Prophecy," a restoration of the spiritual gift of prophecy (I Corinthians 12) or counsel to the Seventh-day Adventist church. Mrs. White had numerous visions which confirmed many Adventist doctrines. When the Edson-Crosier, Bates, and White adherents joined forces, the Seventh-day Adventist denomination was launched.

Although the name "Seventh-day Adventist" denomination was not officially assumed until 1860 at a conference held in Battle Creek, Michigan, nevertheless Seventh-day Adventism had been launched. In 1855, Adventist headquarters were established in Battle Creek and remained there until 1903, when they were transferred to Takoma Park, Washington, D.C.

The three distinctive doctrines of Seventh-day Adventism — the Sabbath, the Sanctuary and the "Spirit of Prophecy" — will be discussed later. The Adventists had a definite theological platform, which for many years remained almost constant. In recent years, however, there has been a definite movement toward a more explicit declaration of belief in the principles of the Christian faith and the tenets of Christian theology. In short, "clarification" and "redefinition" have characterized recent Seventh-day Adventist theological activites.

Today the Seventh-day Adventist denomination numbers over 1,250,000 adult baptized members, while they have over 1,600,000 Sabbath school members throughout the world. There are some 6,300 ordained ministers and more than 3,500 licensed ministers. The Adventists have 44 publishing houses producing literature in approximately 225 languages, while they are preaching and teaching in about 800 languages and dialects. They publish 385 periodicals and more than 60 new books yearly, and have enrolled more than 3,000,000 persons in their Bible study courses offered over the radio. Their *Voice of Prophecy* radio program is heard on 880 stations and is reaching people in some 75 languages. *Faith for Today* their official TV program is heard on 183 stations in the

U.S. and many stations abroad. The *Signs of the Times* and *These Times* their largest missionary magazines have a combined circulation of 420,000 copies a month.

During 1963 Seventh-day Adventists contributed more than $85,000,000 for their church work at home and abroad, while the literature sales of the denomination amounted to $24,000,000. They contributed on the average of over $226 per person. In addition the Adventists maintain 230 medical units employing over 490 doctors in 110 sanitariums and hospitals with 124 clinics and dispensaries. They have numerous medical launches in areas like the Amazon, and welfare projects all over the globe.

It is interesting to note by way of contrast that the average per capita contribution for all denominations in the United States is $48.81! Though still a relatively small denomination, the Seventh-day Adventists are said to have actually more missionaries active on foreign fields than any other mission body except Methodists who have a few over 1,600; the Adventists in excess of 1,500.

To round out the picture where this zealous group is concerned, it should be remembered that Adventists have a working force of more than 46,000 with a total of 12,600 churches organized into 425 conferences and union conferences. The Adventist school system comprising 5,226 schools and colleges employs more than 12,000 teachers. Approximately 295,000 students are attending their schools.

We cannot hope to cover the entire scope of Seventh-day Adventism's historical development in this brief résumé but we see that from meager beginnings in the wake of the *Great Disappointment of 1844* and the collapse of the Millerite movement, the Seventh-day Adventist denomination has pressed forward and expanded until today it constitutes an important albeit controversial segment of American Protestantism.

Although this is but a background sketch, the reader can readily see that in Seventh-day Adventism, religious historians have an interesting subject for study, a subject from which many unusual theological speculations have emerged and continue to emerge.

PSYCHOLOGICAL FACTORS

One of the principal problems in understanding the Seventh-day Adventist movement is to discover the psychological motivation and basis of this thriving denomination of zealots.

I. Early Handicaps

From the beginning, the Adventists were regarded with grave suspicion by the great majority of evangelical Christians, principally because the Seventh-day Adventists were premillennial in their eschatology. That is, they believed that Christ would come before the millennium and so placed themselves squarely in opposition to the predominant post- and a-millennial schools of thought of that era. The *Great Disappointment of 1844* and the collapse of the Millerite movement, naturally brought premillennialism into disrepute. Certain authors of the time considered premillennarians "peculiar" even to the point of condemning premillennialism outright and dubbed as "Adventists" all who held that view of eschatology. This is especially interesting when we consider that premillennialism is an accepted school of thought in eschatology today and that those who hold postmillennial and amillennial views are considered by the premillennarians to be peculiar.

Thus the Adventists started out with two great psychological handicaps: They had incurred disapproval of the group or the main-stream of Christianity and the Millerites from which they sprang had been publicly humiliated by the failure of their chronological calculations. These two factors and the constant jeering by opposing schools of eschatology united the Seventh-day Adventists in a closely-knit group, habitually on the defensive and suspicious of the motives and intentions of other Christians.

Moreover, the Adventists were drawn together by the "special truths" of the Advent message. They were convinced that they had a proclamation for the world — a great "last-day message." Later we shall describe how this attitude widened the chasm between Adventists and Christians of other denominations, so it is sufficient here to note that the Adventists considered themselves a special "remnant people" ordained by God to revive certain neglected truths of the Christian message. Filled with burning zeal to fulfill this mission, they laid themselves open to serious misunderstanding by Christians of other denominations who did not agree with them about the proper day of worship, the state of the dead, and investigative judgment.

Engaged in open conflict with Christians of virtually all denominations, the Adventists retreated into an "exclusivistic shell," despising what they termed "certain antinomian tendencies in contemporary Christian theology." They laid strong emphasis upon man's responsibility to the moral law of God, which eventually brought upon them the label, "Galatianists" or "legalists." Now, as we shall see, there can be little doubt that there was and still is legalism in Adventism, as in other Christian communions; but when we consider these early psychological factors, certain of which still obtain today, their reactions are understandable, though hardly defensible.

Of course the aforementioned "neglected" truths made few friends for the Adventists with Christians of other denominations, mainly because these truths were frequently presented in such manner as to arouse opposition instead of inviting investigation. Seventh-day Adventism has woefully demonstrated many times the old but true adage, "Not what we say but how we say it makes or breaks a case."

II. Identity Concealed

In his book, *Answers to Objections*, F. D. Nichol demonstrates how the psychological defense which Adventists erected in their early days has carried over into modern times. Nichol quotes the charge:

When Seventh-day Adventist ministers go into a community to hold a series of lectures they conceal at first their denominational connection. They thus hope to draw into their audience people who would never have come if they knew Seventh-day Adventists were conducting the meetings. This is a form of deception. There is something the matter with a religious body that is afraid to identify itself as soon as it begins to carry on any activity in a community.

Nichol answers:

Now it is a fact that during most of the history of the Seventh-day Adventist church, the very word Adventist has conveyed to the minds of most people a picture of a deluded band of fanatics sitting on housetops in ascension robes, awaiting the opening of the heavens. This story of ascension robes has become a part of American folklore and has been embalmed in impressive encyclopedias. And the ascension robe story is only part of the fanciful picture that has come to the minds of many when they have heard the word Adventist.

The ascension robe story is a myth, and ninety-nine percent of related stories are likewise myths — as has now been proved — but that has not prevented people from believing them. The net result has been that many people have seen Seventh-day Adventists only through the distorting mists of slanderous myths. This is nothing new in religious history; witness, for example, the early history of the Quakers and the Baptists.

It should not be difficult, therefore, for any reasonable person to see why Adventist ministers through the past years have sought first to cause people to see them simply as Christian preachers before announcing their Adventist connection. After all, we seek to be first, and before all else, Christian preachers of righteousness. Then we hope to build on the timely messages from Bible prophecy that may be described in the words of the Apostle Peter as "present truth" for these last days of earth's history.

It has undoubtedly been true in years past that Adventists could not have gotten a crowd out to hear them in certain cities, at least, if they had revealed their identity at the outset. But we think that that proves not the weakness of the Adventist case, but the strength of distorted ideas founded on fanciful myths. The other side of the picture is that many people, after they have attended Adventist meetings for a time, frankly admit that they have changed their ideas about us and are glad that they first came to the meetings not knowing who was conducting them.

In more recent years our activities have become so much better known that in many places the former distorted picture has been largely corrected. Accordingly, we are increasingly following the plan of announcing at the outset the Adventist sponsorship of the public meetings.[13] That is what we like to do, and what we hope ere long to be able to do everywhere. We are not ashamed of our Adventism, far from it . . . No, we don't want to boast, we simply want to proclaim to the world a message that we earnestly believe should be given at this time. And if, in order to secure an initial hearing, we must at first conceal

the name, we do so for a brief period only with a view to a clear-cut announcement of our Adventist connections a little later in the meetings. Then those who have been coming may decline to come further, if they desire. They generally decide to stay!

Unhappily, as the literature of many objectors to Adventism reveals, it is they who have often been most active in spreading the distorting myths regarding us. And then they are wont to add, as though to prove conclusively their case against us, that we sometimes fail to reveal our Adventist connection at the outset of a series of evangelistic lectures! If they will help us to clear away completely the slanderous myths which folklore has often thrown around the name Adventist, we will be most happy to preface every one of our public meetings with the announcement of its Adventist sponsorship! In the meantime we shall, in such instances and areas as the situation necessitates, follow the precedent set by our Lord's instruction to His disciples as regards the time of disclosing our name (pages 421-22).

Thus we see that some Adventist leaders, at least, maintain the premise that everyone's prejudice against them is based on myths and folklore, and on the fact that they deliberately disguise themselves until they can obtain a hearing and demonstrate that they are Christians. These practices have given rise to the charge of proselyting and it is not without foundation. In general, however, Nichol makes some very good points, though inadvertently he reveals only too clearly that he and many Adventists have been reared in this unhealthy climate of distrust, prejudice and suspicion.

Nichol declares,

If they will help us clear away completely the slanderous myths that folklore has so often thrown around the name Adventist, we will be most happy to preface every one of our public meetings with the announcement of its Adventist sponsorship!

---

[13]Research has revealed that in some cases this is true. However, it is encouraging to note that the *Voice of Prophecy*, the official Seventh-day Adventist radio program, and *Faith for Today*, as well as *It Is Written*, both Seventh-day Adventist TV programs, have publicly identified themselves to offset the charge of concealment. These are singular instances of keeping faith with their statements that they have nothing to hide as Adventists and wish to deceive no one. The literature program has not kept pace with radio or TV and will undoubtedly take time for full identification. In certain instances disclosure of denominational ties has been withheld by denominations other than Seventh-day Adventists, particularly on the mission field and this chiefly because Adventists as well as some other Christian denominations believe that in certain sections of the world where Protestantism, or even Christianity is looked upon with contempt, that it is in harmony with the Word of God that they do not make too prominent their identification in the beginning. This is done to avoid prejudice and false accusations which might hinder the honest in heart from hearing the Gospel of Jesus.

The only difficulty with Nichol's statement is that the burden of proof lies not upon the other denominations, but upon the Adventists themselves. By openly identifying themselves, they can refute these charges of deception and proselyting.

On page 420, Nichol makes the mistake of using passages in the gospel of Matthew (8:4; 9:30; 16:20) where Christ enjoined secrecy, to prove that Adventists are only following Him when they conceal their identity, and he unfortunately tries to establish that such a behavior pattern on the part of Adventists is "honorable." Says Nichol,

> We have yet to hear any devout Christian expressing misgivings and doubts about the ministry of Christ or declaring that He was ashamed or afraid because He concealed His identity for a time. Evidently, then, this much at least may be established at the outset as being proved by these texts; concealing one's identity is not an insult or proof that one is either ashamed or afraid. There may be honorable and altogether reasonable grounds for such concealment.

Although Nichol's argument appears plausible, the cases are not parallel, for over against the incidents which he cites, the Lord Jesus did many miracles in public and taught openly in the Temple as He Himself declared before Caiaphas (John 18:20). But to compare the motives of Adventists with the motives of the Lord Jesus Christ is just a bit more than I am willing to concede.

True, there is much misinformation about Adventist history and theology, but not infrequently it can be traced to unfortunate statements in their own official publications. Although other denominations are likewise guilty, Adventists have largely been outside the main stream of Christian fellowship and so are in an unenviable position. They must go the "second mile" in this respect.

It is evident, then, that because of the opposition and abuse suffered in their early days, and also because of the "special truths" of the Advent message and emphasis upon certain areas of theology, the Adventists have been at a distinct psychological disadvantage and so have tended to band together against other churches. Other denominations, of course, have encouraged this recluse-like behavior

by endless repetition of some of the Millerite myths. These factors, therefore, must be soberly evaluated if we are to understand Seventh-day Adventism.

ADVENTIST THEOLOGY AND CLASSICAL ORTHODOXY

For many years Seventh-day Adventists have been handicapped by the lack of a comprehensive volume which adequately defines their doctrinal position. Many publications clearly set forth certain aspects of Adventism, particularly the writings of F. D. Nichol, L. E. Froom and Ellen G. White, whose role is that of inspired commentator and "messenger" to the Adventist denomination.

Except for the brief statement of fundamentals in the Seventh-day Adventist Yearbook the average Adventist has been somewhat at a loss to explain conflicting theological opinions within his denomination, and even expressions in the writings of Ellen G. White were in certain context so ambiguous as to frustrate even the most devout believer. As a result of this, in 1957 the General Conference of Seventh-day Adventists released the first definitive and comprehensive explanation of their faith, an authoritative volume entitled *Questions on Doctrine.*

This book truthfully presents the theology and doctrine which the leaders of Seventh-day Adventism affirm they have always held. Members of other denominations will find it a reliable source to consult when seeking to understand what the Adventists themselves describe as "the position of our denomination" in the area of church doctrine and prophetic interpretation."[14]

There can be no doubt of the fact that there are conflicting statements in Adventist publications and diverse opinions about certain areas of Adventist theology and interpretation, some of which is quite the opposite of classical orthodox Christianity; but this situation is not peculiar to the Adventist since all Christian denominations have various "wings" in most instances quite vocal, which are a source of constant embarrassment because they represent their own particular interpretations of the denomination's theology as the viewpoint of the denomination itself.

It is therefore unfair to quote any one Adventist writer or a group of writers as representing "the position of our denomination in the area of church doctrine and prophetic interpretation" even though the writings of such persons may in a large area qualify as Adventist theology. One must consult in good faith what the denomination itself represents as its theology and assume that the Seventh-day Adventist theologians know better than non-Adventists the implications and conclusions which they are willing to admit as representative of their church's theology.

This section is divided into several parts, each of which contains statements of the official Adventist position of particular aspects of theology and is thoroughly documented from the primary source material providing questions on doctrine. It is hoped that the reader will weigh carefully the declarations of the Seventh-day Adventist Church as represented by its general conference which alone is empowered to speak for the denomination. They have spoken in *Questions on Doctrine* and their statements should be examined in the light of honest scholarship and Christian ethics.

It is unnecessary to document at great length the fact that Seventh-day Adventism adheres tenaciously to the foundational doctrines of Christian theology as these have been held by the Christian church throughout the centuries. Dr. Anthony Hoekema who believes that Seventh-day Adventism is a non-Christian cult makes this interesting admission, and since Dr. Hoekema is no friend of Adventism, his testimony on this point could hardly be called prejudiced:

. . . I am of the conviction that Seventh-day Adventism is a cult and not an evangelical denomination. . . . It is recognized with gratitude that there are certain soundly Scriptural emphases in the teaching of Seventh-day Adventism. We are thankful for the Adventists' affirmation of the infallibility of the Bible, of the Trinity and of the full deity of Jesus Christ. We gratefully acknowledge their teachings on creation and providence, on the incarnation and resurrection of Christ, on the absolute necessity for regeneration, on sanctification by the Holy Spirit, and on Christ's literal return.[15]

It is puzzling to me, as a student of non-Christian cult systems, how any group can hold the above doctrines in their proper Biblical context which Dr. Hoekema admits the Adventists do and still be a non-Christian cult! However, we shall deal with this aspect of the critics of Adventism at the end of the chapter, therefore, suffice it to say that the Adventists do have

a clean bill of health where the major doctrines of Christian theology are involved.

Lest there be any doubt on the subject, the following quotations taken from *Questions on Doctrine* forthrightly declare the Seventh-day Adventist position in relation to historic Christianity as well as those areas where Adventism differs from the orthodox Christian position.

I. *Inspiration and Authority of the Scriptures*

1. "Seventh-day Adventists believe that 'all Scripture,' both Old and New Testament, from Genesis to Revelation, was 'given by inspiration of God' (2 Tim. 3:16), and constitutes the very word of God — the truth that 'liveth and abideth for ever' (1 Pet. 1:23). We recognize the Bible as the ultimate and final authority on what is truth" (page 26).

2. "Seventh-day Adventists hold the Protestant position that the Bible and the Bible only is the sole rule of faith and practice for Christians. We believe that all theological beliefs must be measured by the living Word, judged by its truth, and whatsoever is unable to pass this test, or is found to be out of harmony with its message, is to be rejected" (page 28).

3. "The eternal heavenly dignitaries — God, and Christ, and the Holy Spirit. . . . We are to cooperate with the three highest powers in heaven, — the Father, the Son and the Holy Ghost, — and these powers will work through us, making us workers together with God" (page 646).

II. *The Nature of Christ*

1. "Jesus Christ is very God, and He has existed with the Father from all eternity" (page 22).

2. "Christ, the Word of God, became incarnate through the miraculous conception and the virgin birth; and He lived an absolutely sinless life here on earth" (page 22).

3. "Christ is called the Second Adam. In purity and holiness, connected with God and beloved by God. He began where the first Adam began. Willingly He passed over the ground where Adam fell, and redeemed Adam's failure" (page 650).

4. "In taking upon Himself man's nature in its fallen condition, Christ did not in the least participate in its sin. He was subject to the infirmities and weaknesses by which man is encompassed. . . . He was touched with the feeling of our infirmities, and was in all points tempted like as we are. And yet He 'knew no sin.' He was

the Lamb 'without blemish and without spot.' . . . We should have no misgivings in regard to the perfect sinlessness of the human nature of Christ" (page 651).

5. "In His human nature He maintained the purity of His divine character. . . . He was unsullied with corruption, a stranger to sin. . . . He was a mighty petitioner, not possessing the passions of our human, fallen natures, but compassed with like infirmities, tempted in all points like as we are" (pages 658-59).[16]

6. "He was perfect, and undefiled by sin. He was without spot or blemish. . . . Jesus, coming to dwell in humanity, receives no pollution" (page 660).

III. The Atonement

1. "Those who teach that a completed atonement was made on the cross view the term in its popular theological sense, but really what is meant by them is that on Calvary the all-sufficient atoning sacrifice of Christ was offered for our salvation. With this concept all true Christians readily and heartily agree. 'We are sanctified through the offering of the body of Jesus Christ, once for all' (Heb. 10:10). Those who view this aspect of the work of Christ as a completed atonement, apply this term *only* to what Christ accomplished on the cross. They do not include in their definition the application of the benefits of the atonement made on the cross, to the individual sinner" (page 342).

2. "Seventh-day Adventists do *not* believe that Christ made but partial or incomplete sacrificial atonement on the cross" (page 349).

3. "Most decidedly the all-sufficient atoning sacrifice of Jesus our Lord was *offered and completed* on the cross of Calvary. This was done for all mankind, for 'he is the propitiation . . . for the sins of the whole world' (1 John 2:2). This sacrificial work will actually benefit human hearts *only* as we surrender our lives to God and experience the miracle of the new birth. In this experience Jesus our High Priest, applies to us the benefits of His atoning sacrifice. Our sins are forgiven, we become the children of God by faith in Christ Jesus, and the peace of God dwells in our hearts" (page 350).

4. "When, therefore, one hears an Adventist say, or reads in Adventist literature — even in the writings of Ellen G. White — that Christ is making atonement[17] now, it should be understood that we mean simply that Christ is now making application

of the benefits of the sacrificial atonement He made on the cross; that He is making it efficacious for us individually, according to our needs and requests. Mrs. White herself, as far back as 1857, clearly explained what she means when she writes of Christ's making atonement for us in His ministry:

" 'The great Sacrifice has been offered and had been accepted, and the Holy Spirit which descended on the day of Pentecost carried the minds of the disciples from the earthly sanctuary to the heavenly, where Jesus had entered by His own blood, to shed upon His disciples the *benefits* of His atonement' " (pages 354-55).

5. *"When the Father beheld the sacrifice of His Son,* He bowed before it in recognition of its perfection. 'It is enough,' He said, 'the Atonement is complete' " (page 663).

IV. The Resurrection

1. "Jesus Christ arose literally and bodily from the grave. He ascended literally and bodily into heaven. He now serves as our advocate in priestly ministry and mediation before the Father" (page 22).

2. "There shall be a resurrection both of the just and the unjust. The resurrection of the just will take place at the second coming of Christ; the resurrection of the unjust will take place a thousand years later, at the close of the millennium (John 5:28, 29; 1 Thess. 4:13-18; Rev. 20:5-10)" (page 14).

V. The Second Coming

1. "[Jesus Christ] will return in a premillennial, personal, imminent second advent" (page 22).

2. "As our denominational name indicates, the second coming of Christ is one of the cardinal doctrines of the Adventist faith. We give it such prominence in our beliefs because it occupies a pivotal place in Holy Scripture, not only in the New Testament, but also in the Old" (page 449).

3. "Jesus will assuredly come the second time. . . . [His] second advent will be visible, audible, and personal. . . . Seventh-day Adventists believe on the evidence of Scripture that there will be one visible, personal, glorious second coming of Christ" (pages 451-52, 459).

VI. The Plan of Salvation

1. "The vicarious, atoning death of Jesus Christ, once for all, is all-sufficient

[16]See Author's Note 1 following XIII. The *"Remnant Church."*

[17]See Author's Note 2 following XIII. The *"Remnant Church."*

for the redemption of a lost race. . . . Man was created sinless, but by his subsequent fall entered a state of ,alienation and depravity. . . . Salvation through Christ is by grace alone, through faith in His blood. . . . Entrance upon the new life in Christ is by regeneration, or the new birth. . . . Man is justified by faith . . . sanctified by the indwelling Christ through the Holy Spirit" (pages 22, 23).

2. "Every person in order to obtain salvation must experience the new birth; . . . this comprises an entire transformation of life and character by the recreative power of God through faith in the Lord Jesus Christ (John 3:16; Matt. 18:3; Acts 2:37-39)" (page 12).

3. ". . . The law of ten commandments points out sin, the penalty of which is death. The law cannot save the transgressor from his sin, nor impart power to keep him from sinning. In infinite love and mercy, God provides a way whereby this may be done. He furnishes a substitute, even Christ the Righteous One, to die 'in man's stead, making 'him to be sin for us, who knew no sin; that we might be made the righteousness of God in him' (2 Cor. 5:21). That one is justified, not by obedience to the law, but by the grace that is in Christ Jesus. By accepting Christ, man is reconciled to God, justified by His blood for the sins of the past, and saved from the power of sin by His indwelling life" (pages 12, 13).

4. "One who truly understands and accepts the teachings of the Seventh-day Adventist Church can assuredly know that he is born again, and that he is fully accepted by the Lord. He has in his soul the assurance of present salvation, and need be in no uncertainty whatsoever. In fact, he may know this so fully that he can truly 'rejoice in the Lord' (Phil. 4:4); and in 'the God of his salvation' (Psalm 24:5)" (page 105).

5. "Nothing we can ever do will merit the favor of God. Salvation is of grace. It is grace that 'bringeth salvation' (Titus 2:11). It is 'through the grace of the Lord Jesus Christ we shall be saved' (Acts 15:11). We are not saved by 'works' (Rom. 4:6; Eph. 2:9; 2 Tim. 1:9), even though they be *good* works. . . . Neither can we be saved by 'law' (Rom. 8:3), nor by the 'deeds' or the 'works' of the law (Rom. 3:20, 28; Gal. 3:2, 5, 10). . . . The law of God was never designed to save men. It is a looking glass, in which, when we gaze, we see our sinfulness. That is as far as the law of God can go with a sinful man. It can reveal his sin but is powerless to

remove it, or to save him from its guilt and penalty and power" (pages 108-9).

VI. *The Spiritual Nature of Man*

1. "Some have maintained that man was created mortal, so far as his body was concerned, but that he possessed an immortal entity called either a 'soul' or a 'spirit.' Others have felt equally certain that man was not in any sense created immortal. They have been convinced that man was not in possession of an ethereal soul, or spirit, which survived death as a conscious entity, apart from the body. . . . We as Adventists believe that, in general, the Scriptures teach that the soul of man represents the whole man, and not a particular part independent of the other component parts of man's nature; and further, that the soul cannot exist apart from the body, for a man is a unit" (page 511, 515).

2. "We as Adventists have reached the definite conclusion that man rests in the tomb until the resurrection morning. Then, at the first resurrection (Rev. 20:4, 5), the resurrection of the just (Acts 24:15), the righteous come forth immortalized, at the call of Christ the Life-giver. And they then enter into life everlasting, in their eternal home in the kingdom of glory. Such is our understanding" (page 520).

VIII. *Punishment of the Wicked*

1. "In the expression 'eternal punishment,' just as in 'eternal redemption' and 'eternal judgment,' the Bible is referring to all eternity — not as of process, but as of *result*. It is not an endless process of punishment, but an effectual punishment, which will be final and forever" (page 540).

2. "We reject the doctrine of eternal torment for the following major reasons: 1. Because everlasting life is a gift of God (Rom. 6:23). The wicked do not possess this — they 'shall not see life' (John 3:36); 'no murderer hath eternal life abiding in him' (1 John 3:15). 2. Because eternal torment would perpetuate and immortalize sin, suffering, and woe, and contradict, we believe, divine revelation, which envisions the time when these things shall be no more (Rev. 21:4). 3. Because it seems to us to provide a plague spot in the universe of God throughout eternity, and would seem to indicate that it is impossible for God Himself ever to abolish it. 4. Because in our thinking, it would detract from the attribute of love as seen in the character of God, and postulates the concept of a wrath which is never appeased. 5. Because the Scriptures teach

that the atoning work of Christ is to 'put away sin' (Heb. 9:26) — first from the individual, and ultimately from the universe. The full fruition of Christ's sacrificial, atoning work will be seen not only in a redeemed people but in a restored heaven and earth (Eph. 1:14)" (page 543).

IX. The Sanctuary and the Investigative Judgment

1. *"Does your teaching of the sanctuary service mean that the work of Christ on Calvary was not an all-sufficient, complete, once-for-all sacrifice — a sacrifice that obtained for us eternal redemption? Or was something subsequently necessary to make the sacrificial work of Christ effective for the salvation of man?*

"To the first part of the question our answer is an unequivocal No. The death of Christ on Calvary's cross provides the only sacrifice by which man can be saved. . . . This 'one sacrifice' (Heb. 10:12), or 'one offering' (verse 14), of Christ was 'for ever' (verse 12), and wrought 'eternal redemption' (Heb. 9:12) for man. This sacrifice was completely efficacious. It provided complete atonement for all mankind, and will never be repeated, for it was all-sufficient and covered the needs of every soul" (pages 356-57).

2. "The expression 'once' or 'once for all,' in connection with the sacrifice of Christ, is deeply significant. . . . 'He died to sin *once for all*' (Rom. 6:10); 'offering of the body of Jesus Christ *once for all*' (Heb. 10:10). He did this not by 'the blood of goats and calves' but by 'his own blood.' He entered *once for all* into the holy place (or, holies), 'thus securing an eternal redemption' for us (Heb. 9:12, R.S.V.).

"The Greek word here translated 'holy place' is *hagia*, and is in the plural form. A correct translation would be 'the holies,' or 'holy places,' as in Hebrews 9:24. This entrance, Scripture teaches, occurred at His ascension to glory (Acts 1), having already finished His sacrificial work on the cross. The word translated 'obtained,' in the Greek is from *heurisko*, and is rendered 'found,' 'procured,' 'gained,' or in R.S.V., 'secured' " (pages 380-81).

3. "Jesus our surety entered the 'holy places,' and appeared in the presence of God for us. But it was not with the *hope* of obtaining something for us at that time, or at some future time. No! *He had already obtained it for us on the cross.* And now as our High Priest He ministers the virtues of His atoning sacrifice to us" (page 381).

4. *"The time of the cleansing of the sanctuary, synchronizing with the period of the proclamation of the message of Revelation 14, is a time of investigative judgment; first, with reference to the dead, and second, with reference to the living.* This investigative judgment determines who of the myriads sleeping in the dust of the earth are worthy of a part in the first resurrection, and who of its living multitudes are worthy of translation (1 Peter 4:17, 18; Dan. 7:9,10; Rev. 14:6, 7; Luke 20:35)" (page 15).

5. "The great judgment scene of heaven will clearly reveal those who have been growing in grace and developing Christ-like characters. Some who have professed to be God's people, but who have disregarded His counsel, will in amazement say to the Lord, 'Have we not prophesied in thy name? and in thy name have cast out devils? and in thy name done many wonderful works?' His reply to such will be brief but emphatic: 'I never knew you: depart from me, ye that work iniquity' (Matt. 7:22, 23)" (page 417).

6. "In view of the principles here set forth, it seems to us abundantly clear that the acceptance of Christ at conversion does not seal a person's destiny. His life record after conversion is also important. A man may go back on his repentance, or by careless inattention let slip the very life he has espoused. Nor can it be said that a man's record is closed when he comes to the end of his days. He is responsible for his influence during life, and is just as surely responsible for his evil influence after he is dead" (page 420).

7. "It is our understanding that Christ as High Priest, concludes His intercessory ministry in heaven in a work of judgment. He begins His great work of judgment in the *investigative* phase. At the conclusion of the investigation the *sentence* of judgment is pronounced. Then as judge Christ descends to *execute* or carry into effect, that sentence. . . . When God's final sentence of judgment is consummated the redeemed will be singing the song of Moses and the Lamb" (page 422).

8. "The blotting of names out of the book of life is, we believe, a work of the investigative judgment. A complete and thorough check of all the candidates for eternal life will need to be completed before Christ comes in the clouds of heaven, for when He appears, the decisions for life or death are already made. The dead in Christ are called to life, and the living followers of Christ are translated (1 Thess. 4:15-17)—the entire citizenry of the ever-

lasting kingdom. There's no time subsequent to the second advent for such decisions" (pages 438-39).

X. The Scapegoat Teaching

1. "Two goats were obviously required, and used, on the Day of Atonement, because there is a *twofold responsibility for sin* — first, my responsibility as the *perpetrator* agent, or medium; and second, Satan's responsibility as the *instigator,* or tempter, in whose heart sin was first conceived.

"Now, concerning my sin, Christ died for *my* sins (Rom. 5:8). . . . He assumed *my* responsibilities, and His blood alone cleanses *me* from all sin. . . . The atonement for *my* sin is made solely by the shed blood of Christ.

"And concerning Satan's sin, and his responsibility as instigator and tempter, no salvation is provided for him. He must be punished for his responsibility. There is no savior, or substitute, to bear his punishment. He must himself 'atone' for his sin in causing men to transgress, in the same way that a master criminal suffers on the gallows or in the electric chair for his responsibility in the crimes that he has caused others to commit. *It is in this sense only that we can understand the words of Leviticus 16:10 concerning the scapegoat, 'to make an atonement with him.'*

"Under criminal law, the instigator, or master mind, may be punished more severely than his agents. . . . Satan is the responsible master mind in the great crime of sin, and his responsibility will return upon his own head. *The crushing weight of his responsibility in the sins of the whole world — of the wicked as well as the righteous — must be rolled back upon him.* Simple justice demands that while Christ suffers for my guilt, *Satan must also be punished as the instigator of sin"* (pages 397-99).

2. "Satan makes no atonement for our sins. But Satan will ultimately have to bear the retributive punishment for his responsibility in the sins of all men, both righteous and wicked. Seventh-day Adventists, therefore, repudiate *in toto* any idea, suggestion, or implication that Satan is in any sense or degree our sin bearer. The thought is abhorrent to us, and appallingly sacrilegious. Such a concept is a dreadful disparagement of the efficacy of Christ and His salvation, and vitiates the whole glorious provision of salvation solely through our Saviour.

"Satan's death, a thousand times over, could never make him a savior in any sense whatsoever. He is the archsinner of the universe, the author and instigator of sin. . . . Only Christ, the Creator, the one and only God-man, could make a substitutionary atonement for men's transgressions. And this Christ did completely, perfectly, and once for all, on Golgotha" (page 400).

XI. The Sabbath and the Mark of the Beast

1. "We believe that the Sabbath was instituted in Eden before sin entered, that it was honored of God, set apart by divine appointment, and given to mankind as the perpetual memorial of a finished creation. It was based upon the fact that God Himself had rested from His work of creation, had blessed His Sabbath, or rest day, and had sanctified it, or set it apart for man (Gen. 2:1-3; Mark 2:27)" (page 149).

2. "We believe that the restoration of the Sabbath is indicated in the Bible prophecy of Revelation 14:9-12. Sincerely believing this, we regard the observance of the Sabbath as a test of our loyalty to Christ as Creator and Redeemer.

"Seventh-day Adventists do not rely upon their Sabbathkeeping as a *means* of salvation or of winning merit before God. We are saved by grace alone. Hence our Sabbath observance, as also our loyalty to every other command of God, is an expression of our love for our Creator and Redeemer. . . .

"We are saved through the righteousness of Jesus Christ received as a gift of grace, and grace alone. Our Lord's sacrifice on Calvary is mankind's only hope. But having been saved, we rejoice that the righteous requirements of the law are fulfilled in the experience of the Christian 'who walks not after the flesh but after the spirit,' and who by the grace of God lives in harmony with the revealed will of God" (pages 153, 190).

3. "*Do Seventh-day Adventists teach in their authorized literature that those who worship on Sunday and who repudiate in its entirety the Seventh-day Adventist teaching as a consequence have the mark of apostasy, or 'the mark of the beast'? Does not Mrs. White teach that those who now keep Sunday already have the mark of the beast?*

"Our doctrinal positions are based upon the Bible and not upon Mrs. White's writings. But since her name has been introduced into the question, an explicit statement from her pen should set the record straight. The following was penned by her in 1899: 'No one has yet received the mark of the beast. The testing time has not yet come. There are true Christians in every church, not excepting the Roman Catholic communion. None are condemned until they have had the light and seen the obligation of the fourth commandment. But *when the decree shall go forth enforcing the counterfeit sabbath,* and the loud cry of the third angel shall warn men against the worship of the beast and his image, the line will be clearly drawn between the false and the true. *Then those who still continue in transgression will receive the mark of the beast'* " (page 183).

4. "To your inquiry, then, as to whether Mrs. White maintained that all those who do not see and *observe* the seventh day as the Sabbath *now* have the 'mark of apostasy,' the answer is definitely No" (page 184).

5. "We hold the firm conviction that millions of devout Christians of all faiths throughout all past centuries, as well as those today who are sincerely trusting in Christ their Saviour for salvation and are following Him according to their best light, are unquestionably saved" (page 184).

XII. *The Question of Unclean Foods*

1. "It is true we refrain from eating certain articles, . . . but not because the law of Moses had any binding claims upon us. Far from it. We stand fast in the liberty with which God has set us free" (page 623).

2. "Our health teaching is not a matter of religious taboos; in fact, it is much more than careful selection in diet. It is, to us, the following of a well-balanced health program. We feel it to be our Christian duty to preserve our bodies in the best of health for the service and glory of God. We believe that our bodies are the temples of the Holy Spirit (1 Cor. 3:16, 6:19; 2 Cor. 6:16), and that whether therefore we eat, or drink, or whatsoever we do, we should 'do all to the glory of God' (1 Cor. 10:31)" (page 624).

XIII. *The "Remnant Church"*

1. *"It is alleged that Seventh-day Adventists teach that they alone constitute the finally completed 'remnant church' mentioned in the book of Revelation. . . . Do Adventists maintain that they alone are the only true witnesses of the living God in our age. . . ?* (page 186).

2. "It is in a spirit of deep humility that we apply this scripture to the Advent Movement and its work, for we recognize

the tremendous implications of such an interpretation. While we believe that Revelation 12:17 points to us as a people of prophecy, it is in no spirit of pride that we thus apply the scripture. To us it is the logical conclusion of our system of prophetic interpretation" (page 191).

3. "But the fact that we thus apply this scripture does not imply in any way that we believe we are the only true Christians in the world, or that we are the only ones who will be saved" (pages 191-92).

4. "Seventh-day Adventists firmly believe that God has a precious remnant, a multitude of earnest, sincere believers, in every church . . ." (page 192).

5. "We believe the majority of God's children are still scattered in this way throughout the world. And of course, the majority of those in Christian churches still conscientiously observe Sunday. We ourselves cannot do so, for we believe that God is calling for a reformation in this matter. But we respect and love those of our fellow Christians who do not interpret God's Word just as we do" (pages 192, 193).

6. "We fully recognize the heartening fact that the host of the true followers of Christ are scattered all through the various churches of Christendom, including the Roman Catholic communion. These God clearly recognizes as His own. *Such do not form a part of the 'Babylon' portrayed in the Apocalypse"* (page 197).

AUTHOR'S NOTE

1. *The Concept of Christ's Sinful Human Nature*

Since almost all critics of Seventh-day Adventism contend that Seventh-day Adventists believe Christ possessed a sinful human nature during the incarnation, a word should be said to clarify this point. These charges are often based on an article in *Signs of the Times,* March 1927, and a statement in *Bible Readings for the Home Circle,* edition of 1944. Regarding the first reference, a critical article states:

> My . . . quotation is from L. A. Wilcox, for many years an editor of *The Signs of the Times,* which according to the latest figures given by the Adventists has been published by them for 82 years. Certainly a statement by an editor of that publication may be considered official. I'm sure that anything that Mr. Wilcox wrote did not just happen to get in. In March 1927 he wrote, "In His (Christ's) veins was the incubus of a tainted heredity like a caged lion ever seeking to break forth and destroy.

Temptation attacked Him where by heredity He was weakest, attacked Him in unexpected times and ways. In spite of bad blood and an inherited meanness, He conquered."

And again in the December 1928 issue of *Signs of the Times* this editor Mr. Wilcox stated: "Jesus took humanity with all its liabilities, with all its dreadful risks of yielding to temptation."[18]

First, L. A. Wilcox was never on the editorial staff of *Signs of the Times*. Moreover, Mr. L. A. Wilcox, who wrote the article, in a letter dated April 26, 1957, states:

The writer of the *Signs* article was a very young man in 1927 and not by any means always felicitous in his phraseology. I know, for I was the writer. The first sentence quoted is crude and shocking and theologically inaccurate, and I was properly spanked for it by Adventist officials, which proves that this article cannot be truly represented as "official" or "authoritative."

It is no more than fair to point out that no man has taught more earnestly or fervently than I as an Adventist minister, the deity of the Lord Jesus Christ, the sinlessness of Christ, salvation by grace, righteousness by faith, the finished work of Calvary, a Christ-centered religion, than I — with the "Amen" of Seventh-day Adventist leadership.

Virtually every critic of Seventh-Day Adventism, including the authors quoted above, also uses a statement quoted from *Bible Readings for the Home Circle* (1944 edition, page 174) — even though in 1945 the statement was expunged by Adventists because it was not in line with official Adventist theology.

A further quotation often seized upon is taken from the book *Desire of the Ages*, by Ellen G. White. On page 117 she says, "Our Savior took humanity, with all its liabilities. He took the nature of man, with the possibility of yielding to temptation." Mrs. White also speaks of "fallen nature." Understandably, not having read all she has written on the subject, these critics conclude that she means that Christ possessed a sinful, carnal, or degenerate human nature. However, Mrs. White's writings clearly indicate that when she speaks of the fallen nature of Christ, she

means the physical properties of the race, which degenerated since the time of Adam who was created perfect without the ravages of sin upon either his physical or spiritual being. Adam did not age before the fall, but Christ was born into the world a true man and with the curse of sin operative upon the physical properties of the human race. For thirty-three years He endured the aging process. He could not have reached the age of thirty-three without organic changes taking place in His body, and were He not subject to the physical decline of the race, he would not have been a true man, "made under the law" (Galatians 4:4). Mrs. White's position has been held by many eminent scholars who have never been accused of being either heretics or non-Christians. Why, then, should she and the Adventists be condemned for holding this view? For centuries Christians have argued about the human nature of Christ. Some have believed that He could have sinned, but did not. Others, including this writer, that He could not have sinned. However, it is a theological issue not likely to be resolved by trite phrases and dogmatic pronouncements.

We have already quoted at length from current official Seventh-day Adventist sources which deny the sinful-nature theory with which critics have relentlessly charged them. Would it not be fairer to consider their publication, *Questions on Doctrine*, released in 1957 and endorsed by the denominational leadership of the Seventh-day Adventist Church, than to cite statements from much older publications that have since been outdated or revised in these respects?

Dr. Anthony Hoekema in his volume, *The Four Major Cults*, falls into the same error as E. B. Jones, Louis Talbot, and other critics of Seventh-day Adventism, and ignores totally the fact that Wilcox publicly and in print (1957) repudiated his position. This fact they all know but seem determined to ignore since Wilcox's statement suits so well their assumption that despite official Adventist statements on doctrine, they, the critics, know more than the Adventists do about their own faith!

2. *The Incomplete Atonement Concept*

It is also often charged that inherent in SDA theology is the unbiblical teaching that "the atonement was not finished on the cross of Calvary." Certain Seventh-day Adventist sources are cited to bolster these charges. For instance, Uriah Smith, a prominent Adventist of the past, stated in his book *Looking Unto Jesus,* "Christ did not make the atonement when He shed His blood upon the cross." Other earlier writers such as J. H. Waggoner have expressed the same thought. He said, "There is a clear distinction between the death of Christ and the atonement" (fn. *The Atonement in the Light of Nature and Revelation,* page 181). Even some later writers like C. H. Watson have been influenced by these early exponents of Adventism. (See *The Atoning Work of Christ.*)

However, a little investigation of these writings would show that Smith and Waggoner wrote eighty years ago. As demonstrated elsewhere in this book this concept has been repudiated by the SDA denomination. The current position of the Seventh-day Adventist denomination — not the opinions of a few scattered writers over a hundred-year period — should be considered in judging this charge of "incomplete atonement."

Current Adventist writings teach that the atonement was completed on the cross; and no less an Adventist than Ellen G. White, writing in the *Review and Herald,* September 21, 1901, stated: "Christ planted the cross between Heaven and earth and when the Father beheld the sacrifice of His Son, He bowed before it in recognition of His perfection. 'It is enough,' He said. 'The atonement is completed.' " In the same periodical, under the date of August 16, 1899, Mrs. White stated, "No language could convey the rejoicing of heaven or God's expression of satisfaction and delight in His only begotten Son that He saw the completion of the atonement."

There are, of course, still extant in certain Adventist publications not yet revised, unfortunate statements like those of Smith and Watson, but the Adventists are aware of this and are taking steps to harmonize all such writings with the true position of the denomination. Many more quotations could be cited, but critics usually overlook the greater number of statements relative to the completeness of the atonement which are readily available in past and present Seventh-day Adventist literature. Nothing could be clearer than the Adventist declaration that:

> When . . . one hears an Adventist say or reads in Adventist literature — even in the writings of Ellen G. White — that Christ is making atonement

now, it should be understood that we mean simply that Christ is now making application of the benefits of the sacrificial atonement He made on the cross; that He is making it efficacious for us individually, according to our needs and requests. Mrs. White herself, as far back as 1857, clearly explained what she means when she writes of Christ's making atonement for us in His ministry:

> "The great Sacrifice had been offered and had been accepted, and the Holy Spirit which descended on the day of Pentecost carried the minds of the disciples from the earthly sanctuary to the heavenly, where Jesus entered by His own blood, to shed upon His disciples the benefits of His atonement."[19]

Is Seventh-day Adventism a Non-Christian Cult?

We earlier mentioned Dr. Anthony Hoekema's book *The Four Major Cults* in which he classifies Seventh-day Adventism as a non-Christian cult system. It is necessary for me to take exception with Dr. Hoekema in this area because, in my opinion, the reasons which Dr. Hoekema gives cannot be justified by the Word of God, historical theology, or present-day practices in denominational Christianity as a whole. To illustrate this point, Dr. Hoekema stated, "I am of the conviction that Seventh-day Adventism is a cult and not an evangelical denomination. In support of this evaluation I propose to show that the traits which we have found to be distinctive of the cults do apply to this movement" (page 389).

Dr. Hoekema then proceeds to list his reasons:

1. An extra-scriptural source of authority (Ellen G. White).
2. The denial of justification by grace alone.
   a. The investigative judgment.
   b. The keeping of the Sabbath.
3. The devaluation of Christ.
4. The group as the exclusive community of the saved.

It is Dr. Hoekema's contention that Ellen White in an extra-Biblical authority in that her counsels are taken to be manifestations of the gift of prophecy (I Corinthians). But granting that the Adventists are entitled to believe that this gift was manifested in Mrs. White as evidence of the charismata (a fact Dr. Hoekema could

[19]*Questions on Doctrine,* pages 354-355.

hardly honestly challenge since the gifts of the Spirit have been and are still manifested in the Christian church), why does he not take into consideration the repeated emphasis of Adventist writers concerning their official pronouncement *Questions on Doctrine* to the effect that they do not consider Mrs. White to be an extra-Biblical authority, but that her writings are only authoritative in those areas where they are in agreement with the Word of God which is the final standard for judging all the gifts of the Spirit.

If the Adventists put Mrs. White's writings on a par with Holy Scripture, if they interpreted the Bible in the light of her writings, and not the reverse, if they willingly admitted this and owned it as their position, then his criticism would be justified, but they do not do so. Dr. Hoekema has apparently ignored what the Adventists say they believe concerning Mrs. White in favor of what he thinks they mean as a result of his deduction from certain of their publications. It is far safer to accept at face value the published statements of a denomination representing its theology particularly if, as in the case of *Questions on Doctrine*, they are answering direct questions bearing on the subject, than it is to rely upon one's own preconceived interpretations as Dr. Hoekema has apparently done in this instance.

It is a serious charge to maintain that any professing Christian group denies justification by grace alone as the basis of eternal salvation; and, if the Adventists were guilty of this, surely there would be ground for considering them as a cultic system. However, literally scores of times in their book *Questions on Doctrine* and in various other publications the Adventists affirm that salvation comes only by the grace of God through faith in Jesus Christ's sacrifice upon the cross.

Why again it is necessary for Dr. Hoekema to question the sincerity of the Adventists in this area and yet accept at face value their other statements concerning their faith in the Scriptures, the Trinity, the full deity of Jesus Christ, creation, providence, incarnation, the resurrection of Jesus Christ, the absolute necessity for regeneration, sanctification by the Holy Spirit and Christ's literal return, is a puzzling inconsistency in his presentation. (See *The Four Major Cults*, page 403.)

Dr. Hoekema insists that the investigative judgment, which is admittedly a literalistic Arminian device, and the keeping of the seventh-day Sabbath, are part of the reasons why he classifies Seventh-day Adventists as cultists, but, in doing this, he makes his Calvinistic interpretation of theology the criterion while ignoring the claims of the Arminian school and of semi-Arminian and semi-Calvinistic theologians, many of whom take strong exception to Dr. Hoekema's pronounced Calvinism. On the basis that Dr. Hoekema would call the Adventists a cult the same charge could be leveled against all devoted Calvinists who consider the Institutes and Calvin's Commentaries every bit as much illumination and guide lines in the study of the Scriptures as the Adventists do where Mrs. White's writings are concerned. In addition to this, the Seventh-day Baptists are Arminian in their theology and keep the seventh-day Sabbath. Are they, too, a non-Christian cult? They certainly have some of Dr. Hoekema's qualifications.

Underscoring his Calvinistic oppositions Dr. Hoekema writes:

Adventists further teach that it is possible for a person through subsequent sinful deeds and attitudes to lose the justification he once received. This teaching implies that one can only be sure of retaining his justification if he continues to do the right kind of deeds and to maintain the right attitudes throughout the rest of his life (page 390).

This on the investigative judgment is clear evidence of Arminianism in which Dr. Hoekema finds sufficient ground to justify the cult label being applied to Adventists. But why just to Adventists? Why not to Pentecostals, Methodists, Anglicans, Episcopalians, Lutherans and others who accept the same Arminian premises, though they have not carried them out for the literalism that the Adventists have in the investigative judgment.

Relative to Sabbatarianism, the fourteenth chapter of Romans justifies the keeping of the seventh-day sabbath or any other day by any Christian who believes he is keeping it unto the Lord. It can become legalistic as Sunday can become legalistic, but merely because the seventh day is honored instead of the first is no ground for the description of "cult."

Dr. Hoekema on page 394 of his volume affirms that:

Seventh-day Adventists do not . . . deny the full deity of Jesus Christ or the doctrine of the Trinity. . . . Seventh-day Adventists today affirm Christ's complete equality with the Father, and the pre-existence of the Son from eternity. . . . Adventists also accept the doctrine of the Trinity, and that of the personality and full deity of the Holy Spirit.

As far as the work of Christ is concerned, Seventh-day Adventists teach the vicarious, substitutionary atonement of Christ. Yet there remains some ambiguity in their teachings on the question of whether the atonement has been finished on the cross, since Mrs. White says on more than one occasion that Christ is making atonement for us today and frequently refers to a "final atonement" after the one completed on the cross. . . .

Dr. Hoekema follows this up by listing five reasons for his feeling that the Adventists "devalue" Christ. Three of these four points involve Arminianism concerning which Dr. Hoekema has an admitted prejudice; the fourth concerns the Sabbath, which is a matter of Christian liberty, unless one presupposes Calvin's interpretation; the fifth reiterates the old accusation that the Seventh-day Adventists believe that "the sins of all men will be laid on Satan just before Christ returns, and that only in this way will sin finally be 'eradicated' or 'blotted out' of the universe" (pages 395 and 396).

Once again, Dr. Hoekema defeats his own case by admitting that the Adventists are soundly orthodox in their christology, hardly a devaluation of Christ!

The implications and deductions which he draws from their Arminianism cannot be considered as evidence against the Adventists, since not only they, but the entire Arminian school of theological interpretation could argue vigorously for the principles which the Adventists lay down.

Finally, the Adventists themselves have repeatedly affirmed that Christ alone vicariously bears the sins of the world and that Satan only bears "his responsibility" for tempting the world to sin.

A careful reading of the book *Questions on Doctrine* which Dr. Hoekema lists in his bibliography in *The Four Major Cults* would have answered his question regarding Mrs. White's usage of the term "making atonement now" and "final atonement."

The Adventists declare forthrightly that whenever terms of this nature are used they understand them to refer to the benefits of the atonement of Christ being shed abroad through the ministry of the Holy Spirit and disown completely any implication or suggestion that the atonement of Christ was not completed upon the cross.

Dr. Hoekema in company with other critics of Adventism has not hesitated to draw upon repudiated sources to underscore the claim that the Adventists devalue Christ. On page 114 of *The Four Major Cults* Dr. Hoekema states:

One of the best known is the statement by L. A. Wilcox to the effect that Christ conquered over sin "in spite of bad blood and an inherited meanness." Though the discussion of this matter in *Questions on Doctrine* implies that the denomination would now repudiate this statement, nowhere in the book are we definitely told that this has been done.

In my book *The Truth About Seventh-day Adventism* conclusive proof was introduced of the total repudiation of that statement by Wilcox himself. Dr. Hoekema lists the book in his bibliography but unfortunately omits reference to Wilcox's repudiation, in order to utilize Wilcox's statement which is not a fair representation of what the Adventist denomination has taught or teaches in this area.

These then are a few of the problems which face the interested student of the puzzle of Seventh-day Adventism, and they must be fairly considered before hastily classifying Adventism as a non-Christian cult.

ELLEN G. WHITE AND THE SPIRIT OF PROPHECY

In most religious movements, one extraordinary and gifted personality dominates the scene, and so it was with Seventh-day Adventism. This dominant personality was, and is today, through her writings, Ellen G. White. She was one of the most fascinating and controversial personages ever to appear upon the horizon of religious history. Her memory and work have been praised by Adventists and damned by many of their enemies since the early years of the movement. Born Ellen Gould Harmon at Gorham, Maine in 1827, and reared a devout Methodist in the city of Portland, Mrs. White was early recognized as an unusual person, for she bore witness to certain "revelations" which she believed she had received from Heaven.

When Ellen was thirteen, the Harmon family came under the influence of the Millerite movement. William Miller delivered a series of addresses in the Casco Street Christian Church in Portland in 1841 and 1842. At the age of seventeen, Ellen embraced the Adventist faith of the

Millerites.[20] Although deeply stirred by Miller's sincerity and his chronological calculations, the Harmon family remained in fellowship with the Chestnut Street Methodist Church of Portland, which in 1843 disfellowshiped them because they believed in the premillennial second advent of Jesus Christ.

Despite her youth, Ellen Harmon passed through trying times, emotionally, physically and spiritually, between 1837 and 1843. In the words of Dr. Froom, "She rebelled against the dismal prospects resulting from an early accident, and its attendant invalidism."[21] In 1840, at a Methodist camp meeting at Buxton, Maine, Ellen Harmon found wonderful deliverance and "her burden rolled from her shoulders," for she experienced great joy in learning that she was truly a child of God, which she publicly confessed afterward by requesting baptism by immersion. Many points still perplexed her, among them the doctrine of the eternal punishment of the wicked, which in subsequent years she surrendered to as well as the concept of conditional immortality and the sleep of the soul while awaiting the resurrection. In December 1844, after The Great Disappointment, while visiting a friend in Portland, Ellen Harmon experienced what she termed her first vision which portrayed the "vindication" of the Advent faith. In that vision she claimed to see the Adventists triumphant over their critics — pressing upward to Heaven in the face of insuperable obstacles.

For many years controversy has raged about Mrs. White and her "revelations," and there are conflicting opinions within and without Adventism regarding her "revelations" and "inspiration," their extent and nature. The position of Ellen White in Adventist teaching, then, is most significant and must be understood if we are to get a proper picture of this people. The writings and counsels of Ellen Harmon (later Ellen G. White by her marriage to James White, a prominent Adventist leader), are termed the "Spirit of prophecy," an expression taken from Revelation 19:10. Adventists believe that in the last days special counsels from God are to be revealed, which neither add to nor contradict Scripture, and that these counsels are primarily for the Seventh-day Adventist denomination. And while following these counsels, they claim they always test them by the Word of God. Finally, they believe that the visions of

Mrs. White, and her counsels to their denomination are the "Spirit of prophecy" for their church.

Through the years, some overzealous Adventist writers have given the impression that everything Mrs. White said, or wrote even in private letters was inspired and infallible. This is decidedly not the official position. The Adventist denomination readily admits that not everything Mrs. White said or wrote was either inspired or infallible, although some individual Adventists still cling to that idea. In this connection we present statements from the new definitive volume on Seventh-day Adventist theology, Questions on Doctrine, in the hope of clearing the way for proper understanding of the life and ministry of Ellen G. White, as viewed by the Seventh-day Adventist church.

I. Seventh-day Adventist Statements — Life and Ministry of Ellen G. White

(Page numbers are in Questions on Doctrine, unless otherwise indicated.)

1. "We do not regard the writings of Ellen G. White as an addition to the sacred canon of Scripture. We do not think of them as of universal application, as is the Bible, but particularly for the Seventh-day Adventist Church. We do not regard them in the same sense as the Holy Scriptures, which stand alone and unique as the standard by which all other writings must be judged" (page 89).

2. "Seventh-day Adventists uniformly believe that the canon of Scripture closed with the book of Revelation. We hold that all other writings and teachings, from whatever source, are to be judged by, and are subject to, the Bible, which is the spring and norm of the Christian faith" (pages 89-90).

3. "I recommend to you, dear reader, the Word of God as the rule of your faith and practice. By that Word we are to be judged" (Ellen G. White, Early Writings, page 78; Questions on Doctrine, page 90).

4. "The Spirit was not given — nor can it ever be bestowed — to supersede the Bible; for the Scriptures explicitly state that the Word of God is the standard by which all teaching and experience must be tested" (The Great Controversy, Introduction, page vii; Questions on Doctrine, page 90).

5. "We have never considered Ellen G. White to be in the same category as the

[20]Ellen G. White, Life Sketches, pages 64-68.

[21]The Prophetic Faith of Our Fathers, Vol. IV, page 978.

writers of the canon of Scripture" (page 90).

6. "It is in . . . the category of messengers [other than the Biblical writers] that we consider Ellen G. White to be. Among Seventh-day Adventists she was recognized as one who possessed the gift of the spirit of prophecy, though she herself never assumed the title of prophetess" (page 91).

7. "Seventh-day Adventists regard her writings as containing inspired counsel and instruction concerning personal religion and the conduct of our denominational work. . . . That portion of her writings, however, that might be classified as predictions, actually forms but a small segment. And even when she deals with what is coming on the earth, her statements are only amplifications of clear Bible prophecy" (page 92).

8. "In His Word, God has committed to men the knowledge necessary for salvation. The Holy Scriptures are to be accepted as an authoritative, infallible revelation of His will. They are the standard of character, the revealer of doctrines, and the test of experience" (pages 92, 93, quoting E. G. W.).

9. "While Adventists hold the writings of Ellen G. White in highest esteem, yet these are not the source of our expositions. We base our teachings on the Scripture, the only foundation of all true Christian doctrine. However, it is our belief that the Holy Spirit opened to her mind important events and called her to give certain instructions for these last days. And inasmuch as these instructions, in our understanding, are in harmony with the Word of God, which Word alone is able to make us wise unto salvation, we as a denomination accept them as inspired counsels from the Lord. But we have never equated them with Scripture as some falsely charge. Mrs. White herself stated explicitly the relation of her writings to the Bible: 'Little heed is given to the Bible, and the Lord has given a lesser light to lead men and women to the greater light' " (Review and Herald, Jan. 20, 1903; Questions on Doctrine, page 93).

10. "While Seventh-day Adventists recognize that the Scripture canon closed nearly two thousand years ago and that there have been no additions to this compilation of sacred books, yet we believe that the spirit of God, who inspired the Divine Word known to us as the Bible, has pledged to reveal Himself to the church through the different gifts of the Spirit. . . . It is not our understanding that these gifts of the Spirit take the place of the Word

of God, nor does their acceptance make unnecessary the Scripture of truth. On the contrary, the acceptance of God's Word will lead God's people to a recognition and a manifestation of the Spirit. Such manifestations will, of course, be in harmony with the Word of God. We know that some earnest Christians have the impression that these gifts ceased with the apostolic church. But Adventists believe that the closing of the Scripture canon did not terminate Heaven's communication with men through the gifts of the Spirit, but rather that Christ by the ministry of His Spirit guides His people, edifying and strengthening them, and especially so in these last challenging days of human history" (pages 93-95).

11. "The Spirit of prophecy is intimately related to the gift of prophecy, the one being the Spirit which indites the prophecy, the other the evidence of the gift bestowed. They go together, each inseparably connected with the other. The gift is the manifestation of that which the Spirit of God bestows upon him whom, according to His own good purpose and plan, He selects as the one through whom such spiritual guidance is to come. . . . Briefly then, this is the Adventist understanding of Ellen G. White's writings. They have been for a hundred years, to use her own expression, 'a lesser light' leading sincere men and women to 'the greater light' " (page 96).

12. "Concerning the matter of church fellowship, we would say that while we revere the writings of Ellen G. White, . . . we do not make acceptance of her writings as a matter for church discipline. She herself was explicit on this point. Speaking of those who did not fully understand the gift, she said: 'Such should not be deprived of the benefits and privileges of the church, if their Christian course is otherwise correct, and they have formed a good Christian character' " (Testimonies, Vol. I, page 328; Questions on Doctrine, pages 96, 97).

13. "We therefore do not test the world in any manner by these gifts. Nor do we in our intercourse with other religious bodies who are striving to walk in the fear of God, in any way make these a test of Christian character" (J. N. Andrews in Review and Herald, Feb. 15, 1870; Questions on Doctrine, page 97).

14. "James White, thrice General Conference president, speaking of the work of Ellen G. White, expressly declares that Adventists believe that God called her 'to do a special work at this time, among this people. They do not, however, make a

belief in this work a test of Christian fellowship' " (*Review and Herald,* June 13, 1871; *Questions on Doctrine,* page 97).

15. "In the practice of the church it has not been customary to disfellowship one because he did not recognize the doctrine of spiritual gifts. . . . A member of the church should not be excluded from membership because of his inability to recognize clearly the doctrine of spiritual gifts and its application to the second advent movement" (F. M. Wilcox, *The Testimony of Jesus,* pages 141-43; *Questions on Doctrine,* page 98).

It may be seen from these quotations that Seventh-day Adventists hold to the restoration of the "gift of prophecy" in the last days of the Christian Church, and that they believe this restoration occurred in the life and ministry of Ellen G. White. The Adventists differ from other churches, then, in that while they hold the Bible to be the unique, complete, infallible, inerrant Word of God, they maintain that in specific contexts Ellen White's writings are to be accepted by Adventists as "testimonies" from the Spirit of God to guide their denominational activities.

Dr. Wilbur M. Smith has summed up the objections of most evangelicals where Seventh-day Adventism emphasis upon Mrs. White and the Spirit of prophecy is involved when he recently observed Mrs. White's place in the new Seventh-day Adventism Bible Commentary.

I do not know any other denomination in all of Christendom today that has given such recognition, so slavishly and exclusively to its founder or principal theologian as has this commentary to the writings of Ellen White. At the conclusion of every chapter in this work is a section headed, "Ellen G. White Comments." For example, on Genesis 28, the blessing conferred upon Jacob, there are less than three pages of comment, but at the end, forty references to the various works of Ellen White. In addition, at the end of the first volume of this commentary is a section again headed, "Ellen G. White Comments," containing eighty columns of material quoted from her writings. There is no section devoted to anyone else, Calvin, Luther, Wesley, or anyone else.

The Preface to this commentary contains the statement: "At the close of each chapter is a cross reference or index to those passages in Ellen G.

White's writings that comment on the various texts in that chapter." And the second sentence followings reads: "The Advent movement has grown strong through the study of the Bible; and it can be said with equal truth that the movement has been safely guided in that study by the light shining from the Spirit of prophecy." I would say that the writers of this commentary believe that "the Spirit of prophecy" has rested *exclusively* upon Ellen G. White, for no one else is so classified in this work.[22]

Dr. Smith is correct in his evaluation of the place of Ellen G. White's writings in the denomination. Seventh-day Adventists are of necessity committed to her visions and counsel because they believe that the Spirit of prophecy rested upon her and upon no other person of their group.

This writer rejects this concept of inspiration but one should carefully note that, for Adventists, "inspiration" in connection with Mrs. White's writings has a rather different meaning from the inspiration of the Bible. Adventists freely admit that the Bible is *objectively* the Word of God, the final authority in all matters of faith and morals. But the writings of Mrs. White cannot be so regarded, and they are the first to say so. Apparently, they have adopted a qualified view of inspiration as related to her writings — "a lesser light to lead men and women to the greater light"—which emphasizes subjective interpretation as the criterion for determining specifically where in Mrs. White's writings the "Spirit of prophecy" has decisively spoken. There is no doubt in my mind that the Adventists are defending a situation which is at best paradoxical and at times contradictory. But this position, as a matter of religious liberty, they are *entitled* to hold so long as they do not make faith in Mrs. White's writings a test of fellowship between themselves and other denominations, and do not attempt to compel other Christians to accept the "testimonies" of Mrs. White as indispensable to a deeper, richer experience of Christian consecration and living.

If Seventh-day Adventists did indeed claim for Mrs. White inspiration in *every* area of her writings, then we might well be cautious about having fellowship with them. However, this they do not do, as I have amply demonstrated from official denominational sources. Since they do not

---

[22]In a letter to the author.

consider Mrs. White's teachings the source of their expositions of faith, the claim that one has only to refute Ellen G. White and her writings, in order to refute Seventh-day Adventism, falls by its own weight.

II. Mrs. White and Her Critics

Through the years a great deal of literature has appeared, criticizing the life and works of Ellen G. White. These criticisms have ranged from the mild judgment that Mrs. White was a sincere but emotionally disturbed mystic, to the charge that she was a "false prophetess" who sought material gain and deliberately plagiarized much of her writing. In the interest of honest investigation and truth, and since it is impossible in a book of this size to analyze all the conflicting data, we shall present some highlights of the controversy, and let the reader determine the validity of these charges.

The inspiration for 90 per cent of the *destructive* personal criticisms leveled against Mrs. White is found in the writings of Dudley M. Canright, an ex-Adventist leader of great ability, and a one time personal friend of Ellen G. White, her husband James, and a great number of prominent Adventist leaders. Canright, one of the most able of the Seventh-day Adventist writers and debaters of his day, left the movement because he lost faith in the inspiration of Mrs. White, and in many doctrines then held by the Adventist Church. While it is true that Canright thrice ceased to preach, his credentials as a minister were never revoked. He finally resigned from the Seventh-day Adventist ministry in 1887 to become a Baptist minister. By Canright's own admission, his personality conflicts with Ellen G. White and her advisers were largely responsible for his turning away from the active ministry at the times mentioned. He, however, apparently maintained close personal relations with James White, Mrs. White's husband, and other prominent Seventh-day Adventist leaders as evident from the correspondence quoted below. Canright rebelled violently against Arianism (the denial of the deity of Christ) and extreme legalism, which existed among some of the early Seventh-day Adventists; and his convictions led him later to write two volumes (*Seventh-day Adventism Renounced*, and *Life of Mrs. E. G. White*), which systematically and scathingly

denounced Seventh-day Adventism theologically and impugned the personal motives and integrity of Mrs. White.

In these two volumes, D. M. Canright laid the foundation for all future destructive criticism of Seventh-day Adventism, and careful research has confirmed the impression that nearly all subsequent similar publications are little more than repetitions of the destructive areas of Canright's writings, buttressed by standard theological arguments. This is especially true of the writings of a former Seventh-day Adventist missionary printer, E. B. Jones, now editor of a small news sheet, *Guardians of the Faith,* who has issued a number of vitriolic pamphlets against Seventh-day Adventism, all of which are drawn almost exclusively from Canright and other critics, and are for the most part outdated and in some cases both scholastically and ethically unreliable.[23] It can be seen, therefore, that what D. M. Canright has written about Ellen G. White is of prime importance as firsthand evidence, and no Seventh-day Adventist apologist, regardless of the scope of his knowledge of Adventism or the breadth of his scholastic learning, can gainsay all that Canright has written.[24]

In the March 22, 1887 issue of the *Review and Herald,* his former brethren wrote of Elder Canright,

We have felt exceedingly sad to part in our religious connection with one whom we have long esteemed as a dear brother. . . . In leaving us he has taken a much more manly and commendable course than most of those who have withdrawn from us, coming voluntarily to our leading brethren and frankly stating the condition of mind he was in. He did this before his own church in our presence and so far as we know has taken no unfair underhanded means to injure us in any way. He goes from our midst with no immoral stain upon his character. He chooses associations more pleasant to himself. This is every man's personal privilege if he chooses to take it.

Writing to Canright on May 22, 1881, from Battle Creek, Michigan, James White, Ellen's husband, stated, "It is time there was a change in the offices of the General Conference. I trust that if we are true and faithful, the Lord will be pleased that we should constitute two of that

---

[23]They contain, however, just enough factual criticism of Adventist teaching to give them an air of respectability, making them doubly deceptive.

[24]Recognizing that some of Canright's criticisms are well taken, I, too, have drawn upon them as *prima facie* sources where thoroughly documented.

Board." In another letter to Canright, dated July 13, 1881, James White said, "Brother Canright, I feel more interest in you than in any other man because I know your worth when the Lord is with you as a laborer." It is apparent, therefore, that Canright was in good standing with the Adventists, despite his later renunciation of Mrs. White's testimonies and the "special truths" of the Adventist message.

In 1951 a carefully documented volume of almost 700 pages was issued by the Review and Herald Publishing Association of Washington, D. C. The author was Francis D. Nichol, leading apologist of the Seventh-day Adventist denomination. This volume, entitled, *Ellen G. White and Her Critics*, attempts a point-for-point refutation of many of the charges made by D. M. Canright in his *Life of Mrs. E. G. White*. Nichol has dug deep into early Adventist history—even beyond Canright's day, but after reading both Nichol and Canright, I have concluded that there is much to be said on both sides. But Canright, we believe, has the edge because he can say, "I was there," or "Mrs. White said . . ." and contradictory contemporary statements are not to be found where many of Canright's charges are concerned.

My own conclusion is that in some areas (particularly theology) Canright's statements are irrefutable, especially with regard to his personal relationships with Mrs. White and the leading members of the Adventist denomination. It is also significant to note that many charges which are based on personal experiences and have been well documented have never been refuted.

By this I do not mean that all of Canright's writing is to be trusted, for many of his criticisms of Mrs. White's activities have been neatly undercut by contemporary evidence unearthed by F. D. Nichol and others. Where Nichol is concerned, "methinks he doth protest too much," and he often goes to extremes to defend Mrs. White. This in my judgment has hurt his case and has proved nothing except that he is a devoted disciple of Mrs. White and therefore strongly biased. Nichol is none the less the most able Adventist apologist.

III. *The Verdict of the Evidence*

After considering all the evidence obtainable, of which the foregoing is only

a part, this writer is convinced that Ellen G. White was a highly impressionable woman, strongly influenced by her associates. That she sincerely believed the Lord spoke to her, none can fairly question, but the evidence set forth in this book gives good reason, we believe, to doubt the inspiration of her counsels, whether Seventh-day Adventists will concede this or not.

My personal evaluation of the visions of Ellen G. White is best summed up in the following statement from a friendly critic. In 1847, at the outset of her work, one of Mrs. White's cousins stated:

I cannot endorse Sister Ellen's visions as of Divine inspiration, as you and she think them to be; yet I do not suspect the least shade of dishonesty in either of you in this matter. I may, perhaps, express to you my belief in the latter without harm—it will, doubtless, result either in your good or mine. At the same time I admit the possibility of my being mistaken. I think that what she and you regard as visions from the Lord are only religious reveries in which her imagination runs without control upon themes in which she is most deeply interested. While so absorbed in these reveries she is lost to everything around her. Reveries are of two kinds: Sinful and religious. In either case, the sentiments in the main are obtained from previous teaching, or study. I do not by any means think that her visions are from the Devil.[25]

If Seventh-day Adventists are to defend their claim for Mrs. White's inspiration, they must explain a number of contradictions in her writings. They would do better to admit, we believe, that she was very human, capable of errors in judgment, subject to lapses of memory, and possessed of the universal human predisposition toward personal sin (Romans 3: 23).

Mrs. White was definitely influenced in some of her writings by time and circumstances, and also by the powerful personalities who surrounded her.[26] Some Adventists maintain that this would in no way prevent her conveying messages from the Lord. However, as I see it, anyone who attempts to prove her divinely inspired or infallible (no informed Adventist holds the latter) must first dispose of the evidence here presented, as well as other evi-

---

[25]Reproduced in *A Word to the Little Flock*, page 29 (1847) by Elder James White.

[26]At various times by Bates, Butler, Haskell, the

"Battle Creek Clique," and of course her husband James White, a much older man, of whom Canright states, "He exercised great influence over her."

dence which space does not admit.[27] F. D. Nichol in *Ellen G. White and Her Critics*, makes a masterful attempt to answer some of these problems, but not all of them can be answered with a good conscience or an airtight defense of Mrs. White and her actions. It does not detract from her stature as a sincere Christian or from the quality of her contribution to insist upon an honest and systematic evaluation of her statements by thinking Adventists, to ascertain just how far Adventists may rightfully maintain that the Lord has "spoken" through Mrs. White. Non-adventists, of course, reject the claims made for Mrs. White and her writings and hope that Adventists will some day amend their questionable view of "Ellen G. White and the Spirit of Prophecy."

After reading the publications of the Seventh-day Adventist denomination and almost all the writings of Ellen G. White, including her *Testimonies*, the writer believes that Mrs. White was truly a regenerate Christian woman who loved the Lord Jesus Christ and dedicated herself unstintingly to the task of bearing witness for Him as she felt led. It should be clearly understood that some tenets of Christian theology as historically understood and the interpretations of Mrs. White do not agree; indeed, they are at loggerheads. Nevertheless, Ellen G. White was true to the cardinal doctrines of the Christian faith regarding the salvation of the soul and the believer's life in Christ. We must disagree with Mrs. White's interpretation of the sanctuary, the investigative judgment, and the scapegoat; we challenge her stress upon the Sabbath, health reform, the unconscious state of the dead, and the final destruction of the wicked, etc. But no one can dispute the fact that her writings conform to the basic principles of the historic Gospel, for they most certainly do. However, we must not assume as many Adventists do that Mrs. White's writings are free from theological and exegetical errors *for they are not*. Although I believe that the influence of Mrs. White's counsels on the Advent denomination parallels the influence of J. N. Darby of the Plymouth Brethren and A. B. Simpson of the Christian and Missionary Alliance, the claim that she possessed a "gift of prophecy" akin to that described in I Corinthians 14 as believed by the Seventh-day Adventist church, I cannot accept.

Many critics of Seventh-day Adventism have assumed, mostly from the writings of professional detractors, that Mrs. White was a fearsome ogre who devoured all who opposed her, and they have never ceased making the false claim that Seventh-day Adventists believe that Mrs. White is infallible, despite the often published authoritative statement to the contrary. Although Seventh-day Adventists do hold Mrs. White and her writings in great esteem, they maintain that the Bible is their only "rule of faith and practice." Christians of all denominations may heatedly disagree with the Seventh-day Adventist attitude toward Mrs. White, but all that she wrote on such subjects as salvation or Christian living characterizes her as a Christian in every sense of the term.

Farther on in this discussion, we shall look at Mrs. White's relations with the Adventist denomination, particularly in the field of theology. Enough has been presented here, however, to show that she was a most interesting personality, far different from the "Sister White" idealized beyond reality in certain Seventh-day Adventist publications.

Dudley M. Canright, the chief critic of Seventh-day Adventism, has, I feel, rendered good service in this respect. He has presented the human side of Mrs. White, from the standpoint of a first-hand friendship which lasted through the formative years of the Seventh-day Adventist denomination. Despite his criticisms of Seventh-day Adventism and Mrs. White, Canright himself never ceased to believe that, despite what he believed to be her errors in theology and her mistaken concept of visions, she was a regenerate Christian. With his brother, Canright attended the funeral of Mrs. White in 1915. His brother describes the occasion thus: "We joined the passing throng, and again stood by the bier. My brother rested his hand upon the side of the casket, and with tears rolling down his cheeks, he said brokenly,

---

[27]We refer to such things as Mrs. White's censure of SDA for purchasing life insurance (*Testimonies*, Vol. I, page 549), a practice most Adventists participate in today; and her counsel regarding eating of meat, although she herself ate meat for almost sixty years (*Ministry of Healing*, pages 312-17). The problem of life insurance is a very clear instance — at least where I am concerned — of the attitude of the SDA Church toward some of Mrs. White's writings, for she definitely stated, "I was shown that Sabbath-keeping Adventists should not engage in life insur-

ance. This is a commerce with the world which God does not approve." No Adventist can deny from the very language used ("I was shown") that this is allegedly a divine dictate, yet SDA's openly engage in the purchase of life insurance, "which God does not approve!" Seventh-day Adventists explain this by declaring that life insurance today is vastly different than when Mrs. White wrote her counsel, but the fact is that up to the time of her death in 1915 she never reversed it and her other counsels stand on the same basis — why not this one?

'There is a noble Christian woman gone!' "[28]

The controversy between Seventh-day Adventist historians and personal recollections of D. M. Canright[29] will probably never be settled this side of Heaven, but beyond question, Canright has left an indelible mark upon the history of both the denomination and Ellen G. White, a woman of great moral fortitude and indomitable conviction. Her influence will doubtless affect the religious world through the Seventh-day Adventist denomination for many years to come.

THE SLEEP OF THE SOUL AND THE DESTRUCTION OF THE WICKED

The doctrine of conditional immortality, commonly called "soul sleep" outside Adventist circles, and its necessary corollary, annihilation,[30] have been cardinal teachings from the beginning of the Seventh-day Adventist Church. They must be dealt with from an exegetical standpoint if the theology underlying the basic premise is to be understood. These positions, incidentally, are held today by the Advent Christian Church, an affiliate of the National Association of Evangelicals, and by outstanding Bible scholars in not a few denominations.

The purpose here is essentially to review the historic position of the Christian church from the days of the apostles to the present, and to examine the teaching of the Scriptures on these subjects. Many noted Christians of the past believed in conditional immortality, among them Martin Luther, William Tyndale, and John Wycliffe, all of whom were competent Greek scholars. Luther even stated that he could not support the doctrine of immortality of the soul, which he called one of the "endless monstrosities in the Roman dunghill of decretals."[31] Tyndale declared that:

in putting them [the souls of the departed dead] in Heaven, hell and purgatory you destroy the arguments wherewith Christ and Paul doth prove the resurrection . . . and again, if the souls be in Heaven, tell me why they be not in as good case as the angels be? And then what cause is there for their resurrection?[32]

However, in his *Commentary on Genesis*, Luther later categorically stated, "In the interim [between death and resurrection], the soul does *not* sleep but is awake and enjoys the vision of angels and of God, and has converse with them."[33]

However, neither preponderance of one opinion, nor the opinions of a few great thinkers can validate theological speculation or interpretation. The Christian Church does not base its belief in the conscious bliss of departed saints on the opinions of individuals, no matter how prominent or learned, but upon the historic, *Biblical foundation of the Christian faith*.

I. Textual Analysis

The Seventh-day Adventist doctrine of the sleep of the soul is best expressed in their own words: "We as Adventists believe that, in general, the Scriptures teach that the soul of man represents the whole man, and not a particular part independent of the other component parts of man's nature; and further, that the soul cannot exist apart from the body, for man is a unit. . . . We, as Adventists, have reached the definite conclusion that man rests in the tomb until the resurrection morning. Then, at the first resurrection (Revelation 20:4, 5), the resurrection of the just (Acts 24:15), the righteous come forth immortalized at the call of Christ, the Lifegiver, and *they then enter into life everlasting*[34] in their eternal home in the kingdom of glory. Such is our understanding."[35]

The key to the preceding statements, of course, is the last phrase of the second

---

[28]W. A. Spicer, *Spirit of Prophecy and the Advent Movement*, page 127.

[29]It has been stated by misinformed Seventh-day Adventists at one time or another that Canright recanted and accepted Seventh-day Adventism shortly before his death. I have examined this story carefully and found it false. Canright did leave the ranks of Adventism at least twice, but returned and preached for them again. In 1887 he left and never returned. He died a Baptist minister, still denouncing the theological deviations of Seventh-day Adventism. As his daughter put it, "Father was more firm in his conviction of the error of their teaching the longer he lived, in spite of Adventist claims that he repudiated his writings against them. I tell you this in anticipation of your having such falsehoods to meet" (*The Christian Standard*, Oct. 16, 1902).

[30]Adventists do not use this term; they prefer "final destruction."

[31]Weimar edition of Luther's *Works*, Vol. VII, pages 131-32.

[32]*An Answer to Sir Thomas More's Dialogue*, Parker's 1850 reprint, Book 4, chapter iv, pages 180-81.

[33]*Works*, XXV, 321.

[34]See also these standard Adventist publications where this erroneous equation is set forth. 1) *In Defence of the Faith*, W. H. Branson, page 239 2) *Desires of Ages*, E. G. White, page 786, paragraph 3 3) *God Speaks to Modern Man*, Arthur Lickey, page 503 4) *Answers to Objections*, F. D. Nichol, page 323, paragraph 325. Thus Adventists speak of having eternal life "now," but they do not emphasize that it is suspended at death hence *not* eternal.

[35]*Questions on Doctrine*, pages 515, 520.

paragraph, "They *then* enter into life everlasting, in their eternal home in the kingdom of glory." Now, the majority of Christians through the centuries have held that this proposition contradicts the teaching of the Word of God contained in the following passages:

1. *I John 5:11-13:* "And this is the record, that God hath given to us eternal life, and this life is in his Son. He that hath the Son hath life; and he that hath not the Son of God hath not life. These things have I written unto you that believe on the name of the Son of God; that ye may know that ye have eternal life, and that ye may believe on the name of the Son of God." In the grammar and context of this passage eternal life (*eionion zoes*) is the present possession of every believer in the Lord Jesus Christ, and if the term *eternal life* does not include *conscious fellowship* then the whole New Testament meaning is destroyed. The Holy Spirit used the present indicative active of the verb *echo*, expressing present, continuous action. Thus we see that the believer, having been regenerated by the Holy Spirit, *already* possesses never-ending life as a continuing *quality* of conscious existence.

2. *John 11:25, 26:* "Jesus said unto her, I am the resurrection and the life: he that believeth in me, though he were dead, yet shall he live: and whosoever liveth and believeth in me shall never die. Believest thou this?" The context here indicates that the Lord Jesus Christ was consoling Martha upon the death of her brother Lazarus. Therefore, the words "life" and "dead" must refer to that particular occasion. To attempt to wrest the meanings of these terms from their expressed context, and to teach that the end of the age is primarily in view or somehow close, is a violation of the grammar and context.

All thorough students of the Word of God, including the Adventists, recognize that in any study of the doctrines of eternal life and immortality, it is vitally essential to apply the hermeneutic principle (comparing all texts on a given subject) of interpretation, and the application of this principle, we believe, leads to the following facts. The root meanings for the words "death" and "life" in the New Testament usage ("death" *thanatos*, in its verb form *apothnesko*, and "life" *zoe* or its verb form *zac*) are respectively "separation or to separate," from communion or fellowship. The Scriptures describe two types of

death, physical and spiritual, the former being the separation of the body from the soul, and the latter being the separation of the soul from God as the result of sin. Also, two kinds of life are spoken of in the New Testament: physical life (*bios*), which is the union or communion of body and soul; and spiritual life (*zoe*), which is the communion or fellowship of the soul with God. These terms we equate with the Greek of the New Testament, and they are essential to an understanding of Christ's words to Martha.

He was assuring her that, despite the physical evidence of death, Jesus, the eternal Word of God, made flesh was Himself the source of life. And, *as such,* He was able to give life, even though death had actually occurred. Let us therefore take His words literally.

Christ's primary purpose was to comfort Martha. And what better comfort could He give than the knowledge that her family's limited concept of life as dependent upon the resurrection was depriving her of the joyous knowledge that the Prince of Life gives to the believer eternal life, unaffected by physical death.

Now let us look carefully at this context with no violation to hermeneutics or grammar, and this great truth becomes clear. John 11:20 tells us that as soon as Martha heard that Jesus was coming to Bethany, she went out to meet him. In verse 21 she greets Him thus: "Lord, if thou hadst been here, my brother had not died." In answer to her obvious affliction and grief Jesus, with divine compassion, stated, "Thy brother shall rise again." Verse 24 indicates, however, that Martha thought He was referring to the resurrection of the dead which will take place at "the last day."

To dispel her confused and grief-instilling concept of life (spiritual life), Jesus gives comfort beyond measure: "I am the resurrection and the life," He declares; "he that believes in me, even though he were dead, yet shall he live, and the one living and believing in me shall never die."

Now it is apparent from the context of verse 25 that Jesus was referring to Martha's brother Lazarus, one who believed in Him and had physically died. Christ's promise is, "yet shall *he* live." But going beyond this, Jesus lifts the veil and reveals that, in the realm of the physically alive, whoever believes in Him shall never experience the greatest of all, terrors, spiritual death.[36]

36Matthew 25:41—separation from God's fellowship.

The Greek is extremely powerful in verse 26 for our Lord deliberately used the double negative, a construction which intensifies with great emphasis that to which it is applied. Jesus *could not* grammatically have been more emphatic in stating that the believer, who is alive both physically and spiritually, can never experience loss of communion of fellowship as a spiritual entity, though his body may "become" dead.

We see, further, that Seventh-day Adventists have no warrant for the idea that death is a state of unconsciousness. The New Testament frequently indicates that the unregenerate man is already "dead," but not even the Adventists would say that he was extinct or unconscious! Some instances of this are: Matthew 8:22, "Let the dead bury their dead"; John 5:25, "The hour is coming and now is, when the dead shall hear the voice of the Son of God, and they that hear shall live"; and Ephesians 2:1, "You hath he quickened, who were dead in trespasses and sins."

Admittedly in the New Testament, death is compared with sleep, but this is recognized by Bible scholars generally as a grammatical metaphor. One does not develop a doctrine from a figure of speech, as conditional immortalists apparently have done, but upon the sound principles of Biblical hermeneutics, contextual analysis, and linguistic exegesis. The application of these principles leads to the one conclusion which the Scripture unreservedly teaches, that *eternal life* is vastly different from "immortality"; although immortality *will* be bestowed upon the believer at the resurrection, *in this life* he already possesses "eternal life," a spiritual quality of existence which will at length be united with the physical quality of incorruptibility which the Bible speaks of as immortality, and "we shall be like him, for we shall see him as he is" (I Corinthians 12; I John 3:2). A study of these words in any Greek lexicon, and of their use in the New Testament, will show that immortality and eternal life are neither identical nor synonymous. For certain Adventist writers therefore to treat these terms as interchangeable is clearly a linguistic impossibility.

3. *II Timothy 1:10:* The Apostle Paul writes that God's eternal purpose "is now made manifest by the appearing of our Saviour Jesus Christ, who hath abolished death, and hath brought *life* and *immor-*

tality to light through the gospel." In this verse "life" (*zoen*) and "immortality" (*aphtharsian*) are clearly distinguished. Life has been bestowed upon the believer at the moment of regeneration by faith in Jesus Christ (I John 5:11, 12); immortality is a future gift, to be bestowed upon the believer's body at the second advent of our Lord, or as Paul expressed it, "This corruptible must put on incorruption (*aphtharsian*), and this mortal must put on immortality" (*athanasian*).

Again in Romans 2:7, the Apostle clearly distinguishes between "eternal life" as a conscious quality of spiritual existence bestowed upon the believer as a gift; and "immortality," which, in this connection in the New Testament refers to the resurrection bodies of the saints or to the nature of God Himself. Thus, God's Word clearly indicates the difference between "life" as spiritual existence, and "immortality," incorruptibility in a body like that of our risen Lord.

4. *Philippians 1:21-23:* "For to me to live is Christ, and to die is gain. But if I live in the flesh, this is the fruit of my labour: yet what I shall choose I wot not. For I am in a strait betwixt two, having a desire to depart, and to be with Christ; which is far better: nevertheless to abide in the flesh is more needful for you."

Seventh-day Adventists say here,

Of course it will be better to be with Christ, but why, it must be asked, should we conclude that the apostle expects immediately upon death to go at once into the presence of Christ? *The Bible does not say so.* It merely states his desire to depart and be with Christ. One might reason that the *implication* is to the effect that being with Christ would be immediately on his departure. But it must be admitted that such is not a necessary implication, and it certainly is not a definite statement of the text. In this particular passage Paul does not tell us *when* he will be with his Lord. In other places he uses an expression similar to one in this passage. For instance, he says, "The time of my departure is at hand" (2 Tim. 4:6). The Greek word used in these two texts, *analuō*, is not used very often in the Greek New Testament, but the word has the meaning "to be loosened like an anchor." It is a metaphor drawn from the loosened moorings preparatory to setting sail.[37]

Now, of all the texts in the New Testament on the state of the believer after the death of his body, this one alone[38] gives us Paul's mind on the subject, so we need to pay strict attention to what he says. In the main, Seventh-day Adventists support their arguments with Old Testament passages, most of which, I maintain, are taken out of context, while ignoring metaphorical usages, implications or deductions. To treat literally such words as "sleep," "death" and "destroy," is I feel, unwarranted. However, in the New Testament, when faced with a positive statement like this one by the Apostle Paul, it seems that they refuse to be literal and insist upon metaphors, deductions and implications. They seem unwilling to accept the Apostle's statement at face value. The noted Adventist author F. D. Nichol, in his book *Answers to Objections,* states that if Philippians 1:21-23 were the only passage about the condition of man in death, he would be forced to acknowledge the accepted Orthodox position. Nichol then attempts to strengthen his argument by taking texts out of context to "prove" that Paul does not *mean* what he most decidedly *says.* With this thought in mind, let us examine the context and grammar of the Apostle's statement for it answers the Seventh-day Adventist contention.

In verse 21 Paul states that to continue to live *is* Christ, and to die "is gain." Since Paul was ordained to preach the Word of God to the Gentiles while enjoying fellowship with the living Christ, what would he gain by death or unconsciousness? According to the Adventist idea, fellowship with Christ would end, and Paul would merely go to sleep until the resurrection. This argument violates both context and grammar.

Verse 23 is grammatically uncomplicated. It is a series of coordinate statements tied together by the conjunctions *kai* and *de.* The phrase "to depart and be with Christ, which is far better" (*eis to analusai kai sun christo einai*) is grammatically devastating to the Seventh-day Adventist position. The preposition *eis* plus the definite article *to* shows "true purpose or end in view" — the strong desire which causes Paul's dilemma. Both infinitives (*analusai* and *einai*) have one construction—they are used with one definite article — so are *one* thought, *one* grammatical expression: literally, "my desire is

to the 'to depart and to be with Christ.' "

In simple English, Paul's one desire has a twofold object: departure and being *with* Christ! If departure did not mean his immediately being with Christ, another construction would have been employed. It therefore seems impossible that soul sleep was in the mind of the Apostle, since he desired to depart *from* his body and to spiritually enjoy the presence of his Lord. The Second Advent could not have been in view in this passage, for the context indicates that Paul expected death — and instantaneous reunion with Christ —*then, not* at the resurrection. There would have been no need of his staying to instruct the Philippians (vs. 24) if he were speaking of the Second Advent, for they would all be glorified together and in need no longer of His presence to strengthen them. Most translators and recognized Greek authorities contend that Philippians 1:21-23 teaches the historic position of the Christian Church, i.e., the conscious presence of the believer with Christ at the death of the body.

As quoted above, the Adventists, in common with all conditionalists, say, but "Why . . . should we conclude from this remark that the Apostle expects, immediately upon death, to go at once into the presence of Christ? The Bible does not say so. It merely states his desire to depart and to be with Christ." We answer that the context of the chapter, the grammatical construction of the verse, and every grammar book on New Testament Greek usage teaches that from the construction utilized the Apostle expected to go *at once* into the presence of his Lord. Nevertheless the Adventists insist, "The Bible does not say so. It merely states his desire to depart and to be with Christ." This statement is not accurate, it is not exegetically sound, and it will not stand the test of contextual criticism. It is only an attempt, I believe, to justify a doctrine that is *not* supported by the Word of God.

In reply to the Adventist statement, "In this particular passage Paul does not tell us *when* he will be with his Lord," we point out that the Apostle categorically states that his desire *is* "to depart." If this departure did not mean immediate presence with Christ, he would have used a different grammatical construction as previously noted; but as it stands, it can have *no other meaning.* In the face of these

<hr />

[38]II Corinthians 5:8 is also a strong passage, but has possible application to the resurrection body and cannot, therefore, be dogmatically adduced to support the historic position — though from a hermeneutic

standpoint it does. The sentence "to be absent from the body and to be at home with the Lord" does however, strongly suggest the intermediate state.

facts, Seventh-day Adventists disregard the preponderance of historical scholarship in favor of the doctrine of "soul sleep."

5. *I Thessalonians 4:13-18:* "I would not have you to be ignorant, brethren, concerning them which are asleep, that ye sorrow not, even as others which have no hope. For if we believe that Jesus died and rose again, even so them also which sleep in Jesus will God bring with him. For this we say unto you by the word of the Lord, that we which are alive and remain unto the coming of the Lord shall not prevent them which are asleep. For the Lord himself shall descend from heaven with a shout, with the voice of the archangel, and with the trump of God: and the dead in Christ shall rise first: then we which are alive and remain shall be caught up together with them in the clouds, to meet the Lord in the air: and so shall we ever be with the Lord. Wherefore comfort one another with these words."

This final passage, I believe, refutes the SDA teaching on the intermediate state of the dead, and is marked by explicit emphasis of construction in the Greek and cannot be ignored by any serious student of the language.

The key is the preposition *sun* which carries the primary meaning of "together with." In verse 14, the Holy Spirit tells us that God intends to bring with Him (*sun auto*), that is, with Jesus at His second advent, believing Christians who have experienced physical death. The physical state of their bodies is described as "sleep," a common metaphor in the New Testament. In every instance where the word "sleep" is used to describe death, it always refers to the *body* and cannot be applied to the soul, especially since "sleep" is never used with reference to the soul. This fact Seventh-day Adventists seem to overlook.

The second use of *sun* is in verse 17, which tells us that believers who survive to the coming of the Lord will be caught up together with them (*sun autois*), that is, with the dead in Christ (*oi nekroi en Christe*) to meet the Lord in the air. Here again, *sun* has no meaning other than "together with"; a fact most difficult for Seventh-day Adventists to explain.

The last use of the preposition *sun* is also in verse 17, "and so shall we ever be with the Lord" (*sun kurio*). It is quite obvious, therefore, that at the Second Advent of Christ those who at death departed to be spiritually with the Lord (Philippians 1:21-23) *return* with Him or "to-

gether with" Him to claim their resurrected, immortal bodies. Simultaneously, their corrupting bodies in the graves, spoken of as "asleep," are instantly metamorphosed or changed and reunited with the returning personalities. This fact is consistently emphasized by continual use of the preposition *sun*, "together with." Since the preposition *sun* means "together with" both times in verse 17, grammatically it cannot mean something altogether different in the same context and parallel usage of verse 14. Therefore, if at Christ's advent our bodies are to go with Him physically (verse 16) it is obvious that the saints who preceded us in death have been with Him from the moment of death, since they accompany Him in His return (verse 14).

A final grammatical point is the Holy Spirit's use of *nekroi* which throughout the New Testament refers primarily to the physical body of man, and only metaphorically to the soul. We see, then, that the corpses (*nekroi*) of the physically dead saints are to be raised and united with their returning souls (verse 14). Not once does the context or grammar indicate that the souls of departed believers are "asleep." Instead, it categorically states that they are "with Jesus" or returning "together with" Jesus.

The great hope of the believer, then, is the joy of personal union with the Lord, and this union, the Apostle Paul tells us, takes place at the death of the body. That this has been the position of the large majority of the Christian church since the times of the apostles, the Adventists have never denied. In I Thessalonians 4, the Apostle Paul was giving comfort to people who were mourning for departed loved ones; and his words carry the undeniable conclusion that they are not "dead" in the usual pagan sense. Although physically dead, they are spiritually alive and with Christ, and are awaiting the day when they will return "together with him," (verse 14) to claim their inheritance of completion, physical immortality or incorruptibility.

II. *"Soul" and "Spirit"*

For a fuller treatment of Adventist teaching on soul sleep, we must discuss briefly the Bible use of "soul" and "spirit." In the Old Testament, the words "soul" and "spirit" are the Hebrew *nephesh* and *ruach*. In the New Testament they are the Greek *psuche* and *pneuma*. Although in the Old Testament *nephesh* and *ruach* frequently refer only to the *principle* of life in both men and animals, in many other places they mean the intellectual and spiritual nature of man. Such verses as Isaiah 57:16, Zechariah 12:1, Isaiah 55:3 and Genesis 35:18,[39] belie the Adventists' criterion for determining the spiritual nature of man. On page 522 of *Questions on Doctrine*, the Adventists list eight Scripture passages about death, to show that at the death of the body, the intellect, will, and spirit of man (*nephesh* and *ruach*) lapse into unconsciousness pending the resurrection. However, seven of these are from the Old Testament, and every one of them refers to the *body*. Adventists lean strongly on the book of Ecclesiastes, especially 9:5-6[40] to substantiate their doctrine. But Ecclesiastes 12:7 tells us that, upon the death of the body, "the spirit [*ruach*] shall return unto God." Unlike the mere principle of life in the animals, man possesses a cognizant, immaterial nature created in God's image.[41]

It is a basic Christian principle, which Adventists share, that the Old Testament must be interpreted by the New Testament, and not the reverse. However, where conditional immortality is involved Adventists do not follow this principle. The New Testament teaches that the immaterial nature of man (soul and spirit) is separate from the body (Matthew 10:28, Luke 8:55, I Thessalonians 5:23, Hebrews 4:12, Revelation 16:3);[42] that it is independent of man's material form, and departs from that form at death, to go either into the presence of the Lord (Philippians 1:23) or into a place of punishment (Luke 16). In Acts 7:59, Stephen committed his spirit (*pneuma*) into the hands of the Lord Jesus Christ. This establishes the fact that the immaterial nature of man is independent of his body; at the same time, the Scripture tells us, "He [Stephen] fell asleep" in death; that

is, his physical body took on the appearance of "sleep." But he as a unit did not die; he merely experienced separation of the soul from the body and he went to be with the Lord, into whose hands he had committed his spiritual nature.

In Luke 23:46 the Lord Jesus Christ said, "Father, into thy hands I commend my spirit." This verse would be meaningless if it applied only to the "Breath of Jesus." The classic example of the penitent thief, who in his last moments believed on the Lord Jesus Christ, is proof that eternal life is a *quality including conscious existence*. It does not terminate with the death of the physical but continues in never-ending personal fellowship with our Lord. "Today shalt thou be with me in paradise," is the guarantee of the Son of God that those who trust Him will never be separated from His presence and fellowship. Seventh-day Adventists, in company with other Conditionalists, attempt to explain this by reading the text, "Verily, verily, I say unto thee today, thou shalt be with me in paradise." The reason is that Christ's statement calls in serious question their doctrine of soul sleep. Moreover, Adventists seem to overlook the important fact that wherever Jesus used the words, "verily, verily, I say unto you," He never qualified them because qualification was unnecessary. It would have been redundant for Jesus to say, "Verily, verily, I say unto you, that is, *today* I am saying unto you. . . ." By this type of interpretation, the Adventists violate the plain sense of one of Christ's favorite expressions of emphasis.

In Matthew 17:3, we see Moses and Elijah with Christ on the Mount of Transfiguration. We know that Moses died (Deuteronomy 34:5), and Elijah was translated (II Kings 2:11). However, it *was* Moses who was communing with our

---

[39]"For I will not contend for ever, neither will I be always wroth: for the spirit should fail before me, and the souls which I have made" (Isaiah 57:16); "The burden of the word of the Lord for Israel, saith the Lord, which stretcheth forth the heavens, and layeth the foundation of the earth, and formeth the spirit of man within him" (Zechariah 12:1); "Incline your ear, and come unto me: hear, and your soul shall live; and I will make an everlasting covenant with you, even the sure mercies of David" (Isaiah 55:3); "And it came to pass, as her soul was in departing, (for she died) that she called his name Ben-oni: but his father called him Benjamin" (Genesis 35:18).

[40]"For the living know that they shall die: but the dead know not any thing, neither have they any more a reward: for the memory of them is forgotten. Also their love, and their hatred, and their envy, is now perished; neither have they any more a portion for ever in any thing that is done under the sun" (Ecclesiastes 9:5, 6).

[41]It is almost universally agreed among Biblical scholars that Ecclesiastes portrays Solomon's apostasy and

is therefore virtually worthless for determining doctrine. It sketches man's life "under the sun" and reveals the hopelessness of the soul apart from God. The conclusion of the book alone mirrors the true revelation of God (chapter 12).

[42]"And fear not them which kill the body, but are not able to kill the soul: but rather fear him which is able to destroy both soul and body in hell" (Matthew 10:28); "And her spirit came again, and she rose straightway: and he commanded to give her meat" (Luke 8:55); "and the very God of peace sanctify you wholly; and I pray God your whole spirit and soul and body be preserved blameless unto the coming of our Lord Jesus Christ" (I Thessalonians 5:23); "For the word of God is quick, and powerful and sharper than any twoedged sword, piercing even to the dividing asunder of soul and spirit, and of the joints and marrow, and is a discerner of the thoughts and intents of the heart" (Hebrews 4:12); "And the second angel poured out his vial upon the sea; and it became as the blood of a dead man: and every living soul died in the sea" (Revelation 16:3).

Lord. Since the Scripture nowhere states that Moses had been raised from the dead for this occasion (Adventists attempt to teach this from the book of Jude, where such an assertion is *not* made), it is evident that the soul of Moses appeared to our Lord. Thus conscious existence is a necessary predicate of the intermediate state.

It is the strong conviction of mine, based upon Scripture, that the doctrine of soul sleep cannot stand in the light of God's revelation. Perhaps the reader will think that there has been too much space given to the meanings of words and the grammar of the Greek New Testament, but this is most essential because the crux of Adventist argument, it seems to me, is a denial of the meaning of terms in their context. For example, they say,

> There is nothing in the word *psuche* [soul] itself that even remotely implies a conscious entity that is able to survive the death of the body. And there is nothing in the Bible use of the word indicating that the Bible writers held any such belief. . . . There is nothing inherent in the word *pneuma* [spirit] by which it may be taken to mean some supposed conscious entity of man capable of existing apart from the body, nor does the usage of the word *with respect to man* in the New Testament in any way imply such a concept. . . . A careful study of all the adjectives used in Scripture to qualify the word "spirit" as applied to man, indicates that *not one* even remotely approaches the idea of immortality as one of the qualities of the human "spirit."[43]

In Matthew 10:28 Jesus Christ apparently believed and taught that the soul was more than "body and breath" as Seventh-day Adventism teaches, for He said, "Fear not them which kill the body, but are not able to kill the soul!"

Seventh-day Adventist writers charge that orthodox theologians have been overly dogmatic about the nature of man while Adventists have maintained a guarded reserve. But Adventists have been equally dogmatic in denouncing the orthodox position. To be dogmatic one should have a sound, scholarly basis for his dogmatism, and such a basis exegetically speaking is conspicuously absent from the historic position of conditional immortalists. As mentioned above, Adventists generally confuse "immortality" with "eternal life." We quite agree that "a care-ful study of all the adjectives used in Scripture to qualify the word 'spirit' as applied to man indicates that not one even remotely approaches the idea of immortality," as our Adventist brethren have stated.[44] But as we have shown, "immortality" refers *only* to the resurrection body of the saints and to the nature of God Himself. Therefore, since the saints are to be clothed with their resurrection bodies at the Second Advent, they do not *now* possess "immortality." For Adventists to confuse "immortality" with "eternal life" and then to argue that "immortality" *means* "eternal life" and is never applied to the spirit, is logical and theological error.

The question of soul sleep, however, should cause no serious division between Christians since it does not affect the foundational doctrines of the Christian faith, or the salvation of the soul. It is merely an area of theological debate, and has no direct bearing upon any of the great doctrines of the Bible. The ground of fellowship is not the condition of man in death but faith in the Lord Jesus Christ, and the love He commanded us to have one for another (John 13:34, 35). Seventh-day Adventists are welcome to hold this doctrine, but when one is faced with such concrete Old Testament instances as Samuel's appearance to Saul (I Samuel 28:18, 19) and such New Testament accounts as those given by the Apostle Paul (II Corinthians 5:8), "To be absent from the body is to be at home with the Lord," or (Philippians 1:23) ". . . to depart and be with Christ, which is far better," it is difficult to see how our Adventist brethren can long substantiate their claim for the "sleep of the soul."

III. Hell and Punishment in New Testament Greek

The grammar of the Greek New Testament teaches unquestionably the doctrine of Hell and eternal punishment. Nowhere is this more pointedly brought out than in the following passages:

1. *Matthew 5:22 and 10:28:* "Whosoever shall say, Thou fool, shall be in danger of hell fire." "Fear him which is able to destroy both soul and body in hell."

In both passages the Greek word *gehenna* portrays a place of punishment for the unsaved. *Gehenna* originally meant the Valley of Hinnom, a garbage dump which smoldered perpetually outside Jerusalem. The rabbis believed that punish-

43*Questions on Doctrine*, pages 514, 517-18.   44*Questions on Doctrine*, page 518.

ment after death could be likened to Gehenna, and often threatened their people with punishment after death. The Lord Jesus Christ, however, pointed out to the unbelieving Jews that those who rejected Him could look forward to everlasting Gehenna. In Matthew 10:28 He coupled *gehenna* with *apolesai*, which Thayer's Greek lexicon defines as "to be delivered up to eternal misery." *Gehenna*, then, symbolizes eternal separation and conscious punishment for the spiritual nature of the unregenerate man. This eternity of punishment is also taught in the Old Testament; e.g., "Their worm shall not die, neither shall their fire be quenched" (Isaiah 66:24).

2. *II Thessalonians 1:8-9:* "In flaming fire taking vengeance on them that know not God, and that obey not the gospel of our Lord Jesus Christ: who shall be punished with everlasting destruction from the presence of the Lord and from the glory of his power."

From the context, especially verse 8, "everlasting destruction" is to be that of "flaming fire," visited upon those who "obey not the gospel of our Lord Jesus Christ." The heart of the problem here is the meaning of the word "destruction," which the Adventists claim is reduction to a state of non-existence (*Questions on Doctrine*, page 14). As a matter of fact, the Greek word *olethros* used here has the clear meaning of "ruining."[45] We see then, that everlasting destruction or "ruination" is the lot of those who know not God. Many people who are not well versed in Greek try to make "destruction" synonymous with "annihilation"; this does violence to New Testament Greek, which supports no such concept. A common illustration will show the fallacy of this idea.

In the course of her work a housewife changes light bulbs and sometimes one drops to the floor and breaks. Of course the bulb has been "destroyed," but no one would say that it had been annihilated, for there is a difference between the *function* of an object and its *nature*. The function of the bulb is to give forth light. When broken, its function is destroyed, but the glass remains, although in fragments, and so does the metal base. Although the bulb has been "ruined" or "destroyed" it certainly has not been "reduced to nothing."

The Bible teaches that unregenerate

men will suffer the eternal wrath of God, and must undergo destruction and ruin of their original function which was "to glorify God and to enjoy Him forever." But the human spirit, created in the image of God (Genesis 1:26,27) remains intact, a spiritual entity of eternal existence, capable of enduring eternally the righteous and just Judge.

3. *Revelation 20:10:* "The devil who deceived them was cast into the lake of fire and brimstone where the beast and the false prophet are, and they will be tormented day and night into the everlasting of the everlasting" (literal translation).

The root meaning of the Greek word *basanizo* is "to torment, to be harassed, to torture or to vex with grievous pain,"[46] and is used throughout the New Testament, to denote great conscious pain and misery, never annihilation or cessation of consciousness. The reader who wishes to pursue this point may look up the following verses where this word is used: Matthew 8:6, 29; Mark 5:7; Luke 8:28; Revelation 14:10, 11. In each place, *basanizo* means conscious "torment." In Revelation 14:10-11, speaking of the followers of the Beast, unmistakably it means torment or punishment, everlasting or never-ceasing.[47]

In Revelation 20:10, Satan, the beast and the false prophet are described as tormented (*basanis thesontai*) "day and night[48] into the everlasting of the everlasting"; so if language means anything at all, in these contexts alone the theory of the annihilation or, as the Adventists say, the final destruction, of the wicked is itself annihilated.

4. *John 3:36:* "He that believeth on the Son hath everlasting life, and he that believeth not the Son shall not see life, but the wrath of God abideth on him."

Our fourth and final grammatical point relative to the doctrine of annihilation is made by coupling Romans 2:8-9 and Revelation 14:10 with John 3:36. Jesus tells us that the one who believes in the Lord Jesus Christ already *has* everlasting life (present tense); and then, of one who "believes not the Son," he states that he "shall not *see* life, but the wrath of God abides on him." The Greek word *menei*, here translated *abide*, appears several times in the New Testament. It carries the idea of continuous action (see John

45Thayer, page 443, on *olethros;* see on *vulnus,* to wound.

46*Ibid.,* page 96b.

47*Ibid.,* page 40, No. 2; also Liddell and Scott on *anapausis.*

48Metaphorical usage clearly indicated in the context — i.e., eternal duration.

1:33, 2:12; 8:31, 15:9). Thus, in John 3:36 the Holy Spirit says that the wrath of God continually abides on the one who "believeth not the Son." Comparing this with Romans 2:8, 9, we see that those who do not obey the truth but do evil are the objects of God's wrath, which Revelation 14:10-11 describes as eternal. "The same shall drink of the wine of the wrath of God . . . and the smoke of their torment ascendeth up for ever and ever: and they have no rest day nor night."

Orges, translated "wrath," appears in each of the verses cited, so there can be no doubt that the same subject is being discussed. It is apparent then that, far from the comparatively blissful prospect of total annihilation, those who "have not the Son of God have not life,"[49] and "the wrath of God continues upon them."[50] God's wrath even now hangs like the sword of Damocles over the heads of those who deny Jesus Christ. It will strike when the rebellious soul goes into eternity and appears before the bar of God's eternal justice.

Seventh-day Adventists should not be ostracized because they cling to this doctrine, since they believe that an undetermined period of punishment will elapse before the actual ultimate destruction of the wicked with Satan and his hosts.

Dr. Francis Pieper, the great Lutheran scholar and author of the monumental *Christian Dogmatics*, states my views in essence when he says:

> Holy Scripture teaches the truth of an eternal damnation so clearly and emphatically that one cannot deny it without, at the same time, rejecting the authority of Scripture. Scripture parallels the eternal salvation of the believers and the eternal damnation of the unbelievers. Whoever therefore denies the one must, to be consistent, deny the other (Matthew 25:46). We find the same juxtaposition and antithesis in other passages of Scripture. This parallelism proves that the term *eternity* in the sense of limited duration as sometimes used in Holy Writ, is inapplicable here. We must take the predicate eternal in its proper or strict sense, a sense of *sine fine* in all Scripture texts which use it to describe the duration and the penalties of the wicked in yonder life (see II Thessalonians 1:9, Matthew 18: 8, Mark 3:29). . . . The Objections

raised in all ages to the endlessness of the infernal punishment are understandable; for the thought of a never-ending agony of rational beings fully realizing their distressing plight is so appalling that it exceeds comprehension. But all objections are based on the false principle that it is proper and reasonable to make our human sentiments and judgments the measure of God's essence and activity.

This is the case in particular with those who contend that an everlasting punishment of a part of mankind does not agree with the unity of God's world plan, or that it is compatible neither with divine love nor with divine justice, who accordingly substitute for eternal damnation eventual salvation by gradual improvement in the next life, or an immediate or later annihilation of the wicked. Against such views we must maintain the general principle that God's essence, attributes and actions exceed our comprehension, that we can therefore not know *a priori* but only from God's revelation in His Word what agrees or conflicts with God's essence and attributes. The nature of eternal damnation consists in eternal banishment from the sight of God or, in other words, in being forever excluded from communion with God. . . . To illustrate the terrible agony setting in with this banishment from the sight of God, the dogmatician points to the agony of the fish removed from its element. But there is this difference; the fish which is removed from its element soon dies, whereas the man who is banished from communion with God must by God's judgment live on, "is guilty of eternal judgment," Mark 3:29.[51]

Seventh-day Adventists would do well to heed Dr. Pieper's observation; they would do well to heed the testimony of the Christian church generally for almost two thousand years; but most important, they should heed the teaching of the Word of God that the soul of man, whether regenerate or unregenerate, exists after the death of the body. The justice of God makes everlasting punishment for the unregenerate and everlasting life for the saved to be two sides of one coin — God's justice and God's love. The Bible then we believe clearly teaches that there is neither authority nor warrant for the doctrines of condi-

[49] I.e., personal communion or fellowship with Christ. Spiritual death is the opposite of eternal life in that the soul is deprived of such communion or fellowship and is conscious of it.

[50] Death (spiritual) far from being unconsciousness is eternal *conscious* endurance of God's just wrath.

[51] Pieper, Francis, *Christian Dogmatics*, pages 544-545, Vol. III.

tional immortality and annihilation. God grant in the fulness of His wisdom that none of His children will persist in setting up their standards as the criterion to determine His perfect righteousness. It is my opinion that Seventh-day Adventists have done just this; first by predicating that a God of love *would not* eternally punish a conscious being, and second by attempting to force the Scriptures into their frame of thought while seeming to ignore context, hermeneutics and exegesis. Their fellow Christians can only pray that they may soon be led to embrace the historic position of the church, which is the antithesis of the sleep of the soul and the annihilation of the wicked.

THE SABBATH, THE LORD'S DAY, AND THE MARK OF THE BEAST

Certainly the most distinctive doctrine promulgated by the Seventh-day Adventist denomination, and one of the two from which they derive their name, is the Seventh-day Sabbath. How Adventists came to hold the Sabbath as the true day of worship, and why they continue to champion it and jealously urge it upon all who worship on Sunday, provides the key to understanding their psychological and theological motivations.

I. *The Sabbath or the Lord's Day?*

Seventh-day Adventists from the beginning have always attempted to equate the Sabbath with the Lord's Day. Their principal method for accomplishing this is to link Mark 2:28 with Revelation 1:10, and thus to undercut one of the strongest arguments against their position, i.e., the Lord's Day as opposed to Sabbath observance.

They reason that since "the Son of Man is Lord also of the Sabbath" (Mark 2:27, 28), when John says he "was in the Spirit on the Lord's day" (Revelation 1: 10), the Sabbath and the Lord's Day must be the same! The weakness of their position is that they base their argument on an English translation instead of on the Greek original. When one reads the second chapter of Mark and the first chapter of Revelation in Greek, he sees that there is no such interpretation inherent in the grammatical structure. The Greek of Mark 2:28 clearly indicates that Christ did not mean that the Sabbath was His *possession* (which the Adventists would like to establish); rather, He was saying that as Lord of all He could do as He pleased on the Sabbath. The Greek is most explicit

here.

Nothing could be clearer from both the context and the grammar. In Revelation 1:10 the Greek is not the genitive of possession, which it would have to be in order to make *te-kuriake* (the Lord's) agree with *hemera* (day). John did not mean that the Lord's Day was the Lord's possession, but rather that it was the day dedicated to Him by the early church, not in accordance with Mosaic law, but in obedience to our Lord's commandment of love.

We may certainly assume that if the Sabbath had meant so much to the writers of the New Testament; and if, as Adventists insist, it was so widely observed during the early centuries of the Christian church, John and the other writers of Scripture would have equated it with the Lord's Day, the first day of the week. Scripture and history testify that they did not, and Adventists have, therefore, little Scriptural justification for their Sabbatarianism.

A. *Testimony of the Fathers*

The Church Fathers provide a mass of evidence that the first day of the week, not the seventh, is the Lord's Day. Some of this evidence is here submitted for the reader's consideration. In company with the overwhelming majority of historians and scholars, we believe that not only the New Testament but the following citations refute Sabbatarianism. We have yet to see any systematic answer to what the Christian church always believed.

1. *Ignatius, Bishop of Antioch,* in the year 110, wrote: "If, then, those who walk in the ancient practices attain to newness of hope, no longer observing the Sabbath, but fashioning their lives after the Lord's Day on which our life also arose through Him, that we may be found disciples of Jesus Christ, our only teacher."

2. *Justin Martyr*[52] (100-165): "And on the day called Sunday, all who live in cities or in the country gather together in one place and memoirs of the apostles or the writings of the prophets are read, as long as time permits. . . . Sunday is the day on which we all hold our common assembly because it is the first day on which God, having wrought a change in the darkness in matter, made the world; and Jesus Christ our Saviour on the same day rose from the dead."

3. *The Epistle of Barnabas* (between 120 and 150): " 'Your new moons and your sabbaths I cannot endure' (Isaiah

[52]Justin also wrote the famous *Dialogue with Trypho,* a Jew, throughout which he refutes Sabbathkeeping as foreign to the gospel of grace and the spirit of Christianity. It is 142 chapters long.

1:13). You perceive how He speaks: Your present sabbaths are not acceptable to me but that which I had made in giving rest to all things, I shall make a beginning of the eighth day, that is a beginning of another world. Wherefore also, we keep the eighth day with joyfulness, a day also in which Jesus rose from the dead."

4. *Irenaeus, Bishop of Lyons* (about 178): "The mystery of the Lord's resurrection may not be celebrated on any other day than the Lord's Day."

5. *Bardaisān* (born 154): "Wherever we be, all of us are called by the one name of the Messiah, namely Christians and upon one day which is the first day of the week we assemble ourselves together and on the appointed days we abstain from food."

6. *Cyprian, Bishop of Carthage* (200-258): "The Lord's Day is both the first and the eighth day."

7. *Eusebius* (about 315): "The churches throughout the rest of the world observe the practice that has prevailed from the Apostolic tradition until the present time so that it would not be proper to terminate our fast on any other day but the resurrection day of our Saviour. Hence, there were synods and convocations of our bishops on this question and they unanimously drew up an ecclesiastical decree which they communicated to churches in all places — that the mystery of the Lord's resurrection should be celebrated on no other than the Lord's day."

8. *Peter, Bishop of Alexandria* (about 300): "We keep the Lord's Day as a day of joy because of Him who arose thereon."

9. *Didache of the Apostles* (about 70-75): "On the Lord's own day, gather yourselves together and break bread and give thanks."

10. *The Epistle of Pliny* (about 112, addressed to the Emperor Trajan): "They [the Christians] affirmed . . . that the whole of their crime or error was that they had been wont to meet together on a fixed day before daylight and to repeat among themselves in turn a hymn to Christ as to a god and to bind themselves by an oath (*sacramentum*) . . .; these things duly done, it had been their custom to disperse and to meet again to take food — of an ordinary and harmless kind. Even this they had ceased to do after my edict, by which, in accordance with your instructions, I had forbidden the existence of societies."[53]

Thus is appears that from apostolic and patristic times, the Christian church observed the Lord's Day or the first day of the week; further, the Jewish Sabbath, in the words of Clement of Alexandria (about 194) was "nothing more than a working day."

In their zeal to establish the authority of the Sabbath, Adventists either reject contrary evidence as unauthentic (and so conflict with the preponderance of scholastic opinion), or they ignore the testimony of the early church. Although they seem unaffected by the evidence, the fact remains that the Christian church has both apostolic and historical support for observing the Lord's Day in place of the Sabbath.

B. *"Authoritative Quotations"*

Recently the Adventist radio program *Voice of Prophecy* circulated a 31-page pamphlet entitled, *Authoritative Quotations on the Sabbath and Sunday.* In it they quoted "leading" Protestant sources to "prove" that Sunday usurped the Sabbath and is a pagan institution imposed by Constantine in 321.

However, many of the sources quoted actually establish what the Adventists flatly deny; i.e., that the seventh-day Sabbath is *not* the Lord's Day or the first day of the week, but is, in fact, the seventh day as its name indicates.

Since the Adventists are willing to quote these authorities to buttress their position in one area, surely they will give consideration to contradictory statements by these same authorities in another:

1. "The Lord's Day did not succeed in the place of the Sabbath. . . . The Lord's Day was merely an ecclesiastical institution. . . . The primitive Christians did all manner of work upon the Lord's Day" (Bishop Jeremy Taylor, *Ductor Dubitantium,* Part 1, Book 2, Chap. 2, Rule 6, Secs. 51, 59).

2. "The observance of the Lord's Day [Sunday] is founded not on any command of God, but on the authority of the church" (*Augsburg Confession of Faith,* quoted in *Catholic Sabbath Manual,* Part 2, Chap. 1, Sec. 10).

3. "But they err in teaching that Sunday has taken the place of the Old Testament Sabbath and therefore must be kept as the Seventh day had to be kept by the children of Israel" (J. T. Mueller,

---

[53]Book 10, epistle 96. Although Pliny does not state to which day of the week he refers, the foregoing quotations corroborate the N.T. record that Christians met on the Lord's Day or the first day of the week to partake of the Lord's Supper, and conduct church

business (Acts 20:7; I Corinthians 16:2). Such was *not* the practice of the early church concerning the Sabbath. See Dr. E. De Pressene, *The Ancient World and Christianity.*

Sabbath or Sunday, pages 15, 16).

4. "They [the Catholics] allege the Sabbath changed into Sunday, the Lord's Day, contrary to the Decalogue as it appears, neither is there any example more boasted than the changing of the Sabbath Day" (Martin Luther, *Augsburg Confession of Faith,* Art. 28, Para. 9).

5. "Although it [Sunday] was in primitive times and differently called the Lord's day or Sunday, yet it was never denominated the Sabbath; a name constantly appropriate to Saturday, or the Seventh day both by sacred and ecclesiastical writers" (Charles Buck, *A Theological Dictionary,* 1830, page 537).

6. "The notion of a formal substitution by apostolic authority of the Lord's Day [meaning Sunday] for the Jewish Sabbath (or the first for the seventh day) . . . the transference to it perhaps in a spiritualized form of the Sabbath obligation established by promulgation of the fourth commandment has no basis whatever, either in Holy Scripture or in Christian antiquity" (Sir William Smith and Samuel Cheetham, *A Dictionary of Christian Antiquities,* Vol. II, page 182, article on the Sabbath).

7. "The view that the Christian's Lord's Day or Sunday is but the Christian Sabbath deliberately transferred from the seventh to the first day of the week does not indeed find categoric expression till a much later period. . . . The Council of Laodicea (A.D. 364) . . . forbids Christians from Judaizing and resting on the Sabbath Day, preferring the Lord's Day and so far as possible resting as Christians" (*Encyclopedia Britannica,* 1899 ed., vol. 23, page 654).

Thus the Adventists have in effect destroyed their argument by appealing to authorities which state unequivocally that the first day of the week is the Lord's Day and that it was observed by the early Christian church from the time of the Apostles.[54]

It should also be carefully noted that in their "Authoritative Quotations" the Adventists overlook the fact that nearly all the authorities argue forcefully for the Lord's Day as the first day of the week, and state that legal observance of the Sabbath terminated at the cross (Colossians 2:16, 17). The Adventists also, in their compilation of quotations appeal even to the Church of Jesus Christ of Lat-

ter-Day Saints (Mormon), and to Fulton Oursler, a Roman Catholic lay writer. The Mormons are a non-Christian cult, a fact which the Adventists admit; and Oursler, a layman, hardly represents the position of Rome.

On page 13 of this same pamphlet, the Adventists make misleading use of the ellipsis. The following is a direct quotation as it appears:

Sunday (*dies-solis,* of the Roman calendar, day of the sun, because dedicated to the sun), was adopted by the early Christians as a day of worship. The sun of Latin adoration they interpreted as the "sun of righteousness." . . . No regulations for its observance are laid down in the New Testament, nor, indeed, is its observance even enjoined. Schaff-Herzog *Encyclopedia of Religious Knowledge,* 1891 ed., Volume 4, Article on Sunday.

Now there is the paragraph as it appears in the *Encyclopedia:*

Sunday (*dies-solis,* of the Roman Calendar, day of the sun because dedicated to the sun), was adopted by the early Christians as a day of worship. The sun of Latin adoration they interpreted as "the sun of righteousness." SUNDAY WAS EMPHATICALLY THE WEEKLY FEAST OF THE RESURRECTION OF CHRIST, AS THE JEWISH SABBATH WAS THE FEAST OF THE CREATION. IT WAS CALLED THE "LORD'S DAY," AND UPON IT THE PRIMITIVE CHURCH ASSEMBLED TO BREAK BREAD (Acts 20: 7, I Corinthians 16:2). No regulations for its observance are laid down in the New Testament, nor, indeed, is its observance even enjoined; YET CHRISTIAN FEELING LED TO THE UNIVERSAL ADOPTION OF THE DAY, IN IMITATION OF APOSTOLIC PRECEDENCE. IN THE SECOND CENTURY ITS OBSERVANCE WAS UNIVERSAL.[55]

Such use of the ellipsis is not uncommon in certain Seventh-day Adventists' writings in connection with the Sabbath, the Lord's Day, etc., and we regret that they resort to it in order to substantiate their position.

In this pamphlet they quote Martin Luther, despite the well known fact that Luther violently opposed Sabbatarianism. His refutation of his Sabbatarian colleague Dr. Carlstadt is a monument to his apolo-

---

[54] See John 20:19, 26; Acts 20:7; I Corinthians 6:1, 2; Revelation 1:10.

[55] Sentences in capital letters were omitted by the writer of the Adventist pamphlet on page 22. This

mutilation of authoritative sources first occurs in *The Present Truth,* Vol. I, No. 9, published in the 1880's. So our Adventist brethren apparently failed to check the quotation's validity.

getic genius. Thus, to quote Luther in order to support the doctrine of the Seventh day suggests that Adventists are not familiar with Luther's theology.

We admire the boldness of our Adventist brethren in their claims for the Sabbath but their boldness is misplaced and leads to a distorted concept of the value of the law of God; for, when a person believes and teaches that "the fourth commandment is the greatest commandment in the Decalogue," it is apparent that he has no understanding of the spirit of the law. Volume IV of the *International Standard Bible Encyclopedia* represents the reasons why the Christian church observes the Lord's Day in preference to the Sabbath, and also clearly states (pages 2629-34) the Seventh-day Adventist position.[56] On page 2633 the Adventists contend: "According to church history the seventh day Sabbath was observed by the early church, and no other day was observed as a Sabbath during the first two or three centuries."

This sentence epitomizes the Adventist propensity for overstating their case; i.e., attempting to read "Sabbath" into "Lord's Day," which all leading authorities confute as we have seen.

II. *Primary Anti-Sabbatarian Texts*

In more than one place, the New Testament comments unfavorably upon the practice of any type of legalistic day keeping. In fact, from the ascension of Christ on, the New Testament and early church observed the first day of the week or the Lord's Day, (Revelation 1:10), as we have endeavored to show. Besides the passages which contrast the Lord's Day with the Sabbath, the apostle Paul, Hebrew of the Hebrews and Pharisee of the Pharisees, the outstanding New Testament authority, apart from our Lord, on the Law of Moses, declared that the Sabbath as "the law" was fulfilled at the cross and was not binding upon the Christian (Colossians 2:16, 17). Since the subject is so vast in scope, the reader is referred to the Bibliography, especially to Dr. Louis Sperry Chafer's *Grace,* and Norman C. Deck's *The Lord's Day or the Sabbath, Which?* These contain excellent refutations of Sabbatarianism. D. M. Canright in *Seventh-day Adventism Renounced* also deals exhaustively and ably with the Sabbath subject.

To narrow the issue down to simple

analysis, we shall review the major New Testament texts, which in context and in the light of syntactical analysis refute the Sabbatarian concept, and substantiate the historic position of the Christian church since the days of the Apostles and the Fathers.[57]

A. *Colossians 2:13-17*

Of all of the statements in the New Testament, these verses most strongly refute the Sabbatarian claim for observance of the Jewish Sabbath. Let us listen to the inspired counsel of Paul, not only the greatest of the apostles, but a Pharisee whose passion for fulfilling the law outdoes that of the most zealous Seventh-day Adventist:

> And you, who were dead in trespasses and the uncircumcision of your flesh, God made alive together with him, having forgiven us all our trespasses; having canceled the bond which stood against us with its legal demands; this he set aside, nailing it to the cross. He disarmed the principalities and powers and made a public example of them, triumphing over them in him. Therefore let no one pass judgment on you in questions of food and drink or with regard to a festival or a new moon or a sabbath. These are only a shadow of what is to come; but the substance belongs to Christ (Colossians 2:13-17 RSV).

This translation, perhaps the best from the Greek text today, contains tremendously important teaching.

First, we who were dead have been made alive in Christ, and have been forgiven all trespasses and sins. We are free from the condemnation of the law in all its aspects, because Christ took our condemnation on the cross. As already observed, there are not two laws, moral and ceremonial, but one law containing many commandments, all perfectly fulfilled by the life and death of the Lord Jesus Christ.

"Therefore," the Apostle Paul boldly declares, "let no one pass judgment on you in question of food and drink or with regard to a festival or a new moon or a sabbath. These are only a shadow of what is to come; but the substance belongs to Christ."

In the face of this clear teaching, Sabbatarians revert to their dual-law theory and argue that Paul is referring only to

---

[56]Bible Question Column in *Signs of the Times,* Jan. 8, 1952.

[57]With few exceptions the church fathers and early historians maintain that Christians gathered together and worshiped on the Lord's Day (Revelation 1:10) or the first day of the week as we have set forth.

observance of the Jewish ceremonial law, not to the Sabbath which, they insist, is a moral precept because it is one of the Ten Commandments. We have seen, however, that the Ten Commandments are but a fragment of the moral law encompassed by the commandment, "Thou shalt love thy neighbor as thyself" (Leviticus 19: 18, Romans 13:9).

Sabbatarians, however, overlook the mass of contradictory evidence and appeal to certain commentators who do not analyze the uses of the word "sabbath," or exegete the New Testament passages where the word occurs. Such commentators are Albert Barnes, *Notes on the New Testament*; Jamieson, Fausset and Brown, *Critical and Explanatory Commentary*; and Adam Clark in his *Commentary*. If a commentator's opinion is not in accord with sound exegesis, it is *only an opinion*, and the commentators named above make no grammatical or textual analysis of the second chapter of Colossians!

Many New Testament commentators try to retain the moral force of the Sabbath (although all of these transfer it to the first day of the week) because it is the subject of the fourth commandment. For this serious theological error there is no warrant in the New Testament. Sabbatarians fail to mention that all the commentators whom they cite repudiate the Sabbath, and most of them teach that the true Sabbath was the Lord's Day (Revelation 1:10), carried over by the early church from apostolic tradition as a memorial to redemption, or the recreation of mankind through the regeneration power of the Holy Spirit. Adventists are therefore without historical or exegetical support when they make the Lord's Day the same as the Sabbath.

With regard to this passage, Adventists maintain that since the word in Colossians 2:16 (*sabbaton*) is in the plural, it means the ceremonial Sabbaths, not the weekly Sabbath, which they contend is still in effect. However, their argument seems to be that Colossians 2:16, 17 refers to sabbaths and feast days which were shadows of things to come, and thus part of ceremonial laws, but that the seventh-day Sabbath is not a shadow of redemption but a memorial of creation and part of the moral law. The leading modern translations, following the best New Testament scholars, render Colossians 2:16 as "a sabbath" or "a sabbath day" not "sabbath days" as in the King James Version. Their

reason for doing this is well stated by W. E. Vine who wrote:

> *Sabbaton* or *sabbata*, the latter the plural form, was transliterated from the Aramaic word which was mistaken for a plural: hence the singular *sabbaton* was formed from it. . . . In the epistles the only direct mentions are in in Colossians 2:16 "a sabbath day" (RV), which rightly has the singular . . . where it is listed among things that were "a shadow of things to come"; i.e., of the age introduced at Pentecost and in Hebrews 4:4-11 where the perpetual *sabbatismos* is appointed for believers: . . . . For the first three centuries of the Christian era the first day of the week was never confounded with the Sabbath; the confusion of the Jewish and Christian institutions was due to declension from apostolic teaching.[58]

Supplementing Dr. Vine's statement is the comment of M. R. Vincent who declared:

> Sabbath days (*sabbaton*), the weekly festivals revised correctly as *day*, the plural being used for the singular. See Luke 4:31 and Acts 20:7. The plural is only once used in the New Testament of more than a single day (Acts 17:2). In the Old Testament, the same enumeration of sacred seasons occurs in I Chronicles 23:31; II Chronicles 2:4; II Chronicles 31:3; Ezekiel 45:17; Hosea 2:11.[59]

As Dr. Vincent points out, the revisers' rendering of *sabbaton* in the singular accords with the use of the word throughout the New Testament. It is significant that in 59 of 60 occurrences in the New Testament, Adventists affirm that they refer to the *weekly* Sabbath; but in the 60th occurrence they maintain it does *not*, although *all* grammatical authorities contradict them.

With regard to Albert Barnes, whom the Adventists delight to quote because he agrees with their interpretation of Colossians two, his comments are demolished by Dean Henry Alford, a truly great Biblical exegete whom the Adventists also frequently quote. Wrote Dean Alford concerning Colossians two:

> Let no one therefore judge you (pronounce judgment of right or wrong over you, sit in judgment on you) . . . in respect of feasts or new moon, or

58*Expository Dictionary of New Testament Words*, pages 311-13.

59*Word Studies in the New Testament*, Commentary on Colossians 2, page 494.

sabbaths (i.e. yearly, monthly, or weekly celebrations). (The relative may refer either to the aggregate of the observances mentioned, or to the *last* mentioned, i.e. the Sabbath. Or it may refer to *all*.) [60]

After making significant comments on the grammar, Dean Alford went even further in his insistence that in verse 17, grammatically speaking, the Apostle Paul contrasts *all* the Jewish laws with their fulfillment in Christ, the former being a shadow, pointing forward to the real substance (*soma*), which was Christ.

Alford summed up his comments thus:

The blessings of the Christian covenant: these are the substance, and the Jewish ordinances the mere type of resemblance, as the shadow is of the living man. . . . We may observe, that if the ordinance of the Sabbath had been, *in any form* of lasting obligation on the Christian church, it would have been quite impossible for the Apostle to have spoken thus. The fact of an obligatory rest of one day, whether the seventh or the first, *would have been directly in the teeth of his assertion here: the holding of such would have been still to retain the shadow, while we possess the substance.* And no answer can be given to this by the transparent special-pleading, that he is speaking only of that which was *Jewish* in such observances: the whole argument being *general,* and the axiom of verse 17 universally applicable. [61]

We see, then, that from a grammatical standpoint if the Adventists insist that Colossians 2:16 refers only to ceremonial sabbaths, they run against the use of the word for weekly sabbaths in the New Testament; and, as Alford points out, if "sabbaths" be allowed, it must include all Sabbaths, weekly, monthly or yearly. On the other hand, if Adventists admit the correction of the revisers and render Colossians 2:16 "a sabbath day," its use in the New Testament still refers almost exclusively (see Acts 17:2) to the weekly Sabbath, which Adventists maintain is permanent, although Paul deliberately classes it with the ordinances which Christ by His death nailed to the cross! (Colossians 2:14).

Dr. J. B. Lightfoot, an acknowledged authority on New Testament Greek, makes this interesting observation:

The word *sabbata* is derived from the Aramaic *shabbatha* (as distinguished from the Hebrew), and accordingly preserves the Aramaic termination of *a.* Hence it was naturally declined as a plural noun, *sabbata, sabbaton.* The New Testament *sabbata* is only once used distinctively as more than a single day, and there the plurality of meaning is brought out by the attached numeral (Acts 17:2). [62]

It is apparent therefore that the use of "sabbath" in the New Testament refutes the Adventist contention that in Colossians two it means Sabbaths other than the weekly Sabbath of the Decalogue. Since it is impossible to retain the "shadow" while possessing the "substance" (Colossians 2:17), the Jewish Sabbath and the handwriting of ordinances "which was contrary to us" found their complete fulfillment in the person and work of the Lord Jesus Christ.

Seventh-day Adventists are also deprived of the support of Albert Barnes, because he admits that if Paul had "*used the word in the singular number, 'the sabbath,' it would then of course have been clear that he meant to teach that that commandment had ceased to be binding and that a sabbath was no longer to be observed.*" [63]

Since Barnes makes this admission, and since modern conservative scholarship establishes the singular rendering of "sabbath" in the New Testament (see RSV, *et al.*), Adventists find even less support for their position.

We conclude our comments on this passage of Scripture by observing that in Numbers 28 and 29 which list the very "ordinances" referred to in Colossians 2:16, 17, the Sabbath is grouped with burnt offerings and new moons (Numbers 28:1-15). Since these offerings and feasts have passed away as the shadow (*skia*), fulfilled in the substance (*soma*) of the cross of Christ, how can the seventh-day Sabbath be retained? In the light of this Scripture alone, I contend that the argument for Sabbath observance collapses, and the Christian stands under "the perfect law of liberty" which enables him to fulfill "the righteousness of the law" by the imperative of love.

B. *Galatians 4:9-11*

But now that you have come to know God, or rather to be known by God,

---

[60] D. H. Alford, *The New Testament for English Readers,* pages 1299, 1300; see his *Commentary on Colossians,* pages 224-25.

[61] *New Testament for English Readers,* page 1300.
[62] *Commentary on Colossians,* page 225.
[63] *Notes on the New Testament,* Colossians 2.

how can you turn back again to the weak and beggarly elemental spirits, whose slaves you want to be once more? You observe days, and months, and seasons, and years! I am afraid I have labored over you in vain (RSV).

Paul's epistle to the Galatians was primarily a massive theological effort to bolster the young church against the Judaizers who added to the gospel of grace "another gospel" (1:6), and sought to "pervert the gospel of Christ" (1:7).

Though steeped in Jewish lore and the law of Moses, Paul steadfastly opposed the Judaizers. The entire epistle to the Galatians is an apologetic against those who would seek to bring the Christian "under the law." After mentioning the errors into which the Galatian church had fallen, Paul, evidently with great disgust, remarks, "You observe days, and months, and seasons, and years! I am afraid I have labored over you in vain" (4:10, 11 RSV). In the Greek the expression "days, and month, and seasons, and years," matches both the Septuagint translation of the ordinances in Numbers 28 and 29, of which all Sabbaths are a principal part, and the ordinances mentioned in Colossians two. Paul was familiar with the Septuagint and quoted it, and the law, including the weekly Sabbaths, was so cherished by the Judaizers of his day that its legalistic observance called forth his strong words. Adventists insist that Paul meant ceremonial feasts and yearly Sabbaths, not the weekly Sabbath; but Paul's language, and the Septuagint translation of Numbers 28 and 29, refutes their objections. It is one thing to interpret your way out of a verse when your interpretation is feasible; it is another to ignore grammar, context, and comparative textual analysis (hermeneutics) as our Adventist friends and others appear to do. To substantiate their interpretation of Paul's statements they do not practice exegesis (taking out of), but eisegesis (reading into) the texts.

After studying Seventh-day Adventist literature, it is my opinion that the overwhelming majority of Seventh-day Adventists do not actually consider themselves "under the law." I believe they fail to realize that by trying to enjoin Sabbath observance upon other members of the Body of Christ, they are in serious danger of transgressing the gospel of grace. To them Paul says,

Tell me, you who desire to be under the law, do you not hear the law? . . . Now before faith came, we were con-

fined under the law, kept under restraint until faith should be revealed. So that the law was our custodian until Christ came, that we might be justified by faith. But now that faith has come, we are no longer under a custodian; for in Christ Jesus you are all sons of God, through faith (Galatians 4:21; 3:23-26 RSV).

Bearing in mind that "the law" in its larger connotation includes the entire Pentateuch, it is apparent from Paul's language that one is "under the law" when he attempts to observe any part of it, because the Christian has been freed from the law. Seventh-day Adventists are doubtless Christians, saved by grace, but we do not find Scriptural warrant for their attempt to enjoin the Sabbath upon their fellow believers.

C. Romans 13:8-10

Owe no one anything, except to love one another; for he who loves his neighbor has fulfilled the law. The commandments, "You shall not commit adultery, You shall not kill, You shall not steal, You shall not covet," and *any other commandment*, are summed up in this sentence, "You shall love your neighbor as yourself." Love does no wrong to a neighbor; therefore love is the fulfilling of the law.

It is really unnecessary to comment extensively upon the foregoing verses since they speak so plainly for themselves.

The Greek word *pleroma*, translated respectively "fulfilled" and "fulfilling" in Romans 13:8, 10 (RSV) appears 90 times in the New Testament and has the same basic meaning. The Apostle Paul surely understood this term; since the Adventists confess the divine inspiration of the Scriptures, they must concede that the Holy Spirit guided his pen. Quoting from the Decalogue upon which the Adventists rely for perpetual Sabbathkeeping, Paul declares, "The commandments . . . are summed up in this sentence, 'You shall love your neighbor as yourself.' Love does no wrong to a neighbor; therefore love is the *fulfilling* of the law." In verse eight the apostle declares, "He who loves his neighbor has *fulfilled* the law"; and since he quotes from the Decalogue as part of the law, the fourth commandment is also fulfilled, not by rigid observance of a given day, but by loving one's neighbor as oneself! Since it is impossible in the Christian context to love one's neighbor at all, apart from loving God as the prerequisite, the issue is clear. The false teaching that love of one's neighbor does not fulfill all the law of God comes from a failure to realize that our love for God and neighbor stems from God's initiating act of love in Christ. This law of love is first enunciated in Leviticus 19:18, which our Lord coupled with the commandment to "love the Lord thy God" (Deuteronomy 6:4), and stated that observance of those two commandments fulfilled "all the law and the prophets."

While our Adventist brethren may seek to escape the implications of Colossians 2:14-17, and to explain away Galatians 4:9-11, in the present passage the Holy Spirit twice declares that love *fulfills* the law. They cannot exempt the Sabbath from this context without destroying the unity of the "Eternal Ten," hence their dilemma.

In Galatians Paul also declares, "The whole law is fulfilled in one word. 'You shall love your neighbor as yourself' " (5:14 RSV). So we see that Paul's theology rested upon the imperative of love. Therefore, it is my conviction that the Holy Spirit, not the Christian church, is the authority for the nullification of all sabbathkeeping. How any student of New Testament Greek could read the unmistakable language of the apostle and then exclude the Sabbath commandment from his argument, passes my understanding.

D. *Romans 14:4-6, 10, 12, 13*

Who are you to pass judgment on the servant of another? It is before his own master that he stands or falls. And he will be upheld, for the Master is able to make him stand. One man esteems one day as better than another, while another man esteems all days alike. Let every one be fully convinced in his own mind. He who observes the day, observes it in honor of the Lord. He also who eats, eats in honor of the Lord, since he gives thanks to God; while he who abstains, abstains in honor of the Lord and gives thanks to God. . . . Why do you pass judgment on your brother? Or you, why do you despise your brother? For we shall all stand before the judgment seat of God; . . . so each of us shall give account of himself to God. Then let us no more pass judgment on one another, but rather decide never to put a stumbling-block or hindrance in the way of a brother (RSV).

In this writer's opinion, and according to Romans 14, the Seventh-day Adventist is entitled to observe the seventh-day Sabbath if he feels that this is what God desires. Further than this, the Holy Spirit adjures us not to "pass judgment" on our fellow Christians regarding such matters as observance of days, and diet. I believe that Seventh-day Adventists, Seventh-day Baptists, and Sabbatarians of other religious groups have the right to worship on the seventh day in the liberty wherein Christ has made us free. It is wrong and unchristian to discriminate against Sabbatarians merely because they "esteem" the Sabbath above the first day of the week, or the Lord's Day. I suggest it is no more legalistic for them to observe the seventh day out of conviction than it is for the Christian church to observe the first day. It is a matter of liberty and conscience.

If Seventh-day Adventists, however, would follow the Biblical teaching of Romans 14 with regard to those who wish to observe Sunday, we would not have the conflict which has been generated by their dogmatic insistence that all should worship on the Sabbath. The sad fact is, however, that all Sabbatarians transgress the very counsels given by the Apostle Paul when he asks,

Who are you to pass judgment on the servant of another? It is before his own master that he stands or falls. And he will be upheld, for the Master is able to make him stand. . . . Why do you pass judgment on your brother? Or . . . why do you despise your brother? For we shall all stand before the judgment seat of God; . . . so each of us shall give account of himself to God. Let us no more pass judgment on one another, but rather decide never to put a stumbling-block or hindrance in the way of a brother (Romans 14:4-13).

Of course Seventh-day Adventists feel that they are called upon to perpetuate or promulgate certain truths which they believe are to be found in the Word of God, and which they believe are to be emphasized in "these last days." Furthermore, the counsels of Ellen G. White, they believe, emphasize the importance of these truths. Granting their basic premise that God has indeed spoken to them concerning Sabbath observance, it is easy to see the source of their zeal. But I feel that there is good evidence that the "spirit of prophecy" is not what they claim; and their "special truths" have, to say the least, questionable theological origins. Non-adventists reject the claims that they make for Mrs. White, and merely because Adventists accept her counsel is no reason for other Christians to feel bound to do so. We repeat—the faith the Adventists place in "the spirit of prophecy" which has endorsed their "special truths," sincere though they may be, does not entitle them to contradict the counsel of the Holy Spirit as revealed in the Word of God. This I believe they have done. I could cite scores of references from contemporary Adventist writers who do indeed pass judgment[64] upon their Christian brothers and upon the Christian church at large, because the latter do not observe the seventh-day Sabbath. It is my opinion in these cases that they neglect the counsel of the Holy Spirit: "One man esteems one day as better than another, while another man esteems all days alike. Let everyone be fully convinced in his own mind. He who observes the day, observes it in honor of the Lord. . . . Happy is he who has no reason to judge himself for what he approves . . . for whatever does not proceed from faith is sin" (Romans 14:5, 6, 22, 23 RSV).

By contending that other members of the Body of Christ should recognize "the spirit of prophecy," Seventh-day Adventists appear to juxtapose the "spirit of prophecy" with the Holy Spirit who says: "Then let us not pass judgment on one another but rather decide never to put a stumbling-block or hindrance in the way of a brother" (verse 13).

There can be little doubt that the great majority of Christians who worship on Sunday would never have discriminated against the Seventh-day Adventists, had the latter not insisted upon "passing judgment" on first-day observance as opposed to Sabbathkeeping. Although motivated by the best intentions and sincere in faith, Adventists have nevertheless put a stumbling-block or hindrance in the way of fellow Christians by their rigid Sabbatarianism. It is indeed unfortunate that such a source of strife exists among Christians.

The fourteenth chapter of Romans is a masterpiece on the subject of Christian liberty, not only in diet but in worship, and in the context of all Paul's writings on the subject it appears that Adventists ignore the plain teaching of Scripture about the observance of days. We ask, should they not be more charitable in the light of I Corinthians 13? They will thus avoid opposition from their fellow Christians.

These four passages from the writings of Paul reflect the position of the historic Christian church from the times of the fathers and the reformers to the leading exegetical commentators of our day. The reader should remember that Adventist arguments, although buttressed by selected Bible passages (sometimes cited out of context), must be studied in the clear light of these four passages which contain the comprehensive New Testament teaching on Sabbatarianism. The early Christian church met upon the *first* day of the week (I Corinthians 16:2). The disciples received the Holy Spirit on the *first* day of the week; collections were taken for the saints on the *first* day of the week, and historic evidence establishes that the *first* day of the week was the Lord's Day, the memorial of the new creation in Christ Jesus which completely fulfilled the law in Christ.

No amount of argument by Adventists can alter these facts, and if we believe the Apostle Paul was inspired by the Holy Spirit it is apparent that we must reject Sabbatarianism. We do not judge Seventh-day Adventists for their Sabbath observance, and they in turn should extend the same charity to their fellow Christians. Only in the recognition of the principles of Romans 14 can true unity in the Body of Christ be realized. There can be no legislation of moral choice on the basis of "special revelation." This we believe is the case in Seventh-day Adventism, for it was Ellen G. White's "Vision" confirming Joseph Bates' "Seal of the Living God" concept as set forth in his pamphlet on the Sabbath that established Sabbatarianism in Seventh-day Adventism. The Bible must be the supreme court of appeal and authority; and the verdict of this court, it appears to me, invalidates the contentions of our Adventist friends.

Author's Note on "The Mark of the Beast"

The subjects of the Seventh-day Sabbath and the Mark of the Beast already have been covered in sufficient detail. However, it is often charged that Adventists teach that salvation depends upon observance of the seventh day as Sabbath, and that the mark of the beast (Revelation 13:16, 17) rests upon all Sunday-keepers. For this reason, the record should be examined.

One ex-Adventist layman writes that there are "characteristic false doctrines of the sect . . . the obligation of seventh-day Sabbath observance on the part of all professing Christians, the 'mark of the

---

[64]Not of a final or eternal nature, however.

beast' for Sunday-keepers." Now if this charge were correct, we too would doubt the possibility of fellowship with Adventists. But such is not the case. Ellen G. White on a number of occasions pointedly denied what is claimed to be the position of the Adventist denomination on this point. Wrote Mrs. White:

No one has yet received the mark of the beast. The testing time has not yet come. There are true Christians in every church, not excepting the Roman Catholic communion. None are condemned until they have had the light and have seen the obligation of the fourth commandment. . . . Sunday-keeping is not yet the mark of the beast, and will not be until the decree goes forth causing men to worship this idol sabbath.[65]

In addition to this quotation, the Adventists have stated:

When Sunday observance shall be enforced by law, and the world shall be enlightened concerning the obligation of the true Sabbath, then whoever shall transgress the command of God, to obey a precept which has no higher authority than that of Rome, will thereby honor popery above God.[66]

To sum up, the Adventists declare,

God surely does not hold men accountable for truth that has not yet come to their knowledge and understanding. . . . We hold the firm conviction that millions of devout Christians of all faiths throughout all past centuries, as well as those today who are sincerely trusting in Christ their Saviour for salvation and are following Him according to their best light, are unquestionably saved. Thousands of such went to the stake as martyrs for Christ and for their faith. Moreover, untold numbers of godly Roman Catholics will surely be included. God reads the heart and deals with the intent and understanding. . . . Seventh-day Adventists interpret the prophecies relating to the beast, and the reception of his work, as something that will come into sharp focus just before the return of our Lord in glory. It is our understanding that this issue will then become a worldwide test.[67]

The statement, then, that Seventh-day Adventists believe that anyone who is a Sunday-keeper *has* the mark of the beast or the mark of apostasy, is made without regard to the facts. Why do these critics attempt to make it appear that Adventists believe that their fellow Christians are lost? The authoritative statements of this denomination are available for all to read. Doubtless some Seventh-day Adventist writers have gone contrary to the teaching of the denomination, but to indict the entire denomination for the excesses of a few is neither ethical nor Christian.

THE SANCTUARY, THE INVESTIGATIVE
    JUDGMENT, AND THE SCAPEGOAT

The foundation of Seventh-day Adventism is its view of prophecy which is of the historic school of interpretation, a school which maintains that prophecy is to be understood in the light of consecutive fulfillment in history. The exaggeration of this idea led William Miller and his followers to teach that the 2300 days of Daniel 8:14 were actually 2300 years. Figuring from 457 B.C., the now verified time of the decree to rebuild Jerusalem (Daniel 9:24),[68] the Millerites thought that 1843 would be the date for the second advent of Jesus Christ. Miller and his followers, among whom were James and Ellen G. White and other prominent Seventh-day Adventists, understood "the sanctuary" of Daniel 8:14 to be the earth which would be cleansed by Christ at the "great and terrible Day of the Lord," which they interpreted as the Second Advent of Christ. We have seen, however, that the Millerites were bitterly disappointed; and when Christ did not appear, Miller himself renounced the system and all resultant movements, including Seventh-day Adventism. But the early Seventh-day Adventists, relying upon the "vision" of Elder Hiram Edson, transferred the location of the sanctuary from the earth to Heaven, and taught that in 1844 Christ went instead into the second apartment of the sanctuary in Heaven (which contemporary Seventh-day Adventists term *the second phase* of His ministry), there to review the cases of those deemed to be worthy of eternal life. This phase of our Lord's ministry the Seventh-day Adventists call the "investigative judgment." It is a unique Arminian type theory intended, I believe, to discipline Christians by the threat of impending judgment and condemnation upon those whose cases are decided upon unfavorably by our Lord. When concluded, the Inves-

[65]*Questions on Doctrine*, pages 183-84.
[66]*Ibid.*, page 178.
[67]*Ibid.*, pages 178, 184-85.

[68]See Dr. Siegfried Horn and Lynn Wood, *The Chronology of Ezra 7*, Review & Herald Pub. Assoc., Washington, D. C.

tigative Judgment will usher in the Second Advent of Jesus Christ, according to the Seventh-day Adventist theology, and the devil, prefigured by the second or scapegoat of Leviticus 16 (Azazel), will bear away unto eternal destruction or annihilation his responsibility for causing sin to enter the universe. James White, a stalwart Seventh-day Adventist leader, when first confronted with the doctrine of the Investigative Judgment, opposed it *in toto*, giving in substance the very arguments put forth by all subsequent ex-Seventh-day Adventists. And it was only after considerable time that James White finally acceded to the doctrine of the Investigative Judgment. There are many critics of Seventh-day Adventism who, when approaching the Sanctuary, Investigative Judgment and Scapegoat concepts, deride and mock the early Adventists and their descendants for accepting such unsupported, extra-Biblical theories, but derision is not the answer, and it should be remembered that Adventists hold these doctrines in sincerity. Therefore, if they are ever to be persuaded of the mistaken nature of their faith, in these areas at least, only the facts of Scripture and the guidance of the Holy Spirit of God will bring it about.

The view of Hiram Edson, described in chapter one, is, so far as this writer is concerned, an attempt to escape the terrible calamity which befell the Millerite movement, and the disappointment and embarrassment that must have followed the failure of the Millerite prophecies and their interpretations of the Book of Daniel. We shall confine ourselves in this chapter, to the salient points of the theological issues raised by these special teachings or doctrines of the Advent message. In the matter of prophetic interpretation, this writer is convinced that the Holy Spirit has wisely veiled from the prying eyes and intellect of man many great truths which will doubtless be revealed toward the end of the age. It is not for us to judge whether the pretorist, historicist, or futurist schools of interpretation are correct, and we ought not overly to concern ourselves with when Christ is coming, whether before, during or after the Great Tribulation. Rather, we ought to be concerned *that* He is coming, because His coming is indeed "the blessed hope of the Christian Church" (Titus 2:13), which hope Adventists and non-Adventists alike who

share the Christian message and faith, anticipate with joy.

I. *The Sanctuary*

Since the Seventh-day Adventists believe that the sanctuary to be cleansed is in heaven (Daniel 8:14), which the Millerites identified as the earth (a regrettable early mistake), we might ask, What is the purpose of the heavenly sanctuary and its cleansing? What are the Adventists really teaching?

The book of Hebrews definitely sets forth a "heavenly sanctuary" of which Christ is the minister (Hebrews 8:1, 2), and the writer of the epistle repeatedly contrasts the Lord Jesus Christ, our risen high priest, with the Aaronic priesthood. He shows that, as a priest after the order of Melchizedek, Christ derives His authority after the power of "an endless life" (Hebrews 7:16), and that He was born *high priest and offering* on Calvary.[69] And this Adventists also emphasizes.[70]

It is futile, therefore, to argue that the word "sanctuary" does not apply to Heaven or something of a heavenly nature, since the Scriptures teach that it does. But the Adventists' error is that they draw from the Scriptures interpretations which cannot be substantiated by exegesis but rest largely upon inference and deduction, drawn from theological applications of their own design.

In their Sanctuary teaching, the Adventists do indeed declare, in the words of Ellen G. White:

> As anciently the sins of the people were by faith, placed upon the sin offering and through its blood transferred in figure to the earthly sanctuary, so in the new covenant the sins of the repentant are by faith placed upon Christ and transferred in fact to the heavenly sanctuary. And as the typical cleansing of the earthly was accomplished by the removal of the sins by which it had been polluted, so the actual cleansing of the heavenly is to be accomplished by the removal or blotting out of the sins that are there recorded.[71]

Here we have the very heart of Seventh-day Adventist teaching relative to the expiation of sin, which is that the sins of believers have been transferred, deposited or recorded in the heavenly sanctuary, and are now being dealt with in the Investigative Judgment.

69Hebrews 7:2, 4-7, 14, 16, 22, 25, 26; 8:1, 2, 6-8, 10; 9:2-12, 14, 23, 24; 26-28; 10:1-10, 12, 19-21.

70*Questions on Doctrine*, pages 377-78, 667.
71*Great Controversy*, pages 421-22.

Let us again listen to Mrs. White:

In the sin offerings presented during the year, a substitute had been accepted in the sinner's stead; but the blood of the victim had not made full atonement for the sin. It had only provided a means by which the sin was transferred to the sanctuary. By the offering of the blood the sinner acknowledged the authority of the law, confessed the guilt of his transgression, and expressed his faith in Him who was to take away the sin of the world; but he was not entirely released from the condemnation of the law. On the day of atonement the high priest having taken an offering for the congregation went into the most holy place with the blood and sprinkled it upon the mercy seat above the table to the law. Thus the claims of the law which demanded the life of the sinner were satisfied. Then in his character of mediator the priest took the sins upon himself and leaving the sanctuary he bore with him the burden of Israel's guilt. At the door of the tabernacle he laid his hands upon the head of the scapegoat, confessed over him all the iniquities of the children of Israel and all their transgressions and all their sins, putting them upon the head of the goat. And as the goat bearing these sins was sent away, they were with him regarded as forever separated from the people.

Mrs. White further stated, "Not until the goat had been thus sent away did the people regard themselves as freed from the burden of their sins.[72]

The Adventist teaching, then, is that Christ as our high priest transferred the sins of believers (i.e., the *record* of sins in Adventist thinking) to the heavenly sanctuary which will be finally cleansed at the conclusion of the great day of atonement, the Investigative Judgment having been concluded. Then the cases of all the righteous having been decided, their sins will be blotted out, followed by the return of the Lord Jesus Christ in glory. Mrs. White made it clear that the sin transferred to the sanctuary in Heaven would remain there until the conclusion of the Investigative Judgment and the subsequent cleansing of the sanctuary.

The blood of Christ, while it was to release the repentant sinner from the condemnation of the law, was not to cancel the sin; it would stand on record

in the sanctuary until the final atonement; so then the type, the blood of the sin offering removed the sin from the penitent but it rested in the sanctuary until the day of atonement.[73]

To substantiate this particular position, Adventists quote Acts 3:19 in the King James Version: "Repent ye therefore and be converted that your sins may be blotted out *when* the times of refreshing shall come from the presence of the Lord."

The chief difficulty with the Adventist contention is that the Greek of Acts 3:19 does *not* substantiate their teaching that the blotting out of sins will take place as a *separate* event from the forgiveness of sins. According to modern translations (the Revised, the American Standard and the Revised Standard Versions), the text should read "Repent therefore and turn again *that* your sins may be blotted out, *that* times of refreshing may come from the presence of the Lord." Peter was urging his listeners to repent, turn from their sins, in order to receive the forgiveness that comes only from the presence of the Lord. This text gives our Adventist brethren no support for their "heavenly sanctuary, investigative judgment" teaching.

II. *Investigative Judgment*

The Bible explicitly declares that when one accepts Christ as Lord, God freely forgives all his sins and ushers him from spiritual death to spiritual life solely on the merits of the perfect life and death of the Lord Jesus Christ. To this Adventists fully agree, and this makes their teaching on Investigative Judgment inconsistent. In John 5:24 the Greek deals a devastating blow to the Seventh-day Adventist concept of Investigative Judgment: "He that hears my word and believes him that sent me has everlasting life and shall not come under *judgment* but is passed from death to life" (literal translation).

Christians, therefore, need not anticipate any Investigatvie Judgment for their sins. True, we shall all appear before the judgment seat of Christ to receive the deeds done in the body (II Corinthians 5: 10), but this has nothing to do with any investigative judgment. It is a judgment for rewards. Several judgments are mentioned in the Bible, but it is my opinion that not one passage substantiates the "investigative judgment" theory—for theory it truly is, relying upon out-of-context quotations and supported by the "spirit of prophecy." They are welcome to this dogma, but faithfulness to New Testament teaching forbids the idea that "the blood of Christ, while it was to release the repentant sinner from the condemnation of the law, was not to cancel the sin; it would be on record in the sanctuary until the final atonement," or "blotting out." The Scriptures clearly teach, "If we confess our sins he is faithful and just to forgive us our sins and to cleanse us from *all* unrighteousness" (I John 1:9). Further evidence of the completeness of the forgiveness of God and the cleansing power of the blood of Christ is found in the first chapter of the book of Hebrews, where the Holy Spirit informs us that Christ as "the image of God," "upholds all things by the word of his power" and that on Calvary He by Himself purged our sins (Hebrews 1:3).

For the word translated "purged" or "purification" the Holy Spirit chose the Greek word *katharismon*, from which we derive *cathartic*. Hence it is said of the Lord Jesus and His sacrifice that He alone, "by himself," gave to our sinful spiritual natures the complete cathartic of forgiveness and purification on the cross. Christians may now rejoice that the Lord Jesus Christ is not engaged in weighing our frailties and failures, for "He knoweth our frame, he remembereth that we are dust" (Psalm 103:14). We cannot, therefore, accept the Adventist teaching on the investigative judgment since we are convinced that it has no warrant in Scripture. We must reject what we believe to be their un-Biblical concept that the sins of believers remain in the sanctuary until the day of blotting out of sins.

Our Adventist brethren, in teaching this doctrine, are overlooking the fact that "the Lord knoweth them that are his" (II Timothy 2:19) and it was no less an authority than the Lord Jesus Christ who declared, "I know my sheep" (John 10:14). The Apostle Paul declares that "Christ died for the ungodly . . . while we were yet sinners Christ died for us . . . when we were enemies we were reconciled to God by the death of his Son" (Romans 5:6, 8, 10). This does not balance with the Seventh-day Adventist teaching of the heavenly sanctuary, the transfer of sins and the investigative judgment. In his epistle to the Colossians the Apostle Paul further declared, Having made peace through the blood of his cross . . . you that were sometime alienated and ene-

mies in your mind by wicked works, yet now hath he reconciled in the body of his flesh through death, to present you holy and unblameable and unreprovable in his sight" (1:20-22). Once again the Holy Spirit declares that we are *now* reconciled through the death of Christ, *having been forgiven all* our trespasses through the blood of the cross (Colossians 2:13).

Seventh-day Adventists, relying upon Daniel 8:14, Daniel 7:9, 10, Revelation 14:7 and 11:18, which refer to "judgment," and "books," attempt to "prove" that the investigative judgment is meant, but examination of each of these texts in context reveals the paucity of the claim. None of these texts has anything to do with any judgment *now* going on. Neither the grammar nor context supports such a contention. One can only base this interpretation on the Adventist premise that the historicist school of prophetic interpretation is the only accurate one, and by accepting the Adventist definition of the sanctuary and judgment. It is significant that non-Adventist Biblical scholars have never allowed these so-called "investigative judgment" interpretations, because there is no Scriptural warrant for them apart from implication and inference.

As mentioned previously, James White at first categorically denied the teaching of the investigative judgment and gave good reasons for his rejection. Although he later embraced this doctrine his objections are still valid:

It is not necessary that the final sentence should be given before the first resurrection as some have taught; for the names of the saints are written in Heaven and Jesus and the angels will certainly know who to raise and gather to the New Jerusalem. . . . The event that will introduce the judgment day will be the coming of the Son of Man to raise the sleeping saints and to change those that are alive at that time.[74]

Relative to the time for the beginning of the great judgment, James White quoted, "I charge thee therefore before God and the Lord Jesus Christ, who shall judge the quick and the dead at [not before] his appearing in His kingdom" (II Timothy 4:1).[75]

Asked when he expected the judgment of Daniel seven to take place, James White stated,

---

[74] *A Word to the Little Flock* (1847), page 24.

[75] James White in the *Advent Review*, August 1850; the brackets are his.

Daniel in the night vision saw that judgment was given to the saints of the most high, but not to mortal saints. Not until the ancient of days comes will the little horn cease prevailing which will not be until he is destroyed by the brightness of Christ's coming.[76]

We see, then, that James White at the beginning rejected the investigative judgment with good reasons. But two more of his statements are quite revealing: He wrote,

The advent angel, Revelation 14:6, 7, saying with a loud voice, "Fear God and give glory to him for the hour of his judgment is come" *does not prove* that the day of judgment came in 1840 or in 1844, nor that it will come prior to the second advent. . . . Some have contended that the day of judgment was prior to the second advent. This view is certainly without foundation in the Word of God.[77]

At that time, James White was on good Biblical ground, but he later forsook this position for the theories and prophetic speculation promulgated by his wife and other influential Adventist leaders. The Lord Jesus Christ Himself placed the judgment after His second advent when He said, "When the Son of man shall come in his glory, and all the holy angels with him, then shall he sit upon the throne of his glory: and before him shall be gathered all nations" (Matthew 25:31, 32). One need only read the following passages to see that the judgments of God upon believers and unbelievers are future events. Notice the language employed:

1. "The quick and the dead" "at His appearing and His kingdom" (Acts 10:42, I Peter 4:5, II Timothy 4:1).

2. "When the Son of Man shall come in his glory . . . he shall set the sheep on his right hand, but the goats on the left" (Matthew 25:31-46).

3. The wheat and the tares: "so shall it be in the end of the world" (Matthew 13:24-30, 36-43).

4. "For we must all appear before the judgment seat of Christ that everyone may receive the things done in the body . . . whether it be good or bad" (II Corinthians 5:10).

5. "So that every one of us shall give account of himself to God" (Romans 14:10-12).

6. "Every man's work shall be made manifest: for the day shall declare it" (I

Corinthians 3:13).

In addition to these verses which unmistakably indicate future judgment, the writer to the Hebrews declares, "As it is appointed unto men once to die, but after this the judgment" (Hebrews 9:27). This, to any non-Adventist, is conclusive evidence that there is no investigative judgment now going on for believers to fear.

Hebrews 4:13 also exposes the faulty concept of investigative judgment: "Neither is there any creature that is not manifest in his sight: but all things are naked and opened unto the eyes of him with whom we have to do." Since our Lord knows the disposition of "cases" allegedly being reviewed in Heaven, what need is there for "investigative judgment"? We believe the Scriptures decidedly do not warrant such a doctrine.

Concluding our comments on the investigative judgment, note that rewards for believers will be meted out *after* the second coming of our Lord, or at "the resurrection of the just," for the resurrection of life (John 5:29, Luke 14:14). Even the Adventists concur in believing that the judgment of the wicked will *not* take place until the end of the millennial age (Revelation 20:11, 12; Matthew 25:31-46). Once again the investigative judgment theory conflicts with the Biblical teaching on judgment regarding both believer and unbeliever. To this writer's mind, the great error of the sanctuary and investigative judgment teachings is the premise that sins confessed by Christians are not fully dealt with until the conclusion of the investigative judgment, a position Scripture will *not* allow.

Adventists, in the opinion of conservative Biblical scholars, not to mention the liberal wing of Protestantism, are only speculating with their sanctuary and investigative judgment theories. Actually, most are agreed that they have created doctrines to compensate for errors in prophetic interpretation. But the very doctrines intended to solve their theological problems have in turn only increased their dilemma — a dilemma which they have yet to solve! Romans 8:1 declares, "There is therefore now no condemnation [i.e. *judgment*, (Greek)] to them who are in Christ Jesus"; and here every Christian's case must rest. We can never be indicted again for our sins nor convicted for them, because Christ has fully paid the penalty. For those who believe in "eternal security" there is *no* judgment for the *penalty* of sin, i.e., eternal separation from God. However, as II Corinthians 5:10 teaches, we shall be judged for how we live as Christians. Seventh-day Adventists, we believe, needlessly subscribe to a doctrine which neither solves their difficulties nor engenders peace of mind. Holding as they do to the doctrine of the Investigative Judgment, it is extremely difficult for us to understand how they can experience the joy of salvation and the knowledge of sins forgiven. This is, however, true of so-called Arminian theology on the whole, which teaches that eternal life, given by God to the believer, is not really eternal in duration. According to this school, it is a conditional life, to be revoked by God when in His sight sufficient transgressions have occurred. Romans 11:29 declares, however, "The gifts and call of God are irrevocable" (RSV). God is fully aware of our past, present and future when He calls and reclaims us; His omniscience is our guarantee of eternal safety.

There is, however, clarification and summary of the doctrine of investigative judgment in *Questions on Doctrine.*

It is our understanding that Christ, as high priest, concludes His intercessory ministry in heaven in a work of judgment. He begins His great work of judgment in the *investigative* phase. At the conclusion of the investigation, the *sentence* of judgment is pronounced. Then as judge, Christ descends to *execute*, or carry into effect, that sentence. For sublime grandeur, nothing in the prophetic word can compare with the description of our Lord as He descends the skies, not as a priest, but as King of kings and Lord of lords. And with Him are all the angels of Heaven. He commands the dead, and that great unnumbered host of those that are asleep in Christ spring forth into immortality. At the same time those among the living who are truly God's children are caught up together with the redeemed of all ages to meet their Saviour in the air, and to be forever with the Lord. . . .

As we have suggested, Seventh-day Adventists believe that at the second coming of Christ the eternal destiny of all men will have been irrevocably fixed by the decisions of a court of judgment. Such a judgment obviously would take place while men are still living on the earth. Men might be quite unaware of what is going on in heaven. It is hardly to be supposed that God would fail to warn men of such an impending judgment and its results. Seventh-day Adventists believe prophecy does foretell such a judgment, and indeed points out the very time at which it was to begin. . . .

When the high priest in the typical service had concluded his work in the earthly sanctuary on the Day of Atonement, he came to the door of the sanctuary. Then the final act with the second goat Azazel, took place. In like manner, when our Lord completes His ministry in the heavenly sanctuary, He, too, will come forth. When He does this, the day of salvation will have closed forever. Every soul will have thus made his decision for or against the divine Son of God. Then upon Satan, the instigator of sin, is rolled back his responsibility for having initiated and introduced iniquity into the universe. *But he* [Satan] *in no sense vicariously atones for the sins of God's people.* All this Christ fully bore, and vicariously atoned for, on Calvary's cross.[78]

It is apparent, then, that for Adventists the investigative judgment is something very real, and they believe that the final blotting out of their sins depends upon the results of that judgment, culminating in the final destruction (annihilation) of the wicked and Satan, typified by the scapegoat of Leviticus 16.

III. *The Scapegoat*

Perhaps no doctrine of Seventh-day Adventism has been more misunderstood than the teaching concerning the scapegoat (Leviticus 16). Because of certain unfortunate choices of words by a few Adventist writers, the impression has been given that Adventists regard Satan as a partial sin-bearer for the people of God. This may be accounted for by the fact that in the early days of Adventism they built much of their theology on the typology of the Mosaic sanctuary, using almost exclusively the phraseology of the King James Version. Hence they got into difficulty when dealing with such involved Old Testament concepts as the scapegoat (Leviticus 16). Not a few scholars, however, support the Seventh-day Adventist concept that Azazel represents Satan. Be that as it may, the important thing is the place of the scapegoat with regard to the atonement of Christ. Do Seventh-day Adventists believe that Satan eventually becomes their vicarious sin-bearer? Not at all! This writer is convinced that the Adventist concept of the scapegoat in connection with the day of atonement, the sanctuary and the investigative judgment is a bizarre combination of prophetic interpretation and typology; but it is by no means the soul-destroying doctrine that many people think it is. Let the Adventists speak for themselves:

We take our stand without qualification on the gospel platform that the death of Jesus Christ provides the *sole* propitiation for our sins (1 John 2:2; 4:10); that there is salvation through no other means or medium, and no other name by which we may be saved (Acts 4:12); and that the shed blood of Jesus Christ *alone* brings remission for our sins (Matthew 26:28). That is foundational.

When Satan tempted our first parents to take and eat of the forbidden fruit, he as well as they had an inescapable responsibility in that act — he the instigator, and they the perpetrators. And similarly, through the ages — in all sin Satan is involved in responsibility, as the originator and instigator, or tempter (John 8:44; Rom. 6:16; 1 John 3:8).

Now concerning my sin, Christ died for *my* sins (Rom. 5:8). He was wounded for *my* transgressions and for *my* iniquities (Isaiah 53). He assumed *my* responsibilities, and His blood alone cleanses *me* from all sin (1 John 1:7). The atonement for *my* sin is made solely by the shed blood of Christ.

Concerning Satan's sin, and his responsibility as instigator and tempter, no salvation is provided for him. He must be punished for his responsibility. . . . He must himself 'atone' for his sin in causing men to transgress, in the same way that a master criminal suffers on the gallows or in the electric chair for his responsibility in the crimes that he has caused others to commit. It is in this sense only that we can understand the words of Leviticus 16:10 concerning the scapegoat, "to make an atonement with him."

Satan is the responsible master mind in the great crime of sin, and his responsibility will return upon his own head. The crushing weight of his responsibility in the sins of the whole world — of the wicked as well as of

the righteous — must be rolled back upon him. Simple justice demands that while Christ suffers for my guilt, Satan must also be punished as the instigator of sin.

Satan makes no atonement for our sins. But Satan will ultimately have to bear the retributive punishment for his responsibility in the sins of all men, both righteous and wicked.

Seventh-day Adventists therefore repudiate *in toto* any idea, suggestion, or implication that Satan is in any sense or degree our sin bearer. The thought is abhorrent to us, and appallingly sacrilegious.

Only Christ, the Creator, the one and only God-man, could make a substitutionary atonement for men's transgressions. And this Christ did completely, perfectly, and once for all, on Golgotha.[79]

To be sure, the Seventh-day Adventists have a unique concept of the scapegoat, but in the light of their clearly worded explanation, no critic could any longer with honesty indict them for heresy where the atonement of our Lord is concerned.[80] The Adventists have stated unequivocally that Jesus Christ is their sole propitiation for sin and that Satan has no part whatsoever in the expiation of sin. This writer agrees that Satan is the master criminal of the universe and that it is axiomatic, therefore, that he should suffer as the instigator of angelic and human rebellion. There are, of course, many interpretations of Leviticus 16 set forth by learned scholars, the great majority of whom are most certainly not Adventists; so at best the question is quite open. The *Abingdon Bible Commentary* (Methodist) relative to Leviticus 16 and the scapegoats states,

On the goats lots are to be cast, one for Jehovah and the other for Azazel. The translation "Dismissal" in the Revised Version margin here (cf. removal in ASV margin) is inadmissible being based on a false etymology. What the word meant is unknown but it should be retained as a proper name of a wilderness demon.[81]

To this statement could be added the opinions of Samuel Zwemer, E. W. Hengstenberg, J. B. Rotherham and J. Russell Howden, the last of whom wrote in the *Sunday School Times* of January 15, 1927,

---

[79]*Questions on Doctrine*, pages 396, 398-400.
[80]See section III. *The Atonement*.

[81]See Author's Note immediately following this section.

The goat for Azazel as it is sometimes misleadingly translated, typifies God's challenge to Satan. Of the two goats, one was for Jehovah signifying God's acceptance of the sin offering; the other was for Azazel. This is probably to be understood as a person being parallel with Jehovah in the preceding clause. So Azazel is probably a *synonym* for Satan.

Although Seventh-day Adventists have no exegetical support for their sanctuary and investigative judgment theories, one thing is certain: they have more than substantial scholastic support for assigning the title "Satan" to Azazel in Leviticus 16 concerning the scapegoat, but where the Scripture does not speak specifically it is far wiser to withhold comment. Many critics, in their zeal to shred Seventh-day Adventism and classify it as "a dangerous non-Christian cult," lay much stress upon the scapegoat teaching. In the light of current Adventist statements concerning their concept of the scapegoat, the misunderstandings of the past have at last been brought out into the open, clarified, and presented in a plausible manner.

Much, much more could be written concerning the Seventh-day Adventist concepts of the sanctuary, investigative judgment and the scapegoat since they are inseparably linked together. But such writers as W. W. Fletcher (*The Reasons for My Faith*) and other ex-Seventh-day Adventists have exhaustively refuted the position of their former affiliation. The reader is urged to consider the Bibliography for additional information on this subject. The saving grace of the entire situation is that the Adventists fortunately deny the logical conclusions to which their doctrines must lead them; i.e., a negation of the full validity of the atonement of Christ which validity they absolutely affirm, and embrace with considerable fervor — a paradoxical situation at best!

Author's Note

We could wish that some of the earlier unrepresentative Seventh-day Adventist statements on the scapegoat teaching had not been made, or better yet, that they were not still circulated in some quarters. However, to ignore their honest current declarations is, I believe, fundamentally unfair. It appears to me to be little more than blind prejudice. One recent review of the book, *Questions on Doctrine,* contains an error frequently found in critical

writings. Imputing to their account a position the Adventists do not hold, the review then proceeds to destroy it as if, in the final analysis, it had both exposed and refuted a pernicious error. While it is true that the Seventh-day Adventists do believe that Azazel, in Leviticus 16, does represent Satan, their interpretation of it is far removed from this reviewer's straw man. After quoting the Seventh-day Adventist statement: "Seventh-day Adventists repudiate *in toto* any idea . . . that Satan is in any sense our sin bearer," this review states "but then two entire chapters are devoted to proving that Satan did bear our sin." It goes on to describe the Adventist position as "repulsive blasphemy" and "unholy twisting of the Scripture. If the Seventh-day Adventists were sound in everything but this and still held this one gross error, we would still have to consider them as an unscriptural cult."[82]

Now with some other portions of this review we are in agreement. But many of the statements show a marked predisposition toward removing various statements from context and placing them together to prove contradiction without respect to their setting. It ignores all the Seventh-day Adventist statements which contradict these out-of-context criticisms. The very chapter alluded to clearly shows that Adventists repudiate the meaning the reviewer has attached to the scapegoat concept. As we have noted, it is regrettable that this teaching has been so stated in some Adventist writings as to give the impression that the scapegoat represents Satan in the vicarious role of sin bearer, but the Adventists have clarified this beyond reasonable doubt in the large majority of their publications.

Questions on Doctrine clarifies the concept of the scapegoat in Seventh-day Adventist theology. For Adventists, when the Lord Jesus Christ returns He will place upon Satan the full responsibility for his role of instigator and tempter to sin. Since Satan caused angels and man to rebel against their creator, Adventists reason that Azazel, the scapegoat of Leviticus 16, is a type of Satan receiving the punishment due him. As we have seen however, Adventists repudiate the idea that Satan is their vicarious sin-bearer in any sense. They point out, and rightly so, that in Leviticus 16 only the first goat was slain as the vicarious offering. The second goat was not killed but was sent into the wil-

[82]*The King's Business,* March 1958, pages 22, 23.

derness to die. Satan similarly bears the weight of guilt and final punishment culminating in the annihilation as the master criminal who has promulgated sin during the period of God's grace toward lost men. To quote the Adventists:

> Satan's death a thousand times over, could never make him a savior in any sense whatsoever. He is the archsinner of the universe, the author and instigator of sin. . . . Only Christ, the Creator, the one and only God-man, could make a substitutionary atonement for men's transgressions. And this Christ did completely, perfectly and once for all on Golgotha.[83]

LAW, GRACE AND SALVATION

In order to understand the Adventist view of law and grace, especially in relation to eternal salvation, we must consider the Adventist antipathy toward antinomianism.

The very word "antinomian" (*anti*, against, and *nomos*, law) describes the conflict between those who believe that not only were the Ten Commandments abrogated at Calvary but even the principles underlying them were "abolished" so that the Christian is not bound by them; and those who believe that the Decalogue is as binding today as when it was given at Sinai.

From the beginning of church history, the great majority of evangelical Christians have been as strongly opposed to antinomianism as are the Adventists. Unfortunately however, the latter have tended to label antinomian anyone who disagrees with their definition of "the law of God." Consequently this has created a great problem in semantics which has disrupted the lines of communication, so to speak, between Adventists and other Christians. Although we believe in obeying the laws of God, and in good works as the evidence of saving faith, we strenuously object to "commandment keeping," to the extent of supposed spiritual superiority. A principal cause of their legalistic tendencies then is the Adventists' abhorrence of antinomianism.

By virtue of the fact that they obey the Fourth Commandment as well as the other nine, Adventists maintain that they alone are God's commandment-keeping church. To be sure, theologians have differed over the nature and extent of the moral law of God, and doubtless the controversy will continue until our Lord comes again. Any group, however, which feels they are the only ones that keep God's commands is likely to foment schism in the Body of Christ.

From their beginning, Adventists have concentrated upon "the law of God," and in *Questions on Doctrine* they devote 34 pages to the exposition of this subject. Although the Adventists repudiate legalism, that is, the doctrine that keeping the law merits salvation, a legalistic spirit does exist in some of their teaching. For example, although denying that the ceremonial law is binding upon Christians, they quote from it to defend their classifying certain foods as "unclean." Although Adventists reject antinomianism, in their desire to avoid the abuses of grace they actually abuse grace by magnifying the letter of the law. How Adventists arrived at this position has been well explained by D. M. Canright (*Seventh-day Adventism Renounced* [chapter xvii]). In one place, Canright sets forth a series of propositions which, in some areas, are exegetically irrefutable, and with which I am in full agreement.

Now let us examine the Adventist claim that the law is binding upon the Christian, as stated in their Fundamental Beliefs, *Questions on Doctrine,* and wherever their writings touch on this subject.

I. *The Principle of Law*

To begin with, we agree to the proposition that the principle underlying the moral laws of God is indeed eternal, and consistent with His character. However, we must distinguish between the principle of the law of God, and the expression of that principle in specific statutes such as those in the Pentateuch. Because Adventists do not seem to make this distinction, it appears to this writer that they relate law to grace, which is an unhealthy practice. They claim that "the Law" was in effect in Eden and during all the centuries thence to Sinai. Wherever the Bible speaks of "commandments" or "law," most Adventists apparently assume that it means the Decalogue. We must, however, clearly differentiate between the *principle* of the law of God and the *function* of the law of God as revealed in the Pentateuch. Not only the Adventists but many historic Protestant groups have failed to make this distinction, and so have been guilty of carrying over into the New Covenant some of the legalistic Jewish functions of the law.

---

[83]*Questions on Doctrine*, page 400.

A. *The Dual Law Theory*

In *Questions on Doctrine*, the Adventists distinguish between "the moral law of God — the Decalogue — and the ceremonial law," setting forth the distinctions in two columns.[84] In column one is the Decalogue which was spoken by God, written by Him on tables of stone, given to Moses and deposited in the Ark. It dealt with moral precepts, revealed sin, and is in effect today. They insist that Christians must "keep the whole law,"[85] (James 2:10) and that we shall be judged by this law (James 2:12). They believe that the Decalogue is established in the life of a Christian by faith in Christ (Romans 3:31), and that Christ magnified the law (Isaiah 42:21), which Paul described as "spiritual" (Romans 7:14).

In column two, Adventists analyze the law of ceremonial ordinances, which were abolished at the cross. They contrast this with "the moral law of God — the Decalogue," stating that the latter was not abolished because it was separate from the ceremonial law. Concerning the ceremonial law, Adventists teach that it was spoken and written by Moses, and given to the Levites who deposited it by the side of the Ark, and that it governed ceremony and ritual. This law prescribed offerings for sins but the apostles gave no commandment to keep it, and the Christian is not bound by it, nor can he be blessed by it. Indeed, they say, "the Christian who keeps this law loses his liberty"; it "was abolished by Christ," and was "the law of a carnal commandment" containing nothing of a moral nature, the Decalogue being "the moral law of God."

Now although there are both moral and ceremonial aspects of the law in the Pentateuch, as well as civil and judicial, nowhere does the Bible state that there is any such juxtaposition of ceremonial with moral law. In fact, the whole Bible teaches that "the law was given through Moses" (John 1:17) and that it is essentially a *unit*, a fact which the Adventists have overlooked. We make this observation after comparing the application of the term "law" in the Old and New Testaments.

To illustrate: As noted above, the Adventists claim that the law of Moses and the Decalogue are separate, the one being ceremonial, the other "the moral law of God." Therefore, although the ceremonial law was abolished at the cross, the moral law remains in effect; and so they insist in "commandment-keeping," not to *earn* salvation, but as it works out in the practice of many, to *retain* salvation. If, however, the ceremonial law and the Decalogue are inextricably bound together, and if both are referred to as "the law," the distinction which the Adventists and others make between them is fictitious. To prove this is to nullify their interpretation concerning "the moral law." Let us examine the Scriptures to see whether such a distinction as they propose can be sustained.

The highest authority on this subject is the Lord Jesus Christ. When speaking of "the law," He alluded to both moral and ceremonial precepts; e.g., Mark 10:19 (moral); and Luke 5:12-14 (ceremonial). The Gospels abound with similar references to "the law," without distinguishing between the moral and the ceremonial, and certainly not teaching that they are separate codes.

We do not mean that the law has no moral and ceremonial aspects, for it has, but they are only aspects, not separate codes or units. They are parts of the one law which "was our schoolmaster to bring us unto Christ, that we might be justified by faith" (Galatians 3:24). The apostle Paul, certainly an authority on "the law," dogmatically affirms that the role of the schoolmaster has *ceased* and that the Christian is "dead to the law." Note, also, that the word "schoolmaster" is in the singular, which destroys the Adventist notion that there is more than one law. If the moral law were separate from the ceremonial law, instead of both being aspects of one law, Paul would have had to write that the *laws* were our *schoolmasters* to bring us to Christ, and that now "we are no longer under *schoolmasters*." But he knew and taught that the law was a unit and that it was perfectly fulfilled as such in the life of our Lord and on the cross of Calvary.

By His perfect life, the Lord Jesus met all the requirements of the moral aspect of the law; by His death, He fulfilled all the ceremonial ordinances which prefigured His incarnation and sacrifice. He Himself said,

> Think not that I am come to destroy the law, or the prophets: I am come not to destroy, but to fulfill. For verily I say unto you, Till heaven and earth pass, one jot or one tittle shall in no wise pass from the law, till all be fulfilled (Matthew 5:17, 18).

---

[84]Pages 130-31.

[85]As a sign of obedience to God.

Which law did Christ fulfill? If he fulfilled only the ceremonial law as the dual law theory states, the moral law is yet to be satisfied. But "Christ is the *end* of the law for righteousness to every one that believeth" (Romans 10:4); and as we have shown, there are no distinct codes such as moral and ceremonial law. The distinction is arbitrary and contradicts the declaration of Scripture that the believer lives by a higher principle: "The law of the Spirit of life in Christ Jesus hath made me free from the law of sin and death" (Romans 8:2).

In order to maintain the dual law theory against the Biblical declaration that the one law has divisions or aspects, Adventists must explain why, in at least 20 passages in the New Testament, a dozen of them in the words of Jesus Christ, the Holy Spirit teaches that there are not two laws, but one; that this law is not only in the five books of Moses but in the Prophets and the Psalms as well. Christ looked upon moral, ceremonial and prophetic precepts as parts of the one law which pointed to His life, ministry, death, and resurrection, as He said to His disciples that first Easter day, "These are the words which I spake unto you, while I was yet with you, that all things must be fulfilled, which were written in the law of Moses, and in the prophets, and in the psalms concerning me" (Luke 24:44).

A study of the passages listed in footnote 86 will convince the reader that the law is one gigantic structure comprised of moral, ceremonial, civil, judicial and prophetic aspects,[86] all of which were grouped by Christ and the apostles under the heading of "the law," and which structure was completely fulfilled in the life and death of the Lord Jesus Christ who instituted the universal principle of divine love as the fulfillment of every aspect and function of the law. Our Lord said,

Therefore all things whatsoever ye would that men should do to you, do ye even so to them: for *this is the law* and the prophets. . . . Thou shalt love the Lord thy God with all thy heart, and with all thy soul, and with all thy mind. This is the first and great commandment. And the second is like unto it, Thou shalt love thy neighbor as thyself. On these two commandments hang

all the law and the prophets (Matthew 7:12; 22:37-40).

Instead of the Adventist belief that the law must be "kept" as a sign of obedience to God, Christ here teaches that the Christian obeys God when he obeys the supreme commandment of love. This teaching is reiterated by the greatest of the apostles, who wrote to the Galatians, "All the law is fulfilled in one word, even in this: Thou shalt love thy neighbor as thyself" (Galatians 5:14). Obviously, if we love our neighbors as ourselves, we do so because we love God with all our hearts, souls, and minds. If we do not so love God, we cannot love our neighbors as ourselves. Thus on this "great commandment" rests the law in all its aspects.

Note the language of these passages, for they indicate the strong emphasis given by our Lord. In Matthew 22:40 Christ uses the Greek word *"holos,"* translated 65 times in the New Testament as "all," 43 times as "whole," twice as "every whit," once "altogether," and once "throughout." With these renditions all lexicons agree, so there can be no linguistic doubt that the all-inclusive principle which binds and seals all aspects of the law into a unit, to be fulfilled in the life of a believer because it has been fulfilled by the Saviour, is once again declared to be "love."

The apostle Paul uses an entirely different word to sum up the unifying principle of the law and the only principle which Scriptures say fulfills it. This is the Greek word *pas.*

In the New Testament *pas* is translated 748 times as "all," 170 times as "all things," 117 times as "every," 41 times as "all men," 31 times as "whosoever," 28 times as "everyone," 12 times as "whole," and 11 times as "every man." We see then how the Holy Spirit rendered linguistically impossible any escape from the clear declaration that the principle of love indeed *fulfills* all the precepts of the law in their *entirety* since the two terms used most frequently in the New Testament to describe inclusiveness were utilized by both Christ and Paul to enunciate this vital issue.

Finally, notice Paul's powerful admonition to the believers at Rome:

Owe no man any thing but to love one another: for he that loveth another

[86] See John 8:17, referring to Deuteronomy 19:15; John 10:34, to Psalm 82:6; John 12:34, to Psalm 72:17 and 102:23-27; John 15:25, to Psalm 35:19 and 69:4; and John 19:7, to Leviticus 24:16. In these passages, moral, ceremonial, and prophetic aspects are all spoken of as "the law." For further Scriptural teaching, the reader is invited to look up Matthew 5:17, 18; 7:12; 11:13; 12:5; 22:36; 23:23; Luke 2:22, 24, 27; 5:17; 10:26; 16:14-17; 24:44; and John 1:45.

hath fulfilled the law. For this, Thou shalt not commit adultery, Thou shalt not kill, Thou shalt not steal, Thou shalt not bear false witness, Thou shalt not covet; *and if there be any other commandment,* it is briefly comprehended in this saying, namely, Thou shalt love thy neighbor as thyself. Love worketh no ill to his neighbor: therefore love is the fulfilling of the law (Romans 13:8-10).

In this context the greatest authority on the law in the New Testament, next to Jesus Christ, used the very emphatic Greek word *etera* which is translated 42 times in the New Testament as "other." Unquestionably the Apostle Paul not only considered the law a unit of which the Decalogue is only a part (quoting five of the Ten Commandments), but he indicated the rest of the law — ceremonial, civil, and judicial — by the word "other." Thus if one is to be a true "commandment-keeper," he has only to obey the divine principle of love, and God looks upon this as fulfillment of "the law." The Holy Spirit does not specify the moral, ceremonial, or civil law. He emphatically states that love is the fulfillment of "the law"; a tremendously important statement, to say the least!

It is significant that in the thirteenth chapter of Romans, after quoting five of the ten commandments which the Adventists steadfastly affirm constitute "the moral law," the apostle conspicuously omits what the Adventists maintain is God's great "seal" — the Sabbath. In fact, the words "any other commandment" must include even the Sabbath in the law of love. Nowhere is this more decidedly emphasized than in the usage of a peculiar term which appears but twice in the New Testament; here in Romans 13:9, and again in Ephesians 1:10. The term in question is the Greek *"Anakephalaioutai"* which in both instances means "to sum up, to repeat summarily, and so to condense into a summary . . . to bring together."[87]

We see then that the Apostle Paul, under the inspiration of the Holy Spirit, taught in both Romans 13:9 and Ephesians 1:10 that as God in the fulness of time intended to "gather together" (KJV) or "sum up" (RSV), those whom He had chosen in Christ, in like manner He has

forever condensed or summed up, comprehended or gathered together, the law in all its aspects and divisions under the all-embracing principle of love. By not adhering strictly to the established laws of sound Biblical interpretations,[88] Seventh-day Adventists seem to have overlooked this fact in the New Testament. In the course of our study of Seventh-day Adventist literature we have been impressed by the fact that some Adventists will cite texts largely out of their context and grammatical structure in what appears to be an attempt to enforce an arbitrary theory of two laws (moral and ceremonial) upon the believer in the age of grace. In so doing, they violate that principle which the Apostle Paul states "sums up or condenses" all of the commandments of the entire law, perfectly fulfilling them under the one heading, "the great commandment," upon which, our Lord declared, "hang all the law and the prophets," the imperative of love.

On page 131 of *Questions on Doctrine* it is stated that the ceremonial law is now "abolished" (Ephesians 2:15); and, "the Christian who keeps this law is not blessed," but "loses his liberty" (Galatians 5:1, 3). Nevertheless, Adventists religiously observe some ceremonial laws, especially with regard to "unclean food." Now, although they deny that their rejection of "unclean" food is based on Mosaic prohibitions, all their literature on the subject appeals to the very law which they insist has been "abolished." Under the covenant of law, nowhere but in the Mosaic ceremonial aspects of the law are people forbidden to eat oysters, clams, lobsters, crabs, reptiles, rabbits, and swine's flesh, but the Adventists still claim the validity of such prohibition. We wish that they would be consistent in following their dual law theory and abandon their "unclean foods" restriction which binds them to what even they admit is an abolished ceremonial teaching; a teaching which they also declare can cause the Christian to "lose his liberty" and miss the blessing of God.[89] Writing on this subject of unclean foods with apostolic authority and in the power of the Holy Spirit, the Apostle Paul unequivocally declared, "Therefore let no one pass judgment on you in questions of food and drink." And he warns Timothy that in the latter days

---

[87]Thayer, *Greek-English Lexicon,* pages 38, 39.

[88]Hermeneutics and exegesis, i.e., comparative study and grammatical analysis of texts.

[89]They vainly endeavor to meet this argument by declaring that these food laws were not ceremonial or typical but laws of hygiene and were in vogue even before the Mosaic dispensation. *Questions on Doctrine,* pages 622-24. But why appeal always to Moses?

some persons will "enjoin abstinence from foods which God created to be received with thanksgiving by those who believe and know the truth. For everything created by God is good, and nothing is to be rejected if it is received with thanksgiving, for then it is consecrated by the Word of God and prayer." Finally he sums it up thus:

I know and am persuaded in the Lord Jesus that nothing is unclean in itself; but it is unclean for any one who thinks it unclean. . . . For the kingdom of God does not mean food and drink but righteousness and peace and joy in the Holy Spirit; he who thus serves Christ is acceptable to God and approved by men.[90]

From these texts it is apparent that Adventists limit their own liberty in Christ by voluntary bondage to ceremonial precepts, and it is the dual law theory which has largely caused their confusion and the consequent error of law-keeping.

For this teaching, which lapses so easily into legalism, we find no Biblical authority since it is demonstrably true that the law of Moses and the Decalogue are a unit described throughout Scripture as "*the* law," and the fact that the Decalogue was written on stones (Exodus 31:18), and the law of Moses written in a book (Exodus 24:4, 7, Deuteronomy 31:24), in no way proves that one is moral and the other ceremonial. As we have seen, the law of Moses, written in a book, and deposited by the Levites by the side of the Ark, deals not only with ceremonial ritual matters, but with those moral precepts contained in the Decalogue itself. One could not be fulfilled, as Christ prophesied and accomplished, and the other left unfulfilled, for then God's sacrificial plan would not have been consummated at Calvary.

B. *"Law" in the New Testament*

When New Testament writers spoke of "the law," they usually meant all five books of Moses,[91] which contain moral, ceremonial and civil ordinances. It was national and applied only to Israel and to anyone who became an Israelite. Nowhere in Scripture is it applied to anyone else. Although the Gentiles, as Paul says, "have not the law," its great moral principle applied to them, so that the Gentiles "do by nature that which is contained in the law"; but they did not come under Law as given to Israel.

Acts 15:23-32 describes how the leaders of the Christian church at Jerusalem, all Jews, were very careful not to impose the demands of the law upon the Gentiles. For them, the complete "law" — moral, ceremonial and civil — had been fulfilled, and the one law to observe now was to love God and your neighbor. St. Augustine remarked "Love God, and do as you please," for if we truly love God with heart, soul, mind and strength, we do only those things which please Him. This is "the law" of the New Testament, the only guide for the Christian. We are "no longer under the law, but under grace," and the function of the "schoolmaster" (Galatians 3:24) has forever and irrevocably ceased.

Let us see how these first Christian leaders solved the problem of "the law":

And they wrote letters by them after this manner; the apostles and elders and brethren send greetings unto the brethren which are of the Gentiles in Antioch and Syria and Cilicia. Forasmuch as we have heard, that certain which went out from us have troubled you with words, subverting your souls, saying, Ye must be circumcised, and keep the law: to whom we gave no such commandment: It seemed good unto us, being assembled with one accord to send chosen men unto you. . . . We have sent therefore, Judas and Silas. . . . For it seemed good to the Holy Ghost, and to us, to lay upon you no greater burden than these necessary things; that ye abstain from meats offered to idols, and from blood, and from things strangled, and from fornication: from which if ye keep yourselves, ye shall do well. Fare ye well (Acts 15:23-25, 27-29).

Since "the law" includes the precepts of the Pentateuch, and certain sections of the Psalms and Prophets, this message to the Gentiles contradicts all dual law teachers who insist that we must for any purpose "keep the law." We know from a comparison of the New Testament with the Old that the Decalogue of itself is not the entire moral law of God, as our Adventist brethren often insist, for there are many other commandments, which are neither *inferred, implied* nor *contained* in the Decalogue but which are just as moral

---

[90]Colossians 2:16; I Timothy 4:3-5; Romans 14:14, 17-18 (RSV).
[91]Compare I Corinthians 14:34, Genesis 3:16; Ro-

mans 7:7, Exodus 20:17; Matthew 22:36-39, Deuteronomy 6:5 and Leviticus 19:18; Matthew 12:5, Numbers 28:9, 10.

as anything appearing in Exodus 20.[92] Although nine of the Ten Commandments are enunciated in the New Testament, we have seen that they are "comprehended, summed up or condensed" in the words of Paul, in the great commandment of love (Romans 13, Galatians 5). So the Adventists have no argument against the total fulfillment of all the law by the life and death of our Saviour.

In Acts 15:24, the leaders of the church in Jerusalem reiterate this principle in their letter to the Gentiles in Antioch, Syria and Cilicia: "Certain which went out from us have troubled you with words, subverting your souls, saying, Ye must be circumcised, and keep the law: to whom we gave no such commandment."

Now although Seventh-day Adventists affirm that law-keeping cannot merit salvation, nevertheless they teach that by breaking the law one forfeits salvation. They invoke a principle which was fulfilled in the life and death of Christ; and in so doing they place themselves in direct opposition to the great law of love enunciated by Christ and the apostles, and are in effect putting "a yoke upon the neck of the disciples, which neither our fathers nor we were able to bear" (Acts 15:10). To those who invoke the law as the criterion of obedience in the Christian life, the Word of God replies, "We gave no such commandment" (Acts 15:24).

Paul's phrase "any other commandment" in Romans 13:9 of course includes abstinence from meats offered to idols, blood, things strangled and fornication, for love of God would enjoin discernment and obedience in all these things.

To support their argument that a Christian must obey the commandments, Adventists and other Christian bodies cite such passages as the following:

If ye love me, keep my commandments. He that hath my commandments, and keepeth them, he it is that loveth me (John 14:15, 21). And hereby we do know that we know him, if we keep his commandments. He that saith, I know him, and keepeth not his commandments, is a liar, and the truth is not in him. . . . And whatsoever we ask, we receive of him, because we keep his commandments, and do those things that are pleasing in his sight. . . . He that keepeth his commandments dwelleth in him and he in him. And hereby we know that he abideth in us by the Spirit which he hath given us. . . . By

this we know that we love the children of God, when we love God, and keep his commandments. For this is the love of God, that we keep his commandments: and his commandments are not grievous (I John 2:3, 4; 3:22, 24; 5: 2, 3).

We too yield to the authority of those verses; but the fallacy of the position lies in the concept that the word "commandments" always refers to the Ten Commandments, which they maintain are "the moral law of God." This claim cannot be substantiated from Scripture, in fact, it is contradicted by the Bible. Let us see how the Lord Jesus and the Apostle John applied the words "commandments" and "law." First, consider the conversation of our Lord with the lawyer in Luke 10: 25-28:

And, behold, a certain lawyer stood up, and tempted him, saying, Master, what shall I do to inherit eternal life?

He said unto him, What is written in the law? how readest thou?

And he answering said, Thou shalt love the Lord thy God with all thy heart, and with all thy soul, and with all thy strength, and with all thy mind; and thy neighbor as thyself.

And he said unto him, Thou hast answered right: this do, and thou shalt live.

Clearly, the Lord Jesus did not subscribe to the Seventh-day Adventist view that "commandment-keeping means keeping all of the Ten Commandments," none of which He mentions in this passage. Christ did not say, "Keep the Ten Commandments, especially the fourth one, and thou shalt live." He said, in effect, "Obey the law of love upon which all the law and the prophets rest, and thou shalt live." This refutes the Adventist claim that when Jesus spoke of commandments he meant *only* the Decalogue.

Among those who listened to our Lord's discourse in the Upper Room was the Apostle John, who records the "new commandment . . . That you love one another as I have loved you" (John 13:34). To this commandment John refers in the passages quoted from his first epistle. Nowhere does he mention the Decalogue or any part of the moral law of God. Instead, he writes:

This is his commandment, That we should believe on the name of his Son Jesus Christ, and love one another, as

[92]See Leviticus 19:18.

he gave us commandment. . . . And this commandment have we from him, That he who loveth God love his brother also (I John 3:23, 4:21).

And in his second epistle he says,

I beseech thee, not as though I wrote a new commandment unto thee, but that which we had from the beginning, that we love one another. And this is love, that we walk after his commandments. This is the commandment, That, as ye have heard from the beginning, ye should walk in it" (II John 5, 6).

What then does John mean when he speaks of "commandment" or "commandments"? In his own words he means:

. . . That which we had from the beginning, that we love one another. And this is love, that we walk after his commandments. This is the commandment, That, as ye have heard from the beginning, ye should walk in it (II John 5, 6).

How different from ironclad obedience to what many, including Adventists, sometimes call "The Eternal Ten"! By "the righteousness of the law," and fulfillment of the law, Christ and all the New Testament writers mean *not* the Ten Commandments but the eternal law of *love*. The motivating power of the universe, love, is to motivate obedience to God. By loving Him and one another, we fulfill all moral law. The chief function of the law was to reveal sin and to "slay" the soul, that righteousness might come by faith, and it was given for the unregenerate, *not* the redeemed: "Knowing this, that the law is not made for a righteous man, but for the lawless and disobedient, for the ungodly and for sinners, for unholy and profane, for murderers of fathers and murderers of mothers, for manslayers" (I Timothy 1:9).

C. The Charge of Pharisaism

By believing they are God's commandment-keeping church, Adventists have exposed themselves to the charge of Pharisaism. Because they monopolize such passages as the following, they give the impression of claiming to be the only people on earth: (1) "Which keep the commandments of God"; (2) "They that keep the commandments of God, and the faith of Jesus"; and, (3) "Blessed are *they that do his commandments*,[93] that they may

have the right to the tree of life, and may enter in through the gates into the city" (Revelation 12:17, 14:12, 22:14).

We admire the desire of our Adventist brethren to obey the commandments of God; but, we ask, what commandments? If they answer, "The Decalogue," we reject their effort to bring us under bondage, for we "are not under the law, but under grace" (Romans 6:14). If some fail to recognize that "the law" of the New Testament is love for God and for one another, and that it fulfills and supersedes all previous embodiments of divine principle, then the issue is clear. Such people speak like "a noisy gong or a clanging cymbal," because they do not give supremacy to the "new" and "great commandment."

Concluding this section on the principle of law, we may sum up our position briefly:

The Adventist insistence that there are two separate codes of laws, the moral and the ceremonial, and that the former is in effect today and the latter was abolished at the cross, finds, we believe, no exegetical or theological basis in Scripture. We have also shown that they select numerous texts out of context and juxtapose them in order to validate their contention. We have seen that the greatest of all commandments is not included in the Decalogue or "the moral law." And yet upon this great commandment, love for the Lord and for one's neighbor, "hang all the law and the prophets." The nineteenth chapter of Leviticus is alone sufficient to refute the dual law theory, for it contains *moral, ceremonial* and *civil* laws sometimes all appearing in the same verse, and yet Leviticus is called by Christ, "the law," as are the other four books of Moses.

The Adventist contention that since the Ten Commandments were spoken by God, inscribed on stone and placed within the Ark, they are superior to the law written by Moses in a book and placed by the side of the Ark, is fallacious. This is true because the book placed by the side of the Ark actually contains *more* moral law than does the Decalogue itself. It is therefore, superior to the Decalogue, at least in scope.

The Bible refutes the Adventist contention that the law was in force in Eden and that it was known to Adam, Noah, Abraham and the patriarchs. Not one

---

[93] All the oldest and best Greek manuscripts of Revelation 22:14 read "They that wash their robes," so the verse gives no support whatever for "commandment-keeping." This fact well-informed Adventists recognize, but a large segment still attempt to utilize certain faulty and incorrect English translations to "prove" their position.

verse of Scripture can be cited free from inference, deduction and implication, that teaches such a doctrine. The Word of God frequently states,

> The law was given by Moses. . . . Did not Moses give you *the law.* . . . If therefore perfection were by the Levitical priesthood, for under it the people received *the law.* . . . The covenant, that was confirmed before of God in Christ, *the law,* which was 430 years after, cannot disannul. . . . The Lord our God made a covenant with us in Horeb. The Lord made not this covenant with our fathers, but with us (John 1:17, 7:19), Hebrews 7:11, Galatians 3:17, Deuteronomy 5:2, 3).

The Adventists' contentions, therefore, concerning the eternal nature of the Decalogue and the time of its application to man, are mere conjecture. Although we admit that the principle of the law was, in effect, written upon the hearts of men by the Holy Spirit, so that they were judged by it (Romans 2), there is a vast difference between the principle of the law and the embodiment of that principle in a given code (Sinaitic-Mosaic), which the Adventists fail to recognize.

Finally, the Old Testament Scriptures all teach the unity of the law. Christ endorsed it, and the Apostles pointed out that its chief purpose was to condemn man and show him his need of redemption that he might come to Christ, the author and fulfiller of *all* the law. We who are "led of the Spirit are not under the law" (Galatians 5:18); for "love is the fulfilling of the law" (Romans 13:10). This love energizes us to "walk not after the flesh, but after the Spirit" that in us "the righteousness of the law might be fulfilled"[94] (Romans 8:4). In Jeremiah 31:31-34 the prophet states that under the new covenant God would write His law "in their inward parts, and write it in their hearts." In II Corinthians 3:3 the Apostle Paul declares that Christians are "the epistle of Christ . . . written not with ink, but with the Spirit of the living God; not in tables of stone, but in fleshy tables of the heart." The motive for obedience to this law is the imperative of Love — "We love him because he first loved us" (I John 4:19).

The great foundational moral law of the universe is therefore declared to be unchanging love. This is vastly different from the national or Mosaic law given only to Israel. That law was designed to be fulfilled, even though it was based upon the eternal principles of the moral character of God (Colossians 2:14-17). And when its fulfillment did take place and the character of God was imputed to the believer and imparted to his life by the power of the indwelling Spirit, the entire Mosaic system passed away; but the eternal principle, its foundation, remained, and is operative today as the law of love, the supreme "commandment" and the only "law" under which the Christian is to live.

The concept of Law in Seventh-day Adventism, then, leads them to the un-Biblical and at times legalistic position that although they are "under grace," by failing to "keep the commandments" they are in danger of coming "under law" again.

The Word of God, however, describes the Christian under grace as "dead to the law" and "alive unto God" (Galatians 2:19), and nowhere is it taught that one can "come alive" again so that the function of the law is resumed.

II. *The Relationship of Grace to Salvation*

Although Adventists lay great stress on "commandment-keeping" and "obedience to the moral law of God as contained in the Ten Commandments," they devote a large portion of their writings to the New Testament doctrine of grace. As we saw earlier, Seventh-day Adventists believe in salvation by grace alone, and vehemently deny that "law" plays any part as a basis for redemption.[95] In their own words,

> Salvation is not now, and never has been, by law or by works; salvation is only by the grace of Christ. Moreover, there never was a time in the plan of God when salvation was by human works or effort. Nothing men can do, or have done, can in any way *merit* salvation.
>
> While works are not a *means* of salvation, good works are the inevitable *result* of salvation. However, these good works are possible only for the child of God whose life is inwrought by the Spirit of God. . . . One thing is certain, man cannot be saved by any effort of his own. We profoundly believe that no works of the law, no deeds of the law, no effort however commendable, and no good works — whether they be many or few, sacrificial or not — can in any way justify the

---

94 Not the embodiment of carnal prohibitions or commandments.

95 See Author's Note immediately following III. *The Author of Salvation.*

sinner (Titus 3:5; Rom. 3:20). Salvation is wholly of the grace; it is the gift of God (Rom. 4:4, 5; Eph. 2:8).[96]

These and many similar clear-cut statements in current authoritative Seventh-day Adventist literature reveal that, despite the "dual law theory" and the peculiar concept that the law is still operative in the life of the believer, Adventists confess the basis of their salvation to be grace, and grace alone, the only basis upon which God deigns to save the fallen children of Adam.

In Chapter 14 of *Questions on Doctrine*, Adventists spell out their allegiance to divine grace as the only channel of salvation: "According to Seventh-day Adventist belief, there is, and can be, no salvation through the law, or by human works of the law, but only through the saving grace of God."[97]

Christians who are familiar with historical theology know that the Adventist position on law, though tinged with legalism, has its roots in the basic Arminian position that one receives salvation as a free gift of God; but, once he has received this gift, the believer is responsible for its maintenance and duration, and the chief means of accomplishing this is "commandment-keeping" or "obedience to *all* the laws of God."

Since Adventists are basically Arminian, we may logically deduce that, in a sense, their salvation rests upon legal grounds. But the saving factor in the dilemma is that by life and by world-wide witness, Adventists, like other so-called Arminians, give true evidence that they have experienced the "new birth," which is by grace alone, through faith in our Lord and His sacrifice upon the cross. One would be callous and uncharitable indeed not to accept their profession of dependence upon Christ alone for redemption, even though there is inconsistency in their theological system.

Some Christians make a great issue of the teaching of "eternal security," and perhaps rightly so because it is an important truth. However, no matter how strongly we may feel about it, our conviction does not entitle us to judge the motives and spiritual condition of other believers in this respect. This is our principal reason for taking the position that Seventh-day Adventists are Christians who believe the historic gospel message. They cannot rightly be called non-Christian cultists or

"Judaizers," since they are sound on the great New Testament doctrines including grace and redemption through the vicarious offering of Jesus Christ "once for all" (Hebrews 10:10) and give evidence of "life in Christ."

For many centuries, there has been much controversy over the juxtaposition of the principles of law and grace in the Scripture. If evangelicals today were asked, "Do you believe that grace and law are in direct opposition?" the answer in most cases would be a strong affirmative. Through the years, confusion has been caused by the abuse of both principles by two groups of equally sincere Christians. One group believes that all law has ceased; the other that the Ten Commandments are still God's standard of righteousness and must be obeyed or salvation is forfeit. What both groups have failed to grasp is that the great conflict is not between law and grace as such; rather, it centers around a proper understanding of their relationship and respective functions.

We have established that love is the ground and source of the doctrine of grace, but the law was necessary to expose the sinfulness of sin and the depth of man's moral depravity. When law becomes the ground of salvation or of restraining the Christian from practicing sin, it intrudes upon the province of grace. When a Christian is not controlled by love, grace is abused and its purpose is nullified. All law is fulfilled by love, as our Saviour and the apostles taught, but the Christian can never please God if he obeys for fear of the law. Life under law binds the soul, for the tendency is for man to obey not because he wants to please God but because he fears God's judgment. Under grace, love works upon the regenerate heart, and what was legalistic duty under law becomes gracious obedience under grace. Actually, grace and love demand more than the law, which to the Pharisees required only outward obedience. Grace commands us to "do the will of God from the heart" (Ephesians 6:6). Seventh-day Adventists declare that they obey the law not out of fear but out of love for God, but it is to be regretted that in a large proportion of their literature on the subject, they declare that the keeping of the law is necessary to *maintain* salvation, and thus they introduce the motive of fear instead of the Biblical inperative of love.

The Apostle John defined the issue

---

[96]*Questions on Doctrine*, pages 141-42. [97]Page 135.

when he wrote, "The law given by Moses, but grace and truth came by Jesus Christ" (John 1:17). As a governing principle, a measure of righteousness, a schoolmaster and an instrument of death, the law was supplanted by grace — the unmerited favor of God. All believers in the Lord Jesus Christ, having passed from death to life through the sacrifice of the Son of God, possess the divine nature and righteousness. Because He first loved us, we are compelled and impelled to love and serve Him. In obedience to the great law of love, the Christian fulfills the *righteousness* of the law (not the law itself; this Christ alone did); and by the transforming power of the indwelling Holy Spirit he will "walk not after the flesh, but after the Spirit" (Romans 8:4).

Seventh-day Adventists believe, we repeat, that they are saved by grace. As "Arminians," however, they are often prone to believe that their remaining saved depends on "commandment-keeping." They are not alone in this error, for it is characteristic of most of those who embrace Arminianism.

III. The Author of Salvation

Because He took our sins upon Himself, in obedience to His Father's will, the Lord Jesus "became the author of eternal salvation unto all them that obey him" (Hebrews 5:8-10). This truth Seventh-day Adventists believe. They strongly assert their belief in the deity of the Lord Jesus Christ, His equality with the Father, and His perfect, sinless human nature, and expound these truths in detail.[98] However, they teach that before his incarnation the Lord Jesus Christ bore the title of Michael the archangel.[99] This interpretation differs greatly from that of Jehovah's Witnesses who believe that Christ was a created being and that "He was a god, but not the almighty God who is Jehovah.[100] The Adventists make this very clear:

> We emphatically reject the idea . . . and the position held by the Jehovah's Witnesses. We do not believe that Christ is a created being. We, as a people, have not considered the identification of Michael of sufficient prominence to dwell upon it at length either in our literature or in our preaching.

. . . We believe that the term "Michael" is but one of the many titles applied to the Son of God, the second person of the Godhead. But such a view does not in any way conflict with our belief in His full deity and eternal pre-existence, nor does it in the least disparage His person and work.[101]

Although a number of authoritative commentators support the Adventist view, the New Testament, I believe, does not warrant this conclusion.[102] Most of the evidence that the Adventists submit is from the Book of Daniel, the rest from the Apocalypse. By comparing such designations as "angel of Jehovah," "angel of the Lord," "Prince," and "Michael," the Adventists conclude that Michael is another title for the Lord Jesus Christ. But Seventh-day Adventists maintain that although he is called "the arch angel" (*archangelos* or "first messenger"), he is *not* a created being since, in the Old Testament, "angel of Jehovah" is a term of Deity. In the light of this, we do not judge them because of their view of Michael, but call the reader's attention to the ninth verse of the book of Jude, which says, "Yet Michael the archangel, when contending with the devil he disputed about the body of Moses, *durst not* bring against him a railing accusation, but said, The Lord rebuke thee."

The word translated *durst* in the King James Bible is the archaic past tense of "dare"; so Michael "did not dare" bring against Satan a railing or blasphemous (*blasphemos*) judgment. The Greek word for "dare" is *tolmao* and appears 16 times in the New Testament, and in the negative always means "not daring through fear of retaliation." Thus if Michael was Christ, according to the Seventh-day Adventists, "He did not dare" to rebuke Satan for fear of retaliation.

Adventists agree that 15 times in the New Testament *"tolmao"* carries the meaning indicated. But, since its use in Jude nine refutes their notion that Michael is a title of Christ, they *reverse* its meaning here! As the Adventists know, none of the commentators to whom they appeal has grammatically analyzed or diagrammed the passage in the Greek or for that matter commented upon exclusive us-

98*Questions on Doctrine*, pages 35-41, 50-65.

99*Ibid.*, pages 71-86.

100*Let God Be True*, pages 34-35, Watch Tower Bible and Tract Society, Brooklyn, N. Y. (1946).

101*Questions on Doctrine*, page 71.

102Matthew Henry, *Commentary;* J. B. Rotherham, *The Emphasized Old Testament;* George Rowlinson, *Pulpit Commentary;* T. Robinson, *Preacher's Homiletic Commentary.*

age of *tolmao* in the Scripture of the New Testament. The agreement of such commentation therefore gives no validity whatever to the Adventists' misuse of *tolmao*. The preincarnate Christ, the *Logos*, having the nature of God (John 1:1), certainly would not refer the creature Satan to God the Father for rebuke. While He was on earth, Christ the Creator rebuked Satan many times.[103] Would He then fear him during His preincarnate life? Scripture belies this.

The Adventist explanation is:

The devil, the prince of evil, could rightly be said to deserve a railing accusation, but to such a thing Michael would not stoop. To say that Michael *could not,* in the sense that He did not have the power or the authority to do so, would not be true. It is not that Michael *could not,* in the sense of being restricted, but rather that He *would not* take such an attitude.[104]

This statement appears to be an attempt to escape the fact that the word "dare" (*tolmao*) in the New Testament always connotes fear, including its use in Jude nine. The text teaches that because Michael did not have the authority to rebuke Satan, "he did not dare" to do so through fear of superior retaliation. There is no implication that Michael's position was so high that he "would not stoop." The context, grammar and root meaning of *tolmao* belie the Adventists' attempt to make this text support their view of Michael. All authorities on Greek grammar agree that the Adventist interpretation violates the classic and New Testament usage of *tolmao.*

Thus the Adventist statement about Michael is neither linguistically nor Scripturally accurate. Although they repudiate the Jehovah's Witnesses' position, they wrest this passage from its true meaning, and read into it their own theory concerning Michael as Christ.

In conclusion, I am convinced of the sincerity of the Adventists' claim to regeneration, and allegiance to the New Testament principle of saving grace. I appreciate their high regard for the law of God, and their desire to obey it. I cannot agree, however, with their insistence upon linking "commandment-keeping" to observance of the ceremonial law, especially with regard to "unclean" foods. I feel, moreover, that they err in saying that Michael is a title of Christ, and I

believe that I have shown that they violate the linguistic and Scriptural meaning of Jude nine.

Author's Note

One of the chief critics of Seventh-day Adventism is a vocal ex-Adventist printer of Minneapolis, a man who has written much against his former church. Writing in *The Sword of the Lord,* August 2, 1957, he bitterly assailed Seventh-day Adventists as willful deceivers. Since his writings are repeatedly quoted by most of the other critics we shall discuss his charge, but in the interest of brevity we shall confine ourselves to one of his chief areas of criticism, law and salvation in Seventh-day Adventist theology.

This critic quotes the book, *Steps to Christ,* by Mrs. Ellen G. White in the following manner: "The condition of eternal life is now just what it has always been . . . perfect obedience to the law of God."

He then maintains that Seventh-day Adventism teaches this and on the surface it appears that he has proved his point; namely that to Adventists salvation is a combination of grace, faith in Christ, plus the keeping of the law. A closer look at the statement in the context from which the critic removed it, however, serves to refute this position. Wrote Mrs. White in the very same context:

We do not earn salvation by our obedience for salvation is the free gift of God to receive by faith. But obedience is the fruit of faith . . . here is the true test. If we abide in Christ and the love of God dwells in us, our feelings, our thoughts, our actions will be in harmony with the will of God as expressed in the precepts of His Holy law. . . . Righteousness is defined by the standard of God's holy law as expressed in the ten precepts given on Sinai. That so-called faith in Christ which professes to release men from the obligation of obedience to God is not faith but presumption. "By grace are ye saved through faith." But "faith if it has not works is dead." Jesus said of Himself before He came to earth, "I delight to do thy will O my God. Yea, thy law is within my heart." And just before He ascended again to Heaven, He declared, "I have kept my Father's commandments and abide in his love." The Scripture says, "Hereby we do know that we know him, if we keep his commandments. He that saith he abides in

---

[103]See Matthew 4:10; 16:23; Luke 4:8; Mark 8:33.

[104]*Questions on Doctrine,* page 80.

him ought also himself to walk even as he walked," because "Christ also suffered for us, leaving us an example, that ye should follow his steps."

The condition of eternal life is now just what it always has been — just what it was in Paradise before the fall of our first parents—perfect obedience to the law of God, perfect righteousness. Since we are sinful, unholy, we cannot perfectly obey a holy law. We have no righteousness of our own with which to meet the claims of the law of God. But Christ has made a way of escape for us. He lived on earth amid trials and temptations such as we have to meet. He lived a sinless life. He died for us and now He offers to take our sins and give us His righteousness. If you give yourself to Him and accept Him as your Saviour, then sinful as your life may have been for His sake you are counted righteous. Christ's character stands in place of your character and you are accepted before God just as if you had not sinned.

So we have nothing in ourselves of which to boast. We have no ground for self exaltation. Our only ground of hope is in the righteousness of Christ imputed to us by His Spirit working in and through us.[105]

In the light of Mrs. White's complete statement on this subject we see that our critic omitted her principal thesis, that we are saved by grace. There are not a few instances of similar carelessness on the part of the writer of this article. The result is that his work is largely discredited and discounted by those who know the proper methods of research.

Seventh-day Adventists are well aware of the law and grace problem and in *Questions on Doctrine* they state:

There has been regrettable misunder-standing as to our teaching on grace, law, and works, and their interrelationships. According to Seventh-day Adventist belief, there is, and can be, no salvation through the law, or by human works of the law, but only through the saving grace of God. This principle, to us, is basic.[106]

Further the Adventists state:

Salvation is not now, and never has been, by law or works; salvation is only by the grace of Christ. Moreover, there never was a time in the plan of God when salvation was by human works or effort. Nothing men can do, or have done, can in any way *merit* salvation.

While works are not a *means* of salvation, good works are the inevitable *result* of salvation. . . . One thing is certain, man cannot be saved by any effort of his own. We profoundly believe that no works of the law, no deeds of the law, no effort however commendable, and no good works — whether they be many or few, sacrificial or not — can in any way justify the sinner (Titus 3:5; Rom. 3:20). Salvation is wholly of grace; it is the gift of God (Rom. 4:4, 5; Eph. 2:8).[107]

Ellen G. White, certainly an authoritative voice in Adventism, summarized it thus:

Christ is pleading for the church in the heavenly courts above, pleading for those for whom he paid the redemption price of his own lifeblood. Centuries, ages, can never diminish the efficacy of this atoning sacrifice. The message of the gospel of His grace was to be given to the church in clear and distinct lines, that the world should no longer say that Seventh-day Adventists talk the law, but do not teach or believe Christ.[108]

---

[105]*Steps to Christ*, pages 36-49 (paperback ed. 1945).

[106]Page 135.

[107]*Questions on Doctrine*, pages 141-42.

[108]*Testimonies to Ministers*, page 92.

UNITARIANISM

The Unitarian Church, or cult, as it might more properly be designated, today numbers over 157,000 persons in the United States, worshiping in some 1,012 churches. Until their merger with the Universalist Church in 1959, Unitarianism had maintained a semi-static relationship of growth, compared with other more missionary minded non-Christian cults, such as Jehovah's Witnesses and the Mormons, but it is on the upswing due to the influencing neo-liberalism and accentuated ecumenical interest.

The central theme of Unitarianism is that there is but one God, a solitary entity, who has revealed Himself through various men and in the Bible, which is considered to be one among a number of divine books. The writings of Buddha, Mohammed, Confucius, Lao and the Vedas and Upanishads are sources of revelation, none of which are infallible, but all of which contribute something to the religious growth and development of mankind. Unitarianism generally affirms that salvation is progressive, and that it is essentially a matter of character development, joined with faith in God and attendant good works, which are counted as means toward an end of final redemption.

To understand Unitarianism the background of history must be utilized to the fullest.

Unitarians generally like to trace their history to apostolic times, especially to the Council of Nicaea (A.D. 325) where the great Arian heresy enunciated a semiunitarian theme by denying the New Testament doctrine of the full deity of Jesus Christ.

Unitarians, however, are notoriously poor historians, and it was not until the fourteenth century that the dogmas now designated as Unitarian, markedly gained any popular support. Of a certainty, some poorly-informed thinkers in the early church adhered to various principles now claimed by Unitarians; but none of the leading theologians of the Christian church ever held to Unitarian teachings, nor do they today. For it is impossible to remain in fellowship with the Christian church and to maintain a Unitarian interpretation of Christian theology.

Unitarians, although they have managed to gain recognition in local church councils in certain areas of the United States (due primarily to a laxity in doctrine on the part of such groups), are refused membership as a body in the National Council of Churches, the World Council of Churches, the National Association of Evangelicals, the American Council of Churches, and by the Roman Catholic and Eastern Orthodox Churches. The term, "Unitarian," and the term, "Christian," are mutually exclusive by definition, historically and theologically.

The first Unitarian writer of note was Martin Cellarium (1499-1564), a friend of Martin Luther, who advanced Unitarian views in 1527. This bold presentation was followed in succession by the anti-Trinitarian positions of Ludwig Haetzer, 1529, Michael Servetus, 1531, who was martyred for his views at Geneva in 1553, and culminated in the work of Fausto Sozini, better known to history as Socinus (1539-1604). Socinus, an Italian by birth, was a nephew of Lelio Sozini, an associate of John Calvin and Philip Melanchthon, whose theology at times wavered, but apparently remained orthodox enough for him to escape martyrdom and to remain in fellowship with Reformed theologians (see the *Encyclopedia Brittanica*, Vol. XXV, XXVI pages 320, 321).

In contrast to his Uncle Lelio, Socinus became an anti-Trinitarian, denying the Trinity and the true deity of Jesus Christ, as do all Unitarians to this day.

Socinianism found strong roots in Hungary, Poland, and Transylvania and eventually spread to Holland, then to England and finally to the United States.

Early in the history of America, the Unitarian faith made itself known through the work of such preachers as Jonathan Mayhew, 1720-1766, pastor of the West Church in Boston, Joseph Priestley, 1794, Hosea Ballou, 1771-1852;

William Ellery Channing, 1803, and Ralph Waldo Emerson, 1838, to mention just a few Unitarians of note.

During the course of its American development, Unitarianism passed through three distinct stages. The first period was 1800-1835. Throughout this era, Unitarianism was subject, in a large measure, to English philosophic rationalism, a semi-supernaturalism and the practice of general philanthropy. The second period of development, 1835-1885, found the Unitarians strongly influenced by German idealism and rationalistic theology flavored by a definite leaning toward mysticism. By 1865 the National Unitarian Conference was organized, and a definite theology was evolved, in which the Unitarians envisioned themselves as disciples of Christ.

The third period of Unitarian illusion began in 1885, and continues on to this day. This period of growth has seen an acceptance of evolution, the empirical methods in religion, higher criticism, the higher recognition of the Universal religion and "an ethical attempt to realize the higher affirmations of Christianity."

These aims were confirmed at the International Congress held by the Unitarians in 1900, and have not undergone any major changes to this day. As was previously noted, the Unitarians merged with the Universalists and have publicly announced that they are not altogether sure whether they can classify themselves as Christians. In fact, some of their leaders have not hesitated to disclaim the title of "Christian," where Unitarian theology is concerned.

THE THEOLOGY OF UNITARIANISM

As its name implies, Unitarianism unequivocally denies the Christian doctrine of the Trinity and by necessity, the Deity of Jesus Christ. During the year 1955, *Look* Magazine sent out a questionnaire to the major religions of the United States, asking specific questions in the context of generally accepted terminology in the realm of Christian theology.

The Unitarian Church selected as its spokesman, the Rev. Carl M. Chorowsky, minister of the First Unitarian Church of Fairfield, Connecticut. Dr. Chorowsky answered the questions of *Look* Magazine with great candor, and with a refreshing directness seldom found in the major, non-Christian cults. His answers are of great value, because they stand as an official statement of Unitarian theology.

Dr. Chorowsky is the author of the following statements, taken from the March 8, 1955, issue of *Look* Magazine, in an article entitled, "What is a Unitarian?"

1. *The Doctrine of God and the Person of Christ.*

In general, a Unitarian is a religious person whose ethic derives primarily from that of Jesus, who believed in One God, not the Trinity. . . . Unitarians hold that the orthodox Christian world has forsaken the real, human Jesus of the Gospel, and has substituted a Christ of dogmatism, metaphysics and pagan philosophy. Because Unitarians refuse to acknowledge Jesus as their Lord and God, they are excluded from the National Council of the Churches of Christ.

Further evidence of the Unitarian attitude toward Jesus Christ, is found in another of Dr. Chorowsky's statements.

Unitarians repudiate the doctrine and dogma of the Virgin Birth. . . . Unitarians do not believe that Jesus is the Messiah, either of Jewish hope or of Christian fanasty. They do not believe He is "God Incarnate," or the Second Person of the Trinity, as the final arbitrator at the end of time, who shall come to judge the quick and the dead.

2. *The Doctrines of Sin and Redemption.*

Unitarians recognize evil and man's responsibility for much of it. . . . Because of the total depravity of man, supposedly, God sent His only begotten Son to the world to die for sinful men. Such doctrine Unitarians find offensive. un-Biblical, even immoral. It is certainly inconsistent with the nature of God or the dignity of man, whom the Eternal One created in the image of God, to love with an everlasting love.

Relative to the doctrine of eternal salvation, Dr. Chorowsky declared:

Unitarians believe in salvation of a character. . . . God's help is not likely to come to those who cast all their burdens on the Lord. There is practical wisdom in the saying, "God helps those who help themselves," . . . if by heaven, you mean an abode of eternal light, where the saved and redeemed enjoy everlasting bliss, and if by hell, you mean the devil's eternal darkness, where the wicked suffer unending torment — then Unitarianism emphatically repudiates such beliefs.

UNITARIANISM AND THE BIBLE

"Do Unitarians believe the Bible is divinely inspired and infallible?" This was one of the key questions addressed to the Unitarian Church, and received the following reply from Dr. Chorowsky:

"No. The doctrine of revelation of the absolute and indisputable authority of the Bible is alien to Unitarian faith and teaching."

It is not necessary to point out that this view of the Scripture is the same view held by reformed Judaism, Christian Science, Unity and a host of other non-Christian cults, all of whom are content to utilize the Scriptures, but in a manner never intended by the authors.

THEOLOGICAL ANALYSIS

To sum up the basic issues of Unitarianism, past and present, three important tenets should be carefully noted by the reader.

First, Unitarianism, while it rejects the authority of the Bible in spiritual, moral and doctrinal matters, paradoxically quotes the Bible repeatedly, and mostly out of context at that, in an attempt to substantiate many of its own teachings.

This fact can be shown easily by perusing any standard Unitarian work, where it will be found that practically every author, without exception, quotes the very Book his religion denies, to establish or to make a point concerning that religion!

Dr. Chorowsky himself makes the mistake, in his answers to *Look* Magazine, relative to the question "Do Unitarians believe in the divinity of Jesus?"

In that particular instance, in his answer he quotes Scripture, although completely out of context, to establish his contention. The question quite naturally arises in the logical mind, Why quote the Bible at all, if you reject nearly every one of the cardinal doctrines it teaches? This, there can be no doubt, Unitarianism does. If Unitarians were truly honest, they would abandon the Scriptures, for it is either reliable or it is not. Why pick and choose whatever parts suit your theology, while denying the hundreds of affirmations within its pages that it is God's Word to man?

The answer must be obvious — Unitarians dare not abandon the Bible outright, though in effect they have, because it is a tried and true badge of religious prestige, useful in attracting the unregenerate man, who has a general respect for the Bible even though he doesn't live up to it or accept the Saviour revealed within its pages. Unitarianism displays a mock reverence for Scripture and for Jesus of Nazareth, although it is clear that it wants no part of His intrinsic Deity, Atoning Death, Bodily Resurrection or triumphant Second Advent.

The Unitarians, it appears, will heap honors upon Christ, but they will not obey His express command:

The Father loveth the Son, and . . . hath committed all judgment unto the Son: that all men should honour the Son, even as they honour the Father (John 5:20-23).

Second, Unitarianism claims to be a form of Christianity, but at the same time it denies the historic doctrines of the Christian Church (the Trinity, Deity of Christ, Virgin Birth, Vicarious Atonement, Bodily Resurrection and Glorious Return of our Lord). All of these are described as "dogmatisms, metaphysics and pagan philosophy," to quote the official view given by Dr. Chorowsky to *Look* Magazine, and which view is also available in numerous official publications.

Dr. Chorowsky further claims that God's plan of redemption as portrayed in the Bible is "offensive, un-Biblical and immoral." This is strange reasoning indeed, coming from those who claim to practice a scientific empirical method of gaining knowledge, and who venerate the great gods, Reason, Logic and Rationalism.

It may be true, and doubtless is in the case of Unitarians, that the redemption of man on the cross by virtue of Christ's atoning sacrifice is "offensive and immoral." But it could hardly be called "un-Biblical!" In fact, Dr. Chorowsky could easily have verified this by consulting any standard concordance to the Bible.

The fact of the matter is, that Christ's vicarious death is referred to not less than 100 times in the New Testament alone, by every major writer (see Matthew 26:28; Mark 14:24; Luke 22:20; John 6:50-55; I Corinthians 11:25; Colossians 1:20; I Peter 1:18,19; Revelation 1:5).

In addition to this, the Bible in countless instances refers directly to the Deity, Virgin Birth, Bodily Resurrection and Second Coming of Jesus Christ, in direct contradiction to Unitarian teachings.

Christianity is more than a way of life, a code of ethics and a pseudo-Christian vocabulary. Christianity is, in its very essence, the Person, Nature and Work of our Lord Jesus, the Eternal Word and Incarnate Son of God, the recognition of whom as personal Saviour and Lord is absolutely essential, the Bible teaches, for entrance into the kingdom of God (John 1:12,3:3; 5:24; 6:37,47; John 14:6; Acts 4:12).

Only the sinner comes to Christ, for He alone of the religious figures of history, could say "Come unto me, all ye that labour and are heavy laden, and I will give you rest" (Matthew 11:28).

This rest, of which our Lord spoke, comes only to those who are willing to cast themselves wholly on the mercy of God. Or, to put it most pointedly, those who would live to please Him, must first please Him to live.

Dr. Chorowsky and the Apostle Peter are at direct variance in this all-important matter of human salvation. For according to Dr. Chorowsky "God's help is not likely to come to those who cast their burdens on the Lord." The Apostle Peter reminds us, however, that above all things we are to cast "all your care upon him, for he careth for you" (I Peter 5:7). If, as in the words of the writer of the epistle to the Hebrews, Jesus Christ is indeed "the same yesterday, to day and for ever" (13:8), and if with the God of the Bible "there is no variableness, neither shadow or turning" (James 1:17), the Unitarian program of "salvation by character" linked by human effort, "God helps those who help themselves," cannot stand the test.

Unitarianism quite literally puts the cart (a moral and ethical life) before the horse (repentance toward God and faith in the Lord Jesus Christ), and is therefore rightly confused, seeing that Unitarians cannot find peace with either God or their fellow man, since "there is no peace, saith the Lord, unto the wicked" (Isaiah 48:22).

In the third chapter of the gospel of John, following Jesus' discourse with Nicodemus, we read:

And this is the judgment, that the light has come into the world, and men loved darkness rather than light, because their deeds were evil (verse 19, RSV).

This is the real reason why Unitarians do not receive Jesus Christ as their Saviour; because despite their affirmation of the necessity of a moral and ethical life and faith in God, good works and the golden rule, etc., by rejecting the historic Christ of Scripture, the God-Man of Revelation, they have indeed demonstrated irrevocably their love of darkness, rather than light, because their deeds are evil. There is no greater evil than to reject Infinite Love, and on the Cross, God who is Love, and who was Love Incarnate, Jesus Christ who "bears in His own body on the tree, our sins."

Jesus Christ was manifested, the Scripture informs us, to bring to ruination the works of the devil and to ruin him who had the authority of death (Hebrews 2: 14). It is a foolish thing indeed, to change the glory of the Immortal God for corruptible things, and to lay up for one's self treasure on earth where the moth and the rust do indeed corrupt and where the thieves do break through and steal.

Unitarians are, in effect, doing this very thing. How then, shall they escape the judgment of Him who is called the Eternal Word, the fulness of God in human form?

Third, Unitarianism desires to escape Biblical teaching that God has indeed committed all judgment unto His Son (John 5:22,23). The obvious reason for this is, that the doctrine of everlasting punishment which Christ will administer at His Second Advent in power, the end of the ages, is a spiritual thorn in the flesh of contemporary Unitarianism.

Dr. Chorowsky and Unitarians in general "emphatically repudiate eternal darkness, where the wicked suffer unending torment."

In this connection, both Peter and Jude declare eternal darkness to indeed be the fate of all who reject Jesus Christ, "God manifest in the flesh" (I Timothy 3:16). And both are agreed that "the mists of darkness" are reserved for such souls "for ever" (II Peter 2:17; Jude 13). The usage of the Greek *ionion* (everlasting) is quite forceful here and cannot be ignored by any thorough student of the Scriptures.

In the light of these facts, the future of Unitarians could hardly be described as bright.

Unitarianism is a product of the deification of Reason, the rejection of Biblical authority and an indescribably fierce pride in one's ability to save himself from the awful penalty of sin. It is one thing for Unitarianism to exercise its prerogative of denial where the foundations of Christianity are involved. But it is quite another to use the Christian Scriptures and abuse numerous contexts therein in order to implement such denials. This is why not a few Christian thinkers have been led to observe that while Unitarianism may be a religion which attempts to exalt reason and rationalism, it is one in which logical consistency is conspicuously absent.

THE ROSICRUCIAN FELLOWSHIP

"May the roses bloom upon your cross," intones the mystical and authoritative voice of the leader, and the echoed response, "And on yours also," from the disciples, probationers and students, making up a typical Rosicrucian Fellowship Center, signals the beginning of another excursion into the metaphysical labyrinths of the 600-year old cult today known as the Rosicrucian Fellowship.

Of all the cult systems under discussion in this book, the Rosicrucians most certainly qualify, along with the spiritists, Theosophists and Swedenborgians, as the most mystically inclined. More than any of the others, they are also devoted to a detailed system of doctrine composed of so many strains of other cult viruses, as to be almost beyond the point of comprehension, much less analysis.

Rosicrucianism is not only an eclectic theological system which mixes pagan mythology with Judaism and Christianity with traces of Hinduism and Buddhism throughout, but it is a system of thinking which seeks to synthesize the basic truths of all religions and absorb them into a master system.

In the literature of Rosicrucianism one will find enormous deposits of symbolism, anthropology, transmigration and even some spiritism.

There is a great similarity in some areas for the vocabulary of theosophy and to the concept that man progresses through many reincarnations, each of which purges him of his preceding sins.

In Rosicrucian theology there exists seven worlds with seven sections or divisions presided over on the highest level by a "universal spirit." All nature, for that matter, all creation, is unified and bears a direct relationship to the cross which represents man's evolutionary past as well as his future destiny. In Rosicrucian theology the cross loses what the Bible describes as its "reproach" and no Rosicrucian stands ready to "go forth therefore unto him without the camp, bearing his reproach" (Hebrews 13:13).

The cross in Rosicrucianism is the mystical symbol of man's evolutionary development past, present and future, and has no true significance as the symbol of what it cost God to redeem the sons of men (Revelation 1:5).

Prominent still, though it has been redefined, the cross stands at the center of Rosicrucianism circled with roses. This creates the concept of the rosy cross.

Man progresses by the mystical number seven, for at seven he possesses a vital body, at fourteen a desire body, at twenty-one a full formation of the mind, though the so-called "dense body" is present at birth.

The mission of the Lord Jesus Christ in Rosicrucian theology was to manifest Himself for the aid of mankind in the evolutionary struggle. Rosicrucian theology relegates Him to the highest manifestation or initiate of the Son. And He, along with Buddha and other great leaders, was revealed to facilitate human progress. Sovereign over all the manifestations is the highest initiate from the Saturn. This is designated the father. The Holy Spirit is known as the highest initiate of the moon. However, neither the Holy Spirit nor the Son have any activity in vicarious atonement or spiritual

428

regeneration which consummates in personal redemption apart from psychic reincarnation.

As one travels through the mazes of Rosicrucian terminology and theology, one encounters the fabulous three heavens which are attained through suffering, silence, thought and eventually the reincarnation wheel. A silver chord allegedly connects the physical or dense body with the spiritual body and at death the chord is broken, releasing the higher nature from the physical. We are told in Rosicrucian literature that Plato was a believer in Rosicrucianism due to his emphasis upon the world soul, and that countless others were secret initiates of Rosicrucian truths. Even the lost continent of Atlantis and the mysterious Lemuran race are included in Rosicrucian speculation. In fact, there is very little that Rosicrucianism does not seek to enfold within its mythological-magical lore, yet everything Christian that it touches suffers violence at its hands.

By the time the average reader of Rosicrucian literature extricates himself or herself from the various Periods (Sun, Moon, Saturn, etc.), ethers, bodies and multiple hypotheses of Rosicrucian philosophy, he is pretty generally impressed with the enormous amount of data the Rosicrucians have amassed as a substitute for the revelations of the Bible. Most always, he is confused by the fact that Rosicrucian terminology and concepts do have a distinct Christian flavor and sound. But somehow or other, the taste is distinctly different!

Mathison is correct when he states, as we previously noted, that "The Rosicrucian Fellowship attempts to explain all history, philosophy and theology, regardless of how diverse the origin, in terms of its own particular world view, which is, at its core, pantheistic." Because of this, it has much in common with other pantheistic cults such as Unity, Christian Science, Theosophy and The Mighty I Am.

It is not our intention in this Appendix to occupy ourselves at great length with the theology of Rosicrucianism which will generate, in the minds of most Christians, a great deal of heat, and very little, if any, light. But since the cult is effective in the Southwestern and Western parts of the United States, and is penetrating the Eastern seaboard and Mid-west with steady effectiveness, as evidenced by the establishment of Rosicrucian Fellowship Centers in key cities throughout the Mid-west and the East, some mention should be made of its history and its theological structure as it affects the Christian doctrine of God, the Person, Nature and Work of Jesus Christ and the destiny of mankind.

HISTORICAL SYNOPSIS

The founder of present day Rosicrucianism was Christianus Rosenkreutz (1378-1484), a German scholar who roundly opposed Roman Catholicism and claimed to be the revealer of the mysteries of the rose cross. From its inception, Rosicrucianism put emphasis upon the occult and the mystical relationship of Christianity to all the great religions of the world. It was by admission, a secret society. It flourished in a day when secret societies were in vogue, and "a century after its origin, Rosicrucianism underwent a recrudescence in connection with Free Masonry, which not only deemed Rosicrucianism genuine, but even borrowed usages and customs from the writings of those who had satirized the fraternity" (*Schaff-Herzog Encyclopedia of Religious Knowledge,* page 97).

In a world which was trying to analyze the meaning of comets, alchemy and Eastern occultism, Rosicrucianism proved to be an attractive alternative to orthodoxy. It was careful to utilize an orthodox Christian vocabulary, however, and to speak out vehemently against Roman Catholicism, Alchemy and dogmatic theology of any type, although it zealously promoted some of the principles of the Protestant Reformation, the theology of which, it might be noted, is the antithesis of Rosicrucian teaching!

Today, there are more than a hundred Rosicrucian centers throughout the world, and the headquarters of the movement to all intents and purposes, is in San Jose, California. The writer visited there in 1961, and obtained valuable information about the methods of the Rosicrucians in propagating their beliefs, as well as additional data about some of the more "spiritual" teachings.

Of all the modern Rosicrucian writers, the best known is the late Max Heindel.

In this age of ecumenicity, the Rosicrucians play heavily upon the notes of "universal brotherhood," publish 2,000,000 copies of their magazines (*The Rosicrucian Digest* and *Rosicrucian Forum*), and maintain "supreme temple of North and South America," which is located in San Jose, California, in Rosicrucian Park.

This group of Rosicrucians identified by the letters A.M.O.R.C. deny being either a religion or a church. They identify themselves as a brotherhood or organization which is attempting to help mankind to master its destiny. This branch of Rosicrucianism in America numbers in excess of 38,000 adherents, presided over by a "supreme secretary," currently, Mr. Cecil Poole. The rival body is under the direction of Mrs. Max Heindel, the late great mentor's widow, who continues to send forth his publications (voluminous and complex) from her headquarters in Oceanside, California.

The major bodies of Rosicrucians do not exceed 100,000 in membership worldwide, but due to a heavy advertising campaign, the zealous propagation of their brotherhood and destiny publications, Rosicrucianism is, in our time, a successful non-Christian cult,

which uses the terminology of Christianity whenever possible (and profitable) to lead the untutored mind into the mazes of a philosophical religion so complex that those who know it best are content to admit readily, the limitations of their own understanding.

ROSICRUCIANISM AND CHRISTIANITY

1. *The Nature of God.*

It is a historic affirmation of Rosicrucianism, that God is an impersonal being, composed of seven spirits, which manifest themselves as a "triune godhead," or, father, son and holy spirit. Lest there be any doubt on the subject, Heindel, in one of his many books, declares:

> . . . The seven spirits before the throne . . . collectively, they are God, and make up the triune godhead . . . the Father is the highest initiate among the humanity of the Saturn. . . . The Son is the highest initiate of the Sun . . . the Holy Spirit (Jehovah) is the highest initiate of the Moon. . . .[1]

In such a semantic jungle, the nature of God, the holy Trinity, or Triune Deity of Biblical revelation undergoes total, if not complete, mutilation. It becomes a type of occult pantheism, culminating in an impersonal spirit-being, who is "collectively" God.

The Rosicrucians believe that the Trinity portrays aspects of God:

> . . . the only begotten, the Word of whom John speaks, is the second aspect of the Supreme Being. This word, and it alone, is begotten of His Father, first aspect before all worlds. . . . Therefore, the Only Begotten is the exalted Being which ranks above all else in the universe, save only the Power aspect, which created it.[2]

For the Rosicrucians, the Holy Spirit is Jehovah, the third aspect of the triune Godhead. But in the sense of Christian theology, these definitions are meaningless, since the Bible declares unequivocally that God is the Father, the Son and the Holy Spirit, three divine Persons,

[1]*The Rosicrucian Cosmo Conception,* pages 376 and 252.

[2]*Ibid.,* page 374.

all sharing the same Nature and Attributes, co-existent, co-equal and co-eternal, and, above all else, personal. The Lord Himself declared:

I AM THAT I AM . . . Thus shalt thou say to the children of Israel, I AM hath sent me unto you (Exodous 3:14).

The Christian doctrine of the Trinity then, cannot be equated with the Rosicrucian caricature of it, although it is significant that the Rosicrucians do usually bend over backward as it were, in an attempt to make their pantheistic theology sound Christian, thus identifying it with the predominant form of religion in the United States which is the Christian religion. They are equally at home among the Buddhists, Hindus or Mohammedans, and can adapt their theology much like chameleons adapt the color of their skins, to the protective coloration of the theological climate in which they find themselves. Such passages as Matthew 28:19; John 14:16 and 26; Luke 1:35; John 1:1 and 14; Colossians 2:9 and Acts 5:3, 4, etc., demonstrate the Christian doctrine of the Trinity beyond reasonable doubt.

2. The Nature and Work of Jesus Christ.

As Rosicrucianism stands opposed to the historic Christian doctrine of the Trinity, so also it opposes the true divinity of the Lord Jesus. Rosicrucianism teaches that Jesus Christ was not Jesus, nor was He the only begotten Son of God. Instead, Jesus was a man, the highest luminary possible. The Christ-spirit was a manifestation of the cosmic Christ and the only begotten is "an exalted being which ranks above all else in the universe, save only the Power aspect which created it." [3]

It is obvious then, that as Christian Science divides Jesus and Christ, into Jesus, an apparent manifestation of manhood indwelled by a Christ-consciousness or idea, so Rosicrucianism employs the same type of spiritual schizophrenia and ends, as does Christian Science and all the Gnostic cults, with a divided Messiah.

In the philosophy of Rosicrucianism, "the Christ spirit which entered the body of Jesus when Jesus Himself vacated it, was a ray from the cosmic Christ. We may follow Jesus back in His previous incarnations and can trace His growth to the present day." [4]

Jesus Christ, in the theology of the Rosicrucians "was a spirit belonging to our human evolution, and so was Gautama Buddha," so that their theology makes no allowance for the incarnation of the only God in the Person of the man from Nazareth (John 1:1, 14, 18).

Christianity and Rosicrucianism can never be reconciled, because the former declares the absolute and unique deity of the central figure of all history, and the latter relegates Him to a pantheon of incarnate deities, or spirits. Our Lord vigorously denied such inferences when He stated, concerning His own mission: "All that ever came before me are thieves and robbers: but the sheep did not hear them" (John 10:8).

The Christ of Holy Scripture cannot be divided and subdivided into pantheistic and Gnostic segments. He refuses to be considered one of many equally good ways, or a mere aspect of the truth. Instead, it is His declaration that He is the Life itself, and as such, the only Way and the Truth. It is folly of the highest order to attempt to equate the Christ of revelation with the Christ of Rosicrucianism. For Heindel's Christ, and the Christ of the "brotherhood," is in reality, one of the "other Jesus" (II Corinthians 11:4), the creation of a fertile imagination and a broad intellect (Heindel) projected into the twentieth century, infused with occult and mystical teachings, and lightly coated with Biblical terminology. He is a clever counterfeit, but he is a counterfeit!

[3] *The Rosicrucian Philosophy*, Max Heindel, page 181 and *The Rosicrucian Cosmo-Conception*, or Mystic Christianity, page 374.

[4] *The Rosicrucian Philosophy*, page 181.

It is unnecessary to point out the Rosicrucian concept of the atonement, since for them it is not vicarious, in the sense that Christ paid the penalty for all sin. The primary reason is that they do not believe that Jesus was *the* Christ.

It is the teaching of Holy Scripture that there is but one God (Deuteronomy 6:4; Galatians 3:20), and that to know Him and Jesus Christ whom He has sent, is to possess life eternal (John 17). The Rosicrucian Fellowship does not know Him; it does not accept His vicarious sacrifice for all sin (Isaiah 53), and substitutes reincarnation for resurrection, teaching that man passes through stages of incarnations, through various spheres of progressive perfection, all a product of cosmic evolution.

THE HISTORY AND DESTINY OF MANKIND

We conclude this brief survey of the Rosicrucian Fellowship by noting that, as its view of God, Christ and Redemption are unbiblical, so also is the Rosicrucian concept of mankind. In the thinking of Rosicrucians, there have been various epics or stages of the development of man upon the earth. For instance, the Negro was known as the Lemurian, or the third of these epics. He was followed by the red race, the yellow race and the white race. The white race, according to the Rosicrucians, were originally Semetic, and were the fifth of the Atlantean race.

Along with this type of occult anthropology, the Rosicrucians would have us believe that Atlantis, a mythical lost continent, brought forth this race, which were the ancestors of those destined to become the fathers of the Aryan race of our day.

For Rosicrucianism, man is evolving into a divine being, and in fact, he is a divine being of sorts, a type of demi-god, in the grand cosmic evolutionary scale. Van Baalen quotes Heindel on this point as saying: "There is endless progress, for we are divine as our Father in heaven, and limitations are impossible" (*The Chaos of Cults,* page 96).

With such a view of man, the Rosicrucians can indeed forge ahead to build an international world brotherhood, because, in their theology, cosmic evolution and the law of progression point ever onward and upward to the eventual salvation of all mankind.

The reader might take into consideration in this connection, the words of the Apostle Paul, who dims somewhat, the Rosicrucian illumination of occult anthropology, when he declared that "the first man (was) Adam" (I Corinthians 15:45).

This is a terse judgment of the concept of progressive races, some of which, according to Rosicrucianism, antidate Adam. Under the inspiration of the Holy Spirit, the Apostle declares that there was only *one* human race, and the father of it is Adam, and that in this man Adam, all have died (Romans 5:12; I Corinthians 15:22) because of sin, Rosicrucians not excepted. All the occult mumbo-jumbo, secret symbols and rosy crosses in creation therefore cannot put "Humpty" Adam together again. There has been only one remedy for sin in all history, and that is divine grace, expressed prophetically before the cross, and experientially after the cross. There can be no substitute for the commands of God, and the Rosicrucian Fellowship would do well to hearken to the words of Him who left as His heritage to mankind, a bloodspattered cross, not one shrouded with roses. It was His promise to His followers that, "Because I live, you will live also." This is the Christ of historic Christianity, and it is His word, not ours that will be the judge of all men, including the Rosicrucian Fellowship "in that day" (II Timothy 1:12, 18).

BIBLIOGRAPHY

BIBLIOGRAPHY

JEHOVAH'S WITNESSES

I. GENERAL

Ball, Francis K. **The Elements of Greek.** New York: Macmillan, 1950.

Bullions, Peter. **Principles of Greek Grammar.** New York: Farmer, Bruce and Company.

Carnell, E. J. **An Introduction to Christian Apologetics.** Grand Rapids: Eerdmans, 1950.

Cole, Marley. **Jehovah's Witnesses, The New World Society.** New York: Vantage Press, 1955.

Davies, Horton. **Christian Deviations.** Philosophical Library, 1954.

Dencher, Ted. **The Watch Tower Versus the Bible.** Chicago: Moody Press, 1961.

Deissman, Adolf. **Light From the Ancient East.** New York: Harpers, 1951.

Finnegan, Jack. **Light From the Ancient Past.** Princeton, N.J.: Princeton Press, 1946.

Gaebelein, Arno C. **The Hope of the Ages.** Our Hope.

Gaebelein, Frank E. **Exploring the Bible.** Van Kampen Press, 1950.

Hamilton, Floyd E. **The Basis of Christian Faith.** New York: Harper, 1949.

Irvine, William C. **Heresies Exposed.** Neptune, N.J.: Loizeaux, 1955.

Knoch, Adolf E. **Concordat Version, New Testament** (Greek Translation). Los Angeles, Calif.: Concordat Publishing Concern, 1931.

Knox, Ronald. **Translation of the Bible.** 3 vols. New York: Sheed & Ward, 1953.

Machen, J. G. **The Origin of Paul's Religion.** Grand Rapids: Eerdmans, 1950; **The Virgin Birth of Christ.** 1950.

MacMillan, A. H. **Faith on the March.** Englewood Cliffs, N.J.: Prentice Hall, 1957.

Martin, W. R., and Klann, Norman H. **Jehovah of the Watchtower.** Grand Rapids: Zondervan, 1955.

Mayer, F. E. **Jehovah's Witnesses.** St. Louis: Concordia Publishing House, 1943.

Moulton, J. H. **A Grammar of New Testament Greek.** (3rd. ed.) Edinburgh: Tavil T. Clark.

Newman, John Henry. **The Arians of the Fourth Century.** Longmans Green, 1911; St. Athanasius, Vol. I & II, 1911.

Pegis, **Basic Writings of St. Thomas Aquinas.** Random House, 1950; **Basic Writings of St. Augustine.** 1950.

Ross, Rev. J. J. **Some Facts and More Facts About the Self-styled Pastor, Charles T. Russell.**

Sanders, J. Oswald. **Heresies Ancient and Modern.** Edinburgh: Marshall, Morgan & Scott, 1954.

Schnell, W. J. **Thirty Years a Watch Tower Slave.** Grand Rapids: Baker, 1956; **Into the Light of Christianity.** 1958.

Souter, Alexander. **The New Testament in Greek.** Oxford, 1947.

Stroup, Herbert Hewitt. **The Jehovah's Witnesses.** New York:

Columbus University Press, 1945.

Thiessen, Henry. **An Introduction to the New Testament.** Grand Rapids: Eerdmans, 1948.

Warfield, Benjamin B. **Christological Studies.** Princeton Press, 1950.

Westcott and Hort. **The New Testament in the Original Greek.** New York: Macmillan, 1885, 1943.

Wilson, Robert Dick. **A Scientific Investigation of the Old Testament.** Philadelphia: Sunday School Times.

Wright, J. Stafford. **Some Modern Religions.** Chicago: Inter-Varsity Press, 1956.

Wulfken, George W. **Let There Be Light** (published by the author).

Yonge, C. D. **An English Greek Lexicon.** London, 1859.

Young, E. J. **An Introduction to the Old Testament.** (rev. ed.) Grand Rapids: Eerdmans, 1958.

Young, G. Douglas. **Grammar of the Hebrew Language.** Grand Rapids: Zondervan, 1951.

Young, Robert. **Annalytical Concordance to the Bible.** New York: Funk & Wagnalls Co., 1919.

MAGAZINE AND NEWS-PAPER ARTICLES

Stewart, E. D. "The Life of Charles Taze Russell," Overland Monthly, Los Angeles, 1917, pp. 126-132.

Davidson, Bill. "Jehovah's Travelling Salesman," Readers Digest, February, 1947.

The Brooklyn Daily Eagle. Back issues, 1912, 1913, 1916.

The Brooklyn Eagle. Back issue, 1942.

The Daily Standard Union, Wednesday, November 1, 1916, page 5.

The Brooklyn Daily Times. November 1, 1916, page 4.

The New York Times. Back issues, 1916.

II. WATCH TOWER BIBLE AND TRACT SOCIETY PUBLICATIONS

Awake (Magazine).

The Emphatic Diaglott. Interlinear Greek-English Translation of the New Testament.

Let God Be True. (rev. ed.) 1952.

Make Sure of All Things. 1953.

The New World Translation of the Christian Greek Scriptures. (rev. ed.) 1951.

The New World Translation of the Hebrew Scriptures. vol. I, 1953.

Russell, Charles T. **Studies in the Scriptures.** vols. I-VII.

The Watchtower (Magazine).

Rutherford, J. F. **The Harp of God; Creation; Religion; The Kingdom; Salvation; Deliverance; Children; Enemies; Light; Government; Why Serve Jehovah?; Jehovah's Witnesses—Why Persecuted?; Religious Intolerance—Why?,** etc.

Rutherford, J. F. **Pamphlets** (most now out of print). International Bible Students Association—

A Great Battle in the Ecclesiastical Heavens. 1915. 64 pages.

Can the Living Talk With the Dead? 1920, 128 pages.

Talking With the Dead. 1920, 155 pages.

Prohibition and the League of Nations. 1920, 59 pages.

Millions Now Living Will Never Die. 1920, 128 pages.

Comfort for the Jews. 1925, 128 pages.

Restoration. 1927, 127 pages.

The Lost Days. 1928, 61 pages.

The Kingdom, The Hope of This World. 1931, 62 pages.

Liberty. 1932.

What Is Truth? 1932.

What You Need. 1932.

Where Are the Dead? 1932.

Who Is God? 1932.

Health and Life. 1932.

Hereafter. 1932.

Home and Happiness. 1932

Keys of Heaven. 1932.

The Kingdom. 1932.

Causes of Death. 1932.

Final War. 1932.

Good News. 1932.

The Crisis. 1933.

Dividing the People. 1933.

Escape to the Kingdom. 1933.

Intolerance. 1933.

Angels. 1934.

Beyond the Grave. 1934.

Favored People. 1934.

His Vengeance. 1934.

His Works. 1934.

Righteous Ruler. 1934.

Supremacy. 1934.

World Recovery. 1934.

Who Shall Rule the World? 1935.

Government. 1935.

Loyalty. 1935.

Universal War Near. 1935.

Choosing Riches or Ruin. 1936.

Protection. 1936.

Armageddon. 1937.

Safety Comfort. 1937.

Uncovered. 1937.

Face the Facts. 1938.

Warning. 1938.

Fascism or Freedom. 1939.

Government and Peace. 1939.

Judge Rutherford Uncovers the Fifth Column. 1940.

Refugees. 1940.

God and the State. 1941.

Books and pamphlets published by the Dawn Bible Student Association—

Our Most Holy Faith, a collection of writings and sermons of "Pastor" Charles Taze Russell, 1948, 719 pages.

Armageddon. 31 pages.

Divine Healing. 31 pages.

Born of the Spirit. 31 pages.

Hope Beyond the Grave. 96 pages.

Does God Answer Prayer? 30 pages.

When a Man Dies. 46 pages.

What Can a Man Pay? 32 pages.

His Chosen People. 62 pages.

Hope For a Fear Filled World. 30 pages.

The Day of Judgment. 32 pages.

Spiritualism. 32 pages.

Our Lord's Return. 48 pages.

The Truth About Hell. 63 pages.

Father, Son, and Holy Spirit. 32 pages.

God and Reason. 96 pages.

Jesus the World Saviour. 32 pages.

God's Plan. 47 pages.

When "Pastor" Russell Died. 70 pages.
Creation.

CHRISTIAN SCIENCE

I. WRITINGS BY MARY BAKER EDDY

Science and Health, With Key to the Scriptures.
Miscellaneous Writings.
Manual of the Mother Church.
Christ and Christmas.
Retrospection and Introspection.
Unity of Good.
Pulpit and Press.
Rudimental Divine Science.
No and Yes.
Christian Science Versus Pantheism.
Message to the Mother Church, June, 1900.
Message to the Mother Church, June, 1901.
Message to the Mother Church, June, 1902.
Christian Healing.
The Peoples' Idea of God.
Poems.
The First Church of Christ, Scientist, and Miscellany.
Christian Science Hymnal, with five hymns written by Mary Baker Eddy. Christian Science Publishing Society, 1909.

II. ADDITIONAL GENERAL BIBLIOGRAPHY

A Complete Concordance to the Writings of Mary Baker Eddy Other Than Science and Health.
A Complete Concordance to Science and Health, With Key to the Scriptures.
The Christian Science Journal.
The Christian Science Sentinel.
The Christian Science Monitor.
Armstrong, Joseph. The Mother Church. C.S.P.S., 1937.
Bates, Ernest Sutherland, and Dittemore, John V. Mary Baker Eddy—The Truth and The Tradition. Alfred A. Knopf, 1932.
Beasley, Norman. The Cross and The Crown, The History of Christian Science. Duell, Sloan & Pearce, 1952.
The Blight That Failed. Charles Scribner's Sons, 1929.
Boltzly, Rev. Oliver D. The Death Pot in Christian Science. The Lutheran Literary Board, 1935.
Dakin, Edwin Franden. Mrs. Eddy. Charles Scribner's Sons, 1929.
Dickey, Adam. Memoirs of Mary Baker Eddy. England: Robert G. Carter, 1927.
Douglass, R. C. Christian Science, A Defense.
Dresser, Horatio W., ed. The Quimby Manuscripts. (1st. ed.) Thomas Y. Crowell Co., 1921.
Gray, James M. The Antidote to Christian Science. Chicago: Moody Press.
Hadden, Robert A. Christian Science and the Christian Scriptures Compared and Contrasted. American Prophetic League, 1952.
Haldeman, Isaac Massey. Christian Science in the Light of Holy Scripture. Fleming H. Revell Co., 1909.
Hanna, Septimus J. Christian Science History. C. S. P. S., 1899.
Haushalter, Walter M. Mrs. Eddy Purloins From Hegel. Boston: A. A. Beauchamp, 1936.

Hawkins, Ann Ballew. Phineas Parkhurst Quimby. published by the author, 1951.
Johnston, Julia Michael. Mary Baker Eddy, Her Mission and Triumph. C.S.P.S., 1946.
Martin, Walter R., and Klann, Norman H. The Christian Science Myth. Grand Rapids: Zondervan, 1956.
Meekan, M. Mrs. Eddy and the Late Suit in Equity. Concord, 1908.
Milmine, Georgine. The Life of Mary Baker Eddy and The History of Christian Science. Doubleday, 1909.
Moore, Rev. A. Lincoln. Christian Science—Its Manifold Attraction. Theodore E. Schulte Publishing Co., 1906.
Paget, Stephen, M.D. The Faith and Works of Christian Science. London, 1909.
Peabody, Frederick W. The Religio-Medical Masquerade. Fleming H. Revell, 1910.
Philips, Jane. Mary Baker Eddy's Early Writings Compared With the Quimby Manuscripts. Pasadena, Calif.: Toujours Publishing Co., 1931.
Powell, Lyman P. Mary Baker Eddy. Macmillan, 1930.
Ramsay, E. Mary. Christian Science and Its Discoverer. C.S.P.S., 1935.
Riddle, T. Wilkinson. Christian Science in the Light of Holy Scripture. London: Marshall, Morgan and Scott, 1931.
Riley, Woodbridge; Peabody, W. Frederick; and Humiston, Charles E. The Faith, the Falsity and the Failure of Christian Science. Fleming H. Revell, 1925.
Sheldon, Henry C. Christian Science So-Called. The Abingdon Press, 1913.
Smith, Clifford P. Historical Sketches. C.S.P.S., 1941.
Snowden, James H. The Truth About Christian Science. Westminster Press, 1920.
Stewart, Herbert. Christian Science—True or False. Belfast: Graham L. Healy, Ltd.
Tenney, Rev. Herbert Melville. Christian Science, Its Truths and Errors. The Burrows Brothers Co., 1888.
Tomlinson, Irving C. Twelve Years With Mary Baker Eddy. C.S.P.S., 1945.
Twain, Mark. Christian Science. Harper, 1907.
Wilbur, Sibyl. The Life of Mary Baker Eddy. C.S.P.S., 1923.
Williamson, Margaret. The Mother Church Extension. C.S.P.S., 1939.
Wittmer, George W. Christian Science in the Light of the Bible. Concordia Publishing House, 1949.
Woodbury, Josephine C. War in Heaven. Boston: S. Usher Printer, 1897.
Christian Science Wartime Activities, 1939-1947. C.S.P.S.
Legal Aspects of Christian Science, 1899. C.S.P.S.

III. NEWSPAPER AND MAGAZINE ARTICLES

Arena Magazine, Selected copy regarding Mrs. Eddy and Christian Science.
Buckley, Dr. J. M. "Dr. J. M. Buckley on Christian Science," North American Review, July, 1901.
Cabot, M.D., Richard C. "100 Christian Science Cures," Mc-

Clures Magazine, Aug., 1908.
"The Deadly Parallel," New York Times, July 10, 1904.
Fishbein, M.D., Morris. "Mary Baker Eddy," Plain Talk, Vol. 1, No. 2, Nov., 1927, pp. 21-26.
McClures Magazine, Selected copy regarding Mrs. Eddy and Christian Science.
The New York Herald Tribune, Article and editorial on Christian Science, Dec. 12 and 13, 1951.
The New York Times, Selected material on Christian Science.
The New York World, Selected material on Christian Science.
Woodbury, Josephine C. "Quimbyism or the Paternity of Christian Science," Arena, May, 1899.
Wright, Livingstone. "How Reverend Wiggin Rewrote Mrs. Eddy's Book," New York World.

MORMONISM

Anderson, Edward H. A Brief History of the Church of Jesus Christ Latter Day Saints. Independence, Jackson County, Mo.: Zion's Printing and Publishing Company, 1928.
Anderson, Einar. Mormonism. Chicago: Moody Press, 1956.
Arbaugh, G. B. Revelation in Mormonism. Chicago: University of Chicago Press, 1932.
Bales, James D. The Book of Mormon? Rosemead, Calif.: Old Paths Book Club, 1958.
Baskin, R. N.: Reminiscences of Early Utah. Salt Lake City: Modern Microfilm Company.
Beadle, J. H. Polygamy, or the Mysteries and Crimes of Mormonism. Philadelphia, Pa.: The National Publishing Company, 1882; Life in Utah or Mysteries and Crimes of Mormonism. 1870.
Bennett, Wallace Foster. Why I Am a Mormon. New York: T. Nelson, 1958.
Berrett, William Edwin, ed. Readings in L. D. S. Church History From Original Manuscripts. (1st ed.) Salt Lake City: Deseret Book Co., 1953.
"Bible and Modern Religions," Interpretation Magazine, vol. X, no. 4 (1956), pp. 440-446.
Book of Commandments. Salt Lake City: Modern Microfilm Company.
Brewer, David L.: Utah Elites and Utah Racial Norms. Salt Lake City: Modern Microfilm Company.
Brigham's Destroying Angel. Salt Lake City: Modern Microfilm Company.
Brodie, Fawn M. No Man Knows My History. New York: Alfred A. Knopf, 1946.
Brodie, Fawn M.: No Man Knows My History. Salt Lake City: Modern Microfilm Company.
Brooks, Juanita (ed.): On the Mormon Frontier, The Diary of Hosea Stout. Salt Lake City: University of Utah Press.
Brooks, Juanita. The Mountain Meadows Massacre. Stanford: Stanford University Press, 1943.
Budvarson, Arthur: The Book of Mormonism — True or False? Grand Rapids: Zondervan Publishing House, 1961. 63 pp.
Call, Lamoni: 2000 Changes in the Book of Mormon. Salt Lake City: Modern Microfilm Company.

Cannon, Frank J.: **Under the Prophet in Utah.** Salt Lake City: Modern Microfilm Company.

Cannon, Frank J. and O'Higgins, Harvey J. **U n d e r the Prophet in Utah.** Boston, Mass.: E. M. Clark Publishing Company, 1911.

Cannon, Frank Jenne. **Brigham Young and His Mormon Empire.** New York: Fleming H. Revell Co., 1913.

Clark, J. A. **Gleanings by the Way.** 1842.

Codman, Jr. **The Mormon Country.** U.S. Publishing Co., 1874.

Corrill, John: **A Brief History of the Church of Christ of Latter Day Saints.** Salt Lake City: Modern Microfilm Company.

Draper, Maurice I. **Christ's Church Restored.** Independence, Mo.: Herald Publishing House, 1948.

Erickson, Ephraim E. **The Psychological and Ethical Aspects of Mormon Group Life.** Chicago: University of Chicago Press, 1922.

Evans, R. C. **One Hundred Years of Mormonism.** Salt Lake City: Deseret News, 1905; **Forty Years in the Mormon Church, Why I Left.** 1920.

Etzenhouser, R., and Phillips, A. B. **Three Bibles Compared.** Independence, Mo.: Herald Publishing Company, 1954.

Folk, Edger E. **The Mormon Monster.** New York: Fleming H. Revell Company, 1900.

Fraser, Gordon H. **Is Mormonism Christian?** Chicago: Moody Colportage Library, 1957.

Gibbs, Josiah F.: **The Mountain Meadows Massacre.** Salt Lake City: Modern Microfilm Company.

Hanson, Klaus: **Quest for Empire.** East Lansing, Michigan: Michigan State University Press.

Hield, Charles R., and Ralston, Russell F. **Baptism for the Dead.** I n d e p e n d e n c e, Mo.: Herald Publishing House, 1953.

History of the Mormons or Latter-Day Saints, Auburn-Derby and Miller, 1852.

Hougey, Hal: **Archeology and the Book of Mormon.** Salt Lake City: Modern Microfilm Company.

Hougey, Hal: **Truth About the 'Lehi Tree-of-Life' Stone.** Salt Lake City: Modern Microfilm Company.

Hunter, Milton R. **The Gospel Through the Ages, Melchizedek P r i e s t h o o d Course of Study.** Salt Lake City, 1945-46.

Ivins, Stanley S.: **The Mose Thatcher Case.** Salt Lake City: Modern Microfilm Company.

Jensen, Andrew: **Plural Marriage.** Salt Lake City: Modern Microfilm Company.

Jonas, Larry: **Mormon Claims Examined.** Salt Lake City: Modern Microfilm Company.

Joseph Smith Begins His Work. Salt Lake City: Modern Microfilm Company. Volume 1.

Joseph Smith Begins His Work, Vol. 2. Salt Lake City: Modern Microfilm Company.

Joseph Smith's Egyptian Alphabet and Grammar. Salt Lake City: Modern Microfilm Company.

Lamb, M. T.: **The Golden Bible.** Salt Lake City: Modern Microfilm Company.

Lee, John Doyle. **A M o r m o n Chronicle.** San Marino, Calif.: Huntington Library, 1955.

Lewis, William. **The Church of Jesus Christ: How Shall I Know It?** Independence, Mo.: Herald Publishing House.

Linn, William Alexander. **The Story of the Mormons.** New York: Macmillan Co., 1902.

Lyford, C. **The Mormon Problem.** New York: Hunt and Eaton, 1866.

Martin, Stuart. **The Mystery of Mormonism.** New York: E. P. Dutton and Company.

Messenger and Advocate. Salt Lake City: Modern Microfilm Company.

Meyer, Eduard. **Ursprung und Geschichte der Mormonen mit Exkursen ueber Anfange des Islams and des Christentums.** 1912.

Millennial Star, Vols. 1-7. Salt Lake City: Modern Microfilm Company.

Mulder, Wm. **Among the Mormons.** New York: Knopf, 1958; "Mormonism's 'Gathering': An American Doctrine with a Difference," **Church History,** xxiii (No. 3, Sept. 1954, 248f.).

Nelson, Dee Jay: **The Joseph Smith Papyri — A Translation and Preliminary Survey.** Salt Lake City: Modern Microfilm Company.

Nutting, J. D. **The Little Encyclopedia of Mormonism.** Cleveland: Utah Gospel Mission, 1927.

O'Dea, Thomas F. **The Mormons.** Chicago: University of Chicago Press, 1957.

Orson Pratt: **The Seer.** Salt Lake City: Modern Microfilm Company.

Orson Pratt's Works. Salt Lake City: Modern Microfilm Company.

Orson Spencer's Letters. Salt Lake City: Modern Microfilm Company.

Pamphlets by Orson Pratt. Salt Lake City: Modern Microfilm Company.

Pearl of Great Price. Salt Lake City: Modern Microfilm Company.

Peck, Reed: **Reed Peck Manuscript.** Salt Lake City: Modern Microfilm Company.

Petersen, La Mar: **Problems in Mormon Text.** Salt Lake City: Modern Microfilm Company.

Petersen, Mark E.: **Race Problems as They Affect the Church.** Salt Lake City: Modern Microfilm Company.

Reiser, A. H. and Marian G. Merkley. **What It Means to Be a Latter-Day Saint, Course of Study for the First Intermediates Dept.** Salt Lake City, 1946.

Revealing Statements By the Three Witnesses to the Book of Mormon. Salt Lake City: Modern Microfilm Company.

Richards, LeGrand. **A Marvelous W o r k and a Wonder.** Salt Lake City: Deseret Book Co., 1950.

Rushton, John W. **The Apostasy and the Restoration.** Independence, Mo.: Herald Publishing House.

Schindler, Harold: **Orrin Porter**

Rockwell; **Man of God, Son of Thunder.** Salt Lake City: University of Utah Press.

Senate Document 189. Salt Lake City: Modern Microfilm Company.

Shook, Charles A. **The True Origin of the Book of Mormon.** Cincinnati, 1914.

Smith, Elbert A. **D i f f e r e n c e s That Persist Between the Reorganized Church of Christ Latter Day Saints and the Utah Mormon Church.** Independence, Mo.: Herald Publishing House, 1943; **The Latter Day Glory; Question Time: Answers to 457 Often-Asked Questions.** 1955.

Smith, Ethan: **View of the Hebrews.** Salt Lake City: Modern Microfilm Company.

Smith, Joseph (ed.): **The Elder's Journal.** Salt Lake City: Modern Microfilm Company.

Smith, Joseph Fielding. **Essentials in Church History.** (11th ed.) Salt Lake City: Deseret News Press, 1946.

Smith, Joseph, Jr. **A Book of Commandments for the Government of the Church of Christ,** organized according to law, on the 6th of April, 1830. Independence, 1833. (Reprinted by the Salt Lake Tribune, 1884.)

Smith, Joseph, Jr. **The Book of Mormon.** Salt Lake City: The Church of Jesus Christ Latter Day Saints, 1952; **Doctrine and Covenants; The Pearl of Great Price.** 1953.

Smith, Lucy: **Joseph Smith's History.** Salt Lake City: Modern Microfilm Company.

Snowden, James H. **The Truth About Mormonism.** New York: George H. Durant Co., 1926.

Spalding, F. S.: **Why Egyptologists Reject the Book of Abraham.** Salt Lake City: Modern Microfilm Company.

Starks, Arthur E. **A Complete Concordance to the Book of Mormon.** Independence, Mo.: Herald Publishing House, 1950.

Stenhouse, T. B. **The Rocky Mountain Saints.** New York: B. Appleton Co., 1873.

Stewart, George. **Priesthood and Church Welfare.** Deseret Book Co., 1939.

Swartzell, William: **Mormonism Exposed.** Salt Lake City: Modern Microfilm Company.

Talmage, James E. **The Articles of Faith.** Salt Lake City: The Church of Jesus Christ Latter Day Saints, 1952.

Tanner, Jerald: **The Negro in Mormon Theology.** Salt Lake City: Modern Microfilm Company.

Tanner, Jerald and Sandra: **Changes in Joseph Smith's History.** Salt Lake City: Modern Microfilm Company.

Tanner, Jerald and Sandra: **Changes in the Pearl of Great Price.** Salt Lake City: Modern Microfilm Company.

Tanner, Jerald and Sandra: **Changes in the Key to Theology.** Salt Lake City: Modern Microfilm Company.

Tanner, Jerald and Sandra: **Joseph Smith and Polygamy.** Salt Lake City: Modern Microfilm Company.

Tanner, Jerald and Sandra: **Joseph Smith's Curse Upon The Negro.** Salt Lake City: Modern Microfilm Company.

Tanner, Jerald and Sandra: **Joseph Smith's Strange Account of the First Vision,** also **A Critical Study of the First Vision.** Salt Lake City: Modern Microfilm Company.

Tanner, Jerald and Sandra: **Mormonism — Shadow or Reality?** Salt Lake City: Modern Microfilm Company.

Tanner, Jerald and Sandra: **The Case Against Mormonism,** Vol. I. Salt Lake City: Modern Microfilm Company.

Tanner, Jerald and Sandra: **The Mormon Kingdom.** Salt Lake City: Modern Microfilm Company.

Tanner, Jerald and Sandra: **The Mormon Papyri Question.** Salt Lake City: Modern Microfilm Company.

3,913 Changes in the Book of Mormon. Salt Lake City: Modern Microfilm Company.

Taylor, John. **The Mediation and Atonement.** The Church of Jesus Christ Latter Day Saints.

Tempel Lot Case. Salt Lake City: Modern Microfilm Company.

Temple Mormonism. Salt Lake City: Modern Microfilm Company.

The Confessions of John D. Lee. Salt Lake City: Modern Microfilm Company.

The Evening and the Morning Star. Salt Lake City: Modern Microfilm Company.

Times and Seasons, Vols. 1-6. Salt Lake City: Modern Microfilm Company.

Tucker, Pomeroy. **Origin, Rise and Progress of Mormonism.** 1867.

Turner, Wallace: **The Mormon Establishment.** Salt Lake City: Modern Microfilm Company.

Walters, Wesley P.: **New Light on Mormon Origins from the Palmyra (N. Y.) Revival.** Salt Lake City: Modern Microfilm Company.

Wardle, James D.: **Selected Changes in the Book of Mormon.** Salt Lake City: Modern Microfilm Company.

Weldon, Roy. **Other Sheep: Book of Mormon Evidences.** Independence, Mo.: Herald Publishing House, 1956.

Westminster Review, Vol. LIX, Jan. and April, 1853, pp. 103-120. New York: Leonard Scott & Co.

Whitmer, John: **John Whitmer's History.** Salt Lake City: Modern Microfilm Company.

Widtsoe, John A. **Priesthood and Church Government.** Deseret Book Company, 1939.

Young, Ann Eliza. **Wife No. 19, A Life in Bondage.** 1876.

Young, Brigham. **Journal of Discourses.** 1901.

SPIRITISM

Butterworth, George W. **Spiritualism and Religion.** New York: Macmillan, 1944.

Doyle, A. Conan. **The History of Spiritualism.** 2 vols.; **Phineas Speaks: Direct Communications in the Family Circle.** London, 1927.

Gray, James M. **Spiritism and the Fallen Angels.** London:

Fleming H. Revell Co., 1920.

Harding, Emma. **Modern American Spiritualism — A Twenty Year Record of the Communion of the World and Spirits.** New York, 1870.

Hill, Arthur J. **Spiritualism—Its History, Phenomena and Doctrine.** New York: George H. Doran & Co., 1919.

Hull, Moses. **Encyclopedia of Biblical Spiritualism.** Chicago: Moses Hull & Co., 1895.

McCabe, Joseph. **Spiritualism— A Popular History From 1847.** London, 1920.

McKnight, Marcus. **Spiritualism.** London, 1950.

Schofield, A. T. **Modern Spiritism—Its Science and Religion.**

Stoddard, Jane T. **The Case Against Spiritualism.** New York: Houghton and Stoughton, 1919.

Wade, Alda Madison. **Evidences of Immortality.** Boston: The Christopher Publishing House, 1956.

Walton, George S. **The Drama of Life After Death.** New York: A. H. Holt & Co., 1932.

PAMPHLETS—

Biederwolf, William E. **Spiritualism Divine? Devilish? or Deception?** Grand Rapids: Eerdmans, 1952.

Froom, Leroy Edwin. **Spiritualism Today.** Washington, D.C.: Review and Herald, 1963.

Wright, The Rev. J. Stanford. **Spiritualism.** London: The Church Book Room Press, 1959.

FATHER DIVINE

Fausset, Arthur H. **Black Gods of the Metropolis.** Philadelphia: University of Pennsylvania Press, 1944.

Harris, Sarah. **Father Divine, Holy Husband.** Doubleday & Co.

Martin, Walter. "Father Divine, King of Cultists," **Eternity Magazine,** Aug., 1955.

THE THEOSOPHICAL SOCIETY

Besant, Anne. **The Ancient Wisdom,** An Outline of Theosophic Teaching. London, 1897; **An Autobiography.** London, 1893.

Blavatsky, Helena P. **The Secret Doctrine.** London, 1893.

Butt, Baseden G. **Madam Blavatsky.** London, 1926.

Kuhn, Alvin B. **Theosophy, A Modern Revival of Ancient Wisdom.** New York: H. Holt & Co., 1930.

Leadbeater, Charles W. **Textbook of Theosophy.** Chicago: The Theosophical Press, 1925.

Olcott, Henry S. **Old Diary Leaves.** An Authentic History of the Theosophical Society. Madras Theosophical Publishing Society, 1935.

Rogers, L. W. **Elementary Theosophy.** (6th ed.) Wheaton, Ill.: The Theosophical Press, 1956.

Sheldon, H. C. **Theosophy and New Thought.** New York, 1916.

Sinnett, Alfred Percy. **The Theosophical Movement 1875-1925** —A History and a Survey. New York: E. P. Dutton, 1925.

Sloan, Ellen M. **Modern Theosophy, Whence, What, Whither?** St. Paul, Minn.: The Way Press, 1922.

Williams, Gertrude Leavenworth. **Priestess of the Occult, Madam Blavatsky.** New York: A. A. Knopf, 1946.

ZEN BUDDHISM

Barrett, William. **Zen Buddhism,** Selected Writings of D. T. Suzuki. Doubleday, 1956.

Chen-Chi-Chang: **The Practice of Zen.** Harper, 1959.

Humphreys, C. **Zen Buddhism.** New York: Macmillan, 1958.

Linssen, Robert. **Living Zen.** New York: Grove Press, 1958.

Ogata, Sohaku. **Zen for the West.** New York: Apollo, William Morrow, 1962.

Suzuki, D. T. **Essays in Zen Buddhism.** 3 vols. London, 1949-51; **An Introduction to Zen Buddhism.** New York: Philosophical Library, 1949; **Manual of Zen Buddhism.** New York: Grove Press, 1960.

Watts, Alan. **The Spirit of Zen.** New York: Grove Press, 1958; **The Way of Zen.** Pantheon, 1957; **The Way of Liberation in Zen Buddhism.** San Francisco: American Academy of Asian Studies, 1955.

SWEDENBORGIANISM

Barrett, B. F. **The Science of Correspondences Elucidated.** Germantown, Pa.: Swedenborg Publishing Assoc., 1909.

Sigstedt, Cyriel O. **The Swedenborg Epic, the Life and Works of Emmanuel Swedenborg.** New York: Twayne, 1952.

Smyth, Julian K. and Wunsch, William. **The Gist of Swedenborg.** Philadelphia: J. B. Lippincott, 1920.

Swedenborg, Emmanuel. **The Complete Works.** Boston: Houghton Mifflin Co., 1907.

Trobridge, G. **Swedenborg: Life and Teachings.** New York: Swedenborg Foundation, 1938.

Vrooman, Hiram. **Science and Theology Co-ordinated.** Chicago: Swedenborg Philosophical Center. (pamphlet)

THE BAHAI FAITH

I. MAGAZINE ARTICLES

Bach, Marcus. "Bahai, A Second Look," **Christian Century,** April 10, 1957.

"We Love All Religions," **Time Magazine,** April 26, 1963.

II. PUBLICATIONS OF BAHAI PUBLISHING TRUST, WILMETTE, ILL.

Abdu'l-Baha. **Some Questions Answered.** (Emphasis on Christianity)

Baha'u'llah. **Gleanings From the Writings of Baha'u'llah.**

Baha'u'llah and Abdu'l-Baha. **The Bahai World Faith.**

Esslemont, J. E. **Baha'u'llah and the New Era.** 1952.

Sears, William. **Release the Sun.**

Shoghi, Effendi. **Promised Day to Come.**

Townshend, George. **The Promise of All Ages.**

Willoughby, John. **All Things Made New.**

THE UNITY SCHOOL OF CHRISTIANITY

Cady, Emilie D. **God a Present Help.** Unity School of Christianity, 1942; **Lessons in Truth.** Kansas City, Mo.: Unity School of Christianity, 1939.

Fillmore, Charles. **Christian Healing.** Unity School of Christianity, 1954 (first published, 1909, 25th printing); **Keep a True Lent.** 1954; **Twelve Powers of Man.** 1943; **Mysteries of Genesis.** 1936; **What Practical Christianity Stands For.** 1939.

Fillmore, Charles and Cora. **Teach Us to Pray.** Kansas City, Mo.: Unity School of Christianity, 1945.

Fillmore, Lowell. **New Ways to Solve Old Problems.** (2nd ed.) Kansas City, Mo.: Unity School of Christianity, 1939.

Fillmore, Myrtle. **Healing Letters.** Lee Summit, Mo.: Unity School of Christianity, 1954 (first published, 1936, 8th printing).

Foulks, Francis W. **Effectual Prayer.** Kansas City, Mo.: Unity School of Christianity, 1949.

Freeman, James Dilett. **The Household of Faith.** Lee Summit, Mo.: Unity School of Christianity, 1951; **The Story of Unity.** 1951.

Metaphysical Bible Dictionary. Lee Summit, Mo.: Unity School of Christianity.

Quimby, Phineas P. **The Quimby Manuscripts.** Edited by Horatio W. Dresser. New York: Julian Press, 1961.

Shanklin, Octavia A. **Selected Studies.** Unity School of Christianity, 1953.

Unity Statement of Faith, Unity School of Christianity.

Wilson, Ernest C. **Have We Lived Before?** Unity School of Christianity, 1953.

SEVENTH-DAY ADVENTISM

I. WRITINGS OF ELLEN G. WHITE

Review and Herald Publishing Association, Takoma Park, Maryland: **The Adventist Home; Child Guidance; Christ's Object Lessons; Counsels on Diets and Foods; Early Writings; Education; Evangelism; Messages to Young People; The Ministry of Healing; Steps to Christ.**

Pacific Press Publishing Association, Mountain View, Calif.: **The Acts of the Apostles; Christian Experience and Teachings; The Desire of Ages; Index to the Writings of Ellen G. White; Patriarchs and Prophets; Prophets and Kings; Testimonies for the Church,** vols. 1-9; **Testimonies to Ministers; Thoughts From the Mount of Blessings.**

II. SEVENTH-DAY ADVENTIST PUBLICATIONS

Anderson, R. A. **The Shepherd Evangelist.** Review and Herald; **Unfolding the Revelation.** Pacific Press.

Andreason, M. L. **The Book of Hebrews.** Review and Herald; **God's Holy Day.** Review and Herald; **The Sabbath.** Review and Herald; **The Sanctuary Service.** Review and Herald; **What Can a Man Believe?**

Pacific Press.

The Bible Made Plain, a series of short Bible Studies for the home circle upon the fundamentals of the Christian faith. Review and Herald.

Bible Readings for the Home, compilation. Review and Herald, 1956.

Bible Readings for the Home Circle. Review and Herald.

Bollman, Calvin P. **Sunday, Origin of Its Observance in the Christian Church.** Review and Herald.

Branson, W. H. **In Defense of the Faith.** Review and Herald.

Bunch, Taylor G. **Behold the Man.** Southern Publishing Assoc.; **The Ten Commandments.** Review and Herald.

Church Manual. Takoma Park, Maryland: General Conference of Seventh-day Adventists.

Cottrell, Roy F. **The True Sabbath.** Southern Publishing Assoc.

Daniels, A. G. **The Abiding Gift of Prophecy.** Pacific Press; **Christ Our Righteousness.** Takoma Park, Maryland: The Ministerial Association of Seventh-day Adventists.

Dixon, Louis J. **Law or Grace.** Southern Publishing Assoc.

Everson, Charles T. **The Rich Man and Lazarus.** Southern Publishing Assoc.; **Who Are the Angels?** Review and Herald.

Froom, Leroy E. **The Coming of the Comforter.** Review and Herald; **Finding the Lost Prophetic Witness.** Review and Herald; **The Prophetic Faith of Our Fathers.** vols. 1-4. Review and Herald.

General Conference Young Peoples Department of Missionary Volunteers pamphlet. **Studies in Bible Doctrine.** Senior Missionary Volunteer. Review and Herald.

Genesis—John. Review and Herald.

Haskell, S. N. **Bible Hand Book.** Review and Herald.

Haynes, Carlyle B. **The Christian Sabbath, Is It Saturday or Sunday?** Southern Publishing Assoc.; **From Sabbath to Sunday.** Review and Herald; **The Gift of Prophecy.** Southern Publishing Assoc.; **Life, Death and Immortality.** Southern Publishing Assoc.; **Seventh-day Adventists, Their Work and Teachings.** Review and Herald; **When a Man Dies.** Review and Herald.

Horn, Sigfried H., and Wood, Lynn H. **The Chronology of Ezra Seven.** Review and Herald.

How to Handle Objections, prepared by the publishing department of The Secretaries of the Southern Union Conference. Southern Publishing Assoc.

Jamison, T. Housel. **A Prophet Among You.** Pacific Press.

Johns, Varner J. **The Secret Rapture and the Antichrist.** Pacific Press.

Lickey, Arthur E. **Fundamentals of the Everlasting Gospel.** Review and Herald.

Marsh, F. L. **Evolution, Creation and Science.** Review and Herald.

Maxwell, Arthur S. **The Coming**

King. Pacific Press; **Your Friends the Adventists.** Pacific Press.

The Ministry (Magazine).

Moseley, Calvin Edwin. **The Lord's Day.** Southern Publishing Assoc.

Nichol, Francis D. **Answers to Objections.** Review and Herald; **The Certainty of My Faith.** Review and Herald; **Ellen G. White and Her Critics.** Review and Herald; **The Midnight Cry.** Review and Herald.

Odom, Robert L. **The Final Crisis and Deliverance.** Southern Publishing Assoc.; **How Did Sunday Get Its Name?** Southern Publishing Assoc.; **Sunday in Roman Paganism.** Review and Herald.

Problems in Bible Translation. Takoma Park, Maryland: General Conference, Seventh-day Adventists.

Reed, W. E. **The Bible, the Spirit of Prophecy and the Church.** Review and Herald.

Review and Herald (Magazine).

Richards, H. M. S. **Hard Nuts Cracked.** Southern Publishing Assoc.

Robinson, D. E. **The Story of Our Health Message.** Southern Publishing House.

Sabbath-School Quarterly (Magazine).

The Seventh-day Adventist Bible Commentary. vols. 1-5.

Seventh-day Adventist Church Directory, United States and Canada. Review and Herald.

Seventh-day Adventist Year Book, 1957. Review and Herald.

Signs of the Times (Magazine).

Smith, Uriah. **Daniel and the Revelation.** vols. 1 and 2. Review and Herald.

Spalding, Arthur W. **Sister White.** Review and Herald.

Spicer, W. A. **Our Day in the Light of Prophecy.** Review and Herald.

Straw, W. E. **Origin of Sunday Observance.** Review and Herald.

These Times (Magazine).

Walker, Allen. **The Law and the Sabbath.** Southern Publishing Assoc.

Werner, A. J. **Fundamentals of Bible Doctrine.** Review and Herald.

Wheeler, Ruth. **His Messenger.** Review and Herald.

Wilcox, F. M. **The Coming Crisis.** Review and Herald; **The Lord's Day, the Test of the Ages.** Pacific Press; **Questions Answered.** Pacific Press.

III. GENERAL

The Advent Herald (Millerite).

The Advent Shield and Review (Millerite). 1844.

Auchincloss, Douglas. ''Peace With the Adventists.'' **Time** Magazine, Dec. 31, 1956. pp. 48-49.

Baer, James E. ''The Seventh-day Adventists,'' Series; ''The Bible and Modern Religions,'' **Interpretation, Journal of** Theology, Jan., 1956.

Barnhouse, Donald Grey. ''Are Seventh-day Adventists Christian?'' **Eternity** Magazine, Sept., 1956.

Biederwolf, Wm. Edward. **Seventh-day Adventism, the Re-**

sult of a Predicament. Grand Rapids: Eerdmans.

Bliss, Sylvester. Memoirs of William Miller. Boston, 1853.

Booth, A. E. Seventh-day Adventism, What Is It? vol. 12, article on William Miller.

Buswell, J. Oliver. The Length of Creative Days. Monograph. New York: Shelton College, 1950.

Canright, D. M. Hard Nuts for Seventh-day Adventists (tract): Life of Mrs. E. G. White. Nashville: B. C. Goodpasture, 1948; Seventh-day Adventism Renounced. B. C. Goodpasture.

Chafer, Louis Sperry. Grace. Van Kampen Press, 1947.

Davies, Horton. Christian Deviations. New York: Philosophical Library. Chapter on Seventh-day Adventism.

Deck, Norman C. The Lord's Day or the Sabbath, Which? Sydney, Australia: Bridge Printery, Ltd.

Dictionary of American Biography. New York: Charles Scribner's Sons.

Dugger, A. F. The Bible Sabbath Defended. Stanbury, Mo.: The Church of God Publishing House.

Dungan, D. R. Sabbath or Lord's Day, Which? Nashville: Harbinger Book Club.

Feinberg, Charles L. The Sabbath and the Lord's Day. Van Kampen Press.

Fletcher, W. W. The Reasons for My Faith. Sydney, Australia: William Brooks & Co., Ltd.

Hulbert, Terry C. "Seventh-day Adventism Weighed in the Balances," The Discerner Magazine, Oct.-Dec., 1956. (This issue a refutation of Seventh-day Adventism.)

Ironside, H. A. What Think Ye of Christ? New York: Loizeaux.

Irvine, Wm. C. Heresies Exposed. New York: Loizeaux.

Jones, E. B. The Answer and the Reasons, eye-opening information regarding Seventh-day Adventism. Oak Park, Ill.: Designed Products; Free Indeed, the author's testimony concerning his deliverance from Seventh-day Adventism. Designed Products; Forty Bible-Supported Reasons Why You Should Not Be a Seventh-day Adventist. Designed Products.

———, "The Historical Background of Seventh-day Adventism," "Seventh-day Adventism and the Gospel of Grace," etc. The Sunday School Times, 1954; "Seventh-day Adventists Counterfeit Gospel," Christian Victory Magazine, Feb., 1952.

Martin, Walter R. "Are Seventh-day Adventists Evangelical?" Christian Life Magazine, Oct., 1956; "Seventh-day Adventism Today," Our Hope Magazine, Nov., 1956; "The Truth About Seventh-day Adventism," series in Eternity Magazine, Oct., Nov., Jan., 1956-57.

Miller, William. Apology and Defense. Aug., 1845 (pamphlet); A Few Evidences of the Time of the Second Coming of Christ (Mss. 1831).

Pickering, Ernest. "Can We Fellowship With Seventh-day Adventists?" The Voice of the Independent Fundamental Churches of America, Oct., 1956.

Pollock, A. J. Seventh-day Adventism Briefly Tested by Scripture. London: The Central Bible Truth Depot.

Putnam, C. E. Legalism and the Seventh-day Question, Can Sinai Law and Grace Coexist? Chicago: The Bible Institute Colportage Assoc.

Rowell, J. B. Seventh-day Adventism Examined. Norwalk, Calif.: Challenge Publishing Co.

"Seventh-day Adventists and the Date of Creation," editorial, The Examiner Magazine, March-April, 1952.

Smith, Oswald J. Who Are the False Prophets? Toronto: The People's Press; Who Are the Seventh-day Adventists and What Do They Teach? Hugh Warren, Wesley Press and Publishing House.

Talbot, Louis T. What's Wrong With Seventh-day Adventism? Grand Rapids: Dunham.

IV. MAGAZINE ARTICLES

Bibliotheca Sacra, April, 1956.

Christianity Today
"What of Seventh-day Adventism?" by Harold Lindsell, Part I, March 31, 1958. Part II, April 14, 1958
"Another Look at Adventism" by Herbert S. Bird, April 28, 1958.
"A Seventh-day Adventist Speaks Back" by Frank H. Yost, July 21, 1958.

Eternity, September, 1956.

Eternity, June, 1958.

King's Business, The, April, 1957.

King's Business, The, March, 1958.

Signs of the Times, January 8, 1952.

Sword of the Lord, The, August 2, 1957.

UNITARIANISM

DeWolf, Harold F. Present Trends in Christian Thought. New York: Association Press, 1960.

Kegley, Charles W., and Bretall, Robert W. The Theology of Paul Tillich. (The Library of Living Theology) New York: Macmillan, 1961.

Kimmel, William, and Clive, Geoffry. Dimensions of Faith. New York: Twayne Publishers, 1959.

Machen, John G. Christianity and Liberalism. New York: Macmillan, 1923; What Is Faith? 1935.

MacKintosh, Hugh Ross. Types of Modern Theology From Schleiermacher to Barth. New York: Scribners, 1937.

Nash, Arnold S. Protestant Thought in the Twentieth Century. New York: Macmillan, 1951.

Scholefield, Harry, ed. Unitarian Universalist Pocket Guide. Boston: Beacon Press, 1963; A Pocket Guide to Unitarianism. 1954.

Wilbur, Earl Morse. A History of Unitarianism. Cambridge, Mass.: Harvard University Press.

THE ROSICRUCIAN FELLOWSHIP

Clymer, R. S. The Boor of Rosicrucae. 3 vols. Quakerstown, Pa.: The Philosophical Publishing Co.

Lewis, Spencer H. Rosicrucian Questions and Answers With Complete History of the Rosicrucian Order. San Jose, Calif.: AMORC.

GENERAL WORKS

Atkins, G. Modern Religious Cults and Movements. New York: Fleming H. Revell Co., 1923.

Bach, Marcus. They Have Found a Faith. New York: Bobbs-Merrill, 1946.

Braden, Charles S. These Also Believe. New York: Macmillan, 1951.

Clark, Elmer T. The Small Sects in America. (rev. ed.) Nashville, Tenn.: Abingdon Press, 1949.

Davies, Horton. The Challenge of the Sects. Philadelphia: Westminster Press, 1961.

Ferguson, Charles. New Books of Revelation. Garden City, N.Y.: Doubleday-Doran, 1929; Confusion of Tongues. 1928.

Ferm, Vergilius. Religion in the Twentieth Century. New York: Philosophical Library, 1948.

Gerstner, John H. The Theology of the Major Sects. Grand Rapids: Baker, 1960.

Martin, Walter R. The Christian and the Cults. Grand Rapids: Zondervan, 1956; The Rise of the Cults. 1955.

Mathison, Richard R. Faiths, Cults and Sects of America. Indianapolis: Bobbs-Merrill, 1960.

Mayer, F. E. Religious Bodies of America. St. Louis, Mo.: Concordia, 1954.

Mead, Frank S. Handbook of Denominations in the United States. (rev. ed.) Nashville: Abingdon, 1956.

Neve, J. L. Churches and Sects in Christendom. Minneapolis: Augsburg, 1952.

Rosten, Leo. A Guide to the Religions of America. New York: Simon and Schuster, 1955.

Sanders, J. Oswald, and Wright, J. Stafford. Some Modern Religions. London: Tyndale Press, 1956.

Schaff, Philip, and Johann Herzog. The New Schaff-Herzog Encyclopedia of Religious Knowledge. 15 vols. Grand Rapids: Baker.

Strong, James. Strong's Exhaustive Concordance of the Bible. New York: Abingdon-Cokesbury Press.

Van Baalen, J. K. The Chaos of Cults. (4th rev. ed.) Grand Rapids: Eerdmans, 1962.

Wyrick, Herbert M. Seven Religious Isms. Grand Rapids: Zondervan, 1940.

INDEX